AQA A-level

For A-level
Years 1 and 2

Economics

Fourth Edition

Ray Powell
James Powell

HODDER
EDUCATION
AN HACHETTE UK COMPANY

Orders: please contact Bookpoint Ltd, 130 Park Drive, Milton Park, Abingdon, Oxon OX14 4SE. Telephone: (44) 01235 827827. Fax: (44) 01235 400401. Email education@bookpoint.co.uk Lines are open from 9 a.m. to 5 p.m., Monday to Saturday, with a 24-hour message answering service. You can also order through our website: www.hoddereducation.co.uk

ISBN: 978 1 5104 5195 7

© Ray Powell and James Powell 2019

First published in 2019 by

Hodder Education,

An Hachette UK Company

Carmelite House

50 Victoria Embankment

London EC4Y 0DZ

www.hoddereducation.co.uk

Impression number   10 9 8 7 6 5 4 3 2 1

Year   2023   2022   2021   2020   2019

Cover photo © vadim.nefedov – stock.adobe.com

Typeset by Integra Software Services Pvt. Ltd., Pondicherry, India

Printed in Italy

A catalogue record for this title is available from the British Library.

Get the most from this book

This textbook has been tailored explicitly to cover the content of the AQA specification for the A-level course. The book is divided into two parts, one covering microeconomics and the other macroeconomics.

The text provides the foundation for studying AQA economics, but you will no doubt wish to keep up to date by referring to additional topical sources of information about economic events. This can be done by reading the serious newspapers, visiting key sites on the internet and reading such magazines as *Economics Review*.

Special features

Key terms
Clear, concise definitions of essential key terms where they first appear and as a list at the end of each section.

Study tips
Short pieces of advice to help you present your ideas effectively and avoid potential pitfalls.

Learning objectives
A statement of the intended learning objectives for each chapter.

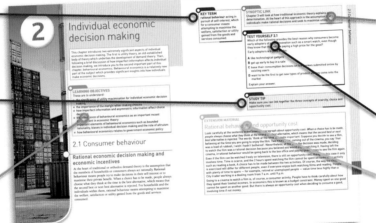

Synoptic links
Connections between different areas of economics are highlighted to help improve your overall understanding of the subject.

Test yourself
Exercises to provide active engagement with economic analysis.

Extension material
Extension points to stretch your understanding.

Case studies
Case studies to show economic concepts applied to real-world situations.

Quantitative skills
Worked examples of the quantitative skills that you will need to develop.

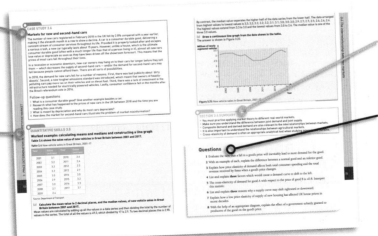

Summaries
Bulleted summaries of each topic that can be used as a revision tool.

Revision questions
Revision questions are provided at the end of each section to help you check your knowledge and understanding of the topics you have covered within each chapter.

Practice questions
There is a section at the back containing questions for you to practise.

Answers are online at: www.hoddereducation.co.uk/AQAEconomics

Contents

1 Microeconomics

Individuals, firms, markets and market failure

Economic methodology and the economic problem

Economics is the study of choice and decision making in a world with limited resources. It tries to explain the economic behaviour of both individuals and groups of people, and the economic relationships between individuals and groups. Related to the noun 'economics' is the verb 'to economise'. In large part, economics is the study of economising — the study of how people make choices about what to produce, how to produce and for whom to produce, in a world in which most resources are limited or scarce. How best can people make decisions on how scarce resources should be allocated among competing uses so as to improve and maximise human happiness and welfare? This is the economic problem, which is the main focus of this introductory chapter.

LEARNING OBJECTIVES
These are to understand:

- important aspects of economic methodology
- the nature and purpose of economic activity
- how resources are used to produce goods and services
- the importance of scarcity, choice and resource allocation
- the significance of production possibility diagrams

1.1 Economic methodology

Economics as a social science

When answering the question 'What is economics?', a good place to start is the fact that economics is a social science. Social science is the branch of science that studies society and the relationships of individuals within a society. Besides economics, psychology, sociology and political science are also social sciences, as are important elements of history and geography.

Psychology studies the behaviour and mental processes of an *individual*. Sociology studies the *social* relationships between people in the context of *society*. By contrast, economics, as the name suggests, studies the *economic behaviour* of both individuals and groups of people, and the *economic relationships* between individuals and groups.

Let us give you two examples of what we mean. Our first example (about *individual behaviour*) is from an important part of economics known as demand theory, which is covered in Chapter 3. The theory addresses consumer behaviour, or how we behave when we go shopping. Why, for example, do people generally buy more strawberries as the price of strawberries falls?

Our second example introduces an important *economic relationship*. Having explained demand, we must go a stage further and look at how consumers interact with firms or producers. Firms supply and sell the goods that consumers buy, and economists call the 'place' in which goods are bought and sold a market. Indeed, before you started this economics course, you may well have heard the words 'supply and demand' and thought that is what economics is about. Well, in large measure that is true, particularly in the early chapters of this book, which cover Unit 1 of the specification.

TEST YOURSELF 1.1
What is economics the study of?

Economics and scientific methodology

The essentials of scientific methodology, in the context of the demand theory we will look at in Chapter 3, are shown in the flowchart in Figure 1.1. Scientists start off by observing some aspect of the universe (in the natural sciences), or some aspect of human behaviour, in the case of the social sciences. In the case of demand theory, the starting point — shown in the uppermost box of Figure 1.1 — is observations of how individual consumers react to changes in the prices of the goods and services they buy. Demand theory then develops from the making of a tentative description, known as a *hypothesis*, of what has been observed. Hypothesis construction is depicted in the second box from the top in the flowchart. In the third box, predictions about human behaviour are deduced from the hypothesis, such as that an individual will always respond to a lower price by demanding more of the good in question.

This prediction is then tested against collected evidence about how individuals behave in the market place (the fourth box from the top). At this stage, the hypothesis becomes a *theory*. (The difference between the two is that whereas a hypothesis is a proposed explanation for something, a theory is when a hypothesis is tested and survives the test.)

At this stage, we are in the bottom left-hand box of Figure 1.1. However, this does not mean that the theory is true in all circumstances. All it says is that the hypothesis has survived the test or tests to which it has been exposed. It might not survive stronger tests, which may not yet have been devised. Scientific method is based on the possibility of *falsification* or *refutation* of a hypothesis.

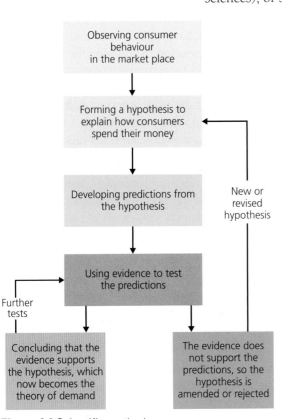

Figure 1.1 Scientific method

If a hypothesis fails to survive the tests to which it is exposed, one of two things can happen. The bottom right-hand box of Figure 1.1 shows the first possibility: outright rejection of the hypothesis. For example, a hypothesis that consumers *always* respond to price cuts by demanding *less* would surely be rejected (as would the hypothesis that consumers *always* respond to a price cut by demanding more of a good). The other possibility, which often occurs in economics, is that the hypothesis is changed, usually by watering it down, so as to make it less deterministic. In the case of demand theory, as the extension material on page 49 in Chapter 3 explains, watering down means that demand theory predicts that *in most but not all cases*, consumers respond to price cuts by demanding more of a good. Watered down in this way, the demand hypothesis survives the tests to which it is exposed, and becomes 'the first "law" of demand'.

TEST YOURSELF 1.2
Give another example of how a theory can be developed from a hypothesis in economics.

3

Social sciences and natural sciences

In 1905, the world-famous physicist, Albert Einstein, developed a theory of gravitation which predicted, among other things, that as it approaches Earth, light from a distant star is 'bent' by the gravitational pull of the sun. However, Einstein's theory could not be tested until 1919 when there was a general eclipse of the sun. The theory survived the 1919 test, although much more recent tests have thrown doubt on parts of it. As is the case with Einstein's theory, natural science theories are usually much 'harder' than the theories associated with 'softer' social sciences such as economics. As we have noted, economic theories often survive only through allowing a significant number of exceptions to their central predictions, which, according to critics, turns the theories into little more than generalisations.

To quote the economist Ha-Joon Chang, economics is not a science like biology is a science. In his book *Economics: The User's Guide*, Chang argues that many economists believe, and tell other people, that economics is a 'value-free' science, like physics or chemistry. However, Chang argues that economics is a fundamentally political and moral subject in relation to choosing the best option. Whereas the particles and compounds studied by natural scientists do not hold political and moral views, human beings who populate the economy do, and so we cannot fully understand the economy without understanding politics and ethics. No economic argument can be free from politics and ethics: for example, the economic case for trying to persuade people to buy fair-trade products.

TEST YOURSELF 1.3
The study of economics can be helped by looking at other relevant social sciences. Can you name three?

Very often economists respond to the criticism that their subject is 'soft' by arguing that they are only concerned with 'positive economics', which they claim is based on quite strict use of scientific methodology. Positive economics is concerned with 'what is' and 'what will happen' if a course of action is taken or not taken. In contrast, 'normative economics' is concerned with 'what *should* or *ought* to be'.

The difference between positive and normative statements

A lot of economics is concerned with what people *ought* to do. This is particularly true of the government. Ought the government to try to reduce unemployment, control inflation and achieve a 'fair' distribution of income and wealth? Most people probably think that all these objectives are desirable. However, they all fall within the remit of normative economics. Normative economics is about value judgements and views, but because people have different views about what is right and wrong, **normative statements** cannot be scientifically tested.

KEY TERMS
positive statement a statement of fact that can be scientifically tested to see if it is correct or incorrect.

normative statement a statement that includes a value judgement and cannot be refuted just by looking at the evidence.

By contrast, a **positive statement** can be tested to see if it is incorrect. If a positive statement does not pass the test, it is falsified. A positive statement does not have to be true, however. For example, the statement that the Earth is flat is a positive statement. Although once believed to be true, the statement was falsified with the growth of scientific evidence. The key point is that positive statements can in principle be tested and possibly falsified, while normative statements cannot. Normative statements include ethical, or moral, judgements. Words such as *ought*, *should*, *better* and *worse* often provide clues that a statement is normative.

To take an economic example, consider the statement 'If the state pension were to be abolished, a million older people would die of hypothermia.' This is a positive statement which could be tested, though few if any people would want to do this. By contrast, the statement 'The state pension ought to be abolished because it is a waste of scarce resources' is normative, containing an implicit value judgement about the meaning of the word 'waste'.

TEST YOURSELF 1.4

Which one of the following is an example of a normative economic statement?

A Increased use of diesel-engine cars will lead to more atmospheric pollution.

B Higher taxes always lead to higher prices.

C The government should spend more on roads.

D Consumers generally act rationally.

How value judgements influence economic decision making and policy

Economists emphasise the distinction between normative and positive economics, but they often forget that the decision to study one over the other is itself a value judgement, and therefore a normative decision. A value judgement is about whether something is desirable or not — if we believe it is more desirable to study what *is* happening in the economy rather than what *ought* to happen, we have made a value judgement. Economics necessarily requires that government ministers make value-based judgements when deciding on economic policies. Despite this, economists often wrongly insist that the subject is value-judgement free.

Several years ago, the then chancellor of the exchequer, the UK government minister in overall charge of economic policy, said: 'Rising unemployment and the recession have been the price that we have had to pay to get inflation down. That price is well worth paying.' Government ministers are seldom as frank as this, knowing that their political opponents and the media will immediately seize on the argument that those in power are uncaring and cynical people. However, the quote does serve to illustrate how decision makers make value judgements when making economic policy decisions.

On occasion, government ministers make decisions on issues such as where a new airport should be located or whether high-speed trains are worthwhile. Before making decisions on issues such as these, the policy-makers know in advance that large swathes of the population will strongly oppose whatever decision is eventually made. To ward off public hostility, government ministers usually create the illusion that the decision-making process is completely scientific and objective. To do this, they hire independent 'experts' to provide advice. But the choice of expert in itself involves a value judgement. Do you choose someone you know in advance is sympathetic to the government's cause, or are you more willing to go for an independent maverick? Whichever way you go, the so-called scientific processes used by the 'experts' to reach their conclusions may be riddled with value judgements. A classic case involved weighing up the costs and benefits of the location of a third London airport, which ultimately depended on putting money values on an hour of a business person's time, and an hour of a holidaymaker's time. It was quickly found that when different values were put on these, the airport location recommended by the experts would have 'lost out' under different costing criteria. (By the time the decision was made in 2016 to choose to build a new

STUDY TIP
Make sure you understand fully how value judgements link to normative statements.

runway at Heathrow rather than to expand Gatwick or Stanstead, the use of cost–benefit analysis had gone out of fashion for UK governments.)

Protest against third runway at Heathrow

The impact of moral and political judgements

Whatever decision is eventually made in the course of framing government economic policy, there will always be winners and losers who gain or suffer as a result of the decision. Governments often claim they have a moral right to make such decisions. They argue that their political manifesto published *before* the previous general election gives them the mandate, supported by the voters, to carry out their policies, regardless of the fact that among the electorate there will inevitably be some losers.

One example is provided by US President Donald Trump's decision in 2018 to implement a 'zero tolerance' policy on illegal immigration into the USA. The policy involved splitting adult illegal migrants from their children, however young they may have been, and keeping the children in wire cages along the US border with Mexico. On humanitarian grounds the policy was so unpopular in the USA that it was quickly abandoned in a policy 'U-turn', though the other parts of Trump's extreme anti-immigrant policy still remained in place.

SECTION 1.1 SUMMARY
- Economic methodology involves the application of tested economic theories to explain real-world economic behaviour.
- It is important to understand the difference between positive and normative statements. A positive statement can be tested to see if it is correct or false; a normative statement is a statement that includes a value judgement which cannot be refuted purely by looking at the evidence.
- A value judgement is about whether something is desirable or not.
- Government ministers make value-based judgements when deciding on economic policies.
- There will always be winners who gain and losers who suffer as a result of government policy decisions.

1.2 The nature and purpose of economic activity

Needs and wants

The production of goods and services to satisfy people's needs and wants is the central purpose of economic activity. A **need** is something people must have, something that they cannot do without. Food provides an example. If people starve, they will eventually die. By contrast, a **want** is something people would *like* to have, but which is not essential for survival. It is not absolutely necessary, but it is a good thing to have. Books provide an example. Some people might argue that books are a need because they think they can't do without them. But they don't need literature to survive. They do need to eat. (It is worth noting that food can be both a need and a want, depending on the type of food. Protein and vitamins are needs, but bars of chocolate are wants. People don't need to eat chocolate to survive.)

Satisfying people's needs and wants means improving **economic welfare**. Welfare is a concept bandied about a lot by economists, but often without a clear indication of what the concept means. Welfare basically means human happiness — anything that makes a person happier improves their economic welfare, though obviously we must ignore activities such as theft where one person becomes better off through stealing from other people. Short-term happiness may be at the expense of long-term happiness. The consumption of more material goods and services *usually* improves economic welfare, though, in the long term, consuming more and more food, and the wrong type of food, can lead to health problems.

> **KEY TERMS**
> **need** something that is necessary for human survival, such as food, clothing, warmth or shelter.
> **want** something that is desirable, such as fashionable clothing, but is not necessary for human survival.
> **economic welfare** the economic well-being of an individual, a group within society, or an economy.

> **STUDY TIP**
> Make sure you can explain the meaning of the term 'economic welfare'.

There are also important elements of human happiness and welfare that have nothing to do with the consumption of material goods. These include quality of life factors, such as the pleasure gained from family and friends or from contemplating a beautiful view.

> **TEST YOURSELF 1.5**
> With an example of each, explain the difference between a need and a want.

The key decisions of what and how to produce

We mentioned at the beginning of this chapter that decisions are made about what to produce, how to produce and who is to benefit from the goods and services produced. How these decisions are made depends upon the nature of the **economic system** within the economy. The set of institutions within which a community decides what, how and for whom to produce is called an economic system. Although the problem of scarcity is fundamental and common to all forms of human society, from humble tribal groupings of hunters or gatherers in the Amazonian forest, to rich national states such as the United States of America, different economic systems have evolved in different societies.

> **SYNOPTIC LINK**
> The key economic concept of scarcity is explained in section 1.4 of this chapter, and also in section 1.3, in the context of scarce environmental resources.

Perhaps the most widely used method of defining and classifying economic systems is according to the way or mechanism through which scarce resources reach the people who eventually consume or use them. Although there are a variety of ways in which wealth and purchasing power can be allocated amongst individuals, including inheritance and other types of gift, theft and luck or chance, such as winning a fortune on the National Lottery, the two mechanisms by which economic systems are defined are the market mechanism (or price mechanism) and the command mechanism (or planning mechanism). An economic system in which goods and services are purchased through the price mechanism in a system of markets is called a **market economy**, whereas one in which government officials or planners allocate economic resources to firms and other productive enterprises is called a **command economy** (or planned economy).

Between these extremes, many economies, particularly those of the developed countries of western Europe such as the United Kingdom, are called **mixed economies**. A mixed economy, as the name suggests, is a mixture of different types of economic system. A mixed economy contains both a large market sector and a large non-market sector in which the planning mechanism operates. Figure 1.2 illustrates mixed economies in relation to planned and market economies.

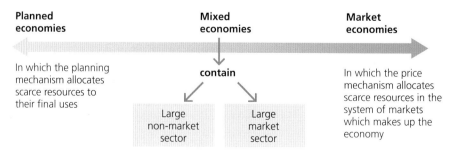

Figure 1.2 Command economies, mixed economies and market economies

KEY TERMS

economic system the set of institutions within which a community decides what, how and for whom to produce.

market economy an economy in which goods and services are purchased through the price mechanism in a system of markets.

command economy (also known as a **planned economy**) an economy in which government officials or planners allocate economic resources to firms and other productive enterprises.

mixed economy an economy that contains both a large market sector and a large non-market sector in which the planning mechanism operates.

TEST YOURSELF 1.6

To what extent is the UK economy a mixed economy?

CASE STUDY 1.1

Allocating resources through the price mechanism and the planning mechanism

In a pure market economy, the price mechanism performs the central economic task of allocating scarce resources among competing uses through the markets which make up the economy. Transport costs and lack of information may create barriers that separate or break up markets. In past centuries, such barriers often prevented markets from operating outside the relatively small geographical area of a single country or even a small region within a country.

However, while some markets exist in a particular geographical location — for example, a street market or until quite recently the London Stock Exchange — many markets do not. In recent years, modern developments have allowed goods to be transported more easily and at lower cost, and have helped in the transmission of market information via telephone and the internet. This has enabled many markets, especially commodity and raw material markets and markets in financial services, to become truly global or international markets functioning on a worldwide basis.

A complete command economy is an economy in which all decisions about what, how, how much, when, where and for whom to produce are taken by a central planning authority, issuing commands or directives to all the households and producers in the society. Such a system could only exist within a very rigid and controlled political framework because of the restrictions on individual decision making that are implied.

In much the same way as a pure market economy, in which the price mechanism alone allocates resources, is a theoretical abstraction, so no economy in the real world can properly be described as a complete or pure planned economy. Before the collapse of the communist political system around 1990, the countries of eastern Europe were centrally planned economies. However, they were not pure planned economies. Production but not consumption was planned. Consumers often had to queue to get consumer goods, whose prices were fixed by the planners. Shortages resulted, which, together with the generally inferior quality of consumer goods, contributed to the breakdown of the command economies.

Some communist countries still exist, namely the People's Republic of China, North Korea, Vietnam and Cuba. However, all these countries, with the exception until recently of North Korea, have encouraged the growth of markets to a greater or lesser extent. They have communist political systems, but they have moved away from being pure command economies. In a sense, China is now more capitalist than the USA and the mixed economies of western Europe. The term 'state-capitalism' is now used to describe much of China's economy.

Follow-up questions

1 Distinguish between a pure market economy and the market sector of a mixed economy.
2 What is the other name of a planned economy?
3 With the help of Chapter 3, explain how the price mechanism allocates scarce resources between competing uses.
4 Why did the command economies of central and eastern Europe, such as the old Soviet Union, break up?

CASE STUDY 1.2

The UK as a mixed economy

The UK economy developed into a mixed economy after the Second World War ended in 1945, when a number of important industries such as coal, rail and steel were nationalised and taken into public ownership. Previously, the 1944 Education Act had extended state provision of education, and the creation of the National Health Service in 1948 did the same for healthcare.

For about 30 years after the end of the Second World War, from the 1940s to the 1970s, the majority of UK citizens (and the major political parties) agreed that the mixed economy was working well. Most people believed that certain types of economic activity, particularly the production and distribution of consumer goods and services, were best suited to private enterprise and the market economy. But people also accepted that utility industries such as gas and electricity should be nationalised, and that important services such as education, healthcare and roads should in part be provided by government, outside the market, and financed through the tax system. In short, a consensus existed around the belief that the mixed economy was right for the UK.

However, from about 1980 onwards, many economists and politicians began to blame the mixed economy for the UK's deteriorating economic performance relative to that of its main competitors in western Europe and Japan. Critics argued that the public and non-market sectors of the economy were inefficient and wealth consuming rather than wealth creating. They had become too big and needed cutting down to size. Critics of the mixed economy argued that a concerted effort should be made to change the nature of the UK economy fundamentally, by increasing private ownership and market production.

Successive governments implemented policies that changed the nature of the mix in favour of private ownership and market forces, at the expense of public ownership and state planning. The UK economy is now much closer to being a pure market and private enterprise economy than it was 45 years ago. The three main policies used to change the nature of the UK economy have been privatisation, marketisation and deregulation, polices which collectively can be called economic liberalisation.

Privatisation involved the sale of state-owned assets such as nationalised industries to private owners. This was often accompanied by marketisation (or commercialisation), whereby prices are charged for goods and services that the state previously provided free of charge. Deregulation, the third aspect of liberalisation, attempts to remove barriers to entry and government red tape and bureaucracy from the operation of markets.

Follow-up questions

1 Critics of the UK economy have called it a 'mixed-up' economy rather than a 'mixed economy'. What do you think they mean?
2 What is meant by the term 'private enterprise'?
3 Distinguish between privatisation and marketisation.
4 Do you think that there is now a case for increasing rather than reducing state ownership of UK industry? Justify your answer.

SECTION 1.2 SUMMARY

- A need is something people must have, something that they cannot do without.
- A want is something people would like to have, but which is not essential for survival.
- How decisions are made about what to produce, how to produce and who is to benefit from the goods and services produced depends upon the nature of the economic system.
- Market economies, command economies and mixed economies are examples of economic systems, defined in terms of whether or not the price mechanism or the planning mechanism allocates scarce resources among competing uses.
- Economic systems can also be defined in terms of who owns the means of production.
- The UK economy is often called a mixed economy, being on the one hand a mix of market and non-market sectors and on the other hand a mix of privately owned and publicly owned sectors.

1.3 Economic resources

For most people, most of the time, increased consumption of material goods is an important part of improving economic welfare. Most of the goods we consume must first be produced. This requires the use of economic resources. These goods are scarce in relation to demand, which gives rise to the need for rationing and economising in their use.

The basic nature of **production** is shown in Figure 1.3. Production is a process, or set of processes, that converts inputs into outputs. The eventual outputs are the consumer goods and services that go to make up our standard of living, though inputs are of course also used to produce the **capital goods** that are necessary for the eventual production of **consumer goods**.

KEY TERMS

production converts inputs or factor services into outputs of goods and services.

capital good (also known as a **producer good**) a good which is used in the production of other goods or services.

consumer good a good which is consumed by individuals or households to satisfy their needs or wants.

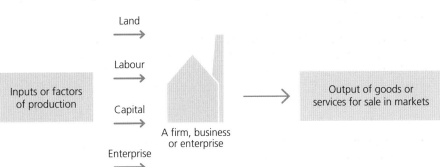

Figure 1.3 The basic nature of production

The factors of production

Economists call the inputs into the production process, which are shown in Figure 1.3, the **factors of production**. Four factors of production are usually identified. These are land, labour, capital and enterprise, the last often being called the entrepreneurial input.

KEY TERM

factors of production inputs into the production process, such as land, labour, capital and enterprise.

STUDY TIP

It is important to understand how factors of production are *inputs* used to produce *output* of goods and services.

Entrepreneurs are different from the other factors of production. They are the people who address the issues introduced earlier, deciding what to produce, how to produce it and for whom to produce it. An entrepreneur decides how much of the other factors of production, including labour, to employ. The costs of employing land, labour and capital, together with the cost of the entrepreneur's own services, become the firm's costs of production. In essence, the entrepreneur is a financial risk taker and decision maker. Profit, which is the entrepreneur's financial reward, results from successful decision making. Entrepreneurial profit is the profit left over after the cost of employing the other factors of production is deducted from the sales revenue gained from selling the goods and services the entrepreneur decides to produce.

The environment as a scarce resource

Environmental resources comprise all the natural resources that are used or can be used in the economic system. These are:

- physical resources, such as soil, water, forests, fisheries and minerals
- gases, such as hydrogen and oxygen
- abstract resources, such as solar energy, wind energy, the beauty of the landscape, good air and clean water

KEY TERMS

renewable resource a resource, such as timber, that with careful management can be renewed as it is used.

non-renewable resource (also known as a **finite resource**) a resource, such as oil, which is scarce and runs out as it is used.

Environmental resources can be split into renewable and non-renewable resources, with the latter further divided into recyclable and non-recyclable resources. **Renewable resources**, which are reproducible and perpetually maintainable, include forests, animals and water. The availability of these resources depends, however, on their management by humans. By contrast, **non-renewable resources**, such as oil, gas and minerals, cannot be regenerated or their regeneration is so slow that the stock of resources cannot meaningfully be increased. These are **finite resources**. Recyclable non-renewable resources such as minerals, paper and glass can be reused in the economic system. In theory, all of these resources can be recycled but it is not always possible and economic to recycle more than a small fraction. Non-recyclable resources such as coal, gas and oil are finite in the sense that, once used, their stock is no longer available for future use.

Oil is a non-renewable resource

TEST YOURSELF 1.7

Distinguish between a non-renewable and a renewable environmental resource.

Environmental resources are part of the factor of production, land. Some environmental resources, such as the air we breathe and the water we drink, are often described as the 'free gifts of nature'. However, this view can be questioned. In most countries and regions where large numbers of people live, clean air and drinkable water are scarce commodities and not the 'free gifts of nature'. Resources which could be put to other uses are used instead to produce clean air and water. The need to get rid of the effects of pollution created by humankind means that clean air and water are scarce and not free. Production and consumption activities taking place in the economy affect and often damage the natural environment.

CASE STUDY 1.3

George Monbiot on how we are trashing the planet

George Monbiot is a British writer known for his environmental, political activism. He writes a weekly column for the *Guardian* newspaper.

In November 2017, George Monbiot published an article about how humankind is trashing planet Earth. He argued that economics teaches us to believe in the holy grail of economic growth. Monbiot argued that 'already we are bursting through the physical limits of the planet that sustains us'. Monbiot rejects the view that, through green consumerism, we can reconcile perpetual growth with planetary survival. One recent article, published in the journal *Environment and Behaviour*, finds that those who identify themselves as conscious consumers use more energy and carbon than those who do not.

The richer we are, the bigger our ecological footprint, regardless of our good intentions. Those who see themselves as green consumers, the paper found, 'mainly focus on behaviours that have relatively small benefits'.

A global growth rate of 3% means that the size of the world economy doubles every 24 years. This causes environmental crises to accelerate at a rate that cannot be sustained.

To read George Monbiot's article in full, access **www.monbiot.com** *and search for 'Everything must go'. You can access all of Monbiot's articles on the same site.*

Follow-up questions

1 What is meant by economic growth?
2 Economists generally seem to think that economic growth is a good thing and that we must always aim for more growth. Explain why you think this is good or bad.
3 Discuss the environmental effect of people choosing to drink bottled water in preference to tap water.
4 Should all of your reading be conducted online without the use of printed textbooks such as this one?

SECTION 1.3 SUMMARY

- Increased consumption of material goods is an important part of improving economic welfare.
- Most of the goods we consume must first be produced.
- This requires the use of economic resources.
- These goods are scarce in relation to demand, which gives rise to the need for rationing and economising in their use.
- Production is a process, or set of processes, that converts inputs into outputs.
- Inputs are called factors of production and are economic resources.
- Land, labour, capital and enterprise (often called the entrepreneurial input) are the factors of production.
- The entrepreneur is the factor of production that decides what to produce, how to produce and for whom to produce.
- Inputs are also used to produce the capital goods that are necessary for the eventual production of consumer goods and services.
- Environmental resources comprise all the natural resources that are used or can be used in the economic system.

1.4 Scarcity, choice and the allocation of resources

Scarcity: the fundamental economic problem

We have already mentioned that we live on a finite planet in which most economic resources are limited. As we have seen, their use usually has to be rationed either by the price mechanism or by the planning mechanism. The **fundamental economic problem** is therefore **scarcity**. In a world of scarcity, people (even the very rich) have limited incomes, which means that they face a budget constraint. When the price mechanism is rationing scarce resources between competing uses, a budget constraint represents all the combinations of goods and services that a consumer may purchase given current prices and their limited income.

> **KEY TERMS**
>
> **fundamental economic problem** how best to make decisions about the allocation of scarce resources among competing uses so as to improve and maximise human happiness and welfare.
>
> **scarcity** results from the fact that people have unlimited wants but resources to meet these wants are limited. In essence, people would like to consume more goods and services than the economy is able to produce with its limited resources.

The need for choice

> **KEY TERM**
>
> **choice** choosing between alternatives when making a decision on how to use scarce resources.

If goods are scarce and incomes are limited, a **choice** or choices have to be made. Consider, for example, a family with a weekly income of £1,200. The family currently spends £350 on housing, £350 on food, £300 on other goods and services, including heating and lighting, and £100 on entertainment. The family's total weekly spending on goods and services is thus £1,100, meaning the family manages to save £100. Suddenly, the cost of housing rises to £550. To avoid getting into debt, and assuming that family income cannot increase, one or more probably unpleasant choices will have to be made. An obvious possibility is to cut down on entertainment, such as visits to the cinema. Other possibilities could be spending less on home heating, buying cheaper food, cutting down on alcoholic drink and stopping saving. Something will have to be given up. Unless the family gets into debt or its income increases, it will have to economise on its spending and saving decisions.

You must also appreciate the fact that, even without an increase in house prices, scarcity means that individuals and households are constantly making choices about how to spend their limited incomes and how to make the best use of their time. A decision to spend more on a holiday, for example, means that a family chooses to spend less on other goods, or to save less.

Choices have an opportunity cost

A need for choice arises whenever an economic agent (for example, an individual, a household or a firm) has to choose between two or more alternatives which are mutually exclusive, in the sense that it is impossible or impractical to achieve both at the same time. In the jargon of economics, an **opportunity cost** is involved.

If you ask friends who haven't studied economics the meaning of the word 'cost', typically they will answer that cost is the money cost either of producing a good or of buying a good. Economists, by contrast, focus on opportunity cost. The opportunity cost of any choice, decision or course of action is measured in terms of the alternatives that have to be given up.

Economists generally assume that people behave rationally. Rational behaviour means people try to make decisions in their self-interest or to maximise their private benefit. When a choice has to be made, people always choose what they think at the time is the best alternative, which means that the second best or next best alternative is rejected. Providing people are rational, the opportunity cost of any decision or choice is the next best alternative sacrificed or forgone. For example, if you choose to spend half an hour watching *EastEnders* on TV, the opportunity cost is the lost opportunity to spend this time reading a magazine or book.

EXTENSION MATERIAL
Rational behaviour and opportunity cost

Look carefully at the sentence in the previous paragraph about opportunity cost: *When a choice has to be made, people always choose what they think at the time is the best alternative, which means that the second best or next best alternative is rejected.* The words 'think at the time' are quite important. Suppose you decide to see a film, believing at the time you are going to enjoy the film. Two hours later, coming out of the cinema, you say 'that was a load of rubbish, I wish I hadn't bothered'. Nevertheless, at the time the decision was made, deciding to watch the film was a rational decision because you believed you would enjoy watching it. Having left the cinema, irrational behaviour would be going back to the box office and paying good money to see the film again.

Even if the film can be watched freely on television, there is still an opportunity cost, though in this case it only involves time. Time is scarce, and the 2 hours spent watching the film cannot be spent on some other activity such as reading a book. A choice has to be made between the two activities. Of course, the way the choice is exercised will differ for different people, even if everyone enjoys both watching films and reading. People with plenty of time to spare — for example, retired or unemployed people — value time less highly than a City trader working in a dealing room from 7 a.m. until 9 p.m.

Going to a cinema to watch a film is, of course, a consumer activity. People have to think carefully about how they spend their limited incomes. In economics this is known as a budget constraint. Money spent on one good cannot be spent on another good. But there is always an opportunity cost when deciding to consume a good, involving time if not money.

TEST YOURSELF 1.10
Give an example of an opportunity cost facing an A-level student when choosing to spend a whole evening playing computer games.

Firms also have to make choices about what and how to produce. Consider a textile manufacturer who can produce either shirts or dresses from the same production line, but not both goods at the same time. In this situation, the opportunity cost of producing more shirts is the number of dresses sacrificed or forgone. Suppose also that both shirts and dresses can be produced using one of two different technologies. These are a labour-intensive technology involving lots of workers but very little capital equipment, and a capital-intensive technology in which there are very few workers but expensive automated capital equipment. Given the budget constraint facing the firm, the opportunity cost of choosing one method of production is the sacrificed opportunity to use the other method.

A further example of opportunity cost arises when a teenager makes a decision about whether to leave school and get a job, or to go to university. Very often this involves the choice between income now and income in the future. Economists call this inter-temporal choice, or choice over time.

SYNOPTIC LINK
Rational and irrational behaviour are key concepts in behavioural economics, described in Chapter 2.

QUANTITATIVE SKILLS 1.1

Worked example: calculating an opportunity cost

A small electrical goods manufacturer can produce either TV sets or radio sets using all its available resources. Table 1.1 shows the different combinations of the two goods the firm can produce.

Table 1.1 Production possibilities for TVs and radio sets

TV sets	Radio sets
0	30
1	29
2	27
3	24
4	20
5	15
6	9
7	0

What happens to the opportunity cost of TV sets in terms of radios, as TV set production increases from zero to seven sets?

If the firm chooses to produce only one TV set, its opportunity cost is one radio set foregone (30 minus 29 radio sets). Performing a similar calculation when TV set production is increased by an extra unit, the opportunity cost of the second TV set is two radio sets. All the opportunity costs are set out in Table 1.2:

Table 1.2 Opportunity costs of producing an extra TV set

1st TV set	1 radio set (30 – 29)
2nd TV set	2 radio sets (29 – 27)
3rd TV set	3 radio sets (27 – 24)
4th TV set	4 radio sets (24 – 20)
5th TV set	5 radio sets (20 – 15)
6th TV set	6 radio sets (15 – 9)
7th TV set	9 radio sets (9 – 0)

The data show an increasing opportunity cost in terms of radio sets forgone as production of TV sets increases.

SECTION 1.4 SUMMARY

- The economic problem is how limited resources are used in relation to people's desires and wants.
- The economic problem results from relative scarcity.
- Scarcity results in the need for choice.
- Whenever a choice has to be made, there is an opportunity cost.
- The opportunity cost of any decision is the next best alternative forgone.
- Economists generally assume that people are rational, choosing the best alternative available.

1.5 Production possibility diagrams

KEY TERMS

production possibility frontier: a curve depicting the various combinations of two products (or types of products) that can be produced when all the available resources are fully and efficiently employed.

technical progress: new and better ways of making goods and new techniques for producing more output from scarce resources.

So far, we have focused mainly on how scarcity and choice may affect firms, families and individuals at the microeconomic level. In much the same way, but on a far grander scale, the economy of the nation as a whole faces a similar need for choice. To explain how the economic problem affects the whole economy, we will use a diagram which you will come across again and again in your economics course — a production possibility diagram.

The key feature of a production possibility diagram is a **production possibility frontier (PPF)** or production possibility curve. A *PPF* illustrates the different combinations of two goods, or two sets of goods, that can be produced with a fixed quantity of resource, providing we assume that all available resources are being utilised to the full. The *PPF* in Figure 1.4 illustrates the different combinations of capital goods and consumer goods that the whole economy can produce when all the economy's resources are employed, with no spare capacity. To put it another way, the *PPF* shows what the economy can produce, assuming that all the labour, capital and land at the country's disposal are employed to the full, and assuming a given state of **technical progress**.

Given that resources and capacity are limited, a choice has to be made about the type of good to produce. Look closely at points *X* and *Y* on the diagram. Point *X* shows the maximum possible output of consumer goods, assuming that the economy only produces consumer goods (i.e. no capital goods are produced). Likewise, point *Y* shows the maximum possible output of capital goods, assuming that the economy only produces capital goods. In fact, points *X* and *Y* show the two extreme production possibilities, since all goods are either consumer goods or capital goods. Finally, the line drawn between points *X* and *Y* in Figure 1.4 is the economy's production possibility frontier. The *PPF* shows all the different combinations of consumer goods and capital goods

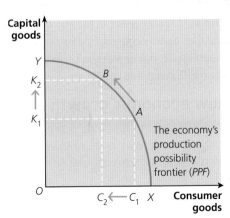

Figure 1.4 Using a production possibility frontier diagram to illustrate the economic problem

17

STUDY TIP
You must learn to draw and interpret production possibility diagrams, which are important in both microeconomics and macroeconomics. At the micro level they can be used to illustrate scarcity, choice, opportunity cost and productive efficiency. At the macro level, they can be used to illustrate economic growth, and full employment and unemployment.

that can be produced, given the assumptions mentioned earlier about full employment of available resources and the state of technical progress. Point A, for example, shows K_1 capital goods and C_1 consumer goods being produced. An increase in capital goods production to K_2, shown at point B, means that consumer goods production falls to C_2. $C_1 - C_2$ is the opportunity cost of producing $K_2 - K_1$ additional capital goods. Whichever combination of capital and consumer goods is actually chosen reflects decisions made in society about allocating scarce resources between competing uses.

QUANTITATIVE SKILLS 1.2

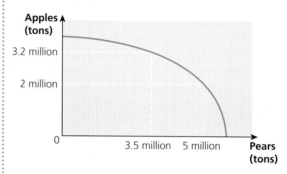

Figure 1.5 Production possibilities for apples and pears

A country is currently producing 3.2 million tons of apples and 3.5 million tons of pears. Calculate the opportunity cost in terms of apples of increasing pear production to 5 million tons.

The opportunity cost of increasing pear production by 1.5 million tons is the sacrifice of 1.2 million tons of apples.

SYNOPTIC LINK
As we explain below, production possibility diagrams can also be used to illustrate economic growth. This is revisited in Chapter 11. Chapter 10 explains another way of illustrating economic growth, in terms of aggregate demand and supply or AD/AS analysis.

Macroeconomic *PPF* diagrams

The production possibility frontier in Figure 1.4 shows the economy *as a whole*, which means that the *PPF* depicts the macro economy. Before we look at some microeconomic production possibility frontiers, we shall explain two important ways in which macroeconomic *PPF* diagrams can be used.

Using a *PPF* diagram to show economic growth

Figure 1.6 shows how a *PPF* diagram can be used to illustrate economic growth. There are two forms of economic growth, which are explained in detail in Chapter 11. These are long-run **economic growth** and short-run economic growth.

Economic growth is defined as the increase in the *potential* level of real output the economy can produce over a period of time: for example, a year. Strictly, this is long-run economic growth, which is not the same as short-run economic growth. If the economy's production possibility

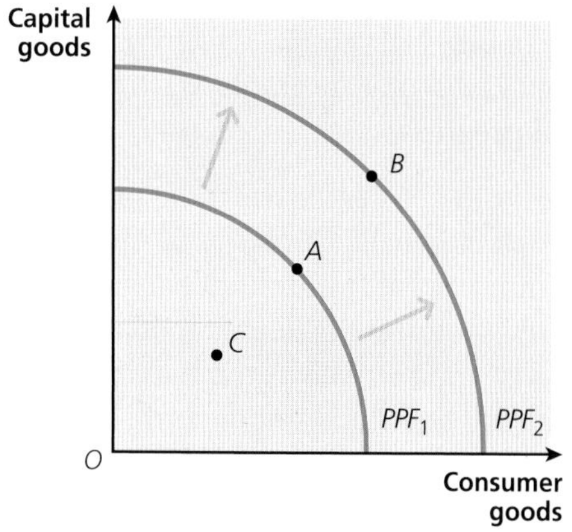

Figure 1.6 Long-run and short-run economic growth

frontier is PPF_1 initially, short-run economic growth is shown by the movement from point C *inside* the frontier to a point, such as point A, *on* the frontier. Long-run economic growth is shown by the *outward* movement of the frontier to PPF_2. The movement from point A to point B depicts long-run economic growth. Short-run growth makes use of spare capacity and takes up the slack in the economy, whereas long-run growth increases total productive capacity.

Using a *PPF* diagram to show full employment and unemployment

As mentioned earlier, all points on a production possibility frontier show full employment of available resources. For a macroeconomic production possibility frontier, this means **full employment** of labour as well as other resources that can be used in the course of production. Thus, points A and B in Figure 1.7 show full employment when the economy's production possibility frontier is in the position indicated. By contrast, a point *inside* the *PPF*, such as point X, shows that some resources, including labour, are not being employed. There is unused capacity in the economy. (Note that if long-run economic growth were to move the *PPF* outward to a new position, points A and B on the 'old' production possibility frontier would now be points of **unemployment**, as they would be located inside the new 'further out' frontier.)

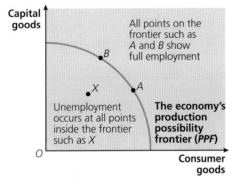

Figure 1.7 Using a production possibility curve diagram to show full employment and unemployment in the economy

Microeconomic *PPF* diagrams

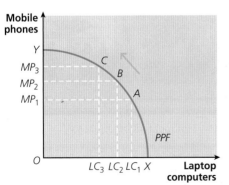

Figure 1.8 The production possibility frontier facing a firm producing mobile phones and laptop computers

Look carefully at the microeconomic production possibility frontier in Figure 1.8. We can tell this is a *microeconomic* diagram because of the labels on the two axes of the graph. The diagram depicts a situation in which a firm can produce both mobile phones and laptop computers from the resources it has available. As in Figure 1.4, points X and Y show the extreme possibilities facing the firm. Point X on the horizontal axis shows the maximum possible output of laptop computers — providing no mobile phones are produced. This means that all available resources are devoted to the production of laptop computers. Conversely, point Y on the vertical axis shows the opposite situation: the maximum possible output of mobile phones when zero laptop computers are produced. As was the case in the macroeconomic production possibility diagrams, all points on the *PPF* between X and Y show different combinations of the two goods being produced between the two extreme possibilities.

We can use Figure 1.8 to explain a number of important economic relationships. These are described overleaf.

Scarcity, resource allocation and choice (revisited)

A *PPF* diagram such as Figure 1.8 shows different possible ways in which scarce resources can be allocated between competing uses. This involves choice. Compared to the **resource allocation** at point *A*, point *B* shows the effect of shifting more resources into the production of mobile phones, with fewer resources being allocated to laptop computer production.

TEST YOURSELF 1.12
Provide another example of a production possibility frontier diagram illustrating a microeconomic idea or concept.

SYNOPTIC LINK
Link the microeconomic use of production possibility frontier diagrams to the coverage of the price mechanism in Chapter 3 and to production, costs and revenue in Chapter 4.

KEY TERM

resource allocation the process through which the available factors of production are assigned to produce different goods and services, e.g. how many of society's economic resources are devoted to supplying different products such as food, cars, healthcare and defence.

Opportunity cost (revisited)

Production possibility diagrams provide a very good way of illustrating opportunity cost. Suppose, for example, that the firm in Figure 1.8 initially produces MP_1 mobile phones and LC_1 laptop computers. This combination of the two goods is shown at point *A* in the diagram. A decision by the manufacturer to increase production of mobile phones from MP_1 to MP_2 means that computer production falls by $LC_1 - LC_2$. Moving from point *A* to point *B* on the curve, the fall in computer production is the opportunity cost of the increase in phone production.

A large company such as Apple must decide how to allocate its resources

Look now at the shape of the *PPF* in Figure 1.8. You can see that the slope of the curve falls, moving up the curve from point *A* to point *B*, and indeed to all other points further up the curve. There is a reason for this. The slope shows the opportunity cost of producing more mobile phones in terms of the laptop computers that have to be sacrificed. When mobile phone production increases from MP_1 to MP_2 laptop computer production falls by $LC_1 - LC_2$. This is the opportunity cost involved. But suppose mobile phone production increases again by the same amount as before (which means that $MP_3 - MP_2$

is the same as $MP_2 - MP_1$). In this situation, shown at point C on the curve, more laptop computers than before have to be given up. $LC_3 - LC_2$ is larger than $LC_2 - LC_1$. The slope of the curve of the production possibility frontier shows that the opportunity cost of producing mobile phones increases as more mobile phones are produced. A greater number of laptop computers have to be sacrificed whenever an extra mobile phone is produced.

Productive efficiency and production possibility diagrams

You will come across the concept of economic efficiency on numerous occasions as you proceed through the course and this book. There are a number of different measures of economic efficiency, one of which is **productive efficiency**. Chapter 5 explains productive efficiency in terms of a firm minimising the average cost of producing a good. In this chapter, we focus on two other ways of explaining the concept, both of which are illustrated by the production possibility curve in Figure 1.9.

Productive efficiency occurs when output is maximised from available inputs. But we know already that a *PPF* shows maximisation of output from available inputs at every point on the curve, though the combination of the two goods (in this case, capital goods and consumer goods) varies at different points on the curve. This means that all points *on* the economy's production possibility frontier shown in Figure 1.9, including points A and B, are productively efficient. By contrast, all points *inside* the *PPF* are productively *in*efficient, including point Z. Productive inefficiency occurs when output is not maximised from available inputs. At point Z, the economy is not employing all the available resources, including, of course, labour. Productive inefficiency is often associated with unemployment.

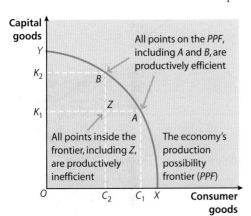

Figure 1.9 Productive efficiency and the economy's *PPF*

Consider now a movement *along* the *PPF* from point A to point B. The diagram is telling us that, when on the *PPF*, more capital goods can be produced only by giving up the production of some consumer goods. This is another way of explaining productive efficiency. Productive efficiency occurs when producing more of one good involves reducing production of other goods. By contrast, when the economy is productively inefficient at point Z, more capital goods *and* consumer goods can be produced by taking up the slack in the economy and making use of idle resources.

TEST YOURSELF 1.13

A production possibility frontier can be used to show all the following **except**:

A all the different combinations of two goods that can be produced from available inputs

B all the productively efficient combinations of output that can be produced from available inputs

C the opportunity cost of producing more of a particular good

D the economic welfare a consumer gains from different combinations of goods

QUANTITATIVE SKILLS 1.3

Worked example: drawing a *PPF* from given data

Draw a production possibility frontier using the data below.

Table 1.3 Production possibility schedule for producing tanks and military aircraft

Tanks	Military aircraft
100	0
90	10
80	20
70	30
60	40
50	50
40	60
30	70
20	80
10	90
0	100

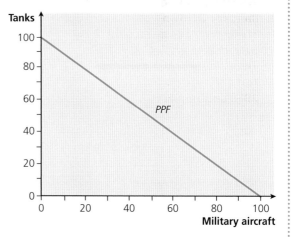

Figure 1.10 *PPF* for tanks and military aircraft

The *PPF* drawn from these data is shown in Figure 1.10.

Unlike all the *PPF*s shown earlier in this chapter, this one shows a constant opportunity cost of 10 military aircraft whenever 10 extra tanks are produced. This means that the *PPF* is a straight line, positioned between the two production possibility extremes of zero tanks and 100 military aircraft, and 100 tanks and zero military aircraft.

TEST YOURSELF 1.14

Suppose the opportunity cost of producing one extra unit of a good in terms of another good sacrificed fell as more of the good was produced. In what way would the shape of the *PPF* differ from those shown in this chapter?

QUANTITATIVE SKILLS 1.4

Interpreting statistical data and performing simple percentage calculations

Table 1.4 shows the proportion of total output exported in selected industries, in January 2010 and January 2019.

Table 1.4 Export proportions for selected manufacturing industries in the UK

Industry	Percentage of total industry output exported, January 2010	Percentage of total industry output exported, January 2019
Alcoholic drinks	14.5	28.6
Petrochemicals	52.9	68.1
Furniture	5.5	10.0
Motor vehicles	39.5	50.6
Computers and electronic and optical products	48.2	58.7
Weapons	9.2	28.1

Source: ONS

(a) **Which industry enjoyed the greatest percentage growth in the proportion of its output exported between January 2010 and January 2019?**
The percentage growth in the proportion of its output exported over the year were for alcohol drinks: 97.2%; petrochemicals: 28.7%; furniture: 81.8%; motor vehicles: 28.1%; computers etc.: 21.8%; weapons: 205.4%. The greatest percentage growth was in weapon exports.

(b) **Is it possible to calculate the actual amount by which petrochemical output changed between January 2010 and January 2019? Explain your answer.**
No. We can calculate the percentage growth but not the actual growth. We need the money value of total output of petrochemicals in January 2010 to enable this calculation to be made..

SECTION 1.5 SUMMARY

- Key economic concepts such as scarcity, choice, opportunity cost, economic growth, and full employment and unemployment, can be illustrated on a production possibility diagram.
- A production possibility frontier illustrates the different combinations of goods that can be produced with a fixed quantity of resources.
- Different economic systems allocate resources between different uses in different ways.
- In a market economy, the price mechanism performs the allocative task.
- The UK economy is a mixed economy, containing a mix of market and non-market sectors, and private and public sectors.
- The nature of the UK mixed economy has changed during the last 40 years.

Questions

1 With an example of each, explain the difference between a positive and a normative statement.

2 What is the fundamental or central economic problem?

3 Relate scarcity to the need to make economic choices and to opportunity cost.

4 Briefly describe the four factors of production.

5 What is a production possibility frontier?

6 Draw a production possibility frontier to illustrate the choice between producing capital goods and consumer goods.

7 Draw a production possibility frontier which illustrates economic growth taking place.

2 Individual economic decision making

This chapter introduces two extremely significant aspects of individual economic decision making. The first is utility theory, an old-established body of theory which underlies the development of demand theory. Then, following a brief discussion of how imperfect information affects individual decision making, we introduce you to the second important part of this chapter, behavioural economics. Behavioural economics is a relatively new part of the subject which provides significant insights into how individuals make economic decisions.

LEARNING OBJECTIVES

These are to understand:

- the significance of utility maximisation for individual economic decision making
- the importance of the margin when making choices
- how imperfect information and asymmetric information affect choice decisions
- the emergence of behavioural economics as an important recent development in economic theory
- important elements of behavioural economics such as bounded rationality, biases in individual decision making and the role of altruism
- how behavioural economics relates to government economic policy

2.1 Consumer behaviour

Rational economic decision making and economic incentives

At the heart of traditional or orthodox demand theory is the assumption that the members of households or consumers always act rationally. **Rational behaviour** means people try to make decisions in their self-interest or to maximise their private benefit. When a choice has to be made, people always choose what they think at the time is the best alternative, which means that the second best or next best alternative is rejected. For households and the individuals within them, rational behaviour means attempting to maximise the welfare, satisfaction or utility gained from the goods and services consumed.

TEST YOURSELF 2.1

Which of the following provides the best reason why consumers become early adopters of a new innovation such as a smart watch, even though they know that they will be paying a high price for the good?

Early adopters are people who:

A like technological gadgets

B get up early to buy in a sale

C base their consumption decisions on the reviews submitted online by existing users

D want to be the first to get new types of product as they come onto the market

Explain your answer.

Utility theory: total and marginal utility, and diminishing marginal utility

What is utility?

Consumers attempt to maximise the welfare or utility they gain from the goods and services they decide to consume. We shall explore this further in the next section, on utility maximisation. In economics, **utility** is usually defined as the pleasure or satisfaction obtained from consumption, and **marginal utility** is the *additional* pleasure or satisfaction obtained from consuming one more unit of something.

TEST YOURSELF 2.2

A family's typical weekly shopping basket might include 'pleasure items' such as packets of crisps and cans of Coca-Cola and other items which fulfil a need and without which life would be more uncomfortable. Are each of the following 'pleasure items' or 'need-fulfilment items'?

• medicine
• chocolate
• daffodil bulbs
• electric light bulbs
• washing-up liquid?

The relationship between total utility and marginal utility

Let us imagine a thirsty child who drinks six glasses of lemonade on a hot sunny afternoon, deriving successively 8, 6, 4, 2, 0 and −2 'units of utility' from each glass consumed. This information is shown in the total and marginal utility schedules in Table 2.1, from which the total and marginal utility curves in Figure 2.1 are plotted. Note that marginal utility is plotted at 'halfway' points.

Table 2.1 Total and marginal utility schedules for lemonade

Glasses of lemonade	Total utility (units of utility)	Marginal utility (units of utility)
0	0	–
1	8	8
2	14	6
3	18	4
4	20	2
5	20	0
6	18	–2

It is important to realise that the total and marginal utility schedules and, likewise, the total and marginal utility curves show exactly the same information, but they show it in different ways. The total utility schedule and the total utility curve show the data cumulatively — for example, when drinking two glasses of lemonade, the thirsty child gains 14 'units of utility' in total. After three glasses, total utility rises to 18 'units of utility', and so on.

In contrast, the marginal utility schedule and the marginal utility curve plot the same data as separate observations, rather than cumulatively. The last unit consumed is always the marginal unit and the utility derived from it is the marginal utility. So, after two drinks, the second glass of lemonade is the marginal unit consumed, yielding a marginal utility of 6 'units of utility'. But when three glasses of lemonade are consumed, the third glass becomes the marginal unit, from which the still partially thirsty child gains a marginal utility of just 4 'units of utility'.

In Figure 2.1, diminishing marginal utility is shown both by the diminishing rate of increase of the slope of the total utility curve drawn in the upper panel of the diagram and by the negative or downward slope of the marginal utility curve in the lower panel. Notice that we have drawn a 'point of satiation' on the diagram, which is reached as the fifth glass of lemonade is drunk. The fifth glass of lemonade yields zero marginal utility. At this point, when marginal utility is zero, total utility is maximised. In the context of food and drink, satiation means being 'full up'. Even if lemonade is free to the consumer, it would be irrational for our 'no-longer-thirsty' child to drink a sixth glass of lemonade. He or she would experience negative marginal utility (or marginal disutility), which is shown by the downward slope of the total utility curve and by the negative position of the lower section of the marginal utility curve.

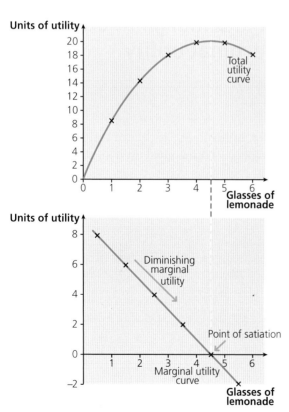

Figure 2.1 An example of total utility and marginal utility curves

QUANTITATIVE SKILLS 2.1

Worked example: calculating marginal utility

An 8-year-old boy decides to enter a competition to see how many jam doughnuts can be eaten in 15 minutes. Table 2.2 shows how many he ate and his total utility schedule.

Table 2.2 Total utility for doughnuts

Jam doughnuts	Total utility (units of utility)	Marginal utility (units of utility)
0	0	
1	6	
2	10	
3	12	
4	12	
5	8	
6	3	

Complete the boy's marginal utility schedule.

The boy's marginal utility schedule is shown in Table 2.3.

Table 2.3 Total and marginal utility for doughnuts

Jam doughnuts	Total utility (units of utility)	Marginal utility (units of utility)
0	0	—
1	6	6
2	10	4
3	12	2
4	12	0
5	8	−4
6	3	−5

KEY TERM

hypothesis of diminishing marginal utility for a single consumer, the marginal utility derived from a good or service diminishes for each additional unit consumed.

The hypothesis (or 'law') of diminishing marginal utility

The numerical examples in Tables 2.1–2.3, and the graph in Figure 2.1, illustrate a famous economic hypothesis, which some would call an economic law: the **hypothesis of diminishing marginal utility**. This simply states that as a person increases consumption of a good — while keeping consumption of other products constant — there is a decline in the marginal utility derived from consuming each additional unit of the good.

TEST YOURSELF 2.3

Explain how traditional economic theory assumes a rational individual will make decisions: for example, when deciding how to respond to a change in a good's price.

SYNOPTIC LINK

In the context of economic methodology, Chapter 1 explained the difference between a hypothesis and a theory. To remind you, whereas a hypothesis is a proposed explanation for something, a theory is when a hypothesis is tested and survives the test.

Adam Smith's diamonds and water paradox

In 1776 the great classical economist Adam Smith wrote about the diamonds and water paradox (or the paradox of value) in his famous book *The Wealth of Nations*. Smith wrote:

> Nothing is more useful than water: but; scarce any thing can be had in exchange for it. A diamond, on the contrary, has scarce any value in use; but a very great quantity of other goods may frequently be had in exchange for it.

In most countries, water has a low price, but a piece of diamond jewellery has a high price. Why does an economy put a much lower value on something vital to sustaining life compared to something that simply looks good? Smith pointed out that practical things that we use every day have a *value in use*, but often have little or no *value in exchange*. On the other hand, some of the things that often have the greatest value in the market or in exchange, such as a drawing by Picasso, have little or no practical use other than, in this case, as ornamentation.

Understanding the diamonds and water paradox comes through first understanding the economic terms 'marginal utility' and 'scarcity'. Scarcity relates to how little of a good there is compared to what people are demanding. Marginal utility is the additional welfare a person gains from using or purchasing an additional unit of the good. People are willing to pay a higher price for goods with greater marginal utility.

Relating this to water and diamonds, water is not scarce in most of the world, which means people can consume water up to the point at which the marginal utility they gain from the last drop consumed is very low. They aren't willing to pay a lot of money for one more drink of water. Diamonds, by contrast, are scarce. Because of their limited supply, the marginal utility typically gained from adding one more diamond to a person's collection is much higher than for one extra drink of water. However, if one is dying of thirst, this paradox breaks down. In this situation, the marginal utility gained from another drink of water would be much higher than the additional satisfaction of owning an extra diamond — at least until the thirst was quenched.

Follow-up questions

1 Define the terms 'scarcity' and 'marginal utility'.
2 Can you think of **two** other goods which generally illustrate the paradox of value?
3 Why are a bottle of water and a diamond priced differently?
4 Is it rational for an individual to trade a diamond for a bottle of water?

Marginal utility and an individual's demand

If lemonade were available completely free (at zero price), it would be rational for our thirsty child to drink exactly five glasses of lemonade in the course of a hot, sunny afternoon. He or she would consume up to the point of satiation, beyond which no further utility can be gained. But because lemonade is an economic good which is scarce in supply and which has an opportunity cost, it is reasonable to assume that the child (or the child's parents) must pay for the drinks. Suppose that the price of lemonade is equal to the marginal utility gained from the fourth glass. In Figure 2.2, the price P_4 represents the opportunity cost of the fourth glass of lemonade: that is, the utility that could be gained if the price were spent on some other good, such as a bar of chocolate. To maximise utility at this price, the thirsty child should drink

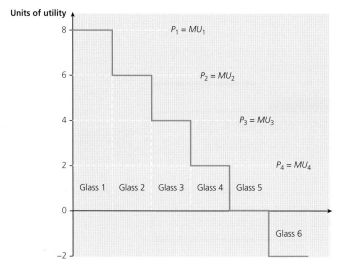

Figure 2.2 Relating marginal utility to changes in price and to the shape of a demand curve

four glasses of lemonade, but no more. It would be irrational to consume a fifth glass at this price, since the extra utility gained would be less than the opportunity cost represented by the price P_4.

Figure 2.2 shows the effect of the price rising from P_4, successively to P_3, P_2 and P_1. These prices equal the marginal utility derived by the child from the third, second and first glasses of lemonade. When the price rises to P_3, our thirsty child reduces demand to three glasses, so as to maximise utility in the new situation. At price P_2 demand is again reduced to two drinks, and so on. The higher the price, the lower the quantity demanded.

SYNOPTIC LINK

This chapter focuses on the individual choices made by consumers or members of households when they decide how much of a good to consume in the economy's goods or product market. In Chapter 6, by contrast, we explain the choices made by members of the same households about how much labour to supply and how much leisure time to enjoy when making decisions in the economy's labour market. In both sets of markets, utility maximisation (explained below) is central to individual economic decision making. In the labour market we assume that workers attempt to maximise the utility derived from the wage and the utility gained from job satisfaction.

Utility maximisation

The assumption of maximising behaviour by economic agents (consumers, workers, firms and even the government) is central to orthodox or traditional economic theory. Economic agents decide their market plans so as to maximise a target objective or goal which is believed to be consistent with the pursuit of self-interest. In demand theory, the objective which households are assumed to wish to maximise is the utility, or satisfaction, obtained from the set of goods and services consumed.

EXTENSION MATERIAL

Maximising versus minimising behaviour

It is worth noting that any maximising objective can always be recast as a minimising objective. Thus a household's assumed objective of *maximising the utility gained from the set of goods and services consumed* can be restated as *minimising the outlay, expenditure or cost of obtaining the same combination or bundle of goods and services*. Whether we set up an assumed objective in maximising or minimising terms depends on our convenience. It is more usual to investigate maximising objectives, but for some purposes a consideration of the minimising principle can shed interesting light on economic behaviour.

Maximisation subject to constraints

If all goods were free, or if households had unlimited income and capacity to consume all goods, a consumer would maximise utility by obtaining all the goods which yield utility, up to the point of satiation. As we have already indicated, satiation occurs when no more utility can be gained from consuming extra units of a good. Any further consumption would yield only disutility at the margin (negative utility, dissatisfaction or displeasure).

However, because of the problem of scarcity, consumers face a number of constraints which restrict the choices they make in the market place. The constraints are:

- **Limited income.** Consumers, even the very rich, do not possess an unlimited income, or stock of wealth that can be converted into income, with which to purchase all the goods and services that could possibly yield utility. Income spent on one good cannot be spent on some other good or service.
- **A given set of prices.** Very often, consumers cannot by their own actions influence the market prices they have to pay to obtain the goods and services they buy. Given this assumption, consumers are 'price-takers' rather than 'price-makers'.
- **The budget constraint.** Taken together, limited income and the set of prices faced impose a budget constraint on consumers' freedom of action in the market place. If we assume that all income is spent and not saved, that there is no borrowing, and that stocks of wealth are not run down, a consumer can only purchase more of one good by giving up consumption of some other good or service, which represents the opportunity cost of consumption.
- **Limited time available.** Even when goods are free, consumer choices must still be made because it is often impossible to consume more than one good at a time or to store more than a limited number of goods for future consumption.

STUDY TIP
The margin is one of the key concepts in A-level microeconomics. Make sure you understand and can define the term and apply the concept.

Importance of the margin when making choices

Along with assumptions such as rational economic behaviour and opportunity cost, the 'margin' is one of the key concepts in traditional or orthodox economic theory. Given consistent tastes and preferences, rational consumers choose between available goods and services in such a way as to try to maximise total utility, welfare or satisfaction derived from consumption of the goods. Along with the relative prices that must be paid for each of the goods, the marginal utilities gained from the consumption of the last unit of each good determine the combination of goods the consumer must choose in order to maximise total utility.

As we shall see in later chapters in Part 1 of this book, in orthodox economic theory, the margin is equally important in other areas of economic choice. For example, we shall see how when firms choose how much of a good to produce and sell, they take account of the marginal sales revenue received from selling the last unit of the good, and the marginal cost of producing the last unit. Generalising across all choice situations, we shall explain how in order to maximise a desired objective, an economic agent must undertake the activity involved up to the point at which the marginal private benefit received equals the marginal private cost incurred. For example, a utility-maximising consumer must choose to consume or demand a good up to the point at which $MU = P$. Marginal utility or MU is, of course, the marginal private benefit derived from consuming the last unit of the good, while the good's price, P, is its opportunity cost in consumption, at the margin.

Can utility be measured?

On several occasions we have referred to 'units of utility' as a unit of measurement for the happiness, pleasure, satisfaction or fulfilment of need which an individual derives from consuming a good or service. However, in real life there is no way in which an individual can mathematically work out the utility to be gained from every unit of a good consumed. Economists have found it impossible to measure directly units of satisfaction, pleasure or fulfilment through which comparisons can be made across individuals.

To get around this problem, the famous economist Paul Samuelson introduced the concept of 'revealed preference'. What revealed preference theory does is work backward from observing how consumers actually behave to observing their preferences. Consumers reveal their preferences by choosing, at given prices and for given levels of income, the bundles or combinations of goods they end up buying.

SECTION 2.1 SUMMARY

- The starting point for understanding individual economic decision making is understanding the nature of rationality and maximising behaviour.
- Economists have traditionally assumed that individuals wish to maximise utility.
- Utility can be thought of as satisfaction, pleasure or fulfilment of need.
- It is important to distinguish between total utility and marginal utility.
- The hypothesis (or 'law') of diminishing marginal utility lies behind the derivation of an individual's demand curve.
- Utility cannot be measured directly.

2.2 Imperfect information

The importance of information for decision making

So far in this chapter, we have assumed that consumers possess perfect information: for example, about the goods that are available to buy, their prices and quality, and about the utility which will be derived from their consumption. Traditional economic theory assumes that if individuals possess perfect information, they will make decisions that maximise their welfare. However, when attempting to maximise total utility, more often than not consumers possess imperfect information. As a result, they make 'wrong' decisions.

A student may spend £100 on a ticket for a rock concert, believing in advance that she will thoroughly enjoy the entertainment. However, she may come out of the stadium in which the event was held believing that she has wasted her hard-earned money and would be far better off if she had spent the £100 on other goods, such as a meal in a high-class restaurant. This is an example of a 'wrong' choice, but it was also a rational choice because she believed in advance that the concert would be good.

In section 8.5 of Chapter 8, we will study how consumers may choose to under-consume a merit good such as education and over-consume a demerit good such as tobacco because they possess imperfect information about the long-term consequences of their choices. We shall investigate the contribution of behavioural economics in the next section of this chapter.

SYNOPTIC LINK
In Chapter 8 we analyse merit goods and demerit goods by examining the information failures households experience when deciding how much to consume of a merit good such as education, or a demerit good such as tobacco.

31

The significance of asymmetric information

KEY TERM

asymmetric information when one party to a market transaction possesses less information relevant to the exchange than the other.

TEST YOURSELF 2.4

Why does asymmetric information give a salesperson an advantage in the market for used cars or in the market for private pensions?

Sometimes, one party to a market transaction, either the buyer or the seller, suffers from imperfect information about the nature of the transaction. **Asymmetric information** arises when either the buyer or the seller involved in a potential transaction knows something that is not observable to the other party. One of the ways in which asymmetric information can manifest itself is through the process known as *adverse selection*, which is a feature of many market transactions. For example, in the sale and purchase of a second-hand computer, the seller of the good knows more about the computer's defects than a potential purchaser. However, to avoid paying too high a price for an inferior product which has lots of defects, potential purchasers often offer low prices on *all* second-hand computers, regardless of the fact that some of the computers are good.

The problem of asymmetric information possessed by buyers and sellers is described in a classic article by George Akerlof on the market for 'lemons' — a 'lemon' being American slang for a poor-quality second-hand car.

CASE STUDY 2.2

The market for lemons

In 2001 George Akerlof was awarded the Nobel prize in economics, largely in response to a 13-page academic paper he published in 1970 titled 'The market for lemons'. Back in 1970, Akerlof found it difficult to get his paper published. Two leading academic journals rejected the paper on the grounds that asymmetric information in the market for second-hand cars was too trivial an economic issue. However, by 2001 things had changed.

On receiving his Nobel prize, Akerlof said:

'Lemons' deals with a problem as old as markets themselves. It concerns how horse traders respond to the natural question: 'if he wants to sell that horse, do I really want to buy it?' Such questioning is fundamental to the market for horses and used cars, but it is also at least minimally present in many market transactions.

Here is an extract from what Akerlof wrote in his 1970 paper:

From time to time one hears either mention of or surprise at the large price difference between new cars and those which have just left the showroom. The usual lunch table justification for this phenomenon is the pure joy of owning a 'new' car.

We offer a different explanation. Suppose that there are just four kinds of cars. There are new cars and used cars. There are good cars and bad cars (which in America are known as 'lemons'). A new car may be a good car or a lemon, and of course the same is true of used cars.

The individuals in this market buy a new automobile without knowing whether the car they buy will be good or a lemon. After owning a specific car, however, for a length of time, the car owner can form a good idea of the quality of this machine.

An asymmetry of information has developed: for the sellers have more knowledge about the quality of a car than the buyers. But good and bad used cars must still sell at the same price, since it is impossible for a buyer to tell the difference between a good and a bad car.

It is apparent that a used car cannot have the same valuation as a new car — if it did, it would clearly be advantageous to trade a lemon at the price of a new car, at a high probability of the new car being a good car. Most used cars traded will be 'lemons', and good used cars may not be traded at all. The 'bad cars tend to drive out the good (in much the same way that bad money drives out the good).'

Follow-up questions

1 Define the term 'asymmetric information'.
2 Explain why a buyer with a good knowledge of car mechanics has an advantage in the market for second-hand cars.
3 Explain, using examples other than those mentioned above, which markets are most affected by the problem of asymmetric information.
4 Discuss to what extent you believe that if the price of a good is too good to be true, you are buying a lemon rather than taking advantage of an opportunity.

> **STUDY TIP**
> You can find out more information about markets for 'lemons' in Case study 3.6 in Chapter 3.

SECTION 2.2 SUMMARY

- Traditional economic theory assumes individuals will make rational choices.
- In reality, individuals have to make decisions based on imperfect information, which makes them prone to making a 'wrong decision'.
- In real world markets the problem of asymmetric information arises when either the buyer or the seller knows something not observable to the other party.

2.3 Aspects of behavioural economic theory

Emergence of behavioural economics

> **KEY TERM**
> **behavioural economics** a method of economic analysis that applies psychological insights into human behaviour to explain how individuals make choices and decisions.

Behavioural economics is a field of study that has attracted a great deal of attention since the beginning of the twenty-first century. Most of the research in the field has come from universities in the USA, but in recent years UK university economics departments have been offering courses in the subject.

Behavioural economics is built on the insights of psychologists seeking to understand human behaviour and decision making. In 2008, economist Richard Thaler and legal scholar Cass Sunstein published *Nudge: Improving Decisions about Health, Wealth and Happiness*, which is a highly accessible overview of behavioural economics. In 2010, the UK government set up the Behavioural Insights Team (BIT), which was initially based in the Cabinet Office in Downing Street. The creation of the BIT, and of a similar body advising the then US president, Barack Obama, marked the growing influence that behavioural economics was having on government policy-makers.

On its website, the BIT writes:

> We coined the term 'behavioural insights' in 2010 to help bring together ideas from a range of inter-related academic disciplines (behavioural economics, psychology, and social anthropology). These fields seek to understand how individuals take decisions in practice and how they are likely to respond to options. Their insights enable us to design policies or interventions that can encourage, support and enable people to make better choices for themselves and society.

33

STUDY TIP

Try to read Thaler and Sunstein's *Nudge: Improving Decisions about Health, Wealth and Happiness*, and also some of the Behavioural Insight Team's publications, which can be accessed on the internet.

The BIT's website is worth reading to find out about projects that the team runs in government. The web address is: **www.behaviouralinsights.co.uk**. You might also access a BIT publication, *Better Choices: Better Deals*, otherwise known as the UK government's consumer empowerment strategy, which recommends how government policy can attempt to influence consumer behaviour. It can be found at **www.gov.uk/government/publications/better-choices-better-deals-behavioural-insights-team-paper**.

TEST YOURSELF 2.5

Which **one** of the following statements is true about how the use of the internet affects consumer behaviour?

A It facilitates the use of price comparison websites.

B It stops consumers comparing prices in stores.

C It always adds to consumer confusion.

D It eliminates the need for consumer choice.

Explain your answer.

EXTENSION MATERIAL

Squaring the circle between traditional and behavioural economic theory

In his excellent book *Predictably Irrational*, Dan Ariely stated that traditional economics is about creating a theory and using it to explain actual behaviour, whereas behavioural economics is about observing actual behaviour and then coming up with a theory.

Traditional theories are often attacked by behavioural economists on the grounds that the simplifying assumptions on which the theories are built are unrealistic. In particular, in the context of what orthodox economists call the 'theory of the firm', behavioural economists query the 'profit-maximising assumption'. This is the assumption that entrepreneurs make business decisions solely on the basis of whether the decisions will lead to larger profits.

However, in a famous essay, 'The methodology of positive economics', published in 1953, the great pro-free-market economist Milton Friedman defended the traditional approach. Friedman wrote: 'Truly important and significant hypotheses will be found to have "assumptions" that are wildly inaccurate descriptive representations of reality, and, in general, the more significant the theory, the more unrealistic the assumptions.'

Friedman rejected testing a theory solely on the realism of its assumptions. He agreed that assumptions such as utility maximisation and profit maximisation are unrealistic. Friedman argued that a theory should be tested and then accepted or rejected on the basis of the validity and fruitfulness of its predictions. If unrealistic assumptions led to wrong conclusions, he would have argued that the theory should be rejected or modified. But if assumptions are unrealistic because of the need to abstract from a complex reality, but still lead to sound predictions which survive scientific testing, they can be justified. In summary, if members of households act 'as if' they are utility maximisers and likewise the entrepreneurs who run firms act 'as if' they are profit maximisers, the predictive power of traditional theories can still be good.

In the traditional theory of the firm, entrepreneurs are assumed to produce and sell output up to the point at which marginal revenue equals marginal cost, yet real-world business people seldom make such decisions when running their businesses. Friedman argued that this does not matter. If Friedman had lived to the present day (he died at the age of 94 in 2006), he might be using similar reasoning to defend traditional economic theory from the attacks of behavioural economists.

STUDY TIP
Make sure you understand the key differences between traditional economic theory and behavioural economics.

SYNOPTIC LINK
The traditional theory of the firm and profit maximisation are explained in depth in Chapters 4 and 5, and scientific methodology is discussed in Chapter 1.

CASE STUDY 2.3

In the April 2010 edition of the Economic Review, *published by Philip Allan for Hodder Education, David Gill presented an overview of interesting developments in behavioural economics. This case study summarises the introduction of David Gill's article.*

Beyond *Homo economicus*

Economists like to simplify the world; in particular they like to simplify people. Most of twentieth-century economics makes a number of standard assumptions about how people behave, which comprise our view of *Homo economicus* or 'economic man'. *Homo economicus* is self-interested: he only cares about himself. He knows the consequences of everything he does. He is rational: he knows what he wants and always acts on these preferences.

This simple model has proved to be exceptionally useful in gaining insights into economic behaviour, especially when consumers and firms interact in large markets. However, the new science of behavioural economics seeks to move beyond *Homo economicus* to a more realistic representation of how people choose and behave. It does so in a number of ways.

First, data collected by economists show a number of so-called 'anomalies' — that is, behaviour which deviates in a consistent manner from that predicted by the model of *Homo economicus*. For example, people appear to be altruistic: they tend to put at least some weight on the wellbeing of others. Another point is that we are generally impatient and lack self-control. Most of us find it difficult to resist immediate temptation, whether it be a chocolate bar at the supermarket checkout counter or an extra hour in bed. Finally, we dislike change. The so-called 'status quo bias' means that we generally like to stick with what we have, unless the incentive to change course is compelling.

Second, research from the field of cognitive psychology paints a picture at odds with that of *Homo economicus*. This research shows that humans often make decisions using simple rules-of-thumb — called *heuristics* — and suffer from many biases when choosing what to do, such as over-confidence, *confirmation bias* (the tendency to search for, and put greater weight on, information that confirms one's preconceptions) and *recency bias* (the tendency to weight recent information and experience more heavily than older information and earlier experiences). Also psychological findings emphasise the fundamental role of emotions in decision making, including, for example, anger, regret, guilt, shame and disappointment.

Third, humans clearly face quite substantial limitations of computation and reasoning. These are particularly important when the environment is complex: for example, when people are interacting strategically, my best action will depend on what others choose to do. An oligopolistic firm deciding what price to set will have to start thinking about what its competitors are going to do.

Follow-up questions

1 How does 'economic man' make decisions?
2 Define the term 'altruism'.
3 Is it rational for an individual to give money to charity or to donate blood?
4 To what extent is the UK mortgage market a complex market?

SYNOPTIC LINK
Oligopolistic pricing behaviour is explained in Chapter 5, pages 144–150.

Bounded rationality

So far in this chapter, we have assumed that when exercising choice, individuals are perfectly rational, in the sense that they make decisions in a context of being fully informed, with perfect logic and aiming to achieve the maximum possible economic gain. However, in real life, individuals are seldom if ever perfectly rational. In the world in which we live, decisions are made in conditions of **bounded rationality**, which means that individuals, however high or low their intelligence, make decisions subject to three unavoidable constraints: imperfect information about possible alternatives and their consequences; limited mental processing ability; and a time constraint which limits the time available for making decisions. In complex choice situations, bounded rationality often results in *satisficing* rather than *maximising* choices.

SYNOPTIC LINK
The difference between firms profit satisficing and maximising is explained in Chapter 5, pages 126–27.

Bounded self-control

Bounded rationality is closely linked to the related concept of **bounded self-control**. Traditional or orthodox economic theory implicitly assumes that when making choices, individuals have complete self-control. Behavioural economists, by contrast, believe that individuals have bounded (or limited) self-control. Making New Year resolutions in the period immediately after Christmas provides many good examples. Having put on weight during the Christmas festivities, people may decide to go for a daily jog early in the morning before going to work each day after 1 January. For many, this may work well for a few days, but the first bout of bad weather often leads to the resolution being broken.

Thinking fast and thinking slow

The Nobel prize-winning psychologist Daniel Kahneman has been one of the most influential figures in the development of behavioural economics. Kahneman introduced economists to the idea that human beings think in two different ways. The first, which Kahneman called System 1 or 'thinking fast', is intuitive and instinctive. Decisions are made quickly and little effort is used to analyse the situation. This is automatic thinking.

The second, which Kahneman called System 2, is 'thinking slow'. In this method of thinking, which is also known as reflective thinking, concentration and mental effort are required to work through a problem before a decision can be made.

For example, when learning to play a new game such as golf, an individual will 'think slow' when deciding on the appropriate golf club to select for a particular stroke, and on how to grip the club and to take a swing at the ball. Because the decision making is relatively slow, involving careful, logical thought about every decision, the process can be tiring. However, the more often the game is played and the more practice is put in, the less golfers have to think about minor decisions. Automatic thinking takes over. Professional golf players often play quickly and instinctively. Through years of repetitive training, their automatic systems have learnt to respond to situations promptly and effectively. In big-game situations they can, of course, suffer if they stop to think. When this happens, they switch back to System 2 or the reflective system, over-thinking the situation, which can mean that bad decisions have disastrous consequences.

Many of our everyday economic decisions are taken by our automatic system. Buying a coffee at a train station, buying groceries in a supermarket and ordering drinks in a bar will often be quick, intuitive decisions. Bigger and more important decisions tend to be taken by our reflective system. Deciding whether to buy a car or a house, and choosing an insurance policy, will normally result from reflective decisions.

Biases in decision making

Behavioural economics argues that quick decisions that people make when exercising choice (automatic thinking) are often heavily biased. This is because decisions are made on the basis of one's own likes, dislikes and past experiences. Psychologists use the term **cognitive bias** to describe this situation. A cognitive bias is a mistake in reasoning or other thought process, often occurring as a result of holding onto one's preferences and beliefs regardless of contrary information. Many kinds of cognitive bias exist, such as confirmation bias which is the tendency to seek only information that matches what one already believes.

'Rules of thumb' are used by humans to help them make sensible decisions based on limited information, but the decisions are prone to cognitive bias. The two common rules of thumb that lead to biases are availability and anchoring.

The availability bias

The **availability bias** occurs when individuals place too much weight on the probability of an event happening because they can recall vivid examples of similar events. For example, after reading several news reports about car thefts, an individual may judge that vehicle theft is much more common than it really is in the local area.

Consider also the economic decision to buy a lottery ticket. The probability of selecting the winning numbers in a draw is outrageously low at over 14 million to 1. It is irrational to believe that buying a ticket is a sound economic decision because the chance of winning the jackpot is so improbable. However, ticket sales for the national lottery between 1 April 2017 and 31 March 2018 were £6.95 billion, an increase of more than £26 million on the previous year. No doubt, when buying a ticket most players do not think about the odds but instead focus on the news stories of people winning the jackpot. The lucky winners of large jackpots are publicised in the national media and their tales are promoted by Camelot, the business that runs the National Lottery. Since its launch in 1994 the National Lottery claims to have created 3,700 millionaires in the UK.

The availability bias often leads to decisions that are not based on logical reasoning. The media report stories that stick in our mind and affect our reasoning process. Humans often believe that the probability of an extreme weather event, such as a hurricane or severe flooding, is more likely than empirical statistical analysis bears out. The market research company Ipsos has published research highlighting how the general public in 14 countries held preconceptions on the make-up of their societies that were significantly detached from the reality. In the UK, for example, the average citizen believed that 24% of the population were immigrants when the real figure is 13% and, likewise, that 24% of the working age population was unemployed when in fact at the time of the research it was less than 7%.

Anchoring

Anchoring is an example of a predictable bias in individual decision making. Most people have a tendency to compare and contrast only a limited set of items. This is called the anchoring effect. A good example is provided by restaurant menus, which sometimes feature very expensive main courses, while also including more (apparently) reasonably priced alternatives. We are lured into choosing the cheaper items, even though their prices are still quite high. When given a choice, we often tend to pick the middle option, believing it is not too expensive, but also not too cheap.

Biases based on social norms

Human beings are social animals and as a result the behaviour of other people influences our own behaviour. By unconsciously learning from the behaviour of other people, **social norms** are established.

Negative social norms include attitudes towards drinking alcohol. Many young adults often drink heavily because they think it is what people of their age are expected to do. By presenting statistical data showing that the majority of young adults do not engage in regular heavy drinking, behavioural economists would seek to *nudge* young drinkers into different patterns of behaviour.

Positive social norms can be seen in the way in which social attitudes have altered toward smoking in the last 30 years. In the 1980s it was socially acceptable to smoke in all public places including libraries, trains and the London Underground. Concerted health campaigns, which provided the general public with better information about the risks of smoking, have altered social attitudes. As a result, people became much more willing to accept laws which restricted their right to smoke. The laws banning smoking in public places are economic sanctions (used by government policy-makers) and not **nudges**. Economic sanctions include restrictions imposed by regulations and/or laws that restrict an individual's freedom to behave in certain ways. Breaking a sanction can lead to punishment.

Critics of behavioural economics point out that sanctions, such as the smoking ban, may be more effective at changing behaviour and improving public health than nudges, which only alter the behaviour of some people. Nevertheless, government reports in Ireland claim that since smoking in public places was banned, people are also less likely to smoke in other people's houses because it is now considered to be socially unacceptable.

KEY TERM

anchoring a cognitive bias describing the human tendency when making decisions to rely too heavily on the first piece of information offered (the so-called 'anchor'). Individuals use an initial piece of information when making subsequent judgements.

TEST YOURSELF 2.6

Explain how individuals use 'rules of thumb' when making decisions.

KEY TERMS

social norms forms or patterns of behaviour considered acceptable by a society or group within that society.

nudges factors which encourage people to think and act in particular ways. Nudges try to shift group and individual behaviour in ways which comply with desirable social norms.

TEST YOURSELF 2.7

Explain how a social norm can lead to less litter and chewing gum being dropped on a street.

SYNOPTIC LINK
See Chapter 8 for a discussion of nudges in relation to environmental market failures.

TEST YOURSELF 2.8

Which one of the following provides the best definition of norms?

Norms are:

A laws that attempt to discourage excessive consumption

B informal rules that govern human behaviour

C formal rules that govern human behaviour

D formal rules about how to buy goods and services

Explain your answer.

Altruism and fairness

KEY TERMS

altruism concern for the welfare of others.

fairness the quality of being impartial, just, or free of favouritism. It can mean treating people equally, sharing with others, giving others respect and time, and not taking advantage of them.

SYNOPTIC LINK
Go back to Chapter 1 to remind yourself of the meaning of normative statements.

Altruism is when we act to promote someone else's wellbeing, even though we may suffer as a consequence, either in terms of a financial or time loss, or by incurring personal risk. Before the development of behavioural economics, economists generally assumed that individuals were not altruistic and acted only in their self-interest. Nevertheless, altruism could still be accommodated within maximising theory — for example, by assuming that individuals derive pleasure as a result of giving to others. More recently, behavioural economists have drawn attention to the fact that for many if not most people, their first impulse is to cooperate with each other rather than to compete. Very young children are frequently observed helping other children around them, out of a genuine concern for their welfare. Animals have also been observed displaying altruism.

Altruistic behaviour often results from people's perceptions of **fairness**. Fairness is a normative term incorporating value judgements, as different people have a range of different views on the meaning of fairness. A popular view is that fairness involves treating people equally or in a way that is right or reasonable.

SECTION 2.3 SUMMARY

- In recent years, behavioural economics has emerged to question many of the assumptions of traditional economic theory.
- Behavioural economists believe that individuals in the real world have bounded rationality.
- An individual's economic decision making may be biased.
- Humans use rules of thumb to help them make decisions based on limited information.
- The two most common rules of thumb that lead to bias are availability and anchoring.
- Social norms can lead people into positive and negative behaviour.
- People are often altruistic and instinctively cooperate rather than compete.
- Most individuals believe in fairness and are concerned with the welfare of others.

39

2.4 Behavioural economics and economic policy

As we mentioned at the beginning of section 2.3, UK and US governments have recently been introducing the insights of behavioural economics into practical policy making. In assessing the impact of behavioural economics on government economic policy making, you need to consider how it might influence the design of a variety of government policies which aim to reduce or eliminate particular economic problems.

At times in this chapter, we have tended to portray traditional or orthodox economics and behavioural economics as if they are completely opposed to each other, implying that if one is correct, the other is inevitably wrong. However, this is a somewhat misguided way of viewing the two very important branches of economic theory. It is better to think of behavioural economics as complementing and improving traditional economic theory by allowing governments and decision-makers to design policy interventions, such as healthcare interventions, to enable them to achieve policy goals more effectively.

As we have seen, behavioural economics argues that individuals are not fully rational in the way traditional economic theory assumes. As a result, they regularly suffer from behavioural biases that make it difficult for them to achieve the results they actually prefer. In this situation, government intervention should aim at helping individuals to achieve an outcome that is in their own best interest.

Choice architecture and framing

Choice architecture

Choice architecture is the term used by behavioural economists to describe how government policy-makers can guide people into making better choices. Government can use behavioural insights to design choice architectures so that citizens are *nudged* to opt for choices that are deemed to be in their best interest, so as to achieve a socially desirable outcome. For example, the layout and design of a canteen affects the menu choices of some individuals when purchasing a meal. Behavioural studies have found that when fruit and salads are placed at the front of a canteen more are bought than when they are placed on the back counters. Consumers are free to choose their meals but the choice architecture nudges individuals into buying healthier food.

Default choice

The **default choice** is a key aspect of choice architecture in which one option is automatically selected unless an alternative is specified. For example, when framing policy on the issue of organ donation, individuals who might donate body organs such as hearts or livers in the event of their death, can be asked whether to 'opt in' or 'opt out' of organ donation. In this context, an 'opt-in' default choice is illustrated by the use of a tick box which, if filled in by a member of the general public, indicates positively that they would like to donate their body organs after their death. Unless the user ticks the box, however, healthcare organisations such as the NHS cannot make use of their organs. This is in contrast with an 'opt-out', where the default position is that the organs can be used to help others survive unless a box has been ticked to indicate that the body parts should *not* be used. Countries that require people to opt out of organ donations generally have a much higher proportion of the population registered to donate than countries that ask people to opt in. For a behavioural economist, the benefits of opt-out over opt-in are clear: the supply of donated organs rises to be closer to the demand for them and the nation's public health improves.

Policy-makers can improve social welfare by designing government programmes that select as a default an option that can be considered in an individual's best long-term interest. A number of examples of this approach have been trialled and introduced by the UK government's Behavioural Insights Team. One of these is automatic pension enrolment.

Signing up to the NHS Organ Donor Register is an opt-in default choice

Framing

People are influenced by how information is presented. **Framing** is the tendency for people to be influenced by the context in which the choice is presented when making a decision. Advertisers have for many years presented consumers with choices in a manner that frames their products in a favourable light. Consider the label on a food product that reads: '90% fat-free'. Would it sell as well if the label read: '10% fat'?

Politicians will often frame (or spin) economic statements in a manner that is favourable to the argument they are trying to make. For example, in December 2014 the then chancellor of the exchequer George Osborne said that the government had more than halved the UK's budget deficit since taking office in May 2010. This message was printed on Conservative Party campaign posters in January 2015. Osborne was trying to frame his government in the voters' mind as one of economic competence. This statement is true if you measure the size of the budget deficit as a ratio of GDP. However, if you measure the budget deficit in money terms, it had only been reduced by around 40% (see Table 2.4).

Table 2.4 UK budget deficit, 2009/10 and 2014/15

Year	UK budget deficit (£bn)	UK budget deficit as a % of GDP
2009/10	153.0	10.2
2014/15	91.3	5.0

Source: OBR

Mandated choices

A variant of default choice is **mandated choice**; this is where people are required by law to make a decision. A mandated or required choice occurs when a choice architect designs a system that forces individuals to make an explicit decision and not merely go ahead with a default position.

An everyday example of a mandated choice outside of government policy is the Microsoft software installation boxes that appear on our computer screens. The Microsoft choice architects force computer users to make choices and select various options before they can move onto the next step and complete the installation process. Most people will choose the recommended settings but they have to make an active decision to do so. Mandated choices work well with simple yes/no decisions but less well with complex decisions.

Restricted choice

Restricted choice means offering people a limited number of options, on the basis that offering too many choices is unhelpful and leads to poor decisions. Most people cannot, or cannot be bothered to, evaluate a large number of choices. The policy of requiring the energy companies to simplify their pricing structures and restrict the number of options offered to consumers is an example of 'restricted choice' in action.

Government policy-makers should consider behavioural insights when designing systems. A well-designed system should make it easier for citizens to pay for government services by setting up direct debits, using accessible language and sending text messages or e-mails to remind people to complete requests. Evidence from the BIT shows that personalised letters increase response rates, whilst asking respondents to sign forms at the top of the page and not the bottom results in more honest answers.

Revisiting nudge theory

As explained earlier, a nudge tries to alter people's behaviour in a predictable way without forbidding any options or significantly changing economic incentives. A nudge is not a legal requirement. Neither is it an economic sanction. Fines, taxes and subsidies are not nudges.

When used as a part of government policy, nudges must be open and transparent to the general public. Governments should be honest with the public and ensure that they explain why they have introduced a nudge, but still allow individuals to make a choice.

Nudges versus shoves

'Nudge' policies seek to lead people by providing them with helpful information and language that then allows them to make an informed choice. By contrast, 'shove' policies instruct people to behave in certain ways, often by responding to financial incentives and disincentives that reward or punish different decisions (see Table 2.5).

Government policies based on traditional economic theories have generally sought to shove people into altering their behaviour rather than to nudge them in the desired direction.

Table 2.5 Nudges versus shoves

Nudge	Shove
• Provides information for people to respond to. • Creates positive social norms. • Opt-out schemes rather than opt-in schemes and default choices. • Active choosing by individuals.	• Uses taxation and subsidies to alter incentives and on occasion, in the case of taxes, to punish people. • Uses fines, laws banning activities and regulations.

> **KEY TERM**
> **restricted choice** offering people a limited number of options so that they are not overwhelmed by the complexity of the situation. If there are too many choices, people may make a poorly thought-out decision or not make any decision.

CASE STUDY 2.4

This case study has been extracted from a paper published by the UK cabinet's Behaviour Insights Team (BIT), published in 2013.

Applying behavioural insights to charitable giving

This paper explores new and innovative ways of increasing charitable giving. It recognises the important indirect benefits of charitable giving that recent behavioural research has begun to explore. This research shows that giving both time and money has large benefits for the wellbeing of the giver as well as the receiver.

Experiments have shown, for example, that individuals are happier when given the opportunity to spend money on others. Similarly, volunteering is associated with increased life satisfaction — not only among volunteers, but also in the wider community. Charitable giving is good for donors, for beneficiaries, and for society at large.

Four behavioural insights

Insight 1 is to **'make it easy'**. One of the best ways of encouraging people to give is to make it easy for people to do so. Making it easy can include:

- giving people the option to increase their future payments to prevent donations being eroded by inflation
- setting defaults that automatically enrol new senior staff into giving schemes (with a clear option to decline)
- using prompted choice to encourage people to become charitable donors

Insight 2 is to **'attract attention'**. Making charitable giving more attractive to an individual can be a powerful way of increasing donations. This can include:

- attracting individuals' attention, for example by using personalised messages
- rewarding the behaviour you seek to encourage, for example through matched funding schemes
- encouraging reciprocity with small gifts

Insight 3 is to **'focus on the social'**. We are all influenced by the actions of those around us, which means we are more likely to give to charity if we see it as the 'social norm'. Focusing on the social involves thinking about:

- using prominent individuals to send out strong social signals
- drawing on peer effects, by making acts of giving more visible to others within one's social group
- establishing group norms around which subsequent donors 'anchor' their own gifts

Insight 4 is that **'timing matters'**. If you get your timing right, it can really help to increase charitable donations. This might include:

- ensuring that charitable appeals are made at the moments when they are likely to be most effective — for example, people are more likely to make a donation in December than January
- understanding that people may be more willing to commit to future (increases in) donations than equivalent sums today

Follow-up questions

1 The BIT paper recommends 'establishing group norms around which subsequent donors "anchor" their own gifts'. Explain the two terms 'group norms' and 'anchor'.
2 Identify, from within the extract, **two** examples of nudge theory being applied.
3 Why is December a better month than January to ask for charitable donations?
4 To what extent can a positive social norm affect the willingness of an individual making a charitable donation?

- Nudge theory, choice architecture and framing lie at the heart of the ways in which behavioural architecture can influence economic policy making.
- Well-designed choice architecture can guide individuals towards making better decisions.
- Governments can improve social welfare by designing government programmes that select a default choice which is seen to be in an individual's best long-term interest.
- Decision making can be influenced when framed in a context.
- Nudge polices seek to lead individuals into making decisions whereas shove polices instruct using the power of the law.

Questions

1 Explain the hypothesis (or law) of diminishing marginal utility.

2 How does traditional economic theory seek to influence individual decision making?

3 Explain how, in traditional economic theory, a rational individual can make a 'wrong' decision.

4 Explain why rational individuals may make satisficing rather than maximising choices.

5 Is it irrational to give money to charity? Discuss.

6 Explain, using examples, how government officials can use framing techniques to make policies more effective.

7 How can governments intervene in markets to help individuals make better choices?

3

Price determination in a competitive market

Chapter 1 introduced you to one of the fundamental economic problems: how to allocate scarce resources between competing uses in conditions in which there are limited resources and unlimited wants. In a market economy, resource allocation is undertaken by the price mechanism operating in the system of markets that make up the economy. This is also true in the 'market sector' of a mixed economy. However, in a mixed economy there is also a 'non-market sector' in which goods and services such as roads and police are produced and delivered to final users 'outside the market'. This chapter focuses on competitive markets in which the price mechanism operates. Chapter 5 examines the less competitive markets of monopoly and imperfect competition, as well as perfectly competitive market structures. The final chapter of Part 1 of this book, Chapter 8, introduces the various market failures in which the price mechanism either does not work at all or produces resource misallocation.

LEARNING OBJECTIVES

These are to understand:

- the nature of demand and supply in a competitive market
- the difference between a movement along a demand or a supply curve and a shift of a demand or a supply curve
- the concept of elasticity and the different elasticities you need to know
- how demand and supply curves are brought together in a supply and demand diagram
- market equilibrium and disequilibrium in a supply and demand diagram
- interrelationships between markets

3.1 The determinants of demand

Demand and markets

Before we explain what determines the level of demand, we shall first examine the nature of a **market** in which the **demand** for, and the **supply** of, goods and services interact with each other.

A market is a voluntary meeting of buyers and sellers in which exchange takes place. Both buyer and seller have to be willing partners to the exchange. Markets do not have to exist in a particular geographical location. Whenever a good or service is voluntarily bought and sold, a market transaction occurs. In the past, market transactions shifted away from open-air street markets to take place in shops. Shops have higher overhead costs, but they offer a permanent site of exchange and a continuing relationship between sellers and buyers. In recent years, the growth of the internet has allowed 24/7 e-commerce. As a result, many markets, especially those in commodities, raw materials and financial services, have become truly global.

Competitive markets occur when there are a large number of buyers and sellers all passively accepting the **ruling market price**, which is set, not by individual decisions, but by the interaction of all those taking part in the market. Highly competitive markets lack entry and exit barriers. This means that new buyers and sellers can easily enter the market without incurring costs. In the same way, buyers and sellers can leave the market if they wish to. Competitive markets also exhibit a high degree of transparency — buyers and sellers can quickly find out what everyone else in the market is doing.

> **KEY TERMS**
> **market** a voluntary meeting of buyers and sellers with exchange taking place.
> **demand** the quantity of a good or service that consumers are willing and able to buy at given prices in a given period of time.
> **supply** the quantity of a good or service that producers are willing and able to sell at given prices in a given period of time.
> **competitive markets** markets in which the large number of buyers and sellers possess good market information and can easily enter or leave the market.
> **ruling market price** (also known as **equilibrium price**) the price at which planned demand equals planned supply.

The relationship between price and quantity demanded

Households and firms operate simultaneously in two sets of markets. The first of these contains the goods markets, in which members of households demand and buy consumer goods and services produced and supplied by firms. But for household demand in the goods market to be an **effective demand** — that is, demand backed up by an ability to pay — households must first sell their labour, or possibly the services of any capital or land they own, in the markets for factors of production. These were briefly mentioned in Chapter 1. Households' roles are therefore reversed in goods markets and factor markets. In this chapter, we ignore factor markets and focus solely on the determinants of demand for consumer goods and services.

> **KEY TERM**
> **effective demand** the desire for a good or service backed by an ability to pay.

What a demand curve shows

A demand curve, such as the one illustrated in Figure 3.1, shows the relationship between the price of a good or service and the quantity of the good or service demanded at different prices. If the price starts off high, for example at P_1, household demand is Q_1. But if the price falls to P_2, quantity demanded increases to Q_2.

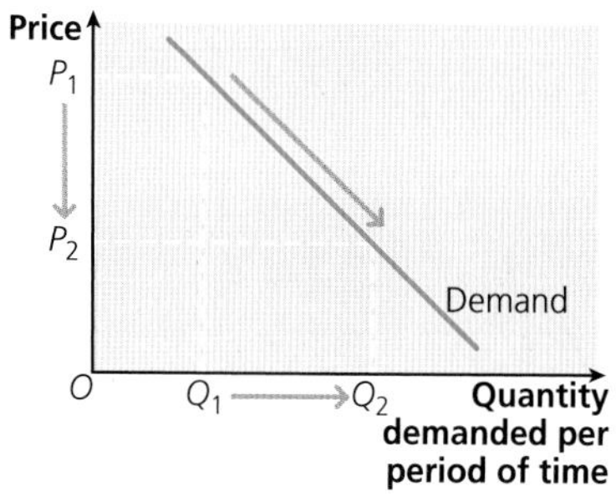

Demand for a good varies according to the time period being considered. For example, weekly demand is different from daily, monthly and annual demand. For this reason, the horizontal axis in Figure 3.1 is labelled 'Quantity demanded per period of time'. It is normal practice to use the

Figure 3.1 A market demand curve

label 'Quantity' on the horizontal axis of a demand curve diagram, as we do in the rest of this book, but this is an abbreviation. It always refers to a period of time.

SYNOPTIC LINK
A microeconomic demand curve, such as the one illustrated in Figure 3.1, looks very similar to a macroeconomic aggregate demand curve, which is explained in Chapter 10. It is vital that you don't confuse the two. Likewise, don't confuse demand with consumption, which is a component of aggregate demand, also explained in Chapter 10.

Market demand and individual demand

KEY TERMS
market demand the quantity of a good or service that all the consumers in a market are willing and able to buy at different market prices.

individual demand the quantity of a good or service that a particular consumer or individual is willing and able to buy at different market prices.

Normally when economists refer to demand, they mean **market demand**. This is the quantity of a good or service that *all* the consumers in the market wish to, and are able to, buy at different prices. By contrast, **individual demand** is the quantity that a particular individual, such as yourself, would like to buy. The relationship between market and individual demand is simple. Market demand is just the sum of the demand of all the consumers in the market.

QUANTITATIVE SKILLS 3.1

Worked example: performing a percentage calculation

1 Calculate to 1 decimal place:
  (a) 14% of £605
  (b) 4% of £4 million
  (c) 0.035% of £800

For question (a), multiply £605 by 0.14, which gives the answer £84.70. Similarly, for question (b), multiply £4 million by 0.04, for which the answer is £160,000, and for question (c) multiply £800 by 0.00035, which gives the answer as £0.28.

2 Express to 2 decimal places:
  (a) 35 as a percentage of 450
  (b) 17 as a percentage of 130
  (c) £6 million as a percentage of £1 billion

For question (a), divide 35 by 450 and convert into a percentage by multiplying by 100. This gives 7.777 recurring, which to 2 decimal places is 7.78%. Repeat the process for questions (b) and (c), which gives the answers 13.08% and 0.60%.

Shifts of a demand curve

Students often confuse a movement *along* a demand curve and a *shift* of a demand curve. A *movement along a demand curve* takes place only when the good's price changes. Provided the demand curve slopes downward, a *fall* in price results in *more* of the good being demanded. This is sometimes called an extension of demand. Likewise, a contraction of demand occurs when a *rise* in price leads to *less* being demanded.

When we draw a market demand curve to show how much of the good or service households plan to demand at various possible prices, we assume that all the other variables that may also influence demand are held unchanged or constant. This is the *ceteris paribus* assumption, which means 'other things being equal'. Among the variables whose values are held constant or unchanged when we draw a demand curve are disposable income and tastes or fashion. Collectively, the variables (other than the good's own price) whose values determine planned demand are often called the **conditions of demand**. A change in a condition of demand shifts the demand curve to a new position.

The conditions of demand

KEY TERM

condition of demand a determinant of demand, other than the good's own price, that fixes the position of the demand curve.

The main conditions of demand are:

- the prices of **substitute goods** (or goods in competing demand) (see pages 55 and 69)
- the prices of **complementary goods** (or goods in joint demand) (see page 55)
- personal income (or more strictly, personal disposable income, after tax and receipt of benefits)
- tastes and preferences
- population size, which influences total market size

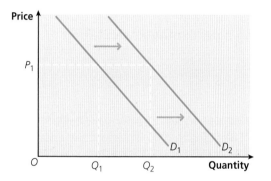

Figure 3.2 The effect of a rightward shift of demand

If any of the conditions of demand change, the position of the demand curve changes, shifting either rightward or leftward. Figure 3.2 illustrates a rightward shift of the demand curve, which is also called an **increase in demand**, showing that more of the good is demanded at all prices. For example, at a price of P_1, the quantity demanded increases from Q_1 to Q_2. Conversely, a leftward shift of demand (known as a **decrease in demand**) causes the quantity demanded to fall at all prices.

Events that might cause a rightward shift of a demand curve include:

- an increase in the price of a substitute good or a good in competing demand (see page 67 on the interrelationship between markets)
- a fall in the price of a complementary good or good in joint demand
- an increase in personal disposable income (but see the explanation of normal goods and inferior goods that follows)
- a successful advertising campaign making people think more favourably about the good
- an increase in population size

TEST YOURSELF 3.2
Household income increases by 3% in a particular year. This causes demand for summer holidays to increase by 5%. Is this an example of an increase in demand or of a movement along a demand curve?

KEY TERMS

substitute goods alternative goods that could be used for the same purpose.

complementary goods when two goods are complements, they experience joint demand.

increase in demand a rightward shift of the demand curve.

decrease in demand a leftward shift of the demand curve.

Normal goods and inferior goods

When disposable income increases, a demand curve shifts rightward, but only if the good is a **normal good**, for which demand increases as income increases. However, some goods are examples of an **inferior good**, for which demand decreases as income increases, and an increase in income shifts the demand curve leftward.

To take an example, private car transport and bus travel are not just substitutes for each other. As people's incomes rise, demand for cars generally increases, while, at the same time, demand for bus travel usually falls. If people respond in this way to changes in income then private transport is a normal good, but certain forms of public transport are inferior goods. For an individual, whether a good is normal or inferior depends on personal income, tastes and, possibly, age. For young children, junk food such as sweets is usually a normal good, but later in life, tastes change and sweets may become an inferior good.

Providing a good is a normal good, an increase in income shifts the good's demand curve to the right. However, if the good is inferior for most people, its demand curve shifts to the left when income increases.

KEY TERMS

normal good a good for which demand increases as income rises and demand decreases as income falls

inferior good a good for which demand decreases as income rises and demand increases as income falls

EXTENSION MATERIAL

Must demand curves always slope downward?

Demand curves don't have to slope downward, though they usually do. However, there are circumstances in which a demand curve may be horizontal or vertical, or indeed slope upward, showing that more is demanded as the good's price increases.

There are a number of possible explanations for upward-sloping demand curves. Some of these are as follows:

- **Speculative demand.** If the price of a good such as housing, shares or a foreign currency starts to rise, people may speculate that in the near future the price will rise even further. In this situation, demand is likely to increase. In the case of house prices, young people who wish to become first-time buyers may scramble to buy houses even when prices are rising, fearing that if they wait, they may never be able to afford to get on the 'housing ladder'.
- **Goods for which consumers use price as an indicator of quality.** Consumers may lack accurate information about the quality of some goods they want to buy, such as second-hand cars and computers. In this situation, a potential buyer may demand more as a good's price rises, believing that a high price means high quality.
- **Veblen goods.** Some companies try to sell their goods based on the fact that they cost more than those of their competitors. Veblen goods, named after the Norwegian economist Thornstein Veblen, are goods of exclusive or ostentatious consumption, or 'snob' goods. They are sometimes called positional goods, though strictly speaking, a positional good is so scarce that few people can ever acquire it. Some people wish to consume Veblen goods, such as Ferrari cars, as a signal of their wealth. The 'reassuringly expensive' advertising campaign for Stella Artois beer is another good example. A few years ago, Interbrew, the Belgian company (now part of AB InBev) that then owned the Stella brand, decided to sell its beer as a premium brand. Interbrew hoped that high prices would attract more customers. However, if you look at the prices of Stella beer today, you will find that AB InBev has now changed tack, selling its beer on a 'stack 'em high, sell 'em fast' principle, at discounted prices.

* Demand means effective demand, based on ability as well as willingness to pay.
* A market demand curve shows how much of a good all the consumers in the market intend to buy at different prices.
* For most goods, demand curves slope downward.
* The conditions of demand fix the position of the demand curve.
* If any of the conditions of demand change, the demand curve shifts to a new position.
* Movements along a demand curve must not be confused with a shift in the position of the curve.

3.2 Price, income and cross elasticities of demand

The meaning of elasticity

KEY TERM
elasticity the proportionate responsiveness of a second variable to an initial change in the first variable.

Whenever a change in one variable (such as a good's price) causes a change to occur in a second variable (such as the quantity of the good that households are prepared to demand), an **elasticity** can be calculated. The elasticity measures the proportionate responsiveness of the second variable to the change in the first variable. For example, if a 5% increase in price were to cause households to reduce their demand by more than 5%, demand would be elastic. In this example, a change in price induces a more than proportionate response by consumers. But if the response were less than a reduction of 5%, demand would be inelastic. And if the change in price were to induce exactly the same proportionate change in demand, demand would be neither elastic nor inelastic — this is called unit elasticity of demand.

Elasticity is a useful descriptive statistic of the relationship between two variables because it is independent of the units, such as price and quantity units, in which the variables are measured.

Although, in principle, economists could calculate a great many elasticities for all the economic relationships in which they are interested, the three demand elasticities you must know are:

* price elasticity of demand
* income elasticity of demand
* cross-elasticity of demand

The following formulae are used for calculating these elasticities:

$$\text{price elasticity of demand} = \frac{\text{percentage change in quantity demanded}}{\text{percentage change in price}}$$

$$\text{income elasticity of demand} = \frac{\text{percentage change in quantity demanded}}{\text{percentage change in income}}$$

$$\text{cross-elasticity of demand} = \frac{\text{percentage change in quantity of A demanded}}{\text{percentage change in price of B}}$$

Price elasticity of demand

KEY TERM

price elasticity of demand measures the extent to which the demand for a good changes in response to a change in the price of that good.

Price elasticity of demand measures consumers' responsiveness to a change in a good's price. (It is sometimes called 'own price' elasticity of demand to distinguish it from cross-elasticity of demand for good A with respect to the price of B, which measures the responsiveness of demand for a particular good to a change in the price of a completely different good.)

STUDY TIP

You should apply elasticity analysis when assessing the effects of a shift of a demand or supply curve. The extent to which the good's price or equilibrium level of output changes depends on the price elasticity of the curve that has not shifted. For example, when the supply curve shifts leftwards, the price elasticity of the demand curve determines the extent to which the good's price and quantity change.

STUDY TIP

Remember that elasticities are calculated by dividing the percentage change in quantity demanded (or supplied) by the percentage change in the variable that caused the change.

TEST YOURSELF 3.3

When the price of a small car is £15,000, there are 100,000 people in the UK who wish to buy it. When the price falls to £10,000, the number wanting to buy the car rises to 200,000. What does this information tell you about the market for small cars in the UK?

Infinite and zero price elasticity of demand

Horizontal and vertical demand curves have constant elasticities at all points on the curve. A horizontal demand curve, such as the demand curve in Figure 3.3(a), is infinitely elastic or perfectly elastic. At the other extreme, the vertical demand curve in Figure 3.3(b) is completely inelastic, displaying a zero price elasticity of demand at all points on the curve. When the price falls, for example from P_1 to P_2, the quantity demanded is unchanged.

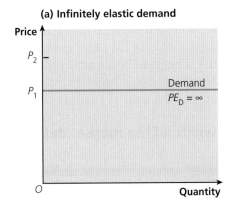
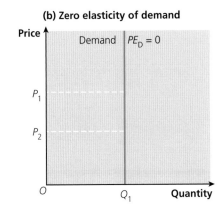

Figure 3.3 Horizontal and vertical demand curves

Figure 3.4 summarises the five demand curves you need to know.

51

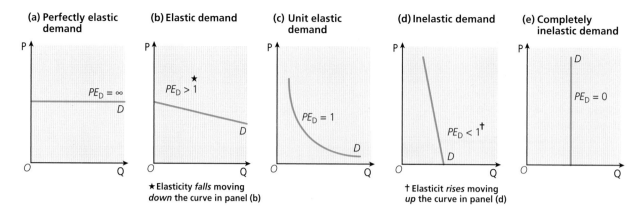

Figure 3.4 Five demand curves you need to know

Factors determining price elasticity of demand

Substitutability

Substitutability is the most important determinant of price elasticity of demand. When a substitute exists for a product, consumers respond to a price rise by switching expenditure away from the good and buying a substitute whose price has not risen. When very close substitutes are available, demand for the product is highly elastic. Conversely, demand is likely to be inelastic when no substitutes or only poor substitutes are available.

Percentage of income

The demand curves for goods or services on which households spend a large proportion of their income tend to be more elastic than those of small items that account for only a small fraction of income. This is because for items on which only a very small fraction of income is spent, particularly for those which are rarely purchased, people hardly notice the effect of a change in price on their income. The same is not true for 'big-ticket' items such as a new car or a foreign holiday.

Necessities or luxuries

It is sometimes said that the demand for necessities is price inelastic, whereas the demand for luxuries is elastic. This statement should be treated with caution. When no obvious substitute exists, demand for a luxury good may be inelastic, while at the other extreme, demand for particular types of basic foodstuff is likely to be elastic if other staple foods are available as substitutes. It is the existence of substitutes that really determines price elasticity of demand, not the issue of whether the good is a luxury or a necessity.

The 'width' of the market definition

The wider the definition of the market under consideration, the lower the price elasticity of demand. Thus the demand for the bread produced by a particular bakery is likely to be more elastic than the demand for bread produced by all bakeries. This is because the bread baked in other bakeries provides a number of close substitutes for the bread produced in just one bakery. And if we widen the possible market still further, the elasticity of demand for bread produced by all the bakeries will be greater than that for food as a whole.

short run the time period in which at least one factor of production is fixed and cannot be varied.

long run the time period in which no factors of production are fixed and in which all the factors of production can be varied.

Time

The time period in question will also affect the price elasticity of demand. For many goods and services, demand is more elastic in the **long run** than in the **short run** because it takes time to respond to a price change. For example, if the price of an electric-powered car falls relative to the price of a petrol-engine car, it will take time for motorists to respond because they will be 'locked in' to their existing investment in petrol-engine cars.

In other circumstances, the response might be greater in the short run than in the long run. A sudden rise in the price of petrol might cause motorists to economise in its use for a few weeks before getting used to the price and drifting back to their old motoring habits.

CASE STUDY 3.1

Elasticity and tobacco taxation

Various studies have calculated the price elasticity of demand for cigarettes of different groups in society such as the young and the old, and men and women.

A World Bank review concluded that price rises of about 10% would on average reduce tobacco consumption by about 4% in richer countries. Smokers in poorer nations tend to be more sensitive to price changes.

Reviewing 86 studies, Gallet and List found a mean price elasticity of –0.48, meaning that, on average, a 10% increase in price will be followed by a decrease in consumption of 4.8%. They also found greater responsiveness among younger people, with an average price elasticity of –1.43 for teenagers, –0.76 for young adults, and –0.32 for adults. They found an average price sensitivity of –0.50 for men and –0.34 for women. Studies have also tended to show greater price sensitivity among low-income groups.

Follow-up questions

1 What is the formula which is used for calculating price elasticity of demand?
2 Name the other two types of elasticity of demand besides price elasticity of demand.
3 Suggest **two** reasons why adult smokers may be less responsive to a rise in the price of cigarettes than teenage smokers.
4 Most of the elasticity statistics quoted above lie between zero and –1. Discuss the significance of this for governments.

QUANTITATIVE SKILLS 3.2

Worked example: performing an elasticity calculation

People's average incomes fall from £1,000 a week to £600 a week. As a result, demand for potatoes increases from 1 million tonnes to 1.2 million tonnes a week. Calculate the income elasticity of demand for potatoes.

The formula for calculating income elasticity of demand is:

$$\text{income elasticity of demand} = \frac{\text{percentage change in quantity demanded}}{\text{percentage change in income}}$$

The percentage change in quantity demanded is +20%. The percentage change in income is –40%. Placing these figures into the formula:

$$\text{income elasticity of demand} = \frac{+20\%}{-40\%} = -0.5$$

The minus sign indicates that the good is an inferior good. The number 0.5 indicates that demand is inelastic.

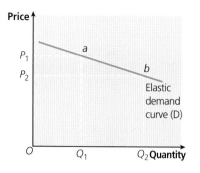

Figure 3.5 The effect of a price fall on total consumer expenditure when demand is elastic

STUDY TIP

Total consumer expenditure is exactly the same as firms' total sales revenue, so if we wish we can state the rule in terms of revenue rather than consumer expenditure.

Price elasticity of demand, total consumer expenditure and firms' total revenue

As an alternative to using the formula to calculate price elasticity of demand between two points on a demand curve, a simple rule can be used to determine the general nature of the elasticity between the two points:

- if total consumer expenditure increases in response to a price fall, demand is elastic
- if total consumer expenditure decreases in response to a price fall, demand is inelastic
- if total consumer expenditure remains constant in response to a price fall, demand is neither elastic nor inelastic, i.e. elasticity = unity (or since the demand curve slopes downward, the elasticity is minus unity or -1)

Consider, for example, Figure 3.5, which shows an elastic demand curve D. At price P_1, total consumer expenditure is shown by the rectangle bounded by P_1, a, Q_1 and O. When the price falls to P_2, the consumer expenditure rectangle changes to the area bounded by P_2, b, Q_2 and O. Clearly, the second of these rectangles is larger than the first rectangle, so total consumer expenditure increases, following a fall in price, when the demand curve is elastic.

EXTENSION MATERIAL

The slope of a demand curve and its elasticity

It is important not to confuse the absolute response indicated by the slope of a curve with the proportionate response measured by elasticity. Take a careful look at the two demand curves in Figure 3.6. In Figure 3.6(a), a straight line (or linear) demand curve has been drawn. Obviously, a straight line has a constant slope. But although the slope is the same at all points on the curve, the elasticity is not.

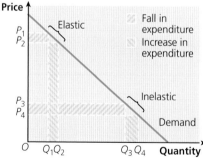

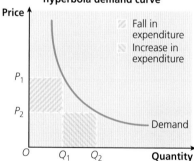

Figure 3.6 Price elasticity of demand and the slope of the demand curve

Moving along a linear downward-sloping demand curve, the price elasticity of demand falls from point to point along the curve. Demand is elastic (or greater than unity) at all points along the top half of the curve. Elasticity equals unity exactly half way along the curve, falling below unity and towards zero along the bottom half of the curve.

If elasticity falls from point to point moving down a linear demand curve, it follows that a non-linear curve (i.e. a curved line) is needed to show the same elasticity at all points on the curve. Figure 3.6(b) shows a demand curve with a constant elasticity of 1 at all points on the curve: that is, elasticity equals unity at all points on the curve. Mathematicians call this a rectangular hyperbola. Whenever the price falls, the proportionate change in quantity demanded exactly equals the proportionate change in price. In this case, consumer expenditure remains unchanged following a rise or fall in price.

Income elasticity of demand

KEY TERM

income elasticity of demand measures the extent to which the demand for a good changes in response to a change in income; it is calculated by dividing the percentage change in quantity demanded by the percentage change in income.

The nature of **income elasticity of demand** — which measures how demand responds to a change in income — depends on whether the good is a normal good or an inferior good.

When disposable income increases, a demand curve shifts rightward, but only if the good is a normal good, for which demand increases as income increases. However, some goods are inferior goods, for which demand decreases as income increases, and an increase in income shifts the demand curve leftward.

Income elasticity of demand is *always* negative for an inferior good and positive for a normal good. This is because the quantity demanded of an inferior good falls as income rises, whereas the quantity demanded of a normal good rises with income.

Normal goods can be further divided into superior goods or luxuries, for which the income elasticity of demand is greater than +1, and necessities, with an income elasticity lying between 0 and +1. Although the quantity demanded of a normal good always rises with income, it rises by a greater percentage for a superior good (such as a luxury car). Conversely, demand for a basic good or necessity such as shoe polish rises by a smaller percentage than income.

The size and sign (positive or negative) of income elasticity of demand affect how a good's demand curve shifts following a change in income.

Cross-elasticity of demand

KEY TERM

cross-elasticity of demand measures the extent to which the demand for a good changes in response to a change in the price of another good; it is calculated by dividing the percentage change in quantity demanded by the percentage change in the price of another good.

Cross-elasticity of demand measures how the demand for one good responds to changes in the price of another good. The cross-elasticity of demand between two goods or services indicates the nature of the demand relationship between the goods. There are three possibilities:

- complementary goods (or joint demand)
- substitutes (or competing demand)
- an absence of any discernible demand relationship

Cars and petrol or diesel fuel, for example, are complementary goods: they are in joint demand. A significant increase in fuel prices will have some effect on the demand for cars, though the effect may not be great. By contrast, private car travel and bus travel are substitute goods. A significant increase in the cost of running a car will cause some motorists to switch to public transport — provided its price does not rise by a similar amount as well.

As with the case of income elasticity of demand, the size and sign (positive or negative) of cross-elasticity of demand affect how a good's demand curve shifts following, in this case, a change in the price of another good. For example, a cross-elasticity of demand of +0.3 for bus travel with respect to the price of running a car indicates that a 10% increase in the cost of private motoring would cause the demand for bus travel to increase by just 3%. For most demand relationships between two goods, cross-elasticities of demand are inelastic rather than elastic, both when the goods are in joint demand and when they are substitutes.

Complementary goods, or goods which are demanded together, such as bicycles and bike lamps, have negative cross-elasticities of demand. A rise in the price of one good leads to a fall in demand for the other good. Suppose, for example that the cross elasticity of demand for bike lamps with respect to the price of new bicycles is –0.51: this tells us that a 10% increase in the price of a new bicycle leads to a 5% fall in the in the demand for bike lamps.

By contrast, the cross-elasticity of demand between two goods which are substitutes for each other is positive. A rise in the price of one good causes demand to switch to the substitute good whose price has not risen. Demand for the substitute good increases. For example, a new bicycle and a new motor scooter are substitutes for each other. If the cross elasticity of demand for a new bicycle with respect to the price of a motor scooter is +0.4, this tells us that a 10% increase in the price of a new motor scooter will lead to a 4% increase in the demand for new bicycles as consumers switch between the two types of private transport.

If we select two goods at random — for example, pencils and suitcases — the cross-elasticity of demand between the two goods will be zero. When there is no discernible demand relationship between two goods, a rise in the price of one good will have no measurable effect upon the demand for the other. The cross elasticity of demand is zero, unless, of course, both items make up an important part of household expenditure.

STUDY TIP
Elasticity basically means responsiveness. Demand elasticities measure how consumers respond to a change in a good's price, income, or the price of another good. You should learn the formulae for each type of elasticity — for example, income elasticity of demand — and avoid making three basic mistakes when using them. The mistakes are:
- missing out the word 'percentage' (or the % sign) from the formula
- writing the formula 'upside down'
- confusing the different elasticities

TEST YOURSELF 3.6
The price of a gaming console for a particular games provider rises by 30%. In subsequent years the demand for games cartridges for this system falls by 10%. What does this tell you about the cross-elasticity of demand between the two products?

SECTION 3.2 SUMMARY
- Elasticity means responsiveness.
- There are three important demand elasticities: price, income and cross elasticity of demand.
- The slope of a demand curve is not the same as price elasticity of demand.
- It is important to understand the determinants of all the elasticities you need to know.
- You must learn all the elasticity formulas, and not confuse them.
- You must be able to interpret elasticity statistics.

3.3 The supply of goods and services

Market supply

Normally when economists refer to supply, they mean market supply. **Market supply** is the quantity of a good or service that all the firms or producers in the market plan to sell at different prices. By contrast, supply by a single firm is the quantity that a particular firm within the market would like to sell. As with demand, the relationship between the two is simple. Market supply is just the sum of the supply of all the firms or producers in the market at different market prices.

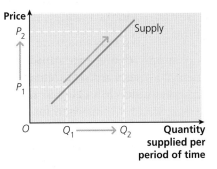

Figure 3.7 A market supply curve

Figure 3.7 shows a market supply curve which indicates that as a good's price rises, more is supplied. If the price starts off low, for example at P_1, firms are willing to supply Q_1. But if the price rises to P_2, planned supply increases to Q_2.

The main reason for upward-sloping supply curves stems from the profit-maximising objective which economists assume firms have. If we assume that a firm always aims to make the biggest possible profit, it follows that a firm will only want to supply more of a good if it is profitable so to do.

For a firm, **profit** is the difference between the **total revenue** the firm receives when selling the goods or services it produces and the costs of producing the goods. Assuming firms do not change their size or scale, the cost of producing extra units of a good generally increases as firms produce more of the good. As a result, it is unprofitable to produce and sell extra units of a good unless the price rises to compensate for the extra cost of production. Rising prices will also encourage new firms to enter the market. The result is the upward-sloping market supply curve we have illustrated.

As with demand, the supply of a good varies according to the time period being considered. Hence the words 'Quantity supplied per period of time' on the horizontal axis in Figure 3.7. In later diagrams, this is shortened to 'Quantity'. But again, as with demand, remember that this is an abbreviation.

Shifts of a supply curve

Earlier in the chapter, we saw that a market demand curve shows how much all the consumers in the market plan to buy at different prices of the good, assuming all the other factors that influence demand remain constant. These 'other factors' were called the conditions of demand and we explained how, if any of them change, the demand curve shifts to a new position.

In exactly the same way, a market supply curve shows the quantities of the good that all the firms in the market plan to supply at different possible prices, assuming the **conditions of supply** remain unchanged. Again, if the *ceteris paribus* assumption no longer holds, one or more of the conditions of supply change and the supply curve shifts to a new position.

The conditions of supply

The main conditions of supply are:

- costs of production, including
  - wage costs
  - raw material costs
  - energy costs
  - costs of borrowing
- technical progress
- taxes imposed on firms, such as VAT, excise duties and the business rate
- subsidies granted by the government to firms

As we have noted, if any of the conditions of supply change, the supply curve shifts to a new position. As with demand, a rightward shift of supply is known as an **increase in supply**, whereas a leftward shift is known as a **decrease in supply**. An increase in wage costs, which for many firms are the most important cost of production, shifts the supply curve leftward (or upward). Firms reduce the quantity of the good they are prepared to supply because production costs have risen. For example, when the price is P_1 in Figure 3.8, a leftward shift of supply from S_1 to S_2 causes the quantity firms are prepared to supply to fall from Q_1 to Q_2. An expenditure tax such as VAT imposed by the government on firms would have a similar effect to an increase in costs of production.

Supply curves also tend to shift rightward when technical progress occurs, reducing production costs, or when firms enter the market. A subsidy given to firms by the government, being similar to a reduction in costs of production, would also shift the supply curve to the right.

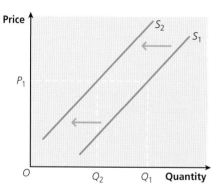

Figure 3.8 A leftward shift of the supply curve

A supply curve shifts leftward (or upward) when the government imposes an expenditure tax such as customs and excise duties or VAT on firms. From a firm's point of view, the tax is similar to a rise in production costs. Firms try to pass the tax on to consumers by increasing the price of the good. For this reason, expenditure taxes provide examples of indirect taxes. The higher price charged means consumers indirectly pay the tax, even though the firms and not the consumers pay the tax to the government.

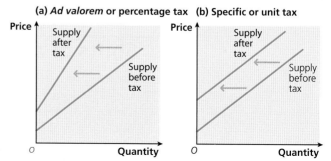

Figure 3.9 An expenditure tax shifting a supply curve

How the supply curve shifts depends on whether the tax that firms are forced to pay is an *ad valorem* tax or a specific tax. In the case of an *ad valorem* tax such as VAT, which is levied at the same percentage rate (e.g. 20%) on the price, the new supply curve is steeper than the old supply curve. This is shown in Figure 3.9(a). If a good is priced at £1, 20% of the price without the tax is 20 pence. However, if the price of a good is £2, the government collects 40 pence of tax revenue for each unit of the good sold.

But in the case of a specific tax or unit tax, such as the excise duty levied on tobacco, the tax levied does not depend on the good's price. Because of this, the new and old supply curves are parallel to each other, separated, as Figure 3.9(b) illustrates, by the size of the tax levied on each unit of the good. When an indirect tax is imposed on a good, the supply curve shifts vertically upwards by the amount of the tax.

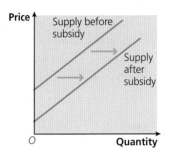

Figure 3.10 A specific or unit subsidy shifting a supply curve

A subsidy given by the government to producers has the opposite effect to an expenditure tax; it shifts the supply curve to the right. In the case of a specific subsidy, which is illustrated in Figure 3.10, the sum of money paid to firms for each unit of the good produced is the same whatever the price of the good and hence the vertical distance between the two supply curves equals the subsidy per unit. By contrast, the size of the subsidy would vary if the subsidy were dependent on the price of the good.

TEST YOURSELF 3.9
Suppose the government subsides private education by giving parents £5,000 a year if their child attends a private school. Would this shift the demand curve for, or the supply curve of, private education? Justify your answer.

SECTION 3.3 SUMMARY

- A market supply curve shows how much of a good all the firms in the market intend to supply at different prices.
- Supply curves usually slope upwards because higher prices lead to higher profits, encouraging existing firms to produce more and attracting new firms into the market.
- The conditions of supply fix the position of the supply curve.
- If any of the conditions of supply change, the supply curve shifts to a new position.
- Movements along a supply curve must not be confused with a shift in the position of the curve.

3.4 Price elasticity of supply

KEY TERM
price elasticity of supply measures the extent to which the supply of a good changes in response to a change in the price of that good.

In contrast to demand elasticities explained earlier in the chapter, there is only one supply elasticity you need to know. This is **price elasticity of supply**, which measures how the supply of a good responds to an initial change in a good's price.

The formula for price elasticity of supply is:

$$\text{price elasticity of supply} = \frac{\text{percentage change in quantity supplied}}{\text{percentage change in price}}$$

Just as with demand curves, you must not confuse the *slope* of a supply curve with its *elasticity*. Upward-sloping *straight-line* (linear) supply curves display the following price elasticities:

- if the supply curve intersects the price axis, the curve is elastic at all points, though elasticity falls towards unity as you move from point to point up the curve

- if the supply curve intersects the quantity axis, the curve is inelastic at all points, though elasticity rises towards unity as you move from point to point up the curve
- if the supply curve passes through the origin, elasticity equals unity (+1) at all points on the curve

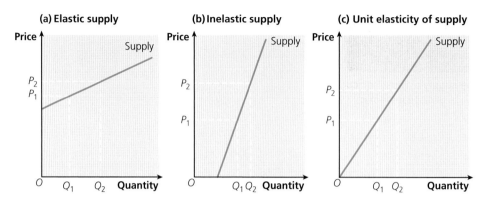

Figure 3.11 Price elasticity of supply and linear supply curves

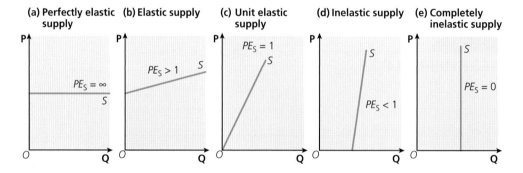

Figure 3.12 The five linear supply curves you should know

TEST YOURSELF 3.10

If the price of a good with a price elasticity of supply of 2.5 increases by 10%, the quantity supplied will:

A fall by 25%

B rise by 25%

C fall by 40%

D rise by 0.4%

Which is the correct answer, and why?

STUDY TIP

You should understand why price elasticity of supply is usually positive and why price elasticity of demand is usually negative.

The factors determining price elasticity of supply

The length of the production period

If firms can convert raw materials into finished goods very quickly (for example, in just a few hours or days), supply will tend be more elastic than when several months are involved in production, as with many agricultural goods.

The supply of most agricultural goods is price inelastic

The availability of spare capacity

When a firm possesses spare capacity, and if labour and raw materials are readily available, production can generally be increased quickly in the short run.

The ease of accumulating stocks

When stocks of unsold finished goods are stored at low cost, firms can respond quickly to a sudden increase in demand. Alternatively, firms can respond to a price fall by diverting current production away from sales and into stock accumulation. The ease with which stocks of raw materials or components can be bought from outside suppliers and then stored has a similar effect.

The ease of switching between alternative methods of production

When firms can quickly alter the way they produce goods — for example, by switching between the use of capital and labour — supply tends to be more elastic than when there is little or no choice. In a similar way, if firms produce a range of products and can switch raw materials, labour or machines from one type of production to another, the supply of any one product tends to be elastic.

The number of firms in the market and the ease of entering the market

Generally, the more firms there are in the market, and the greater the ease with which a firm can enter or leave, the greater the elasticity of supply.

Time

We have already noted that demand is more elastic in the long run than in the short run because it takes time to respond to a price change. The same is true for supply. Figure 3.13 shows three supply curves of increasing elasticity, S_1, S_2 and S_3, which illustrate respectively market period supply, short-run supply and long-run supply.

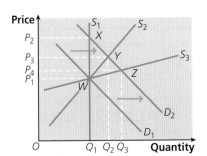

Figure 3.13 The effect of the time period upon price elasticity of supply

- **Market period supply.** The market period supply curve S_1 is shown by a vertical line. S_1 depicts the situation facing firms following a sudden and unexpected rightward shift of demand from D_1 to D_2. When surprised by a sudden increase in demand, firms cannot immediately increase output. In the market period, supply is completely inelastic, and the price rises from P_1 to P_2 to eliminate the excess demand brought about by the rightward shift of the demand curve.
- **Short-run supply.** The higher price means that higher profits can be made, creating the incentive for firms to increase output. In the short run, firms increase output by hiring more variable factors of production such as labour. The short-run increase in output is shown by the movement up the short-run supply curve, S_2. The short-run supply curve is more elastic than the market period supply curve, S_1. In the short run, supply increases to Q_2, and the price falls from P_2 to P_3.
- **Long-run supply.** If firms believe the increase in demand will be long-lasting, and not just a temporary phenomenon, they may increase the scale of production by employing more capital and other factors of production that are fixed in the short run, but variable in the long run. When this happens, firms move along the long-run supply curve S_3. Output rises to Q_3, and the price falls once again, in this case to P_4.

61

In a competitive industry with low or non-existent barriers to entry, elasticity of supply is greater in the long run than in the short run, because in the long run firms can enter or leave the market. Short-run supply is less elastic because supply is restricted to the firms already in the industry.

CASE STUDY 3.2

Housing market elasticities in the UK

UK households have an income elasticity of demand for housing that exceeds +1. However, demand for housing is price inelastic. These demand elasticities, combined with a low price elasticity of supply for housing, push the UK's housing market towards long-term rising prices.

To prevent rapid price rises, new housing would need to have a price elasticity of supply of +10 for supply to equal demand in the long term. But if the price elasticity of supply for new housing remains low, as Table 3.1 shows, house prices will never be stable in the UK when the demand for housing is increasing. Prices are also likely to be unstable when both demand and supply are highly price inelastic.

Table 3.1 Price elasticity of supply in the housing market for different countries

Country	Price elasticity of supply
Canada	+1.2
UK	+0.4
USA	+2.0
France	+0.3
Ireland	+0.6

Follow-up questions

1 State the formula used for measuring price elasticity of supply.
2 Distinguish between the slope and the elasticity of a supply curve.
3 Suggest why the price elasticity of supply of new houses is lower in the UK than in the USA.
4 'To prevent rapid price rises, new housing would need to have a price elasticity of supply of +10 for supply to equal demand in the long term.' Explain this statement.

EXTENSION MATERIAL

A closer look at perfectly elastic demand and supply

Figure 3.14 shows a perfectly elastic demand curve and a perfectly elastic supply curve. (These can also be labelled infinitely elastic demand and infinitely elastic supply.) Although the two parts of Figure 3.14 appear to be identical (apart from the labels), this is misleading. The apparent similarity disguises a significant difference between perfectly elastic demand and perfectly elastic supply. In Figure 3.14(a), demand is infinitely elastic at all prices on or *below* the demand curve, though if the price rises *above* the demand curve (for example, from P_1 to P_2), the amount demanded immediately falls to zero. This is because perfect substitutes are available when demand is perfectly price elastic. Customers cease to buy the good as soon as the price rises *above* the demand curve, switching spending to the perfect substitutes whose prices have not changed.

By contrast, in Figure 3.14(b), supply is infinitely elastic at all prices on or *above* the supply curve, though if the price falls *below* the supply curve (for example, from P_1 to P_2), the amount supplied immediately drops to zero. P_1 is the minimum price acceptable to firms. If they are paid this price (or any higher price), firms stay in the market. The incentive to stay in the market disappears at any lower price and firms leave the market, unable to make sufficient profit.

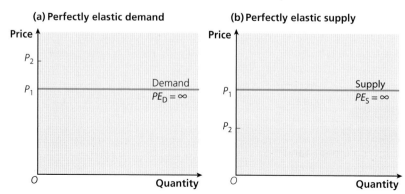

Figure 3.14 Perfectly price elastic demand and supply curves

TEST YOURSELF 3.11

Draw a diagram which shows a demand curve shifting rightward along a supply curve with a zero price elasticity of supply. Explain what happens to the equilibrium price and quantity. Suggest a real-world market which the diagram illustrates.

SECTION 3.4 SUMMARY

- There is only one supply elasticity you need to know: price elasticity of supply.
- The slope of a supply curve is not the same as price elasticity of supply.
- It is important to understand the determinants of price elasticity of supply.
- You must be able to interpret price elasticity of supply statistics.

3.5 The determination of equilibrium market prices

The interaction of demand and supply

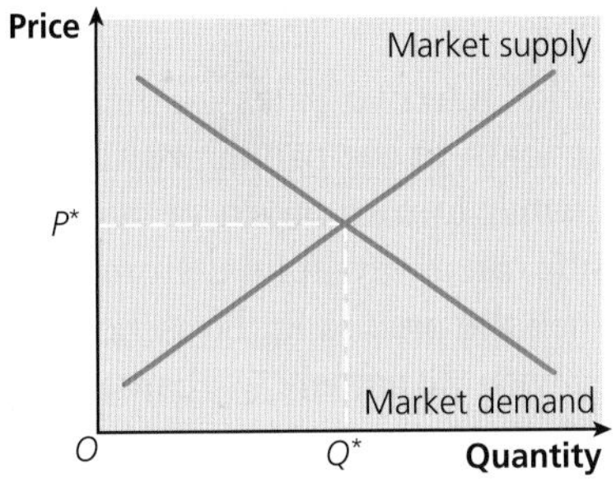

Figure 3.15 Market equilibrium in the tomato market

We now bring together the market demand and market supply curves explained earlier in the chapter to see how the equilibrium price is achieved in a competitive market within the economy. The market we will look at is the tomato market. Its essential features are shown in Figure 3.15.

The market demand curve in Figure 3.15 shows how many tomatoes all the consumers in the market plan to purchase at different prices in a particular period of time. The market supply curve shows how many tomatoes all the farmers and firms in the market wish to supply at different prices in the same time period. The equilibrium market price, *P** in Figure 3.15, is located where the market demand curve for tomatoes intersects or cuts through the market supply curve of tomatoes. We shall now look at the concept of **equilibrium** (and its opposite, **disequilibrium**) in greater depth.

Market equilibrium and disequilibrium

KEY TERMS

equilibrium a state of rest or balance between opposing forces.

disequilibrium a situation in which opposing forces are out of balance.

market equilibrium a market is in equilibrium when planned demand equals planned supply, where the demand curve crosses the supply curve.

market disequilibrium exists at any price other than the equilibrium price, when either planned demand < planned supply or planned demand > planned supply.

The concepts of equilibrium and disequilibrium are important in economic theory and analysis. You should think of equilibrium as a *state of rest* or a *state of balance between opposing forces* and of disequilibrium as a situation of the opposing forces being out of balance. In a market, the opposing forces are supply and demand. **Market equilibrium** in Figure 3.15 occurs where the demand curve and the supply curve cross each other. At price *P**, households *plan* to demand exactly the same quantity of tomatoes that firms *plan* to supply. *P** is therefore the equilibrium price, with *Q** being the equilibrium quantity.

In summary **market disequilibrium** occurs when:

- planned demand < planned supply, in which case the price falls, or when
- planned demand > planned supply, in which case the price rises

Market equilibrium occurs when:

- planned demand = planned supply, in which case the price does not change

SYNOPTIC LINK

Refer back to the mention of 'ruling market price' on page 46.

How excess demand and excess supply lead to changes in price

It is impossible at most prices for both households and firms to simultaneously fulfil their market plans. In Figure 3.16, P_1 is a disequilibrium price for tomatoes because the tomato growers and sellers cannot fulfil their plans at this price. When price is P_1 in Figure 3.16, firms would like to supply Q_2, but households are only willing to purchase Q_1.

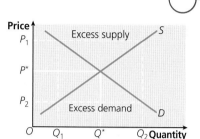

Figure 3.16 Disequilibrium and equilibrium in the tomato market

To explain this further, it is useful to divide the market into two 'sides' — the short side and the long side. When the price is P_1, households, or the people wishing to buy tomatoes, are on the short side of the market, while tomato producers are on the long side. The economic agents on the short side can always fulfil their market plans, but those on the long side cannot. Thus, when the price is P_1, households can purchase exactly the quantity of tomatoes they wish to, namely Q_1. Farmers and other tomato producers, however, are in a different situation. They would like to sell Q_2, but can only sell Q_1, as long as the price remains at P_1. The difference between Q_2 and Q_1 is **excess supply** or unsold stock.

The market is also in disequilibrium at price P_2, because households are unable to buy as much as they wish to at this price. Households would like to buy Q_2 of tomatoes, but they cannot because at this price tomato producers are only willing to supply Q_1. The situation is now reversed compared to P_1. Tomato buyers are on the long side of the market and farmers and tomato sellers are on the short side. In this case, the difference between Q_2 and Q_1 is **excess demand** or unfulfilled demand. Households end up buying Q_1 of tomatoes because this is the maximum quantity that tomato producers are prepared to sell at this price.

How a shift of supply disturbs market equilibrium

Once supply equals demand in a market — for example, at point X in Figure 3.17 — the market remains in equilibrium until an external event hits the market and causes either the market supply curve or the market demand curve to shift to a new position.

Figure 3.17 illustrates what happens in the tomato market when an event such as a bumper harvest causes the supply curve of tomatoes to shift rightward, from S_1 to S_2. Before the shift of the supply curve, P_1 was the equilibrium price of tomatoes. However, once the supply curve shifts, P_1 becomes a disequilibrium price. Too many tomatoes are offered for sale at this price, which means there is excess supply in the market. The excess supply is shown by $Q_2 - Q_1$, or the distance between X and V.

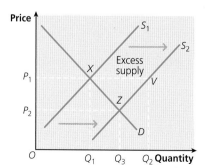

Figure 3.17 The effect of a rightward shift of the market supply curve of tomatoes

To get rid of this unsold stock, tomato producers reduce the price they are prepared to accept. The market price falls from P_1 to P_2, which eliminates the excess supply. In the new equilibrium, planned supply once again equals planned demand, but at the lower equilibrium price of P_2.

TEST YOURSELF 3.13

The equilibrium price for centre court tickets at Wimbledon to watch the men's tennis final is £5,000. The Lawn Tennis Association sells these tickets for £100. What do think happens in the second-hand market for tickets to watch the tennis match?

STUDY TIP

Make sure you can distinguish between a shift of a supply or demand curve, and the adjustment to a new equilibrium along the curve that does not shift.

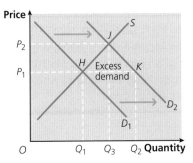

Figure 3.18 The effect of a rightward shift of the market demand curve for tomatoes

How a shift of demand disturbs market equilibrium

Figure 3.18 shows what happens in the market for tomatoes following an increase in consumers' incomes. Tomatoes are usually considered a normal good: that is, a good for which demand increases as income increases. Before the increase in consumers' incomes, the equilibrium price of tomatoes was P_1, determined at the intersection of curves D_1 and S. At this price, planned demand equals planned supply. However, increased incomes shift the market demand curve rightward from D_1 to D_2. Immediately, disequilibrium replaces equilibrium in the market. The rightward shift of demand creates excess demand in the market, as long as the price remains at P_1. Excess demand is shown by $Q_2 - Q_1$, or the distance between H and K.

The market adjustment mechanism now swings into action to get rid of the excess demand. The price increases to P_2 to eliminate the excess demand, and the quantity of tomatoes bought and sold rises to Q_3. In response to the increase in demand from H to K, there is a movement along the supply curve between H and J (an extension of supply) to establish the new equilibrium.

TEST YOURSELF 3.14

There are 30 million customers and 1 million firms producing the good in a particular market in the UK. Explain why you would classify this market as being competitive or uncompetitive.

SYNOPTIC LINK

See Figure 3.8 on page 60, which shows a leftward shift of a supply curve. This could be caused by the imposition of a specific tax or by a cut in a subsidy previously given to firms.

EXTENSION MATERIAL

How the effect of an expenditure tax depends on elasticity of demand

Figure 3.8, earlier in the chapter, can be used to show what can happen when an expenditure tax is imposed on a particular good. The tax shifts the good's supply curve to the left. From the point of view of the firms that produce and sell the good, the tax has the same effect as a rise in costs of production, such as a rise in wage costs. As is the case with cost increases, by raising the price of the good to cover the tax, firms try to increase the price charged to customers by the full amount of the tax. However, their ability to do this depends on price elasticity of demand for the good or service in question.

Figure 3.19 shows that when demand is relatively elastic, consumer resistance means that some, but not all, of a tax (in this case, a specific tax) is passed on to consumers as a price rise. The tax per unit (labelled T in Figure 3.19) is measured by the vertical distance between

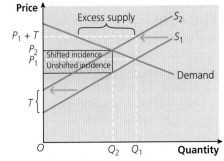

Figure 3.19 Shifting the incidence of a tax when demand is price elastic

65

S_1 (the supply curve before the tax was imposed) and S_2 (the supply curve after the tax was imposed). Immediately after the imposition of the tax, firms may try to raise the price to $P_1 + T$, passing all the tax on to consumers. However, there is excess supply at this price. To get rid of the excess supply, the price falls to P_2. In the new equilibrium, part, but not all, of the tax has been passed onto consumers as a price rise.

The part of the tax passed on to consumers is called the *shifted incidence* of the tax. The rest of the tax (the *unshifted incidence*) is borne by firms or producers. In Figure 3.19, the total tax revenue paid by firms to the government is shown by the rectangle bounded by heavy black lines. The part of the tax rectangle above what was previously the equilibrium price (P_1), shows the shifted incidence of the tax. The part of the tax rectangle below P_1 shows the unshifted incidence.

You should now draw diagrams similar to Figure 3.19, but with perfectly elastic, relatively inelastic and completely inelastic demand curves. The diagrams will show that firms' ability to pass the incidence of a tax on to consumers as a price rise is greatest when demand is completely inelastic, and non-existent when demand is perfectly elastic.

Students often confuse the effect of an increase in an indirect tax imposed on firms with the effect of a direct tax such as income tax imposed on individuals. Whereas a tax imposed on firms shifts the *supply curve* of a good, by reducing consumers' incomes, income tax shifts the *demand curve* for a good. An increase in income tax shifts the demand curve for normal goods leftward, but if the good is an inferior good, the demand curve shifts rightward.

Finally, note that subsidies granted to firms have the opposite effect to taxes imposed on them. Subsidies granted to firms shift the supply curve rightward, showing that firms are prepared to supply more of the good at all prices.

SYNOPTIC LINK

Two examples of equilibrium and disequilibrium in macroeconomics are equilibrium national income and balance of payments equilibrium. Look out for these in Chapters 10 and 14.

TEST YOURSELF 3.15

Distinguish between an expenditure tax and an income tax. Illustrate on a supply and demand graph the possible effect of an increase in both the percentage rate at which VAT is levied on the good and the rate at which income tax is levied, assuming the good is an inferior good.

QUANTITATIVE SKILLS 3.3

Worked example: calculating the equilibrium price of a good
Table 3.2 shows the demand and supply schedules for chocolate bars.

Table 3.2 Demand and supply schedules for chocolate bars

Price per bar (£)	Quantity of bars demanded per week	Quantity of bars supplied per week
0.75	180	240
0.70	200	200
0.65	220	160
0.60	240	120

As a result of a fall in the price of cocoa beans, the supply of chocolate bars rises by 60 bars at all prices. What is the new equilibrium price of chocolate bars?

According to the table, the initial equilibrium price of chocolate bars is 70 pence, at which demand and supply are equal at 200 chocolate bars. If 60 more chocolate bars are supplied at each price, following the fall in the cost of manufacturing the bars, 300 bars are supplied at a price of 75 pence, 260 bars at a price of 70 pence, and 220 bars at a price of 65 pence. This is the new equilibrium price because at this price, demand equals supply at 220 bars. The supply curve has shifted upward by 60 at each price.

STUDY TIP

Many students never really get to grips with microeconomic analysis because they fail to understand the difference between market *plans* and market *action*. Your market plans are what you wish to do when you go shopping. Your market action is what you *end up doing*, i.e. the goods you actually purchase.

CASE STUDY 3.3

Auctions

In theory, an auction provides a quick and efficient method of establishing equilibrium in a market. Auctions have been brought into many people's everyday lives through sites such as eBay. But they also have a long history spanning many different domains. For example, the US government uses auctions to sell Treasury bills and timber and oil leases, Christie's and Sotheby's use them to sell art, and Morrell & Co. and the Chicago Wine Company use them to sell wine.

Each bidder has an intrinsic value for the item being auctioned — he or she is willing to purchase the item for a price up to this value, but not for any higher price.

An auction at Sotheby's

Three types of auction at which a single item is sold are:

1 **Ascending-bid auctions**, also called English auctions. The seller gradually raises the price, bidders drop out until only one bidder remains, and that bidder wins the object at this final price.
2 **Descending-bid auctions**, also called Dutch auctions. The seller gradually lowers the price from a high initial value until the first moment when a bidder accepts and pays the current price. These auctions are called Dutch auctions because flowers have long been sold in the Netherlands using this procedure.
3 **First-price sealed-bid auctions.** In this kind of auction, bidders submit simultaneous 'sealed bids' to the seller. The terminology comes from the original format for such auctions, in which bids were written down and provided in sealed envelopes to the seller, who would open them all together. The highest bidder wins the object and pays the value of her bid.

Follow-up questions

1 What is meant by 'equilibrium in a market'?
2 What type of auction are Sotheby's art auctions?
3 Research another example of a descending bid auction.
4 In the UK, second-hand or used cars are sometimes sold at auction. Describe another way in which second-hand cars are sold.

SECTION 3.5 SUMMARY

- Market equilibrium occurs at the price at which the demand curve crosses the supply curve, i.e. where demand equals supply.
- Disequilibrium occurs when there is either excess demand or excess supply in the market.
- In a competitive market, changes in the market price eliminate excess demand or excess supply; this is how the price mechanism helps to allocate scare resources.

3.6 The interrelationship between markets

So far in this chapter we have looked at how the price mechanism operates in a competitive market. We have seen how shifts of either the demand or supply curve for the good disturb market equilibrium and trigger an adjustment process to establish a new equilibrium.

Shifts of curves are often caused by events taking place in other markets in the economy. On the supply side, they can be caused by a change of price of a good in joint supply (see below). On the demand side, shifts can be caused by a change in price of a good in complementary demand (joint demand) or a substitute good, both of which we have already mentioned. They can also be caused by a change in the price of a good in composite demand, or a good in derived demand, as will be explained below.

Joint supply, joint demand, composite demand and derived demand

Joint supply

Joint supply occurs when production of one good leads to the supply of a by-product. Suppose, for example, that the demand for beef increases, possibly because of rising incomes in developing countries. The slaughter of more cows to meet this demand leads to production of more cow hides, which increases the supply of leather. The interrelationship between the beef and leather markets is shown in Figure 3.20. Note that the price of beef *rises* following the rightward shift of the *demand* curve for beef, but the price of leather *falls* following the rightward shift of the *supply* curve of leather. A rise in the price of the first good leads to a shift of the supply curve of the other good in joint supply. In this example, beef is the main product and leather is the by-product, though the relationship could be reversed.

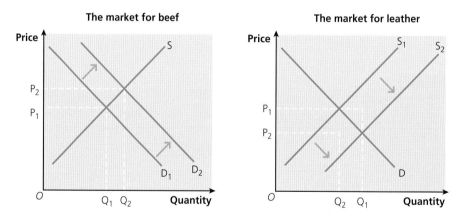

Figure 3.20 The interrelationship between two goods in joint supply

Joint demand

As noted earlier, an increase in the price of a good in joint demand (or a complementary good) has the opposite effect to an increase in the price of a substitute good (or a good in competing demand). For example, Sony games consoles and Sony games cartridges are in joint demand, but Sony and Xbox consoles are in competing demand, so they are substitute goods. Following a significant rise in the price of Sony consoles, demand for them falls, which in turn reduces the demand for Sony games cartridges. The demand curve for Sony cartridges shifts leftward. But the demand curve for Xbox consoles shifts rightward, assuming that consumers consider an Xbox console to be a good substitute for a Sony console.

Composite demand

Students often confuse competing demand, which occurs in the case of substitutes, with *composite demand* and *derived demand*. **Composite demand** is demand for a good which has more than one use. An increase in demand for one use of the good reduces the supply of the good for an alternative use: for example, if more wheat is used for biofuel, less is available for food, unless wheat growing increases.

Derived demand

By contrast, **derived demand** for a good occurs when a good is necessary for the production of other goods. The demand for capital goods such as machinery and raw materials is derived from the demand for consumer goods or finished goods. If the demand for cars falls, so does the demand for engines and gear boxes.

TEST YOURSELF 3.16
With the help of two examples, distinguish between joint demand and composite demand.

STUDY TIP
When you are studying interrelated markets, it is often useful to make use of the concept of cross-elasticity of demand.

KEY TERMS
composite demand demand for a good which has more than one use, which means that an increase in demand for one use of the good reduces the supply of the good for an alternative use. It is related to the concept of competing supply.

derived demand demand for a good or factor of production, wanted not for its own sake, but as a consequence of the demand for something else.

CASE STUDY 3.4

Composite demand and competing supply: biofuels and food

In recent years, high food prices have led experts to warn of the danger of a global food crisis. Many factors have contributed to the price rises, but the growth in production of biofuels has been one of the most important. Much of US maize production goes into biofuels. In 2017/18, 3% of motor vehicle fuels refined in the UK were biofuels, often made from wheat and maize, which are staple foods in the developing world.

Increased demand for biofuels inevitably drives food prices higher, though second- and third-generation biofuels are sourced in other ways: for example, from wood cellulose. Biofuel use is set to grow, and it is still the case that less food is grown as biofuel production increases.

Follow-up questions

1 How are composite demand and competing supply related?
2 Explain how diverting crop production to meet the demand for biofuel is affecting world poverty.
3 Explain **two** causes, other than increased biofuel production, of recent changes in food prices.
4 In your view, are biofuels a source of clean energy or a source of dirty energy?

CASE STUDY 3.5

Digital downloads and streaming replace CDs and DVDs

In 2000, when the first MP3 players were hitting the market, no one anticipated that sales of music downloads would overtake CD and DVD sales. Even when the iTunes store opened in 2003, Apple was only vying for a small market share.

Worldwide streaming revenues were estimated to have risen by 37% to $9.1 billion in 2017, while sales of physical formats dropped 10% to $7.7 billion. Yet within the physical format, sales of traditional vinyl records were staging a recovery.

What are we giving up by adopting the new technology? Booklets, posters and CDs we can hold in our hands, plus music quality (a CD holds far more information than an MP3 file). What are we gaining? Instant satisfaction, convenience and mobile purchasing power.

As sales have moved online, music retail giants like HMV have closed. Now it seems that CDs could be phased out. How will our ways of consuming music evolve as time goes on?

Follow-up questions

1 Over the last 50 years, demand for recorded music switched first from vinyl records to CDs and then to downloading files and on to streamed music. However, vinyl sales are now growing again. Explain **two** reasons for these changes in demand.
2 How would you describe the demand relationship between CDs and MP3 files?
3 Why have many music shops closed in recent years?
4 How have online firms such as Google and Amazon affected UK retail markets in recent years?

EXTENSION MATERIAL

Why prices are often unstable in agricultural markets

In recent history, agricultural markets for foodstuffs and primary products such as rubber have experienced two closely related problems:

- Until recently, there was a long-run trend for agricultural prices to fall relative to those of manufactured goods.
- Prices have fluctuated considerably from year to year.

Agricultural markets are prone to disequilibrium and random shifts of the supply curve from year to year, caused by climatic factors. This leads to unacceptable fluctuations in agricultural prices that, as Chapter 8 explains, may require government intervention to stabilise the price.

The long-run downward trend can be explained by shifts of the demand and supply curves for agricultural products over extended periods of time. This is shown in Figure 3.21, where the equilibrium price for an agricultural product in an early historical period is P_1. Over time, both the demand and supply curves have shifted rightwards. The shift in the demand curve was caused, for example, by rising incomes and population growth, while improved methods of farming increased supply. But for many farm products this shift of supply has greatly exceeded the shift of demand, resulting in a fall to the lower equilibrium price P_2.

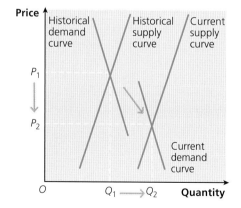

Figure 3.21 The long-run fall in the prices of agricultural products

Since the global recession ended in 2009, we might be seeing the beginning of a long-run trend for food price rises. Can you think of reasons why this might be happening?

The next diagram, Figure 3.22, provides an explanation of fluctuating farm prices. In the diagram, price volatility is caused by random shifts of the short-run supply curve in response to fluctuations in the harvest. Figure 3.22 shows two short-run supply curves: a 'good harvest' supply curve, S_1, and a 'bad harvest' supply curve, S_2. Weather conditions and other factors outside farmers' control shift the position of the supply curve from year to year between the limits set by S_1 and S_2. As a result, market prices fluctuate from year to year within the range of P_1 to P_2.

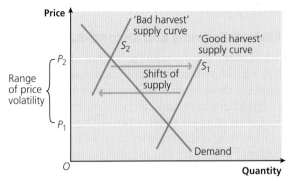

Figure 3.22 Fluctuating agricultural prices caused by shifts of supply

QUANTITATIVE SKILLS 3.4

Worked example: calculating the income elasticity of demand for a good

Table 3.3 shows a price index for food covering the years 2014 to 2018.

Table 3.3 Food price index, 2014–18

Year	Price index
2014	90
2015	100
2016	105
2017	120
2018	110

Which one of the following can be deduced from the data?

A Compared with 2017 the price of food was 10% cheaper in 2018.
B Farmers' revenue from the sale of food rose by 10% in 2015.
C The average price of food increased between 2014 and 2017.
D The price of food rose throughout the period from 2014 to 2018.

This question is testing your understanding of how index numbers are used in economics. Possible answers A, B and D are wrong, leaving C as the correct answer. A is wrong because food was 8.3% cheaper in 2018 not 10% cheaper. To calculate this, you put the change of index points of 10 between the two years as a ratio of 120 and turn this into a percentage. B is wrong because the index numbers do not allow you to calculate farmers' revenue. C is correct because although the price index for food increased in every year between 2014 and 2017, this not true for the change between 2017 and 2018. This means that D is wrong.

CASE STUDY 3.6

Markets for new and second-hand cars

The number of new cars registered in February 2018 in the UK fell by 2.8% compared with a year earlier, making it the eleventh month in a row to show a decline. A car is a consumer durable good, delivering a constant stream of consumer services throughout its life. Provided it is properly looked after and escapes a serious crash, a new car typically lasts about 15 years. However, unlike a house, which is the ultimate consumer durable good (often with a much longer life than that of a person living in it), almost all new cars lose value or depreciate as soon as they have been driven off the showroom forecourt. This means that the prices of most cars fall throughout their lives.

In a recession or economic downturn, new-car owners may hang on to their cars for longer before they sell them — which decreases the supply of second-hand cars — and/or the demand for second-hand cars may fall because people cannot afford them. There are all sorts of possibilities.

In 2018, the demand for new cars fell for a number of reasons. First, there was bad publicity about 'dirty diesels'. Second, a new tougher emissions standard was introduced, which meant that owners of heavily-polluting cars pay more tax on their vehicles and on diesel fuel. Third, there was a lack of investment in the infrastructure needed for electrically powered vehicles. Lastly, consumer confidence fell in the months after the Brexit referendum vote in 2016.

Follow-up questions

1 What is a consumer durable good? Give another example besides a car.
2 Research what has happened to the prices of new cars in the UK between 2018 and the time you are reading this case study.
3 What is meant by depreciation and why do most cars depreciate?
4 How does the market for second-hand cars illustrate the problem of market misinformation?

QUANTITATIVE SKILLS 3.5

Worked example: calculating means and medians and constructing a line graph

Table 3.4 shows the sales value of new vehicles in Great Britain between 2001 and 2017.

Table 3.4 New vehicle sales in Great Britain, 2001–17

Year	Sales (million)	Year	Sales (million)
2001	3.1	2010	2.4
2002	3.2	2011	2.4
2003	3.2	2012	2.5
2004	3.2	2013	2.7
2005	3.0	2014	3.0
2006	2.9	2015	3.2
2007	3.0	2016	3.3
2008	2.7	2017	3.1
2009	2.4		

Source: Department of Transport

(a) **Calculate the mean value to 2 decimal places, and the median values, of new vehicle sales in Great Britain between 2001 and 2017.**

Mean values are calculated by adding up all the values in a data series and then dividing the total by the number of values in the series. The total of all the values is 49.3, which divided by 17 is 2.9. To two decimal places this is 2.90.

By contrast, the median value separates the higher half of the data series from the lower half. The data arranged from highest values to lowest values is 3.3; 3.2; 3.2; 3.2; 3.2; 3.1; 3.1; 3.0; 3.0; 3.0; 2.9; 2.7; 2.7; 2.5; 2.4; 2.4; 2.4. The highest values extend from 3.3 to 3.0 and the lowest values from 3.0 to 2.4. The median value is one of the three 3.0 values.

(b) **Draw a continuous line graph from the data shown in the table.**
The answer is shown in Figure 3.23.

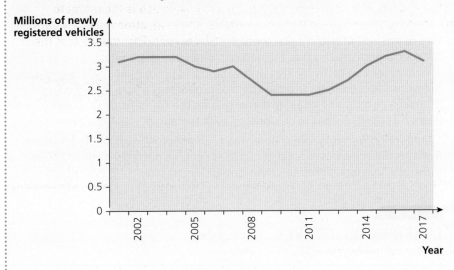

Figure 3.23 New vehicle sales in Great Britain, 2001–17

SECTION 3.6 SUMMARY

- You must practise applying market theory to different real-world markets.
- Make sure you understand the difference between joint demand and joint supply.
- Composite demand and derived demand are also relevant to the interrelationships between markets.
- It is also important to understand the relationships between agricultural markets.
- Cross-elasticity of demand is often an appropriate analytical tool when studying interrelated markets.

Questions

1 Evaluate the view that a fall in a good's price will inevitably lead to more demand for the good.

2 With an example of each, explain the difference between a normal good and an inferior good.

3 Explain how price elasticity of demand affects both total consumer spending and the total revenue received by firms when a good's price changes.

4 List and explain **three** factors which would cause a demand curve to shift to the left.

5 The cross-elasticity of demand for good A with respect to the price of good B is +0.8. Interpret this statistic.

6 List and explain **three** reasons why a supply curve may shift rightward or downward.

7 Explain how a low price elasticity of supply of new housing has affected UK house prices in recent decades.

8 With the help of an appropriate diagram, explain the effect of a government subsidy granted to producers of the good on the good's price.

Production, costs and revenue

This is the first of two chapters which cover an important part of microeconomic theory that economists often call the 'theory of the firm'. This chapter begins by looking at the nature of production, before going on to link production theory to the costs of production a firm incurs when it produces output. The chapter then explains the sales revenue a firm earns when it sells its output to customers, with the aim of making a profit.

The theory covered in this chapter leads seamlessly into Chapter 5, which explains the different market structures such as perfect competition and monopoly in which firms sell their output.

LEARNING OBJECTIVES
These are to understand:

- the meaning of production and the difference between production and productivity, especially labour productivity
- the concepts of specialisation and the division of labour
- how the law of diminishing returns and returns to scale respectively help explain short-run and long-run production theory
- how short-run total, average and marginal cost curves are derived from short-run production theory
- how long-run cost curves are affected by the nature of returns to scale
- economies and diseconomies of scale in the economic long run
- the nature of the revenue curves facing a firm
- how revenue curves are dependent on the type of market structure in which the firm sells its output
- the role of profit in the economy
- how technological change can affect production and costs, and also competitiveness and market structure

4.1 Production

Section 1.3 of Chapter 1 briefly explained the meaning of production and illustrated the basic nature of production in Figure 1.3. The chapter also mentioned the roles of factors of production such as labour, capital and enterprise or the entrepreneurial function in the production process. (An entrepreneur, such as Sir Richard Branson, is both a decision-maker and the bearer of financial risk within a business.)

TEST YOURSELF 4.1
Name four other important entrepreneurs besides Sir Richard Branson.

Before proceeding any further with this chapter, refer back to Chapter 1 and read again what the chapter has to say on **production**.

Now look closely at Figure 4.1, which shows how production theory is the first of the five 'building blocks' of the theory of the firm.

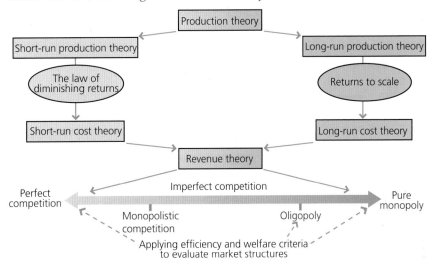

Figure 4.1 The 'building blocks' of the theory of the firm

The flow chart in Figure 4.1 shows that production theory leads into cost theory. Indeed, it is impossible to understand cost theory fully without first understanding the nature of production. The diagram also indicates that short-run cost theory derives from short-run production theory, and likewise long-run cost theory derives from long-run production theory.

Economists call the inputs into the production process the **factors of production**, which are listed in Figure 1.3 in Chapter 1. Four factors of production are usually identified. These are land, labour, capital and enterprise, the last often being called the entrepreneurial input. Land is literally the part of the earth's crust which the firm owns or hires the services of. Labour includes all people employed by the firm who are paid wages or salaries. Capital comprises the capital goods which the firm owns or hires, together with intellectual capital it owns or hires.

Entrepreneurs are different from the other factors of production. They are the people who decide what to produce, how to produce and for whom to produce it. An entrepreneur decides how much of the other factors of production, including labour, to employ. The costs of employing land, labour and capital, together with the cost of the entrepreneur's own services, become the firm's costs of production. Essentially the entrepreneur is a financial risk-taker and decision-maker. Profit, which is the entrepreneur's financial reward, results from successful decision making. Entrepreneurial profit is the profit left over after the cost of employing the other factors of production is deducted from the sales revenue gained from the sale of the goods and services that the entrepreneur decides to produce.

STUDY TIP
Productivity is a key concept in A-level economics. You must know the meaning of labour productivity, and also be aware of the meanings of other types of productivity. Be aware also of the UK's **productivity gap**, which is the difference in productivity levels between the UK and competitor countries.

The meaning of productivity, including labour productivity

Students often confuse productivity with production. While closely related, they do not have the same meaning. For most purposes, **productivity** usually means **labour productivity**, which is output per worker per period of time: for example, per week. However, **capital productivity** or output per unit of capital can also be measured, as can land productivity and entrepreneurial productivity. In reality, of course, all the employed factors of production contribute to both a firm's current level of output and any increase in the level of output.

Minis being produced at the BMW factory in Oxford

Labour productivity or output per worker is extremely significant in manufacturing industries, such as the car industry. In the 1990s and early 2000s, the Rover Car Group (which has since been bankrupted) struggled to survive in the UK car industry. Rover was unable to compete with Japanese car makers such as Nissan and Toyota. Nissan had invested in a then state-of-the-art factory near Sunderland. Labour productivity in the ramshackle Rover factories amounted to only 33 cars per worker per year. By contrast, Nissan produced 98 cars per worker in its then brand-new factory. Given these figures, it is not surprising that the Rover Group, then owned by the German car manufacturer BMW, was forced to stop production of most of its cars in 2005. BMW continued to produce Minis in its high-productivity factories in Oxford.

TEST YOURSELF 4.2
Explain the difference between production and productivity.

QUANTITATIVE SKILLS 4.1

Worked example: interpreting data presented in index number form

Figure 4.2 shows the gross domestic product (GDP) per hour in the G7 countries in 2015 and 2016.

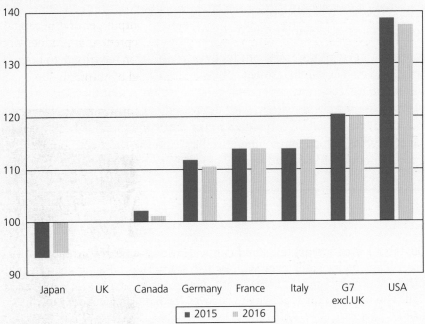

Source: ONS

Figure 4.2 GDP per hour worked in G7 countries, 2015–16

(a) Who are the G7 countries?

As the horizontal axis of the graph indicates, the G7 or Group of Seven countries are Canada, France, Germany, Italy, Japan, the United Kingdom and the United States. G7 is an informal bloc of advanced or high-income industrialised democracies which meets annually to discuss issues such as global economic governance, international security and energy policy. Before 2014 the group, which then included Russia, was known as G8, with the label G7 appearing when Russia was excluded from the group following the country's invasion of the Crimea peninsula, which previously had been part of the Ukraine.

(b) Compare an index number with a percentage number.

Students often confuse data presented in index number form (as in Figure 4.2) with data presented in percentages. The confusion may arise because percentages add up to 100, and the number 100 is the number generally used for the base year in an economic index. (Note: the plural of 'index' is 'indices'.)

(c) Why are there no bars in the graph showing GDP per hour worked in the UK?

The data allow comparisons to be made between GDP per worker in each of the G7 countries. UK GDP per worker is depicted by the index number 100, which is shown by the horizontal line labelled 100. The index number for each of the other G7 countries is either higher or lower than 100. In Italy, for example, the 2015 index number of approximately 114 means that Italian labour productivity was about 14% higher than UK labour productivity, rising to approximately 16% higher in 2016.

Because the data are presented in index number form, we can compare *relative* levels and changes across the G7 countries, but not *absolute* levels and changes. Also, we cannot conclude from the data that Italian workers enjoy higher incomes and living standards than British workers. Although the data *infer* that living standards are higher in Italy than in the UK, this cannot be concluded definitely from the data given here. More evidence is needed to reach this conclusion.

The importance of productivity

In recent years a big problem has adversely affected UK economic performance: the failure of labour productivity to recover from a relatively low level, compared to other countries such as Germany and the USA, in the years following the 2009 recession. This has been the called the 'productivity puzzle'. Why has the UK economy performed less well than competitor countries in increasing labour productivity?

Among the explanations of the productivity puzzle that have been put forward are: inadequate investment in new capital goods, relatively low wages in the UK economy, and employers 'hoarding' rather than laying off workers in the recession, which, with depressed output, inevitably means that labour productivity falls. With regard to the latter argument, the fall in labour productivity has helped employment in the UK in the short run, but the long-run consequences of low productivity growth may be much less favourable.

CASE STUDY 4.1

The UK's productivity puzzle

When the UK entered recession in 2008, labour productivity fell significantly. However, by 2014 UK labour productivity had not recovered to its pre-recessionary 2008 level, with British workers producing about a fifth less for every hour worked than other leading nations. In some years, there was weak recovery, but in other years productivity continued to fall. The failure of productivity to recover from its recessionary low has been called the UK's 'productivity puzzle'.

The UK's 'flexible' labour markets have been very effective in delivering part-time and temporary work, at low cost to employers. In 2014, up to 5.5 million people may have been working on 'zero hours' contracts. At the same time, underemployment (those who would like to work more hours, but cannot do so) has been at record levels. When faced with collapsing markets in the 2008–09 recession, employers — rather than reducing the number of people in work — often tried to cut the wages and hours of those working.

This then led to labour 'hoarding' — keeping workers in employment even though they are in effect producing little or no output. Employers have been reluctant to fire skilled workers, believing that they will be difficult to re-recruit at a later point in the economic upturn. A 2012 survey of private-sector employers by the Chartered Institute of Personnel Development reported that close to a third of businesses had more staff than they needed to fulfil current orders. Most said they were anxious to retain their skills base. From an employer's point of view, it makes sense to let some workers stand idle if this cuts hiring and firing costs and avoids delays in training new workers when demand recovers.

Following a recession, it takes time for firms facing declining demand to shed labour. It also takes time for new, fast-growing sectors to mop up the labour. During this period of flux, too many workers are concentrated in declining industries, with the result that economic output is less than it could be.

Related to this, low labour productivity has been blamed on so-called 'zombie' firms. A 'zombie' firm is an under-performing company, with low labour productivity, which survives because it generates just enough sales revenue to enable interest to be paid on its debts. After previous recessions, banks and other creditors refused to rescue such poorly performing companies, which were allowed to go to the wall. However, this did not happen when the 2008 recession ended in 2009. Very low interest rates or easy credit, accompanied by government exhortations to banks to rescue struggling companies, meant that zombie firms survived. (In 2014, however, the Bank of England dismissed the view that zombie firms provided a significant explanation of low labour productivity.)

What are the consequences of the productivity puzzle? One possibility is that even greater sacrifices may be demanded from those in work, and from those looking for work. If productivity is not improving, reduced labour costs per hour could be achieved by cutting hourly pay. In a 'race to the bottom', UK workers would be pushed to match the lowest competing wages elsewhere in the world. Although the national minimum wage is meant to prevent this happening, there is plenty of evidence that rogue employers flout the law. A better possibility would be to boost productivity. This would require increased investment in newer, more efficient equipment and improved infrastructure. Investment spending on research and development (R&D) might lead to gains over time. However, none of this may happen. In 2014, investment in the UK economy was much lower than it had been in 2008.

Follow-up questions

1 Explain the meaning of a 'flexible' labour market.
2 Find out what has happened to labour productivity in the UK in the 3 years before you read this case study. Has labour productivity recovered?
3 How are 'rogue employers' related to the so-called 'race to the bottom'?
4 Why is raising labour productivity an important policy objective for the UK government?

What is a firm?

> **KEY TERM**
> **firm** a productive organisation which sells its output of goods and/or services commercially.

Before we delve further into the nature of production theory, first in the short run and then in the long run, we shall first get you to consider 'What is a firm?' A **firm** is a business enterprise that either produces or deals in and exchanges goods or services. Unlike non-business productive organisations, such as many charities, firms are commercial, earning revenue to cover the production costs they incur.

EXTENSION MATERIAL

Ronald Coase and the nature of a firm

Way back in 1937, Professor Richard Coase, who much later in 1991 received the Nobel prize in economics for his insights, set out to explain why firms exist. His answer was that firms exist because they reduce transaction costs, such as search and information costs, bargaining costs, costs of keeping trade secrets, and policing and enforcement costs.

Coase then asked, 'Why then don't firms become bigger and bigger? Why isn't all world production carried on by a single big firm?' He gave two main reasons. 'First, as a firm gets larger, there may be decreasing returns to the entrepreneurial function, that is, the costs of organising additional transactions within the firm may rise. Secondly, as the transactions which are organised increase, the entrepreneur fails to make the best use of the factors of production.' At a certain point, the gains from economies of scale are defeated by the costs of bureaucracy.

For further information on Coase and the nature of the firm, and on the different views of later economists, access on the internet the article by Steve Denning, 'Did Ronald Coase get economics wrong?', published in *Forbes* magazine on 25 September 2013.

CASE STUDY 4.2

Japanese manufacturing methods and labour productivity

Until about 30 years ago, most car factories were chaotic places. Modern car factories, by contrast, are much calmer. The difference between the noisy, confused old factory and the smooth-flowing world of the modern ones is the Toyota Production System (TPS), first developed in the 1950s by the Japanese car company. Central to the Toyota Production System, now adopted by all mass car producers, is 'lean manufacturing'.

The aim of lean manufacturing is to combine the best of both craftwork and mass production. It uses less of each input: less labour, less machinery, less space, less time in designing products. Mass production concentrates on reducing defects to a tolerable level. Lean production seeks to eliminate all defects; if something goes wrong, the whole assembly line stops while the fault is identified and put right. An old car factory would have produced a complete afternoon's worth of cars with the same defect. In a lean factory, the mistake is quickly nipped in the bud so that the production of mechanically perfect cars can continue.

Lean manufacturing rejects the old idea of making things in huge batches, which requires holding large buffer stocks of materials and components between each stage of the production process. Now each stage of manufacturing performed in the factory is done on demand. The process eliminates waste by making only as much as is wanted at any given time; gone are the costly piles of work-in-progress that used to litter the factory floor. The change has greatly affected labour productivity.

Follow-up questions

1 Explain how the changes in methods of production mentioned in the passage are likely to have affected labour productivity and costs of production within manufacturing industries.
2 Distinguish between craftwork and mass production.
3 Another feature of Japanese manufacturing methods is known as 'just in time' (JIT). Find out what this means.
4 Research **one** other feature of Japanese manufacturing methods that increases labour productivity.

SECTION 4.1 SUMMARY

* The 'building blocks' of the theory of the firm include production theory, cost theory and revenue theory.
* The key concept in short-run production theory is the law of diminishing returns, also known as the law of diminishing marginal productivity.
* Productivity, which is a key economic concept, is output per unit of input.
* Labour productivity is output per worker.
* Avoid confusing productivity with production. Production is a process or set of processes which converts inputs into outputs.
* A firm is a business enterprise that either produces or deals in and exchanges goods or services.

4.2 Specialisation, division of labour and exchange

The benefits of specialisation and division of labour

KEY TERMS

specialisation a worker only performing one task or a narrow range of tasks. Also, different firms specialising in producing different goods or services.

division of labour this concept goes hand in hand with specialisation. Different workers perform different tasks in the course of producing a good or service.

Over 200 years ago, the great classical economist, Adam Smith, first explained how, within a single production unit or firm (he took the example of a pin factory), output could be increased if workers specialised at different tasks in the manufacturing process.

Smith had established one of the most fundamental of all economic principles: the benefits of **specialisation** or the **division of labour**. According to Adam Smith, there are three main reasons why a factory's total output can be increased if workers perform specialist tasks rather than if each worker attempts all the tasks himself or herself. These are as follows:

- A worker will not need to switch between tasks, so time will be saved.
- More and better machinery or capital can be employed. (Employing 'more of the same' capital is called 'capital widening', while investing in 'state-of-the-art' new technology is called 'capital deepening').
- The 'practice makes perfect' argument that workers become more efficient or productive at the task they are doing, the greater the time spent on the specialist task. However, this advantage can easily become a disadvantage if it involves 'de-skilling' and the creation of boredom and alienation among workers.

Trade and exchange

For specialisation to be economically worthwhile for those taking part in the division of labour, a system of **trade** and **exchange** is necessary. This is because workers who completely specialise cannot enjoy a reasonable standard of living if forced to consume only what they produce. The obvious solution is to produce more than what the worker actually needs, and then to trade the surplus for that produced by others.

KEY TERMS

trade the buying and selling of goods and/or services.

exchange to give something in return for something else received. Money is a medium of exchange.

Several hundred years ago, people living in rural communities within the UK could specialise and then trade whatever they produced through barter. Thus, a farmer might harvest wheat, part of which was then exchanged for services provided by local grain millers and village blacksmiths.

But successful barter requires a 'double coincidence of wants'. Not only must the farmer require the services of the blacksmith; the blacksmith must want the wheat produced by the farmer, and a rate of exchange must be agreed for the two products. As this example suggests, it is reasonably easy to achieve the double coincidence of wants in a small community where people live close to each other and where only a few goods and services are produced and exchanged. However, in modern economies in which a vast number of goods are produced, reliance on barter holds back the growth of the economy. In such economies, barter is an extremely inefficient method of exchange.

These days, when we buy or sell a good or a service, we almost always use money. We finance the transaction either with cash or with a debit card or cheque drawn on a bank or building society deposit. Using money is much more efficient than bartering, as there is no need for a double coincidence of wants. Suppose I want to buy a television set and that I also have a second-hand car I wish to sell. Assuming you wish to buy a second-hand car and have an old TV set you want to get rid of, if we barter the goods, you must want my car and I must want your TV set. We must also agree that the two goods have the same value. But if we use money rather than barter, you pay for my car with money, which I can then use to buy a TV set or whatever I want from somebody else. I could also save the money rather than spend it. Used in this

Our society is becoming increasingly cashless

way, money enables the economy to achieve much greater specialisation and division of labour than is possible with barter.

However, we are increasingly moving towards a 'cashless society' in which credit cards and debit cards, and more recently contactless smartphone payments, are replacing coins and notes as means of exchange. Some economists even believe that so-called cryptocurrencies such as the Bitcoin will replace all current forms of money, though at present this is a minority view. Refer to Chapter 12 on financial markets and monetary policy to find out more about the various forms of money and means of payment.

CASE STUDY 4.3

Adam Smith's pin factory

Adam Smith was an eighteenth-century Scottish philosophy professor, and later customs commissioner, who is often said to be the founder of modern economics. In his book *An Inquiry into the Nature and Causes of the Wealth of Nations*, which was published in 1776, Adam Smith used the example of a local pin factory to explain how the division of labour among workers greatly increases their ability to produce. Here is a slightly abridged version of what Adam Smith wrote:

A workman not educated in the business of pin making could scarce, perhaps, with his utmost industry, make one pin in a day, and certainly could not make twenty. But in the way in which this business is now carried on, one man draws out the wire, another straights it, a third cuts it, a fourth points it, a fifth grinds it at the top for receiving the pin head. The business of making a pin is divided into about eighteen distinct operations. Ten persons could make among them upwards of forty-eight thousand pins in a day. Each person, therefore, making a tenth part of forty-eight thousand pins, might be considered as making four thousand eight hundred pins in a day. But if they had all wrought separately and independently, and without any of them having been educated to this peculiar business, they certainly could not each of them have made twenty, perhaps not one pin in a day.

This great increase in the quantity of work is a consequence of the division of labour. There are three different aspects of this: first, the increase of dexterity in every particular workman; secondly, the saving of the time which is commonly lost in passing from one species of work to another; and lastly, the invention of a great number of machines which enable one man to do the work of many.

Follow-up questions

1 What is meant by the division of labour?
2 What effects does the division of labour have on production and costs?
3 Describe another example, besides pin factories, of firms benefiting from the division of labour.
4 According to Adam Smith, 'This great increase in the quantity of work is a consequence of the division of labour.' Explain **one** way in which this has affected the size of firms.

SECTION 4.2 SUMMARY

- Specialisation occurs in more than one context. These include groups of workers specialising in producing different goods or services, and different workers specialising in different tasks, such as cleaners and managers within a place of work.
- The concept of division of labour goes hand in hand with specialisation, with different workers specialising in different tasks in the course of producing a good or service.
- Trade is the buying and selling of goods and/or services.
- Exchange means to give something in return for something else received.

4.3 The law of diminishing returns and returns to scale

The short run and the long run

In microeconomic theory, the short run is defined as the time period in which at least one of the factors of production is fixed and cannot be varied. This means that the only way in which a firm can produce more in the short run is by adding more variable factors to the fixed factors of production.

In Figure 4.3, the horizontal arrows labelled *A* and *B* show short-run production taking place. By contrast, the movement along the vertical arrow *X* depicts the long run, defined as the time period in which the *scale* of all the factors of production can be changed.

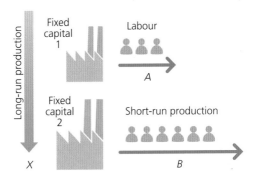

Figure 4.3 Short-run and long-run production

The law of diminishing returns

The law of diminishing returns is a short-run law which states that as a variable factor of production is added to a fixed factor of production, eventually both the marginal returns and then the average returns to the variable factor of production begin to fall.

Table 4.1 shows what might happen in a small musical instrument workshop assembling guitars when the number of workers employed increases from 0 to 10. The first worker employed assembles 1 guitar a day, and the second and third workers respectively add 7 and 10 guitars to the workshop's total daily output. These figures measure the marginal returns (or marginal product) of each of the first three workers employed. The **marginal returns of labour** are the addition to total output brought about by adding one more worker to the labour force.

> **KEY TERM**
>
> **marginal returns of labour** the change in the quantity of total output resulting from the employment of one more worker, holding all the other factors of production fixed.

Table 4.1 Short-run production with fixed capital

	Variable labour										
	0	1	2	3	4	5	6	7	8	9	10
Total returns	0	1	8	18	32	50	64	70	72	68	60
Average returns	–	1	4	6	8	10	10.7**	10	9	7.6	6
Marginal returns		1	7	10	14	18*	14	6	2	−2	−8

* The point of diminishing marginal returns
** The point of diminishing average returns
Note: Total, average and marginal returns are often called total, average and marginal product. For example, in Table 4.1 the 'marginal returns' of labour can be called the 'marginal product' of labour.

In Table 4.1, the first five workers benefit from increasing marginal returns (or increasing marginal productivity). Each additional worker increases total output by more than the amount added by the previous worker. Increasing marginal returns are very likely when the labour force is small. In this situation, employing an extra worker allows the workforce to be organised

83

more efficiently. By dividing the various tasks of production among a greater number of workers, the firm benefits from specialisation and the division of labour. Workers become better and more efficient in performing the particular tasks in which they specialise, and time is saved that otherwise would be lost as a result of workers switching between tasks.

But as the firm adds labour to fixed capital, eventually the **law of diminishing marginal returns** (or 'law of diminishing marginal productivity') sets in. In this example, the law sets in when the sixth worker is employed. The marginal return of the fifth worker is 18 cars, but the sixth worker adds only 14 cars to total output. Diminishing marginal returns set in because labour is being added to fixed capital. When more and more labour is added to fixed plant and machinery, eventually workers begin to get in each other's way and the marginal returns of labour fall, though not often at a labour force as small as six workers.

Note that the impact of diminishing marginal returns does not mean that an extra worker joining the labour force is any less hardworking or motivated than his or her predecessors. (In microeconomic theory we often assume that workers and other factors of production are completely interchangeable and homogeneous.) In the economic short run, as more labour is added to a fixed amount of capital or machinery, the possibilities for further specialisation and division of labour eventually become exhausted.

The law of diminishing returns shown on a diagram

The two panels of Figure 4.4 illustrate the law of diminishing returns. In the upper panel of the diagram, diminishing marginal returns begin to operate at point *A*. Up to this point, the slope of the **total returns** or total product curve increases, moving from point to point up the curve. This shows the labour force benefiting from increasing marginal returns. When diminishing marginal returns set in, the total returns curve continues to rise as more workers are combined with capital, but the curve becomes less steep from point to point up the curve. Point *Y* shows where total returns begin to fall. Beyond this point, additional workers begin to get in the way of other workers, so the marginal returns to labour become negative.

In the lower panel of Figure 4.4, the law of diminishing returns sets in at point *B*, at the highest point on the marginal returns curve. To the left of this point, increasing marginal returns are shown by the rising (or positively sloped) marginal returns curve, while beyond this point, diminishing marginal returns are depicted by the falling (or negatively sloped) marginal returns curve. Likewise, the point of diminishing **average returns of labour** is located at the highest point of the average returns curve at point *C*. Finally, marginal returns become negative beyond point *W*.

It is important to understand that all three curves in Figure 4.4 (and the last three rows in Table 4.1) contain the same information, but the information is used differently in each curve (and row). The total returns curve plots the information *cumulatively*, adding the marginal returns of the last worker employed to the total returns before the worker joined the labour force. By contrast, the marginal returns curve plots the same information *non-cumulatively*, or as separate observations. Finally, at each level of employment, the average returns curve shows the total returns of the labour force divided by the number of workers employed.

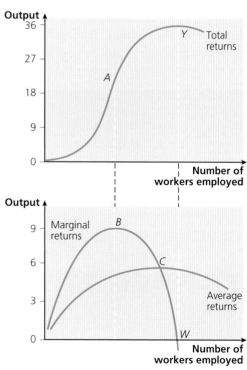

Figure 4.4 Total, marginal and average returns curves

STUDY TIP
Negative marginal returns are not a result of workers' obstinacy or tendency to throw a spanner in the works. Neither are they because the first workers employed are more efficient than those who are employed later. As we said earlier, in the abstract world of microeconomic theory, workers are treated as equally able, homogeneous units.

EXTENSION MATERIAL

The relationship between marginal returns and average returns

The relationship between the marginal returns of labour and the average returns of labour is an example of a more general relationship that you need to know. (Shortly, we shall provide a second example, namely the relationship between marginal costs and average costs of production.)

Marginal and average curves plotted from the same set of data always display the following relationship:

- When the marginal is greater than the average, the average rises.
- When the marginal is less than the average, the average falls.
- When the marginal equals the average, the average is constant, neither rising nor falling.

It is vital to understand this relationship. It does *not* state that an average value will rise when a marginal value is rising; nor does it state that an average value will fall when a marginal value falls. As we saw in Figure 4.4, marginal returns begin to fall as soon as the law of diminishing marginal returns sets in. Nevertheless, as long as marginal returns are greater than the average returns of labour, the latter continue to rise. When marginal returns exceed average returns, the average returns curve is 'pulled up', even when the marginal returns curve is falling. But when the marginal returns curve cuts through the average returns curve (at point C in Figure 4.4), beyond that point the average returns of labour begin to fall. The marginal returns curve cuts through the average returns curve at the latter's highest point. Beyond this point, the marginal returns curve continues to fall, and because marginal returns are less than average returns, they 'pull down' the average returns curve.

The difference between marginal and average returns

Whereas marginal returns are the addition to total output attributable to taking on the last worker added to the labour force, the average returns at any level of employment are measured by dividing the total output of the labour force by the number of workers employed. The average returns of the labour force employed in the guitar workshop are shown by the middle row of data in Table 4.1. Note that in the table, the point of diminishing *average* returns occurs after the sixth worker is taken on, whereas diminishing marginal returns set in after the fifth worker is employed. The relationship between the marginal returns and the average returns of labour is illustrated in the lower panel of Figure 4.4.

Worked example: an example of the relationship between marginal, average and total values

A firm has a fixed amount of capital and land and increases output by employing additional labour according to the schedule in Table 4.2.

Table 4.2 Diminishing returns to labour

Labour	Output
1	20
2	42
3	68
4	93
5	100
6	90

(a) At what level of output do diminishing marginal returns to labour set in?

Diminishing marginal returns set in when the marginal return or marginal productivity falls for an extra worker added to the labour force. The marginal returns of the second worker, which are calculated by subtracting total output when only one worker is employed from total output when two workers are employed, are 22 units of output. Via a similar calculation, the marginal returns of the third worker are 26 units of output. However, diminishing marginal returns set in when a fourth worker is added to the labour force. The marginal returns of the fourth worker are 25 units of output.

(b) At what level of output do diminishing average returns to labour set in?

For each size of labour force, average returns are calculated by dividing total output by the number of workers employed. Average returns when the labour force is 1, 2, 3 and 4 workers are respectively outputs of 20, 21, 22.67 and 23.25, showing increasing average returns. However, when the fifth worker is added to the labour force, marginal returns fall to 7 units of output and average returns fall to 20 units of output. Diminishing *average* returns (falling average output per worker) have now set in.

(c) At what level of output do diminishing total returns to labour set in?

Diminishing *total* returns set in when the addition of an extra worker causes total output to fall. This happens when the sixth worker is added to the labour force. Note that marginal returns are now negative (–10 units of output). The workers are getting in each other's way to such an extent that total output falls.

STUDY TIP

In production theory, students often confuse the law of diminishing returns, which is a short-run law applying when at least one factor of production is fixed, with returns to scale, which relate to the long run when firms can change the scale of all the factors of production. You must avoid this mistake. As we explain shortly, the law of diminishing returns is important for explaining the shape of short-run cost curves, and likewise, returns to scale help to explain the shape of long-run cost curves and the concepts of economies and diseconomies of scale.

Returns to scale

Figure 4.3 earlier in the chapter illustrates the important distinction between returns to a variable factor of production, which occur in the short run, and **returns to scale**, which operate only in the economic long run. Suppose that a firm's fixed capital is represented by **plant** size 1 in the diagram.

KEY TERMS

returns to scale the rate by which output changes if the scale of all the factors of production is changed.

plant an establishment, such as a factory, a workshop or a retail outlet, owned and operated by a firm.

Initially, the firm can increase production in the short run, by moving along the horizontal arrow *A*, employing more variable factors of production such as labour. To escape the impact of short-run diminishing marginal returns which eventually set in, the firm may make the long-run decision to invest in a larger production plant, such as plant size 2. The movement from plant size 1 to plant size 2 is shown by the movement along the vertical arrow *X* in the diagram. Once plant size 2 is in operation, the firm is in a new short-run situation, able to increase output by moving along arrow *B*. But again, the impact of short-run diminishing returns may eventually cause the firm to expand the scale of its operations again in the long run.

Contrasting increasing, constant and decreasing returns to scale

It is important to avoid confusing returns to scale, which occur in the long run when the scale of *all* the factors of production can be altered, with the short-run returns that occur when at least one factor is fixed. With returns to scale there are three possibilities:

KEY TERMS

increasing returns to scale when the scale of all the factors of production employed increases, output increases at a faster rate.

constant returns to scale when the scale of all the factors of production employed increases, output increases at the same rate.

decreasing returns to scale when the scale of all the factors of production employed increases, output increases at a slower rate.

- **Increasing returns to scale.** If an increase in the scale of all the factors of production causes a more than proportionate increase in output, there are increasing returns to scale.
- **Constant returns to scale.** If an increase in the scale of all the factors of production causes the same proportionate increase in output, there are constant returns to scale.
- **Decreasing returns to scale.** If an increase in the scale of all the factors of production causes a less than proportionate increase in output, there are decreasing (or diminishing) returns to scale.

SECTION 4.3 SUMMARY

- The key concept in short-run production theory is the law of diminishing returns.
- The law states that as a variable factor of production is added to a fixed factor of production, eventually both the marginal returns and then the average returns to the variable factor of production begin to fall.
- The key concept in long-run production theory is returns to scale.
- Increasing returns to scale are likely to lead to economies of scale, which are defined as falling long-run average costs, as output increases.
- Decreasing returns to scale are likely to lead to diseconomies of scale, which are defined as rising long-run average costs, as output increases.

4.4 Costs of production

Economics students often confuse production and costs. Production, as previously explained, simply converts inputs into outputs, without considering the money cost of using inputs such as capital and labour. This section of the chapter explains, first, how short-run cost curves are derived from the short-run production theory we have already explained, and second, in a similar way, how long-run cost curves are derived from long-run production theory.

Raw materials are a variable cost, such as Kenco buying coffee beans

Short-run costs

The difference between short-run and long-run costs

We have already defined the short run as the time period in which at least one factor of production is fixed. Short-run costs are made up of fixed costs and the costs incurred when hiring the services of the variable factors of production. These are called variable costs of production. Written as equations:

total cost = total fixed cost + total variable cost

or:

$$TC = TFC + TVC$$

and:

average total cost = average fixed cost + average variable cost

or:

$$ATC = AFC + AVC$$

Long-run costs, by contrast, are always variable costs. Fixed costs don't exist in the economic long run when, as Figure 4.3 showed, a firm can move seamlessly from one size of plant to another.

The difference between fixed and variable costs

In the *short run*, when the inputs divide into fixed and variable factors of production, the costs of production can likewise be divided into fixed and variable costs. **Fixed costs** are the costs a firm incurs when hiring or paying for the fixed factors of production. In the short run, capital is usually assumed to be a fixed factor of production, giving rise to costs which are unchanged in the short run. These include the cost of maintaining a firm's buildings, as well as the initial cost of acquiring buildings such as factory space and offices. By contrast, as the name implies, **variable costs** change as the level of output changes. The costs of hiring labour and buying raw materials are usually regarded as variable costs of production. It is worth remembering that in the *long run*, all costs are variable because the long run is defined as the time period in which all the factors of production can be changed.

The difference between total cost, average variable cost and marginal cost

When a firm increases its output, the **total cost** of production increases. At any level of output, the average cost (or unit cost) is calculated by dividing the firm's total cost of production by the size of output produced. An **average variable cost** curve is shown in the lower panel of Figure 4.5, which also shows the firm's **marginal cost** curve. Marginal cost is the addition to total cost resulting from producing one additional unit of output. We shall shortly explain the shapes of all these cost curves.

> **KEY TERMS**
>
> **fixed cost** cost of production which, in the short run, does not change with output.
>
> **variable cost** cost of production which changes with the amount that is produced, even in the short run.

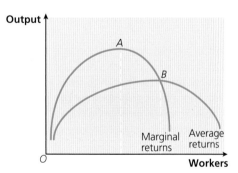

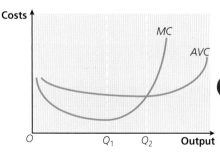

Figure 4.5 Deriving the marginal cost (*MC*) curve and the average variable cost (*AVC*) curve from the marginal and average returns curves

> **KEY TERMS**
>
> **total cost** all the cost incurred when producing a particular size of output.
>
> **average variable cost** total variable cost divided by the size of output.
>
> **marginal cost** addition to total cost resulting from producing one additional unit of output.

The short-run average fixed cost (*AFC*) curve

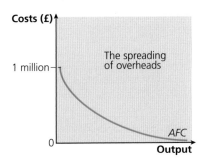

Figure 4.6 A firm's short-run average fixed cost (*AFC*) curve

Fixed costs of production are overheads, such as the rent on land and the maintenance costs of buildings, which a firm must pay in the short run. Suppose, for example, that a car manufacturing company incurs overheads of £1 million a year from an assembly plant it operates. If the plant only managed to produce one automobile a year, **average fixed costs** per car would be £1 million — the single car would bear all the overheads. But if the company were to increase production, average fixed costs would fall to £500,000 when two cars are produced, £333,333 when three cars are produced and so on. The firm's average fixed costs per unit of output fall as output increases, since overheads are spread over a larger output. *AFC* curves *always* slope downwards to the right, as shown in Figure 4.6, with average fixed costs approaching zero at very high levels of output, but never quite equalling zero.

KEY TERM
average fixed cost total cost of employing the fixed factors of production to produce a particular level of output, divided by the size of output: $AFC = TFC \div Q$.

The short-run average total cost (*ATC*) curve

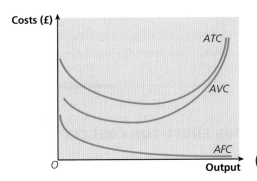

Figure 4.7 Deriving a firm's short-run average total cost (*ATC*) curve

The **average total cost** (*ATC*) curve shown in Figure 4.7 is obtained by adding together at each level of output the *AFC* and *AVC* curves. In the diagram, the firm's average costs of production initially fall as the size of output increases. However, for higher levels of output, beyond the lowest point on the *ATC* curve, average costs usually rise, leading to a U-shaped *ATC* curve.

KEY TERM
average total cost (also known as **average cost**) total cost of producing a particular level of output, divided by the size of output: $ATC = AFC + AVC$.

STUDY TIP
Make sure you practise calculating and plotting average and total costs from given data.

Objective test question: calculating average and total costs from given data

You should be able to calculate average and total costs from given data. This example takes the form of an objective test question in which the data are presented on a graph.

Figure 4.8 shows a firm's average variable costs and average fixed costs of production.

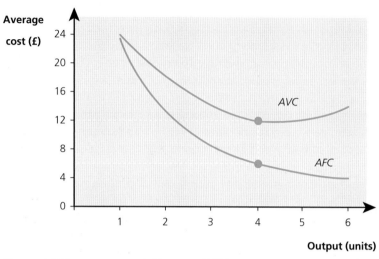

Figure 4.8 The average variable costs (AVC) and average fixed costs (AFC) of production for a firm

The total cost of producing four units is:

A £12   C £48
B £24   D £72

To arrive at the correct answer, which is D, two calculations are required. The first calculation involves adding AVC (£12) to AFC (£6) at an output of four units to arrive at average total cost (ATC), which is £18. The second calculation is multiplying ATC (£18) by output (4) to arrive at total cost, which is £72.

Bringing together the various short-run cost curves

Figure 4.9(a) is similar to Figure 4.7, but with the marginal cost curve added. As we explained earlier, by adding together the AFC and AVC curves, we get the ATC curve. The marginal cost curve cuts through from below *both* the AVC and ATC curves, at the lowest points of these curves. This is a further example of the mathematical relationship between the marginal and average values of a variable, which we explained on page 85.

In Figure 4.9(b), by contrast, the AFC and AVC curves have been left out of the diagram in order to emphasise that the MC curve cuts through the lowest point of the U-shaped ATC curve.

(a) Adding *AFC* to *AVC* to obtain the *ATC* curve

(b) The U-shaped *ATC* curve

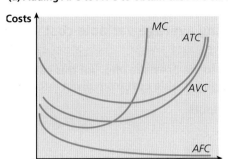

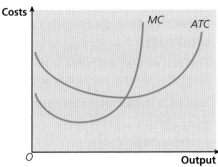

Figure 4.9 The relationships between marginal cost, average fixed cost, average variable cost and average total cost

How factor prices and productivity affect costs and choice of factor inputs

Factor prices are the prices that a firm pays for hiring the different factors of production (capital, labour, etc.). Interest is the factor reward of capital, and wages and salaries are the factor reward of labour. We explained earlier in the chapter that capital productivity is output per unit of capital employed, and labour productivity is output per worker.

Economists generally assume that firms have a single business objective, namely to produce the level of output at which profit can be maximised. The profit-maximising level of output must, of course, be produced at the lowest possible cost for *that particular* level of output. This in turn means that the firm must employ the optimal factor combination when minimising the cost of producing the profit-maximising level of output.

This is where factor prices and productivity come in. If wage levels are low but the price of capital is high, then, provided we ignore labour and capital productivity, labour is more attractive than capital to employ. This suggests that a firm should use a labour-intensive method of production (lots of labour but little capital). Similarly, if labour is expensive to employ but capital is cheap, then cost minimisation is likely to require a capital-intensive method of production (lots of capital but little labour).

This becomes more complicated, however, when we introduce differences in labour and capital productivity into the decision-making process. For example, if wage levels are low but labour productivity is also low, a capital-intensive method of productive method of production can be preferable to labour-intensive production, if the high price of capital is more than offset by high capital productivity.

Capital-intensive production is often accompanied by high wage rates — though with relatively few workers employed. However, if consumers, both at home and abroad, demand more and more of the output produced by capital-intensive firms, employment of labour will also increase. Companies such as Nissan and Toyota, which employ robots rather than workers to produce parts of cars, have provided plenty of evidence of how the greater use of robotised machinery can enable both wage rates and employment to rise in the UK car industry.

Objective test question: calculating average variable cost from given information on total cost

This is a similar objective test question to the previous one, but this calculation works in the opposite direction, asking you to calculate average variable cost from given information on total cost.

Table 4.3 shows total cost at various outputs.

Table 4.3 Total costs of production for a firm

Output	Total cost (£)
0	100
10	115
20	140
30	175
40	220

From the information in the table, we can conclude that the average variable cost at an output of 20 is:

A £2

B £7

C £14

D £120

Only the third and first rows of data are used in the calculation — the data in the other rows are irrelevant or 'background noise'. In row 3, we divide total cost (£140) by the output of 20, arriving at an average total cost of £7. The information in row 1 tells us that total fixed cost is £100. This means average fixed cost is £5 when 20 units of output are produced. Finally, since $AVC = ATC - AFC$, average variable cost is £7 – £5, which is £2. The correct answer is therefore A.

- Short-run cost curves are derived from short-run production theory.
- Long-run cost curves are derived from long-run production theory.
- Short-run costs are made up of fixed costs and variable costs.
- Fixed costs are the costs a firm incurs when hiring or paying for the fixed factors of production.
- Variable costs change as the level of output changes.
- Total costs comprise all the costs incurred when producing a particular size of output.
- Average cost is total cost divided by the size of output.
- Marginal cost is the addition to total cost resulting from producing one additional unit of output.
- The *ATC* and *AVC* curves are U-shaped with the *MC* curve cutting both at their lowest points.

92

4.5 Economies and diseconomies of scale

KEY TERMS

economies of scale as output increases, long-run average cost falls.

diseconomies of scale as output increases, long-run average cost rises.

As a firm grows in size by investing in new plant or buildings, it can benefit from economies of scale. However, beyond a certain size, the firm may eventually suffer from diseconomies of scale. **Economies of scale** are defined as *falling* long-run average costs of production that result from an increase in the size or scale of the firm. Likewise, **diseconomies of scale** are defined as *rising* long-run average costs of production.

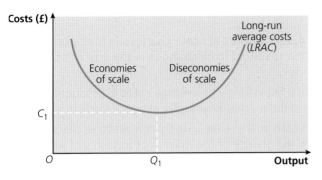

Figure 4.10 A firm's U-shaped long-run average cost (*LRAC*) curve

Figure 4.10, which shows a 'symmetrical' U-shaped *LRAC* curve, has been drawn assuming that economies of scale are followed by diseconomies of scale. In the long run, as already explained, a firm can change the scale of all its factors of production, moving from one size of plant to another. At first sight, the *LRAC* curve appears identical to the short-run *ATC* curve drawn in Figure 4.9(a) and (b). However, the reasons for the U shape of the short-run and the long-run average cost curves are different. The U-shape of the short-run *ATC* curve is explained by the assumption that labour becomes more productive as it is added to fixed capital, before eventually becoming less productive because of the impact of the law of diminishing returns. By contrast, the shape of the long-run average cost curve is explained by two long-run concepts which don't operate in the short run. These are economies and diseconomies of scale.

Figure 4.11 shows a number of short-run average total cost (*SRATC*) curves lying along the *LRAC* curve. Each of the *SRAS* curves, labelled $SRATC_1$ to $SRATC_9$, represents a particular firm size. In the long run, a firm can move from one short-run cost curve to another — for example, from $SRATC_1$ to $SRATC_2$ — with each curve associated with a different scale of capacity that is fixed in the short run. The *LRAC* curve forms a tangent to the *SRATC* curves, each of which touches the *LRAC* curve.

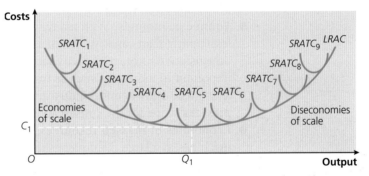

Figure 4.11 A firm's U-shaped long-run average cost (*LRAC*) curve and its related *SRATC* curves

The difference between internal and external economies of scale

The scale economies and diseconomies referred to so far in this chapter have been **internal economies and diseconomies of scale**. To recap, these occur when a firm, or a plant within the firm itself, increases its scale and size. By contrast, **external economies of scale** occur when average or unit costs of production fall, not because of the growth of the firm or plant itself, but because of the growth of the industry or market of which the firm is a part. Likewise, **external diseconomies of scale** occur when average costs of production increase because of the growth of the whole industry or market. The next two sections explain different types of economy and diseconomy of scale.

Internal economies of scale

There are several types of internal economy of scale, as described below.

Technical economies of scale

Technical economies of scale are generated through changes to the 'productive process' as the scale of production and the level of output increase. Technical economies of scale can be caused by:

- **Indivisibilities.** Many types of plant or machinery are indivisible in the sense that there is a certain minimum size below which they cannot efficiently operate.
- **The spreading of research and development costs.** With large plants, research and development (R&D) costs can be spread over a much longer production run, reducing unit costs in the long run.
- **Volume economies.** With many types of capital equipment, costs increase less rapidly than capacity. When a storage tank or boiler is doubled in dimension, its storage capacity increases eightfold. Volume economies are important in industries such as transport, storage and warehousing, as well as in metal and chemical industries where an increase in the scale of plant provides scope for the conservation of heat and energy.
- **Economies of massed resources.** The operation of a number of identical machines in a large plant means that proportionately fewer spare parts need to be kept than when fewer machines are involved.
- **Economies of vertically linked processes.** Much manufacturing activity involves a large number of vertically related tasks and processes, from the initial purchase of raw materials, components and energy through to the completion and sale of the finished product. The linking of processes in a single plant can lead to a saving in time, transport costs and energy.

Managerial economies of scale

The larger the scale of a firm, the greater is its ability to benefit from specialisation and the division of labour within management as well as within the ordinary labour force. A large firm can benefit from a functional division of labour, namely the employment of specialist managers: for example, in the fields of production, personnel and sales. Detail can be delegated to junior managers and supervisors.

Marketing economies of scale

Marketing economies of scale are of two types: bulk-buying and bulk-marketing economies. Large firms may be able to use their market power both to buy supplies at lower prices and also to market their products on better terms negotiated with wholesalers and retailers.

Financial or capital-raising economies of scale

Financial or capital-raising economies of scale are similar to the bulk-buying economies just described, except that they relate to the 'bulk-buying' or bulk-borrowing of funds required to finance the business's expansion. Large firms can often borrow from banks and other financial institutions at a lower rate of interest and on better terms than those available to small firms.

Risk-bearing economies of scale

Large firms are usually less exposed to risk than small firms, because risks can be grouped and spread. Large firms can spread risks by diversifying their output, their markets, their sources of supply and finance and the processes by which they manufacture their output. Such economies of diversification or risk bearing can make the firm less vulnerable to sudden changes in demand or conditions of supply that might severely harm a smaller, less diversified business.

Economies of scope

Economies of scope are factors that make it cheaper to produce a range of products together than to produce each one of them on its own. An example is businesses sharing centralised functions, such as finance or marketing.

TEST YOURSELF 4.4
Explain the difference between technical and managerial economies of scale.

Internal diseconomies of scale

Firms can also suffer from various types or forms of diseconomy of scale, or rising long-run average costs, as they grow in size. These include managerial diseconomies of scale, communication failure, and motivational diseconomies of scale.

Managerial diseconomies of scale

As a firm grows in size, administration of the firm becomes more difficult. Delegation of some of the managerial functions to people lower in the organisation may mean that personnel who lack appropriate experience make bad decisions. This may increase average costs of production.

Communication failure

Communication failure also contributes to managerial diseconomies of scale. In a large organisation there may be too many layers of management between the top managers and ordinary production workers, and staff can feel remote and unappreciated. When staff productivity begins to fall, unit costs begin to rise. As a result, the problems facing the business are not effectively addressed.

Motivational diseconomies of scale

With large firms, it is often difficult to satisfy and motivate workers. Over-specialisation may lead to de-skilling and to a situation in which workers perform repetitive boring tasks and have little incentive to use personal initiative in ways which help their employer.

It is difficult to motivate workers who perform repetitive boring tasks

EXTENSION MATERIAL

Plant-level economies of scale and firm-level economies of scale

So far, we have discussed economies and diseconomies of scale which occur when the whole of a *firm* grows in size. Sometimes, however, *firms* grow larger but without the *plants* they own and operate growing significantly in size. For this reason, it is useful to distinguish between economies of scale that occur at the level of a single plant or establishment owned by a firm and those occurring at the level of the whole firm. In recent years, continued opportunities for further firm-level economies of scale have contributed to the growth of larger firms, but expansion of plant size has been less significant.

The relationship between returns to scale and economies or diseconomies of scale

The link between returns to scale and economies and diseconomies of scale is that increasing returns to scale lead to falling long-run average costs or economies of scale, and likewise decreasing returns to scale bring about rising long-run average costs or diseconomies of scale. The effect of increasing returns to scale on long-run average costs can be explained in the following way: output increases faster than inputs, so if wage rates and other factor prices are the same at all levels of output, the money cost of producing a unit of output must fall. Likewise, with decreasing returns to scale, output increases at a slower rate than inputs, and the money cost of producing a unit of output rises.

There are other reasons for falling long-run average costs besides the impact on costs of increasing returns to scale. These include the effect of 'bulk buying' reducing the cost of raw materials and components.

External economies and diseconomies of scale

As previously mentioned, external economies of scale occur when a firm's average or unit costs of production fall, not because of the growth of the firm itself, but because of the growth of the industry or market of which the firm is a part. Very often, external economies of scale are produced by cluster effects, which occur when a lot of firms in the same industry are located close to each other, providing markets, sources of supply and a pool of trained labour for each other.

External diseconomies of scale occur in a similar way, with the growth of the whole market raising the average costs of all the firms in the industry. As with external economies of scale, external diseconomies can arise from cluster effects. When a large number of similar firms locate close to each other, they not only create benefits which aid all the firms in the cluster; they may also get in each other's way. Competition for labour among the firms may raise local wages, which while being good for workers, increases the unit wage costs of their employers. There may also be an increase in local and regional traffic congestion, which lengthens delivery times and raises delivery costs both for firms and for their customers.

CASE STUDY 4.4

Are economies of scale now less important in the car industry?

In the twentieth century, car manufacturing grew to become perhaps the most important industry in modern industrialised economies. Though car manufacture began in Germany and France, the main growth of car manufacturing in its early years took place in the USA. Henry Ford's adaptation of the <u>moving assembly line</u>, which allowed car factories to benefit from economies of scale, marked the beginning of <u>mass production</u>.

Garel Rhys, director of the Centre for Automotive Industry Research at Cardiff University, has calculated that economies of scale reach their peak at 250,000 cars a year in an assembly plant, although for the body panels the figure could be as high as 2 million.

However, economies of scale in car production are now not as important as they used to be. Reasons for this include: <u>market fragmentation</u>, leading to lower <u>production runs</u>; building cars to order rather than in large-scale batches of identical cars; and new ways of assembling finished cars in which manufacturers such as Toyota are outsourcing more and more of the car to outside suppliers. With car buyers demanding a wider choice of vehicles, production runs have to get smaller.

As car companies produce an ever-wider range of vehicles, so the way cars are made is changing. There is less need for huge, <u>capital-intensive factories</u>, and barriers to entry into the car industry are falling.

Follow-up questions

1 Explain the meaning of each of the concepts underlined in the passage.
2 Describe some of the economies of scale that have contributed to lower average costs in the UK car industry.
3 Name **three** other manufacturing industries in which there are significant economies of scale and indicate in each case the types of economy of scale.
4 Outline **two** ways in which computers and robots have affected methods of production in the car industry.

Economies and diseconomies of scale and the long-run average cost curve

If you refer back to Figures 4.10 and 4.11 you will see symmetrical U-shaped *LRAC* curves, which have been drawn assuming that internal economies of scale are followed symmetrically by internal diseconomies of scale.

However, Figures 4.12 to 4.15 show four other possible shapes of the curve which differ from the symmetrical U-shape shown earlier. Figure 4.12 is a variant of Figures 4.10 and 4.11, but with a horizontal section to the *LRATC* curve inserted between the sections of the curve showing economies and diseconomies of scale. This depicts a situation between outputs Q_1 and Q_2 in which exhaustion of the benefits of economy of scale does not lead immediately to the onset of diseconomies of scale.

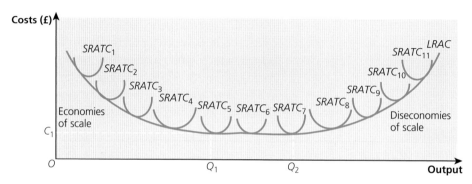

Figure 4.12 A 'three section' long-run average cost curve

Another possibility is illustrated by Figure 4.13: an *LRAC* curve which is horizontal throughout its length. This curve depicts a market or industry in which firms neither benefit from economies of scale nor suffer the consequences of diseconomies of scale.

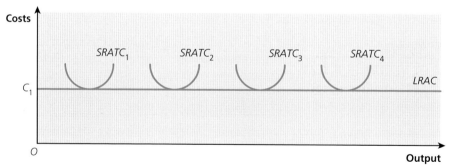

Figure 4.13 Constant long-run average costs

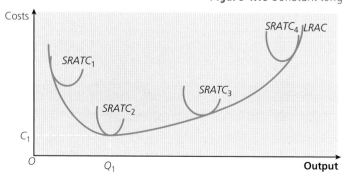

Figure 4.14 An *LRAC* curve showing economies of small-scale production

Figure 4.14 helps to explain why small firms are common in industries supplying services, such as those provided by hairdressers and personal trainers. The markets in which these services are provided typically possess economies of small-scale production. Diseconomies of scale set in early in such industries, leading to a U-shaped *LRAC* curve which is 'skewed to the left'.

By contrast, in Figure 4.15 the *LRAC* curve is 'skewed to the right' of the diagram, showing economies of large-scale production. Diseconomies of scale eventually set in, but only after substantial economies of scale have been achieved.

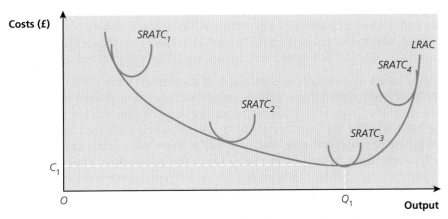

Figure 4.15 An *LRAC* curve showing economies of large-scale production

There are, of course, other factors, apart from the existence or non-existence of scale economies and diseconomies, which contribute to markets containing different sizes of firm. A factor that has been becoming increasingly important in recent decades is firms 'contracting out' the provision of services, previously provided 'in house' by managers and workers employed by the firms themselves, to 'outside' suppliers of the same services. The outside suppliers range from small independent firms such as a local sandwich shop to large-scale specialist firms providing services such as catering, accountancy and ICT maintenance.

All the *LRAC* curves drawn above can be used to show the *average cost-minimising* size of firm. In each case, this is shown at the lowest point on the *LRAC* curve and the *SRAC* curve forming a tangent to the *LRAC* curve at this point. In Figures, 4.10. 4.11, 4.14 and 4.15 there is only one *average cost-minimising* size of firm, located at output Q_1 with average cost C_1. Figures 4.12 and 4.13 are slightly different. Test yourself 4.5 asks why this is so.

TEST YOURSELF 4.5
How many average cost minimising firms are there in Figures 4.12 and 4.13? In each case explain your answer.

TEST YOURSELF 4.6
Apply the mathematical rule of the relationship between the marginal and average values of a variable (see page 85) to Figures 4.12 to 4.15. Copy each of the diagrams and then draw on the diagram the long-run marginal cost curve that fits the diagram.

Long-run marginal costs

Long-run marginal cost (*LRMC*) shows the additional cost incurred if a firm increases output when all the factors of production are variable. The mathematical relationship between *LRMC* and *LRAC* is the same as for *SRMC* and *SRATC*, and your understanding of this is tested in Test yourself 4.6.

When long-run marginal costs fall and are *below* long-run average costs, the *LRAC* curve also falls. Likewise, when long-run marginal costs rise and are *above* long-run average costs, the *LRAC* curve also rises. It follows that when the *LRMC* curve cuts through the lowest point on a *LRAC* curve, the *LRAC* curve must be U-shaped, displaying first economies of scale and then diseconomies of scale.

How internal economies and diseconomies of scale affect particular industries

The following two case studies focus on two industries or markets that are affected by economies and diseconomies of scale.

CASE STUDY 4.5

The rise and fall of London's bendy buses

The end of London's bendy bus experiment has brought shouts of joy from some people. Motorists disliked the long, low monsters getting stuck round narrow crossroads. Cyclists hated the crushing menace they seemed to present. Transport for London found too many fare-dodgers hopping on and off.

'Bendy buses' were used on 12 routes over the decade from 2002 to 2011, but the then mayor of London, Boris Johnson, called them 'cumbersome machines' which were too big for narrow streets and encouraged fare-dodgers. Johnson introduced nearly 500 new double-decker buses, nicknamed 'Boris buses', to replace the 'bendies'. But the 'bendies' could fit 120 on board, while their replacements take only 85. Even if there are plenty of seats available, well over half of them are usually upstairs. Many old people and young mothers with infants don't do stairs and cannot reach the upper deck. They have to be downstairs. The 'bendies' were all downstairs, so their replacement means there has been a massive loss of accessible seats. 'The most accessible bus in London' is now being missed by the old, wheelchair users and mothers with young children.

Follow-up questions

1 Using the concepts of economies and diseconomies of scale, discuss the advantages and disadvantages of bendy buses (a) for Transport for London, the organisation that provided the buses, and (b) for members of the general public.
2 State **one** other example of a supposed innovative form of transport being withdrawn soon after it came into use.
3 Find out whether 'Boris buses' have been successful.
4 Explain **one** way in which public transport could be significantly improved in the UK.

CASE STUDY 4.6

Super-tankers and volume economies of scale

The large super-tankers that are used to transport crude oil across seas and oceans from oil fields to industrial markets benefit significantly from volume economies of scale. However, super-tankers can also suffer from a diseconomy of scale. This is because large super-tankers cannot enter shallow ports. A wider tanker with a shallow draught does not yield as many economies of scale as a conventional super-tanker, but a wider tanker is more flexible and can enter more ports.

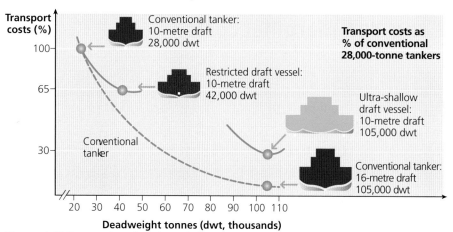

Figure 4.16 Economies of scale and oil tankers

Follow-up questions

1 How could the oil tanker industry be organised to reduce the disadvantages of large super-tankers?
2 What is a volume economy of scale?
3 State **three** examples in other industries of volume economies of scale.
4 Explain how super-tankers sometimes cause *external* diseconomies of scale to occur.

The L-shaped long-run average cost curve

Besides the *LRAC* curves illustrated in Figures 4.10 to 4.15 another possibility is the L-shaped *LRAC* curve drawn in Figure 4.17. This curve, which vaguely resembles the letter 'L', results from the assumption that there are substantial economies of scale, which eventually give way, not to diseconomies of scale, but to a 'flattening out' of long-run average costs. There is evidence of this type of *LRAC* curve in many manufacturing industries involving large-scale production.

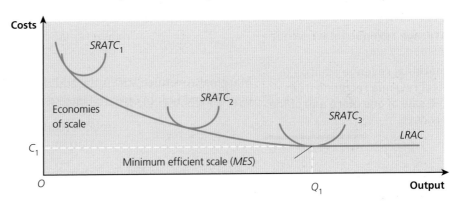

Figure 4.17 An 'L'-shaped *LRAC* curve and minimum efficient scale (*MES*)

The concept of the minimum efficient scale of production

Figure 4.17 also illustrates an important concept in production and cost theory: minimum efficient scale (*MES*). *MES* is the lowest output at which long-run average costs have been reduced to the minimum level that can be achieved, which means that the firm has benefited to the full from economies of scale. In Figure 4.17, all firm sizes to the left of the $SRATC_3$ curve are below minimum efficient scale, incurring higher average costs than can be achieved at the lowest point on $SRATC_3$. By contrast, there would be no further reductions in long-run production costs for any firms producing levels of output above Q_1. In the diagram, the *MES* level of output is Q_1, with average costs minimised at C_1.

SECTION 4.5 SUMMARY

- Economies of scale are associated with falling long-run average costs of production when a firm increases its size of plant.
- Diseconomies of scale are associated with increasing long-run average costs of production when a firm increases its size of plant.
- There are various types of economy of scale including technical, managerial and finance-raising economies.
- There are various types of diseconomy of scale including communicational failure and motivational diseconomy of scale.
- Economies and diseconomies of scale (in cost theory) are often respectively caused by increasing and decreasing returns to scale (in production theory).
- It is important not to confuse internal and external economies and diseconomies of scale.
- Likewise, it is important not to confuse short-run and long-run cost curves.
- In some industries, there are substantial economies of scale, which eventually give way to a 'flattening out' of long-run average costs. In these industries, there is a minimum efficient scale of production.

4.6 Marginal, average and total revenue

KEY TERMS

total revenue all the money received by a firm from selling its total output.

average revenue total revenue divided by output.

marginal revenue addition to total revenue resulting from the sale of one more unit of the product.

Revenue is the money that a firm earns when selling its output. **Total revenue** (*TR*) is all the money a firm earns from selling the total output of a product. By contrast, at any level of output, **average revenue** (*AR*) is calculated by dividing total revenue by the size of output. Stated as an equation:

$$\text{average revenue} = \frac{\text{total revenue}}{\text{output}} \text{ or } AR = \frac{TR}{Q}$$

Marginal revenue (*MR*) is the addition to total revenue resulting from the sale of one more unit of output. Stated as an equation:

$$\text{marginal revenue} = \frac{\Delta \text{ total revenue}}{\Delta \text{ output}} \text{ or } MR = \frac{\Delta TR}{\Delta Q}$$

where Δ is the symbol used to indicate the changes in total revenue and the change in total output.

STUDY TIP

The Greek delta symbol Δ is used by mathematicians as the symbol for a change in the value of a variable over a range of observations. The word 'marginal' means the change in the value of a variable when there is one more unit of the variable, so Δ is the symbol that indicates this change. It is used in the formulae for marginal product and marginal cost, as well as for marginal revenue.

Average revenue and the firm's demand curve

Figure 4.18 shows the demand conditions facing a high-street retailer of electrical goods in a particular week. If the firm sets the price of microwave ovens at £500, 20 customers want to buy an oven. Total sales revenue is £10,000 and average revenue per oven sold is £500. However, by reducing the price to £300, the retailer can sell 60 ovens. Total revenue is now £18,000 and average revenue is £300. The point to note is that at each level of sales, the average revenue the retailer earns is the same as the price charged. This is always the case when the price charged is the same for all the units of output being sold. Hence, in these conditions, the demand curve facing the firm is also its average revenue (*AR*) curve.

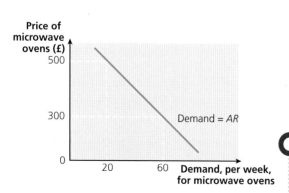

Figure 4.18 The demand curve facing a firm when it decides how much output to sell

STUDY TIP

Make sure you understand that the demand curve for a firm's output is the same as the average revenue curve facing the firm.

The relationship between average and marginal revenue

To understand the relationship between marginal and average *revenue* curves you should start by re-reading the explanation in the extension material on page 85 about the relationship between marginal and average *returns*. (Indeed, the relationship is the same for all marginal and average values of two variables, provided they are plotted from the same data set: for example, marginal and average cost plotted from cost data.)

Marginal and average curves plotted from the same set of data always display the following relationship:

- When the marginal is greater than the average, the average rises.
- When the marginal is less than the average, the average falls.
- When the marginal equals the average, the average is constant, neither rising nor falling.

The nature of a firm's revenue curves depends on the competitiveness of the market structure in which the firm sells its output. The final row of Figure 4.1 at the start of this chapter sets out the four market structures that we shall explain in greater detail in Chapter 5. Two of these are **perfect competition** and **monopoly**. The marginal and average revenue curves are different in these market structures.

Average revenue and marginal revenue in perfect competition

A perfectly competitive market is defined by a number of conditions or characteristics that the market must possess. These conditions, which we shall revisit in Chapter 5, are:

- a very large number of buyers and sellers
- all buyers and sellers possess perfect information about what is going on in the market
- consumers can buy as much as they wish to purchase and firms can sell as much as they wish to supply at the ruling market price set in the market as a whole
- an individual consumer or supplier cannot affect the ruling market price through its own actions
- an identical, uniform or homogeneous product
- no barriers to entry into, or exit from, the market in the long run

Taken together, the six listed conditions tell us that a perfectly competitive firm, which is depicted in Figure 4.19(a), faces a perfectly elastic demand curve for its product. The demand curve facing the firm is located at the ruling market price, P_1, which itself is determined through the interaction of market demand and market supply in Figure 4.19(b). Note that the horizontal axis in Figure 4.19(b) shows millions of units of output being produced. This is because Figure 4.19(b) depicts the whole market, comprising very large numbers of both consumers and firms. In equilibrium, where market demand equals market supply, the ruling market price is P_1, and the equilibrium quantity is Q_1 millions of units. In Figure 4.19(a), the horizontal axis is labelled 'hundreds', to reflect the fact that in perfect competition a single firm is only a tiny part of the total market.

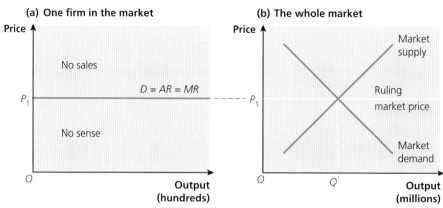

(a) One firm in the market

Price

No sales

$D = AR = MR$

P_1

No sense

O

Output
(hundreds)

(b) The whole market

Price

Market supply

P_1

Ruling market price

Market demand

O Q'

Output
(millions)

Figure 4.19 Average revenue and marginal revenue curves in perfect competition

The assumption that a perfectly competitive firm can sell whatever quantity it wishes at the ruling market price P_1, but that it cannot influence the ruling market price by its own action, means that a firm in a perfectly competitive markets is a passive **price-taker**.

The labels '*No sales*' and '*No sense*' placed on Figure 4.19(a), respectively above and below the price line P_1, help to explain why a perfectly competitive firm is a price-taker. '*No sales*' indicates that if the firm raises its selling price above the ruling market price, customers desert the firm to buy the identical products (perfect substitutes) available from other firms at the ruling market price. '*No sense*' refers to the fact that, although a perfectly competitive firm *could* sell its output below the price P_1, doing so is inconsistent with the profit-maximising objective. No extra sales can result, so selling below the ruling market price inevitably reduces both total sales revenue and therefore profit, given the fact that the firm can sell any quantity it wants at the ruling market price.

It follows from this that the ruling market price facing each firm in the market is both the firm's average revenue curve and its marginal revenue curve. If each unit of the good is sold at a price of £1 (average revenue), selling an extra unit of the good always increases total revenue by £1 (marginal revenue). The horizontal price line is also the perfectly elastic demand curve for the firm's output. It is perfectly elastic because the goods produced by all the firms in the market, being uniform or homogeneous, are perfect substitutes for each other. In summary, for a firm, $D = AR = MR$, as depicted in Figure 4.19(a).

Average revenue and marginal revenue in monopoly

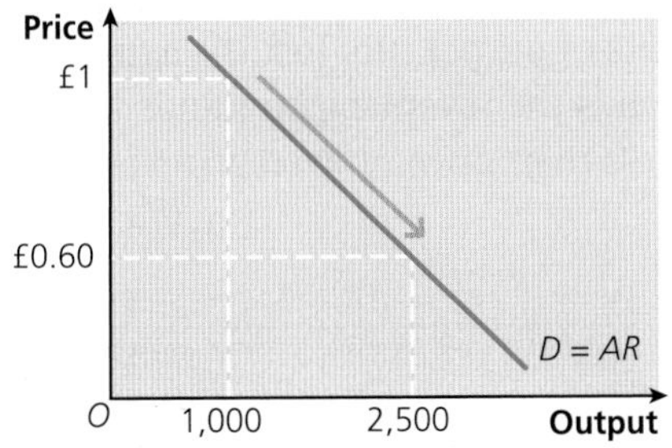

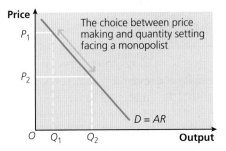

Figure 4.20 Price equalling average revenue (*AR*) in monopoly

It is worth repeating that the demand curve facing a perfectly competitive firm, besides being located at the ruling market price, is also the firm's *AR* curve and its *MR* curve. By contrast, the demand curve for a monopolist's output is the monopolist's *AR* curve, but it is *not* the monopolist's *MR* curve.

To understand why the market demand curve is the monopolist's average revenue (*AR*) curve, consider Figure 4.20, which shows two prices, £1 and £0.60, which can be charged by a monopolist for the good it produces.

At a price of £1, 1,000 units are demanded. At this price, the monopolist's total revenue is £1,000. Average revenue, or total revenue divided by output ($TR \div Q$), is £1, which is of course the same as price. This is the case at all prices: the price charged for all units of the good and average revenue are always the same. For example, if the monopolist sets the price at £0.60, 2,500 units of the good are demanded; total sales revenue is £1,500 and average revenue ($TR \div Q$) is £0.60. The downward-sloping market demand curve facing the monopolist is therefore the firm's average revenue (*AR*) curve.

KEY TERMS

price-maker when a firm faces a downward-sloping demand curve for its product, it possesses the market power to set the price at which it sells the product.

quantity-setter when a firm faces a downward-sloping demand curve for its product, it possesses the market power to set the quantity of the good it wishes to sell.

The downward-sloping *AR* curve can affect the monopoly in two different ways. If the monopolist is a **price-maker**, choosing to set the price at which the product is sold, the demand curve dictates the maximum output that can be sold at this price. For example, if the price is set at P_1 in Figure 4.21, the maximum quantity that can be sold at this price is Q_1. But if the monopolist cuts the price it charges to P_2, sales increase to Q_2. Alternatively, if the monopolist is a **quantity-setter** rather than a price-maker, the demand curve dictates the maximum price at which a chosen quantity of the good can be sold. If the monopolist wants to sell Q_2, the market demand curve shows that the maximum price at which this quantity can be sold is P_2. To summarise, if the monopolist sets the price, the market demand curve dictates the maximum quantity the firm can sell. Conversely, if the monopolist sets the quantity, the market demand curve determines the maximum price the firm can charge. However, for any one good it produces, a firm cannot be a price-maker and a quantity-setter at the same time.

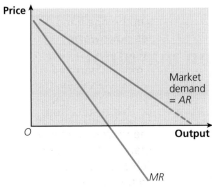

Figure 4.21 The choice between price making and quantity setting facing a monopolist

However, to understand why marginal revenue and average revenue are *not* the same in monopoly, you must remember that when the *marginal* value of a variable is less than the *average* value of the variable, the *average* value falls.

Because the market demand curve or average revenue curve falls as output increases, the monopolist's marginal revenue curve *must* be below its average revenue curve. Figure 4.22 shows the relationship between the *AR* and the *MR* curves. You should see, however, that the *MR* curve is not only below the *AR* curve — it has also been drawn twice as steep. This is always the case whenever the *AR* curve is a downward-sloping straight line.

Figure 4.22 Monopoly average revenue (*AR*) and marginal revenue (*MR*) curves

The next diagram, Figure 4.23, explains in more depth the relationship between *AR* and *MR* curves in monopoly. The monopolist initially charges a price of P_1 and sells the level of output Q_1. However, to increase sales by an extra unit to Q_2, the downward-sloping *AR* curve forces the monopolist to reduce the selling price to P_2. This reduces the price at which *all* units of output are sold. Total sales revenue increases by the area *k* in Figure 4.23, but decreases by the area *h*. Areas *k* and *h* respectively show the revenue

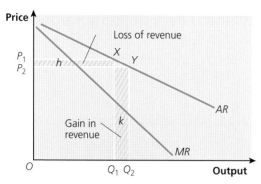

Figure 4.23 Explaining a monopolist's marginal revenue (*MR*) curve

gain (namely, the extra unit sold multiplied by price P_2) and the revenue loss resulting from the fact that, in order to sell more, the price has to be reduced for *all* units of output, not just the extra unit sold. Marginal revenue, which is the revenue gain minus the revenue loss (or $k - h$), must be less than price or average revenue (area k).

SYNOPTIC LINK
A monopoly is explained in detail in Chapter 5, while Chapter 6 applies the related concept of monopsony to labour markets.

EXTENSION MATERIAL

Elasticity and revenue curves

We mentioned earlier in the chapter that the horizontal price line facing a perfectly competitive firm is also the perfectly elastic demand curve for the firm's output. The explanation for this lies in the word 'substitutability'. When studying elasticity, you learnt that the availability of substitutes is the main determinant of price elasticity of demand. In perfect competition, because of the assumptions of a uniform product and perfect information, the output of every other firm in the market is a *perfect substitute* for the firm's own product. If the firm tries to raise its price above the ruling market price, it loses all its customers.

In monopoly, by contrast, provided the demand curve is a straight line as well as downward sloping, price elasticity of demand falls moving down the demand curve. Demand for the monopolist's output is elastic in the top half of the curve, falling to be unit elastic

exactly half way down the curve, and inelastic in the bottom half of the curve. This is shown in Figure 4.24. Demand is elastic between *A* and *B*, unit elastic at *B*, and inelastic between *B* and *C*.

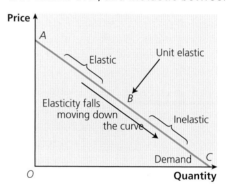

Figure 4.24 Price elasticity of demand and a monopolist's demand or average revenue (*AR*) curve

SYNOPTIC LINK
We shall revisit the significance of elasticity in the next chapter, when comparing profit maximisation with revenue maximisation.

The relationship between marginal revenue and total revenue

Marginal revenue measures the change in total revenue that results from an increase in the quantity of goods sold. It indicates how much revenue increases for selling an additional unit of a good or service. Marginal revenue is also shown by the *slope* of the total revenue curve. Increasing marginal revenue can be shown by the total revenue curve becoming steeper. Falling marginal revenue is shown by the total revenue curve becoming less steep as sales increase. And finally, constant marginal revenue means that the slope of

STUDY TIP
Make sure you practise calculating and plotting average, marginal and total revenue from given data.

the total revenue curve is unchanged as sales increase. Look back to Figure 4.4 on page 84 of this chapter. This illustrates the relationship between marginal returns and total returns, another example of the relationship between the marginal and the total values of a variable. The relationship between marginal costs and total cost provides a third example.

SECTION 4.6 SUMMARY

- Revenue is the money that a firm earns when selling its output.
- Total revenue is all the money a firm earns from selling the total output of a product.
- Average revenue is calculated by dividing total revenue by the size of output.
- Marginal revenue is the addition to total revenue resulting from the sale of one more unit of the product.
- The demand curve facing the firm is also its average revenue curve.
- The nature of a firm's revenue curves depends on the competitiveness of the market structure in which the firm sells its output.
- In perfect competition, the average and marginal revenue curves are horizontal.
- In monopoly, the average revenue curve slopes downward, with the marginal revenue curve below the average revenue curve.

4.7 Profit

Profit is the difference between total revenue and total costs

KEY TERM
profit the difference between total sales revenue and total cost of production.

Students often confuse profit and revenue, mistakenly believing that the two terms have the same meaning. In fact, profit and revenue are different. **Profit** is the difference between the sales revenue the firm receives when selling the goods or services it produces and the costs it incurs when producing these goods or services.

total profit = total revenue − total costs

In some circumstances, total costs of production may exceed total sales revenue, in which case there is a loss. Think of a loss as being *negative* profit.

KEY TERM
profit maximisation occurs at the level of output at which total profit is greatest.

We have already mentioned that economists generally assume that firms have a single business objective: **profit maximisation**. This means producing the level of output at which profit (revenue minus costs) is greatest. (Firms may also have other objectives, such as survival, growth and increasing their market share. And as we have seen in Chapter 2 on individual economic decision making, behavioural economists question the assumption of traditional economic theory that individuals, both as consumers and as entrepreneurs, are rational decision-makers who endeavour to maximise their utility.)

107

The difference between normal and abnormal (supernormal) profit

When explaining profit maximisation, we shall apply two profit concepts, used frequently by economists undertaking microeconomic analysis, but rarely used outside the field of microeconomic theory. These are *normal profit* and *abnormal profit*.

Normal profit is the minimum level of profit necessary to keep incumbent firms in the market, rewarding the time, decision making and entrepreneurial risk taking 'invested' into production. However, the normal profit made by incumbent firms, or firms already established in the market, is insufficient to attract new firms into the market. Economists treat normal profit as an opportunity cost, which they include in firms' average cost curves. In the long run, firms unable to make normal profit leave the market. Normal profit varies from one industry to another, depending on the risks facing firms. **Abnormal profit**, or **supernormal profit**, by contrast, is extra profit over and above normal profit.

KEY TERMS

normal profit the minimum profit a firm must make to stay in business, which is, however, insufficient to attract new firms into the market.

abnormal profit (also known as **supernormal profit** and **above-normal profit**) profit over and above normal profit.

STUDY TIP
Avoid confusing normal profit with another abstract microeconomic term: normal good. You came across normal goods when studying demand theory in Chapter 3.

QUANTITATIVE SKILLS 4.5

Worked example: calculating revenue and profit

Table 4.4 provides information about the short-run output, costs and revenue of a firm.

Table 4.4 Short-run output, costs and revenue

Output per week	Total revenue (£000s)	Total cost (£000s)
0	0	10
1	20	14
2	38	19
3	54	28
4	68	44
5	80	80
6	90	93

From the information in the table, calculate:

(a) **marginal revenue when output per week increases from 4 to 5 units**
The marginal revenue, which is the change in the total revenue, is £80,000 − £68,000, which is £12,000.

(b) **the level of output at which the firm would make normal profit but not abnormal profit**
Assuming that normal profit is being treated as a cost of production, the firm makes normal profit, but not abnormal profit, when total revenue equals total cost. This is at a level of output of 5 units per week.

(c) **the profit-maximising level of output per week**
Profits are maximised at the level of output at which ($TR − TC$) is greatest. This is at a level of output of 3 units per week, when total profit equals £54,000 − £28,000, which is £26,000.

The role of profit in a market economy

In the long run, and in the absence of entry barriers, abnormal profit performs the important economic function of attracting new firms into the market. Not only do rising profits, and the hope of higher profits in the future, provide business incentives for managers within a firm to work harder to make the business even more profitable, they also create incentives for other firms to enter the market. Abnormal profit acts as a 'magnet' attracting new entrants into a market or industry. As Chapter 5 explains, if market entry is easy and/or relatively costless, new firms joining the market should lead to an increase in market supply. In competitive markets, the entry of new firms triggers a process which reduces both abnormal profit and prices, with the latter benefiting consumers.

However, when entry barriers are high and monopoly or highly imperfect competition exists in a market, profit may simply reward inefficient producers. This is a form of market failure in which the 'producer is king' rather than the consumer, and in which 'producer sovereignty' rather than 'consumer sovereignty' exists.

Except when monopolies make large profits by exploiting their consumers, profit can be an indicator of economic efficiency. Large profits might mean that firms have succeeded in eliminating unnecessary costs of production and are also using the most efficient production processes.

Profit performs other roles in a market economy. These include the creation of worker and shareholder incentives. Profit also influences the allocation of resources, it is an efficiency indicator, and it is a reward for innovation and for risk taking. Finally, profits provide an important source of business finance.

The creation of worker incentives

Some companies use profit-related pay and performance-related pay to increase worker motivation, in the hope that workers will work harder and share the objectives of the business's managers and owners. This can, however, be counterproductive if ordinary workers see higher management and company directors enjoying huge profit-related bonuses, while they receive a pittance.

The creation of shareholder incentives

High profit generally leads to high dividends or distributed profit being paid out to shareholders who own companies. This creates an incentive for more people to want to buy the company's shares. As a result, the company's share price rises, which makes it cheaper and easier for a business to raise finance.

Profits and resource allocation

High profits made by incumbent firms in a market create incentives for new producers to enter the market and for existing firms to supply more of a good or service. Likewise, loss making, or perhaps a failure to make abnormal profits, creates incentives for firms to leave markets and to deploy their resources in more profitable markets.

Profit as a reward for innovation and risk taking

As we explain in the final section of this chapter, innovation is an improvement on something that has already been invented, which thus turns the results of invention into a useful product. If entrepreneurs believe that innovation can result in high profits in the future, the incentive to innovate increases. As we can never be sure of future profits, risks are involved. However, successful risk taking leads to high profits.

TEST YOURSELF 4.7

How may increases in economic efficiency and economic welfare be promoted through this process?

Profit as a source of business finance

Instead of being distributed to the business's owners as a form of income, profit can be retained within the business. Retained profits are perhaps the most important source of finance for firms undertaking investment projects. High profits also make it easier and cheaper for firms to use borrowed funds as an important source of business finance.

CASE STUDY 4.7

The John Lewis economy

John Lewis PLC is a generally successful retailing company which shares its profits with all its workers and makes them part-owners, within the business, of the John Lewis Partnership. The Partnership offers its employees indirect ownership of the company. Like a mutual business such as a building society, John Lewis PLC has no external shareholders. Instead members of the Partnership are granted some voting rights at board level plus a slice of the profits, which are added to their salaries each year.

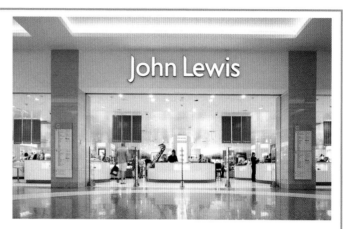

John Lewis employees do not directly own shares in the business. By contrast, most listed companies offer shares to employees as part of remuneration. Government ministers have claimed that employee share ownership is key to improving company profit and productivity.

The John Lewis Partnership is the largest employee-owned business in the UK. But as it stands, the employee-owned sector is not currently large enough to bring about a wholesale change in the character of the British business model.

In recent years John Lewis has been less successful than it was a few years ago. Profits have fallen, so worker remuneration has also fallen. Plans for a John Lewis economy that would inspire businesses to share ownership with their staff have also been undermined by the removal of government support services offered to such businesses.

Follow-up questions

1 Explain the term 'profit sharing'.
2 Outline one advantage and one disadvantage of profit sharing and co-ownership for the United Kingdom economy.
3 Find out more details of the economic performance of John Lewis PLC in recent years.
4 The passage states that John Lewis is a PLC and mentions listed companies and mutual businesses. Explain the meaning of these terms.
5 Why is John Lewis generally considered to be an unusual form of PLC?

SECTION 4.7 SUMMARY

- Profit is not the same as revenue.
- Profit is revenue minus cost.
- In traditional economic theory, but not necessarily in behavioural theory, firms are assumed to be profit maximisers.
- Normal profit is the minimum profit a firm must make to stay in business, which is, however, insufficient to attract new firms into the market.
- Abnormal profit is profit over and above normal profit.
- Profit has various roles in a market economy, including creating incentives and rewarding innovation and risk taking.

4.8 Technological change

Most people have a general idea of what technology means, but they nevertheless find it difficult to give the term a precise definition. Here, however, is one snappy definition: whereas science is concerned with how and why things happen, technology focuses on *making things happen*. Thus, technology is knowledge put to practical use to solve problems facing human societies.

Technological change, by contrast, involves changing existing technologies, hopefully for the better, and the development of completely new technologies, both to improve existing *products* and the *processes* involved in making the products, and to develop completely new products and processes. In the economic sphere, this leads to the development of completely new markets, to changes in market structure, and also to the destruction of some existing markets.

> **KEY TERM**
> **technological change** a term used to describe the overall effect of invention, innovation and the diffusion or spread of technology in the economy.

Technological change and technical progress

The word 'technology' is often associated with technical progress. However, the term 'technical progress' has two rather different meanings. On the one hand, in a normative or value-judgement context, 'technical progress' implies that technological change is fundamentally about increasing economic welfare and making people happier. For example, although the development and use of the motor car has several important drawbacks, such as the harm resulting from road accidents and environmental pollution, for the most part, through making it much easier for most people to travel, cars and buses have significantly improved human welfare.

But in a narrower sense, unrelated to welfare considerations, 'technical progress' means applying scientific and engineering knowledge, as it develops, to produce goods which are more efficient and work better, regardless of whether these are good for society. In this narrower meaning, technical progress includes the development of distinctly harmful goods such as chemical weapons, which, when used, have a devastating effect on human welfare.

> **KEY TERMS**
> **invention** making something entirely new; something that did not exist before at all.
> **innovation** improves on or makes a significant contribution to something that has already been invented, thereby turning the results of invention into a product.

The difference between invention and innovation

Invention is about creating new ideas for products or processes. **Innovation**, by contrast, converts the results of invention into marketable products or services. Many inventions fail to see the light of day because they have no practical use. It is innovation, rather than invention, that is really important for the success of a firm.

In an article in *Huffpost* most recently published on 6 December 2017, the American entrepreneur Tom Grasty distinguishes between invention and innovation in the following way:

In its purest sense, invention can be defined as the creation of a product or introduction of a process for the first time. Innovation, on the other hand, occurs if someone improves on or makes a significant contribution to an existing product, process or service. Consider the microprocessor. Someone invented the microprocessor. But by itself, the microprocessor was nothing more than another piece on the circuit board. It's what was done with that piece — the hundreds of thousands of products, processes and services that evolved from the invention of the microprocessor — that required innovation.

If ever there were a poster child for innovation it would be former Apple CEO Steve Jobs. And when people talk about innovation, Jobs' iPod is cited as an example of innovation at its best. But let's take a step back for a minute. The iPod wasn't the first portable music device (Sony popularized the 'music anywhere, anytime' concept 22 years earlier with the Walkman); the iPod wasn't the first device that put hundreds of songs in your pocket (dozens of manufacturers had MP3 devices on the market when the iPod was released in 2001); and Apple was actually late to the party when it came to providing an online music-sharing platform (Napster, Grokster and Kazaa all preceded iTunes).

So, given those sobering facts, is the iPod's distinction as a defining example of innovation warranted? Absolutely. What made the iPod and the music ecosystem it engendered innovative wasn't that it was the first portable music device. It wasn't that it was the first MP3 player. And it wasn't that it was the first company to make thousands of songs immediately available to millions of users. What made Apple innovative was that it combined all of these elements — design, ergonomics and ease of use — in a single device, and then tied it directly into a platform that effortlessly kept that device updated with music.

Apple invented nothing. Its innovation was creating an easy-to-use ecosystem that unified music discovery, delivery and device. And, in the process, they revolutionized the music industry.

The effect of technological change on economic performance

Through its diffusion into the economy, technological change affects methods of production, productivity, efficiency and firms' costs of production. We shall now look at each of these in turn.

Methods of production

Throughout human history, technological change has affected methods of production. The mid-twentieth century witnessed the growing use of automobiles. We are now living in the 'computer age'. Computers, which were first developed in the 1940s, are now widely used in manufacturing (for example, when computer-controlled robots build cars), in distribution (for example, in the online sale of books by Amazon), and as consumer goods in themselves. And hidden within many goods that are not themselves computers, such as washing machines and cars, are microprocessors that control how the good functions.

Closely allied to the changes in production has been the change in recent decades from mechanised to automated production. As a simplification, mechanisation means that human beings operate the machines that are used to produce goods. Automation, by contrast, means that machines operate other machines — for example, a computer-controlled robot operating a welding tool to weld together the body panels of a car. Both mechanisation and automation have often been accompanied by assembly-line production, allegedly first introduced by Henry Ford in 1908.

Productivity

Earlier in this chapter on page 76, we reminded you of the meaning of *productivity*. We defined productivity as output per unit of input, though it can also be considered as output per unit of time. We also said that when economists talk about productivity, they usually mean *labour productivity*. Technological change generally increases labour productivity. This has usually been the case following the introduction of both mechanised and automated production methods. However, in the case of automation and the use of computers in production, there have been several well-publicised examples in organisations such as the National Health Service of very expensive computer systems that have failed to work properly and which, in extreme cases, have had to be scrapped. In these cases, labour productivity may fall rather than increase, at least until the system can be made to work properly.

> **STUDY TIP**
>
> Make sure you don't confuse *production* with *productivity*. The two concepts are closely related, but production refers to total output, whereas productivity is output per unit of input.

CASE STUDY 4.8

The failure to produce paperless records of patient care in the NHS

On 18 September 2013, the parliamentary Public Accounts Committee published a report on the Dismantled National Programme for IT in the National Health Service. Although officially 'dismantled', the National Programme continues in the form of separate component programmes which are still racking up big costs.

Launched in 2002, the National Programme was designed to reform the way that the NHS in England uses information. While some parts of the National Programme were delivered successfully, other important elements encountered significant difficulties. In particular, there were delays in developing and deploying the detailed care records systems. Following three reports on the National Programme by both the National Audit Office and the Public Accounts Committee, and a review by the Major Projects Authority, the government announced in September 2011 that it would dismantle the National Programme but keep the component parts in place with separate management and accountability structures.

The public purse is continuing to pay the price for failures by the department and its contractors. The department's original contracts totalled £3.1 billion for the delivery of care records systems to 220 trusts in the north, midlands and east. The full cost of the National Programme is still not certain. The department's most recent statement reported a total forecast cost of £9.8 billion. However, this figure did not include potential future costs.

The benefits to date from the National Programme are extremely disappointing. The department's benefits statement reported estimated benefits to March 2012 of £3.7 billion, just half of the costs incurred to this point. The benefits include financial savings, efficiency gains and wider benefits to society (for example, where patients spend less time chasing referrals). However, two-thirds of the £10.7 billion of total forecast benefits were still to be realised in March 2012.

After the sorry history of the National Programme, the Public Accounts Committee was sceptical that the department could deliver its vision of a paperless NHS by 2018. Making the NHS paperless will involve further significant investment in IT and business transformation.

Follow-up questions

1 Research on the internet to find out what has happened to the NHS's plan to introduce paperless patient records in the period since September 2013.
2 Find out about and investigate another example of a computer systems disaster in either the public sector or the private sector.
3 What are the functions of the National Audit Office and the Public Accounts Committee of the House of Commons, and the Major Projects Authority?
4 What is meant by the 'public purse'?

Efficiency

As we explain in Chapter 5, economists recognise a number of types of economic efficiency. Two of these are productive efficiency and dynamic efficiency. **Productive efficiency** centres on minimising average costs of production. **Dynamic efficiency** measures the extent to which productive efficiency increases over time, in the economic long run. Dynamic efficiency results from improvements in products and services, innovation and the process of creative destruction.

Technological change generally improves both productive efficiency and dynamic efficiency. As a general rule — though there are exceptions, one of which is illustrated by Case study 4.4 — technological change leads to improvements in both productive and dynamic efficiency. By increasing productivity, over time technological changes shift both short-run and long-run cost curves downward, thereby improving both productive and dynamic efficiency.

Costs of production

It follows from what we have written about technological change generally improving both productivity and efficiency that it also reduces costs of production, in the short run but especially in the long run. This is because the long run is the time period in which firms can invest in new capital equipment and technology which they hope will reduce costs of production.

EXTENSION MATERIAL

Some other effects of technological change

A theme running through this section on technological change is that, particularly in recent years, technological change has been highly significant in the development of new products and new markets, and the destruction of existing markets. To explain this further, it is useful to introduce the concepts of *disruptive* innovation and *sustaining* innovation.

A disruptive innovation is an innovation that helps create a new market, but in so doing eventually disrupts an existing market over a few years or decades, thereby displacing an earlier technology. Disruptive innovation often improves a product or service in ways that the market did not initially expect. It creates new goods or services for a different set of consumers in a new market which competes with the established market. By doing so, it eventually lowers prices in the existing market. By contrast, a sustaining innovation does not create new markets but develops existing markets, enabling firms within them to offer better value and often to compete against each other, sustaining improvements.

According to Harvard University business professors Joseph L. Bower and Clayton M. Christensen, one of the most consistent patterns in business is the failure of leading companies to stay at the top of their industries when technologies or markets change. Writing back in the 1990s, Bower and Christensen gave the example of the US company, Xerox, which at the time had dominated the photocopier market, losing market share to the Japanese company, Canon, in the small photocopier market.

Bower and Christensen ask why it is that companies like Xerox invest aggressively — and successfully — in the technologies necessary to retain their current customers, but then fail to make certain other technological investments that customers of the future will demand. The explanation they offer is that companies that dominate an existing technology are in danger, as disruptive innovation occurs, of remaining too close to their existing body of customers. All too often existing customers reject the goods produced by a new technology because it does not address their needs as effectively as a company's current products. The large photocopying centres that represented the core of Xerox's customer base at first had no use for small, slow table-top copiers produced by Xerox's new technology. Result: Canon stepped in, quickened the speed of the copiers, and took over the market.

CASE STUDY 4.9

The impact of the smartphone on Kodak and the traditional camera industry

In September 2013, the American camera company Kodak emerged from the bankruptcy it had been in for nearly 2 years. Since 2000, demand for Kodak's most successful product, camera film, which once ranked among the most profitable consumer products ever invented, had been in rapid decline. To make matters worse, Kodak's management had grossly underestimated the speed of the collapse.

This was all due to the development of digital cameras, and later smartphones. Global sales of traditional photographic film and paper dropped like a stone. Up to that point, the boxes of film that Kodak produced had been highly profitable. New entrants were deterred by the high costs of entry to this capital-intensive market and Kodak enjoyed profit margins that might have been as high as 50%.

Kodak Ektra

But in the first few months of this century, a technology change began that was to wreck one of the most lucrative business models of the last century and threaten Kodak's very existence. In 1999, only 5% of new cameras sold in the USA were digital. By the end of 2000, this had changed dramatically. By 2003, now being accused of ignoring the revolution until it was too late, Kodak cut tens of thousands of jobs at its capital-intensive film factories and announced a new digital strategy.

In 2016, Kodak sold its first smartphone, the Ektra, with a design based on the iconic 1941 Kodak Ektra 35mm camera. Kodak was aiming to establish a nostalgic niche in a highly competitive market dominated by Apple's iphone and Samsung smartphones. Kodak said it wanted to make the Ektra for people with 'artistic-oriented hobbies, interests, passions'. However, Kodak's Ektra smartphone was badly reviewed, and despite significant price cuts and upgrades, sales were poor. So far, Kodak has failed to establish its niche in the smartphone market.

Disruptive digital technology has caused the crash of many business models since 1999 — but few quite so rapid as the fate that befell Kodak. Within a matter of months, the once hugely profitable camera film market had given way to the surge of digital cameras and smartphones.

Follow-up questions

1 Find out fuller details of what has happened to Kodak since the company emerged from bankruptcy in 2013.
2 In what way have smartphones, which were first marketed in 2007, affected the market for digital cameras?
3 Research statistics for camera sales in a recent year by visiting **www.statista.com** Construct a pie chart to show the sales of different camera manufacturers.
4 Similarly, research statistics for smartphone sales in a recent year. Construct a pie chart to show the sales of different smartphone manufacturers.

The influence of technological change on the structure of markets

Case study 4.9 on Kodak provides a good example of the influence of technological change on the structure of markets. It describes how, when cameras transmitted the images they photographed onto chemical film, very high entry barriers into the chemical film market led to Kodak's domination of the market. By contrast, entry into the digital camera market is relatively easy. Hence the camera film market, dominated by Kodak, was close to a monopoly, whereas the digital camera and smartphone markets are closer to a much more competitive form of market, **monopolistic competition**, which we explain in Chapter 5.

Technological change does not always, however, lead to more competitive market structures. In some industries, technological change has led to outcomes in which very large firms dominate. This happens if technological change leads to capital indivisibilities, which occur when very large quantities of capital equipment are required for one unit of a good to be produced. It is not economically feasible for firms to use smaller units of capital to produce their goods. This means that small firms cannot compete in the market.

A good example is the jumbo jet industry. The technological change which enabled very large jet airliners to be produced led to an outcome in which, in the western world, the American Boeing Corporation and the European Airbus consortium are the only two jumbo jet manufacturers. In Chapter 5, we shall call this situation a **duopoly**.

> **KEY TERMS**
>
> **monopolistic competition** a market structure in which firms have many competitors, but each one sells a slightly different product.
>
> **duopoly** two firms only in a market.

How the process of creative destruction is linked to technological change

The term **creative destruction** was first coined in 1942 by the Austrian economist Joseph Schumpeter to describe how capitalism, which dominates the economic system in which we live, evolves and renews itself over time. (Capitalism is the name given to the parts of the economy in which the means of production or capital are privately owned. In the UK, public limited companies or PLCs are the dominant form of capitalist business enterprise.)

In his book *Capitalism, Socialism, and Democracy*, Schumpeter wrote: 'The opening up of new markets, foreign or domestic…incessantly revolutionises the economic structure from within, incessantly destroying the old one, incessantly creating a new one. This process of Creative Destruction is the essential fact about capitalism.' Schumpeter also stated that 'The essential point to grasp is that in dealing with capitalism we are dealing with an evolutionary process.'

Creative destruction is strongly related to the processes through which technological change and innovation affect the ways in which businesses behave. It describes a process in which economic growth occurs in the economy as a result of new innovations creating more economic value than that being destroyed by the decline of the technologies the new innovations replace. Over time, societies that allow creative destruction to operate grow more productive and richer; their citizens benefit from new and better products and higher living standards. Creative destruction is central to the ways in which free-market economies and mixed economies develop and change over time.

> **KEY TERM**
>
> **creative destruction** capitalism evolving and renewing itself over time through new technologies and innovations replacing older technologies and innovations.

CASE STUDY 4.10

Apple and creative destruction

On 1 April 1976, Apple Computer Inc. was incorporated by three 'techno-geeks', Steve Jobs, Steve Wozniak and Ron Wayne. Twenty-one years later in 1997, Steve Jobs, having left Apple following disputes about business strategy, rejoined the company and remained in charge until his death in 2011. (In 2007, Jobs had renamed the company Apple Inc. to reflect the fact that Apple had diversified away from computers into the iPod, the iPhone, the iPad and iTunes.)

Over this period, and particularly since 2001 when the iPod was first marketed, Apple had a crushing effect on specific competitors. According to Barry Ritholtz, writing in the *Washington Post* shortly after Jobs' death from pancreatic cancer, this was creative destruction writ large. Ritholtz argued that Jobs remade entire industries according to his unique vision. From music to film, mobile phones to media publishing and computing, Jobs' impact has been enormous.

Today, the triple threat of iPod/iPhone/iPad has left behind a wake of overwhelmed business models, confounded managements and bereft shareholders. The businesses which have been destroyed, or left as mere rumps of their former selves, include Hewett-Packard (HP), Nokia and Blackberry. According to Ritholtz, HP's printer business might still have some ink left in its cartridges, but its PC operations are hurting, gutted by sales of the iPad. HP's tablet entry, the TouchPad, was an unmitigated disaster, unable to compete with the iPad.

In 2007, the Finnish company Nokia totally dominated the mobile phone market. Many people thought that Nokia's lead was more or less insurmountable. But what has happened since is a reminder of just how quickly and completely the market power of a previously 'dominant' tech firm can disappear. Following the introduction of Apple's iPhone in 2007, both Nokia and Blackberry began a rapid decline.

Under a headline 'Once-cool Blackberry fails to keep pace with rivals', China's *Morning Post* described how Blackberry, an early mover in the high-end mobile phone market, lost market share mainly to Apple's iPhone and to smartphones powered by Google's Android operating system. While Blackberry was considered perhaps the hippest if not the largest mobile phone maker several years ago, the company quickly lost momentum as it failed to keep pace with innovations from rivals. Gerry Purdy, an analyst at Compass Intelligence, said that 'The one gigantic issue facing Blackberry was the delay in getting into the smartphone market. And that was three years after the iPhone was released. So that's six years. The market was moving too fast.' Blackberry was too complacent, having become 'blinded' to competitive threats.

Even software giant Microsoft has suffered from Apple's innovation and marketing. Once Apple's main competitor in computer manufacturing and software, Microsoft has become vulnerable on multiple fronts. It has missed nearly every major trend in technology in recent years. Microsoft still has its cash cows Windows and its Office suite of products, but the company could lose out significantly to Apple in the next few years.

Follow-up questions

1 What is meant by 'creative destruction'?
2 This case study was written at the time of Steve Jobs' death in 2011. Find out what has happened to Nokia's and Blackberry's smartphone businesses in the years since then.
3 Cathode-ray television-tube manufacturers, video rental shops, high-street travel agents and bookshops have all in recent years been victims of creative destruction. Research how this has happened in one of these industries and explain why you think consumers may or may not have benefited from the process.
4 The marketing of smartphones by ICT companies such as Apple has contributed to the growth of social media. Explain how social media have been affecting more traditional forms of media such as newspapers and television.

> ### SECTION 4.8 SUMMARY
>
> - The ways in which firms operate are affected by technological change, which encompasses the processes of invention, innovation and diffusion of technology in the economy.
> - In the long run, capitalism develops through a process known as creative destruction, through new technologies and innovations replacing older technologies and innovations.
> - Technological change involves changing existing technologies, hopefully for the better, and the development of completely new technologies, both to improve existing products and the processes involved in making the products, and to develop completely new products and processes.
> - Technical progress means applying scientific and engineering knowledge, as it develops, to produce goods which are more efficient and work better.
> - Innovation improves on or makes a significant contribution to something that has already been invented, thereby turning the results of invention into a product.
> - Technological change affects methods of production, productivity, efficiency and firms' costs of production.
> - Technological change has been very significant in the development of new products and new markets, and the destruction of existing markets.
> - Creative destruction is a process through which capitalism evolves and renews itself over time through new technologies and innovations replacing older technologies and innovations.

Questions

1 Why is it important first to understand production theory in order to understand cost theory?

2 Distinguish between the short run and the long run.

3 Explain the mathematical relationship between the marginal and the average values of a variable.

4 State the law of diminishing returns.

5 What is the difference between the marginal returns to a variable factor of production and returns to scale?

6 Distinguish between internal and external economies of scale.

7 Why are a firm's revenue curves dependent on the competitiveness of the market structure in which it exists?

8 Define the term 'profit'.

9 Distinguish between technological change and technological progress.

5

Perfect competition, imperfectly competitive markets and monopoly

Chapter 4 has already introduced you to the two market structures of perfect competition and monopoly, and briefly mentioned the imperfectly competitive market structures of monopolistic competition and oligopoly that lie between the two extremes on the market structure spectrum. This chapter draws on the information about cost and revenue curves explained in Chapter 4 to explain profit maximisation in perfect competition and monopoly. After evaluating these two market structures using efficiency criteria, the chapter then looks at the two intermediate market structures of monopolistic competition and oligopoly. The order in which we cover the different market structures differs from how they are set out in the A-level specification. This is because we believe that it is easier to appreciate the nature of monopolistic competition and oligopoly after first understanding monopoly. The chapter concludes with an explanation of the pricing policies, such as price discrimination, that firms may use in imperfectly competitive market structures, followed by comparison of perfect competition and monopoly markets in terms of the welfare criteria of consumer surplus and producer surplus.

LEARNING OBJECTIVES
These are to understand:

- profit maximisation in different market structures
- whether perfect competition is more efficient than monopoly
- how monopolistic competition and oligopoly are forms of imperfect competition
- the use of concentration ratios to define oligopoly in terms of market structure
- oligopoly in terms of market behaviour or conduct, in the context of interdependence among oligopolists
- the difference between competitive and collusive oligopoly
- why and how firms undertake price discrimination
- the different forms of economic efficiency
- how dynamic efficiency relates to the process of creative destruction and how firms compete in real-world markets
- the welfare criteria of consumer surplus and producer surplus and how they can be used to evaluate the different market structures

5.1 Market structures

Market structure can be defined in terms of the organisation and other characteristics of a market. Important features of market structure include:

- the number of firms in the market
- the market share of the largest firms, which as we later explain can be measured with the use of concentration ratios
- the nature of the costs incurred by the firms in the market
- the nature of the sales revenue earned by firms in the market
- the extent to which there are barriers to entry to, and exit from, the market
- ease of access to information about what is going on in the market
- the extent to which firms in the market undertake product differentiation and adopt different price-setting procedures
- the ways, if any, in which firms are affected by buyers' behaviour in the market

The spectrum of competition

In the context of markets, the word 'spectrum' encompasses the range of market structures which lie between the two extremes of perfect competition and monopoly. Figure 5.1 is similar to the lower part of Figure 4.1 in Chapter 4. However, Figure 5.1 contains more information about each of the market structures that we explain in this chapter.

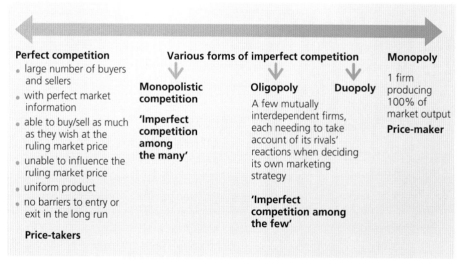

Figure 5.1 The spectrum of market structures

Distinguishing between different market structures

The number of firms in a market

Factors such as the number of firms in the market, the degree of product differentiation and ease of entry are used to distinguish between different market structures. A requirement for a market to be perfectly competitive is a large number of buyers and sellers, while at the other extreme pure monopoly is defined by the fact that there is just one firm in the market.

Perfect competition is in fact an abstract theoretical extreme rather than a real-world market structure. It is impossible for markets to display simultaneously all the conditions, listed in Figure 5.1, which are necessary for perfect competition to exist. Since any violation of the conditions of perfect competition immediately renders a market imperfectly competitive, even the most competitive markets in the real economy are examples of imperfect competition rather than perfect competition. The best we can say is that some of the highly competitive markets in the world we live in approximate to perfect competition, but nevertheless they are not perfectly competitive.

At the other extreme, pure monopoly does exist, though it is more accurate to say that market structures *dominated* by one firm are much more common than pure monopoly. In the UK, water companies provide examples of pure monopoly. Depending on where you live, there is only one company supplying tap water to your house or flat. For example, if you live in central London, you must buy your tap water from Thames Water — it is impossible to shop around and buy your water from an alternative supplier. To nit-pick, you could of course buy bottled water instead of tap water, but this would not be a realistic choice for non-drinking uses of water, such as taking a shower or washing a car. And even if in other industries a firm appears to be a pure monopoly, the availability of substitute products and foreign competition through which overseas firms compete with the dominant domestic firm weaken the firm's monopoly power.

Almost all real-world firms are therefore better described as imperfectly competitive, located between the two extremes of perfect competition and pure monopoly. As Figure 5.1 indicates, monopolistic competition is often described as imperfect competition among the many, which means that, as in perfect competition, there are a large number of firms in such markets. However, unlike perfect competition, many real-world markets display the characteristics of monopolistic competition which we explain later in this chapter. Typical examples are high-street coffee shops and newsagents.

We shall also examine oligopoly later in the chapter. In oligopoly, there are only a few firms in the market, at least in terms of large firms, though often the large firms coexist with a number of smaller firms. Figure 5.1 describes oligopoly as 'imperfect competition among the few'. As we explain later in the chapter, concentration ratios are used when oligopoly is defined in terms of market structure, while interdependence among the firms that make up the market is a main characteristic when oligopoly is defined in terms of market behaviour.

Market entry barriers

Market structure is also affected by the ease of entry into (and exit from) the market. In the short run, when at least one factor production (usually assumed to be capital) is fixed, firms cannot enter or leave the market, whatever the market structure. In the long run, by contrast, when all the factors of production are variable, firms can enter or leave competitive markets. However, at the other end of the market spectrum, pure monopoly is protected by **entry barriers** in the long run as well as in the short run, while in an oligopolistic market there may still be significant entry barriers in the long run.

In pure monopoly, entry barriers are permanent in the sense that if they are removed, the entry of new firms, attracted by the monopolist's abnormal

KEY TERM
entry barriers obstacles that make it difficult for a new firm to enter a market.

profit, immediately means the monopoly is destroyed. (At this point, it is worth noting that an efficient monopolist, making normal profit, will not attract new entrants into the market.) However, building on the concepts of technological change and creative destruction introduced in Chapter 4, later in this chapter we shall be explaining how the development of competing new products and technologies weakens and often destroys the monopoly power of dominant firms whose power was previously seen as impregnable.

An entry barrier is a cost of production which must be borne by a firm that seeks to enter an industry, but is not borne by businesses already in the industry. Closely related to entry barriers are **exit barriers**, which make it difficult for an established or incumbent firm to leave a market.

KEY TERM

exit barriers obstacles that make it difficult for an established firm to leave a market.

TEST YOURSELF 5.2
Explain two examples of (a) natural barriers to market entry; (b) artificial barriers to market entry; and (c) sunk costs.

EXTENSION MATERIAL

Limit pricing and predatory pricing

Firm may set the prices at which they sell their goods to create an artificial barrier to market entry. This is when they set limit prices or, in a more extreme case, predatory prices. When natural barriers to market entry are low or non-existent, incumbent firms (that is, firms already in the market) may set low prices, known as limit prices, to deter new firms from entering the market. Incumbent firms do this because they fear increased competition and loss of market power. With limit pricing, firms already in the market sacrifice short-run profit maximisation in order to maximise long-run profits, achieved through deterring the entry of new firms.

Should limit pricing be regarded as an example of a competitive pricing strategy, which reduces prices and the supernormal profits enjoyed by the established firms in the market? Or is limit pricing basically anti-competitive and best regarded as an unjustifiable restrictive practice? The answer probably depends on circumstances, but when limit pricing extends into predatory pricing, there is a much clearer case that such a pricing strategy is anti-competitive and against consumers' interest.

Whereas limit pricing deters market entry, successful use of predatory prices removes recent entrants to the market. Predatory pricing occurs when an established or incumbent firm deliberately sets prices below costs to force new market entrants out of business. Once the new entrants have left the market, the established firm may decide to restore prices to their previous levels.

Product differentiation

In Chapter 4, we defined a firm as a productive organisation that sells its output of goods or services commercially. Many decades ago, when economists were first putting together the theory of the firm and developing the model of perfect competition, not only did they regard firms as one-product business organisations, they assumed that within a market, all firms produce a uniform or homogeneous product. (This is one of the conditions of perfect competition listed in Figure 5.1.)

While there are a large number of small firms in the UK economy today, relatively few produce just a single good or service. Most firms — particularly large and medium-sized business enterprises, but also small businesses — undertake varying degrees of **product differentiation**. Firms often produce a range of relatively similar products, some of which compete with each other, but others

KEY TERM

product differentiation the marketing of generally similar products with minor variations or the marketing of a range of different products.

of which are aimed at differentiated market segments. Mobile phones provide examples of both. Apple is well known for introducing two new smartphones roughly every year: a 'high-end' and a slightly more basic (and cheaper) model. However, Apple continues to manufacture and sell 'last year's model'. As a result, the latest models — at the time of writing, the iPhone 6 models — compete with earlier models which Apple still sells, such as the iPhone 5 and the iPhone 4. Samsung, which is Apple's main rival in the smartphone market, differentiates its phones in a similar way, but launches its new phones more frequently and in a wider variety of options than its American competitor.

SECTION 5.1 SUMMARY

- Market structures provide the framework in which businesses exist.
- Different market structures display different degrees of competitiveness.
- There are two main types of entry barrier making it difficult or preventing a new firm from entering a market: natural barriers and artificial (or man-made) barriers.
- Sunk costs cannot be recovered if a firm decides to leave a market.
- Firms of all sizes undertake varying degrees of product differentiation.

5.2 The objectives of firms

Profit maximisation

We have already mentioned, particularly in Chapter 2 when describing how behavioural economics questions many of the assumptions of traditional economic theory, how traditional theory assumes that the owners and entrepreneurs who run firms have only one business objective: to produce the level of output at which profit is maximised.

For all firms, whatever their business objective(s):

total profit = total revenue − total cost

Profit maximisation requires that a firm produces the level of output at which $TR - TC$ is maximised, whatever the market structure in which the firm produces and sells its output. Given the profit-maximising objective, if the firm succeeds in producing and selling the output yielding the biggest possible profit, it has no incentive to change its level of output.

The profit-maximising rule ($MR = MC$)

It is generally more useful to state the condition for profit maximisation as:

marginal revenue = marginal cost, or $MR = MC$

$MR = MC$ means that a firm's profits are greatest when the addition to sales revenue received from the last unit sold (marginal revenue) equals exactly the addition to total cost incurred from the production of the last unit of output (marginal cost).

Imagine, for example, a market gardener producing tomatoes for sale in a local market, but unable to influence the ruling market price of 50p per kilo. At any size of sales, average revenue is 50p, which also equals marginal revenue. Suppose that when the horticulturalist markets 300 kilos of tomatoes, the cost of producing and marketing the 300th kilo is 48p. If the tomato grower decides not to market the 300th kilo, 2p of profit is sacrificed. Suppose also that total costs rise by 50p and 52p respectively when a 301st kilo and a 302nd kilo are marketed. The sale of the 302nd kilo causes profits to fall by 2p, but the 301st kilo of tomatoes leaves total profits unchanged: it represents the level of sales at which profits are exactly maximised.

To sum up, when:

- $MR > MC$, profits rise when output increases
- $MR < MC$, profits rise when output reduces

So only when $MR = MC$, at the level of output Q_1 in Figure 5.2, are profits maximised.

When $MR > MC$ or $MR < MC$ the firm fails to maximise profit. To maximise profit, the firm must change its level of output until it reaches the point at which $MR = MC$. Once this is reached, the firm has no incentive to change output, unless some event disturbs either costs or revenues.

It is important to understand that firms in *all* market structures (perfect competition, monopoly and imperfectly competitive markets such as monopolistic competition and oligopoly) can only maximise profit when marginal revenue equals marginal cost. $MR = MC$ is a universal condition that must be met for profit maximisation to occur, whatever the market structure.

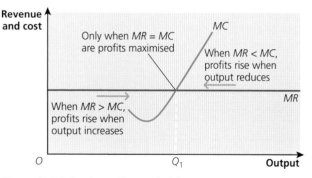

Figure 5.2 A firm's profit-maximising output occurs when $MR = MC$

TEST YOURSELF 5.3
Distinguish between profit maximisation and revenue maximisation.

The divorce of ownership from control

In a firm, the entrepreneur is the decision-maker and financial risk-taker, providing answers to such standard economic questions as *what, how, how much, where* and *when* to produce. In many small firms, the owner of the business

KEY TERM

divorce of ownership from control the owners and those who control the firm (managers) are different groups with different objectives.

TEST YOURSELF 5.4

Who owns a UK public limited company (PLC)?

is the entrepreneur, so ownership and control lie with the same person. But this is generally not true for larger businesses, where there is a **divorce of ownership from control**. Medium-sized and large companies are often owned by thousands of shareholders, though the majority of shares are usually owned by a relatively small number of financial institutions such as pension funds and insurance companies. However, management decisions are made by executive directors, who are members of the company's corporate board and employed by the company, and by other managers or executives whom they in turn employ.

In theory, the directors of a public company who exercise the entrepreneurial function are answerable to the shareholders. This means that, in the event of bad performance and a failure to maximise profit, the directors can be voted out of office. In practice, however, this seldom happens.

How divorce of ownership from control may affect firms' objectives, conduct and performance

Perhaps the most important problem resulting from the divorce between ownership and control is the possibility that directors and managers will pursue an agenda of their own, which is not in the interests of the shareholders as a body. This is an example of what is known as the principal–agent problem, or agency problem, where shareholders are the principals and managers are the agents. The problem stems from the fact that shareholders, who in a company are the owners of the business, may have an objective (profit maximisation) which differs from the objectives of the managers they employ. Rather than maximise profits, managers or business executives, who possess a monopoly of technical knowledge about the actual running of the company, concentrate on achieving managerial objectives such as maximising their career prospects or creature-comforts.

Conflicts of interest arise between agents and principals when the incentives which affect their behaviour are not the same. The agent bears the cost of fulfilling the task delegated by the principal, but the agent does not usually receive the full benefit of their actions. This destroys the incentive for the agent to put the same effort into the task that would be the case if the agent were acting solely on their own behalf. Related to this is the fact that agents may take on excessive risk if they enjoy the benefits of doing so, but not the costs. For example, when managers take on excessive risk in the event of success they are rewarded with high bonuses, but in the event of failure the owners of the business end up losing a lot of money. This illustrates the problem of 'moral hazard', which occurs when one person takes more risks because someone else has agreed to bear the burden of those risks.

There are two important reasons why an agent can get away with not acting in the best interest of the principal. Firstly, the cost to the principal of sacking or punishing the agent may be too high relative to any benefit the principal will enjoy. Secondly, information asymmetry may result from the fact that the agent knows more than the principal about what is going on in the business. It is often difficult or even impossible for shareholders to know whether the directors and managers they employ are acting in their best interests. For example, if a company reports disappointing profits, shareholders may find it difficult to judge whether the blame stems from managerial laziness and incompetence, or whether the poor results are due to adverse economic factors outside management control.

Various methods can be used to realign the incentives facing the owners of a business and the directors and managers they employ. These include profit-related pay and paying managers partly by giving them company shares (executive stock options). These are financial 'carrots', but 'sticks' such as dismissal can also be used. (However, the threat of dismissal is somewhat weakened by the fact that all too often unsuccessful managers are 'rewarded for failure' with large financial pay-offs when they leave the business.)

Possible business objectives other than profit maximisation

In the context of the principal–agent problem, we have already mentioned the pursuit by the managers who run a business of objectives such as maximising management status and power. Another business objective is to provide good customer service and quality of product, both in terms of the product itself and in the provision of good-quality and reliable after-sales service. These objectives, which are particularly important for socially minded owners and managers, are not in themselves inconsistent with the profit-maximising objective. Very often they are best seen as means towards an end, the end being the achievement of some other business objective such as profit maximisation.

Growth maximisation and survival as business objectives

'Growth for growth's sake' is another possible business objective, though usually the continuing growth of a business is best viewed as a means of achieving economies of scale and their associated cost reductions. Growth can contribute to managerial prestige. It can also be a means of achieving monopoly power by knocking out smaller competitors. In the case of the proprietors of newspapers and television stations, growth is a means of increasing political influence.

At the other extreme, loss-making businesses, and those that fear their low level of profits might turn into losses, often see survival as a primary business objective. This is most common when the economy is hit by recession. Businesses hope they can ride out the adverse effects of economic downturn, survive and continue to grow once the worst is over.

Sales revenue maximisation

Firms may also try to maximise sales revenue, particularly when managerial pay is linked to revenue rather than profit. Students often confuse profit maximisation with revenue maximisation, but the two concepts are different. As we have explained, profit maximisation occurs at the level of output at which the difference between a firm's total sales revenue (TR) and its total costs of production (TC) is greatest. This is also the level of output at which marginal revenue equals marginal cost ($MR = MC$). By contrast, revenue maximisation occurs at the level of output at which marginal revenue is zero.

The difference between profit maximisation and revenue maximisation is shown in Figure 5.3. The profit-maximising level of output Q_1 is located below point X where $MR = MC$. By contrast, the revenue-maximising level of output Q_2 is located at point Z, where $MR = 0$. Providing the AR and MR curves slope downward to the right, the profit-maximising level of output is always below the revenue-maximising level of output.

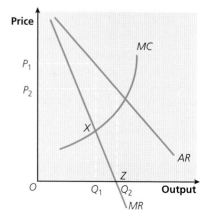

Figure 5.3 Profit maximisation and revenue maximisation when a firm's AR curve slopes downward

QUANTITATIVE SKILLS 5.1

Worked example: profit maximisation

At its present level of output an entrepreneur determines that its marginal cost is £36 (and on the rising portion of the curve), and its marginal revenue is £42 (on a downward-sloping *MR* curve).

The firm will maximise profits or minimise losses by:

A increasing price while keeping output constant
B decreasing price and increasing output
C decreasing both price and output
D increasing both price and output

The correct answer is B. Since $MR > MC$ at the firm's *current* level of output, profits rise when the firm increases its level of output. The question tells us that the firm has a downward-sloping *MR* curve. This means that its AR curve also slopes downward. Since AR is the same as price, whenever the firm increases output, it has to accept a lower price. (If you refer back to Figure 5.3, the firm would initially be producing an output level below and to the left of Q_1. By increasing output to Q_1, price would fall and profit would increase up to Q_1, but fall thereafter.)

The satisficing principle

As we saw in Chapter 2, behavioural economists argue that it is too crude to view individuals and firms simply as utility and profit maximisers. With regard to the nature of production, behavioural economists see the firm as an organisation comprising coalitions of different groups within the firm, each possessing different group objectives. The different groups, often called *stakeholders* in the business, may each have a different vested interest in terms of how the business performs.

Different stakeholder groups have different views on what the company should be doing. Managers, for example, may seek prestige, power and high salaries. Besides wanting higher wages, workers may be looking for improved job security and working conditions. In their desire to achieve higher profits, shareholders may try to keep down wages and managerial salaries. Differing goals or aspirations can result in group conflict. Management may try to resolve conflict between the different interest groups by replacing the profit-maximising objective with **satisficing**. Satisficing, which means achieving a satisfactory outcome rather than the best possible outcome, may help to resolve the conflict between managers' and shareholders' objectives. While trying to maximise executive creature-comforts such as managerial status, salaries, fringe benefits and career structures, a company's board of directors must keep shareholders happy. According to this theory, managers maximise their own objectives, but subject to the constraint of delivering a satisfactory level of profit for shareholders.

However, attempting to satisfice so as to satisfy the aspirations of as many groups within the firm as possible means compromise and the possible setting of minimum rather than maximum targets. Satisficing is particularly likely for monopolies and firms in imperfectly competitive markets protected by entry barriers. In these circumstances, in seeking an easy life, a firm's managers may content themselves with satisfactory profit, combined with a degree of

KEY TERM
satisficing achieving a satisfactory outcome rather than the best possible outcome.

TEST YOURSELF 5.5
Explain why one of the five possible answers to the following question is correct and why the other four answers are wrong.

A firm engaged in satisficing behaviour is most likely to:

A maximise profits

B maximise revenue

C produce at an output different from that of a profit-maximising firm

D maximise sales

E minimise costs

127

inefficiency or unnecessary costs, which could in principle be eliminated. In highly competitive markets, by contrast, firms that are initially content with satisfactory profits and a degree of inefficiency might be forced by the entry of new, more competitive firms to eliminate unnecessary costs. In order to survive, firms end up 'as if' they are profit maximisers, even though they may appear, at first sight, to be satisficing or pursuing some other business objective.

SECTION 5.2 SUMMARY

- Traditional theory assumes that the owners and entrepreneurs who run firms have only one business objective: to produce the level of output at which profit is maximised.
- Profit is maximised at the level of output at which $MR = MC$.
- In large businesses, there is often divorce of ownership from control.
- Firms may have business objectives other than profit maximisation, such as growth maximisation and sales maximisation.
- Firms may be satisficers rather than maximisers, aiming for satisfactory rather than maximum profits.

5.3 Perfect competition

Mention has been made of perfect competition on several occasions both in this chapter and in Chapter 4. To recap, perfect competition does not actually exist in real-world economies because it is impossible to meet simultaneously all the six conditions listed in Figure 5.1. Nevertheless, perfect competition plays a significant role in the traditional theory of the firm because it provides a yardstick against which the desirable and undesirable properties of real-world markets can be measured. For example, we shall use perfect competition as a benchmark against which to judge whether monopoly functions efficiently or inefficiently, and the extent to which resource misallocation occurs in monopoly.

CASE STUDY 5.1

The 'invisible hand' of the market

In 1776, in his book *An Inquiry into the Nature and Causes of the Wealth of Nations*, the economist Adam Smith wrote:

Adam Smith

> An individual neither intends to promote the public interest, nor know how much he is promoting it. He intends only his own gain, and he is in this, as in many other cases, led by an invisible hand to promote an end which was no part of his intention. It is not from the benevolence of the butcher, the brewer, or the baker that we expect our dinner, but from their regard to their own interest. We address ourselves, not to their humanity but to their self-love.

Smith was making the argument, repeated ever since by economists of a free-market persuasion, that the pursuit of individual self-interest in the market economy leads to outcomes which are in the common good or public interest — providing that the markets are free and competitive. Consumers benefit from individualistic behaviour in competitive markets because prices and profits end up being lower than would be the case if the markets were dominated by a few large firms.

Follow-up questions

1 Outline **one** way in which consumers can benefit from a lack of competition in a market.
2 Describe **one** circumstance, apart from when there is little or no competition in a market, in which the pursuit of self-interest may be undesirable in the economy.
3 When may cooperation between individuals be preferable to individualistic economic behaviour?
4 Does the 'invisible hand' of the market always lead to markets performing well?

The importance of self-interest

Economists generally regard competitive markets as desirable. However, the desirable properties of competitive markets (namely economic efficiency, welfare maximisation and consumer sovereignty) do not result from any assumption that business people or entrepreneurs in competitive industries are more highly motivated or public spirited than monopolists. Traditional economic theory assumes that everyone is motivated by self-interest and by self-interest alone. This applies just as much to firms in competitive markets as it does to monopolies. Entrepreneurs in competitive industries would very much like to become monopolists, both to gain an easier life and also to make bigger profits. Indeed, from a firm's point of view, successful competition means eliminating competition and becoming a monopoly. But in perfect markets, market forces (Adam Smith's invisible hand of the market) and the absence of barriers to entry and exit prevent this happening.

Imagine, for example, a situation in which a firm in a perfectly competitive industry makes a technical breakthrough which reduces production costs. For a short time the firm can make significant profits. But because, in highly competitive markets, market information is available to all firms, other firms within the market and new entrants attracted to the market can also enjoy the lower production costs.

Ultimately, of course, consumers benefit from lower prices brought about by technical progress and the forces of competition, but it is market forces, and not some socially benign motive or public spirit on the part of entrepreneurs, that accounts for the optimality of a highly competitive market as a market structure.

CASE STUDY 5.2

How the use of mobile phones can make markets more competitive

For a market to be competitive, buyers and sellers need accurate information about supply and demand. Before the use of mobile phones, fishermen in southern India lacked information about prices being charged for newly caught fish in other fishing villages along the coast. This lack of adequate information about conditions of supply and prices being charged led to small, separated and relatively uncompetitive fish markets.

If a fisherman made a good catch, other fishermen operating out of his home port and fishing in the same area would also catch a lot of fish. But when all the fishing vessels sailed back home, fish prices in the local village fish market would slump because of excess supply.

Another possibility was to sail down the coast after the catch was made, in the hope that in other villages fish catches were less bountiful and prices were therefore better. But, because of high fuel prices and uncertainty about what might be happening elsewhere, fishermen generally chose to return to their own village. This was wasteful because oversupply led to fish being thrown away, even though they might have been sold in slightly more distant fish markets. Another result was that there were wide variations in fish prices in different fishing villages.

However, after mobile phones had been introduced in southern India, while they were still at sea fishermen began to call markets all along the coast to find out where prices were highest. Having obtained this information, fishermen were now prepared to market their fish further afield, despite the fuel costs involved. The number of unsold fish that previously had been thrown back into the sea fell dramatically. Fish prices also fell. The 'law of one price' was operating — there was now a single price along the coast for more or less identical fish. By improving the exchange of information between fishermen, mobile phone technology has therefore contributed to the growth of a larger and much more competitive market.

Follow-up questions

1 Explain how the case study illustrates how better information on the part of buyers or sellers improves the way a market functions.
2 Name **two** UK markets that have been made more competitive as a result of the growing use of mobile phones.
3 Describe **one** economic disadvantage resulting from the use of mobile phones.
4 What is the 'law of one price' mentioned in the passage?

Short-run profit maximisation in perfect competition

At this stage, you should refer back to Chapter 4, page 102 and look again at Figure 4.19. The two graphs in the diagram illustrate how each firm in a perfectly competitive market passively accepts the ruling market price, which becomes each firm's average revenue (AR) and marginal revenue (MR) curve. The third condition of perfect competition tells us that a perfectly competitive firm can sell as much as it wishes at the market's ruling price. But how much will it actually wish to produce and sell? Providing we assume that each firm's business objective is solely to maximise profit, the answer is shown in Figure 5.4.

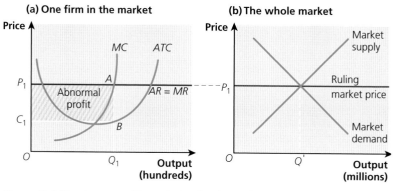

Figure 5.4 Short-run profit maximisation in perfect competition

As in Figure 4.19, Figure 5.4(b) shows how the ruling market price (P_1) is determined at the intersection of the demand and supply curves in the market as a whole. When beamed horizontally into Figure 5.4(a), the ruling market price becomes the average revenue (AR) curve and the marginal revenue (MR) curve facing each firm in the market. However, in Figure 5.4(a), we have added the perfectly competitive firm's average total cost (ATC) and its marginal cost (MC). Point A in Figure 5.4(a) (at which MR = MC) locates the profit-maximising level of output Q_1, with the firm's output shown in hundreds of units. At this level of output, total sales revenue is shown by the area OQ_1AP_1 (output multiplied by average revenue or price). Total cost is shown by the rectangular area OQ_1BC_1 (output multiplied by average cost). Abnormal profits (measured by subtracting the total cost rectangle from the total revenue rectangle) are shown by the shaded area C_1BAP_1.

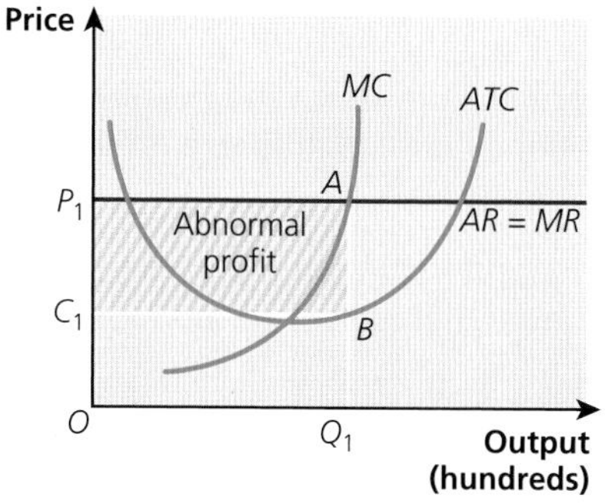

In Figure 5.5, the graph is the same as Figure 5.4(a), but presented without any information about what is going on in the market as a whole. The diagram enables you to focus on a firm's short-run profits in conditions of perfect competition, especially the positions of the cost and revenue curves and the abnormal profit rectangle.

Figure 5.5 A perfectly competitive firm maximising profit in the short run

TEST YOURSELF 5.6
Explain the difference between the short run and the long run.

Long-run profit maximisation in perfect competition

Referring back to the list of the conditions of perfect competition, you will see that although firms cannot enter or leave the market in the short run, they can do so in the long run. Suppose that in the short run, firms make abnormal profit, as we have just illustrated in Figures 5.4 and 5.5. In this situation, the ruling market price signals to firms outside the market that abnormal profits can be made, which provides an incentive for new firms to enter the market.

Figure 5.6 shows what might happen next. Initially, too many new firms enter the market, causing the supply curve to shift to the right to S_2 in Figure 5.6(b). This causes the price line to fall to P_2, which lies below each firm's ATC curve. When this happens, firms make a loss (or *subnormal profit*). However, just as abnormal profit creates the incentive for new firms to enter the market, subnormal profit has the opposite effect of causing some firms to leave the market.

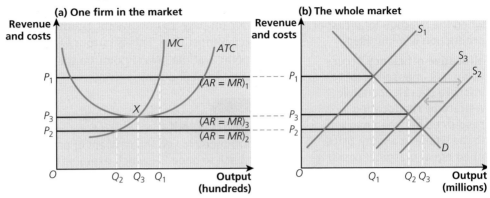

(a) One firm in the market

(b) The whole market

Figure 5.6 Perfect competition in the long run

When the price line lies below the ATC curve in Figure 5.6(a), and firms start leaving the market, the market supply curve shifts to the left in Figure 5.6(b). This causes the market price to rise. Eventually, the price settles at P_3, where, as Figure 5.6(a) shows, surviving firms make normal profit only. In this situation, each firm produces the level of output, measured in hundreds of units, immediately below point X in the diagram.

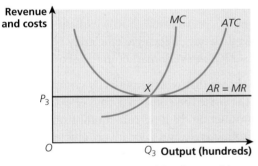

Figure 5.7 A perfectly competitive firm making only normal profit in the long run

Figure 5.7 is similar to Figure 5.6(a), but only shows the price line P_3. In the diagram, a firm's total revenue and also its total cost are shown by the rectangle OQ_3XP_3. The entry of new firms into the market, attracted by short-run abnormal profits, has whittled away these profits to produce a long-run outcome in which surviving firms make normal profit only. (Remember, normal profit is treated as a cost of production, and is not shown explicitly in the diagram.) Since only normal profit is made, there is no incentive for firms to enter or leave the market.

TEST YOURSELF 5.7

A perfectly competitive firm can be described as a 'passive price-taker'. Explain what this means. What would happen in the short run and in the long run if a perfectly competitive firm tried to sell its output at a price above the ruling market price for the good the firm is producing?

131

Perfect competition and the efficient allocation of resources

On page 114 of Chapter 4 we stated that there are a number of types of economic efficiency. One of those which we identified is **productive efficiency**, which we first introduced in Chapter 1. We explained that for a particular firm in the market, the productively efficient level of output is the one immediately below the lowest point on the firm's ATC curve, at which the average cost per unit of output is minimised.

KEY TERMS

productive efficiency for the economy as a whole occurs when it is impossible to produce more of one good without producing less of another. For a firm it occurs when the average total cost of production is minimised.

allocative efficiency occurs when it is impossible to improve overall economic welfare by reallocating resources between markets. In the whole economy, price must equal marginal cost ($P = MC$) in every market.

In this chapter we introduce another type of efficiency, **allocative efficiency**, and discuss the extent to which perfect competition is both productively and allocatively efficient. Later in the chapter, we shall apply the same analysis to the three other market structures you need to know: monopoly, monopolistic competition and oligopoly.

Productive efficiency and perfect competition

Figure 5.7 on page 131 shows the productively efficient level of output in perfect competition. This is output Q_3, which is located immediately below point X at the lowest point on the ATC curve. This is the average cost minimising level of output.

SYNOPTIC LINK

We introduced to you the concept of productive efficiency in Chapter 1. Refer back to page 21, which explains productive efficiency for the whole economy. When the economy is producing on its production possibility frontier, it is impossible to produce more of one good without producing less of another. All points on the economy's production possibility frontier are productively efficient.

Allocative efficiency and perfect competition

Allocative efficiency occurs when it is impossible to improve overall economic welfare by reallocating resources between industries or markets (assuming an initial distribution of income and wealth). As we shall shortly explain under the heading 'A further look at allocative efficiency', allocative efficiency is achieved when price equals marginal cost ($P = MC$) in every market in the economy.

Now look again at Figure 5.7. This shows that when a perfectly competitive market is in long-run equilibrium, the price the consumer pays (P_3) does indeed equal the marginal cost of production. In long-run equilibrium, a perfectly competitive firm is both productively and allocatively efficient, though when economies of scale are possible, which perfectly competitive firms cannot achieve, this is no longer the case.

But will perfect competition achieve an efficient allocation of resources?

To recap, Figure 5.7 shows the long-run equilibrium of a perfectly competitive firm. The firm appears to be productively efficient because it produces at the lowest point on the ATC curve, and it appears to be allocatively efficient because $P = MC$.

However, this conclusion must be qualified in a number of significant ways. Productive efficiency combined with allocative efficiency occurs only if:

● All the firms in the market benefit from all the available economies of scale. This is unlikely because each firm produces only a tiny part of total market output. Each firm is likely to be well below minimum efficient scale (*MES*).
● There are perfectly competitive markets for *all* goods and services, including future markets, and $P = MC$ simultaneously in each and every market. To take this point further, *every* firm in *every* market *throughout the world* must be producing where $P = MC$. This is an impossible outcome to achieve, even if all the conditions of perfect competition could be met.
● There are no externalities, negative or positive.

SYNOPTIC LINK

Refer to Chapter 8 for an explanation of externalities.

How competitive is perfect competition?

Although perfect competition is an abstract and unreal market structure, it is interesting to consider the forms competition might take in a perfectly competitive market economy. The first point to note is that price competition, in the form of price wars or price cutting by individual firms, would not take place. In perfect competition, all firms are passive price-takers, able to sell all the output they produce at the ruling market price determined in the market as a whole. In this situation, firms cannot gain sales or market share by price cutting. Other forms of competition, involving the use of advertising, packaging, brand-imaging or the provision of after-sales service to differentiate a firm's product from those of its competitors, simply destroy the conditions of perfect competition. These are the forms of competition which are prevalent, together with price competition, in the imperfectly competitive markets of the real economy in which we live.

So the only form of competition, both available to firms and also compatible with maintaining the conditions of perfect competition, is cost-cutting competition. Cost-cutting competition is likely in perfect competition because each firm has an incentive to reduce costs in order to make abnormal profit. But even the existence of cost-cutting competition in a perfect market can be questioned. Why should firms finance research into cost-cutting technical progress when they know that other firms have instant access to all market information and that any abnormal profits resulting from successful cost cutting can only be temporary?

Think also of the nature of competition in a perfect market, from the perspective of a typical consumer. The choice is simultaneously very broad and very narrow. The consumer has the doubtful luxury of maximum choice in terms of the number of firms or suppliers from whom to purchase a product. Yet each firm is supplying an identical good or service at exactly the same price. In this sense, there is no choice at all in perfect competition.

A further look at allocative efficiency

As we noted earlier, allocative efficiency occurs when $P = MC$ in all industries and markets in the economy. To explain this further, we must examine closely both P and MC. The price of a good, P, is a measure of the value in consumption placed by buyers on the last unit consumed. P indicates the utility or welfare obtained at the margin in consumption. This is the good's opportunity cost in consumption. For example, a consumer spending £1 on a bar of chocolate cannot spend the pound on other goods. When buying the chocolate bar, other goods or services are sacrificed. At the same time, MC measures the good's opportunity cost in production: that is, the value of the resources which go into the production of the last unit, in their best alternative uses.

Suppose that all the economy's markets divide into two categories: those in which $P > MC$ and those in which $P < MC$. In the markets where $P > MC$, households pay a price for the last unit consumed which is greater than the cost of producing the same unit. The high price discourages consumption, so we conclude that at this price the good is under-produced and under-consumed. Conversely, in the second set of markets, in which $P < MC$, the value (P) placed on the last unit consumed by households is less than the MC of the resources used to produce the last unit. The price is too low, encouraging too much consumption of the good; thus at this price the good is over-produced and over-consumed.

Now suppose resources can be taken from the second group of markets where $P < MC$ and reallocated to the former group of markets in which $P > MC$. Arguably, total consumer welfare or utility will increase as reallocation of resources takes place. As the reallocation proceeds, prices tend to fall in those markets *into which* resources are being shifted and prices tend to increase in the markets *from which* resources are being moved. Eventually,

KEY TERM

allocative inefficiency occurs when $P > MC$, in which case too little of a good is produced and consumed, and when $P < MC$, in which case too much of a good is produced and consumed.

as prices adjust, P equals MC in all markets simultaneously. Beyond the point at which $P = MC$ in all markets, no further reallocation of resources between markets can improve consumer welfare (assuming, of course, that all the other factors which influence welfare, such as the distribution of income, remain unchanged). The outcome, in which $P = MC$ in all markets, is allocatively efficient.

It follows that **allocative inefficiency** occurs when $P > MC$ or $P < MC$. For any given employment of resources and any initial distribution of income and wealth amongst the population, total consumer welfare can increase if resources are reallocated from markets where $P < MC$ into those where $P > MC$, until allocative efficiency is achieved when $P = MC$ in all markets.

SECTION 5.3 SUMMARY

- It is necessary to understand the six conditions which must be met for a market to be perfectly competitive.
- No real-world market meets all these conditions but perfect competition provides a yardstick against which the desirable and undesirable properties of real-world markets can be measured.
- In perfect competition short-run equilibrium, firms make abnormal or supernormal profits.
- In perfect competition long-run equilibrium, the entry of new firms has brought the price down until surviving firms make normal profits only.
- Subject to certain conditions such as a lack of possible economies of scale, in long-run equilibrium, firms are productively efficient and allocatively efficient.

5.4 Monopoly and monopoly power

To remind you again, at this point we are departing from precisely following the specification sequence, by explaining the topic of 'Monopoly and monopoly power' before we explain the two intermediate market structures of monopolistic competition and oligopoly.

The meaning of monopoly

As we noted earlier in the chapter, pure **monopoly** means one firm only in a market. We quoted regional water companies in the UK as an example. However, the word 'monopoly' is often used in a much looser way to describe any market in which there is a dominant firm, but in which there are also smaller firms. In this and the following sections of this chapter, we shall be looking solely at pure monopoly.

KEY TERM

monopoly one firm only in a market.

SYNOPTIC LINK

Chapter 6 compares *monopsony* or a single *buyer* in the economy's labour markets with *monopoly* or a single *seller* in the economy's goods markets.

Short-run and long-run profit maximisation in monopoly

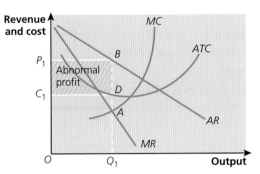

Figure 5.8 Profit maximisation in monopoly

The profit-maximising or equilibrium level of output in monopoly is shown in Figure 5.8. As in perfect competition, the equilibrium output Q_1 is located at point A, where $MR = MC$. It is worth repeating that $MR = MC$ is the condition that must be met to maximise profit for any firm, whatever the market structure. However, in monopoly, point A does not show the profit-maximising price, which is located at point B on the demand curve or AR curve above point A. P_1 is the maximum price the monopolist can charge and succeed in selling output Q_1.

You will notice that Figure 5.8 does not distinguish between *short-run* and *long-run* profit maximisation in monopoly. This is because a monopoly is protected by barriers to entry, which prevent new firms entering the market to share in the abnormal profit made by the monopolist. Entry barriers enable the monopolist to preserve abnormal profits in the long run as well as in the short run. By contrast, in perfect competition abnormal profits are temporary, being restricted to the short run. Indeed, in monopoly, abnormal profit is often called *monopoly profit*. A monopolist has the **monopoly power** to preserve profit by keeping competitors out.

EXTENSION MATERIAL

Entry and exit barriers and related concepts

Monopolies and firms in oligopolistic markets use entry barriers to protect the firm's position and power in the market. There are two main types of entry barrier: natural barriers and artificial (or man-made) barriers.

Natural barriers

Economies of scale, which provide a **natural barrier** to market entry, mean that established large firms produce at a lower long-run average cost, and are more productively efficient, than smaller new entrants, who become stranded on high-cost short-run average cost curves. Indivisibilities, which provide examples of technical economies of scale, prevent certain goods and services being produced in plants below a certain size. Indivisibilities occur, for example, in metal smelting and oil refining industries. **Sunk costs** are another natural entry barrier. Sunk costs, which cannot be recovered if a firm decides to leave a market, therefore increase the risk and deter entry.

Artificial barriers

In contrast to natural barriers, which are also known as *innocent* barriers, **artificial barriers** (which are also known as *strategic barriers*) are the result of deliberate action by incumbent firms to prevent new firms from entering the market. Strategic entry barriers include:

- **Patents.** Acquire patents, which provide legal protection for an invention, for all the variants of a product that they develop.
- **Product differentiation.** By differentiating their products, which then become protected by intellectual property and trade mark legislation, firms protect themselves from 'copy-cat' market entrants.
- **High levels of expenditure on advertising and marketing.** Established firms can make it difficult for new competitors by spending heavily on advertising and marketing, which are irrecoverable expenditures and a form of sunk cost if the firm decides to leave the market.
- **Benefiting from 'first mover' advantage.** By being first into a market, 'first-movers' such as Apple can establish themselves, build a customer base and make it difficult for later arrivals to compete.
- **Limit pricing and predatory pricing.** Limit pricing occurs when firms already in the market reduce prices so that they only just make normal profit, in order to deter or limit the entry of new competitors. Predatory pricing goes one stage further — occurring when an established or incumbent firm deliberately sets prices below costs to force new market entrants out of business.

KEY TERMS

monopoly power (also known as **market power**) the ability of a monopoly to raise and maintain price above the level that would prevail under perfect competition. Market power can also be exercised, usually to a lesser degree, by firms in oligopoly and monopolistic competition.

natural barriers barriers to market entry caused by geography. For example, if one firm has control of a resource essential for a certain industry, other firms are unable to compete in the industry.

sunk costs costs that have already been incurred and cannot be recovered.

artificial barriers (also known as **strategic barriers**) 'man-made' barriers to market entry, e.g. patent protection.

CASE STUDY 5.3

Patents and drug companies

Without patents, drugs companies would be dead. When rivals try to breach those patents, multinational drug companies react ferociously. They bring in lobbyists. They bring in lawyers. Often — by their own admission — they bring in private detectives.

'Intellectual property protection is critical to an industry like ours,' said the chairman of Britain's largest drug company, GlaxoSmithKline. 'If someone can come along the next day and copy [your invention], then no one would ever put any money into R&D.'

He added: 'If we believe people are undermining our intellectual property we have to deal with it by getting the information. Of course we — and I'm sure all other companies — use professional people who work, within the law, to get that information.' Private detective agencies are often used. Pfizer admits to using private detectives: 'They know the loops in the law.' The 'loops' are many. Private detectives raid rubbish bins, track down former employees and prepare 'sting operations' by luring adversaries into doing business with fake companies.

In developed countries, the multinational drug companies are protected by strong patent laws. But in India, China and South America, where respect for intellectual property has never been engrained, the task facing drug companies in protecting their patents is far harder.

Follow-up questions

1 What is a patent?
2 Name **two** other types of intellectual property right in addition to patents.
3 Governments in poor developing countries often claim that their citizens cannot afford the prices charged for medicines by companies such as GlaxoSmithKline and Pfizer. Do you agree that drug prices should be lower in poor countries? Justify your answer.
4 Describe how technical progress has been eroding the power of music industry companies to protect their intellectual property.

SECTION 5.4 SUMMARY

- In monopoly, entry barriers prevent the entry of new firms from competing away abnormal profit. Abnormal profit exists in monopoly in the long run as well as in the short run.
- As in all market structures, profits are maximised at the level of output at which $MR = MC$.
- A monopoly faces a downward-sloping demand curve (the market demand curve), which is the monopoly's average revenue (AR) curve.
- The monopoly's marginal revenue (MR) curve is positioned below the AR curve.
- Monopoly must not be confused with monopoly power. Monopoly firms possess the power to restrict output and raise the price, but imperfectly competitive firms possess a degree of monopoly power.

Possible advantages of monopoly

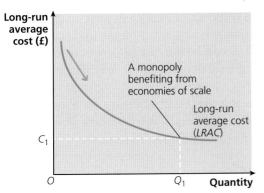

Figure 5.9 How economies of scale may justify monopoly

The possible advantages of monopoly result from two sources: economies of scale and dynamic efficiency. When substantial economies of scale are possible in an industry, monopoly may lead to a better outcome than competition. Figure 5.9 illustrates a natural monopoly, described in the extension material below. Because of limited market size, there is insufficient room in the market for more than one firm benefiting from full economies of scale.

In Figure 5.9, economies of scale are shown by the downward-sloping long-run average cost curve. By assumption, a monopoly is able to produce output Q_1 at a long-run average cost (or unit cost) of C_1, whereas competitive firms are unable to produce this output without destroying the competitive market.

A further advantage of monopoly, which we explain further in section 5.11, is that compared to perfect competition a monopoly can use its abnormal profit to fund research and development (R&D), which then leads to better ways of making existing products and to the development of completely new products.

> **TEST YOURSELF 5.8**
> Explain the main efficiency concepts that economists use when analysing and evaluating different market structures such as perfect competition and monopoly.

EXTENSION MATERIAL

Natural monopoly

A pure natural monopoly can occur when, for climatic or geological reasons, a particular country or location is the only source of supply of a raw material or foodstuff. However, we usually use the term 'natural monopoly' to describe a situation in which there is only room in the market for one firm benefiting to the full from economies of scale. In the past, utility industries such as water, gas, electricity and the telephone industries were regarded as natural monopolies. Because of the nature of their product, utility industries experience a particular marketing problem. The industries produce a service that is delivered through a distribution network or grid of pipes and cables into millions of separate businesses and homes. Competition in the provision of distribution grids is extremely wasteful, since it requires the duplication of fixed capacity, therefore causing each supplier to incur unnecessarily high fixed costs.

Possible disadvantages of monopoly

The main disadvantage of monopoly is that it may lead to productive inefficiency and allocative inefficiency. The latter results in resource misallocation. We explained above that a possible advantage of monopoly is that in the long run average costs may fall to be lower than those in perfect competition as a result of a monopoly's ability to benefit from economies of scale and to innovate. The counter-argument is that, protected from competitive pressures, a monopoly may *profit-satisfice* rather than *profit-maximise* and be content with satisfactory profits and an easy life.

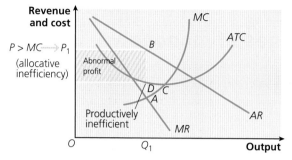

$P > MC \longrightarrow P_1$
(allocative inefficiency)

Figure 5.10 Productive and allocative inefficiency in monopoly, assuming an absence of both economies of scale and successful innovation

In the absence of any benefits associated with economies of scale and successful innovation, Figure 5.10 shows that a monopoly is likely to be both productively inefficient and allocatively inefficient. Productive inefficiency occurs because average total costs are shown at point D on the diagram and not at point C, which would be the case in perfect competition. The profit-maximising level of output Q_1 is also allocatively inefficient because price (shown at point B) is greater than marginal cost (shown at point A). In summary, for allocative efficiency to occur, price must equal marginal cost ($P = MC$). In monopoly, however, $P > MC$ as Figure 5.10 shows.

EXTENSION MATERIAL

X-efficiency and X-inefficiency

X-efficiency occurs when a firm successfully eliminates all unnecessary costs of production it might otherwise have incurred. X-inefficiency, by contrast, means that unnecessary production costs still persist.

Look back at Figure 5.7 which shows that in long-run equilibrium a perfectly competitive firm is both productively efficient (minimising ATC) and allocatively inefficient (producing where $P = MC$). It is also X-efficient, since competitive market forces have eliminated any unnecessary costs of production which in the short run the firm had previously incurred.

Now look at Figure 5.8 which shows the equilibrium level of output in monopoly at Q_1, with the price at P_1. The firm is productively inefficient (average costs are not minimised at point D) and it is also allocatively inefficient ($P > MC$). The monopoly is producing too little and selling at too high a price.

However, a monopoly may choose to be X-inefficient rather than X-efficient. To understand this, look closely at Figure 5.11. This diagram is the same as Figure 5.8, but with point Z added. If the monopoly produces the level of output Q_1, without incurring unnecessary costs, its average costs per unit of output are shown at point D, which is located on the ATC curve. However, if the monopolist produces at point Z rather than at point D, unnecessary average production costs are incurred, equal per unit to the distance between Z and D. The monopoly may be able to survive perfectly happily, enjoying an 'easy life', and making *satisfactory* rather than *maximum* profits. This is because entry barriers protect monopolies. As a result, the absence or weakness of competitive forces means unnecessary costs very often persist in monopoly and in other imperfectly competitive markets. In this situation, the monopoly ends up producing 'off' its average cost curve at a point such as Z, which means that it is X-inefficient as well as productively and allocatively inefficient.

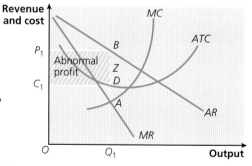

Figure 5.11 X-inefficiency and monopoly

TEST YOURSELF 5.9
Explain the difference between productive efficiency and allocative inefficiency.

5 PERFECT COMPETITION, IMPERFECTLY COMPETITIVE MARKETS AND MONOPOLY

138

CASE STUDY 5.4

Natural monopoly in the UK water industry

In 1989 the UK water industry, which had previously been run largely by publicly owned authorities, was sold to private owners. To start with, UK-owned PLCs, whose share prices were quoted on the London Stock Exchange, became responsible for the provision of drinking water and the treatment of sewage. However, in the 30 or so years since their privatisation, most of the water companies have been bought by foreign owners.

The largest water company, Thames Water, which serves the London region, provides a case in point. Initially, the Australian bank Macquarie borrowed £2.8 billion to buy Thames Water. Then, according to the journalist Nick Cohen writing in the *Spectator* in September 2017, Macquarie loaded £2 billion of Cayman Islands debt on to Thames Water and its customers, despite giving assurances to the water regulator Ofwat that it would do no such thing. This allowed Macquarie to take its profits. According to Martin Blaiklock, an infrastructure consultant, Macquarie's investors received returns of 15–19% over 11 years, twice the expected level, leaving behind £2 billion of debt for Thames Water's customers to bear.

Now Thames Water is owned by a Kuwaiti investment fund and a Canadian pension fund. But when pressed by the BBC to say that they would not seek to imitate Macquarie and extract exorbitant returns from a captive market, they refused to answer the question.

In 2017 the *Financial Times* described water privatisation as 'an organised rip-off'. The *FT* posed the rhetorical question: 'How hard can it be to be the chief executive of a privatised British water company?' The paper answered its own question by stating that the company's customers are determined by geography, and its prices set by the industry regulator. Pretty much all the company has to do is to make sure its sewage plants work and to keep the public waterways clear of human waste.

But after loading Thames Water with debt and flooding the Thames Valley with excrement, Thames Water's then chief executive received a 60% pay rise in 2015. At the time of the sell-off of the publicly owned water authorities in 1987, the then-Conservative government argued that greater competition would significantly increase efficiency within the water industry. However, in the 30 or so years since the sell-off, there is very little evidence that efficiency has improved. Many argue the opposite, that efficiency has deteriorated, particularly with regard to the pollution that the water companies discharge into the environment.

Follow-up questions

1 Why is Thames Water a natural monopoly?
2 Why is it difficult if not impossible to increase competition in the water industry?
3 Assess the case for taking the water companies back into public ownership.
4 Find out how much the chief executives of water companies are paid. Do you think that they are over-paid? Justify your answer.

QUANTITATIVE SKILLS 5.2

Worked example: profit maximisation and market structure

Firm X is maximising profit in the long run, and the following data are known about its cost and revenue structure:

- marginal costs = £400
- average costs = £450
- marginal revenue = £400
- average revenue = £500

Firm X could be operating in all the market structures listed below except one. Which is the exception?

Market structures: perfect competition; monopoly; monopolistic competition; oligopoly.

In the data, $MR = MC$, so we know the firm is making the maximum profit. However, $MC < AC$, so the firm is producing on the downward-sloping section of the AC curve. Also, since $MR < AR$, the AR curve slopes downward. All this is consistent with long-run profit maximisation in monopoly, monopolistic competition and oligopoly, but not with perfect competition, for which the following has to hold: $MR = MC = AC = AR$. Perfect competition is the answer.

5.6 Monopolistic competition

The meaning of monopolistic competition

In significant respects, monopolistic competition resembles both perfect competition and monopoly.

Monopolistic competition resembles perfect competition in the following ways:

- As in perfect competition, there are a large number of firms in the market.
- In the long run there are no barriers to entry or exit.
- As a result, the entry of new firms, attracted by short-run abnormal profits, brings down the price each firm can charge until only normal profits are made in the long run.

Monopolistic competition also resembles monopoly in the following ways:

- Each firm faces a downward-sloping demand curve. This results from the fact that each firm produces a slightly different product — differentiated by such features of modern production and marketing as style, design, packaging, branding and advertising. The goods produced by the various firms provide *partial* but *not perfect* substitutes for each other. The resulting 'product differentiation' in the market means that each firm possesses a degree of monopoly power over its product. Unlike in perfect competition, if a firm raises its price, it does not lose *all* its customers because there is brand loyalty.
- Each firm's marginal revenue (*MR*) curve is below its average revenue (*AR*) curve, which of course is the demand curve for the firm's output.

> **STUDY TIP**
>
> Students often wrongly believe that monopolistic competition is closer to pure monopoly than it is to perfect competition. In reality, monopolistically competitive markets, characterised by a large number of small to medium-sized firms competing against each other by differentiating the goods or services they produce and sell, are closer to perfect competition.

Short-run profit maximisation in monopolistic competition

Short-run profit maximisation in monopolistic competition is illustrated in Figure 5.12, which is very similar to profit maximisation in monopoly, illustrated earlier in Figure 5.8. However, in monopolistic competition the demand or average revenue curve represents demand for the goods produced by just *one* firm within the market rather than demand for the output of the *whole* market. And because the other firms within the market produce *partial* though *not perfect* substitutes, the demand curve facing the firm is likely to be rather more elastic at the prices each firm may decide to set than would be the case in pure monopoly.

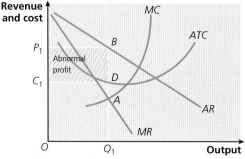

Figure 5.12 Short-run profit maximisation in monopolistic competition

The profit-maximising level of output, Q_1, is located below point A on the diagram, where $MR = MC$, and the abnormal profits made by the firm in the short run are shown by the rectangular area C_1DBP_1.

Long-run profit maximisation in monopolistic competition

The absence of barriers to entry or exit in the long run is of great importance in the theory of monopolistic competition. Long-run profit maximisation in monopolistic competition is different in an important respect from profit maximisation in monopoly. In the long run, the entry of new firms causes the demand curve or AR curve facing an established firm to shift leftward or inward. The leftward shift may result from the introduction of new substitute products, attracting some customers away from the existing firms. Long-run profit maximisation is achieved when the AR curve just touches (or forms a tangent to) the firm's ATC curve, thereby removing the firm's abnormal profit. This is shown in Figure 5.13, at point B immediately above level of output Q_1. Since only normal profit is made, total sales revenue and total costs of production are both shown by the rectangle OQ_1BP_1. Note also that the point of tangency between the AR and ATC curves occurs immediately above point A, which determines the profit-maximising level of output Q_1 where $MR = MC$.

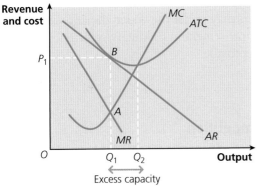

Figure 5.13 Long-run profit maximisation in monopolistic competition

STUDY TIP
It is worth remembering that in all market structures — perfect competition, monopoly and all types of imperfect competition — the profit-maximising level of output occurs where $MR = MC$.

TEST YOURSELF 5.10
Describe the ways in which monopolistic competition resembles perfect competition and the ways in which it resembles pure monopoly.

Evaluating monopolistic competition

We have just explained that, as in perfect competition, the market mechanism eliminates abnormal profits in monopolistic competition and brings about a long-run profit-maximising price which equals the average cost of production ($P = ATC$). Nevertheless, in the absence of any economies of scale, monopolistic competition is both allocatively and productively inefficient in comparison with perfect competition. As in monopoly, $P > MC$ and the firm is producing above the lowest point on its ATC curve.

Indeed, because in the long run a firm in monopolistic competition must be producing a level of output less than the output at which average total costs reach their lowest point, the productive inefficiency in monopolistic competition takes the form of excess capacity, measured by the difference in Figure 5.13 between Q_1 (the profit-maximising level of output) and Q_2, the productively efficient level of output, which is located below the lowest point on the *ATC* curve. However, as in perfect competition, long-run profit maximisation and freedom of entry in monopolistic competition mean that firms are forced to produce on their average cost curves. They must eliminate any unnecessary costs; otherwise they will fail to make normal profits.

At the same time, product differentiation increases the range of choice available to the consumer. It can be argued that monopolistic competition can in fact improve economic welfare. The economist Kelvin Lancaster argued that the number of differentiated products increases until the gain to consumers in choice from adding one more products to the market exactly equals the loss resulting from having to produce less of the existing products at a higher cost. According to this argument, monopolistic competition does not necessarily result in economic waste. Consumers may prefer the wider choice available in monopolistic competition to any improvement in productive efficiency that alternative market structures might provide.

QUANTITATIVE SKILLS 5.3

Worked example: profit maximisation in monopolistic competition

Table 5.1 provides information about the price, total revenue, total costs and marginal costs for haircuts on a particular day in a barber's shop operating in monopolistic competition.

Table 5.1 Revenue and costs for a barber's shop

Number of haircuts per day	Price (£)	Total revenue (£)	Marginal revenue (£)	Total costs (£)	Marginal costs (£)
0	11	0		5	–
1	10	10			2
2	9	18			3
3	8	24			6
4	7	28			8
5	6	30			9

From the information in the table:

(a) fill in the missing information in the marginal revenue and total costs columns
The answer is shown in Table 5.2 below.

Table 5.2 Revenue and costs for a barber's shop: completed version

Number of haircuts per day	Price (£)	Total revenue (£)	Marginal revenue (£)	Total costs (£)	Marginal costs (£)
0	11	0	–	5	–
1	10	10	10	7	2
2	9	18	8	10	3
3	8	24	6	16	6
4	7	28	2	24	8
5	6	30	1	33	9

(b) calculate the profit-maximising price of haircuts
Profit maximisation occurs at the level of output 3 haircuts per day, at which *MR* = *MC*. This is when the price of a haircut is £8 and both *MR* and *MC* are £6. (Note that total profit is the same at 2 haircuts per day, with the third haircut having zero effect on total profit.)

Is advertising a barrier to market entry or does it promote competition?

Advertising can be divided into informative advertising and persuasive
advertising. As the name suggests, *informative advertising* increases competition
because it provides consumers and producers with useful information about
goods and services which are available to buy, and about the different goods
that different firms are producing.

By making the demand curve for a product less price elastic, *persuasive
advertising*, by contrast, often reduces competition. In effect, customers
become 'captive customers' who are unwilling to buy a cheaper substitute
good. Persuasive advertising tries to make people believe that a product is a
'must-have' product. Little information about the good itself is provided: for
example, its price. Instead, advertisements focus on how ownership or use
of the product will improve the consumer's feelings of self-worth and/or the
image portrayed to other people.

People who drink Coca-Cola may
be unwilling to drink a cheaper
substitute

Persuasive advertising often goes hand in hand with *saturation advertising*.
Monopolies and other large firms use saturation advertising to prevent small
firms entering the market. The small firms are unable to enter the industry
because they cannot afford the minimum level of advertising and other forms
of promotion for their goods which are necessary to persuade retailers to stock
their products. The mass advertising, brand imaging and other marketing
strategies of large established firms effectively crowd out newcomers from the
market place. Supermarkets are often unwilling to stock goods produced by
new entrants to the market because their products are insufficiently advertised.

Price competition

Price competition takes place when a firm reduces prices in order to sell more
of a good or service. Increased sales can occur in two different but interrelated
ways. In the first, consumers switch from other markets where prices are
higher and buy this good instead. In the second, consumers switch from
buying similar goods from rival firms *within the same market* to buy the good
from the firm that has cut its price.

It is sometimes argued, though without much evidence, that competitive
firms do not like to use price competition because it leads to self-defeating

SYNOPTIC LINK
The coverage of price competition in this chapter links with earlier analysis of the role of prices in a market economy in Chapter 3.

price wars, which ultimately only benefit consumers. However, there are a number of ways in which firms undertake price competition, particularly in markets dominated by just a few firms. Besides limit pricing and predatory pricing, which we have already described, firms, especially those in monopolistic competition and competitive oligopoly, may undertake special offer pricing. Firms introduce temporary 'special offer' prices on some of the goods they are selling. Supermarket pricing provides many examples of this, including offering certain goods for sale at discounted prices for a limited period of time.

Non-price competition

In the absence of, or in addition to, price competition — through which firms try to gain market share and/or protect their existing sales by cutting their prices — firms in imperfectly competitive markets, both in monopolistic competition and in oligopoly, are likely to undertake various forms of *non-price competition*. These include:

- marketing competition, including obtaining exclusive outlets such as tied public houses and petrol stations through which breweries and oil companies sell their products
- the use of persuasive advertising, product differentiation, brand imaging, packaging, fashion, style and design
- quality competition, including the provision of point-of-sale service and after-sales service

SECTION 5.6 SUMMARY

- Monopolistic competition is 'imperfect competition among the many'.
- Monopolistic competition resembles perfect competition in that abnormal profits can be made in the short run but not in the long run.
- In the long run, the entry of new firms competes away abnormal profits.
- Monopolistic competition resembles monopoly in that each firm faces a downward-sloping demand curve (and *AR* curve).
- In the long run, firms in monopolistic competition are allocatively efficient, but not productively efficient.
- However, consumers benefit from the choice offered by a large number of firms selling slightly differentiated products.

5.7 Oligopoly

The meaning of oligopoly

The prefix *oligo* attached to a word is taken from the Greek word *olígos*, meaning few. In a literal sense, therefore, an oligopoly is a market or industry containing a few firms. This is the way oligopoly is defined as a form of market structure. However, there is a problem with this method of definition. How many or how few firms should there be for oligopoly to exist? Do 10 firms make up an oligopoly but 11 firms do not? And what about a market in which there are, say, seven very large firms, but also scores or even hundreds of small firms or minnows?

Market structure and concentration ratios

As we have just noted, oligopoly can be defined in terms of market structure and a limited number of firms in a market. We shall look at how concentration ratios are used to identify oligopoly in highly concentrated market structures.

A **concentration ratio** can provide a good indicator of an oligopolistic market structure. For example, a five-firm concentration ratio shows the percentage or share of output in an industry produced by the five largest firms in the industry. Figure 5.14 enables us to calculate the five-firm concentration ratio among the seven largest banks in the UK banking industry reported in March 2018. The five-firm concentration ratio was 89%, though we should note that many other smaller UK banks such as Metro Bank and Tesco Bank are not included in the data.

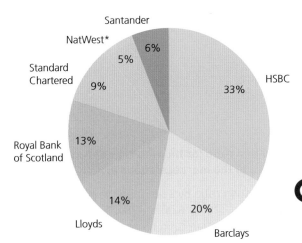

*NatWest is a subsidiary of the Royal Bank of Scotland Group

Figure 5.14 Market shares in the UK banking industry, March 2018 (% of total bank assets)

> **KEY TERM**
>
> **concentration ratio** measures the market share (percentage of the total market) of the biggest firms in the market. For example, a five-firm concentration ratio measures the aggregate market share of the largest five firms.

> **CASE STUDY 5.5**
>
> ### Competition in the UK supermarket industry
>
> Writing in an October 2014 edition of *Management Today*, Alastair Dryburgh explained why, in his view, Tesco cannot compete with Aldi and Lidl. The management expert argued that if Tesco wanted to return to health, it had to give up the idea that it could win by being the cheapest. Tesco was losing out to 'hard discounter' retailers like Aldi and Lidl.
>
> Some commentators were arguing that Tesco should cut prices by more than it had done in the past in order to compete, but Dryburgh believed that this would be a suicidal move. Aldi had stated publicly that its intention was to remain at least 15% cheaper than Tesco. Aldi has always been well placed to meet this target: its whole business has been designed to be lower cost than the competition.
>
> In February 2017 Aldi stocked only around 1,500 lines, as against Tesco's 60,000. Around 90% of those lines are own brands. The package sizes are designed to make optimum use of the shelves, and the goods are delivered in shelf-ready packaging. Dryburgh argued that a company cannot compete on price with other firms which have systematically designed their businesses to be lower cost — it would be like British Airways deciding to compete on price with Ryanair.
>
> Follow-up questions
> 1 Suggest **two** forms of non-price competition that Tesco might use to regain market share from 'hard discounter' retailers.
> 2 Tesco's largest supermarkets have usually been built outside of town and city centres. However, along with other supermarket companies, since 1994 Tesco has invested in convenience stores such as Tesco Express in high-street locations and in suburban shopping parades. Why have supermarket companies such as Tesco chosen to invest in convenience stores?
> 3 Research the prices charged in Tesco superstores and convenience stores. Are the prices charged similar or different? Suggest **one** reason for any price differences.
> 4 Research Tesco's recent business strategy and comment on its success or failure.

QUANTITATIVE SKILLS 5.4

Worked example: calculating a concentration ratio

Table 5.3 shows the usage-based market share of internet web browsers in Europe in a recent year.

Table 5.3 Market share of internet web browsers

Web browser market	Market share (%)
Internet Explorer	62.0
Mozilla Firefox	28.4
Apple Safari	4.3
Google Chrome	2.8
Opera	2.2
Others	0.3

Calculate the four-firm concentration ratio for the web browser market in Europe and comment on the nature of the market structure.

We calculate the four-firm concentration ratio by adding up the percentage market shares of the four leading firms. This is 62.0% + 28.4% + 4.3% + 2.8%, which equals 97.5%. The concentration ratio tells us that the European web browser market is an oligopoly, at least as defined by market structure. The data provide no evidence as to whether or not it is a competitive or collusive oligopoly, though in the absence of evidence discovered by monopoly regulators, such as the Competition and Markets Authority in the UK, it is probably a competitive oligopoly.

TEST YOURSELF 5.13
Distinguish between monopolistic competition and oligopoly.

KEY TERM
market conduct the pricing and marketing policies pursued by firms. This is also known as market behaviour, but is not to be confused with market performance, which refers to the end results of these policies.

TEST YOURSELF 5.14
What is the difference between market structure and market conduct?

Oligopoly and market behaviour

As already mentioned, oligopoly is best defined, not only by market structure or the number of firms in the market, but also by **market conduct**, or the behaviour of the firms within the market. An oligopolistic firm affects its rivals through its price and output decisions, but its own profit can also be affected by how rivals behave and react to the firm's decisions. Suppose, for example, the firm reduces its price in order to increase market share and boost profit. Whether the price reduction increases or reduces the firm's profit depends on the reactions of the other firms.

Interdependence and uncertainty in oligopoly

Competitive oligopoly exists when the rival firms are interdependent in the sense that they must take account of each other's reactions when forming a market strategy, but independent in the sense that they decide their market strategies without cooperation or collusion. As a result, uncertainty is a characteristic of competitive oligopoly; a firm can never be completely certain of how rivals will react to its price, marketing and output strategy. If the firm raises its price, will the rivals follow suit or will they hold their prices steady in the hope of gaining sales and market share?

Non-collusive oligopoly, collusive oligopoly and cartels

As we noted in the previous paragraph, in competitive oligopoly, firms act independently in the sense that they do not form agreements with each other. This is also known as non-collusive oligopoly. The uncertainty facing

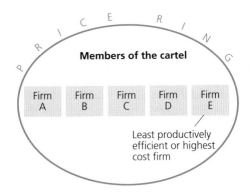

Figure 5.15 A cartel or price ring

competitive oligopolists can be reduced and perhaps eliminated by the rival firms colluding together — for example, by forming a **cartel** or price ring. In Figure 5.15, five firms jointly agree to charge a price to keep Firm E, which is the least efficient firm, in the market. In a competitive market, Firm E would have to reduce costs or go out of business. Cartel agreements enable inefficient firms to stay in business, while other more efficient members of the price ring enjoy abnormal profit. By protecting the inefficient and enabling firms to enjoy an easy life protected from competition, cartels display the disadvantages of monopoly (high prices and restriction of choice). However, this is usually without the benefits that monopoly can sometimes bring, namely economies of scale and improvements in dynamic efficiency.

TEST YOURSELF 5.15
Why may firms in highly concentrated markets decide to form a cartel?

KEY TERM
cartel a collusive agreement by firms, usually to fix prices. Sometimes there is also an agreement to restrict output and to deter the entry of new firms.

Collusion versus market cooperation

Although forming a cartel can achieve a better outcome than competitive behaviour for oligopolistic firms, the result is unlikely to be good for consumers. For this reason, cartel agreements are usually illegal and judged by governments as being anti-competitive and against the public interest. Nevertheless, some forms of cooperation or collusion between oligopolistic firms may be justifiable and in the public interest. These include joint product development (such as the Ford Fiesta and Mazda 2 cars, both built using many shared components between 1974 and 2015), and cooperation to improve health and safety within the industry or to ensure that product and labour standards are maintained. Such examples of industry collaboration, or overt collusion, which is in full public view, are normally deemed to be good, in contrast to price collusion, which is regarded as bad. Price collusion and other market-rigging agreements almost always take place in secret. This is covert collusion. Tacit collusion, by contrast, occurs when there is 'an understanding' without any explicit agreement between the firms.

STUDY TIP
Collusive or cooperative behaviour enables firms to reduce the uncertainty they face in imperfectly competitive markets. However, some forms of collusion — for example, on joint development of products or ensuring industry safety standards — are in the public interest.

TEST YOURSELF 5.16
The chairpersons of firms tendering for a government contract attend a secret meeting and verbally agree with each other to fix a higher price than if there were independent bids. What sort of collusion is this? Justify your answer.

147

Joint-profit maximisation in collusive oligopoly

Joint-profit maximisation, which is illustrated in Figure 5.16, occurs when a number of firms decide to act as a single monopolist, yet keep their separate identities. Oligopolistic firms undertake joint-profit maximisation in the belief that it can lead to higher profits for all the firms taking part. The monopoly *MC* curve depicted on the right-hand side of the diagram is the sum of the identical *MC* curves of three firms (one of which is shown on the left of the diagram). The three firms share an output of 750 units, determined on the right of the diagram where the industry *MR* and *MC* curves intersect. Each firm charges a price of £10, which, as the diagram shows, is the maximum price consumers are prepared to pay for 750 units of the good. The monopoly output of 750 units is well below 1,000 units, which would be the output if the industry were perfectly competitive. The shaded area in the right-hand panel shows the efficiency or welfare loss caused by the cartel raising the price to £10 and restricting output to 750 units. In this example, the members of the cartel split the 750 units equally, each firm producing 250 units. The shaded area on the left of the diagram shows the abnormal profit made by each firm.

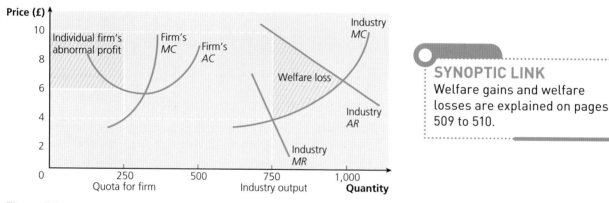

Figure 5.16 Joint-profit maximisation by members of a cartel

SYNOPTIC LINK
Welfare gains and welfare losses are explained on pages 509 to 510.

Although there is an incentive for firms to collude to maximise their joint profits, there is also an incentive for each member of the cartel to cheat on the agreement. The marginal cost of producing the 250th unit of the good is only £4, yet for the firm (but not the whole industry) the marginal revenue received from selling one more unit is £10 (that is, the price set by the cartel). One member of the cartel can increase its profit at the expense of the other firms by secretly selling an output over and above its quota of 250 units at a price less than £10, but greater than the marginal cost incurred (£4). This is an example of a divergence between individual and collective interest. The firms' collective interest is to maintain the cartel so as to keep total sales down and the price up. But each firm can benefit by cheating on the agreement — providing all the others do not cheat.

The kinked demand curve model

The kinked demand curve theory can be used to illustrate how a competitive oligopolist may be affected by rivals' reaction to its price and output decisions. The theory was originally developed to explain alleged price rigidity and an absence of price wars in oligopolistic markets.

Suppose an oligopolist initially produces output Q_1 in Figure 5.17, selling this output at price P_1. In order to anticipate how sales might change following a price change, firms need to know the position and shape of the demand and revenue curves for their products. But in imperfectly competitive markets, firms lack accurate information about these curves, particularly at outputs significantly different from those currently being produced. This means that the demand curve or *AR* curve in Figure 5.17 is not necessarily the correct or *actual* demand curve for the oligopolist's output. Instead, it represents the firm's *estimate* of how demand changes when the firm changes the price it is charging.

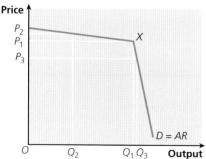

Figure 5.17 The kinked demand curve

When *increasing* price from P_1 to P_2, the oligopolist expects rivals to react by keeping their own prices stable and not following suit. By holding their prices steady, rivals try to gain profit and market share at the firm's expense. This means that the oligopolist expects demand to be *relatively elastic* in response to a price increase. The rise in price from P_1 to P_2 is likely to result in a *more than proportionate fall in demand* from Q_1 to Q_2.

Conversely, when *cutting* its price from P_1 to P_3, the oligopolist expects rivals to react in a very different way, namely by following suit immediately with a matching price cut. In this situation, because the market demand curve for the products of all the firms slopes downward, each firm will benefit from *some* increase in demand. However, the oligopolist fails to gain sales from rivals *within* the market. This means the oligopolist expects demand to be less elastic, and probably *inelastic*, in response to a price cut. The fall in price from P_1 to P_3 may result in a *less than proportionate increase in demand* from Q_1 to Q_3. The oligopolist therefore expects rivals to react *asymmetrically* when price is raised or lowered.

In Figure 5.17, the oligopolist's initial price and output of P_1 and Q_1 intersect at point X, or at the kink at the junction of two demand curves of different elasticity, each reflecting a different assumption about how rivals may react to a change in price. If when price is raised, demand is elastic, and when price is cut, demand is inelastic, any change in price will reduce the oligopolist's total revenue. In this situation, the oligopolist fears that both a price increase and a price cut are likely to reduce total profit. Given this fear, the best policy may be to leave price unchanged.

EXTENSION MATERIAL

Developing the kinked demand curve theory

By developing the theory a little more, we can explain a second reason why prices may tend to be stable in oligopoly. As Figure 5.18 illustrates, a mathematical discontinuity exists along the vertical line drawn above output Q_1. For the demand and average revenue curves, the discontinuity occurs at the 'kink' where the curves intersect. But for the marginal revenue curves, which are twice as steep as the AR curves with which they are associated, the discontinuity is the 'gap' between the two MR curves, shown by the distance B to C.

Suppose initially the firm's marginal cost curve is MC_1, intersecting the MR curve at point A, which is positioned in the middle of the vertical section. The diagram shows that the MC curve can rise or fall within the vertical section of the MR curve, without altering the profit-maximising output Q_1 or price P_1. But if marginal costs rise above MC_2 at point B or fall below MC_3 at point C, the profit-maximising output changes. In either of these circumstances, the oligopolist would have to set a different price to maximise profits, providing of course that the AR curve accurately measures demand for the firm's product at different prices. Nevertheless, the oligopolist's selling price remains stable at P_1 as long as the marginal cost curve lies between MC_2 and MC_3, despite quite considerable changes in marginal costs.

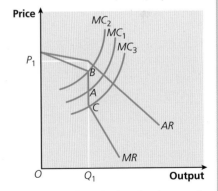

Figure 5.18 Developing the theory of the kinked demand curve

Criticisms of the kinked demand curve theory

There are a number of weaknesses in the theory we have just described. Although at first sight it is attractive as a neat and apparently plausible explanation of price stability in conditions of oligopoly, few economists now accept the kinked demand theory of oligopoly pricing.

First, it is an incomplete theory, since it does not explain how and why a firm chooses in the first place to be at point *X* in Figure 5.17. Second, the evidence provided by the pricing decisions of real-world firms gives little support to the theory. Competitive oligopolists seldom respond to price changes in the manner assumed in the kinked demand curve theory. It is more reasonable to expect a firm to test the market — that is, to raise or lower its selling price to see if rivals react in the manner expected. If rivals do not, then the firm must surely revise its estimate of the shape of the demand curve facing it. Research has shown fairly conclusively that oligopoly prices tend to be stable or sticky when demand conditions change in a predictable or cyclical way, but that oligopolists usually raise or lower prices quickly and by significant amounts, both when production costs change substantially, and when unexpected shifts in demand occur.

> **STUDY TIP**
> Students often wrongly believe that the kinked demand curve provides a complete theory of oligopoly. It is actually a very doubtful theory, but it does illustrate how oligopolists are interdependent and affected by uncertainty.

The advantages and disadvantages of oligopoly

The term 'oligopoly' covers a range of more narrowly defined market structures, ranging from pure duopoly (two firms only in a market), to markets which combine quite a large number of firms, a few dominant, but many very small and without much market power. It also ranges from competitive or non-collusive oligopoly to cartels in which member firms collude together, often to reduce competition. The following list of advantages and disadvantages is not relevant for all oligopoly market structures.

Possible advantages of oligopoly

- Just like a monopoly, firms benefit from economies of scale in oligopoly, which means they can become more dynamically efficient and can pass on cost cuts as low prices to consumers.
- With only a few firms available from which to buy, it will be easy for consumers to compare and choose the best option for their needs. Oher markets may offer too much choice, leading to confusion among consumers. Behavioural economists sometimes make this point.
- Provided that there is a degree of competition, oligopolists continuously innovate and develop new and better products.

Possible disadvantages of oligopoly

- Again, just like a monopoly, oligopolies restrict output and raise prices (and profit), compared to a more competitive market. Firms may satisfice, content with an easy life.
- As we have noted, cartels are a bad form of market structure, combining the disadvantages of monopoly (high prices, productive and allocative inefficiency and lack of choice) with few if any of the benefits.
- Small, competitive and innovative firms may find it difficult to enter the market.
- Ultimately, as in monopoly, the producer rather than the consumer ends up 'being king', with producer sovereignty rather than consumer sovereignty ruling the market.

Price leadership, price agreements and price wars

Price leadership

Because overt collusive agreements to fix the market price, such as cartel agreements, are usually illegal, imperfectly competitive firms often use less formal or tacit ways to coordinate their pricing decisions. An example of covert collusion is **price leadership**, which occurs when one firm becomes the market leader and other firms in the industry follow its pricing example.

Price agreements

We have already seen earlier in the chapter how members of a cartel often fix the prices that all the members of the cartel charge by forming a price ring. **Price agreements** can also be made between firms and their suppliers, and between firms and their customers. In both these cases, a price agreement is usually good for a specified period of time, such as 6 months.

Price wars

Price wars, which take place both in monopolistic competition and in oligopoly, may be started accidently or may be instigated deliberately to damage competitors. Whereas price leadership usually involves quite friendly relations between the companies involved, price wars — as the name indicates — centre on price cutting aimed at the very least at increasing market share, and in the extreme at forcing rival firms out of business. Consumers may of course benefit from a price war, at least in the short run, though if firms are driven out of the market, the monopoly power of the surviving firms increases, which is likely to be to the detriment of consumers.

CASE STUDY 5.6

Discounting in the book market

Many years ago, UK law allowed manufacturers to decide the prices at which retailers sold their goods. If a shop tried to undercut or discount a set price, the manufacturer could stop supplying the good to the retailer. As a result, price competition between firms selling similar goods hardly existed and manufacturers made excessive profits. This was a restrictive practice known as *retail price maintenance*.

Eventually the law was changed in an effort to promote more competition. However, manufacturers then set recommended retail prices (RRPs), which they hoped shops would abide by.

Selling at recommended retail prices became especially important in book publishing, where very little price discounting took place. Paperback books were generally sold at the prices printed by the publishers on the covers. Small bookshops justified the lack of price competition on the grounds that consumers benefited, both from bookshops surviving in small towns and from a much wider selection of books being on display.

However, the law was eventually changed. Large book chain stores such as Waterstones began to sell books at prices well below the publishers' recommended prices. Small bookshops could not compete and many closed down. However, large stores themselves were now facing increasing competition from the growth of the online retailer, Amazon. Many people now pop into bookshops, not to buy books, but to browse, before going home to order the books they want online.

The picture is different in France. French law fixes book prices with the result that readers pay the same whether they buy online, from a big high-street chain, or from a small bookseller. Extensive discounting is banned, although 5% discounts are allowed. Result: there are between 2,500 and 3,000 independent bookshops in France, compared with fewer than 1,000 in the UK. Most small French towns have at least two bookshops and there is a wide choice of books on display.

The French government says that the banning of discounts of more than 5% has saved its independent bookstores from the ravages of free-market capitalism that hit the UK when it abandoned fixed prices. Nevertheless, the owners of French bookshops still argue they cannot compete with Amazon, even with Amazon's discounts limited to 5%, because the online retailer provides free postage and free fast delivery deals on top of the discount. Consumers can also bypass French law by ordering books online in countries such as Belgium.

A French culture minister has said: 'Everyone has had enough of Amazon, which by dumping practices, slashes prices to get a foothold in markets, only to raise them as soon as they have established a virtual monopoly...the book and reading sector is facing competition from certain sites using every possible means to enter the French and European book market...it is destroying bookshops.'

Follow-up questions

1 Explain how the changing nature of competition in the book market illustrates the process of creative destruction.
2 Do you agree that the growth of Amazon has been good for consumers? Justify your answer.
3 Conduct some research to find out whether the number of specialist bookshops has declined in the town or area in which you live.
4 Many people are worried about the decline of 'high street' shopping in the UK. Do you agree that this is a problem? What, if anything, can be done to reverse this decline?

SECTION 5.7 SUMMARY

- Oligopoly is imperfect competition 'among the few'.
- High concentration ratios are often used to define oligopoly.
- It is usually more useful to define oligopoly by interdependence and reactive behaviour.
- It is also useful to distinguish between collusive and competitive oligopoly.
- Oligopolists sometimes collude to reduce uncertainty and to increase monopoly profit.
- The theory of the kinked demand curve, which is often used to model competitive oligopoly, illustrates the effects of uncertainty and interdependence in oligopoly, but the theory has a number of weaknesses.
- Just like a monopoly, firms benefit from economies of scale in oligopoly, which means they can become more dynamically efficient and can pass on cost cuts as low prices to consumers.
- Provided that there is a degree of competition, oligopolists continuously innovate and develop new and better products.
- Again, just like a monopoly, oligopolies restrict output and raise prices (and profit), compared to a more competitive market. Firms may satisfice, content with an easy life.
- Collusive oligopoly in the form of a cartel is a bad form of market structure, combining the disadvantages of monopoly (high prices, productive and allocative inefficiency and lack of choice) with few if any of the benefits.

5.8 Price discrimination

The meaning of price discrimination

KEY TERM

price discrimination charging different prices to different customers for the same product or service, with the prices based on different willingness to pay.

Price discrimination involves firms charging different prices to different customers for the same product or service, based on differences in the customers' ability and willingness to pay. Those customers who are prepared to pay more are charged a higher price than those who are only willing to pay a lower price. In the main form of price discrimination, the different prices charged are not based on any differences in costs of production or supply. However, in one form of price discrimination, bulk buying, consumers buying larger quantities are charged lower prices than consumers purchasing smaller quantities of the good.

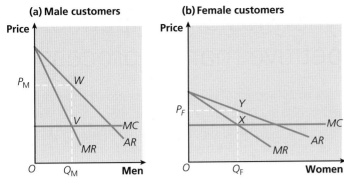

(a) Male customers

(b) Female customers

Figure 5.19 Price discrimination when a firm charges different prices to two groups of customers

When this happens, different costs of supply may be involved. Bulk purchases generally have lower average costs of production than smaller purchases.

In Figure 5.19 a night club divides its market into male and female customers, each with a different elasticity of demand at each price of admission. At all the prices that could be charged for entry into the club, female demand is more elastic than male demand. For both men and women, the downward-sloping demand curves in Figure 5.19 show average revenue, but not marginal revenue. In each case, the MR curve is twice as steep as the AR curve. The diagrams also assume that the marginal cost incurred when an extra person enters the club is always the same. This is shown by the horizontal MC curve.

To maximise profit, MR must equal MC in both male and female sub-markets. As the diagrams show, this means that men pay a higher price for admission than women, namely P_M, with women paying the lower entry price of P_F. With the different prices being charged, Q_M males and Q_F females are allowed into the club. The point to note is that the different prices charged result from the different male and female price elasticities of demand. Profit is maximised when more price-sensitive female customers pay less to enter the club than the less price-sensitive males. Note that when profit maximising, the MR received from the last man and woman admitted are the same. If this were not the case, the club could increase profit by changing the numbers of men and women admitted.

The conditions necessary for price discrimination

Successful price discrimination requires that the following conditions are met:

- It must be possible to identify different groups of customers or sub-markets for the product. This is possible when customers differ in their knowledge of the market or in their ability to shop around. Some customers may have special needs for a product and competition among oligopolists may vary in different parts of the market. In some geographical areas and for some products, a firm may face many competitors, whereas in other parts of the market the firm may be the sole supplier.
- At any particular price, the different groups of customers must have different price elasticities of demand. In these circumstances, total profits are maximised by charging a higher price in a market in which demand is less elastic.
- The markets must be separated to prevent seepage. Seepage takes place when customers buying at the lower price in one sub-market resell in another sub-market at a price which undercuts the oligopolist's own selling price in that market. In the European car market, car manufacturers have often charged higher prices for a vehicle in the UK market than in mainland Europe. One reason for this has been the fact that UK motorists demand right-hand drive cars in contrast to cars in mainland Europe which are left-hand drive. However, seepage occurred when specialist car importers bought cars on the Continent to resell in the UK market, thereby undercutting the prices the car manufacturers recommended for the UK market.

5.9 The dynamics of competition and competitive market processes

Traditionally, economists have thought of competition as price competition that leads to consumers benefiting from lower prices and more choice. And in a process which is akin to the 'survival of the fittest', the economy also benefits from the weeding out of high-cost, productively inefficient firms.

However, in imperfectly competitive real-world markets, firms do not just compete on the basis of price, but that competition will, for example, also lead firms to strive to improve products, reduce costs and improve the quality of the service provided. As we saw in section 5.6 on monopolistic competition, imperfectly competitive firms undertake various forms of non-price competition, such as marketing competition, product differentiation, and the use of brand imaging, packaging, fashion, style and design competition. All of these are used to make firms more dynamically efficient and attractive to customers. Non-price competition may also enable innovative and entrepreneurial firms to enter markets more easily.

But on the other hand, business decisions which at first sight may appear to be competitive and in consumers' interests are in fact 'anti-competitive' in the sense that they aim to increase the market power of already dominant firms. This view of competition is closely linked to the process of creative destruction, mentioned in Chapter 4 and earlier in this chapter, and also in the extension material that follows. Creative destruction, which is part of the process through which capitalist economies change over time and become more dynamically efficient, has become the centrepiece for modern thinking on how economies evolve.

EXTENSION MATERIAL

Profit and loss in perfect competition

Figure 5.20 shows a firm facing different prices in a perfectly competitive market. If initially the price is P_1, in order to maximise profit, each firm produces output Q_1 which is located below point A on the diagram where $MR = MC$. At this price, all firms make abnormal profit.

However, abnormal profit attracts new firms into the market, which causes the price to fall. As the price falls, some abnormal profit continues to be made, providing the ruling price remains above P_2, which is *break-even price*. Below P_2, the price line is below ATC and losses are now made.

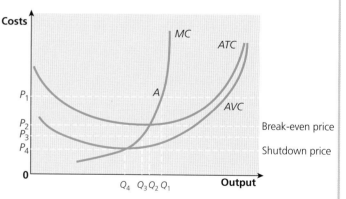

Figure 5.20 Firm facing different prices in a perfectly competitive market

Providing however that the price is lower than P_2 but higher than P_4, firms make losses in the short run, but these losses are smaller than would be the case if the firms produce no output at all.

This is because in the short run, firms incur fixed costs of production. If they produce zero output, each firm's loss equals fixed cost.

By producing the output at which $MR = MC$, firms can do better than this. For example, at price P_3 in Figure 5.20 a firm earns enough revenue to more than cover its variable costs of production. As it can now pay off a *part* of its fixed costs, it is better producing and selling *some* output, thereby incurring a loss *smaller* than would be the case if it produced nothing at all. If, however, the price falls *below* P_4, in the long run the firm should sell its capital assets and shut down. By so doing, the firm reduces its loss to zero. Price P_4 is called *shutdown price*.

CASE STUDY 5.7

How Apple competes

Nearly 40 years ago, when the Apple Macintosh personal computer was launched, all rival computers were square boxes and most of them were battleship grey. Not much thought was given to design. But the introduction of the Apple Mac changed things completely.

The first way in which Apple separated itself from the crowd was to 'think different'. Apple's main method of competition is to create new products, and new categories of products, which did not exist before. Examples over the years include innovation in the markets for MP3 and MP4 players, smartphones, tablets and, of course, computers. By not being much bothered about what its competitors do, Apple has broken the mould with all these products and has set industry standards.

Apple also competes through the management style the company has had since its inception. In rival companies, competitive decisions take a very long time to make because they have to be approved by many committees, all of which feed into the decision-making process. Apple is not like this. All decisions are made by a single executive committee. This leads to an almost seamless roll-out of new products, and the ability to launch a new product which nobody else had thought of almost every other year.

The third way in which Apple sets itself aside from its competitors is design. It is said that 'great design principles are pervasive in the Apple DNA'.

Unless Apple's competitors start innovating on their own, Apple will continue to have at least a 2-year lead over them. Tim Bajarin, the president of Creative Strategies Inc., believes that thanks to Apple's ability to 'think different', its management style and its design DNA, the company will keep its competitors following it instead of leading the market forward themselves.

Follow-up questions

1 Explain how Apple's success illustrates the dynamics of competition and competitive market processes.
2 Research how Apple has marketed new products in the years between when this book was published (2019) and your reading of the case study.
3 Apple designs computers and other electronic devices but Apple products are manufactured in China and in other low-wage countries. President Donald Trump has argued that such manufacturing should be returned to the USA. Argue the case for and against this.
4 Do you think that Apple will eventually decline due to the process of creative destruction?

SECTION 5.9 SUMMARY

- Both consumers and firms benefit from price competition.
- However, firms in imperfectly competitive market structures also benefit from various forms of non-price competition.
- These may sometimes be 'anti-competitive' in that they increase the market power of dominant firms.
- However, innovative, entrepreneurial firms may also benefit.
- And through the process of creative destruction, dynamic efficiency and economic performance may improve.

KEY TERM

contestable market a market in which the potential exists for new firms to enter the market. A perfectly contestable market has no entry or exit barriers and no sunk costs, and both incumbent firms and new entrants have access to the same level of technology.

5.10 Contestable and non-contestable markets

Much of the debate about the best way to deal with the problems posed by market concentration and monopoly power now centres upon the need to deregulate and remove barriers to market entry. This debate reflects the growing influence of **contestable market** theory. Until about 40 years ago, government approaches to the abuse of monopoly power involved an ever-increasing extension of government regulation into the activities of private-sector firms. Increased intervention was justified by the belief that regulatory powers must be strong enough, first, to countervail the growing power of large business organisations and, second, to make monopolies behave in a more competitive fashion.

At the time, monopoly was normally defined by the number of firms in the market and by the share of the leading firms, measured by a concentration ratio. The basic dilemma facing the policy-makers centred on how to reconcile the potential gains of large-scale productive efficiency with the fact that lack of competitive pressure can lead to monopoly abuse and consumer exploitation.

However, in contestable market theory, monopoly power is dependent not on the number of firms in the market or on concentration ratios, but rather on the ease or difficulty with which new firms may enter the market. Industrial concentration is not a problem, provided that an absence of barriers to entry and exit creates the ability for new firms to enter and contest the market. *Actual* competition in a market is not essential. The threat of entry by new firms or *potential* competition is quite enough, according to contestable market theory, to ensure efficient and non-exploitative behaviour by existing firms within the market.

In recent years, contestable market theory has had a major impact upon UK monopoly policy. The theory implies that, provided there is adequate potential for competition, a conventional regulatory policy is superfluous. Instead of interfering with firms' pricing and output policies, the government should restrict the role of monopoly policy to discovering which industries and markets are potentially contestable. Deregulatory policies should be used to develop conditions in which barriers to entry and exit are minimised, to ensure that reasonable contestability is possible. Appropriate policies suggested by the theory of contestable markets include removal of:

- licensing regimes for public transport and television and radio transmissions
- controls over ownership, such as exclusive public ownership
- price controls that act as a barrier to entry, such as those which used to be practised in the aviation industry

A reduction of price controls in the aviation industry has increased competition

Sunk costs and hit-and-run competition

For a market to be perfectly contestable, there must be no barriers to entry or exit and hence no sunk costs. Sunk costs, as described earlier, are costs incurred when entering a market that are irrecoverable should the firm decide to leave the market. *Sunk costs* must not be confused with *fixed costs*, although some sunk costs are also fixed costs. Suppose a firm invests in new machinery when it enters the market. This is a fixed cost, but if the machinery can be sold at a good price to another firm, it is not a sunk cost. In this situation, the cost can be recovered if the firm decides to leave the market. By contrast, if the machinery has no alternative use and a cost of disposal rather than a second-hand value, investment in the fixed capital is a sunk cost. Another sunk cost might be expenditure on advertising to establish the firm in the market. If market entry is unsuccessful and the firm decides to leave, the expenditure cannot be recovered.

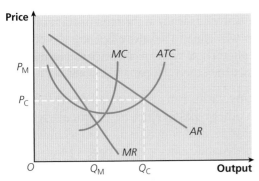

Figure 5.21 A monopoly setting a contestable price P_C to prevent the market being contested

Because sunk costs are unrecoverable and therefore make exit from a market costly, they discourage **hit-and-run competition**. Hit-and-run competition occurs when a firm temporarily enters a market to share in the abnormal profit being made by firms already in the market, and then leaves when abnormal profits have been competed away. As such, it is a feature of a contestable market. And just as *potential* ease of entry makes a market contestable, so the threat of hit-and-run competition can be sufficient to keep prices and profits at their lowest possible levels, thereby increasing consumer surplus. This situation is shown in Figure 5.21, which illustrates how a monopolist facing the threat of potential market entrants reacts by reducing the selling price from P_M to P_C, with the result that only normal profits are made. (This pricing policy is basically the same as limit pricing.)

TEST YOURSELF 5.17

Explain why one of the five possible answers to the following question is correct, but the other four are wrong.

Abnormal profits being made by a perfectly competitive firm in the short run would disappear in the long run because of:

A firms engaging in large-scale advertising

B allocative inefficiencies

C differentiated goods

D freedom of entry into this market

E high sunk costs

SECTION 5.10 SUMMARY

- In contestable market theory, monopoly power is dependent not on the number of firms in the market or on concentration ratios, but rather on the ease or difficulty with which new firms may enter the market.
- In a contestable market, the potential exists for new firms to enter the market.
- A perfectly contestable market has no entry or exit barriers and no sunk costs, and both incumbent firms and new entrants have access to the same level of technology.
- Potential competition is enough to ensure efficient and non-exploitative behaviour by existing firms within the market.
- Contestable market theory now has a major impact on UK monopoly policy.
- For a market to be perfectly contestable, there must be no sunk costs.
- Hit-and-run competition occurs when a new firm enters the market, makes profits and then quickly leaves, given that there are no or low barriers to exit.

5.11 Market structure, static efficiency, dynamic efficiency and resource allocation

KEY TERM

static efficiency efficiency (e.g. productive and allocative efficiency) at a particular point in time.

With the exception of the explanation of static efficiency which follows, this section provides a summary of key concepts explained earlier in the chapter, and on occasion in Chapters 1 and 4. So far in this chapter we have examined different market structures in terms of whether or not they are productively and allocatively efficient. In Chapter 1 we defined productive efficiency as the minimisation of average costs and earlier in this chapter we defined allocative efficiency as occurring when price equals marginal costs ($P = MC$). These types of efficiency can be thought of as **static efficiency**, which is efficiency measured at a particular point of time.

Monopolies and imperfectly competitive firms can also benefit from dynamic efficiency, which is improvements in other types of efficiency, particularly productive efficiency, that occur over time, and which result from technical progress and innovation. We defined dynamic efficiency on page 114 of Chapter 4. Monopolies can make abnormal profit, which in this context is also called monopoly profit, in the long run as well as in the short run. This profit can achieve improvements in dynamic efficiency through funding research and development (R&D) and product innovation.

Improvements in dynamic efficiency change the allocation of resources within the economy. Resources shift away from high-cost industries into lower-cost industries, and into better ways of making existing products and the development of completely new products.

SECTION 5.11 SUMMARY

- Static efficiency is productive and allocative efficiency measured at a particular point of time.
- Earlier sections of the chapter explained that in long-run equilibrium, perfect competition is both productively and allocatively efficient.
- Monopolistic competition is allocatively efficient in the long run, but not productively efficient.
- Dynamic efficiency is improvements in productive efficiency occurring over time.
- Monopoly and oligopoly are likely to be dynamically efficient.

5.12 Consumer and producer surplus

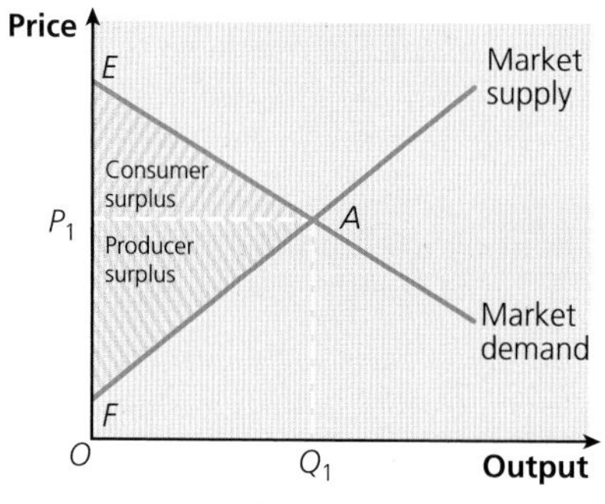

Figure 5.22 Consumer surplus and producer surplus

In this final section of the chapter, we use the concepts of consumer surplus and producer surplus as welfare criteria with which to evaluate the market structures of perfect competition and monopoly.

Consumer surplus is the difference between the *maximum price* a consumer is prepared to pay and the *actual price* he or she has to pay. In a competitive market illustrated in Figure 5.22, the total consumer surplus enjoyed by all the consumers in the market is measured by the triangular area P_1EA. Consumer welfare increases whenever consumer surplus increases — for example, when market prices fall. Conversely, however, higher prices reduce consumer surplus and welfare.

Producer surplus, which is a measure of producers' welfare, is the difference between the *minimum price* a firm is prepared to charge for a good and the *actual price* charged. In Figure 5.22, the producer surplus enjoyed by all the firms in the market is measured by the triangular area P_1FA.

KEY TERMS
consumer surplus a measure of the economic welfare enjoyed by consumers: surplus utility received over and above the price paid for a good.

producer surplus a measure of the economic welfare enjoyed by firms or producers: the difference between the price a firm succeeds in charging and the minimum price it would be prepared to accept.

STUDY TIP
It is important to understand consumer surplus and producer surplus in order to analyse how economic welfare may be affected by events that raise or lower the price of a good.

SYNOPTIC LINK
You will come across consumer surplus and producer surplus in Chapter 10 when analysing the effect of an import duty or tariff on economic welfare.

Figure 5.23 shows how consumer surplus falls, and producer surplus increases, when the perfectly competitive industry is transformed into a monopoly — provided we assume that neither economies of scale nor dynamic efficiency improvements result from the transformation: that is, assuming that the marginal costs under monopoly and perfect competition are the same.

As Figure 5.23 shows, industry output in perfect competition is determined at point A, with output at Q_1 and price at P_1. However, monopoly equilibrium is determined at point B where $MR = MC$. (Note that the *marginal cost curve* in *monopoly* is the same curve as the *market supply curve* in *perfect competition*.) The diagram illustrates the standard case against monopoly, namely that compared to perfect competition, monopoly restricts output (to Q_2) and raises price (to P_2).

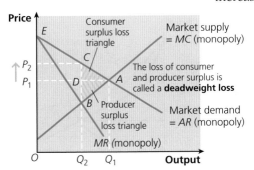

Figure 5.23 Consumer surplus and producer surplus in monopoly

We can use Figure 5.23 to illustrate how consumer surplus and producer surplus (and hence economic welfare) are affected by a monopoly replacing perfect competition. By raising the price from P_1 to P_2 the monopoly gains some of the consumer surplus that would have existed under perfect competition. The reduction in consumer surplus is equal to the rectangular area P_1P_2CD. This means that producer surplus (in the form of monopoly profit) increases at the expense of consumer surplus. Over and above this transfer, however, there is a net loss of economic welfare caused by the fact that the amount bought and sold falls to Q_2. The welfare loss or **deadweight loss** is shown by the two shaded triangular areas in Figure 5.23, which depict the loss of consumer surplus (the top triangle) and the loss of producer surplus (the bottom triangle). The deadweight loss is evidence of market failure in monopoly.

KEY TERM
deadweight loss the loss of economic welfare when the maximum attainable level of total welfare fails to be achieved.

SYNOPTIC LINK
Chapter 8 discusses why the existence of monopoly may lead to market failure.

TEST YOURSELF 5.18

Explain why one of the four possible answers to the following question is correct and why the other three are wrong.

A decrease in the production costs of LCD television screens through the development of new technology is most likely to:

A raise price and decrease producer surplus

B maintain the existing price and increase consumer surplus

C lower price and increase consumer surplus

D maintain the existing price and decrease producer surplus

Consumer surplus and price discrimination

Firms undertaking price discrimination usually benefit from the practice, but their customers generally suffer. What is an advantage to firms or producers is a disadvantage for consumers. Figure 5.24 shows how consumer surplus falls when different prices are charged to different customers. Because consumer surplus is a measure of consumer welfare, consumers end up being worse off as a result of price discrimination. By contrast, the firms undertaking the price discrimination benefit. Their profits and producer surplus increase as a result of the transfer of consumer surplus away from their customers.

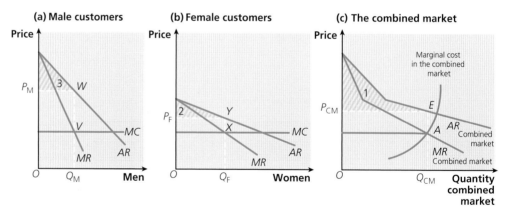

Figure 5.24 Price discrimination and the transfer of consumer surplus

As Figure 5.24 illustrates, price discrimination allows firms to increase profit by taking consumer surplus away from consumers and converting it into additional abnormal profit. Figure 5.24(a) and (b) are the same as Figure 5.19(a) and (b) on page 153. However, Figure 5.24(c) has been added to show the combined market with the male and female average revenue curves added together. The male and female marginal revenue curves have also been added together. Note that for the combined market (but *not* the male and female sub-markets considered separately), the marginal cost curve slopes upward, depicting the impact of the law of diminishing returns.

In the absence of price discrimination, all consumers pay the same price, namely P_{CM} shown in Figure 5.24(c). Without price discrimination, consumer surplus

TEST YOURSELF 5.19

'Increasing consumer surplus is always good but increasing producer surplus is always bad.' Evaluate this statement.

is shown by the shaded area (labelled 1) above P_{CM} in panel (c). But with price discrimination, when male customers are charged price P_M and female customers P_F, consumer surplus falls to equal the shaded areas labelled 3 and 2 in Figure 5.24(a) and (b). The firm's profit has increased by transferring consumer surplus from consumers to the producer. Producer welfare (or producer surplus) has increased at the expense of consumer welfare (or consumer surplus).

EXTENSION MATERIAL

Price discrimination: the limiting case

So far we have explained price discrimination where discriminating firms divide the market into a number of different market segments. This is also called third-degree price discrimination. Here we shall look at first-degree price discrimination, which is also called 'perfect' price discrimination. It is the limiting case of price discrimination. First-degree price discrimination is illustrated in Figure 5.25. (There is also another type of price discrimination called second-degree price discrimination. This occurs when the price charged varies according to quantity demanded. With 'bulk buying', larger quantities are available at a lower price per unit — a 'bulk-buying' discounted price.)

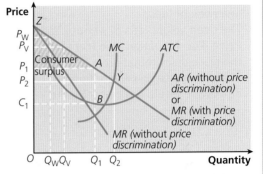

Figure 5.25 Price discrimination: the limiting case, when each customer is charged the maximum price he or she is prepared to pay

Figure 5.25 illustrates a situation in which *all* the consumer surplus is transferred into producer surplus or producer welfare. Every customer is charged the maximum price he or she is prepared to pay. Figure 5.25 is basically the same as Figure 5.8 on page 135, which shows monopoly equilibrium. In the absence of price discrimination, the firm produces the level of output Q_1 where $MR = MC$ and all customers are charged the price P_1. Abnormal profit is shown by the rectangle C_1BAP_1, and consumer surplus by the triangular area P_1AZ.

Now consider what happens when the firm charges each customer the maximum price he or she is prepared to pay. Customer Q_V depicted in the diagram is charged price P_V, customer Q_W is charged P_W, and so on. In this situation, there may be as many prices as there are customers. Because each customer is paying the maximum price he or she is prepared to pay, all the consumer surplus is transferred away from consumers to the firm, thereby boosting monopoly profit.

In summary, price discrimination leads to a loss of consumer surplus or consumer welfare. Firms exploit producer sovereignty and monopoly power, charging most consumers higher prices than would be charged in the absence of price discrimination. For these reasons, price discrimination is usually regarded as undesirable.

However, Figure 5.25 also shows how *some* consumers at least, often the poorest consumers, can benefit from price discrimination. Each time the firm sells to one more customer, total sales revenue rises by the extra units sold multiplied by the price the customer pays. Because different customers are charged different prices, charging a high (or low) price to one customer does not affect the prices charged to other customers. In the absence of price discrimination, the firm's AR curve continues to be the demand curve the firm faces, with the firm's MR curve located below the demand (or AR) curve. But when each customer is charged the maximum price he or she is prepared to pay, the demand curve is now the same as the firm's MR curve. The profit-maximising level of output, where $MR = MC$, shifts to Q_2, located at point Y in Figure 5.25. Customers who would refuse to buy the good at price P_1 buy the extra output because the prices they are charged are lower than P_1. As a result, most consumers end up paying a price which is higher than P_1 (the profit-maximising price in the absence of price discrimination), but some consumers pay a lower price. The lowest of all the prices charged is P_2, which is the price charged to the marginal, and perhaps the poorest, customer.

Consider also a situation in which a firm cannot make enough profit to stay in business unless some consumer surplus is taken from consumers and transferred to the producer. Market provision of healthcare by a doctor in an isolated village or very small town is an example. When charging the same price to all her patients, a doctor cannot earn enough income to continue to provide the service. Without an increase in income, the doctor will move to a larger city and local medical care will no longer be available in the village. But with price discrimination, the rich pay a higher price than the poor. Everybody gets some benefit, and a needed service is provided.

- The welfare concepts of consumer surplus and producer surplus can be used in the analysis of price discrimination and different market structures.
- Consumer surplus is the difference between the maximum price a consumer is prepared to pay and the actual price he or she has to pay.
- Producer surplus, which is a measure of producers' welfare, is the difference between the minimum price a firm is prepared to charge for a good and the actual price charged.
- When perfect competition is replaced by monopoly, some of the consumer surplus that existed under perfect competition is transferred to the monopoly.
- This means that producer surplus (in the form of monopoly profit) increases at the expense of consumer surplus. Over and above this transfer, however, there is a net loss of economic welfare which is called a deadweight loss.
- The deadweight loss of welfare is evidence of market failure in monopoly.
- Price discrimination also transfers consumer surplus away from consumers and toward firms undertaking the price discrimination.
- However, price discrimination can enable firms to supply goods and services to poorer customers who otherwise would not be profitable to serve.

Questions

1 Explain why profit is maximised when $MR = MC$ both in perfect competition and in monopoly.

2 Explain why firms in real-world markets use methods of competition other than price competition.

3 Do you agree that perfect competition, if it existed, would always be preferable to monopoly? Justify your answer.

4 Distinguish between monopoly and monopoly power.

5 What is a cartel and why are cartels usually regarded as bad for the economy?

6 How can the process of creative destruction be related to changing market structures?

7 What is monopoly deadweight loss? Illustrate the concept on a diagram.

8 Explain how (a) firms and (b) consumers can benefit from price discrimination.

The labour market

This chapter reintroduces the analysis which occupied Chapter 3, namely the role of the price mechanism in allocating scarce resources between competing uses. However, unlike Chapter 4, which looked solely at markets for goods, or markets for outputs, this chapter focuses on the price mechanism and the labour market, which is a market for a factor of production or input into the production process. An important part of this chapter is the analysis of perfect competition and imperfect competition in the labour market. The imperfectly competitive labour market that we shall examine is an example of monopsony. The chapter explains the similarities between, but also the differences that separate, perfect competition in the economy's goods market, studied in Chapter 5, and in its labour market. The chapter concludes by examining how trade unions, the national minimum wage and wage discrimination affect labour markets.

LEARNING OBJECTIVES
These are to understand:

- the similarities between labour markets and goods markets, but also the differences between these two sets of markets
- the demand for labour as a derived demand
- the demand for labour in a perfectly competitive labour market
- the supply of labour in a perfectly competitive labour market
- how wage rate and the level of employment are determined in a perfectly competitive labour market
- the similarities of and differences between a monopsony labour market and a monopoly goods market
- how wage rate and the level of employment are determined in a monopsony labour market
- the impact of trade unions on wage rates and employment
- the national minimum wage
- the effects of wage discrimination and other forms of discrimination in labour markets

6.1 The demand for labour

The labour market and the goods market

Much of the theory we explain in this chapter, including the theory of the demand for labour, is really just the price theory you have already studied in the goods market of an economy, operating in the labour market. A labour market is an example of a factor market — that is, a market in which the services of a factor of production are bought and sold. Markets for land, capital goods and entrepreneurial skill are the other factor markets.

As Figure 6.1 shows, households and firms function simultaneously in both sets of markets, but their roles are reversed. Whereas firms are the source of supply in a goods market, in a factor market firms exercise demand for factor services

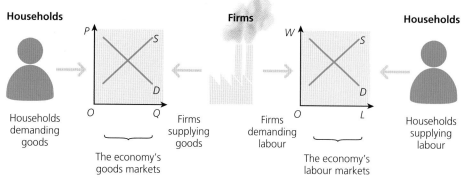

Households   **Firms**   **Households**

Households demanding goods — Firms supplying goods

The economy's goods markets

Firms demanding labour — Households supplying labour

The economy's labour markets

Figure 6.1 The goods market and the labour market, which is one of the economy's factor markets

supplied by households. The incomes received by households from the sale and supply of factor services contribute in large measure to households' ability to demand the output supplied by firms in the goods market. To exercise demand, which requires an ability to pay as well as a willingness to pay, households need an income, and for most people this requires the sale of their labour services in a labour market.

The relationship between households and firms in the two markets is essentially circular. In goods markets, finished goods and services flow from firms to households, who spend their incomes on the goods. In labour markets, members of households earn the incomes they spend on goods by selling labour to their employers.

SYNOPTIC LINK

The relationship between households and firms in the economy's labour markets is central to the circular flow of income, which is explained in Chapter 10.

The demand for labour as a derived demand

KEY TERM

derived demand demand for a good or factor of production, wanted not for its own sake, but as a consequence of the demand for something else.

A firm demands labour only if profits can be increased by employing more workers. But this assumes that households in goods markets demand the goods and services that workers are employed to produce. This means that a firm's demand for labour is a **derived demand** — it is derived from the demand for goods. Assuming a profit-maximising objective on the part of firms, there can be no demand for labour in the long run unless the firms employing labour sell the outputs produced for at least normal profit in the goods market.

STUDY TIP

Make sure you understand the difference between derived demand and composite demand. If in doubt, see Chapter 3.

TEST YOURSELF 6.1

Name two goods or services other than labour for which demand is a derived demand.

Marginal productivity theory and the demand for labour

The marginal physical product of labour

KEY TERM

marginal physical product of labour the addition to a firm's total output brought about by employing one more worker.

To understand a firm's demand curve for labour, we begin by explaining the **marginal physical product of labour** (MPP_L). Rather confusingly, this term is just another name for the marginal returns (or marginal product) of labour,

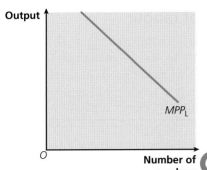

Figure 6.2 The marginal physical product of labour

which we explained in Chapter 4. MPP_L measures the amount by which a firm's total output rises in the short run (holding capital fixed), as a result of employing one more worker. In Chapter 4, we explained how the law of diminishing returns or diminishing marginal productivity operates as a firm employs more labour when capital is held fixed.

The law of diminishing returns is illustrated in Figure 6.2, which shows the marginal product of labour falling as additional workers are hired by the firm.

SYNOPTIC LINK

Figure 6.2 assumes that labour suffers from diminishing marginal physical productivity whenever more labour is added to fixed capital. In other words, the possibility that at a low level of demand for labour, there could be an increasing marginal physical productivity of labour is ignored. We are assuming that the marginal physical product of labour falls whenever an additional worker is employed. Compare Figure 6.2 to Figure 4.4 in Chapter 4, which is not based on this assumption.

QUANTITATIVE SKILLS 6.1

Worked example: calculating the marginal physical product of labour

Using the total physical product data in Table 6.1, calculate the marginal physical product of labour of workers employed assembling wheelbarrows in a particular week.

Table 6.1 Total physical product of labour

Size of labour force	Total physical product of labour (wheelbarrows per week)
0	0
1	5
2	12
3	21
4	31
5	40
6	46
7	50
8	51
9	51
10	49

The marginal physical product of labour measures the change in the total physical product of labour when an additional worker is added to the labour force. For the first worker employed, the answer is calculated by subtracting the total physical output when no workers are employed from the total physical product of labour when one worker is employed. This is 5 – 0, which is 5. For the second worker, the answer is 12 – 5, which is 7. Likewise, for the 3rd, 4th, 5th, 6th, 7th, 8th, 9th and 10th workers, their marginal physical productivities are respectively: 9, 10, 9, 6, 4, 1, 0 and –2.

(If you were to plot this information on a graph, the slope of the marginal physical productivity curve would resemble the marginal returns curve drawn in the lower panel of Figure 4.4 in Chapter 4. This is because the total physical product schedule in Table 6.1 assumes that the wheelbarrow manufacturing business initially benefits from the increasing marginal productivity of labour before diminishing marginal returns sets in.)

The marginal revenue product of labour

The falling MPP_L curve in Figure 6.2, which is also drawn in Figure 6.3(a), shows the *physical* output produced by an extra worker — measured, for example, in automobiles or loaves of bread, or whatever goods or services the firm produces. To convert the marginal *physical* product of labour into the **marginal revenue product of labour** (MRP_L), the MPP of labour must be multiplied by marginal revenue (MR), which is the addition to the firm's total sales revenue resulting from the sale of each of the extra products in the goods market. Assuming a perfectly competitive goods market (as well as a perfectly competitive labour market), MR is identical to the good's price, and is shown by the horizontal MR curve in Figure 6.3(b).

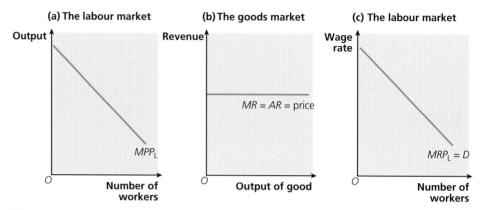

Figure 6.3 Deriving the MRP_L curve from the MPP_L curve

The marginal revenue product curve of labour, which is shown in Figure 4.3(c), can be explained with the use of the following equation:

marginal physical product × marginal revenue = marginal revenue product of labour

or:

$MPP_L \times MR = MRP_L$

Under perfect competition, since $MR = AR$ in the goods market where a firm sells its output, then in the labour market:

$MRP_L = MPP_L \times price$

TEST YOURSELF 6.2

Distinguish between the marginal physical productivity and the marginal revenue productivity of labour.

Deriving the *MRP* curve of labour when the goods market is imperfectly competitive

Assuming perfect competition in the goods market in which the firm sells its output, the slope of the *MRP* curve in Figure 6.3(c) is explained solely by the diminishing marginal physical product of labour: that is, by the law of diminishing returns.

However, if output is sold in an imperfectly competitive goods market, the marginal revenue product of labour declines faster than in a perfectly competitive goods market. This is because in imperfectly competitive goods markets, the marginal revenue earned from selling an extra worker's output also falls as output increases. The firm faces a downward-sloping demand curve for its products and, therefore, it has to reduce the price of the product in order to sell the extra output the worker produces. In this situation, there are *two* reasons for the MRP_L curve to fall as employment increases.

SYNOPTIC LINK
Refer back to Chapter 4 for explanations of the slope of the *MR* curve in perfectly competitive and monopoly goods markets.

TEST YOURSELF 6.3
Using the answers to Quantitative skills 6.1, calculate the marginal revenue productivity of each of the ten workers, given the assumption that, however many wheelbarrows are produced, their price is always £60.

What a demand curve for labour shows

The demand curve for labour shows the relationship between the wage rate and number of workers employed. The lower the wage rate, the more labour a single employer, or all the employers, within a labour market will be willing to take on or hire.

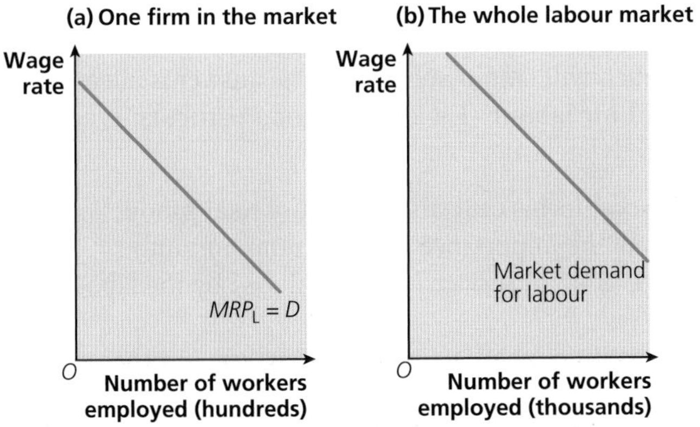

Whenever there is more than one employer in the labour market, the market demand curve for labour is in a different position from a single firm's demand curve for labour. Figure 6.4(a) shows a *firm's* demand curve for labour in a perfectly competitive labour market. In such a market, the *market* demand curve for labour, which is shown in Figure 6.4(b), would simply be the addition of the demand curves for labour of each of the firms that make up the market. Since each firm's demand for labour would be shown by the MRP_L curve facing the firm, the market demand curve for labour would be the horizontal sum of all the MRP_L curves.

(a) One firm in the market

(b) The whole labour market

Figure 6.4 The *market* demand curve for labour in panel (b) is the sum of each *firm's* demand curve for labour in panel (a)

TEST YOURSELF 6.4
Suggest two other causes of a rightward shift in the demand for labour.

STUDY TIP
Don't confuse a *movement* or *adjustment along* a demand curve for labour with a *shift* of the demand curve for labour. In the former case, a fall in the wage rate relative to the price of capital causes more labour to be demanded because workers become relatively cheaper than capital to employ. Factor substitution occurs with labour replacing capital in the production process. In the latter case, an increase in the derived demand for labour leads to more labour being demanded at all wage rates, causing a rightward shift in the demand curve for labour.

KEY TERM
elasticity of demand for labour proportionate change in demand for labour following a change in the wage rate. The elasticity can be calculated by using the following formula:
proportionate change in quantity of labour demanded/proportionate change in the wage rate

Shifts of the market demand curve for labour in different labour markets

The market demand curve for labour can shift to the right or left for a number of reasons. (A rightward shift is called an *increase* in demand for labour and a leftward shift is a *decrease* in demand for labour.) Reasons for this include:

- **A change in labour productivity.** As explained earlier, a firm's demand curve for labour is the *MRP* curve of labour facing the firm. It follows from this that if labour productivity increases, more labour is demanded at each wage rate and the firm's demand curve for labour shifts to the right. The same is the case when marginal revenue increases. (Remember, the demand for labour is a *derived demand*. If demand increases for the good that labour produces, raising the price of the product, the demand for labour curve shifts to the right.) And if a firm's demand curve for labour shifts to the right, the market demand curve for labour, which is the sum of each firm's demand curve for labour, must also shift to the right.

- **A change in technology.** Changes in technology can cause the demand curve for labour to shift, in some cases to the right, but in other cases to left.
  - If technical progress makes labour more productive relative to other factors of production, firms are likely to substitute labour for other factors of production, in which case the demand curve for labour shifts to the right. Technical progress is also likely to improve productive and dynamic efficiency, which reduce the cost of making the product; if this leads to lower prices and higher demand for the product, it is also likely to increase the demand for labour.
  - However, technical progress can also have the opposite effect by causing firms to substitute capital for labour. For example, a switch to automated methods of production, which increases the productivity of capital relative to labour, may reduce the demand for labour, thereby causing the demand curve for labour to shift to the left. Technical progress can also increase the demand for certain types of labour at the expense of workers with other skills, who may lose their jobs. The technological unemployment which results is a part of the process of creative destruction which we described in Chapter 4, page 116.

The elasticity of demand for labour

If the wage rate increases, but nothing else that might affect the demand for labour changes, by how much will employment fall? The answer is affected by firms' **elasticity of demand for labour**. The demand for a particular type of labour is likely to be relatively inelastic:

- when the relevant wage cost forms only a small part of total production costs (this has been called 'the importance of being unimportant')
- when the demand for the good or service being produced by the labour is inelastic
- when it is difficult to substitute other factors of production, or other types of labour, for the labour currently employed
- in the short run, rather than the long run, since it often takes time for employers to adjust the method of production

QUANTITATIVE SKILLS 6.2

Worked example: calculating the effect of a wage increase on employment

You are a labour market analyst providing advice to a trade union, whose members are unskilled workers currently being paid £10 an hour for their work. The union, which is pushing for a wage increase of 50p per hour, wants to know what will happen to the employment of its 20,000 members who currently have jobs. Your research tells you that the employer's wage elasticity of demand for unskilled workers is −10.

Assuming that everything else in the economy remains unchanged, calculate the effect of an increase in the wage rate by 50p per hour on the employment of the union members.

Given that the wage rate initially is £10 an hour, the proposed wage rate increase of 50p pence an hour is a 5% increase. The formula for the employer's wage elasticity of demand for labour is:

$$\text{wage elasticity of demand for labour} = \frac{\text{percentage change in quantity of labour demanded}}{\text{percentage change in the wage rate}}$$

% change in quantity of labour demanded = 5% × −10 = −50%

Given that 20,000 unskilled union members currently have jobs, the data indicate that half of them (10,000 union members) may lose their jobs.

STUDY TIP

Remember to avoid confusing the *slope* of a demand or supply curve with its *elasticity*.

CASE STUDY 6.1

Labour shortages in the fruit-picking market

In the summer of 2018, three out of five soft fruit growers were struggling to recruit the 30,000 seasonal staff needed. And with a shortage of seasonal laborers to pick the fruits, a trend exacerbated by the fall in inward migration of fruit pickers from central Europe caused by the Brexit vote, there were growing fears that many soft fruits would be left to rot on their stems. Growers said that they expected the position to be worse in future years. The labour market was definitely tightening.

Romanian grape pickers at a Kent vineyard

Soft fruit production in Britain grew by 131% between 1998 and 2018, largely as a result of an increase in home-grown strawberries, which are now protected from bad weather by plastic sheeting. The industry was worth more than £1.2 billion in 2018. The staff shortage was not restricted to fruits, with the entire horticultural sector buffeted by Brexit and improvements in labour markets in eastern Europe. As unemployment has fallen in Bulgaria and Romania, the number of people applying to work in England's fields has dropped, with Britain's impending departure from the European Union now amplifying the trend.

It has led to uncertainty over future immigration rules, while fears of encountering a growing hatred of immigrants and a weakened British currency — resulting in less money to send home — have also deterred arrivals. One fruit picker said that her friends don't go to the United Kingdom any more, but to Italy and Germany. The labour squeeze is occurring despite workers being mostly paid at the national living wage of £7.83 an hour and some given airline tickets, housing support and productivity bonuses.

The prospect of British fruit pickers replacing foreign workers is remote. 'We had two British applicants this year, in six months,' said the boss of one recruitment agency, adding that there was absolutely no appetite for the jobs among British workers.

Farmers are calling on the government to open the immigration system to more seasonal workers from countries outside the EU, as Germany, Spain, Portugal and Ireland have already done. Britain, whose citizens voted to leave the European Union to put a brake on European immigration, is ironically perhaps the only member country to recruit only within the EU.

Without government intervention, the impact of the labour shortage on the soft fruit industry could be devastating. A third of British producers had already decided to scale back investment, while others were looking at expanding in different countries.

Follow-up questions

1 Why is the demand for fruit pickers highly seasonal?
2 What is meant by the statement 'The labour market was definitely tightening'?
3 Explain why the national living wage paid at £7.83 an hour apparently had no effect on the labour shortage.
4 Evaluate the effect of the 2016 Brexit vote on the agricultural labour market in the UK.

SECTION 6.1 SUMMARY

- A labour market is an example of a factor market — that is, a market in which the services of a factor of production are bought and sold.
- In labour markets, members of households earn the incomes they spend on goods by selling labour to their employers.
- The demand for labour is a derived demand.
- Assuming perfect competition, the marginal revenue product curve is the firm's demand curve for labour.
- The elasticity of demand for labour is the proportionate change in the demand for labour following a change in the wage rate.
- The market demand curve for labour is the horizontal sum of the MRP_L curves facing all the firms in the labour market.
- The market demand curve for labour can shift to the right or left for a number of reasons.
- The reasons include a change in labour productivity and a change in technology.

6.2 Influences on the supply of labour to different labour markets

The market supply of labour

Just as the market demand curve for labour shows how much labour all the firms in the labour market plan to demand at different wage rates, so the market supply curve of labour shows how much labour all the workers in the labour market plan to supply at different wage rates. Figure 6.5 below shows the market supply curve of labour.

The graph shows how many hours of labour workers plans to supply — for example, at different hourly wage rates — in a particular occupation in a particular week. The diagram depicts a situation in which workers respond to an increase in the hourly wage rate from £7 to £15 by increasing the total number of hours they are prepared to work from 1 million hours to 1.5 million hours per week.

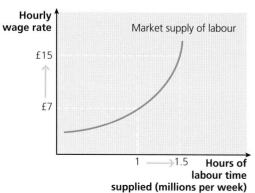

Figure 6.5 A market supply curve of labour in a particular week

Monetary and non-monetary considerations

The money wage rate on offer is the first of two factors which influence the amount of labour that workers are willing to supply. The second factor is the utility or economic welfare derived from other aspects of working, sometimes called the non-monetary benefits (these include what is popularly known as job satisfaction or, if negative, job dissatisfaction).

Different types of work yield different amounts of job satisfaction and dissatisfaction. When a worker enjoys the job, the net advantage of work is greater than the welfare yielded by the wage. In this situation, the worker is willing to work for a money wage lower than the wage that would be acceptable if there were no satisfaction from the work itself. But for some workers, work such as routine assembly-line work in factories and heavy manual labour is unpleasant, yielding job dissatisfaction.

> **SYNOPTIC LINK**
> For most people, both money and leisure time are affected by the law of diminishing marginal utility, which is explained in Chapter 2 on page 27.

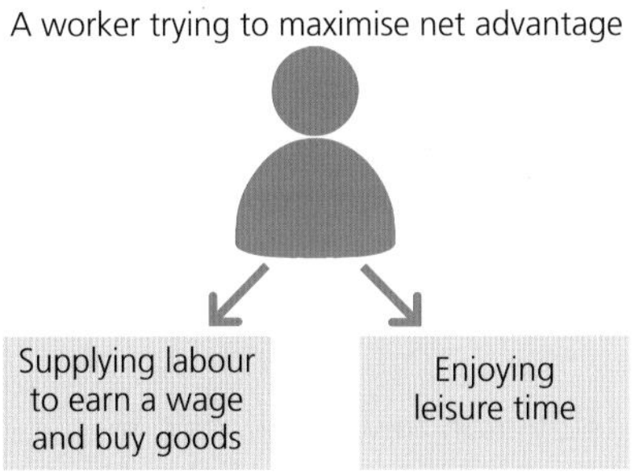

A worker trying to maximise net advantage

Supplying labour to earn a wage and buy goods

Enjoying leisure time

Figure 6.6 The choice between supplying labour and enjoying leisure time

The supply of labour for this type of employment reflects the fact that the hourly wage rate must be high enough to compensate for the unpleasantness (or sometimes the danger) of the job.

Figure 6.6 shows a worker who is free to decide how many hours to work each day or each week, choosing between supplying more labour or enjoying more leisure time. As more labour time is supplied at a particular hourly wage rate, the extra income yields less and less extra satisfaction for the worker. But because there are only 24 hours in the day, the decision to supply more labour simultaneously means the decision to enjoy less leisure time. In this situation, each extra hour of leisure sacrificed is accompanied by an increasing loss of economic welfare. At the margin, to maximise personal welfare, a worker must supply labour up to the point at which:

$$\text{utility of welfare from the last unit of money earned} = \text{utility or welfare from the last unit of leisure time sacrificed}$$

In this situation, the marginal private benefit received by a worker from supplying labour equals the marginal private cost incurred from giving up leisure time. Provided personal preferences remain stable, there is no incentive for the worker to supply more labour at the *going* hourly wage rate.

However, a *higher* hourly wage will provide an incentive to work more hours. With a higher wage rate, at the margin, the welfare derived from the wage becomes greater than the welfare derived from the last unit of leisure time enjoyed. To maximise personal welfare at the higher wage rate, the worker would be expected to supply more labour and enjoy less leisure time. The result is the upward-sloping labour supply curve shown earlier in Figure 6.5. An increase in the wage rate from £7 an hour to £15 an hour increases the number of hours worked in the labour market from 1 million hours to 1.5 million hours.

Individual workers job choice depends on the utility they expect to derive from the money wage rate and job satisfaction or dissatisfaction in different occupations. However, given that the non-monetary advantages usually change slowly, a rise in the wage in an occupation should lead to an increase in the supply of labour.

SYNOPTIC LINK

At this point in the course, it is a good idea to remind yourself of the meaning of opportunity cost. As Chapter 1 explains, the opportunity cost of any choice, decision or course of action is measured in terms of the alternatives that have to be given up. There is an opportunity cost whenever a person decides to work. The opportunity cost of supplying one more hour of labour time (in order to earn money) is the hour of leisure time sacrificed. Because of the time constraint resulting from the fact that there are only 24 hours in a day, a decision to supply one more hour of labour time means that the worker chooses one hour less of leisure time. Labour time and leisure time are substitutes for each other, and working longer hours eats into leisure time.

CASE STUDY 6.2

Who should be paid more, MPs or newsreaders?

Economics teachers often ask their students to ponder on whether workers employed in pleasant occupations, such as television celebrities, should be paid more than those in disagreeable occupations, such as road sweepers. If job satisfaction or dissatisfaction were to be the only factor determining wages, the road sweeper would be paid more. However, more often than not, other factors, related to supply and demand, productivity, learned skills and innate ability, tend to override the job satisfaction factor and explain why television celebrities are paid more than road sweepers.

A few years ago, a government minister asked: 'should MPs be paid more than television newsreaders?' In a follow-up poll, 45% of the general public said 'yes' and 55% voted 'no'. Former Conservative MP Michael Portillo, now a TV presenter of programmes about railway journeys, argued that:

Low pay will discourage good people from becoming MPs, especially if we are now going to denigrate their outside earnings too, even though that's how TV presenters boost their salaries. The present exchange rate is approximately one Jonathan Ross equals 100 MPs. It is a topsy-turvy world where we pay top journalists more to comment occasionally on what the prime minister does than we pay him to do his job 24/7.

Replying 'no', Ken Livingstone, an ex-mayor of London and former Labour MP, said:

Far too many people are paid too much for what they do. In 1979, Britain's top 10% of earners were paid four times as much as the bottom 10%. By 2018 that figure had doubled to at least ten times as much. Is Britain more than twice as well run as it was 40 years ago? Is the output of television twice as good as in the 1970s? Are our politicians and bankers twice as honest? It's time for a dramatic reduction in top salaries across the board, not just those of TV presenters.

Follow-up questions

1 Do you believe that both MPs and TV newsreaders are paid too much? Use economic theory to justify your argument.
2 Name **two** other groups of workers who you think are paid too much. Justify your answer.
3 Name **two** other groups of workers who you think are paid too little. Justify your answer.
4 Should relative wage and salary rates be determined solely by market forces? Again, justify your answer.

TEST YOURSELF 6.6
Suggest two other factors which might cause the market supply curve of labour to shift to the right.

Shifts of the market supply curve of labour

Changes in the non-monetary factors affecting the supply of labour shift both an individual worker's supply curve of labour and the market supply curve of labour to a new position. These factors include the benefits of job security, promotion prospects, good working conditions, holiday entitlement and other psychological benefits of work. Improvements in these benefits will shift the supply curve of labour to the right. A deterioration in these benefits shifts the supply curve of labour to the left. Generalising, if people decide they value leisure more highly, they will work fewer hours at each wage rate, and the supply curve for labour will shift to the left. If they decide they want more goods and services rather than leisure time, the supply curve is likely to shift to the right.

Other factors that can shift the supply curve of labour include:

- **Changes in income.** It is reasonable to assume that leisure time is a normal good for most people, so a rise in income increases the demand for leisure time, which in turn causes the supply curve of labour to shift to the left. However, for a few people, leisure time might be an inferior good. For them, higher income reduces their demand for leisure time and they end up supplying more labour.
- **Changes in population.** A rise in population, perhaps caused by immigration, increases the supply of labour; a reduction lowers it. A fall in the number of people of working age causes the labour supply curve to shift to the left, except perhaps when this is offset by those who have reached retirement age deciding to work longer in order to finance their eventual retirement.
- **Changes in expectations.** Likewise, if older people expect to live longer yet become less optimistic about their future pensions, this could increase the labour supply. A rise in the proportion of people staying on in further and higher education will tend to reduce the supply of labour.

SYNOPTIC LINK
At this point you might refer back to Chapter 3 and refresh your understanding of normal goods and inferior goods.

The elasticity of supply of labour

The factors which determine the wage **elasticity of supply of labour** include the following:

KEY TERM
elasticity of supply of labour proportionate change in the supply of labour following a change in the wage rate. The elasticity can be calculated by using the following formula:

proportionate change in quantity of labour supplied/ proportionate change in the wage rate

- The supply of unskilled labour is usually more elastic than the supply of a particular type of skilled labour. This is because the training period of unskilled labour is usually very short, and any innate abilities required are unlikely to be restricted to a small proportion of the total population.
- Factors which reduce the occupational and geographical mobility of labour tend to reduce the elasticity of labour supply.
- The supply of labour is also likely to be more elastic in the long run than in the short run.
- The availability of a pool of unemployed labour increases the elasticity of supply of labour, while full employment has the opposite effect.

QUANTITATIVE SKILLS 6.3

Worked example: calculating the wage elasticity of supply

Fearing a shortage of labour, a firm that wants to expand, and which currently employs 1,000 workers, increases the wage it pays to all its workers from £10 per hour to £15 per hour. As a result, 500 workers apply for jobs at the firm.

What is the wage elasticity of supply of labour with respect to the stated wage rate increase?

The formula needed to calculate the correct answer is:

$$\text{wage elasticity of supply of labour} = \frac{\text{percentage change in quantity of labour supplied}}{\text{percentage change in the wage rate}}$$

$$= +50\%/+50\% = +1$$

Thus, between these two hourly wage rates the wage elasticity of supply of labour is unitary: that is, equal to 1.

SECTION 6.2 SUMMARY

- The market supply curve of labour slopes upward, showing that workers plan to supply more labour as the wage rate rises.
- The supply of labour is affected by non-monetary considerations or rewards as well as by monetary considerations or rewards.
- Non-monetary rewards include job satisfaction.
- Changes in non-monetary rewards shift the supply curve of labour to a new position.
- Likewise, changes in income, population size and expectations shift the position of the supply curve of labour.
- The opportunity cost of working is the leisure time forgone.
- The elasticity of supply of labour is the proportionate change in the supply of labour following a change in the wage rate.

6.3 Perfectly competitive labour markets

In this section, we bring the demand for, and supply of, labour together and explain the determination of relative wage rates and levels of employment in perfectly competitive labour markets.

A perfectly competitive *labour* market, if it were to exist, would have to meet all of the following conditions at the same time. As would be the case in a perfectly competitive *goods* market, a perfectly competitive labour market would have to contain a large number of buyers and sellers, each unable to influence the ruling market price (in this case, the ruling market wage), and operating in conditions of perfect market information. Employers and workers would be free to enter the labour market in the long run, but an individual employer or firm could not influence the ruling market wage through its independent action.

Just as in a perfectly competitive goods market, it is impossible for all these requirements to be met simultaneously. It follows that perfectly competitive labour markets do not exist in the real world. Some labour markets, such as the market for fruit pickers in a region or district where there are a very large number of orchards, *approximate* to perfect competition, but nevertheless they are not perfectly competitive.

SYNOPTIC LINK
Refer back to Figure 5.1 in Chapter 5, which lists the six conditions which would have to be met for perfect competition to exist.

How the ruling market wage affects perfectly competitive firms

In Chapter 5, we explained how a firm in a perfectly competitive goods market would be able to sell as much as it wanted at the ruling market price, meaning that the firm faces a perfectly elastic demand curve which is also the firm's average and marginal revenue curve. Each firm is a passive price-taker at the ruling price determined in the market as a whole, choosing the quantity to sell, but not the price.

A very similar situation would exist for a firm employing workers in a perfectly competitive labour market, except that now the firm could *buy* as much labour as it wanted to employ at the ruling market wage. To state this another way, each employer would face a perfectly elastic *supply* of labour curve in a perfectly competitive labour market. Figure 6.7 illustrates why.

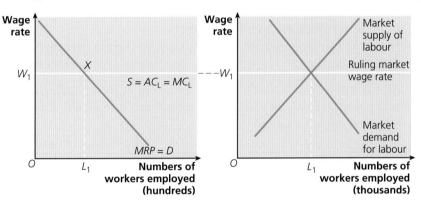

(a) One firm in the market **(b) The whole labour market**

Figure 6.7 A perfectly competitive labour market

In a perfectly competitive labour market, each employer would have to passively accept the ruling market wage. The ruling wage, determined in Figure 6.7(b), is also the perfectly elastic supply curve of labour facing each of the firms in the labour market. This means it is also the **average cost of labour** (AC_L) curve and the **marginal cost of labour** (MC_L) curve facing each firm in the labour market. This is shown in Figure 6.7(a). At the ruling market wage, each firm would be a passive price-taker, able to hire as many workers as it wished to hire at the ruling market wage, but unable to influence the ruling wage by its own actions.

KEY TERMS
average cost of labour total wage costs divided by the number of workers employed.

marginal cost of labour the addition to a firm's total cost of production resulting from employing one more worker.

Equating MRP_L with the wage rate

To maximise profit when selling the output produced by labour, each firm would have to demand labour up to the point at which:

the addition to sales revenue resulting from employment of an extra worker = the addition to production costs resulting from the employment of an extra worker

or:

$$MRP_L = MC_L$$

The marginal revenue product of labour (MRP_L) is the marginal benefit accruing to the employer when hiring an extra worker. Likewise, the marginal cost of labour (MC_L) is the marginal private cost incurred by each firm. Since, in a perfectly competitive labour market, the marginal cost of labour would always equal the wage paid to the workers, the perfectly competitive firm's level of employment or demand for labour at each wage rate would be where:

$$MRP_L = W$$

Point X in Figure 6.7(a) shows the number of workers that a firm would be willing to employ at a ruling wage rate W_1. Consider what would happen if the firm were to employ a labour force larger than L_1. Additional workers would add more to total costs of production than to total revenue, and so total profit would fall. Conversely, with a workforce below L_1, the MRP of the last worker is greater than the wage, and the total profit would increase if more workers were employed.

Summarising:

- If $MRP > W$, more workers should be hired.
- If $MRP < W$, fewer workers should be employed.
- If $MRP = W$, the firm is employing the number of workers consistent with profit maximisation.

As the MRP curve shows each firm's demand for labour at each possible wage rate, including wage rate W_1, the MRP curve facing each firm would in fact be the firm's demand curve for labour.

TEST YOURSELF 6.8
What is meant by profit maximisation?

The role of market forces in determining relative wage rates

In a perfectly competitive labour market, each employer would be just one among many in the market, able to hire however many workers it wished to employ, provided only that the ruling market wage was offered to all employees taken on.

Look again at Figure 6.7(b). This shows the equilibrium market wage W_1 determined where the market demand curve for labour intersects the market supply curve of labour. Once market forces, operating in the whole labour market, have established the ruling market wage, each worker in the labour market is a passive wage-taker at the market-determined wage rate.

Refer back also to Case study 5.2 in Chapter 5, which mentions the 'law of one price'. The law says that identical goods should sell for the same price in two separate markets, the more nearly perfect both markets are. Applied to the labour market, this means that if labour markets were perfectly competitive and in equilibrium, workers with the same skills and performing similar tasks would be paid the same wage rates.

Of course, in the real world this does not happen. Real-world markets are imperfectly competitive to a greater or lesser extent. And even if most of the conditions of perfect competition were met, different skills and productivities, together with changes in demand for different groups of workers, would mean that differences in wage rates would persist.

SECTION 6.3 SUMMARY

* In this section we have brought together the demand for, and supply of, labour so as to explain the determination of relative wage rates and levels of employment in perfectly competitive labour markets.
* To understand a perfectly competitive labour market, you need to appreciate the similarities of such a market to a perfectly competitive market for a good such as wheat, but also the differences between goods and labour markets.
* The supply curve of labour facing an individual firm in a perfectly competitive labour market is the horizontal line depicting a perfect elasticity of supply, determined by the interaction of supply and demand in the market as a whole.
* For a firm in a perfectly competitive labour market, this horizontal line is also the average cost of labour (AC_L) and the marginal cost of labour (MC_L).
* To maximise profit when selling the output produced by labour, each firm would have to demand labour up to the point at which the addition to sales revenue resulting from employment of an extra worker equalled the addition to production costs resulting from the employment of an extra worker.

KEY TERMS

monopsony there is only one buyer in a market.

monopsony power the market power exercised in a market by the buyer of a good or the services of a factor of production such as labour, even though the firm is not a pure monopsonist.

TEST YOURSELF 6.9
Explain the difference between monopsony and monopoly.

TEST YOURSELF 6.10
Why are many UK labour markets better described as monopsonistic rather than as pure monopsonies?

6.4 Imperfectly competitive labour markets

Just as is the case with markets for goods, all real-world labour markets are imperfectly competitive to a lesser or greater degree. At one extreme, some labour markets approximate to perfect competition, but at the opposite extreme are monopsonistic labour markets.

Monopsony means a single buyer, just as monopoly means a single seller. In a pure monopsonistic labour market, workers cannot choose between alternative employers, since there is only one firm or employer available to hire their services. However, pure monopsonistic labour markets are extremely rare. The armed services are perhaps the nearest example of a pure monopsony, though even here we can nit-pick by arguing that soldiers can sell their labour services to foreign-based militias or to the police or security guard firms. Nevertheless, many large firms exercise a high degree of **monopsony power** in the labour market in which they hire their workers.

Monopsony power refers to a situation in which there are dominant employers but not pure monopsony. In the provision of health care, the National Health Service has considerable monopsony power, though the existence of private hospitals shows that the NHS is not a pure monopsony.

CASE STUDY 6.3

Recession, recovery and the UK jobs market

When the UK economy entered recession in 2008, many UK companies, including the plant manufacturers JCB, began to sack workers. Those workers who still had jobs feared they would soon be made redundant. To try to prevent further lay-offs, union members at JCB offered to work for lower wages. However, wage reductions did not work. In fact, JCB sacked even more workers as orders for bulldozers and other construction plant dried up. As a manufacturer of capital goods, JCB was especially vulnerable to changes in demand for the machinery it produces.

However, by 2018, JCB was creating jobs again as the UK economy recovered from recession. In June 2018 the company announced an investment of more than £50 million in a new British plant which it hopes will create hundreds of jobs. Many of the workers JCB hires are agency workers and lack the guarantee of continuous employment. However, JCB says that most of its full-time employees have entered through some period of temporary work and proved their worth. With an improving economy, the company has taken them on. And as a result of investing in its training academy, JCB has recently created 100 jobs for teenage apprentices. But JCB is creating far more jobs by investing in factories in Brazil and India. A company spokesman has said, 'Growth for JCB anywhere is good for JCB and a significant number of the machines are still made here in the UK and shipped around the world.'

Follow-up questions

1 What is a capital good, and why are companies such as JCB especially vulnerable to changes in demand?
2 With the help of a demand curve for labour, explain why JCB laid off workers in 2008.
3 Explain why companies such as JCB, whose clients are building companies, are especially likely to lay off workers in a recession.
4 In what way does the information in the case study illustrate the globalisation process?

The determination of relative wage rates and levels of employment in a monopsony labour market

Various factors such as monopsony power, trade unions and imperfect information contribute to imperfections in a labour market. We shall examine the role of trade unions in the next section of this chapter. In this section we look at monopsony and monopsony power.

Although in some ways a monopsonistic labour market resembles a monopolistic goods market, there are also significant differences. In much the same way that the market demand curve facing a monopoly supplier of a good is the monopolist's average revenue curve, so in a monopsonistic labour market, the market supply curve of labour is the firm's average cost of labour curve. The AC_L curve shows the different wage rates that the monopsony must pay to attract labour forces of different sizes. For example, Figure 6.8 shows a monopsonistic employer hiring five workers at an hourly wage rate or AC_L of £10. As the diagram shows, the hourly wage per week must rise to £11 to attract a sixth worker into the firm's labour force.

Figure 6.8 In a monopsony labour market, the MC_L curve lies *above* the AC_L or supply curve

SYNOPTIC LINK
If you refer back to Chapter 4, page 105, you will see that for a similar reason, in the goods market, a monopolist's *MR* curve is *below* its *AR* curve.

TEST YOURSELF 6.11
What is monopsony power?

The supply or AC_L curve facing the monopsony shows the wage that has to be paid to *all* workers at each size of the labour force, to persuade the workers to supply their services. However, in a monopsony labour market, the AC_L curve is *not* the marginal cost of labour curve (MC_L). To attract an extra worker, the monopsony must raise the hourly wage rate and pay the higher wage to all the workers. In this situation, the marginal cost of labour incurred by employing an extra worker is the change in total amount by which the wage bill rises, not just the wage rate paid to the additional worker hired. The MC_L curve of labour illustrated in Figure 6.8 is positioned *above* the AC_L (or supply) curve.

In Figure 6.8, the MC_L incurred per hour by employing the sixth worker is £16, made up of the £11 wage rate paid to the sixth worker, plus the £1 extra that now has to be paid to each of the five workers already employed before the sixth worker joined the labour force.

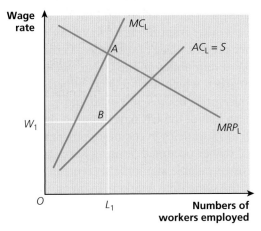

Figure 6.9 The determination of the wage rate and the level of employment in a monopsony labour market

Figure 6.9 shows how the equilibrium wage and the equilibrium level of employment are determined in a monopsonistic labour market. As in the case of a perfectly competitive employer in the labour market, the monopsonist's level of employment is determined by the point where $MRP_L = MC_L$. This occurs at point A in Figure 6.9, with L_1 workers being hired.

However, the wage rate is determined at point B on the supply curve (and AC_L curve), which lies below point A. The monopsony wage rate (W_1 in Figure 6.9) is therefore less than the marginal revenue product of labour. At point B, L_1 workers are willing to work for an hourly wage rate of W_1. Although the monopsony could pay a wage rate higher than W_1, it has no need to do so. Why pay more, when W_1 attracts all the workers the monopsony wants to hire? Indeed, if the monopsony were to pay a wage higher than W_1, it would inevitably incur unnecessary production costs and fail to maximise profits when selling its output in the goods market. Profit maximisation requires that L_1 workers are employed and a wage of W_1 is paid.

Reasons for wage differences in imperfectly competitive labour markets

TEST YOURSELF 6.12
Explain how the wage rate would be determined in an imperfectly competitive labour market.

In imperfectly competitive labour markets, wage differences in different labour markets are often substantial. Five reasons for this are:

- **Disequilibrium trading.** Economies are subject to constant change, such as the development of new goods and services and improved methods of production or technical progress. Patterns of demand also change. Because market conditions are always changing, labour markets — like other markets — are usually in disequilibrium rather than in equilibrium. Although market forces tend to equalise wages in competitive labour markets, at any point in time disparities exist, reflecting the disequilibrium conditions existent at the time.
- **Imperfect market information.** As the name implies, imperfectly competitive labour markets are characterised by imperfect market information. Workers sometimes lack accurate information on rates of pay, not only in other labour markets, but also within the industry in which they are selling their labour. Likewise, employers lack information about

TEST YOURSELF 6.13
State two examples of occupational immobility of labour and two examples of geographical immobility of labour.

wage rates in other labour markets and also, on occasion, within their own industries. Imperfect market information also contributes to the immobility of labour, which is described below.

- **Occupational immobility of labour.** This occurs when workers are prevented, by either natural or artificial barriers, from moving between different types of job. Workers are obviously not homogeneous or uniform, so differences in natural ability may prevent or restrict movement between jobs. Artificial or 'man-made' barriers also prevent workers from moving between labour markets. These barriers include membership qualifications imposed by professional bodies such as accountancy associations, and trade union restrictive practices such as closed shops, which restrict employment to union members. Non-members may find it difficult or impossible to join the trade union, though such practices are now illegal in the UK.

- **Geographical immobility of labour.** This occurs when factors, such as ignorance of job opportunities, family and cultural ties, and the financial costs of moving or travel, prevent a worker from filling a job vacancy located at a distance from his or her present place of residence. Perhaps the most significant cause of geographical immobility in the UK in recent years has been the state of the housing market, which itself reflects imperfections in other factor markets. During house price booms, low-paid and unemployed workers in the northern half of the UK have found it difficult or impossible to move south to fill job vacancies in the more prosperous southeast of England. The prices of owner-occupied housing have soared and there has been very little housing available at affordable rents in either the private or the public sector. At the same time, workers living in their own houses in the southeast may be reluctant to apply for jobs elsewhere in the country, for fear that they will never be able to afford to move back to southern England.

- **Discrimination.** Various forms of racial, religious, age and gender discrimination affect both the demand for and the supply of labour. On the demand side, employers may be unwilling to employ certain types of labour, while on the supply side, workers may refuse to work alongside other workers they perceive to be different.

SYNOPTIC LINK
Discrimination in a labour market is explained in more detail in section 6.7.

SECTION 6.4 SUMMARY
- Real-world markets are imperfectly competitive to a greater or lesser extent.
- A monopsony is the only buyer of labour in an imperfectly competitive labour market.
- In monopsony, the wage rate and the level of employment are likely to be lower than in a perfectly competitive labour market.
- Wage differences in different labour markets can be caused by disequilibrium trading, imperfect market information, the occupational immobility of labour, the geographical immobility of labour, and discrimination in the labour market.

6.5 The influence of trade unions in determining wages and levels of employment

A **trade union** is an association of workers formed to protect and promote the interests of its members. A major function of a union is to bargain with employers to improve wages and other conditions of work. In the analysis which follows, we shall regard a trade union as a monopoly supplier of labour, which is able to keep non-members out of the labour market and also to prevent its members from supplying labour at below the union wage rate. Of course, in real life a union may not necessarily have the objectives specified above, and even if it does, it may not be able to achieve them.

In labour markets where trade unions are strong and possess significant bargaining power, wage rates are usually determined through a process known as **collective bargaining**. This term refers to a situation in which unions bargain with employers, with the unions negotiating collectively on behalf of their members. Sometimes bargaining takes place with a single employer, while on other occasions it may be with a number of employers in the labour market. The market wage rate is determined through the bargaining process, with the employers then deciding how many workers to employ at this wage rate.

However, many UK employers are now reluctant to recognise and bargain with the unions to which their employees belong. A number of factors are responsible for the shift in the balance of power in the labour market away from trade unions and toward employers. Two of the factors are a series of Employment Acts which have restricted the legal rights of trade unions, and the impact of globalisation and international competition upon British labour markets. UK trade unions remain powerful only in industries which are protected from international competition, such as London Transport, the rail industry and other areas of public sector employment.

The decline of collective bargaining in the UK means that more and more rates of pay, including those of teachers, are now 'employer determined' on a 'take-it-or-leave-it' basis.

TEST YOURSELF 6.14
Describe one other condition of work that a trade union might bargain to improve besides those mentioned above.

The effect of introducing a trade union into a previously perfectly competitive labour market

Figure 6.10 shows the possible effects which may result from workers organising a trade union in a labour market that had previously been perfectly competitive. A first point to make is that the market would immediately become imperfectly competitive! It can be seen that, without a trade union, the competitive wage rate is W_1. After the workers join the union, through collective bargaining it negotiates a rise in the minimum wage rate acceptable to union members to W_2. Without the union, the market supply of labour curve is the upward-sloping line labelled $S = AC_L$. With the union, the market

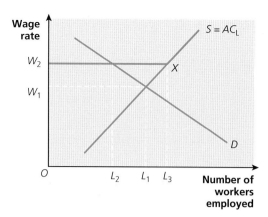

Figure 6.10 The effect of introducing a trade union into a previously competitive labour market

SYNOPTIC LINK

In Chapter 11, the type of unemployment shown in Figure 6.10 is called classical, or real-wage, unemployment.

STUDY TIP

The effects shown in Figure 6.10 can also be used to explain the effect of a national minimum wage imposed above the wage rate that would be determined by market forces.

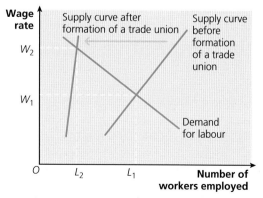

Figure 6.11 A trade union shifting the market supply curve of labour

supply of labour curve is the kinked line W_2XS. For all sizes of labour force to the left of, or below, L_3, the supply curve of labour is horizontal or perfectly elastic, lying along the wage W_2 set by the trade union. If employers wish to hire a labour force larger than L_3 (and to the right of point X), a wage higher than W_2 has to be offered. Beyond L_3, the supply curve of labour slopes upward because higher wage rates are needed to attract more workers.

At the wage level set by the union, employers only wish to hire L_2 workers. However, L_3 workers are willing to work at this wage rate. This means there is excess supply of labour and unemployment in the labour market. More workers wish to work than there are jobs available. The resulting unemployment is shown by the distance $L_3 - L_2$. However, the fall in employment compared to the competitive equilibrium is $L_1 - L_2$.

The effect described above is sometimes used to justify the argument that any attempt by a union to raise wages must inevitably be at the expense of jobs, and that if unions are really interested in reducing unemployment, they should accept wage cuts. However, many economists — especially those of a Keynesian and left-of-centre persuasion — dispute this conclusion. They argue, first, that it is unrealistic to assume that conditions of demand for labour are unchanged. By agreeing to accept technical progress, by working with new capital equipment and new methods of organising work and by improving the skills of their members, a union can ensure (with the cooperation of management) that the *MRP* curve of labour shifts to the right. In these circumstances, increased productivity creates scope for both increased wages and increased employment. Higher wages may encourage firms to adopt improvements in productivity to pay for the higher wages but, on the other hand, some unions may resist the changes in working practices that lead to increased productivity.

Second, both wages and employment can rise when a union negotiates for higher wages in firms producing in an expanding goods market. In these conditions, increased demand for output creates increased demand for labour to produce the output. Indeed, rising real wages throughout the economy are likely to increase the aggregate demand for the output of all firms producing consumer goods because wages are the most important source of consumption expenditure in the economy.

So far, we have assumed that trade unions try to increase pay by preventing union members supplying labour at wage rates below the rate set by the union. Figure 6.11 illustrates a second way in which much the same result can be achieved. In this case, the trade union establishes a *closed shop*, which keeps non-union workers out of the labour market. The union-controlled entry barrier shifts the supply curve of labour to the left, and increases the inelasticity of the curve. A similar effect can be achieved by unions and professional associations that insist on long periods of training before the worker is formally qualified, during which time only very low wages are paid. Employment falls from L_1 to L_2, and the wage rate rises to W_2. The advantage to the union, and its members who are employed, is that there is no pool of unemployed workers who would be willing to work for lower wages — that is, there is not an excess supply of labour.

The effect of introducing a trade union into a monopsony labour market

The assertion that unions raise wages at the expense of jobs is heavily dependent on the assumption that, before the union was formed, the labour market was perfectly competitive (it is worth remembering that *no* real-world labour market can meet all the conditions of perfect competition). In the case of a monopsonistic labour market, it is possible for a union to raise *both* the wage rate and employment, even without the *MRP* curve shifting rightward. This is illustrated in Figure 6.12. If the monopsonistic labour market is non-unionised, the equilibrium wage rate is W_1 and the level of employment is L_1.

The introduction of a trade union into a monopsonistic labour market has the same effect on the labour supply curve as would be the case if the labour market were to be perfectly competitive. In Figure 6.12, when the union sets the wage rate at W_2, the kinked line W_2XS becomes the labour supply curve (and also the AC_L curve). But in monopsony, W_2XS is *not* the marginal cost of labour curve. The MC_L curve is the double-kinked line W_2XZV. The double kink is explained in the following way.

Provided the monopsony employs a labour force smaller than or equal to L_2, the MC_L of employing an extra worker equals both the AC_L and the union-determined wage of W_2. But beyond L_2 and point X, the monopsony must offer a higher wage in order to persuade the members of an enlarged labour force to supply their labour. In this situation, with all the workers now being paid the higher wage rate, the marginal cost of labour increases significantly and there is a discontinuity, X to Z, in the MC_L curve; to the right of L_2 the MC_L curve lies above the AC_L curve. The upward-sloping line ZV drawn in Figure 6.12 shows the MC_L of increasing employment above the level L_2.

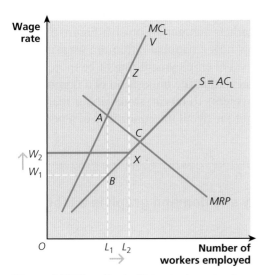

Figure 6.12 The effect of introducing a trade union into a monopsony labour market

This means there is a discontinuity, shown by the vertical distance from point X to point Z, between the horizontal section of the MC_L curve (for levels of employment at or below L_2 and point X) and the upward-sloping section of the curve (ZV) to the right of point X. In the absence of a union, the level of employment is L_1, determined at point A (with point B determining the wage rate W_1). But when the union sets the wage rate at W_2, employment rises to L_2, which is the level of employment at which the *MRP* curve intersects the gap or discontinuity in the MC_L curve at point C, between X and Z. The union has managed to increase both the wage rate and the level of employment.

SECTION 6.5 SUMMARY

- A trade union is an association of workers formed to protect and promote the interests of its members.
- A major function of a union is to bargain with employers to improve wages and other conditions of work.
- We have assumed that a trade union is a monopoly supplier of labour, which is able to keep non-members out of the labour market and also to prevent its members from supplying labour at below the union wage rate.
- Free-market economists argue that if a union raises the wage rate above the perfectly competitive wage rate, unemployment increases.
- In monopsony, a trade union may be able to increase both the wage rate and the level of employment toward the perfectly competitive levels.
- A national minimum wage can have the same effect.

The effects of a national minimum wage upon labour markets

The explanation in the previous section, of how a trade union can increase both the wage rate and the level of employment, can also be used to analyse the effect of a **national minimum wage** (NMW) set by the government. As we have already noted, if we assume a perfectly competitive labour market, Figure 6.10 can be adapted to show how a national minimum wage set above the market-clearing wage rate leads to a loss of jobs and unemployment. The same may be true if labour markets are highly competitive without being perfectly competitive. But if labour markets are monopsonistic, Figure 6.12, which likewise can be adapted to show how a national minimum wage can increase both the wage rate and the level of employment, might be more appropriate. However, this does not mean that the imposition of a minimum wage will *never* lead to a fall in employment. To repeat, some labour markets are very competitive even if they do not satisfy all the conditions of a perfectly competitive labour market.

> **KEY TERM**
>
> **national minimum wage** a minimum wage or wage rate that must by law be paid to employees, though in many labour markets the wage rate paid by employers is above the national minimum wage.

QUANTITATIVE SKILLS 6.4

Worked example: plotting and interpreting data on a supply and demand graph in a labour market

The figures in Table 6.2 relate to the demand for, and supply of, gardeners at different hourly wage rates. The demand and supply schedules are in thousands of workers.

Table 6.2 The labour market for gardeners

Wage rate (£ per hour)	Supply$_1$	Demand$_1$	Supply$_2$
5	40	160	100
7	60	150	110
9	80	140	120
11	100	130	130
13	120	120	140
15	140	110	150
17	160	100	160

(a) **Calculate the market wage rate and employment level for gardeners when the demand schedule is Demand$_1$ and the supply schedule is Supply$_1$.**

The only hourly wage rate at which demand equals supply is £13.00. This is the equilibrium market wage rate, with the equilibrium level of employment being 120,000.

(b) **The supply schedule now becomes Supply$_2$, but the demand schedule does not change. What happens to the equilibrium wage rate and level of employment?**

The only hourly wage rate at which demand equals supply is £11.00. This is the equilibrium market wage rate, with the equilibrium level of employment being 130,000.

(c) **Suppose the government now sets a national minimum wage at £13 per hour. How much unemployment would this create among gardeners?**

The Given that the supply schedule is still Supply$_2$, the national minimum wage rate of £13.00 has been set above the equilibrium market wage, which leads to 20,000 unemployment.

The advantages and disadvantages of a national minimum wage

SYNOPTIC LINK
See the coverage of government intervention in markets in Chapter 11.

A national minimum wage only really affects labour markets where, before its introduction, the market-determined wage rate is below the NMW rate. This, of course, includes markets where wages are depressed through monopsony power. When the national minimum wage rate is set below wage rates determined by free-market forces, then, just like any other minimum price law, it has no effect on the market.

Supporters of a national minimum wage argue that a 'wage floor' can be justified on the grounds that it reduces exploitation by employers of low-paid workers. As we have mentioned, many real-world labour markets, particularly those for low-paid unskilled workers, resemble the monopsony labour market shown earlier in Figure 6.9. In Figure 6.13 we have redrawn Figure 6.9, but with wage rate W_2 added to the diagram. This is the wage rate, determined at point C in the diagram, where the market demand for labour, depicted by the MRP curve, would equal the market supply of labour in a perfectly competitive labour market.

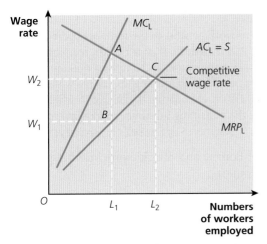

Figure 6.13 Comparing market wage rates in perfect competition and monopsony

Figure 6.13 illustrates the fact that in an imperfectly competitive labour market, the employer or employers use their market power to drive down the wage rate below the competitive rate of W_2 to the lower rate of W_1. Trade unions might, of course, create a situation in which the monopsony power of the buyers of labour (the employers) is matched by the monopoly power of the sellers of labour (the unions). This might restore the wage rate to W_2. But if this does not happen, a national minimum wage is deemed necessary, according to its supporters, to eliminate or reduce labour market exploitation of low-paid workers.

Exploitation of low-paid workers also increases poverty. Supporters of the national minimum wage believe that an NMW, set at a 'fair' level, should be a vital part of government policy which aims to prevent 'rogue' employers driving wage rates down to 'poverty rates'. (See Chapter 7 and the extension material on page 187.) By redistributing income from employers toward low-wage workers, a national minimum wage reduces income inequality as well as poverty.

Most of the evidence collected since national minimum wages were first introduced suggests that 'wage floors' either slightly increase or slightly decrease employment. Either way they do not result in mass unemployment. Recent studies generally conclude that, although there probably are unemployment effects, such effects are extremely slight. By raising the incomes of low-paid workers with only a slight impact on employment, according to this view, the benefits of national minimum wages far outweigh the costs.

SYNOPTIC LINK
A national minimum wage also boosts aggregate demand (see Chapter 10) because low-paid workers spend almost all of their incomes on consumer goods and services, rather than saving their income as richer people often do.

Economists who believe in the virtues of a free-market economy, subject to the minimum possible level of government intervention, argue that the disadvantages of a national minimum wage exceed any possible advantages. In a briefing paper, 'The minimum wage: silver bullet or poisoned chalice?', published in 2014 by the Institute of Economic Affairs (IEA), a pro-free-market 'think tank', Ryan Bourne and J. R. Shackleton argued that:

There is evidence of reduced working hours in response to NMW increases. International research suggests many of the negative effects operate after a long time period through reducing new job creation.

Employment impacts of increases in the minimum wage are likely to disproportionately affect the young, the unskilled, the long-term unemployed and those in lower productivity regions. There is evidence that minimum wages lead firms to replace lower-skilled and less experienced younger workers with older workers. The 18–24 year old unemployment rate has risen from 11.5% in April 1999 (when the NMW was introduced) to 17.9% today. And of those unemployed within this age group, the proportion out of work for more than 12 months has risen from 14.4% in 1999 to 31.8% in 2013.

Claims employers are 'subsidised' by in-work benefits in the form of tax credits have some truth, but are exaggerated. Nearly a third of all tax credit recipient households do not have an adult in paid employment and a further million households work fewer than 30 hours per week. Reforming tax credits would be a better means (than raising the NMW) of eliminating the degree to which tax credits subsidise the employers of the remaining full-time workers in receipt of credits.

(It is well worth reading the whole of Bourne and Shackleton's briefing paper, which you can access on the IEA website.)

CASE STUDY 6.4

Should we have a national minimum wage?

A few years before the national minimum wage was introduced in the UK in April 1999 by a Labour government, in 1994 the National Bureau of Economic Research in the USA published a research article written by David Card and Alan B. Krueger. The article was titled 'Minimum wages and employment: a case study of the fast food industry in New Jersey and Pennsylvania'.

Card and Krueger summarised their research as follows:

On April 1, 1992 New Jersey's minimum wage increased from $4.25 to $5.05 per hour. To evaluate the impact of the law we surveyed 410 fast food restaurants in New Jersey and Pennsylvania before and after the rise in the minimum wage. Comparisons of the changes in wages, employment, and prices at stores in New Jersey relative to stores in Pennsylvania (where the minimum wage remained fixed at $4.25 per hour) yield simple estimates of the effect of the higher minimum wage.

Our findings challenge the prediction that a rise in the minimum wage reduces employment. Relative to stores in Pennsylvania, fast food restaurants in New Jersey increased employment by 13 percent. We also compare employment growth at stores in New Jersey that were initially paying high wages (and were unaffected by the new law) to employment changes at lower-wage stores. Stores that were unaffected by the minimum wage had the same employment growth as stores in Pennsylvania, while stores that had to increase their wages increased their employment.

Card and Krueger's conclusions were seized on by British economists and politicians who supported the introduction of the national minimum wage. At the time, the British Conservative Party, then in opposition, opposed its introduction. However, by 2010 Conservative prime minister David Cameron, who initially opposed the national minimum wage, publicly stated that it 'turned out much better than many people expected'. This cautious acceptance of the minimum wage among policy-makers is now reflected throughout the developed world, where few countries remain without a statutory wage floor.

However, many economists continue to oppose a national minimum wage, arguing that it distorts free markets and creates unemployment. In 2011 Karthik Reddy, in an article commissioned by the IEA, concluded that:

> Far from having positive effects for the working poor, the implementation of the minimum wage in the UK is likely to have had a negative effect on employment. The minimum wage has been routinely raised at a rate greater than inflation, resulting in a tremendous increase in the real value of the minimum wage. This rise is particularly problematic for workers during times of recession. The present government could alleviate the difficulties of the minimum wage by resisting the urge to raise it further and gradually allow inflation to reduce its real value. A slow death of the wage floor would stimulate employment and permit Britain to regain a competitive edge.

Follow-up questions

1 Using appropriate diagrams, analyse and compare the effect of a national minimum wage rate in competitive and monopsonistic labour markets.
2 Are Card and Krueger's conclusions compatible with Figure 6.12? Justify your answer.
3 Distinguish between the national minimum wage (NMW) and the national living wage (NLW).
4 At what rates is the national minimum wage set at the time you read this case study?

EXTENSION MATERIAL

The national living wage replaces the national minimum wage

Students have often confused the official *national minimum wage* (NMW) with the concept of a *living wage*. The NMW was introduced by a Labour government in 1999, and then continued by the Coalition government elected in 2010. The Conservative government which replaced the Coalition government in 2015 then bowed to popular pressure and replaced the national minimum wage with a national living wage (NLW) in 2016, but only for workers aged 25 and older.

Both the NMW and latterly the NLW have been increased in most years by an amount more or less in line with the inflation rate measured by the consumer prices index (CPI). The government decides their levels after taking advice from the Low Pay Commission.

When it was first introduced, the NMW rate was £3.60 per hour (£3.00 for 18- to 21-year-olds). In July 2015, the adult NMW rate was £6.50 per hour. The most recent increase in the adult NMW for workers aged 21 to 24 took place in April 2018, with the rate rising to £7.38 per hour those workers. At the same time the NLW was increased to £7.83 per hour. At the time of its introduction, the NLW was set at £7.20 per hour, for both full-time and part-time workers. The various levels for both the NLW and the NMW in 2018 were as shown in Table 6.3.

Table 6.3 National living wage and national minimum wage rates, April 2018

Age group	Hourly rate (£)
National living wage (25+)	7.83
National minimum wage (21–24)	7.38
National minimum wage (18–20)	5.90
National minimum wage (16–17)	4.20

Source: HM Treasury

Table 6.4 shows the actual level of the NMW and the NLW for workers aged 25 and over between 2017 and 2018 and forecasts for both between 2019 and 2022. It would be a good idea for you to check the current levels of both the NMW and the NLW at the time when you read this extension material.

Table 6.4 National minimum wage and national living age rates for workers aged 25 and over, 2017–22 (projected)

	Hourly rate (£)					
	2017	2018	2019	2020	2021	2022
National minimum wage	7.05	7.38	7.57	7.76	7.97	8.21
National living wage	7.50	7.83	8.20	8.57	8.82	9.09

Source: OBR

QUANTITATIVE SKILLS 6.5

Worked example: nominal and real values

Between 2010 and September 2017 most workers employed in the UK public sector saw their nominal wage rates increase by 1% per year. This pay cap was largely abolished in July 2018, though the government said that any pay increases above 1% a year would have to be self-financing. The rate of inflation, measured by changes in the consumer prices index (CPI) in the 12 months before July in each year, was 4.4% in 2011, 2.6% in 2012, 2.8% in 2013, 1.6% in 2014, 0.1% in 2015, 0.6% in 2016, 2.6% in 2017 and 2.3% in 2018.

How did real wages paid to public-sector workers experiencing a 1% annual pay cap change between July 2011 and July 2018? Briefly comment on your answers.

The change in the real wage rate in each year equals the change in the nominal wage rate minus the rate of inflation. This means that, according to the data, the change in the real wage rate was –3.4% in 2011, –1.6% in 2012, –1.8% in 2013, –0.6% in 2014, +0.9% in 2015, +0.4% in 2016, –1.6% in 2017 and –1.3% in 2018.

Because the CPI inflation rate was higher than the 1% pay cap in all but two of the years, according to the data, public-sector real wages fell in most of these years; 2015 and 2016 were the only years in which public-sector real wages increased slightly.

6.7 Discrimination in the labour market

The nature of wage discrimination

KEY TERM

wage discrimination paying different workers different wage rates for doing the same job.

TEST YOURSELF 6.15

Distinguish between the national minimum wage (NMW) and the national living wage (NLW).

STUDY TIP

You should understand the similarity between *wage discrimination* in the labour market where a firm hires its labour and *price discrimination* in the goods market where the firm sells its output.

In imperfectly competitive labour markets, employers often possess sufficient market power to reduce the total wage bill through undertaking **wage discrimination**, which involves paying different workers different wages for doing the same job. Figure 6.14 illustrates the effect of wage discrimination introduced into a previously competitive labour market. We shall assume that in the absence of wage discrimination, all workers are paid the same wage, W_1, determined by supply and demand. Employers' total wage costs are shown by the rectangle OW_1AL_1.

But if, instead of paying W_1 to all workers, employers pay each worker the minimum he or she is prepared to work for, the total wage bill falls to equal the shaded area $OBAL_1$. Employers thus gain at the expense of workers, which is one reason why firms pay, and trade unions resist, discriminatory wages whenever possible.

Wage discrimination can also occur when a group of workers is systematically paid a wage that is below their *MRP*. This occurs when employers successfully exploit their monopsony power in the labour market, as illustrated in Figures 6.12 and 6.13.

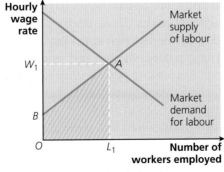

Figure 6.14 Wage discrimination

189

Bringing together wage discrimination and price discrimination

In the case of perfect price discrimination (often called first-degree price discrimination), a firm charges different prices to different customers for the same good, with the same marginal cost of production, so that each customer pays the maximum price he or she is prepared to pay. The entire consumer surplus that customers would otherwise enjoy is transferred to the firm, enlarging the firm's profit.

With perfect wage discrimination, the firm pays each worker the minimum wage the worker is prepared to accept, without transferring their employment elsewhere. The part of the wage that workers would otherwise get is transferred to the firm, once again boosting profit.

In real life, wage discrimination is most likely to occur in imperfectly competitive labour markets. From an imperfectly competitive firm's point of view, the best possible outcome is simultaneous price discrimination in the goods market where it sells its output and wage discrimination in the labour markets where it hires its workers. Profit is boosted from two directions at once.

Can you think of reasons why such simultaneous exploitation seldom takes place?

A condition necessary for wage discrimination

Successful wage discrimination, through which employers pay different wage rates to different groups of workers, requires employers to be able to identify and separate different groups of workers supplying the same type of labour. This is possible when workers differ in their knowledge of the labour market and in their ability to shop around among employers.

Types of wage discrimination

So far we have defined wage discrimination in terms of employers paying workers the minimum they are prepared to work for, without focusing on issues of gender, ethnicity and other aspects of discrimination. There are many kinds of discrimination. We shall look at gender discrimination as an example, but it is worth researching how other groups are discriminated against, too.

Gender discrimination

Along with race discrimination, gender discrimination is significant. In recent years, although women have accounted for an increasing share of total employment in the UK, women's pay often continues to be lower than men's pay, despite the fact that equal pay legislation has been in place since 1972. The pay gap between men and women is at risk of widening for the first time on record, a leading pay equality campaign group has warned. In November 2017, the Fawcett Society said that progress has stalled in closing the gender pay gap, which stood at 14.1% — the same as it was in 2015 and 2016. The pressure group stated that if the gap closes at the rate it has since 2012, it won't reach zero until a century later in 2117. The gap is higher in the private sector, at 17.1%, but it has fallen by 4.3 percentage points since 2011. In the public sector it has stayed flat at just above 14%. Fawcett research published earlier in 2017 found that the mean aggregate pay gap for Pakistani and Bangladeshi women was 26% and for black African women it was 24%.

Women are almost twice as likely (1.8 times more likely) to receive the lowest pay — with 221,000 women earning less than the statutory minimum wage, 100,000 more women than men.

A second survey, the 2017 Gender Salary Survey, undertaken by the Chartered Management Institute (CMI) found that the gender pay gap stood at 26.8%, with male managers on average out-earning female peers by £11,606 a year — £3,000 more than previously thought.

There are several reasons why women earn less than men:

- Women work predominantly in low-paid industries and occupations. Within many occupational groups, women are paid less than men. This is often because women are under-represented in the higher-paid posts within an occupation, though it is also the case that many women are paid less for doing the same job.
- Discrimination against women in labour markets may contribute to these circumstances. In addition, women are disproportionately highly represented in industries where the average size of firm and plant is small. These industries tend to pay lower wages and offer fewer promotion prospects than large firms and large industries. Such industries are also seldom unionised. Indeed, within all industries, women workers traditionally have been less unionised than men.
- This relates to another reason why women earn less than men: on average, their attachment to the labour force is weaker. Each year of work experience raises the pay of both men and women by an average 3%. Yet if women leave the labour force, usually to look after young children, their potential pay falls by 3% for each year involved. For example, consider a man and woman who enter employment with equal potential and after 8 years the woman leaves the workforce in order to raise a family. If she re-enters the labour force 8 years later, she will be 16 years, in pay terms, behind the man.
- The higher labour turnover of women also imposes costs on the employer — for example, the costs of training replacement workers. This may reduce the incentive for employers to train female workers. Similarly, some women may have less incentive to spend time and money on their own education and training if they expect the benefits that they will eventually receive to be less than the costs initially incurred.

Figures 6.15 and 6.16 illustrate how gender discrimination may affect labour markets. In Figure 6.15 the demand curve for female workers, shown as 'Demand with discrimination', lies to the left of their marginal revenue product curve. This results in Q_2 women being employed, with each being paid an hourly wage rate of W_2. Without gender discrimination, female employment would be Q_1, with the wage rate at W_1.

If gender discrimination takes place in one labour market, other labour markets in which no discrimination is taking place will also be affected. In these markets, as Figure 6.16 shows, the supply curve of female workers increases as a direct result of discrimination taking place in the first labour market. Female employment increases from Q_1 to Q_2, and the female wage rate falls from W_1 to W_2.

> **STUDY TIP**
> Be aware that there are a number of different types of discrimination operating in different labour markets.

> **TEST YOURSELF 6.16**
> Name three ways in which wage discrimination can occur in a labour market.

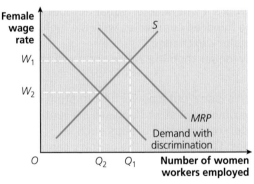

Figure 6.15 How gender discrimination may affect a labour market

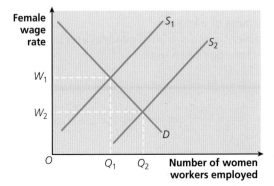

Figure 6.16 The effect of gender discrimination in one market upon female employment and wage rates in other labour markets

Glass ceiling for women replaced by reinforced concrete as progress stalls

The so-called glass ceiling that prevents women progressing in the workplace is more like 'reinforced concrete', Nicola Brewer, the chief executive of the Equality and Human Rights Commission (EHRC), has warned:

> We always speak of a glass ceiling. These figures reveal that in some cases it appears to be made of reinforced concrete. We need radical change to support those who are doing great work and help those who want to work better and release talent.

> Young women's aspiration are in danger of giving way to frustration. Many of them are now excelling at school and achieving great things in higher education. And they are keen to balance a family with a rewarding career. But workplaces forged in an era of stay-at-home mums and breadwinner dads are putting too many barriers in the way — resulting in an avoidable loss of talent at the top.

Labour MP Dawn Butler

There are fewer women MPs in Westminster. However, 208 female MPs were elected during the 2017 General Election — a record high and 32% of all MPs. This was up from 191 in the 2015 election and the highest proportion of any UK election to date. The UK government's target of 25% female membership by 2015 has now been reached.

The EHRC has likened women's progress to a snail's pace. According to the commission, a snail could crawl:

- nine times round the M25 in the 55 years it will take women to achieve equality in the senior judiciary
- from Land's End to John O'Groats and halfway back again in the 73 years it will take for equal numbers of women to become directors of FTSE 100 companies (FTSE 100 is the hundred companies with the highest market capitalisation whose share prices are quoted on the London stock exchange.)
- the entire length of the Great Wall of China in 212 years, only slightly longer than the 200 years it will take for women to be equally represented in Parliament

The commission's report argued that its findings are not just a 'women's issue' but a powerful symptom of a wider failure. The report asked in what other ways old-fashioned, inflexible ways of working are preventing the UK from tapping into talent — whether that of women or other under-represented groups such as disabled people, ethnic minorities and those with caring responsibilities. IT argued that the country cannot afford to go on marginalising or rejecting talented people who fail to fit into traditional work patterns.

Follow-up questions

1 What is meant by a 'glass ceiling'?
2 Do 'glass ceilings' adversely affect other groups in society, such as ethnic and religious minorities and old people, or does discrimination take different forms against these groups of people?
3 Research up-to-date statistics on women's representation in Parliament since the 2015 general election, and whether the government's 25% target for female company directors has been met.
4 Are there any occupations in which men experience a 'reverse glass ceiling?

CASE STUDY 6.6

A real-world example of wage discrimination: Ford car workers in 1968 and after

In 2010 the film *Made in Dagenham* was released, to be followed in 2014 by a West End musical with the same name. The two events drew to popular attention the important story of how UK law was changed by the action of women employed at Ford's Dagenham car plant in the East End of London in 1968 and in the years thereafter. Here is part of the real story of *Made in Dagenham*.

Back in 1968, the idea of a male breadwinner bringing in a 'family wage' legitimised lower pay for women. However, in that year, women sewing machinists in Ford's car plant in Dagenham took a stand for equal pay in a strike that stopped production for 3 weeks. The Ford strike, which captured the attention of Barbara Castle, the secretary of state for labour, led to the 1970 Equal Pay Act.

The demand of the Ford women had originally been to regrade their jobs from unskilled B grade to semi-skilled grade C. At the time, Ford graded its workers according to a skilled male rate, a semi-skilled male rate, an unskilled male rate and a women's rate. The women's rate of pay was only 87% of the unskilled male rate. However, a grade C rating was only achieved in 1984, following a second strike. Even then, given the fact that Ford's seamstresses were skilled rather than semi-skilled workers, they continued to be underpaid.

Follow-up questions

1 Find out whether wage differences between male and female workers are greater in the private sector than in the public sector.
2 What is the difference between skilled, semi-skilled and unskilled work? Give an example of each of these types of work.
3 Research details about the extent to which women workers remain underpaid in the UK today.
4 As part of the process of globalisation, car production has moved away from Europe and North America to countries such as China and South Korea. What effect worldwide do you think this might have had on female pay?

SECTION 6.7 SUMMARY

- In monopsony, a trade union may be able to increase both the wage rate and the level of employment toward the perfectly competitive levels. A national minimum wage can have the same effect.
- From 2016 onward, for adults the national living wage (NLW) replaced the national minimum wage (NMW).
- Perfect wage discrimination occurs when workers are paid the minimum wage rates they are prepared to accept.
- Gender discrimination means that women often earn less than men.

Questions

1 What is meant by 'role reversal' in the contexts of the goods market and the labour market in an economy?

2 Explain **three** factors that are significant in determining a firm's demand for labour.

3 Explain the shape of a market supply curve of labour.

4 What is a perfectly competitive labour market?

5 Distinguish between the elasticity of demand for labour and the elasticity of supply of labour.

6 How is the wage rate determined in a monopsony labour market?

7 Evaluate the view that when trade unions raise wages they inevitably reduce levels of employment.

8 Assess whether gender wage discrimination has been significantly reduced in the UK in recent years.

7

The distribution of income and wealth: poverty and inequality

The way the labour market operates, which was analysed in Chapter 6, contributes significantly to inequalities in the distribution of income. This chapter builds on this analysis, covering also wealth inequalities and causes of poverty, which result partially from income and wealth inequalities.

As the experience of many poor countries shows, unregulated market forces tend to produce highly unequal distributions of income and wealth, which many economists believe to be an important form of the market failures investigated in Chapter 8. However, a minority of economists disagree. Extreme pro-free-market economists sometimes argue that people who end up poor deserve to be poor. According to this view, the market does not fail; it simply creates incentives that cause people to generate income and wealth which end up benefiting most of the population. They also argue that attempts by governments to redistribute income and wealth from the rich to the poor usually end up, through the distortion of personal incentives, in government failure which harms national economic performance. Nevertheless, the mainstream economic view is that some form of intervention to moderate the extreme inequalities that would occur in a completely free-market economy is desirable. The arguments are about the *extent* to which governments should intervene to reduce inequality, and the methods of intervention.

For households at the bottom of the income distribution, severe income inequalities are an important cause of poverty (although, as mentioned above, pro-free market economists argue that the resulting incentives provide a route out of poverty). However, poverty has causes other than those associated with income inequality, and we shall examine these later in the chapter.

While this chapter explains inequalities and poverty in a microeconomic way, they reappear in Part 2 of the book, first in the discussion of macroeconomic problems and policies, and later in Chapter 13 when, for example, investigating the role of fiscal policy in both creating and trying to solve inequalities and poverty.

These are to understand:

- the nature and causes of inequalities in the distribution of income and wealth in the UK
- how government policies such as progressive taxation, transfers and the national minimum wage attempt to make the distribution of income more equal
- the meaning of poverty
- absolute poverty and relative poverty
- the main causes of poverty in the UK
- how progressive taxation relates to fiscal drag and to the poverty and unemployment traps

7.1 The distribution of income and wealth

The difference between income and wealth

The **distribution of income** measures how personal or household income is distributed among different income groups in society, such as between rich and poor. The term is also used to measure other forms of distribution — for example, between people living in different parts or regions of the economy, between different generations (such as the old and the young), and between men and women. Measures of income distribution can also be extended to the international distribution of income between countries — with countries at different stages of economic development having not only different total levels of income, but also different distributions between rich and poor — and also between different regions, age groups and gender.

Likewise, the **distribution of wealth** measures how personal or household wealth is distributed among different groups in society. Again, the distribution between rich and poor (and the intermediate groups which separate rich and poor) is most often considered, though economists sometimes focus on differences in regional, age group and gender distributions of wealth.

Together with other members of the general public, economics students often confuse the two words, **income** and **wealth**. The main difference between them is that income is a *flow* whereas wealth is a *stock*. Personal wealth is the stock, or historical accumulation, of everything you own that has value. For those households with at least one working member, wage and salary payments into the household's bank account are an inward flow of income, whereas, for an owner-occupying household, the house they live in, minus any outstanding mortgage debt, usually forms a large part of their household wealth.

To recap, your personal income is the *flow* of money you receive hourly, weekly, monthly or annually, some of which (the part that you *save*) can add to your personal wealth. As we shall see, this is one of the links between income and wealth. A second link operates in the opposite direction — the wealthier you are, the more investment income or unearned income you are likely to earn, which adds to your total income. Indeed, the rich benefit from a virtuous circle: wealth increases income, which allows the wealthy to save, and saving

KEY TERMS

distribution of income how income is divided between rich and poor, or between different groups in society, e.g. on a regional, age or gender basis.

distribution of wealth how wealth is divided between rich and poor, or between different groups in society, e.g. on a regional, age or gender basis.

income personal or household income is the flow of money a person or household receives in a particular time period.

wealth personal wealth is the stock of everything that a person or household owns at a particular point in time which has value.

195

adds to wealth, and so on. By contrast, many of the poor suffer a vicious circle: low income means the poor have to borrow, borrowing adds to personal debt, income is then spent on debt repayment, consumption falls, and any wealth the poor possess disappears.

TEST YOURSELF 7.1

Which of the following is a form of income rather than a form of wealth?

(a) A national savings certificate; (b) housing benefit received by poor families; (c) an inheritance; (d) interest paid to the owner of a government bond; (e) prize money won by a gambler; (f) a dividend paid to a shareholder.

QUANTITATIVE SKILLS 7.1

Worked example: quintiles and deciles

Figure 7.1 shows quintile data for the distribution of UK income, and Figure 7.2 shows decile data for the median household total wealth in the UK.

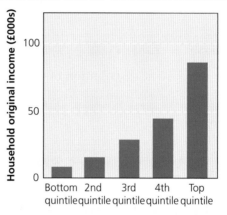

Source: ONS

Figure 7.1 Household original income and inequality in the UK, by quintile, 2017

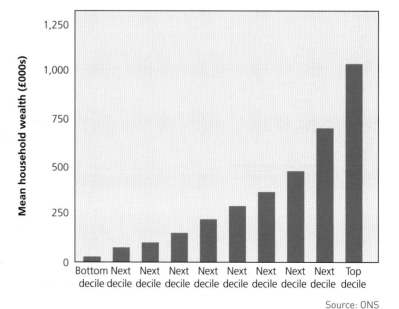

Source: ONS

Figure 7.2 Median household total wealth, by decile, 2016

Explain what is meant by a quintile. Describe two other quantiles that economists often use when they present data.

Note that the Annex to the A-level specification states that you must understand and use the terms 'mean' and 'median' and relevant quantiles.

As the second part of the question implies, a quintile is an example of a quantile. A quantile is a portion of a total amount divided into sub-groups. Total income in Figure 7.1 has been divided into five equal-sized groups, or fifths. These are quintiles. Other commonly used quantiles are quartiles (the total is divided into four groups, or quarters); deciles (the total is divided into ten groups, or tenths); vigintiles (the total is divided into 20 groups, or twentieths); and finally, percentiles (the total is divided into 100 groups, or hundredths).

SYNOPTIC LINK
Chapter 10 explains national income and national wealth in a macroeconomic context.

TEST YOURSELF 7.2
What is a decile?

EXTENSION MATERIAL

How the World Bank classifies countries according to income per capita

The World Bank classifies world economies into four groups: low income; lower-middle income; upper-middle income; and high-income. Income is measured using gross national income (GNI) per capita, in US dollars. In July 2017 the bank updated the thresholds for each classification as shown in Table 7.1.

Table 7.1 The World Bank's 2017 thresholds for classification of countries by income

Threshold	GNI/capita (current US$)
Low income	< 1,005
Lower-middle income	1,006–3,955
Upper-middle income	3,956–12,235
High income	> 12,235

The UK is, of course, a high-income country with GNI per capita (according to the World Bank) of $40,530 in 2016. Turkey is an upper-middle-income country (GNI per capita $10,930 in 2016); Bolivia is a lower-middle-income country (GNI per capita of $3,130 in 2016); while in sub-Saharan Africa the Democratic Republic of Congo is a low-income country (GNI per capita of $450 in 2016).

SYNOPTIC LINK
Chapter 15 provides further details of income groups in the context of the United Nations Human Development Index.

197

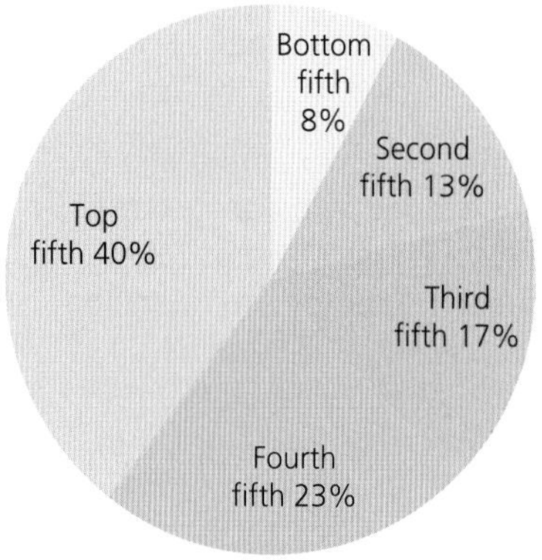

Source: The Equality Trust

Figure 7.3 How income was shared in the UK in 2018 (note the figures do not add up to 100% due to rounding)

Factors which influence the distribution of income and wealth

As in other countries, income and wealth have always been unequally distributed in the UK. Even when economic growth creates full employment, the incomes of the rich tend to increase faster than those of the poor. For this reason, fast economic growth may actually widen income differences, though those at the bottom of the pile can still end up *absolutely* better off.

Factors influencing the distribution of income

Figure 7.3 shows that in 2018 the top fifth of UK households received 40% of total household income, whereas the bottom fifth received only 8%. The data relate to income after taxes have been deducted and welfare benefits received. A large number of factors influence the distribution of income, as described below.

Factors of production

An important factor is the distribution of national income between the different factors of production: land, labour, capital and entrepreneurs. The owners of large land holdings, such as country estates or large parts of the West End of London, receive large incomes in the form of rent. This puts large landowners in the top income quintiles shown in Figure 7.1. The share of national income of landlords and owners of capital has grown, whereas labour's share has fallen. After being largely stable in many countries for decades, the share of national income paid to workers has been falling since the 1980s. Chapter 3 of the April 2017 edition of the *World Economic Outlook* published by the International Monetary Fund (IMF) finds that this trend is driven by rapid progress in technology and global integration.

Across the world, labour's share of worldwide incomes was 62% in the early 2000s, down from over 66% in the early 1990s. One reason for this is that wages have not been rising as fast as productivity and hence labour's share of national income has fallen. Many of the owners of capital, including entrepreneurs, receive their income in the form of dividend payments on the shares they own. Profits and entrepreneurial incomes have risen at the expense of wages and salaries, although the salaries received by top business executives have also grown much faster than wages.

The distinction between earned and unearned income

Earned income includes wages, salaries, other forms of employee compensation, and self-employment income. Unearned income is income derived from sources other than employment, including interest and investment income (such as dividend income paid to shareholders). The various determinants of wages discussed in Chapter 6 can be used to explain differences in earned incomes. By contrast, differences in unearned income depend primarily on inequalities in the distribution of wealth.

Wage and salary differentials

Within the labour market, the difference between the wages and salaries of those at the top and those at the bottom have widened. To an extent this can be explained by standard supply and demand theory. Figure 7.4(a) shows a high hourly wage rate in the market for airline pilots, while Figure 7.4(b)

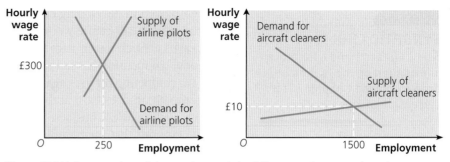

Figure 7.4 Using supply and demand to explain differences in rates of pay in different jobs

shows a much lower wage rate in the market for aircraft cleaners. Two of the main factors contributing to this difference in hourly wage rates are the differences in labour productivity, which determine the relative positions of the demand curves for pilots and for cleaners, and the different slopes and positions of the supply curves.

The labour productivity of an airline pilot is significantly higher than that of an aircraft cleaner. The demand for pilots is less wage elastic than the demand for cleaners. Similarly, because of factors such as long training periods, the supply of airline pilots is lower and more inelastic with respect to changes in their salaries. By contrast, the supply of airline cleaners is higher at any given wage and more wage-rate elastic. The cleaners are unskilled and do not require much training. As a result, an increase in the wage paid to airline cleaners greatly increases the number of workers willing to clean aircraft. Because of these factors, and others we have not considered, pilots' salaries end up being much higher than the wages received by the workers who clean their aircraft. In Figure 7.4, pilots are paid £300 an hour, whereas cleaners earn £10 an hour, which is just above the national living wage.

Globalisation and the international migration of workers

Globalisation and the international migration of workers have also widened the differences between the wages and salaries paid to different groups of workers. In the UK, low-paid workers are in competition, both with incoming migrants from poorer parts of the world, and with overseas-based

A call centre in Mumbai

SYNOPTIC LINK
See Chapters 1 and 6 for more information on the factors of production and Chapter 14 for discussion of globalisation.

workers employed in developing countries, to which UK employers have outsourced jobs. A call-centre worker, serving the UK market but employed in India, earns a much lower wage than a similar worker employed in the UK. International competition has led to falling wages in UK labour markets where workers are competing for jobs against similar workers in other countries. Similar competition does exist at the high end of labour markets too, but in this case, well-paid UK business executives often succeed in raising their pay on the grounds that their employers must match the 'rate for the job' established in richer countries such as the USA. If their pay does not rise, they argue, they will move to better-paid jobs in other countries.

CASE STUDY 7.1

Causes of declining labour share of income

According to an IMF blog published on 12 April 2017 from which this case study has been taken, labour's share of income declines when wages grow more slowly than productivity, or the amount of output per hour of work. The result is that a growing fraction of productivity gains has been going to capital. And since capital tends to be concentrated in the upper ends of the income distribution, falling labour income shares are likely to raise income inequality.

In advanced economies, labour income shares began trending down in the 1980s. They reached their lowest level of the past half-century just prior to the 2008 global financial crisis and have not recovered materially since. Labour income shares now are almost 4 percentage points lower than they were in 1970.

Despite more limited data, it is also the case that labour shares have declined in emerging markets and developing economies since the early 1990s. This is especially true for the larger economies in this group. In China, for example, despite impressive gains in poverty reduction over the past two decades, labour shares still fell by almost 3 percentage points.

Indeed, as growth remains sub-par in many countries, an increasing recognition that the gains from growth have not been broadly shared has strengthened a backlash against economic integration and bolstered support in favour of inward-looking policies. This is especially the case in several advanced economies.

In advanced economies, about half of the decline in labour shares can be traced to the impact of technology. The decline was driven by a combination of rapid progress in information and telecommunication technology, and a high share of occupations that could be easily be automated.

Follow-up questions

1 Distinguish between labour and capital.
2 What is meant by an inward-looking policy?
3 The case study states that 'labour's share of income declines when wages grow more slowly than productivity'. Why should this be so?
4 In 2014 the French economist Thomas Piketty published an important book on the distribution of income between labour and capital. Access Pikkety's lectures on YouTube: for example, 'New thoughts on capital in the twenty-first century'.

STUDY TIP
Make sure you can apply the theory of the labour market explained in Chapter 6 to the factors determining the distributions of income and wealth.

Inequality in the distribution of wealth

While Figures 7.1 and 7.3 both show that the distribution of income in the UK is unequal, Figure 7.2 when compared to Figure 7.1 indicates that the distribution of wealth is significantly more unequal than the distribution of income.

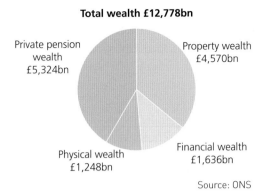

Total wealth £12,778bn

Private pension wealth
£5,324bn

Property wealth
£4,570bn

Financial wealth
£1,636bn

Physical wealth
£1,248bn

Source: ONS

Figure 7.5 Breakdown of the types of wealth owned by UK households, 2016

According to the Resolution Foundation, a UK think tank whose aim is to improve the standard of living of low- and middle-income families, the spreading of property wealth across the UK in the mid-1990s and mid-2000s contributed to a decade-long fall in wealth inequality. However, that trend has now gone into reverse.

The UK's record £11.1 trillion of wealth in 2014 was distributed far less equally than earnings or household income. Currently, one in ten adults own around half of the nation's wealth, with the top 1% owning 14% of UK wealth. By contrast, 15% of adults have no or negative wealth.

The Office for National Statistics (ONS) defines total net wealth as the sum of four components: net property wealth, physical wealth, net financial wealth and private pension wealth, although it does not include rights to state pensions. These are shown in Figure 7.5 for 2016.

As we mentioned earlier, wealth is a 'stock' concept rather than a 'flow'; it is measured at a particular point in time. Income, which refers to the flow of resources received over a period of time, allows wealth to be accumulated, but similarly, wealth is capable of producing flows of income either in the present or — as in the case of pension wealth — in the future.

QUANTITATIVE SKILLS 7.2

Worked example: calculating percentages to two decimal places

Figure 7.5 shows the relative contribution of each of the four wealth components to aggregate total wealth in the UK in 2016. Calculate to two decimal places the percentage contribution of each of the four components of wealth to total wealth in 2016.

In 2016, the two components making the largest contribution to aggregate total wealth were private pension wealth and net property wealth (accounting for 41.67% and 35.76% respectively). Financial wealth made up 12.80% of the total wealth in 2016 and physical wealth (other than property wealth, e.g. cars) made the smallest contribution of the four components (9.77%).

STUDY TIP

These days, UK data, particularly in macroeconomics but also in microeconomic topics such as the distributions of income and wealth, are increasingly expressed in trillions of pounds. Make sure you understand the difference between a trillion, a billion and a million.

Factors influencing the distribution of wealth

The factors influencing the distribution of wealth are closely linked to the factors which influence the distribution of income. Indeed, as we have already mentioned, high incomes lead both to a large amount of saving taking place, and to spending on items such as expensive houses, both of which add to household wealth. By contrast, households living on small incomes can afford neither to save nor to purchase houses, which appreciate rather than depreciate in value.

Some of the other factors that influence the distribution of wealth are described below.

The ability to benefit from capital gains

A capital gain occurs when the value of an asset such as a house increases. Most consumer durable goods, such as cars and television sets, depreciate in value over the years after they are purchased. By contrast, the value of land and property generally increases, at least in the UK. Share prices also tend to rise in the long run, though they can also fall in value. On the whole, the already wealthy own the most expensive houses, often also owning more than one house, and they are the main owners of shares. The least wealthy often rent rather than own the houses they live in, and seldom own shares.

Private pension assets

Property and financial assets such as shares are generally forms of marketable wealth, accounting together for 48.57% of the household wealth in 2016, shown in Figure 7.5. However, as Figure 7.5 shows, in 2016 private pension assets, which are generally non-marketable, made up 41.67% of total household wealth. Until quite recently, company pension schemes were not available for many low-paid UK workers, and neither did low-paid workers contribute to private pension schemes sold, for example, by insurance companies such as Standard Life. This has meant that many low-paid workers have expected their retirement income to be provided solely by the state pension, which on its own is little more than a poverty income. (Case study 7.5 on page 219 explains the new automatic enrolment scheme which the UK government has introduced to extend private pensions to low-paid workers.)

Inheritance, gifts and luck

In popular parlance, wealthy families are often divided into 'new wealth' and 'old wealth'. Entrepreneurs who have built up large personal fortunes, often starting from scratch, through founding their own businesses and successful risk taking, fall into the category of 'new wealth'. By contrast, 'old wealth' includes people who inherit wealth through the luck of having been born into very rich families, rather than through exercising entrepreneurial skills. Members of the landed aristocracy who pass wealth-holdings from generation to generation are 'old wealth'. 'Old wealth' can, of course, lead to 'new wealth' — for example, when the sons and daughters of rich families use their expensively acquired education and inherited wealth as the platform on which to develop entrepreneurial skills. Likewise, 'new wealth' can create 'old wealth', when for example the fortunes of the newly rich are passed on to the next generation.

Wealth taxation versus taxation of income

In the UK, a much larger fraction of the government's tax revenue comes from taxation of income than from the taxation of wealth. Wealth is lightly taxed and there are many loopholes through which the already wealthy can legally avoid paying wealth taxes such as inheritance tax. The wealthy can also afford to employ accountants and financial advisers who minimise the tax they are liable to pay, and in this way the wealthy become even wealthier.

KEY TERMS

equality when everyone is treated exactly the same. A completely equal distribution of income means that everybody has the same income.

equity when everyone is treated fairly.

The difference between equality and equity in relation to the distribution of income and wealth

The terms **equality** and **equity** are often used interchangeably, which can be confusing. Although the concepts are related, they are not the same. Complete equality in the distribution of income is achieved when each person receives exactly the same amount of income. The degree of inequality is indicated by the extent to which people's incomes differ. Equity is when people are treated fairly, but differently, having taken into account their different circumstances. Very few people would argue that it would be equitable if everyone received the same income, irrespective of their efforts and the contribution they make to society. It is when people start to discuss how much inequality is fair that the arguments usually begin.

Equity, which means fairness or justness, is a *normative* concept, which cannot be measured. Different people form different value judgements on what is equitable or inequitable. By contrast, equality is a *positive* concept. A positive statement, such as the view that the incomes received by everyone in the economy are the same, can be tested against the evidence to see if it is true or untrue. As we shall shortly explain, it is possible to measure the degrees of equality and inequality in the distributions of income and wealth.

SYNOPTIC LINK
We first described positive and normative statements in Chapter 1 on page 4.

TEST YOURSELF 7.3
Which of the following are normative statements?

A The distribution of wealth is more unequal than the distribution of income.

B The rich deserve to be rich.

C Inequalities can be measured.

D Governments ought to give more help to the poor.

EXTENSION MATERIAL

Horizontal and vertical equity

Government intervention in the economy, which treats people in the same circumstances equally, obeys the principle of *horizontal equity*. Horizontal equity occurs when households with the same income and personal circumstances (for example, number of children) pay the same income tax and are eligible for the same welfare benefits. *Vertical equity* is much more controversial, since it justifies taking income from the rich (on the grounds that they do not need it) and redistributing it to the poor (on the grounds that they do need it). The distribution of income after taxation and receipt of transfers is judged by many to be more equitable than the distribution of income before taxes have been paid and transfer payments received. (In this context, a *transfer* or *transfer payment* is a payment of money for which goods or services are not received in exchange. Governments use transfer payments, such as pensions, as means of income redistribution by giving out money as a part of their social welfare programmes.)

However, achieving greater vertical equity can conflict with another principle of intervention, the *benefit principle*, which argues that those who receive most benefit from government spending (for example, motorists benefiting from roads) should pay the most in taxes.

STUDY TIP
Make sure you understand the difference between equity and efficiency.

The Lorenz curve and Gini coefficient

Economists use **Lorenz curves** and the **Gini coefficient** to measure inequality. A Lorenz curve measures *the extent* to which the distribution of income (or wealth) is equal or unequal. The degree of inequality is measured by a Gini coefficient statistic.

> **KEY TERMS**
>
> **Lorenz curve** a graph on which the cumulative percentage of total national income or wealth is plotted against the cumulative percentage of population (ranked in increasing size of share). The extent to which the curve dips below a straight diagonal line indicates the degree of inequality of distribution.
>
> **Gini coefficient** measures the extent to which the distribution of income or wealth among individuals or households within an economy deviates from a perfectly equal distribution.

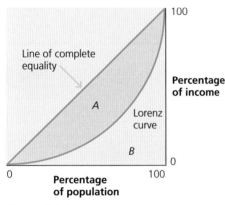

Figure 7.6 A Lorenz curve

The Lorenz curve in Figure 7.6 shows population on the horizontal axis, measured in cumulative percentages from 0% to 100%. The vertical axis shows the cumulative percentage of income received by the population. If incomes were distributed equally, the Lorenz curve would lie along the diagonal line in the diagram. The nearer the Lorenz curve is to the diagonal, the more equal is the distribution of income.

The Gini coefficient measures the area between the Lorenz curve and the diagonal as a ratio of the total area under the diagonal. In terms of the diagram, the Gini coefficient is calculated using the following formula:

$$\text{Gini coefficient} = \frac{\text{area } A}{\text{area } A + \text{area } B}$$

The lower the value of the Gini coefficient, the more equally household income is distributed. If the Lorenz curve were to lie along the 45-degree line in Figure 7.6, every household would have exactly the same income and the Gini coefficient would be zero. At the other extreme, if one person received all the income and everybody else no income, the Lorenz curve would be the reverse L-shape lying along, first, the horizontal axis, and then the right-hand vertical axis in the diagram. Between these two extremes, Lorenz curves closer to the line of complete equality show greater equality (and Gini coefficients approaching zero), while Lorenz curves further away from the diagonal display greater inequality (and Gini coefficients approaching 1).

Figure 7.7 shows how the Gini coefficient for equivalised disposable income changed in the UK between 1977 and 2015. (Equivalised income is a measure of household income that takes account of the differences in a household's size and composition. It is used for the calculation of poverty.) Measured in this way, inequality of disposable income increased in the 1980s, and then fell in the early 1990s. After a slight increase around the millennium, it fell again from around 36% in 2001 to just under 32% in 2015. Inequality was at its lowest for 30 years.

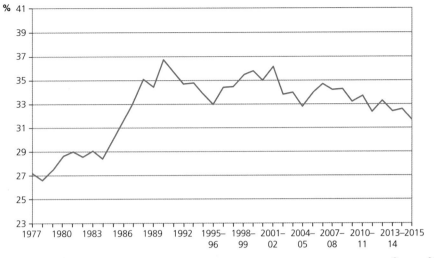

Source: ONS

Figure 7.7 Gini coefficient for equivalised disposable income, UK, 1977–2015

TEST YOURSELF 7.4
Table 7.2 shows the distribution of income (by quintile) in country X and country Y. Plot Lorenz curves for the two countries.

Table 7.2 Income distributions by quintile

	Percentage of total disposable income	
Quintile	Country X	Country Y
1st	5	4
2nd	10	6
3rd	15	25
4th	20	30
5th	50	4
Total	100	35

TEST YOURSELF 7.5
Which **two** of the following are most likely to reflect a move towards a more equal distribution of income? Explain your answer.

A The share of total income going to the bottom 50% of income earners rises from 30% to 40%.

B The share of total income going to the top 15% of income earners rises from 60% to 62%.

C The Gini coefficient rises towards 1.

D The Gini coefficient falls towards 0.

The likely benefits and costs of more equal distributions of income and wealth

It is sometimes argued, particularly by economists who favour government intervention in markets, that more equal distributions of income and wealth can lead to faster economic growth. The fruits of faster growth can then be used to improve living standards and the economic welfare of most or all the population. The logic behind this argument is that people on low incomes and who possess little wealth generally spend all or most of their incomes on consumption and save very little, or nothing at all. Increased spending on consumer goods and services increases aggregate demand in the economy, which promotes economic growth. By contrast, the better-off spend a smaller fraction of their incomes on consumption, which leads to slower growth. Inequality can also mean that the talents of some people in society are wasted or, at least, not fully exploited. Inequality in income usually means that there is also inequality of opportunity.

However, economists of a more pro-free-market persuasion generally reject this view of the world, partly on the grounds that it takes no account of incentives and disincentives. They argue that the **progressive taxation** of higher incomes and wealth, combined with the transfer of taxed income to the less well-off, in the form of welfare benefits, significantly reduces the incentives to work hard, both among the better-off and among the poor. Reducing incentives to effort and enterprise reduces, rather than increases, the rate of economic growth. Extreme pro-free-market analysts argue that to make the poor better off *eventually*, inequality must first be increased rather than reduced. By incentivising those already in work to work harder, and the unwaged welfare benefit claimants to search for jobs, faster economic growth can be achieved. In the long run, the low-waged benefit even though in the short run their incomes fall.

Taken to the extreme, however, widening income and wealth inequalities undoubtedly increases poverty, at least in the short run. Most people in the UK seem to subscribe to a consensus view that there should be a certain amount of redistribution, compared to the outcome that would be achieved in a complete free-market situation. This redistribution is necessary for moral reasons and also to maintain social cohesion within society. The debating issues are, first, where to draw the line when redistributing income and wealth, and second, what methods should be used to achieve the degree of redistribution desired.

KEY TERM

progressive taxation a tax is progressive when, as income rises, a greater proportion of income is paid in taxation. The term can be applied to a particular tax such as income tax or to taxation in general.

TEST YOURSELF 7.6

If a country's Gini coefficient fell from 0.9 to 0.7 over a 5-year period, what would this tell you about the distribution of income within the country?

STUDY TIP

Make sure you understand, first, the difference between income and wealth, and second, the difference between equal and equitable.

CASE STUDY 7.2

The case for and against a flat tax

A 'flat tax' is the same as a proportional tax. Pro-free-market economists in the USA and elsewhere have been arguing the case for a 'flat tax' for decades. In 1994, Estonia became the first country in Europe to introduce a flat tax, replacing the existing three tax rates on personal income, and another on corporate profits, with one uniform rate of 26%. Other countries in central and eastern Europe have since followed suit, some introducing flat tax rates as low as 12 or 13%. In the UK, the Conservatives have flirted with but not taken up the idea. The UK Independence Party (UKIP) is most in favour of flat taxation and has discussed the rate at which it should be set.

Tallinn, the capital of Estonia

The main case for flat taxes is that fewer brackets are simpler to administer, with one tax bracket being the simplest of all. If a pure flat income tax were to be introduced in the UK, Her Majesty's Revenue and Customs (HMRC) would take the same amount from the first pound earned by a taxpayer as would be taken from the last pound earned. As a result, many high-income earners want flat taxes to be introduced.

Rory Meakin, who is the research director at the pro-free-market lobby group, the Taxpayers' Alliance, is in favour of flatter taxes and a much simpler tax system. Meakin argues:

> Britain's tax code is one of the longest in the world. By 2013, UK tax handbooks were extending to over 17,000 pages, three times longer than in 1997. We have a basic rate, a higher rate and an additional rate of income tax, with a different set of rates for dividends and yet another for savings.

> There's no need for taxes to be so maddeningly complex. Complexity also makes the tax system both economically and socially destructive. Quite apart from the money it sucks out of the productive economy, it's economically damaging for two reasons. First, it requires an army of clever accountants and tax lawyers to navigate the system for businesses and an opposing battalion of bureaucrats to monitor all those rules and rates. Second, it means that the public just doesn't understand how the tax system operates, which, among other things, risks discouraging people with new commercial ideas from starting new businesses. That means opportunities are lost and fewer jobs are created. And it's socially damaging because the confusion leads to suspicion that others are getting away with something, directly leading to distrust of the whole system.

> We need to sweep away all that complexity and replace the current system of taxation with lower, simpler and more proportionate taxes which are easier to understand, with fewer loopholes and exemptions.

By contrast, Richard Murphy, head of the anti-poverty Tax Research partnership, which is funded by the anti-poverty Joseph Rowntree Charitable Trust, is against flat taxes. Murphy believes that the view that flat taxes are simple and would raise tax revenue is a myth, as is the view that a great deal of the cost of administering the tax system could be eliminated. This would only be true if taxes were scrapped along with the money they raise. This provides the real clue to what flat taxes are all about. It is not chance that flat taxes are always promoted by people who also argue for small government and massive cuts in public spending.

Follow-up questions

1 Find out the difference between a flat tax or proportional tax, a progressive tax and a regressive tax.
2 Giving an example of each, explain the difference between tax avoidance and tax evasion.
3 Supporters of flat taxation believe that flat taxes would reduce tax avoidance and tax evasion. Explain why you agree or disagree with this view.
4 Evaluate the case for massive cuts in public spending in the UK.

QUANTITATIVE SKILLS 7.3

Worked example: calculating the mean and the median

The 12 fellow students in your economics class have told you that in a typical week their household incomes are £480; £750; £300; £250; £1,000; £600; £400; £500; £800; £520; £550; and £450. Your own household income is £570. What is the mean household income and the median household income in your class?

The mean and the median are two kinds of 'average', with the mean being the most commonly recognised. The mean household income can be calculated by adding up the household incomes (in this case £7,170) and dividing this number by 13 (the total number of households in this example, as your household is included as well as those of your fellow students). The mean value for all 13 households is approximately £551.54.

The 'median' is the 'middle' value in the list of numbers. To find the median, you should list the numbers in numerical order (£250; £300; £400; £450; £480; £500; £520; £550; £570; £600; £750; £800; and £1,000), and then locate the middle value. In this example, the median value is £520.

STUDY TIP
Make sure you understand the links between equality and inequality on the one hand and poverty on the other hand.

SECTION 7.1 SUMMARY

- The distribution of income measures how personal or household income is distributed among different income groups in society, such as between rich and poor.
- The distribution of wealth measures how personal or household wealth is distributed among different groups in society.
- Inequalities in the distribution of UK income and wealth have widened over recent decades but have narrowed slightly since 2010.
- Inequalities in the distribution of wealth have always been wider than those in the distribution of income.
- An important factor influencing the distribution of income is the shares of national income going to different factors of production.
- Other factors affecting the distribution of income include the shares of earned and unearned income, the widening of earnings differences between workers at the top and bottom of the pay league table, and the effect of globalisation and the international migration of workers.
- Factors influencing the distribution of wealth include the ability to benefit from capital gains, ownership of private pension assets, the roles of inheritance, gifts and luck, and the different effects of wealth and income taxation.
- Equality must not be confused with equity or fairness.
- Economists use Lorenz curves and the Gini coefficient to measure inequality.
- A Lorenz curve measures *the extent* to which the distribution of income (or wealth) is equal or unequal.
- The degree of inequality is measured by a Gini coefficient statistic.
- Economists who favour government intervention in markets believe that more equal distributions of income and wealth can lead to faster economic growth. The fruits of faster growth can then be used to improve living standards and the economic welfare of most or all the population.
- Economists of a pro-free-market persuasion believe that government intervention reduces the incentives to work hard, both among the better-off and among the poor.

7.2 The problem of poverty

Poverty is the state of being extremely poor and not having enough money or income to meet basic needs including food, clothing and shelter. The World Bank describes poverty in the following way:

> Poverty is hunger. Poverty is lack of shelter. Poverty is being sick and not being able to see a doctor. Poverty is not having access to school and not knowing how to read. Poverty is not having a job, is fear for the future, living one day at a time.

Poverty is caused both by a low real national income relative to a country's total population size and by inequalities in the distributions of income and wealth. The former leads to *absolute* poverty for many if not most of a country's inhabitants, whereas the latter causes *relative* poverty. These terms are explained below.

The difference between relative and absolute poverty

Absolute poverty

The Joseph Rowntree Foundation defines **absolute poverty** in the following way:

> A poverty level that does not change over time, in terms of the living standard that it refers to. It stays the same even if society is becoming more prosperous. An absolute poverty line thus represents a certain basic level of goods and services, and only rises with inflation to show how much it would cost to buy those goods and services.

Relative poverty

Relative poverty is suffered by a household if its income is below a specified proportion of the average income for all households For example, in the UK, the 'poverty line' has usually been set at 60% of median income. The charity Barnardo's says:

> Relative poverty defines 'poverty' as being below a relative poverty threshold. It classifies individuals or families as 'poor' not by comparing them to a fixed cut-off point, but by comparing them to others in the population under study.

TEST YOURSELF 7.7

The inability to satisfy basic food needs is part of the definition of:

A relative poverty

B obesity

C absolute poverty

D idleness

Explain why statement C provides the correct answer and why the other statements are wrong.

How the Conservatives tried to redefine child poverty

On 1 July 2015, Iain Duncan Smith, the then secretary of state for work and pensions, announced that he intended to repeal the 2010 Child Poverty Act, which committed the government to a target of eradicating child poverty in the UK by 2020. The government wanted to get rid of the definition of relative poverty in the 2010 Act (anyone in a household beneath 60% of median income), to abandon all the 2010 targets, and to introduce a new definition of relative poverty, embracing work and education levels in the family.

The work and pensions secretary wanted to remove a statutory duty to publish levels of UK household income as part of the welfare reform. However, following fierce opposition led by the Child Poverty Action Group (CPAG) and the House of Lords, the government did a 'U-turn' and accepted that the material deprivation measures should remain protected.

Follow-up questions

1 Explain the difference between relative poverty and absolute poverty.
2 Access the Child Poverty Action Group's website and find out more detail about what has happened to Duncan Smith's proposals since 2015.
3 Explain why you agree or disagree with the proposed new definition of child poverty which has now been abandoned.
4 The growth in the number of people sleeping on the streets is a symptom of growing poverty in the UK. Between 2010 and 2018, rough-sleeping estimates showed an increase of 165%. Evaluate one way in which rough-sleeping could be reduced.

The causes and effects of poverty in the UK

For the most part, UK poverty is relative rather than absolute, although many homeless people living in cardboard boxes in town centres are absolutely as well as relatively poor. Three of the main causes of relative poverty in the UK are old age, unemployment and the low wages of many of those in work.

Old age and poverty

Old age causes relative poverty largely because, as we have seen, many old people rely on the state pension and lack a private pension. Before the early 1980s, the state pension rose each year in line with the increase in national prosperity delivered by economic growth and higher real earnings. However, pensions then moved away from being index-linked to average earnings, to be linked instead to the rate of inflation, measured at first by changes in the retail prices index (RPI). Pensions no longer rose in line with the general increase in the standard of living and pensioners' living standards were in effect kept at their 1980 level. Old people who were reliant solely on the state for their income became increasingly worse off compared to people in work.

In 2011, the Coalition government introduced what is known as the 'triple lock'. The government said that the state pension would now rise in line with either earnings, or CPI (consumer prices index) inflation, or a 2.5% increase, whichever is the greatest. Shortly afterwards, the government considered switching back to linking pension increases solely to rises in average earnings, thus ending the annual inflation-linked rise in benefits. In contrast to earlier decades when the rate of increase in average earnings exceeded the rate of inflation, by 2013 earnings were rising by around 1% a year, which was lower than the rate of inflation — which, at the time, was nearer to 2%. By 2015, average earnings were rising by slightly more than the then low rate of inflation. Following a dip around the time of the Brexit vote in 2016, by 2018 average earnings had resumed their slight increase. However, whatever is likely to happen in the future, unless supplemented from other sources of income, the state pension will continue to be very much a poverty income.

Unemployment and poverty

Unemployment benefits are generally lower than the pay workers received before losing their jobs. An increase in unemployment therefore increases poverty. In 2013, as part of the policy of cutting public spending, the Coalition government introduced a limit on the total amount of benefit that most people aged 16 to 64 can claim. This limit may further increase poverty, though this effect could be offset by a continuing rapid fall in unemployment. Absolute poverty can best be reduced by fast and sustained economic growth and by creating jobs. This may also reduce relative poverty. Economic growth can also create the wherewithal, if the electorate and state are so minded, to increase the real value of the state pension and unemployment benefits. Possibly in part due to the political power of the so-called 'grey vote', the government may be more minded to increase the real value of the state pension than of unemployment benefits.

Low wages and poverty

When discussing the nature of both absolute and relative poverty in the UK, we must distinguish between the low-waged and the unwaged, who are unemployed. The low-waged, unlike the unwaged, are workers with jobs, albeit jobs in which their hourly and weekly earnings are low. The low-waged include many unskilled workers, together with skilled workers who have lost their jobs in industrial sectors such as manufacturing and coal mining, and who have had to accept employment in low-waged, unskilled jobs. The low-waged poor are almost always relatively poor rather than absolutely poor. In contrast, some of the unwaged, including homeless people living on the street, fall into the category of the absolutely poor. The national minimum wage, which we explained in Chapter 6, was an attempt to reduce the poverty of the low-waged. The national living wage has now taken on this mantle.

> **TEST YOURSELF 7.8**
> How does the education that people receive affect the chances of whether they are rich or poor?

The effects of poverty in the UK

According to the Child Poverty Action Group (CPAG), poverty damages childhoods, life chances and eventually all in society. It is a direct cost to government resulting from additional demands placed on services and benefits for the poor, as well as reduced tax receipts.

Educational deprivation

In terms of education deprivation, the CPAG argues that children from poorer backgrounds lag at all stages of education. For example, by the age of 3, poorer children are estimated to be, on average, 9 months behind children from more wealthy backgrounds. By the end of primary school, pupils receiving free school meals are estimated to be almost three terms behind their more affluent peers. This gap grows to over five terms by the age of 14, and by 16, children receiving free school meals achieve 1.7 grades lower at GCSE.

Health deprivation

The CPAG says that poverty is also associated with a higher risk of both illness and premature death. Children born in the poorest areas of the UK weigh, on average, 200 grams less at birth than those born in the richest areas. Children from low-income families are also more likely to die at birth or in infancy than children born into richer families. They are more likely to suffer chronic illness during childhood or to have a disability. Poorer health over the course of a lifetime has an impact on life expectancy: professionals live, on average, 8 years longer than unskilled workers.

The effect of poverty on communities

Children living in poverty are almost twice as likely to live in bad housing. This has significant effects on both their physical and mental health, as well as their educational achievement. Fuel poverty also affects children detrimentally as they grow up. Low-income families sometimes have to make a choice between food and heating. Children from low-income families often forgo activities that most children would take for granted. They miss school trips; can't invite friends round for tea; and can't afford a one-week holiday away from home.

Besides having serious effects on children, poverty adversely affects other groups in society, particularly pensioners whose sole income is the state pension. For example, the elderly are the main group in society suffering from fuel poverty. Though in 2016 energy prices fell for a time, falling energy prices generally turn out to be a short-term 'blip', soon to be replaced by the 'normal service' of rising prices in response to global resource depletion. During 2017 energy companies announced a wave of price hikes that pushed up prices right across the board. Old-age poverty and the fact that the old are living for longer lead to other adverse effects on society — for example, elderly 'bed-blockers' continuing to occupy hospital wards after they have been successfully treated, simply because they have nowhere else to go.

SECTION 7.2 SUMMARY

- Poverty is caused both by a low real national income relative to a country's total population size and by inequalities in the distributions of income and wealth.
- The former leads to absolute poverty for many if not most of a country's inhabitants, whereas the latter causes relative poverty.
- Absolute poverty is a condition characterised by severe deprivation of basic human needs, including food, safe drinking water, sanitation facilities, health, shelter, education and information. It depends not only on income but also on access to services.
- Relative poverty occurs when income is below a specified proportion of average income: for example, below 60% of median income.
- Relative poverty is more significant than absolute poverty for most of the poor in the UK, except the destitute.
- Old age, unemployment and low wages are important causes of poverty in the UK.
- The Child Poverty Action Group believes that poverty damages childhoods, life chances and eventually all in society. It leads to health and education deprivation and to the breakdown of communities.
- The old form a significant part of the poor.

7.3 Government policies to alleviate poverty and to influence the distribution of income and wealth

Poverty and the tax and benefits system

Poverty is seldom caused directly and immediately by taxation and the benefits system. However, through a process known as fiscal drag (which will be explained shortly) and through cuts in welfare benefits, poverty can increase. Making taxation more progressive and increasing welfare benefits reduces poverty and inequalities in the distribution of income, at least in the short run. However, as we have already mentioned, pro-free-market economists believe that, in the drive to reduce inequality, these changes worsen labour market incentives, competitiveness and economic growth. They may lead to a culture of welfare dependency where some people are long-term unemployed and are reluctant to look for work. According to this view, in the long run, low incomes may fail to grow, and poverty may increase. If true, government intervention in labour markets in an attempt to reduce poverty results in government failure.

STUDY TIP
Make sure you understand the concepts of market failure and government failure, which are explained in Chapter 8.

EXTENSION MATERIAL

Universal benefits versus means-tested benefits

Government welfare benefits paid to the poor and to other groups in society can be divided into: national insurance benefits, such as state pensions; universal benefits; and means-tested benefits. The winter fuel payment, which in 2018 ranged between £100 and £300, depending on personal circumstances, is a universal benefit: it is paid to all pensioner households who claim the benefit, irrespective of household income. Winter fuel payment is also untaxed. (Pensioners 'opt in' to claim winter fuel payment. However, some behavioural economists argue that rich pensioners who currently claim the payment should be 'nudged' or encouraged to opt out of continuing to claim the benefit, on the grounds that they do not need it.)

Over the years, UK governments have sought to replace universal benefits with means-tested benefits. This is because, as is the case with the winter fuel payment, benefits that are not means-tested are usually expensive to provide and go to people who do not need them. (The growth of means-tested benefits also reflects the fact that other benefits, including national insurance benefits, have not been increased in line with earnings.) However, universality means that people who do need the benefits usually end up receiving them. With means testing, by contrast, people who need a benefit, particularly the elderly poor, may be too proud to claim the benefit, or be put off by the amount of form filling needed to prove eligibility.

With means-tested benefits, people's ability to claim a benefit is determined by their income and their outgoings (or 'means'). Means-tested benefits are more efficient than universal benefits in the sense that taxpayers' money is less likely to be given to people who do not need the benefit. However, as we shall shortly see in the context of the poverty and unemployment traps, means testing can create unintended disincentive effects which prevent the low-waged from working harder and the unwaged (or unemployed) from seeking employment.

At the time of writing in July 2018, since 2015 the Conservative government has been 'rolling out' Universal Credit (UC) to replace a number other means-tested benefits, including Housing Benefit, Income Support and income-related Jobseeker's Allowance, which is the main benefit paid to the unemployed. Originally announced in 2013, the introduction of Universal Credit has been dogged by very expensive ICT problems (themselves a waste of taxpayers' money), and it will be several years before the Credit has fully replaced the separate benefits we have just listed.

The effects of taxes and benefits on household income, 2016/17

A household is a group of people, such as a family, who are living together in a house or flat. According to the Office for National Statistics, in 2016/17 before direct taxes were paid and cash benefits received, the richest fifth had an average original income 12 times larger than the poorest fifth — £88,800 per year compared with £7,400. When direct taxes and cash benefits were included, income was shared less unequally between households — the income of the poorest fifth of households increased by £6,000 to £13,400, and the income of the richest fifth decreased by £18,100 to £70,700.

Consequently, the ratio of income of the richest fifth to the poorest fifth fell from 12 to 1, to 5 to 1. The inclusion of indirect taxes (such as alcohol duties and value added tax) and benefits-in-kind (for example, state education and the National Health Service) further reduces this ratio to less than 4 to 1.

This fall in the ratio of income between the richest fifth and the poorest fifth of households is explained by comparing the composition of taxes and benefits of these two groups of households. The poorest fifth of households received relatively larger amounts of both cash benefits and benefits-in-kind in 2016/17. Richer households, on the other hand, paid higher amounts in taxes — both direct and indirect.

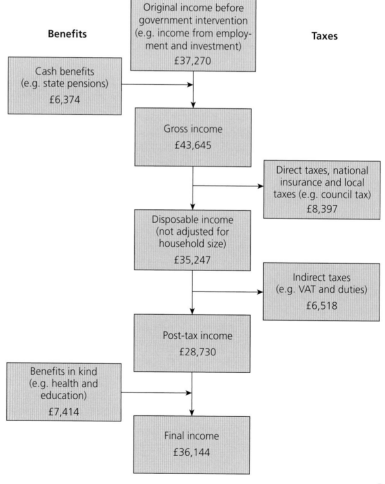

Source: ONS

Figure 7.8 Average household income, cash benefits received, including benefits in kind, and taxes paid, 2016/17

214

There are five stages, illustrated in Figure 7.8 for the tax year 2016/17, through which taxes and benefits affect the distribution of income. These are as follows:

1 Household members begin with income from employment, private pensions, investments such as the shares they own, and other non-government sources. This is referred to as 'original income'.
2 Households then receive income from cash benefits. The sum of cash benefits and original income is referred to as 'gross income'.
3 Households then pay direct taxes. Income after direct taxes have been subtracted from gross income is called 'disposable income'.
4 Indirect taxes are then paid on spending on goods and services. Disposable income minus indirect taxes is referred to as 'post-tax income'.
5 Households finally receive a benefit from services provided by the government (benefits in kind). Post-tax income plus benefits in kind is referred to as 'final income'.

TEST YOURSELF 7.10
What is meant by the terms 'original income' and 'disposable income'?

SYNOPTIC LINK
Government policies to deal with poverty are examples of fiscal policy. See Chapter 13 for detailed discussion of the UK government's fiscal policy.

QUANTITATIVE SKILLS 7.4

Worked example: plotting data on a bar chart
Table 7.3 shows workers in poverty by employment types for the financial years from 2009/10 to 2016/17.

Table 7.3 Workers in poverty by employment type (millions)

Year	Full-time employed	Full-time self-employed	Part-time employed or self-employed
2009/10	1.26	0.52	1.27
2010/11	1.28	0.53	1.32
2011/12	1.36	0.52	1.36
2012/13	1.21	0.50	1.47
2013/14	1.36	0.59	1.39
2014/15	1.39	0.57	1.54
2015/16	1.42	0.57	1.49
2016/17	1.51	0.55	1.72

Source: ONS

Plot the data on a bar chart.

The answer is shown in Figure 7.9.

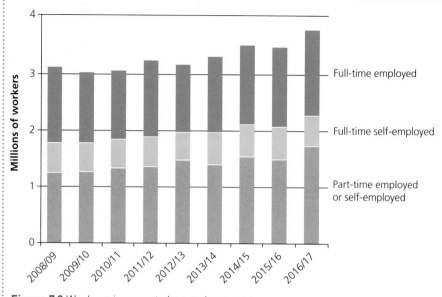

Figure 7.9 Workers in poverty by employment type

There are various ways of using bar graph or charts. For answering the question, we have used a stacked bar chart. Stacked bar charts are a way of showing information about different sub-groups of the main categories.

Fiscal drag, poverty and low pay

The UK tax system has affected poverty partly through a process known as fiscal drag. Fiscal drag occurs in a progressive income tax system when the government fails to raise tax thresholds (or personal tax allowances) to keep pace with inflation. Figure 7.10(a) shows an income pyramid with the rich at the top and the poor at the bottom, and with the tax threshold fixed at an income of £10,000. In this example, a person with an income of £9,900 is just below the threshold and pays no income tax.

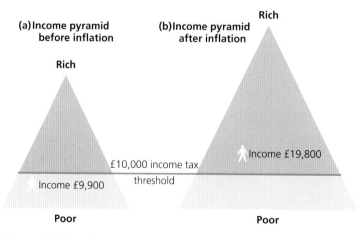

Figure 7.10 How fiscal drag brings people on low income into the tax net

Suppose that over the next few years both prices and all money incomes exactly double. In the absence of taxation and assuming there are no benefits available, real incomes would remain unchanged, with households no better or worse off. But if the government fails to increase personal tax allowances in line with inflation (that is, to raise the tax threshold to £20,000), a doubling of the person's money income to £19,800 means that £9,800 of income is now taxable. The individual concerned is now worse off in real terms.

The new situation is shown in Figure 7.10(b). Inflation has dragged the low-paid worker across the basic tax threshold and into the tax net. In a similar way, higher-paid workers are dragged deeper into the tax net if the higher 40% and 45% **marginal tax rates** remain unadjusted for inflation.

In recent years in the UK, the Coalition government and more recently the Conservative government have tried to reduce relative poverty among the low-paid by raising income tax thresholds by more than the rate of inflation, taking the basic tax threshold to £11,850 in 2018. The government's ambition is to raise the basic tax threshold to £12,500 by 2020, but this may not happen because the government needs to find new tax revenue to pay for increased spending on the NHS. However, the increases in the personal tax allowance, or tax threshold, that have been made have taken a significant number of the low-paid out of the income tax net and 'clawed back' some of the fiscal drag that had taken place in earlier years.

The earnings trap or poverty trap

Fiscal drag is one of the causes of the poverty trap. As there are a number of ways in which the poor can be trapped in poverty, this particular trap, which traps the *low-waged* in relative poverty, is perhaps better called 'the earnings trap'. It affects people in employment on low rates of pay, rather than the unemployed who are *unwaged*. Another cause of poverty affecting the homeless stems from the fact that to get a job they need a home, but to get a home they first need a job.

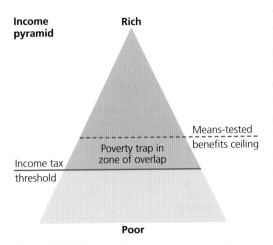

Figure 7.11 The earnings trap or poverty trap

The immediate cause of the earnings trap is the overlap, illustrated in Figure 7.11, between the income tax threshold (the level of income at which income tax starts to be paid) and the means-tested welfare benefits ceiling (the level of income at which means-tested benefits cease to be paid). When welfare benefits are means-tested, a person's right to claim the benefit is reduced and eventually tapers away or disappears completely, as income rises. By contrast, a universal benefit is claimed as of right and is not dependent on income, although the state may decide to 'claw back' universal benefits that are taxable.

Low-paid workers caught within the zone of overlap in Figure 7.11 not only pay income tax and national insurance contributions on each extra pound earned; they also lose part or all of the right to claim benefits. Thus low-paid workers and their families whose income falls within this zone of overlap become trapped in relative poverty, since any increase in their pay results in little or no increase (and in extreme cases a fall) in their disposable income.

The effective marginal rate of taxation of workers in poorly paid occupations is high when the loss of means-tested benefits is added to deductions through income tax and national insurance contributions. Calculated in this way, the marginal tax rates of the low-paid can be much higher (often around 70% and in extreme cases over 100%) than the top 45% rate currently paid by the better-off on income (in 2018) above £150,000. Moreover, since the low-paid are generally employed in occupations yielding little job satisfaction or scope for legal tax avoidance, it can be argued that disincentives to work imposed by the UK tax and benefits system affect the poor at the lower end of the income pyramid much more than they affect the better-off.

The poverty trap can be eliminated by getting rid of the zone of overlap in the income pyramid illustrated in Figure 7.11. The income tax threshold could be raised to take low-waged households out of the tax net. Means-tested benefits could be completely replaced by universal benefits, though this is unlikely to happen. The national living wage rate might also reduce poverty by being raised to a higher rate than is currently planned in an attempt to prevent employers paying 'poverty wages'. However, raising the NLW could be counterproductive if unemployment increases as a result. At the time of its introduction, the Conservative government said that the NLW might lead to a loss of 60,000 jobs, which implies that a higher NLW rate would lead to even more job losses. However, the government also said that continuing economic growth would create many more jobs.

> **TEST YOURSELF 7.12**
> Why is the poverty trap best called an earnings trap?

CASE STUDY 7.4

Universal Credit has probably placed more families in the poverty trap

When Universal Credit was announced in 2013, the UK government stood accused that its changes to the tax and benefits system risked penalising almost 2 million low earners. A report by the anti-poverty campaigning group, the Joseph Rowntree Foundation, suggested that with many left to deal with a more complex benefits system than before, Universal Credit could see people worse off in work and struggling to manage their finances. The report stated that, while 'making work pay' is the key aim of Universal Credit, many households are set to be worse off, or only marginally better off.

The report also raised serious concerns about a 'one-size-fits-all' IT-based delivery system and about potential IT failures which could quickly lead to backlogs, poor service and complaints.

However, the government claimed that in monetary terms, 3.1 million households would be entitled to more benefits as a result of the introduction of Universal Credit, while 2.8 million households would be entitled to less. Iain Duncan Smith, the secretary of state for work and pensions who introduced Universal Credit, said that across all households, there would be an average household gain of £16 per month.

One of the principal goals of Universal Credit is to ensure that additional earnings will always leave families better off and to avoid 'cliff edges' in incomes. In the foreword to the Universal Credit White Paper, Iain Duncan Smith said:

> At its heart, Universal Credit is very simple and will ensure that work always pays and is seen to pay. Universal Credit will mean that people will be consistently and transparently better off for each hour they work and every pound they earn.

But in 2018 the introduction of a £7,400 earnings ceiling, which limited a family's right to claim free school meals for their children, created a serious cliff edge that actually increased family proverty. According to the Children's Society, the effect of the cliff edge is illustrated in Figure 7.12.

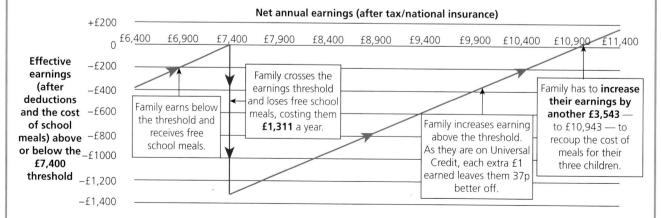

Source: Children's Society and Child Poverty Action Group

Figure 7.12 The free school meals 'cliff edge' and poverty trap for a family with three children

Follow-up questions

1 Explain how Figure 7.12 illustrates the 'cliff edge' described in the case study.
2 Find out whether, at the time you read this case study, the 'roll out' of Universal Credit has been completed.
3 Compare a universal benefit with a means-tested benefit.
4 Discuss whether Universal Credit has reduced the poverty trap, or increased poverty and drawn more families into the trap. To help your answer, access the web page **https://fullfact.org/education/free-school-meals-and-universal-credit/** which investigates the claim by the Children's Society quoted in the case study and illustrated in Figure 7.12.

The unemployment trap

The poverty trap, described earlier, affects the low-waged in jobs rather than the unemployed who are unwaged. It is important not to confuse the poverty trap or earnings trap with the unemployment trap. The unemployment trap is closely related to the earnings trap, since both affect the poor and result from the nature of the tax and benefits systems. But people caught in the unemployment trap are out of work — at least in terms of officially declared employment. The unemployment trap contains unwaged social security claimants who choose unemployment. This is because they decide they are better off out of work, living on benefits, than in low-paid jobs paying income tax and national insurance contributions (NICs), and losing some or all of their right to claim means-tested benefits.

One link between the earnings trap and the unemployment trap is the underground economy — the hidden or informal economy in which people work, usually for cash payments, while failing to declare income and sometimes fraudulently claiming social security benefits. Low-paid workers in employment can escape the earnings trap by giving up declared work in order to claim unemployment benefits, while receiving income from undeclared work in the underground economy. The underground economy is sometimes called the 'black economy'.

CASE STUDY 7.5

Enrolling low-paid workers into workplace pension schemes

As they approach retirement, some workers wrongly believe that their entitlement to a state pension will provide them with more than just a 'poverty income'. As a result, until recently too many have chosen not to opt into private pension plans. Two further factors have contributed to under-enrolment. In the first place, many low-paid and often young workers saw that contributing to a private pension scheme would leave them with even less of their already meagre incomes to spend on everyday living. Better to adopt a 'live-now, pay-later' approach to life and to spend now and not bother to save.

In the second place, private pension schemes were until recently often based on the 'opt-in' principle. Lethargy and inertia meant that too few workers bothered to join a private pension scheme.

Drawing on the insights of behavioural theory which we explained in Chapter 2, this is now changing. The UK government has introduced, since 2012, a system of automatic workplace pension contributions, in which a slice of workers' pay packets is diverted to savings pots to pay for their eventual pensions. Employers are obliged to pay in as well, and the government also adds a little extra through tax relief.

The new system, called automatic enrolment, is an important example of 'nudge' theory being taken on board in government policy. Unless employers already provide 'in-house' workplace pension schemes (which have traditionally been available mostly for the better-paid professional workers), workers are now being automatically enrolled in workplace pension schemes — unless they choose to 'opt out'.

The 'opt-out' scheme was gradually introduced between 2012 and 2018. It is expected that relatively few eligible workers will decide to opt out. Once again, this is partly due to lethargy, but workers also know opting out will lead to the loss of employers' contributions. Workers below the age of 22 will still have to opt in, as will part-time workers. Since the pension contributions of low-paid workers are generally small, the value of their pensions was expected to be £6,549.40 a year in 2018/19 compared to £6,360 a year in 2017/18. When the private pensions have been added to the state pension, the retirement incomes of previously low-paid workers will still be relatively low compared to the more fortunate pensioners. Automatic enrolment may also have the unintended consequence of hastening the introduction by so-called rogue employers of more casual part-time employment and zero-hours employment contracts.

Follow-up questions

1 Explain the difference between 'opting in' and 'opting out' in the context of a pension scheme.
2 What is a zero-hours employment contract?
3 Distinguish between the state pension and a private pension.
4 Why is pension automatic enrolment an example of the behavioural economics concept of 'nudge'?

SYNOPTIC LINK
Case study 7.5 illustrates how the insights of behavioural economics covered in Chapter 2 can be used to evaluate the effects of government economic policy.

The consequences of government policies which affect poverty and the distribution of income and wealth

We have made passing reference to some of these consequences in earlier sections of this chapter. Among the points we have made are:

● Redistributive policies can make the distributions of income and wealth more equal and reduce relative poverty. Many would argue that such policies are equitable. However, by reducing incentives to work hard and to be entrepreneurial, redistributive polices may have adverse unintended consequences, such as slower economic growth and loss of international competitiveness.
● Redistributive policies can alleviate child poverty, old-age poverty and fuel poverty, but these aims have been only partially achieved.
● Arguably, faster economic growth provides the main avenue for reducing absolute poverty, and perhaps also relative poverty, but according to pro-free-market economists, wider inequalities in the distributions of income and wealth may be necessary if fast growth is to be achieved and sustained.
● Some fiscal measures, used to try to reduce poverty and narrow inequalities in the distribution of income, have resulted in the development of the poverty and unemployment traps.

SECTION 7.3 SUMMARY

- In the past, governments have used progressive taxation and transfers to the poor as the main methods of making the distribution of post-tax income more equal.
- Fiscal drag occurs in a progressive income tax system when the government fails to raise tax thresholds (or personal tax allowances) to keep pace with inflation.
- Fiscal drag contributes to the existence of a poverty trap or earnings trap, and also to an unemployment trap.
- It is important to understand the difference, and also the relationship, between the poverty trap (or earnings trap) and the unemployment trap.
- The poverty trap affects people in employment on *low rates of pay*, rather than the unemployed who are *unwaged*.
- The unemployment trap contains unwaged social security claimants who choose unemployment.
- Government intervention to reduce poverty may lead to government failures that make matters worse.
- Pro-free-market economists focus on the disincentive effects of progressive taxation and transfers, whereas interventionist economists argue that the policies are necessary if post-tax income inequalities and poverty are to be reduced.

Questions

1 Describe how inequalities in the distribution of income and wealth have changed in recent years.

2 Evaluate the view that progressive taxation and transfers should not be used to reduce income inequalities and poverty.

3 Evaluate the view that the government should rely on market forces to determine the distribution of income and wealth in the UK, and should reduce direct intervention in the economy which has aimed at making the UK more equal.

4 Explain the difference between absolute and relative poverty.

5 Do you agree that faster economic growth which is needed to reduce poverty necessarily requires that the distribution of income becomes less equal? Justify your answer.

8

The market mechanism, market failure and government intervention in markets

Earlier chapters have explained how markets work. This chapter adds another dimension by introducing and explaining the four functions that prices perform in a market economy, or in the market sector of a mixed economy. It then explains how, when one or more of these four functions breaks down, market failure occurs.

The next sections look in some detail at the main forms of market failure: public goods, externalities, and merit and demerit goods. Externalities and merit and demerit goods are analysed with the help of the concepts of marginal private and external cost and benefit. The chapter also looks at environmental externalities, property rights and information failures associated with market failure. We then explain how income and wealth inequalities are a form of market failure.

In developed countries such as the UK, the existence of market failure leads to government intervention in the economy to make markets function better, and in some cases to replace the market with state provision of goods and services. The last parts of the chapter introduce some 'industrial policy' issues. These are government competition policy, public ownership versus the privatisation of industries and services, and the regulation and deregulation of markets.

LEARNING OBJECTIVES

These are to understand:

- the four functions that prices perform and how markets and prices affect resource allocation
- the meaning of market failure
- the difference between a private good and a public good
- the difference between a merit good and a demerit good
- how externalities lead to market failure
- the concepts of marginal private, external and social cost and benefit
- how these concepts are used to analyse externalities, and merit and demerit goods
- how to apply the concept of allocative efficiency to market failure
- a number of environmental market failures
- the importance of property rights in the public policy response to externalities
- merit and demerit goods in the context of information failures
- how monopoly may lead to market failure and resource misallocation
- how income and wealth inequalities lead to market failure
- the ways government intervention in the economy tries to correct market failure and why it may fail

8.1 How markets and prices allocate resources

The functions of prices

Earlier chapters have provided lots of information about the role of prices in a market economy or in the market sector of a mixed economy. So far, however, we have not drawn attention to the precise functions that prices perform. These are:

- the signalling function
- the incentive function
- the rationing function
- the allocative function

Prices signal information

Prices provide information that allows buyers and sellers in a market to plan and coordinate their economic activities. This is the **signalling function of prices**. Here is an example. Most Friday afternoons, a woman visits a local street market to buy fruit and vegetables for her family. She wants to buy both strawberries and raspberries. On reaching the market, she looks at the prices displayed by the market vendors on white tabs stuck into each tray of produce. The prices charged, which may not be the same at all the market stalls, provide vital information about what to buy.

Prices create incentives

The information signalled by *relative* prices, such as the price of strawberries relative to the price of raspberries, creates incentives for people to alter their economic behaviour. A higher price in a market creates incentives for producers to supply more of a good or service because they believe that larger profits can be made. As Figure 8.1 shows, the incentive function of a price rise is shown by an extension of supply along the market supply curve, S, depicted by a movement up the left-hand arrow in the diagram. Likewise, falling prices reduce profits and thence the incentive to supply the product. Either way, this is the **incentive function of prices** in operation. Similarly, in labour markets, rising wages create the incentive for people to acquire new skills and supply their labour services, while falling wages reduce these incentives.

The rationing function of prices

Figure 8.1 also illustrates the **rationing function of prices**. At price P_1, the price rises to get rid of the excess demand shown in the diagram. The rising price, reflecting the strength of consumer preferences and consumers' ability to pay, rations demand for the good. The rationing function of prices is depicted by the movement up the right-hand arrow in the diagram, which shows a contraction of demand along the demand curve D. Demand contracts until excess demand is eliminated. In a similar way, rising wages in a labour market ration firms' demand for labour.

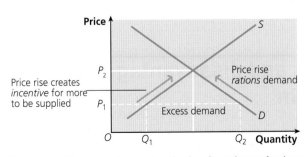

Figure 8.1 The incentive and rationing functions of prices

Prices and resource allocation

The rationing function of prices is related to, but not quite the same as, the **allocative function of prices**. The rationing function distributes scarce goods to those consumers who value them most highly. By contrast, the allocative function directs resources between markets, away from the markets in which prices are too high and in which there is excess supply, towards the markets where there is excess demand and price is too low.

How prices coordinate the decision making of buyers and sellers

If you refer back to Case study 5.1, you will see a brief reference to the *invisible hand of the market*, an idea first used by the great classical economist, Adam Smith. Smith believed that if markets are highly competitive, approximating to what is now called perfect competition, both firms and consumers will passively accept the market prices set by the interaction of supply and demand in the market as a whole.

In a pure market economy, prices and markets alone perform the central economic task of allocating scarce resources between competing uses, but markets are also important, and usually dominant, in mixed economies. In both these types of economies, prices coordinate the decision making of buyers and sellers through their responses to the incentive function of prices which we have described, and then on through the rationing and allocative functions of prices.

Producers use the most efficient methods of production available to them to cut costs in pursuit of their business objective of profit maximisation. Consumers buy from sellers who charge the lowest price. Firms also switch productive resources into markets that maximise their return. All this takes place automatically through the invisible hand of the market.

The advantages and disadvantages of the price mechanism

Advantages

Arguably, the operation of the price mechanism in competitive markets has the advantage of promoting consumer sovereignty, in the sense that the goods and services produced are those that consumers have voted for when spending the pounds in their pockets. When consumer sovereignty exists, 'the consumer is king' (or queen). Firms and industries that produce goods other than those for which consumers are prepared to pay, do not survive in highly competitive markets.

Providing it operates in this way, through cost reduction the price mechanism leads to a productively efficient allocation of resources.

And by redistributing resources into the production of goods and services that people wish to buy, the price mechanism achieves an allocatively efficient outcome.

Disadvantages

As the name suggests, imperfectly competitive markets are characterised by asymmetric market information and market power, both of which favour firms or producers rather than consumers. In extreme cases, as in monopoly, the operation of the price mechanism leads to an outcome in which firms exploit their producer sovereignty. The goods and services available for consumers to buy are determined by the firms rather than by consumer preferences expressed in the market place.

Even if producer sovereignty is not exercised on a 'take-it-or-leave-it' basis by a monopoly, the highly imperfectly competitive firms may still possess sufficient market power to manipulate consumer wants through such marketing devices as persuasive advertising. In these situations, the producer rather than the consumer is 'king'.

The price mechanism is 'value neutral' in that it has no regard for equality and the fairness or otherwise of the allocation of buying power between different income groups. And as we shall see in the next section, the unfettered operation of the price mechanism may lead to a number of significant market failures.

The case for and against extending the operation of the price mechanism into new areas of activity

Pro-free-market economists believe that markets and the price mechanism work well and that government intervention in the economy works badly. Many also take the view that because of the risk of government failure which produces an outcome worse than market failure, the price mechanism should be extended into parts of the economy previously dominated by state provision of goods and services and the operation of the command mechanism or planning mechanism.

However, other economists, whom we shall call interventionist economists, take the opposite view, believing that markets often perform badly and that government intervention and the planning mechanism can often improve on the free operation of the price mechanism. We shall go deeper into this debate in section 8.10 on government failure.

- Prices perform four functions in markets: signalling information, creating economic incentives, rationing scarce resources and allocating them between competing uses.
- Prices signal information that allows buyers and sellers in a market to plan and coordinate their economic activities.
- The information signalled by *relative* prices creates incentives for people to alter their economic behaviour.
- Rising prices ration demand for a product.
- Changing relative prices allocate scarce resources away from markets exhibiting excess supply, and into markets in which there is excess demand.
- Prices coordinate the decision making of buyers and sellers through their responses to the incentive function of prices, and then on through the rationing and allocative functions of prices.
- The operation of the price mechanism in competitive markets has the advantage of promoting consumer sovereignty.
- When consumer sovereignty exists, 'the consumer is king'. Firms and industries that produce goods other than those for which consumers are prepared to pay, do not survive in highly competitive markets.
- In imperfectly competitive markets and monopoly, the operation of the price mechanism leads to an outcome in which firms exploit their producer sovereignty. In these situations, 'the producer is king'.
- The price mechanism is 'value neutral' in that it has no regard for equality and the fairness or otherwise of the allocation of buying power between different income groups.

KEY TERMS

market failure when the market mechanism leads to a misallocation of resources in the economy, either completely failing to provide a good or service or providing the wrong quantity.

complete market failure a market fails to function at all and a 'missing market' results.

partial market failure a market does function, but it delivers the 'wrong' quantity of a good or service, which results in resource misallocation.

missing market a situation in which there is no market because the functions of prices have broken down.

8.2 The meaning of market failure

Market failure occurs whenever a market leads to a misallocation of resources. It occurs whenever the market mechanism or price mechanism performs badly or unsatisfactorily, or fails to perform at all. It is useful to distinguish between **complete market failure**, when the market simply does not exist, and **partial market failure**, when the market functions, but produces the 'wrong' quantity of a good or service. In the former case, there is a '**missing market**'. In the latter case, the good or service may be provided too cheaply, in which case it is over-produced and over-consumed. Alternatively, as in monopoly, the good may be too expensive, in which case under-production and under-consumption result.

Relating market failure to the functions of prices

In section 8.1, when explaining how the price mechanism distributes scarce resources between alternative uses in a market or mixed economy, we introduced the four functions that prices perform in such economies. To recap, these are: signalling information; creating incentives to influence people's behaviour; allocating scarce resources between competing uses; and rationing the demand for goods and services.

Ignoring the possibility that market failure can be associated with inequalities in the distribution of income, we can say that when all four of these functions perform well, markets also work well and market failure is either non-existent or trivial. However, when one or more of the four functions of prices significantly breaks down, market failure occurs. You will see in sections 8.3 and 8.4 how, in the case of pure public goods and externalities, the price mechanism breaks down completely. If an alternative method of provision does not exist, none of the public good is produced and there is complete market failure. In the case of an externality such as pollution, firms (and indeed consumers) that generate pollution simply dump it on other people (whom we call third parties). There is no market in which the unwilling consumers of pollution can charge producers for the discomfort they suffer. The lack of a market means there is no incentive for the polluter to pollute less. Hence, again, there is market failure.

TEST YOURSELF 8.1
Do you agree that a highly unequal distribution of income is a market failure? Justify your answer.

SECTION 8.2 SUMMARY

- Market failure occurs when the market mechanism leads to a misallocation of resources in the economy, either completely failing to provide a good or service or providing the wrong quantity.
- Complete market failure occurs when a market fails to function at all and a 'missing market' results.
- When all four of the functions of prices perform well, markets also work well and market failure is either non-existent or trivial.
- However, when one or more of the four functions of prices significantly breaks down, market failure occurs.

8.3 Private goods, public goods and quasi-public goods

Private goods

Most goods are **private goods**, which possess two defining characteristics.

KEY TERMS

private good a good, such as an orange, that is excludable and rival.

excludable good people who are unprepared to pay can be excluded from benefiting from the good.

rival good when one person consumes a private good, the quantity available to others diminishes.

- The owners can exercise private property rights, preventing other people from using the good or consuming its benefits. A pure private good is **excludable** — for example, a shopkeeper can prevent people from consuming the goods on display in her shop, unless they are prepared to pay for them. (Shoplifters, of course, try to get round this exercise of private property rights!)
- The second property of a pure private good is that it is **rival**. Rivalry can be illustrated in the context of a good such as chocolate. If you eat a bar of chocolate, other people cannot eat it and gain its benefits. In this sense, people are rivals. (Rivalry is sometimes called diminishability. When one person consumes a private good, such as a sweet or a banana, the quantity available to others diminishes.)

227

Public goods

A **public good** exhibits opposite characteristics to those of a private good, as it is non-excludable and non-rival. It is these characteristics that lead to market failure.

A lighthouse, or rather the beam of light provided by a lighthouse, is an example of a public good. Suppose an entrepreneur builds the lighthouse shown in Figure 8.2, and then tries to charge each ship that passes in the night and benefits from the beam of light. Providing ships pay up, the service can be provided commercially through the market.

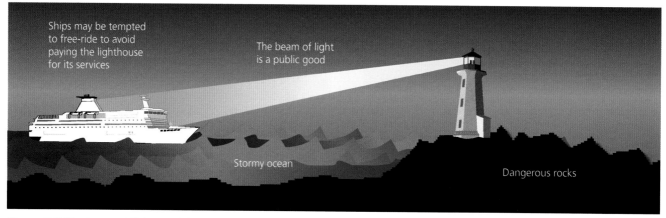

Ships may be tempted to free-ride to avoid paying the lighthouse for its services

The beam of light is a public good

Stormy ocean

Dangerous rocks

Figure 8.2 The beam of light provided by a lighthouse is a public good

However, the market is likely to fail. The appearance of one more ship near the lighthouse does not prevent other ships from sailing in the area. Non-rivalry thus occurs. It is also impossible to exclude free-riders (in this case, ships that benefit without paying). Because of non-excludability, it may be impossible to collect enough revenue to cover costs. If too many ships decide to 'free-ride', profits cannot be made and the incentive to provide the service through the market disappears. The market thus fails to provide a service for which there is an obvious need. There is then a need for alternative provision by the government in its public spending programme, or possibly by a charity (such as Trinity House in the UK).

Other examples of public goods

Other examples of public goods include national defence, police, street lighting, roads, and television and radio programmes. To take one of these, national defence is non-rival in the sense that receiving the benefits of national defence (for example, greater peace of mind) does not reduce the benefits available to other people. National defence is also non-excludable because providing the benefits for one means providing the benefits for all.

To explain this further, consider a situation in which the state does not provide national defence. Instead, the government lets individual citizens purchase in the market the defence or protection they want. But markets only provide defence when entrepreneurs can successfully charge prices for the services they supply. Suppose an aspiring citizen, who believes a fortune can be made in the defence industry, sets up a company, Nuclear Defence Services Ltd, with the aim of persuading the country's residents to purchase the services of nuclear missiles strategically located around the country. After estimating the money value of the defence received by each individual, Nuclear Defence

Services Ltd bills each household accordingly and waits for the payments to flow in…

But the payments may never arrive. As long as the service is provided, every household can benefit without paying. Nuclear Defence Services Ltd cannot provide nuclear defence only to the country's inhabitants who are prepared to pay, while excluding the benefit from those who are not prepared to pay. Withdrawing the benefit from one means withdrawing it from all. But all individuals face the temptation to consume without paying, or to free-ride. If enough people choose to free-ride, Nuclear Defence Services Ltd makes a loss. The incentive to provide the service through the market thus disappears. Assuming, of course, that the majority of the country's inhabitants believe nuclear defence to be necessary (that is, a good rather than a 'bad'), the market fails because it fails to provide a service for which there is a need. The result is a missing market.

TEST YOURSELF 8.3

Explain why D is the correct answer to the following question, and why A, B and C are incorrect.

When applied to a public good, 'non-rival' means that:

A there is a single monopoly supplier of the good

B the resources used in the good's production could not have been used to produce other goods

C if the good is provided for one person, it must be provided for everybody else

D consumption of the good by one person does not reduce the amount of the good available to others

---

EXTENSION MATERIAL

'Goods' and 'bads'

A good such as a loaf of bread provides benefits to the person or persons who consume it. Consumer goods yield usefulness or utility, and sometimes pleasure and satisfaction. (Using economic jargon, we say that the consumption of consumer goods increases economic welfare.)

In everyday language, we generally use the word 'bad' as an adjective: for example, a bad film or a bad football match. However, economists also use the word as a noun. In this usage, an economic 'bad' is the opposite of a good, yielding disutility, dissatisfaction or displeasure. For most people, consumption of a bad such as rotten meat reduces rather than increases economic welfare.

Likewise, a 'public bad' is the opposite of a public good. An example of a public bad is rubbish or garbage. The production of public bads such as garbage leads to a free-rider problem, though the problem is subtly different from the one that occurs in the case of public goods. People are generally prepared to pay for the removal of garbage, to avoid the unpleasantness otherwise experienced. However, payment can be avoided by dumping the bad in a public place or on someone else's property.

In the UK, local authorities generally empty household dustbins without charging for each bin emptied. Suppose this service is not provided, and private contractors remove rubbish and charge households £1 for each dustbin emptied. To avoid paying £1, some households may decide to dump their waste in the road or in neighbours' dustbins. (Builders' skips provide a good example of this practice. A household hiring a skip is well advised to fill the skip as quickly as possible, before the rest of the street takes advantage of the facility.) If too many households free-ride, it is impossible for the private contractor to make a profit, and a service for which there is a need is no longer provided. Hence the case for free local authority provision, financed through taxation.

CASE STUDY 8.1

The Seattle stomp

For several years some US local authorities have been charging households for emptying their dustbins, arguing that if rubbish disposal is free, people produce too much garbage. The obvious economic solution is to make households pay the cost of disposing of their waste. That will give them an incentive to throw out less and recycle more (assuming that local governments provide collection points for suitable materials). Several US cities have started charging households for generating rubbish. The common system is to sell tags which householders attach to rubbish bags or bins. In effect, the price of a tag is the price the household pays for creating another bag of rubbish.

In Charlottesville, Virginia, households were charged 80 cents for each tag they bought. Following the introduction of pricing, the number of garbage bags collected fell sharply, by 37% over the first five months. However, this was largely due to a practice nicknamed the 'Seattle stomp' — a frantic dance first noticed when Seattle introduced rubbish pricing. Rather than buy more tags, households simply crammed 40% more garbage into each bag. But this is inefficient as compacting or crushing is better done by machines at landfill sites than by households. The weight of rubbish collected at Charlottesville (a better indicator of disposal costs than volume) fell by a modest 14%, while in nearby cities with no pricing scheme, it fell by 3.5%.

More significantly, people resorted to illegal dumping or fly-tipping rather than paying to have their rubbish removed. Fly-tipping may have accounted for 30–40% of the reduction in collected rubbish. There was a 15% increase in the weight of materials recycled, suggesting that people chose to recycle free rather than pay to have their refuse carted away. But cities with garbage-pricing policies are likely to have 'greener' citizens who recycle more in any case. Once this effect is removed, it appears that pricing rubbish collection has no significant effect on recycling. Also, people throw out more rubbish in richer towns than in poorer ones. The rich not only have more trash to remove, but their time is too valuable to be spent recycling or dumping.

Follow-up questions

1 Why do most local councils in the UK empty household dustbins without charging a price for the service?
2 Evaluate the case for charging a price for emptying dustbins.
3 What is meant by fly-tipping?
4 What policies might a behavioural economist recommend to reduce fly-tipping?

Quasi-public goods

KEY TERM

quasi-public good a good which is not fully non-rival and/or where it is possible to exclude people from consuming the product.

TEST YOURSELF 8.4

Using an example, explain the difference between a pure public good and a quasi-public good.

Public goods can be divided into pure public goods and **quasi-public goods**. National defence and police are examples of pure public goods — defined as public goods for which it is impossible to exclude free-riders. However, most public goods (street lighting, roads, television and radio programmes, and also lighthouses) are really quasi-public goods (also known as non-pure public goods).

Methods can be devised for converting the goods into private goods by excluding free-riders (for example, electronic pricing of road use). Quasi-public goods can be provided by markets, but the second property of non-rivalry or non-diminishability means there is a case for providing all public goods free in order to encourage as much consumption as possible. Provided we assume the lack of a capacity restraint, for public goods and quasi-public goods, the optimal level of consumption occurs when they are available free of charge. (However, capacity constraints, resulting from factors such as the limited ability of roads to carry cars and the limited bandwidth of airwaves, means that there is also a case for charging for public goods such as roads and airwaves to deal with the problem of congestion.)

The significance of technological change

Roads provide one of the best examples of a good which has changed over the years from being regarded as a pure public good to now being thought of as a quasi-public good. Until quite recently, except in the case of motorways where limited points of access meant that toll gates could be installed, it was deemed impractical to charge motorists for the use of ordinary roads.

This has now changed. Technological change makes it feasible for the government or local authorities to use electronic pricing to charge *all* motorists for road use. The charges can also be varied at different times of day to create incentives for car drivers to shift their travel patterns from rush hour to non-rush hour. There is a case for *not* charging a price when roads are uncongested and thus largely non-rival, but for charging for road use as soon as the problem of congestion and road rivalry occurs. So why are there so few road pricing schemes? After all, we are happy to pay for most goods and to pay different prices at different times of day: for example, for watching a movie at a cinema. The answer to this question probably lies in the political power of the motoring lobby. Politicians fear they will not get re-elected if they try to bring in road pricing schemes.

> **SYNOPTIC LINK**
> You can read more about technical change and technical progress in section 4.8 of Chapter 4.

CASE STUDY 8.2

Sixteen years of the London congestion charge

In February 2019, the London congestion charge was 16 years old. At the time of its introduction, many economists believed that the congestion charge marked the triumph of economic common sense over narrow self-interest. Economists confidently believed that many other cities, both in the UK and abroad, would rush to adopt London-style road pricing. In the event, this did not happen. In November 2008, Manchester voters were asked to approve the introduction of a city-centre congestion charge and they voted against it.

What have been the possible benefits and costs of the London congestion charge? In 2003 the idea of charging car users to drive around the capital was met with near-apocalyptic warnings from motoring groups and newspapers such as the *Daily Mail*. The charge would 'destroy' the city's commercial heart and cause 'total gridlock', warned some. It would 'cause misery to thousands of commuters across the capital', said Conservative Greater London Authority's transport spokesman. 'Londoners will suffer conditions worse than cattle trucks on their morning commute into work,' she added.

Since it was introduced in 2003, however, the charge, which has risen from £5 through £8 to its present level of £11.50, has not caused gridlock. Rather, it has resulted in a slight reduction in traffic levels. But while car numbers are down, the number of private hire vehicles — minicabs and Ubers — is up. Trips by taxi and private hire vehicles as the main mode of the journey increased by 9.8% between 2015 and 2016 alone — and 29.2% since 2000. Today, more than 18,000 different private hire vehicles enter the congestion charging zone each day, with peaks on Friday and Saturday nights. This has reduced the speed of traffic through the city centre, which in turn has affected the bus network.

Follow-up questions

1 Why have other cities, in Britain and the rest of the world, not rushed to follow London's example and introduce a congestion charge?
2 What policies have cities in other countries introduced to try to reduce road congestion?
3 Do you agree that road use should be priced? Justify your answer.
4 It has been said that the real aim of the London congestion charge is to reduce air pollution rather than traffic congestion: for example, by giving exemption to electrically powered cars. Do you think these two objectives are compatible? Justify your reasoning.

SECTION 8.3 SUMMARY

- A private good is a good or service, such as an apple, that is excludable and rival.
- Excludability occurs when people who are unprepared to pay can be excluded from benefiting from a good or service.
- Rivalry occurs when one person consumes a private good or service and the quantity available to others diminishes.
- A public good is a good or service, such as a radio programme, that is non-excludable and non-rival.
- Examples of public goods include national defence, police, street lighting, roads, and terrestrial television and radio programmes.
- Public goods can be divided into pure public goods and quasi-public goods.
- Roads provide an example of a good which has changed over the years from being regarded as a pure public good to now being thought of as a quasi-public good.
- For public goods and quasi-public goods, the optimal level of consumption occurs when they are available free of charge — providing there is no capacity constraint.

8.4 Positive and negative externalities in production and consumption

What are externalities?

Externalities exist when there is a divergence between private and social costs and benefits. Essentially, an **externality** is a special type of public good or public 'bad' which is 'dumped' by those who produce it onto other people (third parties) who receive or consume it, whether or not they choose to. The key feature of an externality is that there is no market in which it can be bought or sold — externalities are produced and received outside the market, providing another example of a missing market.

Positive and negative externalities

The provider of an external *benefit* (or **positive externality**), such as a beautiful view, cannot charge a market price to any willing free-riders who enjoy it, while conversely, the unwilling free-riders who receive or consume external *costs* (or **negative externalities**), such as pollution and noise, cannot charge a price to the polluter for the bad they reluctantly consume.

Externalities and property rights

A **property right** is the exclusive authority to determine how a resource is used, whether that resource is owned by government or by individuals. The owner of a house, for example, has the right to live in the house, to let others such as the members of their family live in the house without paying rent, to rent the property to a tenant, or to sell the house to a new owner. In modern capitalist economies, the legal system gives house owners the power to exercise private property rights in one or other of these ways.

However, when externalities are generated, the right to exercise private property rights can disappear. For example, the owner of a beautiful house

> **KEY TERM**
> **externality** a public good, in the case of an external benefit, or a public bad, in the case of an external cost, that is 'dumped' on third parties outside the market.

> **KEY TERMS**
> **positive externality** an external benefit that occurs when the consumption or production of a good causes a benefit to a third party, where the social benefit is greater than the private benefit.
>
> **negative externality** an external cost that occurs when the consumption or production of a good causes costs to a third party, where the social cost is greater than the private cost.
>
> **property right** the exclusive authority to determine how a resource is used.

which is visible from the public highway cannot prevent passers-by from enjoying the positive externality of the view of the house. The owner might be able to build a high wall to obstruct this view, or even to destroy the house, but in most situations, passers-by can free-ride: in other words, enjoy the benefits without paying.

The free-rider problem

Earlier, we briefly mentioned the **free-rider problem** in the extension material on 'goods' and 'bads'. We have seen that the owner of a pure public good cannot exclude people who are unprepared to pay from gaining the benefits of the good. These people can free-ride, gaining the benefits without paying, Likewise, the provider of an external *benefit* (or positive externality), such as a beautiful view, cannot charge a market price to any willing free-riders who enjoy it, while conversely, the unwilling free-riders who receive or consume external *costs* (or negative externalities), such as pollution and noise, cannot charge a price to the polluter for the bad they reluctantly consume. With both public goods and externalities, the free-rider problem is a cause of market failure.

The free-rider problem occurs when non-excludability leads to a situation in which not enough customers choose to pay for a good, preferring instead to free-ride, with the result that the incentive to provide the good through the market disappears and a missing market may result.

Externalities can be generated by firms in the course of producing the goods they eventually sell in a market, or they can be generated by households and individuals when they consume goods. The former are known as *production* externalities, while the latter are *consumption* externalities. We shall look at these in turn.

Production externalities

Negative production externalities

Consider the power station illustrated in Figure 8.3, which discharges pollution into the atmosphere in the course of producing electricity. We can view a negative **production externality** (or external cost) such as pollution as being that part of the true or real costs of production which the power station evades by dumping the bad on others: for example, the people living in the houses and the businesses in the commercial forestry industry. The price that the consumer pays for the good (electricity) reflects only the money costs of production, and not all the real costs, which include the external costs (including the eyesore or visual pollution also shown in the diagram). In a market situation, the power station's output of electricity is thus under-priced. The allocative function of prices has once again broken down — under-pricing encourages too much consumption of electricity, and therefore over-production of both electricity and the spin-off, pollution.

> **KEY TERM**
> **free-rider problem** a free rider is someone who benefits without paying as a result of non-excludability. Customers may choose not to pay for a good, preferring instead to free ride, with the result that the incentive to provide the good through the market disappears.

> **STUDY TIP**
> Make sure you understand the difference between negative and positive externalities, and between production and consumption externalities, and can give examples of all of these.

> **KEY TERM**
> **production externality** an externality (which may be positive or negative) generated in the course of producing a good or service.

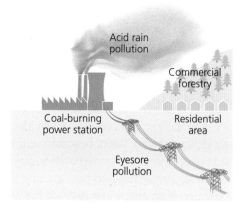

Figure 8.3 The discharge of negative production externalities by a power station

Positive production externalities

Figure 8.4 shows again the power station previously illustrated in Figure 8.3, but in this case the production of electricity yields positive production externalities (or external benefits) rather than negative externalities. We have assumed that the power station discharges warm (but clean) water into the lake adjacent to the power station. Warmer temperatures increase fish stocks,

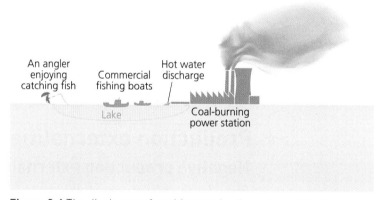

Figure 8.4 The discharge of positive production externalities by a power station

and commercial fishing boats and private anglers then benefit. Unless it owns the lake, the power station company cannot charge the fishermen for the benefits they are receiving. (You might, of course, query our assumption that the water discharge creates positive rather than negative externalities. In all likelihood, disruption of a local ecosystem might cause negative externalities, such as algae pollution.)

Consumption externalities

Negative consumption externalities

We are all probably familiar with the annoying experience of going to the cinema and having our pleasure disrupted by the ringing of mobile phones or the noisy eating of popcorn by the person sitting a few seats away. These are examples of negative **consumption externalities**, unwillingly received by a cinema goer as a result of consumption activities undertaken by other members of the audience. There are many examples of similarly

KEY TERM

consumption externality an externality (which may be positive or negative) generated in the course of consuming a good or service.

annoying externalities — walking through litter and chewing gum dropped by pedestrians, being splashed by inconsiderate motorists, and reluctantly listening to 'head-banger' music discharged through open windows by 'boy racers' as they drive their souped-up BMWs too close to us on the pavement.

Positive consumption externalities

A good example of a positive consumption externality is the pleasure gained by a passer-by walking past beautiful buildings and household gardens in a residential area. At this point, it is also worth noting that a negative consumption externality suffered by one person may be a positive consumption externality for somebody else.

Consider also a situation when a person pays to watch a Premier League football match. The football fan would gain less pleasure from watching the match if the stadium were empty than if soaking up the 'atmosphere' generated by other chanting fans in a packed stadium. Much the same happens in restaurants. Prospective diners walk past empty or nearly empty restaurants, preferring instead to queue for a table at an already full eatery. Maybe they think the food is better, but despite having to wait longer for their food, what they also enjoy is the 'atmosphere' generated by other diners.

Summary: different types of externality

As we have explained, externalities divide into negative externalities and positive externalities (which are also known as external costs and benefits). Table 8.1 lists the possible types of externality and gives examples of negative externalities (costs) and positive externalities (benefits) for each.

Table 8.1 Examples of the different types of externality

Type of externality	Negative externalities	Positive externalities
Pure production externalities *(generated and received in production)*	Acid rain pollution discharged by a power station which harms a nearby commercially run forest	A farmer benefiting from drainage undertaken by a neighbouring farmer
Pure consumption externalities *(generated and received in consumption)*	Noisy music at a party disturbing neighbouring households	Households benefiting from the beauty of neighbouring gardens

How externalities lead to the 'wrong' quantity of a good being produced and consumed

We mentioned earlier that when negative externalities are generated in the course of production, part of the true or real costs of production are not borne by the producer, instead being dumped on others. This means that, even in competitive markets, if *negative production* externalities are generated, goods end up being too cheap or under-priced. The market has created the wrong incentives. Because prices under-reflect the true costs of production, which include the cost of the negative externalities, too much of the good ends up being produced and consumed.

The opposite happens when firms generate *positive production* externalities. Prices end up being too high, leading to the 'wrong' quantity of the good being produced and consumed. Once again, the market has created the wrong incentives, which discourages consumption. In this case, prices over-reflect the true costs of production. Not enough of the good ends up being produced and consumed.

In much the same way, when *negative* and *positive consumption* externalities are generated, markets are distorted and the wrong quantity of a good is produced and consumed. This is explained in section 8.5 on merit and demerit goods.

EXTENSION MATERIAL

Establishing markets for trading private property rights

In 1960, Professor Ronald Coase argued that if markets can be created for private property rights, government intervention to correct market failures may not be necessary. Coase used the example of wood-burning locomotives, which in nineteenth-century America frequently set fire to farmers' fields. If farmers possess the property right to prevent crops being destroyed, they can sell the right to the railway companies. By contrast, if the railway companies possess the property right to emit sparks, farmers could pay the companies to reduce emissions.

Coase argued that in both cases the outcome might be the same. If farmers have a right to stop the sparks, but emitting sparks is worth more to the railway than stopping the sparks is worth to the farmers, the railway will buy the right to emit sparks from the farmers, and the damage continues. But if the railway companies have the right to emit sparks, and this right is worth more to them than to the farmers, the right will not be sold, and the damage again continues. In this example, initial ownership of property rights has no effect on the amount of resources devoted to suppressing sparks. The ability to trade property rights ensures the same outcome in either case.

This theory, which is known as the Coase theorem, has greatly influenced the free-market approach to market failures. Indeed, most economists now accept that governments should try to work *with the market* rather than *against the market* through regulation.

The tragedy of the commons

Critics of the private ownership of property rights do not generally want to abolish those rights. Instead, they wish to transfer property rights from private ownership to government ownership. However, the worst-case scenario is when private property rights are abolished and replaced by 'common ownership', but without any form of government control that aims to achieve the 'common good'.

In 1968, in an article titled 'The tragedy of the commons', Garrett Hardin told the following story (we have adapted Hardin's story into our own words):

> In Britain before the eighteenth century, much farmland was open common land on which farmers could graze as many animals as they wished, for free.
>
> As long as poaching and disease keep the numbers of animals below the carrying capacity of the land, common land grazing works well. However, it was in a herdsman's self-interest to graze more and more animals, since his gain, the money earned from selling slaughtered additional animals, would exceed any loss incurred from the gradual deterioration of the common. The herdsman would receive all the proceeds from the sale of an

Garrett Hardin

additional animal, but the effects of over-grazing would be shared by all the herdsmen.

A rational herdsman would therefore conclude that the only sensible course for him to pursue was to add another animal to his herd. But each herdsman would then be locked into a system that compelled him to increase his herd without limit — in a world that is limited. Another animal would be added to the grazing land, and then another, and then another... But this would be the conclusion reached by each and every rational herdsman sharing the common. Therein is the tragedy. Freedom of the commons brings ruin to all.

A few years later in 1974, Hardin used the following example to illustrate the tragedy of the commons. Satellite photos of northern Africa showed an irregular dark patch over an area of 390 square miles. Ground-level investigation revealed a fenced area inside of which there was plenty of grass. Outside, the ground cover had been devastated. Hardin argued that the explanation was simple. The fenced area was private property, subdivided into sections. Each year, the owners moved their animals to a new section. Fallow periods of four years gave the pastures time to recover from the grazing. The owners did this because they had an incentive to take care of their land. But no one owned the now barren land outside the fenced-off area. This land being open to nomads and their herds, the tragedy of the commons was taking its toll.

> **SYNOPTIC LINK**
> Refer back to the section on 'Externalities and property rights' on page 232.

CASE STUDY 8.3

Has the fishing industry fallen victim to the tragedy of the commons?

Nearly 50 years ago, environmentalists sounded the first warnings about the Earth's natural resources running out. Some of the fears then voiced, it was later shown, were groundless. For some resources such as oil, the market mechanism has encouraged consumers to economise and producers to search for and to develop new sources of supply.

But with fish it may be different. Unless stocks are managed tightly by all concerned with fishing, they may well collapse, and soon another 'tragedy of the commons' will have been played out. It happens because people think they can take a limitless amount of the Earth's 'free gifts', such as the atmosphere or the sea, or now, we are realising, fish.

For centuries these apparently free goods had no prices attached to them and so there was nothing to impose restraint on their use. And for centuries, nothing harmful happened, such is the seemingly limitless bounty of the Earth. But on a finite globe, the limits logically have to be reached at some stage. A fish stock can make what is known as an 'equilibrium shift'; it can change under pressure to a new level of stable numbers much lower than they were before. Intensive fishing pressure may take out many of the bigger fish so that breeding slows down in a cumulative process, until virtually no new 'recruits' to the breeding stock are coming through.

In the early 2000s it was widely argued that the decline in the North Sea might be irreversible if very stringent measures were not taken. A further problem then detected was the possible advent of global warming: as the sea waters warm, cod seem to be moving further north to cooler waters where they prefer to spawn. But at the time, there was little doubt that fishing pressure was the main threat.

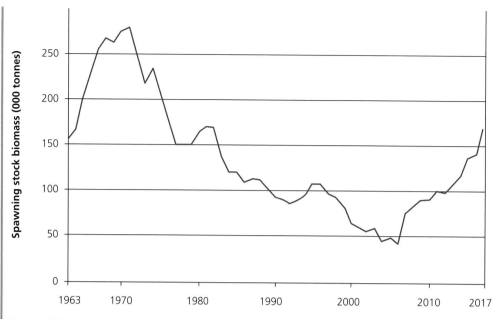

Figure 8.5 North Sea cod stocks, 1963–2017

However, as Figure 8.5 shows, these fears may be ungrounded — at least in the North Sea. The graph shows that, although the spawning stock biomass (SSB) of North Sea cod (the fish stock population capable of reproducing) had fallen dramatically from around 1970 until 2006, since then the SSB has recovered and by 2017 it had reached its highest level for 35 years.

Follow-up questions

1 Do you agree that the depletion of North Sea cod stocks prior to 2006 was an example of the tragedy of the commons?
2 Find out whether stocks of North Sea cod have continued to recover up to the time you have read this case study.
3 State two other environmental resources which might be suffering a tragedy of the commons.
4 Research whether the recovery of North Sea cod stocks should be regarded as a success for the European Union's Common Fisheries Policy.

Environmental market failures

Some of the market failures we have discussed result from the discharge of negative externalities into the environment. Such environmental externalities often involve pollution of land, sea, rivers and air, and the externalities associated with road use and congestion. We have described how coal-burning power stations discharge sulphur dioxide pollution into the atmosphere, and also the 'eyesore' pollution caused by unsightly buildings and electricity transmission lines. Later in the chapter we shall explain how governments can attempt to correct such market failures through taxation, regulation including outright bans, or a combination of these approaches. Governments are also increasingly making use of behavioural 'nudges' to reduce environmental market failures such as those caused by the dumping of plastic into rivers and oceans. The A-level specification also emphasises that exam candidates should appreciate the relevance of the 'tragedy of the commons' for environmental market failures.

The Green Deal

Between 2010 and 2013 the Behavioural Insights Team (BIT) worked with the Department of Energy and Climate Change (DECC) and the Department for Communities and Local Government (DCLG) to launch the government's flagship environmental policy: the Green Deal.

For years governments have offered subsidies on green products such as energy-saving light bulbs and loft installation. Traditional economic policies, which create incentives by reducing the price of products, have had limited success. The Behavioural Insights Team has used its understanding of the behavioural factors that determine household decision making to develop policies that encourage energy-saving behaviour among households and firms.

Choosing small rewards today rather than large rewards in the future

It is reasonable to assume that households will invest in energy-saving measures in their homes that reduce heating costs. New boilers, floor, wall and loft installation, double or triple glazing, energy-efficient external doors and other improvements insulate buildings so that they retain heat and bring down energy bills. However, many households decide against undertaking such spending because they are unwilling to pay large upfront costs today for benefits which will arrive in small instalments spread over many years. When left to themselves without any policy 'nudges' that might change their way of thinking, households prefer small rewards *today* rather than much larger rewards *in the future*.

The Green Deal was designed to change household behaviour. It did this by helping households pay for the upfront costs of investing in energy-efficiency measures. Private sector companies, charities and local authorities paid for the upfront cost of energy-efficiency products and installation. Households then paid back these costs through their electricity bills. However, the repayment costs were not as high as they otherwise might have been because the households were benefiting from the energy-saving investments that reduced their electricity bills. The Green Deal rested on the assumption that, over the years ahead, household energy bills, which include the repayment costs, would not be higher than would have been the case if no energy-saving measures had been undertaken. In the long run, when the loan had been paid off, households would experience significantly lower energy bills and gain all the benefit.

The behavioural economic insight is that by deferring the cost of energy-saving measures, the government could encourage individuals to invest in products that improve the efficiency of the nation's housing stock and reduce carbon emissions.

Evaluating the Green Deal

In 2015, the newly elected Conservative government ended the Green Deal. Demand for the Green Deal had been exceptionally high. When the Green Deal Home Improvement Fund (GDHIF) was launched in June 2014, it spent its entire year's £120 million budget within 6 weeks. The GDHIF provided 20,000 households with vouchers to pay for energy-saving improvements on their homes. In December 2014 the DECC released a further £24 million which was taken up within 24 hours.

Consumer groups generally supported the Green Deal but they raised three main criticisms. First, a *Which?* magazine investigation found that the quality of the assessments conducted by Green Deal assessors varied widely. Some assessors produced good assessments of the energy-saving measures required in a property, but others failed to identify problems correctly and produced flawed reports. This was a systems failure that is likely to occur in any policy programme introduced by either public- or private-sector organisations.

Second, households who signed up for the Green Deal might eventually have to pay higher energy bills once the repayment costs had been added in.

Third, the Green Deal was extremely complex and charged a rate of interest of up to 10.8% APR. Households might have done better by paying for home improvements upfront themselves, or through personal loans.

The end of the Green Deal

As mentioned, in July 2015 the newly elected Conservative government announced the end of the Green Deal, which had been introduced with great fanfare by the previous Coalition government. The Department for Energy and Climate Change said it had decided to end the Green Deal in order to protect taxpayers, citing low take-up and concerns about industry standards. The opposition Labour Party argued that government policy to improve energy efficiency had been a 'failure'. Roger Harrabin, the BBC environment analyst, said:

> The decision has caused anger — not because anyone really likes the Green Deal, but because it is being scrapped without a replacement in sight. The home insulation industry says it will create huge uncertainty for firms while the government works out what the replacement policy should be. There is no doubting the need for a scheme to finance improvements in home energy. The UK has some of the worst-insulated housing stock in Europe, and saving energy is by far the cheapest way of the UK cutting carbon emissions and bringing people out of fuel poverty. The government is accused of lacking ambition in this area: last parliament it prompted the insulation of 5 million homes. This parliament it aims to improve just 1 million.

However, in 2017 the Green Deal was relaunched — but this time provided by the private sector through a new Green Deal Finance Company.

Follow-up questions

1 Explain why 'traditional economic policies', which create incentives by reducing the price of products, have had limited success.
2 Research what has happened to government energy policy in the UK since the announcement to scrap the Green Deal.
3 Find out how successful the relaunched Green Deal has been.
4 Describe **one** other way in which households can be encouraged to conserve energy within their homes.

Case study 8.4 on the Green Deal describes a recent, but partially aborted, government approach to a possible environmental market failure. Contrast this with Case study 8.5, which describes a much older market failure that occurred over half a century ago in London.

CASE STUDY 8.5

The great smog of 1952

Smog is a mixture of smoke and other pollutants, and of fog. Smog occurs when climatic conditions trap air above cities and industrial areas, which prevents the dirty air from dispersing. It was the Clean Air Act of 1956 which cleared most of the smoke out of our city air. It is not surprising the Clean Air Act was passed, because the London smog of 1952 was the most deadly weather-related catastrophe in Britain for some 150 years. Figure 8.6 shows the amount of smoke emitted and the number of deaths in London between 1 and 15 December 1952.

Nevertheless, while sulphur dioxide pollution has decreased, at least in the lower atmosphere, and soot has largely disappeared, other less visible, but still toxic, chemicals are being emitted, particularly by motor vehicles which are powered by petrol and diesel fuel. Arguably, the most damaging pollutant is nitrous oxide, which is emitted unseen into the atmosphere by human activities such as agriculture, fossil fuel combustion, wastewater management and industrial processes. Nitrous oxide molecules stay in the atmosphere for an average of 120 years before disintegrating. The impact of one pound of nitrous oxide on warming the atmosphere is over 300 times that of one pound of carbon dioxide.

There have been many other examples of serious air pollution in recent years. Rapid industrialisation and automobile ownership have led to serious smog problems in cities in China and India. In September 2015, the Volkswagen emissions scandal, so-called 'dieselgate', began. A US regulator found that Volkswagen had intentionally programmed diesel engines to activate their emissions controls only during laboratory emissions testing, but with up to 40 times more pollution being emitted in real-world driving conditions.

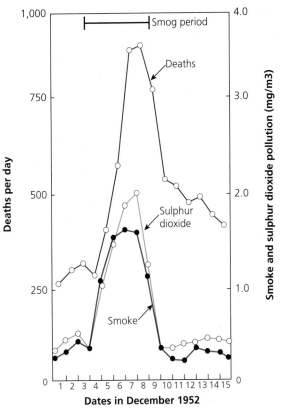

Figure 8.6 The effect of the London smog in 1952

Follow-up questions

1 Analyse **two** ways in which a government can intervene to bring about cleaner air.
2 In recent years, many UK families have installed wood-burning stoves in their houses. Use the internet to find out whether the use of these stoves is causing atmospheric pollution in UK towns and cities.
3 Motor vehicle emissions break clean-air laws in the streets of many British cities. Should all vehicles be banned from currently polluted streets? Justify your answer.
4 Find out what punishments have been levied on the Volkswagen car group in the USA and in other countries.

The concepts of marginal private, external and social costs and benefits

To explain the nature of externalities in greater depth, we need to apply the marginal analysis we used in the context of utility theory in Chapter 2 and in the explanation of marginal returns, cost and revenue in Chapter 4.

At the heart of microeconomic theory lies the assumption that, in a market situation, an economic agent considers only the private costs and benefits resulting from its market actions, ignoring any costs and benefits imposed on others. For the agent, private benefit maximisation occurs when:

marginal private benefit (MPB) = marginal private cost (MPC)

However, social benefit maximisation, which maximises the public interest or the welfare of the whole community, occurs when:

marginal social benefit (MSB) = marginal social cost (MSC)

Orthodox or traditional economic theory usually assumes that households and firms seek to maximise their private benefit or self-interest, net of costs, and not the wider social interest of the whole community. They ignore the effects of their actions on other people. However, when externalities are generated, costs and benefits are inevitably imposed on others, so maximising net private benefit no longer coincides with the maximisation of net social benefit.

Social benefit is defined as private benefit plus external benefit. As a result:

marginal social benefit = marginal private benefit + marginal external benefit

($MSB = MPB + MEB$)

Likewise, social cost is defined as private cost plus external cost, which means that:

marginal social cost = marginal private cost + marginal external cost

($MSC = MPC + MEC$)

SYNOPTIC LINK
Refer back to Chapters 2 and 4 which first introduced the way marginal analysis is used in economic theory.

QUANTITATIVE SKILLS 8.1

Worked example: calculating social costs and benefits
Table 8.2 shows the costs and benefits of building a new shopping mall.

Table 8.2 Costs and benefits of building a shopping mall

Private costs	£10 million
External costs	£20 million
Private benefits	£8 million
External benefits	£25 million

Calculate the social costs and the social benefits and then decide whether building the shopping mall is worthwhile, first for society, and second for the property developer.

Social cost is calculated as follows:

social cost = private cost + external cost

and likewise social benefit is calculated as:

social benefit = private benefit + external benefit

Social cost is therefore £30 million, while social benefit is £33 million. Since the social benefit exceeds the social cost by £3 million, the shopping mall is worthwhile for society at large. However, it is not worthwhile for the property developer, whose private costs exceed private benefits by £2 million.

TEST YOURSELF 8.5
Explain why B is the correct answer to the following question, and why A, C and D are incorrect.

Which one of the following creates an incentive for firms to reduce pollution?

A An increase in negative externalities when firms increase their output

B A tax levied on polluting firms

C Subsidies paid to firms that increase their levels of production

D The removal of regulations imposed on polluting firms

Using marginal analysis to show how negative production externalities cause market failure

We shall now return to the example of pollution emitted by a fossil-fuel burning power station. We initially assumed that when a coal-burning power station generates electricity, only negative externalities are discharged and there are no positive externalities. Given this simplification, the marginal private benefit accruing to the power station from the production of electricity, and the marginal social benefit received by the whole community, are the same and shown by the downward-sloping curve in Figure 8.7. But, because pollution is discharged in the course of production, the marginal social cost of electricity production exceeds the marginal private cost incurred by the power station. In the diagram, the MSC curve is positioned above the MPC curve. The vertical distance between two curves shows the marginal external cost (MEC) at each level of electricity production.

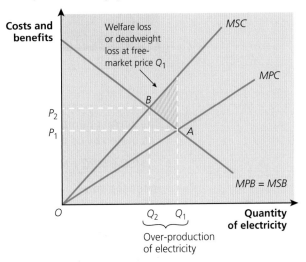

Figure 8.7 A coal-burning power station generating pollution (a negative production externality)

The power station maximises private benefit by producing output Q_1, where $MPC = MPB$. Q_1 is immediately below point A in Figure 8.7. However, the socially optimal level of output is Q_2, where $MSC = MSB$. Q_2 is immediately below point B in Figure 8.6. The privately optimal level of output is thus greater than the socially optimal level of production. To put it another way, market forces over-produce electricity by the amount $Q_1 - Q_2$. The market fails because the power station produces the wrong quantity of the good: namely, too much electricity. At the free-market price of P_1, electricity is too cheap. The price would have to rise to P_2 to bring about the socially optimal level of consumption.

The shaded area in Figure 8.7 illustrates the 'loss' of welfare or deadweight loss (DWL), which exists at the free-market output, Q_1 (where $MPC = MPB$), all the way back to the socially optimum output, Q_2. This is because for units Q_2 to Q_1, the social cost of producing each unit of electricity is greater than the benefit society derives from each unit produced — that is, $MSC > MSB$. Society would be better off if these units, Q_2 to Q_1, were not produced and the resources were transferred to the production of other products. When production takes place at the socially optimal output (where $MSB = MSC$), the DWL is eliminated.

243

QUANTITATIVE SKILLS 8.2

Worked example: calculating private, social and external costs

Table 8.3 shows the costs incurred when producing different quantities of a chemical. Some of the cells in the table are blank.

Table 8.3 Costs incurred in chemical production

Output of chemicals (tonnes per week)	Marginal private cost (£000)	Marginal social cost (£000)	Marginal external costs (£000)
500	100		20
600		160	30
700	160	200	

Copy the table and insert the correct numbers in the blank spaces.

The completed version is shown in Table 8.4.

Table 8.4 Costs incurred in chemical production: completed version

Output of chemicals (tonnes per week)	Marginal private cost (£000)	Marginal social cost (£000)	Marginal external costs (£000)
500	100	**120**	20
600	**130**	160	30
700	160	200	**40**

The correct numbers to insert in the three blank spaces should be calculated by using the following equation:

$$MSC = MPC + MEC$$

In the top row: **£120,000** = £100,000 + £20,000

In the middle row: £160,000 = **£130,000** + £30,000

In the bottom row: £200,000 = £160,000 + **£40,000**

(Note: remember to include the thousands and the £ sign in your answers.)

Using marginal analysis to show how positive production externalities cause market failure

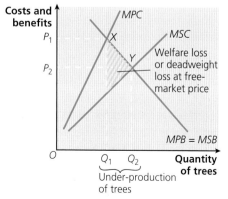

Figure 8.8 A commercial forestry company generating positive production externalities

Whereas *negative* production externalities (illustrated in Figure 8.7) lead to the marginal social costs of production exceeding marginal private costs of production, when *positive* production externalities are generated, the marginal social costs of production lie *below* the marginal private costs incurred by the producers of the good or service. This is illustrated in Figure 8.8, which shows the costs incurred when a commercial forestry company plants trees.

The positive production externalities generated by tree planting include improved water retention in the soil and a carbon sink effect, whereby trees absorb greenhouse or global-warming gases from the atmosphere. As stated, positive production externalities such as these mean that the *MSC* curve is positioned below the *MPC* curve. The vertical distance between the two curves shows a *negative* marginal external cost (MEC) at each level of tree planting. (A *negative* marginal *external cost* is exactly the same as a *positive* marginal *external benefit* enjoyed by society as a whole.)

The shaded area in Figure 8.8 illustrates the 'loss' of welfare or deadweight loss (DWL), which exists at the free-market output, Q_1 at point X (where MPC = MPB), all the way forward to the socially optimum output, Q_2. When production takes place at the socially optimal output (where MSB = MSC) at point Y, the DWL is eliminated. This is sometimes referred to as a 'welfare gain'. There is a net gain in social welfare if the trees between Q_1 and Q_2 are planted because the MSB is greater than the MSC for each of these trees up to the point at which MSB = MSC.

In order to maximise its private benefit, the commercial forestry plants Q_1 trees. (This is the free-market level of output.) Q_1 is immediately below point X, where MPC = MPB. However, Q_1 is less than the socially optimal level of output Q_2, located below point Y, where MSC = MSB. Figure 8.8 illustrates the fact that, when positive production externalities are generated, the market fails because too little of the good is produced and consumed. Under-production and under-consumption are depicted by the distance $Q_2 - Q_1$.

> **STUDY TIP**
> Note that in Figure 8.8 the 'spillover' benefits generated by production (positive external benefits) are depicted as a 'negative external cost'. The planting of trees reduces the costs imposed on society by pollution and hence the total cost to society of planting the trees is less than the cost to the firm.

QUANTITATIVE SKILLS 8.3

Worked example: marginal costs and the benefits of vaccination

Table 8.5 shows some of the costs a consumer incurs and the benefits received by her family and also by society when her young child receives a measles vaccination.

Table 8.5 Costs and benefits of a vaccination

Marginal private cost of the vaccination (£)	Marginal private benefit resulting from the vaccination (£)	Marginal social benefit resulting from the vaccination (£)
20	100	1,000

(a) **What is the marginal external benefit resulting from the vaccination?**
Using the equation MSB = MPB + MEB, the marginal external benefit received by society from the vaccination of a child is £900.

(b) **Suppose evidence shows that a fraction of children who are vaccinated suffer brain damage as a result of receiving the treatment. This creates a marginal social cost for society of £1,200 per vaccination. On the basis of these figures, should the health service recommend that children be vaccinated?**
Given the extra information, the marginal social cost of each vaccination exceeds the marginal social benefit by £200. Marginal social benefit is £1,000, but marginal social cost is £1,200. On the basis of these figures alone, the health service should not recommend that children are vaccinated.

CASE STUDY 8.6

Road pricing

In recent years the issue of whether or not to charge motorists for the use of roads has entered public debate. The issue centres largely on road *congestion*, rather than on pollution, because fuel taxes are a better way of reducing the environmental pollution caused by vehicles burning fossil fuels. Since 2003 motorists have been charged for driving in central London during business hours, and a private sector firm owns and runs a section of toll motorway north of Birmingham. Electronic pricing has become technically possible and is likely *eventually* to be used in future road-charging schemes. However, in the short term, the power of the motoring lobby, which argues that motorists should enjoy the freedom to use of the public highway without charge, is likely to delay the widespread introduction of road pricing, at least in the UK.

The case for and against road pricing brings together issues concerning both public goods and negative externalities. Roads are a good example of a quasi-public good, since toll booths or electronic pricing can be used to exclude free-riders. Road use also results in the discharge of negative externalities. The extent to which negative externalities are produced depends in part upon whether the road is congested or uncongested. During peak periods, a rise in the number of road users increases the journey time of other road users. A negative externality is generated.

In the following analysis, we shall assume that commercial vehicles, but not private cars, use the road. This means that all the negative externalities unleashed by road users are negative production externalities. However, road congestion could also legitimately be treated as a negative consumption externality — if generated by the use of private cars.

Given our simplifying assumption, Figure 8.9 illustrates the benefits and costs resulting from an extra commercial vehicle using the road, first when the road is uncongested, and then when road congestion has set in. The diagram shows the flow of traffic (for example, the number of commercial vehicles travelling on the road per hour) on the horizontal axis and the cost per journey on the vertical axis.

When the traffic flow is less than F_1, an extra vehicle on the road does not impose any negative externalities or external costs upon other road users — provided we ignore the pollution emitted by the vehicles. In this situation, road use should be free, to encourage the allocatively efficient or socially optimal level of use. For levels of traffic flow between zero and F_1, the marginal social cost of road use equals the marginal private cost borne by vehicles and their owners ($MSC = MPC$). But once the road becomes congested (at flows of traffic greater than F_1), this is no longer the case, and there is a case for road pricing to provide the incentive to reduce road use.

For traffic flows above F_1, each commercial vehicle driven on the road adds to traffic congestion, and all road users then suffer from increased journey times and the frustration of being stuck on a congested road. Beyond F_1, the marginal social cost of motoring is greater than the marginal private cost incurred by the last commercial vehicle to drive on the road ($MSC \rightarrow MPC$). But in the absence of road pricing, when deciding whether or not to drive on the road, road users consider only the private cost of motoring and not the external cost dumped on others. Providing there is no charge for road use, commercial vehicles are driven up to traffic flow F_2 (at point h). At F_2, the marginal private benefit of driving the vehicle equals the marginal private cost ($MPB = MPC$). At this point, the private cost incurred by the marginal vehicle to use the road is C_1, but this is less than the social cost of the marginal journey, which includes the marginal cost of congestion caused by the marginal vehicle but suffered by other road users. At traffic flow F_2, the marginal external cost of congestion imposed on other road users is shown by the distance ($k - h$).

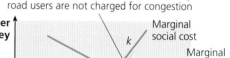

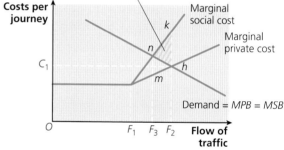

Figure 8.9 The benefits and costs of driving on an uncongested and a congested road

A misallocation of resources is the result. Commercial vehicles make more journeys than they would, had their owners or drivers borne the full social cost of using their vehicles. The shaded triangle bounded by the points n, k and h measures the welfare loss suffered by society at the privately optimal traffic flow F_2, where $MPB = MPC$.

Arguably, there is a case for road pricing when roads become congested. Allocative efficiency is improved when a motorist is charged a price equal to the marginal external cost imposed on other road users, as a result of the journey. The optimal congestion charge would be ($n - m$), which measures the marginal external cost of a journey at the socially optimal level of road use, F_3. Some congestion still occurs at F_3, but it is less than at F_2, and the owners or drivers of commercial vehicles pay for the congestion they generate. The congestion charge or road price internalises the externality. Journeys that are worth undertaking in the absence of a congestion charge are not worthwhile once the appropriate charge is imposed.

Follow-up questions

1 What is meant by the socially optimal level of road use?
2 Do you agree that fuel taxes are the best way of reducing the environmental pollution caused by vehicles burning fossil fuels? Justify your answer.
3 The passage states that electronic pricing has become technically possible. If this is the case, why have very few road-pricing schemes been introduced in the UK?
4 Suggest **two** other ways in which the environmental pollution caused by road traffic could be reduced.

Negative externalities and allocative efficiency

In Chapter 5, we explained how a perfectly competitive economy can, in theory at least, achieve a state of allocative efficiency when it brings about an outcome in which $P = MC$ in all the markets that make up the economy. However, allocative efficiency could only occur if:

● there were competitive markets for all goods and services, including future markets
● there were no economies of scale
● markets were simultaneously in equilibrium

However, it is impossible for markets throughout the economy — or indeed throughout the world economy — to meet all these conditions, so allocative efficiency is an abstract rather than a real-life concept. And in the context of market failure, we can now add a fourth requirement for allocative efficiency to be achieved:

● when $P = MC$ there would have to be no externalities, negative or positive

If we ignore the four bullet points set out above, in the long run, profit maximisation occurs in a perfect market at the price at which $P = MPC$. In the absence of externalities, this also means that the price equals the marginal social cost (MSC) of production: $P = MSC$. But as we have seen, when the production of a good causes pollution, external costs are generated, with the result that $MSC > MPC$. This means that when $P = MPC$, $P < MSC$.

To achieve allocative efficiency, price must equal the *true* marginal cost of production: that is, the marginal social cost and not just the marginal private cost. But in a market situation, profit-maximising firms are assumed only to take account of private costs and benefits. When externalities exist, therefore, the market mechanism fails to achieve an allocatively efficient outcome.

To put it another way, firms evade part of the true or real cost of production by dumping the externality on third parties. The price that the consumer pays for the good reflects only the private cost of production, and not the true cost, which includes the external cost. The firm's output is thus under-priced, encouraging too much consumption. A misallocation of resources results: too much consumption, and hence too much production, means that too many scarce resources are being used by the industry that is producing the negative externalities.

STUDY TIP
While the specification states that you 'should be able to illustrate the misallocation of resources resulting from externalities in both production and consumption', the concept of allocative inefficiency is not mentioned in the context of market failures. However, you should understand that resource misallocation means that there is an allocatively inefficient use of resources.

QUANTITATIVE SKILLS 8.4

Worked example: calculating an allocatively efficient price

The marginal private cost of producing an extra unit of a good is £15 and the marginal external cost resulting from the pollution incurred in the course of production is £3 for each extra unit.

Assuming no other externalities in consumption or production, all other things being equal, what price should achieve an allocatively efficient level of production and consumption of the good?

All other things being equal, the allocatively efficient level of production and consumption requires that price equals marginal social cost ($P = MSC$), with $MSC = MPC + MEC$. For this good, the MSC of producing an extra unit is £18 (£15 + £3), so a price of £18 is needed to ensure that the level of production and consumption of the good is allocatively efficient.

Note: in this example, since there are no externalities in consumption, the price of the product reflects the marginal social benefit (MSB) derived from the last unit of the product that is produced and consumed. Hence $P = MSC$ is equivalent to $MSB = MSC$.

CASE STUDY 8.7

Allocative efficiency and rail fares

Motorists in cities pay substantially less than the costs they create when driving their vehicles. The greater the congestion, the truer this is. The extra cost or, as economists would call it, the marginal social cost of an extra vehicle coming onto a road is quantifiable. Wherever there is congestion, the marginal social cost will be greater than the marginal private cost, since the marginal costs to the motorist of using the road are additional vehicle costs, which include the cost of petrol or diesel fuel, and the costs of wear and tear and time. The motorist does not have to take into account the costs imposed on other road users and on pedestrians.

On the other hand, if rail transport in cities is required to cover costs, it will be over-priced relative to users of urban roads, since rail users will be required to cover all the costs, both private and external, that they create, while road users will not. The effect of this difference in pricing policy is an inefficient distribution of traffic between road and rail. Less traffic travels by rail, especially at peak times, than is efficient. Similarly, there is too much traffic on the roads.

One way of getting prices right would be to raise the price of urban road use until both public and private road transport covered their true costs. But if we accept that it is politically imprudent or undesirable to raise the cost of using roads to a level where marginal social costs are covered, one can attempt to get the allocatively efficient relationship between road and rail by the opposite course of action: by keeping rail fares lower than they would be if the railways charged the full market price. This is the essence of the case for rail subsidies.

For this case to be proven, the traffic that the railways divert from the roads must reduce congestion by an amount sufficient to justify the rail subsidies required. Underlying this is the proposition that users of city roads pay less through taxation for using them than covers the full social cost of their use.

Follow-up questions

1 Define the term 'marginal social cost'.
2 The passage suggests that subsidising rail fares can establish the allocatively efficient relationship between the prices paid for road and rail use. Explain this statement.
3 Why does allocative inefficiency result in resource misallocation?
4 Outline the case against subsidising rail fares.

8.5 Merit and demerit goods

Merit goods

Merit goods are not the same as public goods. As we have seen, public goods are defined by two characteristics: they are non-excludable and non-rival. Because of these characteristics, a market may fail to provide a pure public good such as national defence. By contrast, markets can and do provide merit goods such as healthcare and education but, arguably, they under-provide. While public goods can result in a missing market or *complete* market failure, merit goods (and also their opposite, demerit goods) lead to *partial* market failure. As goods such as private healthcare and private education clearly show, markets provide merit goods, but they provide the 'wrong' quantity.

KEY TERM

merit good a good, such as healthcare, for which the social benefits of consumption exceed the private benefits. Value judgements are involved in deciding that a good is a merit good.

STUDY TIP
Students often assert that any good that is 'good for you' is a merit good. Make sure you can explain why this assertion is wrong.

KEY TERMS

information failure occurs when people make wrong decisions because they do not possess or they ignore relevant information. Very often they are myopic (short-sighted) about the future.

social benefit the total benefit of an activity, including the external benefit as well as the private benefit. Expressed as an equation: social benefit = private benefit + external benefit.

STUDY TIP

You should understand that merit goods are private goods; they are excludable and rival, even though they are often provided by the public sector.

A merit good has two important characteristics: positive externalities in consumption and **information failures** which distort a consumer's choice on what is the privately optimal level of consumption.

- **Merit goods and positive externalities.** When a person consumes a merit good such as healthcare, the resulting positive externalities benefit other people. An obvious example is that healthy people seldom spread diseases. The **social benefit** enjoyed by the wider community is greater than the private benefit enjoyed by the healthy person.
- **Merit goods and information failures.** For a merit good such as healthcare, the long-term private benefit of consumption exceeds the short-term private benefit of consumption. But when deciding how much to consume, individuals take account of short-term costs and benefits, ignoring or undervaluing the long-term private costs and benefits. In the UK, Open University students, whose ages range from 22 to well over 70, have been known to say: 'If only I had got my qualifications when I was younger; unfortunately I did not value education when I was at school.'

Education and healthcare are the best-known examples of merit goods. However, many goods can be classified as merit goods, though you must avoid the temptation that many students succumb to, to define any good that is 'good for you' as a merit good. Most consumer goods are good for you, but economists don't classify them as merit goods. Besides education and healthcare, other examples of merit goods, most people would argue, are car seatbelts, crash helmets, public parks and museums. Nevertheless, the classification of merit and demerit goods depends upon value judgements — what one person regards as a merit good, for example opera, may be viewed by another person as a demerit good.

TEST YOURSELF 8.6

Explain why C provides the correct answer to the following question, and why A, B and D are incorrect.

A difference between a merit good and a public good is that:

A a merit good is always provided by the private sector whereas a public good is always provided by the government

B a merit good has a cost attached to it, whereas a public good is provided without cost to anybody

C consumption of a merit good reduces the amount available for others whereas an individual's consumption of a pure public good leaves unaffected the amount available for others

D a merit good is limited in supply whereas the supply of public goods is infinite

Positive consumption externalities and merit goods

A merit good, such as education or healthcare, is a good or service for which the social benefits of consumption enjoyed by the whole community exceed the private benefits received by the consumer. Consumption by an individual arguably produces positive externalities that benefit the wider community. The community benefits from an educated (and civilised) population, and a healthy population means there are fewer people to catch diseases from.

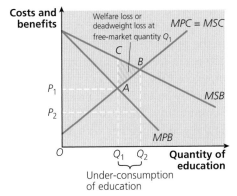

Figure 8.10 Under-consumption of a merit good in a free market

If educational services were to be provided solely through the market, and at market prices, too few people would benefit from education. In Figure 8.10, the privately optimal level of consumption is Q_1, determined at point A, where $MPC = MPB$. This is below the socially optimal level of consumption, Q_2. The socially optimal level of education lies below point B on the diagram, located where $MSC = MSB$. According to this analysis, free-market provision of merit goods leads to under-consumption. The MSB of units of education between Q_1 and Q_2 is greater than the MSC of these units. Producing and consuming these units will add to the welfare of society.

Suppose that the government reacts by providing a **subsidy** which reduces the price of education to P_2. At the subsidised price, consumption of education rises to the socially optimal level of Q_2. The market failure has now been corrected.

STUDY TIP
Make sure you practise drawing graphs such as the ones in Figures 8.7, 8.8, 8.10 and 8.11.

KEY TERM
subsidy a payment made by government or other authority, usually to producers, for each unit of the subsidised good that they produce. Consumers can also be subsidised: for example, bus passes given to children to enable them to travel on buses free or at a reduced price.

CASE STUDY 8.8

Museums as merit goods

Museums perform the important cultural function of conserving, interpreting, researching and displaying heritage. Museums have a mix of ownership patterns. For example, over 40% of UK museums are governed by public authorities, with the rest privately owned, mostly on a non-profit basis. Museums cover a wide range of institutions of varying size and reputation, ranging from internationally renowned institutions such as the British Museum to a large number of relatively small, often locally focused museums.

The funding of museums remains a source of considerable debate. Government subsidy or provision may be justified on the basis that museums generate external benefits: for example, knowledge acquired by a visitor may be passed on to others. Museums may also be regarded as merit goods, generating a better educated and informed public and collective pride.

Government subsidy of museums may also be justified on the grounds that the subsidy would encourage consumption. The case against government subsidy is that it may encourage inefficiency, leading to government failure through favouring well-off visitors who can afford to pay. It is also a cost to the taxpayer.

Follow-up questions
1 Do you agree that a museum is a merit good? Justify your answer.
2 Some argue that if entry to museums is free, people will not value what museums have to offer. Explain why you agree or disagree.
3 'Some people believe that when free, museums attract the wrong sort of visitor, namely homeless people looking for warmth. Entry prices should be used as a rationing device so that only people who genuinely want to see what a museum has to offer are admitted.' Should prices be used as a rationing device in this way?
4 In the USA, many museums and art galleries are funded by rich philanthropists such as the Getty Museum in Los Angeles. Should British museums be funded by rich individuals rather than by the state?

251

Demerit goods

As their name suggests, **demerit goods** are the opposite of merit goods. The **social costs** to the whole community which result from the consumption of a demerit good, such as tobacco or alcohol, exceed the private costs incurred by the consumer. This is because consumption by an individual produces negative externalities that harm the wider community. The *private* cost can be measured by the money cost of purchasing the good, together with any health damage suffered by the person consuming the good. But the *social* costs of consumption also include the cost of the negative externalities. These include, for example, costs imposed on other people from passive smoking and road accidents caused by drunken drivers, together with the cost of taxes raised to pay for the care of victims of tobacco- and alcohol-related diseases.

As is the case with merit goods, there are two main characteristics of a demerit good, the first centring on externalities, and the second on information failures that affect the good's consumption. With the first characteristic, the benefit the smoker or drinker derives from consumption is greater than the benefit to society. The second characteristic is based on the distinction between the short-term and long-term net benefit derived by the person consuming a demerit good.

- **Demerit goods and negative externalities.** When a person consumes a demerit good such as tobacco, negative externalities are generated which are unpleasant or harmful for other people. People unwillingly breathe in the fumes the smoker discharges, with eventual harmful effects on their health. (This is the problem of passive smoking.) Smelly clothing is a more trivial example of a negative externality in consumption that is caused by smoking. Hence, the marginal social benefit is less than the marginal private benefit.
- **Demerit goods and information failures.** When teenagers first get the 'habit' of smoking, drinking or drug taking, they may either ignore the long-term private costs they may suffer later in life, or downplay the significance of these costs. Either way, young people tend to be short-sighted with respect to the costs of consuming demerit goods. A person who started drinking as a teenager may regret the decision later in life when suffering an alcohol-related illness. Hence, the long-run net benefit of consuming a demerit good is less than the short-run benefit.

Merit and demerit goods and value judgements

The left-hand and right-hand columns of Table 8.6 list a number of goods that are accepted by most people as clear-cut examples of merit goods or demerit goods. However, for the goods listed in the middle column — for example, contraception — the position is less clear. Because people have different values and ethics (often related to their religions), contraception and abortion are viewed by some people as merit goods, but by others as demerit goods. Whether a good is classified as a merit good or a demerit good, or indeed as neither, thus depends on the value judgements of the person making the classification.

Table 8.6 Merit and demerit goods, and less clear-cut cases

Merit good	Merit or demerit goods?	Demerit goods
Education	Contraception	Tobacco
Healthcare (e.g. vaccination, preventative dental care, HIV testing)	Abortion	Alcohol
Crash helmets	Sterilisation	Narcotic drugs, such as heroin and crack cocaine
Car seatbelts		Pornography
Museums and public parks		Prostitution

Finally, remember that value judgements are being made when describing particular goods as merit goods (or demerit goods). It is also worth noting that under-provision of merit goods and over-provision of demerit goods may also result from the imperfect information that consumers possess, which can lead — for example, in the case of demerit goods — to failure to give adequate weight to the long-term consequences of consuming a good such as tobacco. We shall explore the effects of imperfect information a little later in the chapter.

SYNOPTIC LINK

The importance of value judgements when distinguishing between merit and demerit good provides an important example of the distinction between positive statements and normative statements, a distinction first explained in Chapter 1. To recap, a positive statement is a statement of fact or a statement that can be tested to see if it is right or wrong. For example, statements that the Earth is round and that the Earth is flat are both positive statements, though scientific evidence shows that the second statement is wrong. By contrast, a normative statement is a statement of opinion, involving a value judgement. Thus, a statement that the Earth *ought* to be flat is normative.

Are there such things as demerit goods and merit goods?

Some economists, usually of a pro-free-market persuasion, question whether any goods are demerit goods or merit goods. These economists are libertarians who believe that individuals are the best judges of what is bad or good for them. People should be free, within the law, to smoke or drink themselves to death, or to prevent their children being vaccinated against measles. According to this view, it is not the state's role to intervene in individual behaviour, except when the pursuit of self-interest harms other people. For example, the state should prevent motorists from exercising the freedom to drive on the wrong side of the road.

Anti-libertarians, however, do not accept this view of individual freedom of choice. They argue that over-consumption of demerit goods and under-consumption of merit goods invariably leads to other people being harmed and that the libertarian argument is specious. Taxation, subsidy and regulation are fully justified as means of altering individual behaviour.

Lying somewhat in between these two approaches are the insights of behavioural economists, who argue that individuals should be given as much choice as possible in deciding what is good for them, but that governments should use appropriate policies to 'nudge' them in the direction deemed socially optimal.

Using marginal analysis to show how negative consumption externalities cause over-consumption of demerit goods

In the same way as the consumption of merit goods generates positive externalities which benefit the wider community, the consumption of demerit goods leads to the dumping of negative externalities on others.

According to the first characteristic of a demerit good given on page 252, the consumption of goods such as tobacco and alcohol by an individual leads to the dumping of negative externalities on other individuals or third parties. Figure 8.11 shows that too much tobacco is consumed when bought at market prices unadjusted by taxes or by a minimum price law. At least in the short term, the privately optimal level of consumption is Q_1, where $MPC = MPB$. This is greater than the socially optimal level of consumption, Q_2, located where $MSC = MSB$. Free-market provision of demerit goods therefore leads to over-consumption, and hence over-production of tobacco.

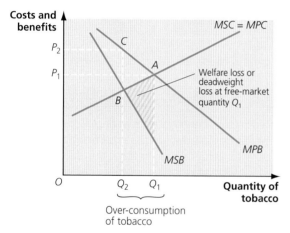

Figure 8.11 How over-consumption of a demerit good occurs in a free market

Because the negative externalities in this example are generated when people smoke (for example, the smoke breathed in by passive smokers who do not enjoy the fumes they inhale), the externalities are *consumption* externalities rather than *production* externalities. As a result, the marginal social benefit (MSB) curve of the whole community lies below the marginal private benefit (MPB) curve of the smokers themselves, with the distance between the two curves showing the negative externality.

To bring about the socially optimal level of consumption at Q_2, an indirect tax equal to the distance between points B and C in Figure 8.11 could be imposed, which would increase the price of tobacco to P_2. The tax needs to be set equal to the marginal external cost (MEC) of consumption at the socially optimal level of consumption (Q_2).

STUDY TIP

It is important to understand that the costs imposed by consumers on society (the negative externalities) are depicted in Figure 8.10 as negative benefits. Thus, the distance between points B and C on the graph can be interpreted either as the marginal external cost of smoking or as the negative external benefit of smoking at the socially optimal level of smoking, Q_2. The two are the same. For example, if someone is smoking at a party, the pleasure derived from the event by non-smokers is reduced; hence the cumulative benefit to all the party-goers is less than the pleasure derived by the smoker.

Note also that, for the socially optimal level of smoking to be zero (in which case a ban might be imposed on smoking), the MSB curve in Figure 8.10 would need to positioned well to the left of the curve in the diagram, intersecting the MSC curve at zero quantity.

SYNOPTIC LINK
Taxes and government spending are used in the government's fiscal policy. Along with monetary policy, fiscal policy is usually considered to be a macroeconomic topic. As such, fiscal policy is explained in some depth in Chapter 13. Nevertheless, taxes imposed on firms and subsidies, which are part of government spending, also have microeconomic dimensions.

TEST YOURSELF 8.7

Table 8.7 shows the marginal private and external benefits and the marginal private and external costs of two products at their free-market equilibrium levels of output.

Table 8.7 Private and external costs and benefits of products W and Z

	Product W (£)	Product Z (£)
Marginal private benefit	400	140
Marginal external benefit	100	80
Marginal private cost	400	140
Marginal external cost	180	60

Taking into account the information provided in the table, for each of the products W and Z, is there a case for increasing the level of output above the free-market output, or is there a case for reducing the level of output so that it is below the free-market output?

CASE STUDY 8.9

Smoking yourself 'fit'

Strange as it seems, early cigarette advertisements, such as the Kensitas advert from 1929 (see the photo on the left), often boasted the 'health benefits' of smoking, claiming 'relief' from asthma, wheezing, hay fever and obesity. In 1946 the American tobacco company Camel ran a series of adverts claiming that Camel were the 'doctor's choice' (see the photo on the right).

1929 Kensitas magazine advert (left) and 1946 Camels magazine advert (right)

By the 1950s, research began to link smoking to cancer. Worldwide, tobacco use causes more than 5 million deaths per year, and current trends show that tobacco use will cause more than 8 million deaths annually by 2030, largely through the growth of smoking in developing countries.

Cigarettes (and other tobacco products) and alcoholic drink are the two best-known examples of demerit goods. These days, governments in countries such as the UK either ban tobacco and drinks advertising, or severely regulate what the adverts can show. This has not always been the case, as the examples of advertisements for Kensitas and Camel cigarettes show.

Tobacco and drinks companies want to make their products appealing to young people, possibly in the hope that if teenagers develop the habit, they will be hooked on cigarettes and alcohol for the rest of their lives. To combat claims that the industry has been acting in an irresponsible way, the UK firms that produce alcoholic drinks have set up a public relations organisation, the Portman Group, to monitor adverts that might bring the drinks industry into disrepute.

Follow-up questions

1 Most economists agree that tobacco is a demerit good. Why is this so?
2 Why do governments in countries such as the UK and USA now ban advertisements like these?
3 Is self-regulation by trade bodies such as the Portman Group the best way of discouraging consumption of demerit goods? Justify your answer.
4 Find out how successful e-cigarettes have been in reducing consumption of nicotine.

Merit and demerit goods and the information failure

Some economists argue that under-consumption of merit goods and over-consumption of demerit goods stem not so much from the externalities that consumption generates, but from an information failure. Many people become addicted to demerit goods in their teenage years. Because of peer-group pressure and related factors, teenagers are heavily influenced by factors relating to lifestyle and personal circumstances, while at the same time ignoring, downplaying or being myopic about how their addictions may affect them many years ahead. Individuals take account of *short-term* costs and benefits, but ignore or undervalue the *long-term* private costs and benefits.

For most merit goods, the long-term private benefit of consumption exceeds the short-term private benefit. But, as is the case with demerit goods, when deciding how much to consume, individuals often take account only of short-term costs and benefits. Preventative dentistry provides a good example. Many people ignore the long-term benefit of dental check-ups, and decide not to consume the service. Their decisions are influenced by factors such as the price charged by the dentist and the unpleasantness of the dental experience. Unfortunately, they may end up later in life with rotten teeth or gum disease, saying: 'If only I had visited the dentist more often when I was younger.'

SYNOPTIC LINK
Section 2.2 of Chapter 2 discusses the importance of information for decision making and the effect of asymmetrical information.

Merit goods and uncertainty, moral hazard and adverse selection

Uncertainty about future long-term benefits and costs contributes to under-consumption of merit goods. For example, a person does not know in advance when, if ever, the services of a specialist surgeon might be needed. Sudden illness may lead to a situation in which a person cannot afford to pay for costly surgery, if provided solely through a conventional market.

One market-orientated solution is for private medical insurance to pay for the cost of treatment at the time when it is needed. However, private medical insurance often fails to pay for treatment for the chronically ill or for the poor. Private insurance may also fail to provide medical care for risk-takers in society who decide not to buy insurance, as distinct from risk-averters, who are always the most ready customers for insurance.

Like all private insurance schemes, healthcare insurance suffers from two further problems, both of which lead to market failure. These are the problems of **moral hazard** and adverse selection. Moral hazard is demonstrated by the tendency of people covered by health insurance to be less careful about their health because they know that, in the event of accident or illness, the insurance company will pick up the bill. Adverse selection relates to the fact that people whose health risks are greatest are also the people most likely to try to buy insurance policies. Insurance companies react by refusing to sell health policies to those who most need private health insurance. For those to whom they do sell policies, premium levels are set sufficiently high to enable the companies to remain profitable when settling the claims of customers facing moral hazard or who have been adversely selected.

Public collective provision, perhaps organised by private sector companies but guaranteed by the state and funded by compulsory insurance, may be a better solution. Both private and public collective-provision schemes are a response to the fact that the demand or need for medical care is much more predictable for a large group of people than for an individual.

KEY TERM

moral hazard the tendency of individuals and firms, once insured against some contingency, to behave so as to make that contingency more likely.

SYNOPTIC LINK

Moral hazard is mentioned in the specification in the context of the regulation of the financial system in Chapter 12 on financial markets and monetary policy. Make sure you understand the concept both in the context described in this chapter of persons covered by health insurance failing to look after their health and also the context described in Chapter 12 of banks making risky investments because they know that if an investment goes wrong, they will be bailed out by the government and/or the central bank.

TEST YOURSELF 8.8

With the use of examples, explain the difference between a merit good and a public good.

SECTION 8.5 SUMMARY

- Markets provide merit goods such as healthcare and education but generally they under-provide.
- When a person consumes a merit good, the resulting positive externalities benefit other people.
- The long-term private benefit resulting from consuming a merit good exceeds the short-term private benefit of consumption.
- When a person consumes a demerit good, the resulting positive externalities harm other people.
- The social costs to the whole community which result from the consumption of a demerit good, such as tobacco or alcohol, exceed the private costs incurred by the consumer.
- Some economists believe that under-consumption of merit goods and over-consumption of demerit goods stem not so much from the externalities that consumption generates, but from an information failure.

8.6 Market imperfections

The effect of imperfect and asymmetric information

Whereas all consumers and firms would possess perfect information about what is happening in a perfectly competitive market, the same is not true in monopoly and imperfect competition. For example, in the context of an oligopolist's kinked demand curve, we explained in Chapter 5 how firms in imperfectly competitive markets are likely to lack accurate information about how their rivals, namely other firms in the market, may react to their pricing decisions. To get rid of the resulting uncertainty, imperfectly competitive firms may be tempted to collude. If cartels are formed, this can lead to an outcome which displays the disadvantages but not the advantages of monopoly. As the next section explains, by restricting output and raising prices, monopoly is a form of market failure.

Refer back also to Case study 3.6 on markets for second-hand cars in Chapter 3. This illustrates the effects of asymmetric information on market outcomes. The sellers of second-hand cars possess more information about the quality of the cars than prospective buyers. By driving down the prices of good quality cars below what they would otherwise be, the market is distorted, which results in a form of market failure.

> **SYNOPTIC LINK**
> Chapters 3 and 5 provide examples of the effects of asymmetric information and imperfect information.

Why the existence of monopoly may lead to market failure

We also saw in Chapter 5 how, compared to competitive markets and in pursuit of excess profit, monopolies are likely to restrict market output and raise prices. The result is consumer exploitation. Prices end up being too high, with too few of society's scarce resources being allocated to the market in which the monopoly is producing. However, as Chapter 5 also explains, sometimes the benefits of monopoly can exceed the costs, in which case there is no market failure.

> **SYNOPTIC LINK**
> Refer back to section 5.5 in Chapter 5, and read the discussion on the advantages and disadvantages of monopoly.

> **STUDY TIP**
> Make sure you can link the analysis of market failure to the reasons why monopoly and market imperfections provide examples of market failure: for example, the statement in Chapter 5 that the existence of deadweight loss provides evidence of market failure in monopoly.

> **TEST YOURSELF 8.9**
> With the help of a diagram, explain why a monopoly restricts output and raises its selling price above the price that would be charged by a firm in a perfectly competitive market.

Why the immobility of factors of production can lead to market failure

An important cause of market failure is the immobility of factors of production, which can involve either geographical or occupational immobility. We summarise below the issues of **immobility of labour**.

We have already explained on page 183 some of the causes of the occupational and geographical immobility of labour. As we state there, occupational immobility of labour arises when workers lack the skills to move between different types of employment, and because expensive and time-consuming training may be necessary if workers are to switch. The need to gain recognised professional qualifications acts as an important cause of occupational immobility, especially when workers want to move between different countries. To protect their own workers, governments often fail to recognise other countries' professional qualifications.

We also stated that geographical immobility of labour occurs when geographical barriers between markets prevent labour moving from one area to another to find employment. Especially important are immigration laws which act as a barrier to the international mobility of labour between countries.

All these causes of immobility of labour lead to unemployment and a waste of scarce resources, and contribute to market failure in factor markets.

TEST YOURSELF 8.10

Give one example of the occupational immobility of labour and one example of the geographical immobility of labour.

CASE STUDY 8.10

Taxi wars

Until quite recently, the London taxi market, in which cabs could be hailed or flagged down in the street, was dominated by black cabs. Entry into the black cab driving profession was strictly limited by the needs, first, to spend several years gaining the 'knowledge' of all the streets in the centre of the country's capital city, and second, to be granted a cab-driver's licence, which were deliberately kept in short supply.

Competition first emerged from mini-cabs, but they had to be pre-booked by phoning or visiting a mini-cab company's office, and then hoping that the car would show up. But a new form of competition has emerged which threatens to destroy the black cab market. Passengers are no longer subject to the availability of a black cab or a pre-booked mini-cab. They can now make use of a smartphone app that essentially puts a taxi in their pocket whenever they need one, in any major city in the world.

By reducing barriers to labour market entry, smartphone technology is destroying the monopoly power of black cab drivers. Since the launch of the Uber app in 2009, there has been a massive power shift in the cab market. Uber and other web-based cab booking services are accessed via smartphones. The service connects passengers with vetted, private drivers who pick up their customers within minutes and take them to where they want to go. When the booking is made, the passenger's location is pinpointed with the GPS on their phone. The passenger chooses the kind of car they need, checks the estimated price of the journey, and is then told how long they will need to wait for their car to arrive. They see a photo of the driver, their name and a contact phone number. When arriving at their destination, passengers don't need to hand over cash as payment automatically takes place via a credit card. Next day an e-mail is sent to the passenger with a breakdown of the costs, and passengers are not expected to tip their driver.

Follow-up questions

1 Before Uber entered the market, in what ways did black cab companies possess monopoly power?
2 Explain the effect of the Uber app on labour mobility in the cab trade.
3 In 2017, Transport for London (TfL) refused to renew Uber's licence to operate in London. Why did TfL do this, and what has happened since?
4 Describe **one** other example of smartphone technology improving labour market mobility.

SECTION 8.6 SUMMARY

- Consumers and firms do not possess perfect information about what is happening in an imperfectly competitive market.
- Firms in imperfectly competitive markets are likely to lack accurate information about how their rivals, namely other firms in the market, may react to their pricing decisions.
- To get rid of the resulting uncertainty, imperfectly competitive firms may be tempted to collude, and in some cases to form cartels.
- A cartel has the disadvantages but not the advantages of monopoly. As the next section explains, by restricting output and raising prices, monopoly is a form of market failure.
- Immobility of labour is the inability of labour to move from one job to another, either for occupational reasons (e.g. the need for training) or for geographical reasons (e.g. the cost of moving to another part of the country).
- Geographical immobility of labour occurs when workers find it difficult or impossible to move to jobs in other parts of the country or in other countries for reasons such as higher housing costs in locations where the jobs exist.

8.7 Competition policy

The theoretical background to competition policy

Two important points to remember about perfect competition are:

- In the absence of economies of scale, perfect competition would be more productively and allocatively efficient than monopoly.
- In perfect competition, the 'consumer is king' and consumer sovereignty rules, whereas monopoly leads to the manipulation of consumers and the exploitation of producer sovereignty. By restricting output and raising prices, monopoly results in a net welfare loss as well as a transfer of consumer surplus into producer surplus and monopoly profit.

But even though perfect competition does not actually exist in real world economies, when firms operate in markets where a high degree of competition prevails, many economists believe that this helps to prevent the abuses that can occur when firms possess a significant degree of monopoly power.

As its name implies, **competition policy** is the part of government economic policy which tries to make the imperfectly competitive and monopolistic markets of the real world more competitive. The aims of competition policy include preventing the exploitation of monopoly power, reducing costs of production, improving efficiency, getting rid of excessive profit so that prices reflect costs of production, and removing entry and exit barriers which separate markets.

Competition policy does recognise, however, that there are two main circumstances in which monopoly may be preferable to small firms producing in a competitive market:

- When the size of the market is limited but economies of scale are possible, monopolies can produce at a lower average cost than smaller, more competitive firms.
- Under certain circumstances, firms with monopoly power may be more innovative than firms that are not protected by entry barriers. When this is the case, monopoly may be more dynamically efficient than a more competitive market.

The three different parts of UK competition policy

As noted in the key term definition above, competition policy in the UK comprises policy toward monopoly, mergers and restrictive trading practices.

Monopoly policy

Since there are few, if any, pure monopolies in the UK, monopoly policy might better be called 'oligopoly policy' or policy toward highly concentrated markets dominated by just a few firms. Of the three main elements of competition policy we examine in this chapter, monopoly policy is the one with the longest history, dating back well over half a century to the establishment of the Monopolies Commission in 1948. The Monopolies Commission later became the Competition Commission, which in turn in 2013 was rebranded as the **Competition and Markets Authority** (CMA). The CMA began operations in 2014. The CMA is not restricted solely to the investigation of pure monopoly. It also investigates mergers that might create a new monopoly or a highly concentrated market structure.

A cost–benefit approach to monopoly policy

Because economists recognise that monopoly can be either good or bad depending upon circumstances, UK policy has always been based on the view that each case must be judged on its merits. If the likely costs resulting from the reduction of competition exceed the benefits, monopoly should be prevented, but if the likely benefits exceed the costs, monopoly should be permitted. Ongoing regulation is needed to make sure that firms, particularly large firms, continue to act in the public interest.

KEY TERM
competition policy the part of the government's microeconomic policy and industrial policy which aims to make goods markets more competitive. It comprises policy toward monopoly, mergers and restrictive trading practices.

KEY TERM
Competition and Markets Authority government agency responsible for advising on and implementing UK competition policy.

STUDY TIP
The label 'monopoly policy' is slightly misleading as very often the policy is aimed at oligopolies or concentrated markets rather than at pure monopoly.

The Competition and Markets Authority

As already noted, since 2014 UK monopoly policy has been implemented by the Competition and Markets Authority (CMA). The CMA was formed through the merger of two older government agencies, the Office of Fair Trading (OFT) and the Competition Commission (CC). Since 2017, the CMA has been responsible to a government ministry, the Department for Business, Energy and Industrial Strategy (BEIS).

The CMA uses market structure, conduct and performance indicators to scan or screen the UK economy on a systematic basis for evidence of monopoly abuse. Concentration ratios provide evidence of monopolistic market structures. Market conduct indicators such as consumer and trade complaints allow the CMA to monitor anti-competitive business behaviour. When the CMA discovers evidence of monopoly that it believes is likely to be against the public interest, it investigates further. Until recently, the main issue to be decided was the relatively narrow one of whether particular trading practices undertaken by the investigated firm(s) were in the public interest. The 'public interest' was fairly vaguely defined. The 2002 Enterprise Act changed this, introducing competition-based tests to replace the public interest test. The tests centre on whether any features of the market (which include structural features and conduct by firms or customers in the market) prevent, restrict or distort competition.

Alternative approaches to the problem of monopoly

Ever since the start of competition policy 70 years ago, the UK has adopted a regulatory and investigatory approach to the problem of monopoly. Relatively few firms and takeover bids are actually investigated. The policy rationale is that the possibility of a CMA investigation creates sufficient incentive for most large firms to behave well and to resist the temptation to exploit monopoly power in ways that are against the public interest.

However, although the CMA has adopted a 'watchdog investigatory/regulatory' role, a number of other strategic approaches could, in principle, be used to deal with the problem of monopoly. These include:

- **Compulsory breaking up of all monopolies ('monopoly busting').**
  Many free-market economists believe that the advantages of competitive and free markets, namely economic efficiency and consumer sovereignty, can be achieved only when the economy is as close as possible to perfect competition. In itself, monopoly is bad and impossible to justify. The government should adopt an automatic policy rule to break up monopolies wherever they are found to exist. UK policy-makers have seldom, if ever, adopted a monopoly-busting approach, although, as we have explained, powers do exist that allow the government to order the break-up of an established monopoly.
- **Use of price controls to restrict monopoly abuse.** Although price controls have been used by UK governments at various times to restrict the freedom of UK firms to set their own prices, this policy has only been used in a limited way in recent years. Under the influence of free-market economic theory, price controls have fallen out of favour.
- **Taxing monopoly profits.** As well as controlling prices directly, the government can tax monopoly profit to punish firms for exploiting their monopoly power and making excessive profit. Monopoly taxes have not

generally been used in the UK, except on a few occasions — for example, on the 'windfall' gain that landlords receive when the land they own is made available for property development. Similarly, windfall profits received by banks from high interest rates have been subject to a special tax. Also, in the late 1990s, the incoming Labour government imposed a windfall tax on profits of the privatised utilities.

- **Rate of return regulation.** In the USA, the regulators have imposed maximum rates of return on the capital that the utility companies employ. In principle, these act as a price cap, as the utilities are fined if they set prices too high and earn excessive rates of return. However, in practice, instead of increasing productive efficiency, rate of return regulation often has the opposite effect. This type of intervention has the unintended consequence of encouraging utility companies to raise costs so that raising prices does not lead to higher profits and hence they comply with the rate of return regulation. The higher costs, which are the result of the productively inefficient use of resources, may allow the managers of the business to have an easier life. Monopolies are especially likely to allow costs to rise when protected by high entry barriers.

- **State ownership of monopoly.** In the past, UK Labour governments have sometimes regarded the problem of monopoly as resulting solely from private ownership and the pursuit of private profit. At its most simplistic, this view leads to the conclusion that the problem of monopoly disappears when the firms are nationalised or taken into public ownership. Once in public ownership, the monopolies are assumed to act solely in the public interest.

- **Privatising monopolies.** Opposing state ownership, past Conservative governments argued that state ownership produces particular forms of abuse that would not be experienced if the industries were privately owned. These include a general inefficiency and resistance to change, which stem from the belief by workers and management in the state-run monopolies that they will always be bailed out by government in the event of a loss. According to the Conservative view, monopoly abuse occurs in nationalised industries, not from the pursuit of private profit, but because the industries are run in the interest of a feather-bedded workforce that is protected from any form of market discipline. It is also alleged that interference by governments for social and political reasons made it difficult for nationalised industries to operate efficiently. The Conservatives believe that the privatisation of state-owned monopolies should improve efficiency and commercial performance, because privatisation exposes the industry to the threat of takeover and the discipline of the capital market. In some cases, privatisation has also subjected previously state-owned monopolies to competition.

- **Deregulation and the removal of barriers to entry.** Most economists believe that privatisation alone cannot eliminate the problem of monopoly abuse; it merely changes the nature of the problem to private monopoly and the commercial exploitation of a monopoly position. In recognition of this problem, the privatisation of the telecommunication, gas and electricity monopolies was accompanied by the setting up of the regulatory bodies Ofcom and Ofgem, operating in addition to the CMA. One method of exposing monopolies — including the privatised utility industries — to increased competition is to use deregulatory policies to remove artificial barriers to entry. We explain deregulation in greater detail later in the chapter.

TEST YOURSELF 8.11
What is meant by a 'cost–benefit' approach to the problem of monopoly?

SYNOPTIC LINK

In section 5.10 of Chapter 5, we explained that in recent years, contestable market theory has had a major impact on UK monopoly policy. We described how the theory implies that, provided there is adequate potential for competition, a conventional regulatory policy is superfluous. The government's main role should be to discover which industries and markets are potentially contestable. The growing influence of contestable market theory has been accompanied by the introduction of deregulatory policies that are meant to develop conditions in which there are reduced barriers to entry and exit or a complete absence of such barriers.

For a market to be perfectly contestable, barriers to entry must disappear and there must be no sunk costs. As we explained in Chapter 5, sunk costs are costs incurred, when entering a market, that are irrecoverable should the firm decide to leave the market.

Merger policy

Whereas a government's monopoly policy deals with established monopoly, or markets already dominated by large firms, merger policy is concerned with takeovers and mergers that might create a new monopoly. Strictly, a merger involves the voluntary coming together of two or more firms, whereas a takeover is usually involuntary, at least for the victim being acquired through a hostile takeover. However, the term 'merger policy' is used to cover all types of acquisition of firms, friendly or hostile, willing or unwilling.

Until quite recently, the government itself decided whether to refer merging companies to the compatition authorities for investigation. This laid the government open to the criticism that, when deciding against a merger reference, it was bending to the lobbying power of big business and engaging in political opportunism. However, the CMA now makes virtually all merger references. The CMA keeps itself informed of all merger situations that might be eligible for investigation on public interest grounds. Currently, a takeover or merger is eligible for investigation if it is expected to lead to a substantial lessening of competition (SLC).

European Union merger policy

The European Commission, which is the executive body of the EU, has long had powers to prevent and control mergers in member countries, but before 1990 the commission did not apply these powers systematically. The EU merger policy, which is the main part of EU competition policy, is based on the principle of *subsidiarity*, which delegates policy as much as possible to national governments. Member countries continue to use national policy to deal with smaller mergers, but the European Commission adjudicates on larger mergers with a community dimension. As with UK merger policy, nearly all the commission's criteria for assessing whether a merger is justified are competition-related, showing again the influence of contestable market theory. In 2018, it remains to be seen whether the EU's monopoly and merger policies will have any jurisdiction over UK competition policy if the UK exits the EU.

CASE STUDY 8.11

European Competition Commissioner fines Google €4.3 billion

In July 2018, the European Competition Commissioner Margrethe Vestager fined Google €4.3 billion for abusing its market dominance with the Android operating system, which powers most of the world's mobile phones. Vestager said:

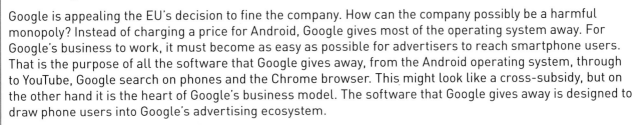

> Our case is about three types of restrictions that Google has imposed on Android device manufacturers and network operators to ensure that traffic on Android devices goes to the Google search engine. In this way, Google has used Android as a vehicle to cement the dominance of its search engine. These practices have denied rivals the chance to innovate and compete.
>
> In particular, Google:

- has required manufacturers to pre-install the Google Search app and browser app (Chrome), as a condition for licensing Google's app store (the Play Store);
- made payments to certain large manufacturers and mobile network operators on condition that they exclusively pre-installed the Google Search app on their devices; and
- has prevented manufacturers wishing to pre-install Google apps from selling even a single smart mobile device running on alternative versions of Android that were not approved by Google.

Google is appealing the EU's decision to fine the company. How can the company possibly be a harmful monopoly? Instead of charging a price for Android, Google gives most of the operating system away. For Google's business to work, it must become as easy as possible for advertisers to reach smartphone users. That is the purpose of all the software that Google gives away, from the Android operating system, through to YouTube, Google search on phones and the Chrome browser. This might look like a cross-subsidy, but on the other hand it is the heart of Google's business model. The software that Google gives away is designed to draw phone users into Google's advertising ecosystem.

Follow-up questions

1 Find out how Google has grown since the business was founded in 1998.
2 Microsoft, the dominant company in the PC era, and Google, the dominant company in the internet era, have both benefited greatly from cross-subsidy and from network effects.
3 Find out what is meant by a network effect and by cross-subsidy.
4 Do you believe that Google is a harmful monopoly? Justify your reasoning.

Restrictive trading practices policy

Restrictive trading practices undertaken by firms in imperfect product markets can be divided into two broad kinds: those undertaken independently by a single firm, and collective restrictive practices that involve either a written or an implied agreement among two or more firms.

Independently undertaken restrictive practices include:

- decisions to charge discriminatory prices (see section 5.8)
- the refusal to supply a particular resale outlet
- full-line forcing, whereby a supplier forces a distributor that wishes to sell one of its products to stock its full range of products

A cartel agreement, in which firms come together to fix or rig the price of a good, is the most commonly known example of a collective restrictive trading practice.

Both independently undertaken and collective restrictive trading practices are now dealt with by the Competition and Markets Authority (CMA). The CMA usually asks the firm or firms involved to drop the practice voluntarily on the grounds that it is anti-competitive. A cartel agreement is usually banned, unless the firms involved persuade the CMA that the agreement is in the public interest — for example, to protect the public from injury.

> **SECTION 8.7 SUMMARY**
> - Monopoly leads to the manipulation of consumers and the exploitation of producer sovereignty.
> - By restricting output and raising prices, monopoly results in a net welfare loss as well as a transfer of consumer surplus into producer surplus and monopoly profit.
> - Competition policy is the part of government economic policy which tries to make the imperfectly competitive and monopolistic markets of the real world more competitive.
> - The aims of competition policy include preventing the exploitation of monopoly power, reducing costs of production, improving efficiency, getting rid of excessive profit so that prices reflect costs of production, and removing entry and exit barriers which separate markets.
> - The Competition and Markets Authority (CMA) is the government agency responsible for advising on and implementing UK competition policy.
> - The three parts of UK competition policy are monopoly policy, mergers policy and restrictive trading practices policy.
> - The CMA adopts a cost–benefit approach to competition policy.

8.8 Public ownership, privatisation, regulation and deregulation of markets

Public ownership

> **KEY TERM**
>
> **public ownership** ownership of industries, firms and other assets such as social housing by central government or local government. The state's acquisition of such assets is called nationalisation.

Publicly owned or state-owned industries are also known as *nationalised industries*. Although there were nationalised industries in the UK in the nineteenth and early twentieth centuries, the main period of nationalisation occurred in the years after the Second World War. From 1945 until 1951 and then intermittently from 1964 until 1979, whenever Labour governments had control of the UK economy, industries such as coal mining, the railways and the steel industry were taken into **public ownership**. Labour governments justified nationalisation on the grounds that effective state planning required public ownership of the 'commanding heights' of the economy. Public ownership was essential for efficient operation of key industries which were regarded as too important to be left to the vagaries of private ownership and market forces.

As well as being an instrument of socialist planning and control of the economy, public ownership was used (as we explained in the previous section) as a method of regulating the problem of monopoly — in particular, the problem of natural monopoly in the utility industries.

Since 1979 very few new industries have been taken into public ownership in the UK. However, there have been two examples of *temporary* nationalisation. The first of these was the complete or partial nationalisation of the Northern Rock, Lloyds, RBS and HBOS banks. This was a response to the financial crisis which hit the UK economy (and also the wider world economy) in 2007 and 2008. Because of the extreme adverse effects that bank collapses would have on other industries and consumers, banks were regarded as 'too important to fail'. Those that were in danger of failing were either nationalised or merged. The decision to take banks into public ownership was made for pragmatic rather than ideological reasons. The intention was always, particularly under the Conservative-led Coalition government, to sell the nationalised banks back to the private sector as soon as they became financially viable.

The other industry taken into temporary public ownership was the east coast railway service. The nationalisation of this service and its eventual return to the private sector, and subsequent renationalisation, are discussed in Case study 8.12.

TEST YOURSELF 8.12

Do you agree that public ownership leads to the creation of state monopolies? Justify your argument.

CASE STUDY 8.12

East Coast Rail returns to private hands, before being renationalised again

In March 2015, the *Guardian* newspaper reported that train services on the mainline between London and Edinburgh were once again being operated by a private firm after more than 5 years under state control, reigniting the row over ownership of the railway.

East Coast trains were rebranded as Virgin Trains East Coast. Under the management of a joint venture between two private sector companies, Stagecoach and Sir Richard Branson's Virgin, a private-sector organisation took over the running of the railway on an 8-year franchise.

The previous private operators of the east coast railway line failed to meet their financial commitments. A small government-owned company, Directly Operated Railways, stepped in to run trains on the mainline in late 2009 after the previous franchisee, National Express, walked away when revenues fell during the financial crisis.

In its 5 years as East Coast, the state-run firm gave several millions of pounds in profits to the Treasury. In the last 2 years in which it operated, East Coast was one of two state-owned firms to make a net contribution to government coffers, paying in more to the government than it received in subsidy or indirect grants.

The success of the nationalised East Coast trains led to calls to keep the line in state hands. The general secretary of the Trades Union Congress (TUC), Frances O'Grady, said that sale to the private sector would be a 'costly mistake'. She said: 'By taking East Coast out of public ownership the government is passing the profits to Stagecoach and Virgin shareholders, instead of using the cash to reduce rail fares and improve services for passengers.'

However, in June 2018, the east coast rail service was temporarily renationalised because the private owners Virgin and Stagecoach could no longer meet the promised payments in the £3.3 billion contract. With a reminder of its name before nationalisation in 1948, the new operator has been rebranded as the London and North Eastern Railway.

Follow-up questions

1 When was Virgin Trains East Coast set up?
2 What were the reasons for the Conservative government granting the company a franchise to operate trains?
3 What happened to the company in June 2018?
4 Do you agree that other privately owned operators of UK railway companies should also be renationalised? Justify your answer.

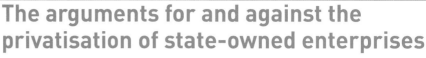

> **KEY TERM**
> **privatisation** the transfer of assets from the public sector to the private sector.

The arguments for and against the privatisation of state-owned enterprises

Privatisation involves the transfer of publicly owned assets to the private sector. In the UK, this has usually involved the sale to private ownership of nationalised industries and businesses that were previously owned by the state and accountable to central government. Between 1981 and 2015 more than 16 major industries were privatised and state ownership of industries was transformed from the ownership of major parts of the British economy to becoming a mere rump. Although the main privatisations involved the sale of nationalised firms and industries, other state-owned assets such as land and socially owned housing have also been privatised.

The case for privatisation

Arguments used to justify privatisation include:

● **Revenue raising.** Privatisation, or the sale of state-owned assets, provides the government with a short-term source of revenue, which at the height of privatisation was at least £3–4 billion a year. But obviously an asset cannot be sold off twice.

● **Reducing public spending and the government's borrowing requirement.** After 1979, Conservative governments aimed to reduce public spending and government borrowing. When the state successfully sold loss-making industries such as the Rover Group, public spending on subsidies fell. Government borrowing also falls if private ownership returns the industries to profitability, since corporation tax revenue is boosted and the state earns dividend income from any shares that it retains in the privatised company, providing that the privatised firms remain British.

● **The promotion of competition.** Privatisation has been justified on the grounds that it promotes competition through the break-up of monopoly. At the time of their privatisation, industries such as gas and electricity were natural monopolies. But the growth of technology-driven competition, together with the removal of barriers to entry by regulating agencies such as Ofgem, has significantly increased competition.

● **The promotion of efficiency.** For free-market economists, this is perhaps the most important justification for privatisation. Supporters of privatisation believe that public ownership gives rise to special forms of inefficiency which disappear once an industry moves into the private sector. The culture of public ownership makes nationalised industries resistant to change. Through exposure to the threat of takeover and the discipline of the capital market, the privatisation of a state-owned monopoly should improve the business's efficiency and commercial performance.

● **Popular capitalism.** The promotion of an enterprise culture was an important reason for privatisation in the UK. Privatisation extended share ownership to employees and other individuals who had not previously owned shares, and thus added to the incentive for the electorate to support the private enterprise economy. Privatisation has generally proved popular with voters, so governments, both Conservative and then Labour, saw no point in abandoning a winning programme.

The case against privatisation

Privatisation has the following possible disadvantages:

- **Monopoly abuse.** Opponents of privatisation have argued that, far from promoting competition and efficiency, privatisation increases monopoly abuse by transferring socially owned and accountable public monopolies into weakly regulated and less accountable private monopolies.
- **Short-termism wins over long-termism.** Many of the investments that need to be undertaken by the previously nationalised industries can only be profitable in the long term. There is a danger that under private ownership, such investments will not be made because company boards concentrate on the short-termism of delivering dividends to keep shareholders and financial institutions happy. Under-investment in maintaining the rail track and in technically advanced trains by the privatised railway companies is said to provide an example. However, there is a counter-argument that under public ownership, the government starved the nationalised industries of investment funds in order to keep government borrowing down.
- **Selling the 'family silver'.** Opponents of privatisation argue that if a private sector business were to sell its capital assets simply in order to raise revenue to pay for current expenditure, it would rightly incur the wrath of its shareholders. The same should be true of the government and the sale of state-owned assets. Taxpayers should not sanction the sale of capital assets owned on their behalf by the UK government to raise revenue to finance current spending on items such as wages and salaries. In reply, supporters of the privatisation programme argue that, far from selling the family silver, privatisation merely returns the family's assets to the family: that is, from the custody of the state to direct ownership by private individuals.
- **The free-lunch syndrome.** Opponents of privatisation claim that state-owned assets have been sold too cheaply, encouraging the belief among first-time share buyers that there is such a thing as a free lunch. This is because the offer price of shares in newly privatised industries was normally pitched at a level which guaranteed a risk-free capital gain or one-way bet at the taxpayer's expense. Arguably, this encourages the very opposite of an enterprise economy.

Regulation and deregulation of markets

Regulation

> **KEY TERM**
> **regulation** the imposition of rules and other constraints which restrict freedom of economic action.

Economic **regulation** involves the imposition of rules, controls and constraints which restrict freedom of economic action in the market place. There are two types of regulation: external regulation and self-regulation. Both types of regulation can be imposed by law. When this is the case, a failure to comply with a regulation means breaking the law. Court cases may follow which could lead to the imposition of fines or even imprisonment.

- External regulation, as the name suggests, involves an external agency laying down and enforcing rules and restraints. The external agency may be a government department such as the Department for Business, Innovation and Skills, or a special regulatory body or agency set up by government, such the Competition and Markets Authority.
- By contrast, self-regulation or voluntary regulation involves a group of individuals or firms regulating themselves — for example, through a professional association such as the Law Society or the British Medical Association.

269

Regulation and market failure

Competition can sometimes bring about a situation in which social costs and benefits are not the same as the private costs and benefits incurred and received by the people actually undertaking the market activity. As explained earlier in the chapter, the over-production of externalities such as environmental pollution, and the under-consumption of education, healthcare and other merit goods provide familiar examples of divergence between private and social costs and benefits. Governments use regulation to try to correct such market failures and to achieve a socially optimal level of production and consumption. Monopoly is also a form of market failure, and regulation is used to limit and deter monopoly exploitation of consumers.

Other examples of government regulation aimed largely at reducing the social costs of market activity include health and safety at work, anti-discrimination and safeguards of workers' rights, and consumer protection legislation. Much of this regulation is concerned with the adequate provision of information for customers and workers, and the setting of quality standards for the production of goods. Such regulation may affect advertising standards, consumers' rights of redress when purchasing faulty goods, and workers' rights in the event of discrimination or unfair dismissal.

Advantages of government regulation: a summary

In a narrow sense, regulation is necessary to protect:

- consumers from harmful products and to maintain quality standards
- workers from labour market exploitation
- the environment
- children and old people from exploitation and abuse
- people from self-harm

More broadly, regulation is necessary to enable markets to perform well and to limit the damage caused by market failures.

Deregulation

Deregulation involves the removal of any previously imposed regulations that have adversely restricted competition and freedom of market activity. During the last 35 years, significant deregulation has taken place in the UK and the USA. Systems of regulation built up during the early post-1945 period have on occasion been completely abandoned, while in other cases they have been watered down or modified. The UK government has removed the protected legal monopoly status enjoyed, for example, by bus companies, airlines and commercial television and radio companies. Access to BT's distribution network of land lines has been given to competitors in the telecommunications industry, and private power companies have been allowed to rent the services of the national electricity and gas distribution grids.

There are two main justifications of deregulation:

- the promotion of competition and market contestability through the removal of artificial barriers to market entry
- the removal of 'red tape' and bureaucracy which imposes unnecessary costs on economic agents, particularly businesses

---

STUDY TIP

While there is a strong case for removing many regulations, such as those that unnecessarily raise costs of production and consumer prices, many regulations can be justified on the grounds that they protect people from, for example, the abuse of monopoly power and harmful externalities.

KEY TERM

deregulation the removal of previously imposed regulations.

TEST YOURSELF 8.13

With examples of each, distinguish between deregulation and privatisation.

Disadvantages of government regulation: a summary

In a narrow sense, deregulation is necessary to get rid of:

- unnecessary bureaucracy and 'red tape'
- compliance costs
- interference in individual economic decision making

More broadly, deregulation enables markets to function more efficiently and to incur lower costs. The justification of deregulation is based on the assumption that government intervention in a market economy must be kept to a minimum and that individuals know better than governments what is in their self-interest.

Deregulation and the theory of contestable markets

Much of the justification for the policies of deregulation and economic liberalisation that have been pursued in recent years has been provided by the theory of contestable markets, which was explained earlier in the chapter and in Chapter 5. Contestable market theory argues that the most effective way to promote competitive behaviour within markets is not to impose ever-more regulation upon firms and industries, but to carry out the opposite process of deregulation.

According to this view, the main function of deregulation is to remove barriers to entry, thereby creating incentives both for new firms to enter and contest the market and for established firms to behave in a more competitive way. Under the influence of the theory of contestable markets, governments have sought to remove or loosen all regulations whose main effect has been to reduce competition and to create unnecessary barriers to market entry.

Regulatory capture

Another theory that has had some influence upon the trend towards deregulation is the theory of **regulatory capture**. This theory argues that regulatory agencies created by government can be 'captured' by the industries or firms they are intended to oversee and regulate. Following capture, the regulatory agencies begin to operate in the industry's interest rather than on behalf of the consumers whom they are supposed to protect. A classic case of regulatory capture occurred when the director general of Oflot, the agency which regulates the national lottery, was caught accepting free air tickets and other 'sweeteners' from one of the lottery companies he was supposed to regulate.

Regulatory capture can also occur without the regulator behaving inappropriately. For example, the inevitable close contacts between the regulator and the regulated may mean that the regulator becomes predisposed to accepting the views of the organisations being regulated rather than those of the consumer. Also, the regulator often relies on the regulated organisations to provide much of the information which it uses to make its judgements; the information supplied may be biased.

Even if regulatory capture does not take place, the supporters of deregulation argue that much regulatory activity is unnecessary and ultimately burdensome upon industry and consumers. Once established, the regulators have an incentive to extend their role by introducing ever more rules and regulations, since it is in this way that they justify their pay and their jobs. Regulation acts both as an informal 'tax' upon the regulated, raising production costs and consumer prices, and also as an extra barrier to market entry, restricting competition.

KEY TERM

regulatory capture occurs when regulatory agencies act in the interest of regulated firms rather on behalf of the consumers they are supposed to protect.

TEST YOURSELF 8.14

Describe one other example of alleged regulatory capture besides the example we have given.

The regulation of the privatised utility industries

As we have explained, deregulatory policies have been implemented alongside privatisation in liberalising the UK economy. In the 1980s and 1990s, UK governments realised that once industries such as telecommunications, gas, water and electricity were privatised, there was a danger they might abuse their monopoly position and exploit the consumer. For this reason, special regulatory agencies such as Ofgem, which now regulates the gas and electricity industries, were set up at the time of privatisation to act as watchdogs over the performance of the utilities in the private sector. Initially, industry-specific regulatory bodies were created, but some of these agencies have been merged and now cover more than one industry.

The establishment of regulatory agencies such as Ofrail at a time when governments have actively been pursuing a policy of deregulation and economic liberalisation created a rather strange paradox and a source of possible conflict. On the one hand, by setting markets free, deregulation reduces the role of the state; on the other hand, new watchdog bodies, such as Ofgem, have extended the regulatory role of government and its agencies.

However, successive governments have argued that there need be no conflict between regulation and deregulation. This is because the regulatory bodies are themselves actively involved in deregulating the industries they oversee — for example, by enforcing the removal of barriers that prevent the entry of new firms. Recent technological progress has made it increasingly possible for new firms to enter the utility industries, particularly in the telecommunications industry. By introducing competition into markets that were previously dominated by established companies such as BT and British Gas, new market entrants have eroded the natural monopoly position previously enjoyed by the privatised utilities.

Supporters of the liberalisation programme hope that the watchdog agencies will prove so successful that eventually these regulatory bodies can wither away, when the markets they oversee have become sufficiently competitive. However, at best this is likely to be a long process. Although new firms are beginning to compete in the markets previously completely dominated by state-owned utilities, established companies like British Gas are still dominant. Their continuing market power means that, certainly for the next few years, the regulatory bodies set up at the time of privatisation must continue as a surrogate for competition. Some commentators argue that, far from withering away, the new regulatory agencies may gradually extend their powers and functions. Free-market critics of economic regulation believe that the UK regulatory system provides a classic example of a growing bureaucracy.

SECTION 8.8 SUMMARY

- Publicly owned or state-owned industries are also known as nationalised industries.
- Labour governments justified nationalisation on the grounds that effective state planning required public ownership of the 'commanding heights' of the economy.
- Public ownership was regarded as essential for efficient operation of key industries which were regarded as too important to be left to the vagaries of private ownership and market forces.
- Public ownership was also used as a method of regulating the problem of monopoly — in particular, the problem of natural monopoly in the utility industries.
- Since 2009, there has been temporary nationalisation of some banks and the east coast railway service.
- Regulation is the imposition of rules and other constraints which restrict freedom of economic action.
- Governments use regulation to correct market failures so as to achieve a socially optimal level of production and consumption.
- Regulation is used to limit and deter monopoly exploitation of consumers.
- Regulatory agencies such as Ofwat have been created to regulate privatised utility industries and the railways.
- The theory of regulatory capture argues that regulatory agencies created by government can be 'captured' by the industries or firms they are intended to oversee and regulate.
- Following capture, the regulatory agencies begin to operate in the industry's interest rather than on behalf of the consumers whom they are supposed to protect.
- Deregulation is the removal of previously imposed rules deemed to harm economic performance.

8.9 Government intervention in markets

The reasons against and for government intervention in markets

To understand why governments intervene in markets in economies such as the UK, it is useful to divide economists (and politicians) into two different groups: those who believe that unregulated markets generally work well, and those who argue that markets are prone to market failure. The former group are non-interventionists who want to leave as much as possible to market forces, while the latter group believe that government intervention can make markets work better.

- **Pro-free market economists** see a market economy as a calm and orderly place in which the market mechanism, working through incentives transmitted by price signals in competitive markets, achieves a better or more optimal outcome than can be attained through government intervention. In essence, risk-taking business men and women, who will gain or lose through the correctness of their decisions in the market place, know better what to produce than civil servants and planners cocooned by risk-free salaries and secured pensions. And providing that markets are sufficiently competitive, what is produced is ultimately decided by the wishes of consumers, who know better than governments what is good for them. According to this philosophy, the correct economic function of government is to act as 'night-watchman' by maintaining law and order, providing public goods and possibly merit goods when the market fails, and generally ensuring a suitable environment in which 'wealth-creating' firms can function in competitive markets, subject to minimum interference and regulation.
- **Interventionist economists**, by contrast, believe that all too often markets are uncompetitive, characterised by monopoly power and producer sovereignty, and prone to other forms of market failure. Additionally, uncertainty about the future and lack of correct market information are destabilising forces. By intervening in the economy, especially to correct market failures, the government 'knows better' than unregulated market forces. It can anticipate and counter the destabilising forces existent in markets, achieving a better outcome than is likely in an economy subject to market forces alone.

Correcting market failures

There are various methods open to a government for correcting, or at least reducing, market failures. At one extreme, the government can abolish the market, using instead the command or planning mechanism, financed from general taxation, for providing goods and services. At the other extreme, the government can try to influence market behaviour by providing information, and by exhorting and 'nudging' firms and consumers to behave in certain ways (for example, not to use plastic bags). Between these extremes, governments can impose regulations to limit people's freedom of action in the market place, and use taxes and subsidies, price ceilings and price floors to alter prices in the market in order to change incentives and economic behaviour.

Government provision of public goods and merit goods

Because of the free-rider problem which we explained on page 233, markets may fail to provide pure public goods such as national defence and police services. When free-riding occurs, the incentive function of prices breaks down. If goods are provided by a market, people can free-ride rather than pay a price, so the firms that are trying to sell the goods cannot make a profit. Given that there is a need for public goods, as we have seen, governments often step into the gap and provide the goods, financing the provision out of general taxation.

Just as governments discourage the production and consumption of negative externalities and demerit goods, in much the same way they try to encourage the production and consumption of positive externalities and merit goods. The government may choose to regulate or to try to change the prices of merit goods and other goods and activities which yield external benefits. In the latter case, subsidies are often used to encourage production and consumption.

Regulation, on the other hand, can force consumers to consume merit goods. The government may require people to be vaccinated against disease and to wear seatbelts in cars and crash helmets on motorbikes.

In the UK, education is both compulsory and completely subsidised, from 2015 at least for children between the ages of 5 and 18. Low-income families would be in an impossible situation if required to pay for education as well as to send their children to school. Subsidies can, of course, be paid to private providers of education and healthcare: namely, to private schools and private hospitals. However, in the UK, education and healthcare are also provided by the state, forming an important part of public spending. Nevertheless, private sector provision is growing. One reason for growing private-sector provision of merit goods lies in the fact that state provision does not necessarily mean good-quality provision.

SYNOPTIC LINK
Reread the earlier sections of this chapter on the various forms of market failure.

Forcing firms and consumers to generate positive externalities

The state can impose regulations that force firms and consumers to generate positive externalities. Local authority bylaws can require households to maintain the appearance of properties, and the state may order landowners to plant trees. In this situation, it is illegal *not* to provide external benefits for others.

Government intervention, negative externalities and demerit goods

There are two main ways in which governments can intervene to try to correct the market failures caused by negative externalities and demerit goods. As with positive externalities and merit goods, the government can use quantity controls or regulation. Alternatively, or in addition, it can use taxation.

Regulation and the correction of market failures

Governments use regulations, including compulsory consumption, and subsidies to enforce or encourage production of positive externalities and the consumption of merit goods.

Regulation can directly influence the quantity of the externality that a firm or household can generate, and the level of consumption of a demerit good such as tobacco. In its most extreme form, regulation can be used to ban completely, or criminalise, the generation of negative externalities such as pollution or the sale and consumption of a demerit good such as heroin. However, it may be impossible to produce a good or service such as electricity in a coal-burning power station without generating at least some of a negative externality. In this situation, banning the externality has the perverse effect of preventing production of a good (for example, electricity) as well as the bad (pollution). Because of this, quantity controls that fall short of a complete ban may be more appropriate. These include maximum emission limits and restrictions on the time of day or year during which the negative externality can legally be emitted. In the case of 'milder' demerit goods, smoking can be banned in public places, while shops would break the law by selling alcohol to younger teenagers.

Taxation and the correction of market failures

Until recently, governments have been more likely to use regulation rather than taxation to reduce negative externalities such as pollution and congestion. Indeed, in the past, it was difficult to find examples of pollution taxes outside the pages of economics textbooks, possibly because politicians feared that pollution taxes would be too unpopular. But in recent years, governments have become more prepared to use congestion and pollution taxes. This reflects growing concern, among governments and the public alike, of environmental issues such as global warming and the problems posed by fossil fuel emissions and other pollutants. It may also reflect both the growing influence of green or environment pressure groups, such as Friends of the Earth, and a growing preference to tackle environmental problems with market solutions rather than through regulation.

Completely banning negative externalities and demerit goods is a form of market replacement rather than market adjustment. By contrast, because **taxes** placed on goods affect incentives which consumers and firms face, they provide a market-orientated solution to the problems posed by negative externalities and demerit goods. Taxation compensates for the fact that there is a missing market in the externality. In the case of pollution, the government calculates the money value of the negative externality, and imposes this on the firm as a pollution tax. This is known as the 'polluter must pay' principle. The pollution tax creates an incentive, which was previously lacking, for less of the bad to be dumped on others. By so doing, the tax internalises the externality. The polluting firm must now cover all the costs of production, including the cost of negative externalities, and include these in the price charged to customers. By setting the tax so that the price the consumer pays equals the social cost of producing another unit of the good generating the negative externality, resource allocation in the economy is improved. However, a pollution tax, like any tax, itself introduces new inefficiencies and distortions into the market, associated with the costs of collecting the tax and with creating incentives to evade the tax illegally: for example, by dumping pollution at night to escape detection. This is an example of government failure which is explained in the final section of this chapter.

> ## KEY TERM
> **tax** a compulsory levy imposed by the government to pay for its activities. Taxes can also be used to achieve other objectives, such as reduced consumption of demerit goods.

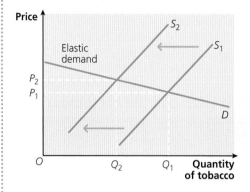

Figure 8.12 The effect of imposing a tax on tobacco when demand is elastic

Pollution permits

Until quite recently, the main choice of policy for dealing with the problem of pollution was between regulation and taxation. As we have explained, the former is an interventionist solution whereas taxation, based on the principle that the polluter must pay, has been seen as a more market-orientated solution, but nevertheless one which required the government to levy and collect the pollution tax. In the 1990s, another market-orientated solution started in the USA, based on a trading market in permits or licences to pollute. More locally to the UK, the EU Emissions Trading Scheme is now the centrepiece of European efforts to cut emissions.

A permits to pollute scheme (for electricity) still involves regulation: for example, the imposition of maximum limits on the amount of pollution that coal-burning power stations are allowed to emit, followed by a steady reduction in these ceilings in each subsequent year (say, by 5%). But once this regulatory framework has been established, a market in traded pollution permits takes over, creating market-orientated incentives for the power station companies to reduce pollution because they can make money out of it.

A tradable market in permits to pollute works in the following way. Energy companies able to reduce pollution by more than the law requires sell their spare permits to other power stations that, for technical or other reasons, decide not to, or cannot, reduce pollution below the maximum limit. The latter still comply with the law, even when exceeding the maximum emission limit, because they buy the spare permits sold by the first group of power stations. But, in the long run, even power stations that find it difficult to comply with the law have an incentive to reduce pollution, so as to avoid the extra cost of production created by the need to buy pollution permits.

Price ceilings or maximum price laws

Perhaps the simplest ways in which a government can impose a price control is through the use of a **price ceiling** or a price floor. Suppose, for example, that in a particular market — say, the market for bread — the government imposes a price ceiling or maximum legal price, shown as P_1 in Figure 8.13. Because the price ceiling has been imposed below the free-market equilibrium price of P^*, it creates excess demand, shown by the distance between Q_1 and Q_2. In a free market, market forces would raise the price and eliminate the excess demand. But, because the price ceiling prevents this happening, there is no mechanism in the market for getting rid of excess demand. Rather than rationing by price, households are rationed by quantity. Queues and waiting lists occur, and possibly bribery and corruption, through which favoured customers buy the good but others do not. It is also worth noting that price ceilings interfere with the incentive function of prices, in the sense that the ceilings prevent prices from rising to attract new firms into the market.

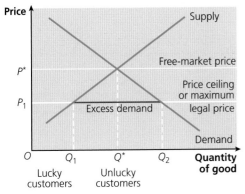

Figure 8.13 The effect of a maximum price control or price ceiling

> **KEY TERM**
>
> **price ceiling** a price *above* which it is illegal to trade. Price ceilings, or maximum legal prices, can distort markets by creating excess demand.

The emergence of an informal or shadow market (sometimes called a black market) is also likely. Secondary markets emerge when primary markets (or free markets) are prevented from working properly. A secondary market is a meeting place for lucky and unlucky customers. In the secondary market, some lucky customers, who bought the good at price P_1, resell at a higher price to unlucky customers unable to purchase the good in the primary market.

Price floors or minimum legal prices

> **KEY TERM**
>
> **price floor** a price *below* which it is illegal to trade. Price floors, or minimum legal prices, can distort markets by creating excess supply.

Sometimes governments impose minimum price laws or **price floors**. For a minimum price law to affect a market, the price floor must be set above the free-market price. Figure 8.14 illustrates the possible effect of the national minimum wage imposed in UK labour markets. A national minimum wage rate set at W_1 (which is *above* the free-market wage rate of W^*) creates an excess supply of labour, thereby causing unemployment equal to the distance between L_1 and L_2. It may also cause rogue employers to break the law: for example, paying 'poverty wages' to vulnerable workers such as illegal immigrants. Note also that whereas a price ceiling imposed above the free-market price in Figure 8.13 would have no effect on the price at which bread is traded in the market, a national minimum wage set below the free-market wage rate in Figure 8.14 would have no effect on unemployment. This is the situation in many UK labour markets.

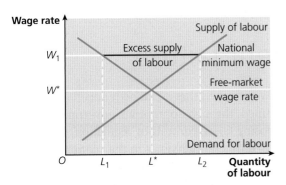

Figure 8.14 The possible effect of the UK national minimum wage

As with price ceilings, price floors interfere with the incentive function of prices. This is because falling prices cause inefficient or high-cost firms to leave the market. A price floor prevents this from happening.

TEST YOURSELF 8.16
With the help of appropriate diagrams, relate the effects of maximum and minimum legal prices to the concepts of excess supply and excess demand.

STUDY TIP
Make sure you can describe and explain at least three ways in which government intervention can affect the price of a good or service.

QUANTITATIVE SKILLS 8.5

Worked example: calculating the effect of a price ceiling

Figure 8.15 shows how the imposition of a price ceiling distorts a market.

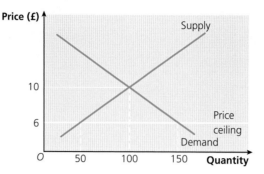

Figure 8.15 Price ceiling

Calculate the total amount spent on the good, first at market equilibrium price, and then when the price ceiling is in place.

At any price which might be charged for the good, the money value of the good bought and sold is calculated by multiplying price by quantity ($P \times Q$). At the good's equilibrium or market-clearing price of £10, 100 units of the good are bought and sold, so the amount spent on the good is £1,000. However, when a price ceiling of £6 is imposed, only 50 units of the good are bought and sold. The money spent on the good falls to £300, even though consumers would like to buy 150 units of the good at this price.

SECTION 8.9 SUMMARY

- Pro-free market and interventionist economists hold different views on when governments should intervene in markets.
- Reasons for intervention include the correction of market failures, which includes government provision of public goods and merit goods and forcing or incentivising firms and consumers to generate positive externalities.
- Methods of intervention include regulation and taxation, the imposition of price ceilings and price floors, and the introduction of pollution permits.

8.10 Government failure

KEY TERM
government failure occurs when government intervention reduces economic welfare, leading to an allocation of resources that is worse than the free-market outcome.

When explaining market failure, we assumed that it can be reduced or completely eliminated, once identified, through appropriate government intervention: for example, by imposing taxes, controls or regulation. But there is another possibility. When the government intervenes in the economy to reduce or correct market failure, its intervention may lead to the appearance of other forms of resource misallocation. When this happens, **government failure** occurs.

We saw earlier that governments often provide free state education because they wish to increase consumption of what they perceive to be a merit good.

If you refer back to Figure 8.10, you will see that the socially optimal level of provision of education, Q_2, is higher than Q_1, the amount of education which markets would probably provide. However, government intervention does not in itself ensure that Q_2 is eventually provided. Since it makes decisions on the basis of imperfect information, the government may not know what is the socially optimal level of education. Some people argue that free state education leads to over-provision because people want to consume the quantity available when zero price is charged for education. If this is the case, governments may create, rather than remove, market distortions. Some people also believe that the quality of state education is poorer than that of private market-based education. If this is the case, it is a further example of government failure.

Reasons for government failure

The pursuit of conflicting policy objectives

A good example is provided by government investment decisions. When governments wish to expand the economy, they may give the go-ahead to long-term investment projects such as the building of new roads, which they then cancel because of the perceived need to contract the economy. Very often government decisions can be criticised for favouring short-termism at the expense of long-termism.

Administrative costs

There are also administrative costs to consider. Government intervention in the economy to correct market failure may create unnecessary layers of bureaucracy, which create costs which taxpayers have to pay. If so, this is a government failure. Examples are the high costs the UK government incurred when deciding whether or not to permit the construction of a third runway at Heathrow airport, or to expand Gatwick or Stansted, or to build a completely new airport in the Thames estuary. Many free-market economists believe this is unnecessary government expenditure, but more interventionist economists believe the expenditure is fully justified because it leads to better eventual government decisions.

The 'law of unintended consequences'

At this point, it is appropriate to introduce the 'law of unintended consequences'. This 'law', which has become very fashionable in recent years, predicts that, whenever the government intervenes in the market economy, effects will be unleashed which the policy-makers had not foreseen or intended. Sometimes the unintended effects may be advantageous to the economy, while in other instances they may be harmful but relatively innocuous. In either of these circumstances, government intervention can be justified on the grounds that the social benefits of intervention exceed the social costs and therefore contribute to a net gain in economic welfare. But if government activity — however well intentioned — triggers harmful consequences which are greater than the benefits that the government intervention is supposed to promote, then government failure results.

STUDY TIP
It is important to avoid confusing government failure with market failure.

TEST YOURSELF 8.17
With examples of each, explain the difference between government failure and market failure.

279

Examples of possible government failure

Government price controls create black markets

In section 8.9, we explained how a price ceiling or maximum price law can create excess demand in a market, which is then relieved through trading in an informal or shadow market: in other words, a black market. Price ceilings are normally put in place to protect consumers from high prices. However, the rising price of a product may simply reflect market forces and the changing nature of supply or demand in the market. A higher price might be needed to create incentives for consumers to economise and for firms to divert more scarce resources into producing the good. The price ceiling may prevent this happening. The controlled price can send out the wrong signals and create the wrong incentives, thus contributing to resource misallocation. And since it may be a criminal activity to break the price law, black markets are sometimes characterised by corruption and the threat of the use of illegal force.

However, economists of a free-market persuasion often justify black markets on the grounds that they do the job that the primary market should do: that is, equate demand with supply. A price ceiling prevents the primary market from working properly. Arguably, the touts and dealers who act as middlemen in the black market or underground economy contribute to better resource allocation, although their contribution would not be needed if there were no price controls. A black market or secondary market only comes into existence because price controls distort the primary market.

CASE STUDY 8.13

The landfill tax and government failure

Government policies that aim to reduce the discharge of negative externalities can also lead to government failure. Almost every economic activity produces waste: for example, household rubbish and the waste created by building and construction. A large proportion of UK waste is either incinerated (which discharges pollutants into the atmosphere) or collected by local government and placed in landfill sites. Landfill also causes pollution, and a further problem arises as all the available landfill sites fill up.

In 1996, the UK government imposed a landfill tax which it hoped would create jobs and reduce waste. But to evade the tax, rogue building contractors and some households began to fly-tip and to dump rubbish in public places and on other people's land. This was an unintended and adverse consequence of a tax that was intended to improve the environment.

Many blame the controversial landfill tax for the rise in organised unauthorised dumping. The tax increased the costs of taking waste to licensed sites by up to a third. The cost of getting rid of one truckload of rubble could be as high as £400. Finding alternative dumping grounds, where off-loading a lorry costs little or nothing, allows the unscrupulous to make a fortune. But the cost to the environment is immense.

Research published in 2011 by the Countryside Alliance uncovered the enormous scale of illegal fly-tipping in England and Wales. Figures obtained under the Freedom of Information Act reveal that illegal fly-tipping cost taxpayers over £40 million in 2010. At least 656,000 incidents of unlawful rubbish dumping were recorded in England and Wales between April 2010 and March 2011, which works out at 75 incidents of fly-tipping every hour — more than one per minute!

At the time, the cost of clearing the waste alone was just under £25 million, yet only one in 50 cases led to a prosecution. In cash-strapped rural local authorities, the rate of prosecutions dropped to just 3 in every 1,000. If waste is dumped on private land, the owners, irrespective of having no part in the fly-tip, have a duty of care and are bound by law to clear it up in their own time and at their expense.

The chief executive of the Countryside Alliance said, 'With the Coalition Government raising the landfill tax and with more cuts coming to council budgets, this problem is only going to get worse.'

More than 1 million incidents of fly-tipping were dealt with by councils in England in 2016/17, costing taxpayers £58 million to clear up.

Follow-up questions

1 Relate fly-tipping to the concept of negative externalities.
2 Do you agree that landfill illustrates both market failure and government failure? Justify your answer.
3 In Singapore, littering fines range from $300 to $1,000 for first-time offenders. The fine rises up to $5,000 for third-time offenders with the possibility of facing time in prison. Do you think that similar fines should be imposed in the UK on people who are caught fly-tipping?
4 How might nudge theory be used to discourage people from dropping litter or fly-tipping?

QUANTITATIVE SKILLS 8.6

Worked example: calculating price elasticity of demand

Between 2015 and 2019 a government increased its tax on waste disposal. Table 8.8 shows the changing price of waste disposal at a landfill site.

Table 8.8 Price of waste disposal

Year	£ per tonne of waste
2015	10
2016	11
2017	12
2018	13
2019	14

If the quantity of landfill space demanded fell by 10% between 2015 and 2019, calculate from the data the price elasticity of demand for landfill space.

If the quantity demanded fell by 10% and the price per tonne rose by 40%, the price elasticity of demand for landfill space was:

−10%/+40%

which is −0.25. According to the data, since the elasticity statistic (ignoring the minus sign) was less than 1 or unity, the demand for landfill space was inelastic with respect to the change in price.

- Governments use regulations, including prohibition, and taxation to prevent or reduce production of negative externalities and to reduce consumption of demerit goods.
- Governments use regulations, including compulsory consumption, and subsidies to enforce or encourage production of positive externalities and the consumption of merit goods.
- Along with public goods, merit goods such as education are often provided by governments.
- A price ceiling imposed below the free-market price distorts the market and creates excess demand.
- Governments impose price floors or minimum legal prices, such as the national minimum wage, to prevent prices falling below desired levels.
- Governments may create, rather than remove, market distortions.
- Government failure occurs when government intervention in markets fails to correct market failure and/ or leads to outcomes worse than the intervention was meant to correct. Like market failure, government failure is associated with a misallocation of resources.
- Government failure can result from government decisions made on the basis of inadequate information; as a result of conflicting objectives; and from the administrative costs of government intervention. It is also associated with the unintended consequences of government intervention in markets.

Questions

1 Do you agree that government policies which aim to correct market failure are always successful? Justify your answer.

2 Evaluate different forms of government intervention to deal with the problems caused by negative externalities.

3 Evaluate the view that if merit goods are provided free by the state, the socially optimal level of consumption is always achieved.

4 Explain how monopoly may lead to market failure.

5 Using the concept of elasticity, explain why taxing demerit goods may be relatively ineffective in reducing their consumption.

6 With the help of an appropriate diagram, explain how a maximum legal price may distort a market.

7 Using examples, explain the difference between market failures resulting from inefficiency and those resulting from inequity.

8 Do you agree that markets can be relied upon to reduce the problems of environmental pollution? Justify your answer.

9 Evaluate the advantages and disadvantages of privatisation.

Microeconomics key terms

abnormal profit (also known as **supernormal profit** and **above-normal profit**) profit over and above normal profit.

absolute poverty a condition characterised by severe deprivation of basic human needs, including food, safe drinking water, sanitation facilities, health, shelter, education and information. It depends not only on income but also on access to services.

allocative efficiency occurs when it is impossible to improve overall economic welfare by reallocating resources between markets. In the whole economy, price must equal marginal cost $(P = MC)$ in every market.

allocative function of prices changing relative prices allocate scarce resources away from markets exhibiting excess supply and into markets in which there is excess demand.

allocative inefficiency occurs when $P > MC$, in which case too little of a good is produced and consumed, and when $P < MC$, in which case too much of a good is produced and consumed.

altruism concern for the welfare of others.

anchoring a cognitive bias describing the human tendency when making decisions to rely too heavily on the first piece of information offered (the so-called 'anchor'). Individuals use an initial piece of information when making subsequent judgements.

artificial barriers (also known as **strategic barriers**) 'man-made' barriers to market entry, e.g. patent protection.

asymmetric information when one party to a market transaction possesses less information relevant to the exchange than the other.

availability bias occurs when individuals make judgements about the likelihood of future events according to how easy it is to recall examples of similar events.

average cost total cost divided by the size of output

average cost of labour total wage costs divided by the number of workers employed.

average fixed cost total cost of employing the fixed factors of production to produce a particular level of output, divided by the size of output: $AFC = TFC \div Q$.

average returns of labour total output divided by the total number of workers employed.

average revenue total revenue divided by output.

average total cost (also known as **average cost**) total cost of producing a particular level of output, divided by the size of output: $ATC = AFC + AVC$.

average variable cost total cost of employing the variable factors of production to produce a particular level of output divided by the size of output: $AVC = TVC \div Q$.

behavioural economics a method of economic analysis that applies psychological insights into human behaviour to explain how individuals make choices and decisions.

bounded rationality when making decisions, individuals' rationality is limited by the information they have, the limitations of their minds, and the finite amount of time available in which to make decisions.

bounded self-control limited self-control in which individuals lack the self-control to act in what they see as their self-interest.

capital good (also known as a **producer good**) a good which is used in the production of other goods or services.

capital productivity output per unit of capital.

cartel a collusive agreement by firms, usually to fix prices. Sometimes there is also an agreement to restrict output and to deter the entry of new firms.

choice choosing between alternatives when making a decision on how to use scarce resources.

choice architecture a framework setting out different ways in which choices can be presented to consumers, and the impact of that presentation on consumer decision making.

cognitive bias is a systematic error in thinking that affects the decisions and judgements that people make.

collective bargaining a process by which wage rates and other conditions of work are negotiated and agreed upon by a union or unions with an employer or employers.

command economy (also known as a **planned economy**) an economy in which government officials or planners allocate economic resources to firms and other productive enterprises.

Competition and Markets Authority government agency responsible for advising on and implementing UK competition policy.

competition policy the part of the government's microeconomic policy and industrial policy which aims to make goods markets more competitive. It comprises policy toward monopoly, mergers and restrictive trading practices.

competitive markets markets in which the large number of buyers and sellers possess good market information and can easily enter or leave the market.

complementary goods when two goods are complements, they experience joint demand.

complete market failure a market fails to function at all and a 'missing market' results.

composite demand demand for a good which has more than one use, which means that an increase in demand for one use of the good reduces the supply of the good for an alternative use. It is related to the concept of competing supply.

concentration ratio measures the market share (percentage of the total market) of the biggest firms in the market. For example, a five-firm concentration ratio measures the aggregate market share of the largest five firms.

condition of demand a determinant of demand, other than the good's own price, that fixes the position of the demand curve.

condition of supply a determinant of supply, other than the good's own price, that fixes the position of the supply curve.

constant returns to scale when the scale of all the factors of production employed increases, output increases at the same rate.

consumer good a good which is consumed by individuals or households to satisfy their needs or wants.

consumer surplus a measure of the economic welfare enjoyed by consumers: surplus utility received over and above the price paid for a good.

consumption externality an externality (which may be positive or negative) generated in the course of consuming a good or service.

contestable market a market in which the potential exists for new firms to enter the market. A

perfectly contestable market has no entry or exit barriers and no sunk costs, and both incumbent firms and new entrants have access to the same level of technology.

creative destruction capitalism evolving and renewing itself over time through new technologies and innovations replacing older technologies and innovations.

cross-elasticity of demand measures the extent to which the demand for a good changes in response to a change in the price of another good; it is calculated by dividing the percentage change in quantity demanded by the percentage change in the price of another good.

deadweight loss the name given to the loss of economic welfare when the maximum attainable level of total welfare fails to be achieved.

decrease in demand a leftward shift of the demand curve.

decrease in supply a leftward shift of the supply curve.

decreasing returns to scale when the scale of all the factors of production employed increases, output increases at a slower rate.

default choice an option that is selected automatically unless an alternative is specified.

demand the quantity of a good or service that consumers are willing and able to buy at given prices in a given period of time.

demerit goods goods, such as tobacco, for which the social costs of consumption exceed the private costs. Value judgements are involved in deciding that a good is a demerit good.

deregulation the removal of previously imposed regulations.

derived demand demand for a good or factor of production, wanted not for its own sake, but as a consequence of the demand for something else.

diseconomies of scale as output increases, long-run average cost rises.

disequilibrium a situation in which opposing forces are out of balance.

distribution of income how income is divided between rich and poor, or between different groups in society, e.g. on a regional, age or gender basis.

division of labour this concept goes hand in hand with specialisation. Different workers perform different tasks in the course of producing a good or service.

distribution of wealth how wealth is divided between rich and poor, or between different groups in society, e.g. on a regional, age or gender basis.

divorce of ownership from control the owners and those who control the firm (managers) are different groups with different objectives.

duopoly two firms only in a market.

dynamic efficiency measures improvements in productive efficiency that occur in the long run over time.

economic growth the increase in the *potential* level of real output the economy can produce over a period of time.

economic system the set of institutions within which a community decides what, how and for whom to produce.

economic welfare the economic well-being of an individual, a group within society, or an economy.

economies of scale as output increases, long-run average cost falls.

effective demand the desire for a good or service backed by an ability to pay.

elasticity the proportionate responsiveness of a second variable to an initial change in the first variable.

elasticity of demand for labour proportionate change in demand for labour following a change in the wage rate. The elasticity can be calculated by using the following formula:

proportionate change in quantity of labour demanded/proportionate change in the wage rate

elasticity of supply of labour proportionate change in the supply of labour following a change in the wage rate. The elasticity can be calculated by using the following formula:

proportionate change in quantity of labour supplied/proportionate change in the wage rate

entry barriers obstacles that make it difficult for a new firm to enter a market.

equality when everyone is treated exactly the same. A completely equal distribution of income means that everybody has the same income.

equilibrium a state of rest or balance between opposing forces.

equity when everyone is treated fairly.

excess demand when consumers wish to buy more than firms wish to sell, with the price below the equilibrium price.

excess supply when firms wish to sell more than consumers wish to buy, with the price above the equilibrium price.

exchange to give something in return for something else received. Money is a medium of exchange.

excludable good people who are unprepared to pay can be excluded from benefiting from the good.

exit barriers obstacles that make it difficult for an established firm to leave a market.

external diseconomy of scale an increase in long-run average costs of production resulting from the growth of the market or industry of which the firm is a part.

external economy of scale a fall in long-run average costs of production resulting from the growth of the market or industry of which the firm is a part.

externality a public good, in the case of an external benefit, or a public bad, in the case of an external cost, that is 'dumped' on third parties outside the market.

factors of production inputs into the production process, such as land, labour, capital and enterprise.

fairness the quality of being impartial, just, or free of favouritism. It can mean treating people equally, sharing with others, giving others respect and time, and not taking advantage of them.

firm a productive organisation which sells its output of goods and/or services commercially.

fixed cost cost of production which, in the short run, does not change with output.

framing how something is presented (the 'frame') influences the choices people make.

free-rider problem a free rider is someone who benefits without paying as a result of non-excludability. Customers may choose not to pay for a good, preferring instead to free ride, with the result that the incentive to provide the good through the market disappears.

full employment when all who are able and willing to work are employed.

fundamental economic problem how best to make decisions about the allocation of scarce resources among competing uses so as to improve and maximise human happiness and welfare.

geographical immobility of labour when workers are unwilling or unable to move from one area to another in search of work.

Gini coefficient measures the extent to which the distribution of income or wealth among individuals or households within an economy deviates from a perfectly equal distribution.

government failure occurs when government intervention reduces economic welfare, leading to an allocation of resources that is worse than the free-market outcome.

hit-and-run competition occurs when a new entrant can 'hit' the market, make profits and then 'run', given that there are no or low barriers to exit.

hypothesis of diminishing marginal utility for a single consumer, the marginal utility derived from a good or service diminishes for each additional unit consumed.

immobility of labour the inability of labour to move from one job to another, either for occupational reasons (e.g. the need for training) or for geographical reasons (e.g. the cost of moving to another part of the country).

incentive function of prices prices create incentives for people to alter their economic behaviour, e.g. a higher price creates an incentive for firms to supply more of a good or service.

income personal or household income is the flow of money a person or household receives in a particular time period.

income elasticity of demand measures the extent to which the demand for a good changes in response to a change in income; it is calculated by dividing the percentage change in quantity demanded by the percentage change in income.

increase in demand a rightward shift of the demand curve.

increase in supply a rightward shift of the supply curve.

increasing returns to scale when the scale of all the factors of production employed increases, output increases at a faster rate.

individual demand the quantity of a good or service that a particular consumer or individual is willing and able to buy at different market prices.

inferior good a good for which demand decreases as income rises and demand increases as income falls

information failure occurs when people make wrong decisions because they do not possess or they ignore relevant information. Very often they are myopic (short-sighted) about the future.

innovation improves on or makes a significant contribution to something that has already been invented, thereby turning the results of invention into a product.

internal economies and diseconomies of scale changes in long-run average costs of production resulting from changes in the size or scale of a firm or plant.

invention making something entirely new; something that did not exist before at all.

joint supply when one good is produced, another good is also produced from the same raw materials, perhaps as a by-product.

labour productivity output per worker.

law of diminishing marginal returns (also known as **the law of diminishing marginal (and average) productivity**) a *short-term* law which states that as a variable factor of production is added to a fixed factor of production, eventually both the marginal and average returns to the variable factor will begin to fall.

long run the time period in which no factors of production are fixed and in which all the factors of production can be varied.

Lorenz curve a graph on which the cumulative percentage of total national income or wealth is plotted against the cumulative percentage of population (ranked in increasing size of share). The extent to which the curve dips below a straight diagonal line indicates the degree of inequality of distribution.

mandated choice people are required by law to make a decision.

marginal cost addition to total cost resulting from producing one additional unit of output.

marginal cost of labour the addition to a firm's total cost of production resulting from employing one more worker.

marginal physical product of labour the addition to a firm's total output brought about by employing one more worker.

marginal returns of labour the change in the quantity of total output resulting from the employment of one more worker, holding all the other factors of production fixed.

marginal revenue addition to total revenue resulting from the sale of one more unit of the product.

marginal revenue product of labour the money value of the addition to a firm's total output brought about by employing one more worker.

marginal tax rate the tax rate levied on the last pound of income received. The term can be applied solely to income taxes or to all the taxes that a person or business pays.

marginal utility the additional welfare, satisfaction or pleasure gained from consuming one extra unit of a good or service.

market a voluntary meeting of buyers and sellers with exchange taking place.

market conduct the pricing and marketing policies pursued by firms. This is also known as market behaviour, but is not to be confused with market performance, which refers to the end results of these policies.

market demand the quantity of a good or service that all the consumers in a market are willing and able to buy at different market prices.

market disequilibrium exists at any price other than the equilibrium price, when either planned demand < planned supply or planned demand > planned supply.

market economy an economy in which goods and services are purchased through the price mechanism in a system of markets.

market equilibrium a market is in equilibrium when planned demand equals planned supply, where the demand curve crosses the supply curve.

market failure when the market mechanism leads to a misallocation of resources in the economy, either completely failing to provide a good or service or providing the wrong quantity.

market structure the organisational and other characteristics of a market

market supply the quantity of a good or service that all the firms in a market plan to sell at given prices in a given period of time.

merit good a good, such as healthcare, for which the social benefits of consumption exceed the private benefits. Value judgements are involved in deciding that a good is a merit good.

missing market a situation in which there is no market because the functions of prices have broken down.

mixed economy an economy that contains both a large market sector and a large non-market sector in which the planning mechanism operates.

monopolistic competition a market structure in which firms have many competitors, but each one sells a slightly different product.

monopoly one firm only in a market.

monopoly power (also known as **market power**) the ability of a monopoly to raise and maintain price above the level that would prevail under perfect competition. Market power can also be exercised, usually to a lesser degree, by firms in oligopoly and monopolistic competition.

monopsony there is only one buyer in a market.

monopsony power the market power exercised in a market by the buyer of a good or the services of a factor of production such as labour, even though the firm is not a pure monopsonist.

moral hazard the tendency of individuals and firms, once insured against some contingency, to behave so as to make that contingency more likely.

national minimum wage a minimum wage or wage rate that must by law be paid to employees, though in many labour markets the wage rate paid by employers is above the national minimum wage.

natural barriers barriers to market entry caused by geography. For example, if one firm has control of a resource essential for a certain industry, other firms are unable to compete in the industry.

need something that is necessary for human survival, such as food, clothing, warmth or shelter.

negative externality an external cost that occurs when the consumption or production of a good causes costs to a third party, where the social cost is greater than the private cost.

non-renewable resource (also known as a **finite resource**) a resource, such as oil, which is scarce and runs out as it is used.

normal good a good for which demand increases as income rises and demand decreases as income falls

normal profit the minimum profit a firm must make to stay in business, which is, however, insufficient to attract new firms into the market.

normative statement a statement that includes a value judgement and cannot be refuted just by looking at the evidence.

nudges factors which encourage people to think and act in particular ways. Nudges try to shift group and individual behaviour in ways which comply with desirable social norms.

occupational immobility of labour when workers are unwilling or unable to move from one type of job to another, e.g. because different skills are needed.

opportunity cost the cost of giving up the next best alternative.

partial market failure a market does function, but it delivers the 'wrong' quantity of a good or service, which results in resource misallocation.

perfect competition a market that displays the six conditions of: a large number of buyers and sellers; perfect market information; the ability to buy or sell as much is desired at the ruling market price; the inability of an individual buyer or seller to influence the market price; a uniform or homogeneous product; and no barriers to entry or exit in the long run.

plant an establishment, such as a factory, a workshop or a retail outlet, owned and operated by a firm.

positive externality an external benefit that occurs when the consumption or production of a good causes a benefit to a third party, where the social benefit is greater than the private benefit.

positive statement a statement of fact that can be scientifically tested to see if it is correct or incorrect.

poverty the state of being extremely poor and not having enough money or income to meet basic needs.

price agreement an agreement between a firm, similar firms, suppliers or customers regarding the pricing of a good or service.

price ceiling a price *above* which it is illegal to trade. Price ceilings, or maximum legal prices, can distort markets by creating excess demand.

price discrimination charging different prices to different customers for the same product or service, with the prices based on different willingness to pay.

price elasticity of demand measures the extent to which the demand for a good changes in response to a change in the price of that good.

price elasticity of supply measures the extent to which the supply of a good changes in response to a change in the price of that good.

price floor a price *below* which it is illegal to trade. Price floors, or minimum legal prices, can distort markets by creating excess supply.

price leadership the setting of prices in a market, usually by a dominant firm, which is then followed by other firms in the same market.

price-maker when a firm faces a downward-sloping demand curve for its product, it possesses the market power to set the price at which it sells the product.

price-taker a firm which is so small that it has to accept the ruling market price. If the firm raises its price, it loses all its sales; if it cuts its price, it gains no advantage.

price war occurs when rival firms continuously lower prices to undercut each other.

private good a good, such as an orange, that is excludable and rival.

privatisation the transfer of assets from the public sector to the private sector.

producer surplus a measure of the economic welfare enjoyed by firms or producers: the difference between the price a firm succeeds in charging and the minimum price it would be prepared to accept.

product differentiation the marketing of generally similar products with minor variations or the marketing of a range of different products.

production converts inputs or factor services into outputs of goods and services.

production externality an externality (which may be positive or negative) generated in the course of producing a good or service.

production possibility frontier a curve depicting the various combinations of two products (or types of products) that can be produced when all the available resources are fully and efficiently employed.

productive efficiency for the economy as a whole occurs when it is impossible to produce more of one good without producing loss of another. For a firm it occurs when the average total cost of production is minimised.

productivity output per unit of input.

productivity gap the difference between labour productivity, e.g. in the UK and in other developed economies.

profit the difference between total sales revenue and total costs of production.

profit maximisation occurs at the level of output at which total profit is greatest.

progressive taxation a tax is progressive when, as income rises, a greater proportion of income is paid in taxation. The term can be applied to a particular tax such as income tax or to taxation in general.

property right the exclusive authority to determine how a resource is used.

public good a good, such as a radio programme, that is non-excludable and non-rival.

public ownership ownership of industries, firms and other assets such as social housing by central government or local government. The state's acquisition of such assets is called nationalisation.

quantity-setter when a firm faces a downward-sloping demand curve for its product, it possesses the market power to set the quantity of the good it wishes to sell.

quasi-public good a good which is not fully non-rival and/or where it is possible to exclude people from consuming the product.

rational behaviour acting in pursuit of self-interest, which for a consumer means attempting to maximise the welfare, satisfaction or utility gained from the goods and services consumed.

rationing function of prices rising prices ration demand for a product.

regulation the imposition of rules and other constraints which restrict freedom of economic action.

regulatory capture occurs when regulatory agencies act in the interest of regulated firms rather on behalf of the consumers they are supposed to protect.

relative poverty occurs when income is below a specified proportion of average income, e.g. below 60% of median income.

renewable resource a resource, such as timber, that with careful management can be renewed as it is used.

resource allocation the process through which the available factors of production are assigned to produce different goods and services, e.g. how many of society's economic resources are devoted to supplying different products such as food, cars, healthcare and defence.

restricted choice offering people a limited number of options so that they are not overwhelmed by the complexity of the situation. If there are too many choices, people may make a poorly thought-out decision or not make any decision.

returns to scale the rate by which output changes if the scale of all the factors of production is changed.

rival good when one person consumes a private good, the quantity available to others diminishes.

ruling market price (also known as **equilibrium price**) the price at which planned demand equals planned supply.

satisficing achieving a satisfactory outcome rather than the best possible outcome.

scarcity results from the fact that people have unlimited wants but resources to meet these wants are limited. In essence, people would like to consume more goods and services than the economy is able to produce with its limited resources.

short run the time period in which at least one factor of production is fixed and cannot be varied.

signalling function of prices prices provide information to buyers and sellers.

social benefit the total benefit of an activity, including the external benefit as well as the private benefit. Expressed as an equation: social benefit = private benefit + external benefit.

social cost the total cost of an activity, including the external cost as well as the private cost. Expressed as an equation: social cost = private cost + external cost.

social norms forms or patterns of behaviour considered acceptable by a society or group within that society.

specialisation a worker only performing one task or a narrow range of tasks. Also, different firms specialising in producing different goods or services.

static efficiency efficiency (e.g. productive and allocative efficiency) at a particular point in time.

subsidy a payment made by government or other authority, usually to producers, for each unit of the subsidised good that they produce. Consumers can also be subsidised: for example, bus passes given to children to enable them to travel on buses free or at a reduced price.

substitute goods alternative goods that could be used for the same purpose.

sunk costs costs that have already been incurred and cannot be recovered.

supply the quantity of a good or service that producers are willing and able to sell at given prices in a given period of time.

tax a compulsory levy imposed by the government to pay for its activities. Taxes can also be used to achieve other objectives, such as reduced consumption of demerit goods.

technological change a term used to describe the overall effect of invention, innovation and the diffusion or spread of technology in the economy.

total cost all the cost incurred when producing a particular size of output.

total returns of labour total output produced by all the workers employed by a firm.

total revenue all the money received by a firm from selling its total output.

trade the buying and selling of goods and/or services.

trade union a group of workers who join together to maintain and improve their conditions of employment, including their pay.

unemployment when not all of those who are able and willing to work are employed.

utility the satisfaction or economic welfare an individual gains from consuming a good or service.

variable cost cost of production which changes with the amount that is produced, even in the short run.

wage discrimination paying different workers different wage rates for doing the same job.

want something that is desirable, such as fashionable clothing, but is not necessary for human survival.

wealth personal wealth is the stock of everything that a person or household owns at a particular point in time which has value.

2

Macroeconomics
The national and international economy

The measurement of macroeconomic performance

This is the first of the seven remaining chapters in the book covering macroeconomics. The subject area of the previous eight chapters in Part 1 of the book on microeconomics describes, explains and analyses the 'little bits' of the economy: for example, individual markets, firms and industries. By contrast, macroeconomics looks at 'the economy as a whole', or in aggregate. Consider the question 'what determines the price of bread?' This is a microeconomic question, focusing on supply and demand in a single market *within* the economy. By contrast, 'what determines the average price level of *all* goods and services?' is a macroeconomic question. Similarly, 'what determines the annual rate of change of the overall price level, i.e. the rate of inflation?' is a macroeconomic rather than a microeconomic question. This and similar questions relating to the levels and rates of change of economic variables such as output, consumption, investment, and exports and imports, lie at the heart of macroeconomics.

LEARNING OBJECTIVES
These are to understand:

- the main objectives of macroeconomic policy
- how the ranking of the policy objectives has changed over time
- policy trade-offs and conflicts
- the range of data used to measure the performance of an economy
- how index numbers are used to show changes in key economic variables
- the uses of national income data

9.1 The objectives of government economic policy

A **policy objective** is a target or goal that a government wishes to achieve or 'hit'. Since the Second World War, governments in mixed economies such as the UK have generally had the same broad range of objectives. These are to:

- achieve economic growth and improve living standards and levels of economic welfare
- create and maintain full employment or low unemployment

KEY TERM
policy objective a target or goal that policy-makers aim to 'hit'.

- limit or control inflation, or to achieve some measure of price stability
- attain a satisfactory balance of payments, usually defined as the avoidance of an external deficit which might create an exchange rate crisis

Economic growth

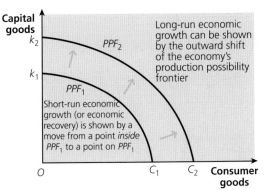

Figure 9.1 Short-run and long-run economic growth

You first came across economic growth in Chapter 1 when learning about production possibility curves. As a recap, Figure 9.1, which is much the same as Figure 1.6 in Chapter 1, will remind you of the distinction between short-run and long-run economic growth. **Short-run economic growth**, which occurs when there are unemployed resources (including labour) or 'slack' in the economy, is when there is a movement from a point *inside* the economy's production possibility frontier to a point *on* the frontier. Short-run growth is also called economic recovery. **Long-run economic growth**, by contrast, results from an outward movement of the production possibility frontier, from PPF_1 to PPF_2 in Figure 9.1.

Figure 9.2 shows what happened to the annual rate of growth of real **gross domestic product (real GDP)** (as distinct from **nominal GDP**) in the UK and in the **eurozone** between the first quarter of 2007 and the end of the first quarter of 2018. For the UK, the data for 2007 show the final year of the long economic boom that preceded the 2008/09 **recession**. Negative economic growth occurred in the recession which ended midway through 2009, since when there has been continuous but slow recovery in the UK. The eurozone, by contrast, entered a second recession in 2012. Since the Brexit referendum in June 2016, GDP growth has fluctuated in both the UK and in the eurozone, but has generally been less than 1% a year. At the time of writing in June 2019, the UK had still not left the EU. Indeed, fear of the adverse consequences of a 'no deal' Brexit had led UK firms and households to stockpile goods such as medicines and car parts (by firms) and food (by households). Stockpiling perversely boosted short-term growth in the UK.

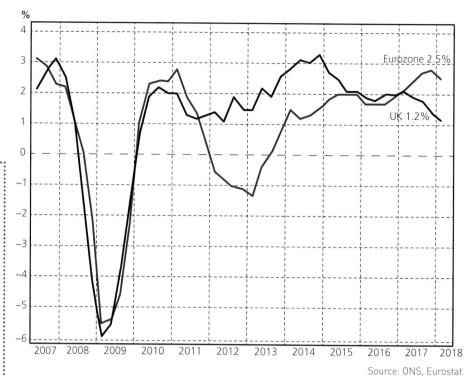

Source: ONS, Eurostat

Figure 9.2 Year-on-year economic growth in the UK and the eurozone, quarter 3, 2007 to quarter 1, 2018

> **STUDY TIP**
> Make sure you appreciate that economic growth is always measured in *real* rather than in *nominal* terms. You must understand the difference between real GDP and nominal GDP. (Nominal GDP is also called money GDP.) The difference between the two is that nominal GDP is real GDP multiplied by the average current price level for the year in question.

CASE STUDY 9.1

The Great Depression in the 1930s

These days, a recession is defined in the UK (though not in the USA) as a fall in real GDP which lasts for at least 6 months. However, a depression (or slump) is a vaguer term, best thought of as a very deep and long recession. (According to an old joke, a downturn is when your neighbour loses his job, a recession is when you lose your own job, and a depression is when economists lose their jobs!)

The 1920s was a period of growing national prosperity in the USA. Nevertheless, the Great Depression, when it arrived in 1929–30, was steeper and more protracted in the USA than in other industrial countries. The US unemployment rate rose higher and remained higher longer than in any other Western country. US real GDP

A soup kitchen in Chicago during the great depression

fell by 9.4% in 1930 and the US unemployment rate climbed from 3.2% to 8.7%. In 1931, real GDP fell by another 8.5% and unemployment rose to 15.9%. But 1932 and 1933 were the worst years of the Great Depression. By 1932, real GDP had fallen in the USA by 31% since 1929 and over 13 million Americans had lost their jobs. The US economy began the first stage of a long recovery in 1934: real GDP rose by 7.7% and unemployment fell to 21.7%.

Follow-up questions

1 What is meant by negative economic growth?
2 Find out how a recession is defined in the USA. (Search on the internet for an article, published in the *Independent*, titled 'Economists who make the recession call', by Stephen Foley.)
3 Research the details of the recession the UK experienced in 2008–09. When did recovery from recession start, and what is the state of the economy at the time you are reading this book?
4 What is an economic recovery? Is the UK experiencing a recovery on the date you are reading this case study?

QUANTITATIVE SKILLS 9.1

Worked example: calculating the mean and median values

Using the data in Table 9.1, calculate the mean value, to 2 decimal places, and the median value, of the annual change in gross value added (GVA) per head in the UK regions in 2016.

Table 9.1 Annual changes in GVA per head in UK regions, 2016 (%)

London	3.7
South East	1.9
East of England	3.0
West Midlands	3.0
East Midlands	2.1
Yorkshire and Humber	1.4
South West	3.3
North West	2.9
North East	0.7
Scotland	2.4
Wales	3.5
Northern Ireland	2.8

Source: ONS, December 2017

Gross value added (GVA) is a term used in the UK's national accounts to measure the contribution to the economy of each individual producer, industry or sector in the United Kingdom. It is used in the estimation of GDP. Table 9.1 shows the percentage changes that occurred in *nominal* GVA per head for the 12 planning regions into which the UK is divided, for the year 2016.

With a set of data such as this, the mean and the median are two measures of average values. The mean is the value obtained by dividing the sum of the percentage changes by the number of regions. Thus:

3.7% + 1.9% + 3.0% +3.0% + 2.1% + 3.3% + 2.9% +0.7% + 2.4% + 3.5% + 1.4% + 2.8% = 30.7%

30.7% ÷ 12 = 2.56%

So 2.56 is the mean value, to two decimal points.

By contrast, the median value is the 'middle number' in the sorted list of numbers. The sorted list, ranging from highest to lowest, is:

3.7%   3.5%   3.5%   3.0%   3.0%   2.9%   2.8%   2.4%   2.1%   1.9%   1.4%   0.7%

As the sorted list contains 12 numbers (one for each of the UK's 12 planning regions), the middle numbers are the sixth and seventh numbers in the list, with five numbers above and five below their value. Dividing the sum of the sixth and seventh numbers (2.9% and 2.8%) by two, the median value of 2.85% is obtained.

Full employment and unemployment

There are different definitions of **full employment**, two of which we briefly explain in this chapter. First is the so-called Beveridge definition. In 1944, a famous White Paper on employment policy, written by William Beveridge (an economist at the London School of Economics, who later became Lord Beveridge), effectively committed modern governments to achieving full employment. In the White Paper, Beveridge defined full employment as occurring when unemployment falls to 3% of the labour force.

> ## KEY TERM
>
> **full employment** according to Beveridge's definition, full employment means 3% or less of the labour force unemployed. According to the free-market definition, it is the level of employment occurring at the market-clearing real-wage rate, where the number of workers whom employers wish to hire equals the number of workers wanting to work.

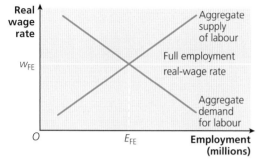

Figure 9.3 Full employment in the economy

Partly because they regard Beveridge's 3% definition as too arbitrary and lacking any theoretical underpinning, free-market economists favour a second definition of full employment. For them, full employment occurs in the economy's aggregate labour market at the market-clearing real-wage rate, where the number of workers willing to work equals the number of workers whom employers wish to hire. In Figure 9.3, this is shown where the aggregate supply curve of labour intersects the aggregate demand curve for labour. The full employment wage rate is w_{FE} and the full employment level of employment is E_{FE}.

Figure 9.3 could be interpreted as showing that when full employment occurs, there is absolutely no unemployment. However, in the real economy in which we live, this is not the case. Beveridge's definition of full employment accepts this fact. There will always be *some* unemployment, simply because the economy is constantly changing, with some jobs disappearing while new jobs are created. Chapter 11 describes and explains some of the main types of unemployment that economists recognise.

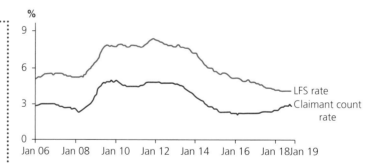

Figure 9.4 Changes in LFS unemployment and claimant count unemployment in the UK, January 1996 to January 2019

> ## KEY TERMS
>
> **claimant count** the method of measuring unemployment according to those people who are claiming unemployment-related benefits (Jobseeker's Allowance).
>
> **Labour Force Survey** a quarterly sample survey of households in the UK. Its purpose is to provide information on the UK labour market. The survey seeks information on respondents' personal circumstances and their labour market status during a period of 1–4 weeks.

Two methods have been used to measure unemployment in the UK. One of these, the **claimant count**, has recently been dropped by the UK government as an official measure of unemployment because it is increasingly a poor proxy for overall unemployment levels. The second measure, the **Labour Force Survey** (LFS) measure is favoured by government and is the official measure of unemployment. As Figure 9.4 illustrates, the LFS measure has been higher than the claimant count measure.

> ## STUDY TIP
>
> Make sure you appreciate how the LFS measure of unemployment is constructed.

> ## SYNOPTIC LINK
>
> Employment and unemployment are explained in Chapter 11 on economic performance.

CASE STUDY 9.2

UK economy: unemployment figures explained by the ONS

People often question the way the Office for National Statistics (ONS) compiles the unemployment figures. Caron Walker, director of collection and production for the ONS, explains how and why it is done:

The answers lie with the Labour Force Survey, the huge continuous survey that ONS uses to measure unemployment (along with employment and economic inactivity). The unemployment figures use an internationally agreed definition.

To count as unemployed, people have to say they are not working, are available for work and have either looked for work in the past four weeks or are waiting to start a new job they have already obtained. Someone who is out of work but doesn't meet these criteria counts as 'economically inactive'.

Each quarter the LFS covers 100,000 people in 40,000 households chosen randomly by postcode. That's about one in 600 of the total population. The results are then weighted to give an estimate that reflects the entire population. Our survey has a very large sample size compared, for example, with opinion polls, which often sample around 1,000 people. Even so, in any survey there is always a margin of uncertainty, in this case around plus or minus 3% for the unemployment level.

The other measure of joblessness — the claimant count — is published for each single month. It doesn't suffer from the limitations of sample size and sampling frame because it derives from the numbers of Jobseeker's Allowance (JSA) claimants recorded by Jobcentre Plus, so a monthly figure is possible right down to local level. But because many people who are out of work will not be eligible for JSA, it is a narrower measure of unemployment; it is usually much lower than the LFS measure. And it's not comparable with other countries' data, unlike the LFS measures which use internationally agreed definitions.

Follow-up questions

1 Research what has happened to the UK unemployment figures since the January 2019 figures shown in Figure 9.4.
2 How is the Labour Force Survey (LFS) measure of unemployment constructed?
3 The article by Caron Walker was published in 2013. What has happened to the UK claimant count since then?
4 Find out what has been happening to the level of unemployment in the part of the UK in which you live.

TEST YOURSELF 9.2

Who publishes the UK unemployment statistics each month?

Price stability

KEY TERMS

inflation a persistent or continuing rise in the average price level.

deflation a continuing tendency for the average price level to fall.

disinflation when the rate of inflation is falling, but still positive.

Inflation is a general rise in average prices (a rise in the price level) across the economy. This must not be confused with a change in the price of a particular good or service within the economy. Goods' prices rise and fall all the time in a market economy, reflecting consumer choices and preferences, and changing costs. If the price of one item — say, a particular model of car — increases because demand for it is high, this is not inflation. Inflation occurs when most prices are rising by some degree across the whole economy. A change in the price of one good may of course lead to a change in the measured rate of inflation, particularly if spending on the item makes up a significant fraction of total consumer spending.

Achieving absolutely stable prices is not necessarily the same as controlling the rate of inflation. Absolute price stability requires a zero annual rate of inflation, with the average price level neither rising nor falling from year to year. Although a zero rate of inflation has occasionally been achieved, it is extremely rare. Much more usually, in the UK at least, controlling inflation means

297

achieving a low inflation rate rather than absolute price stability. For most of the last two decades, successive UK governments have aimed to achieve a 2% inflation rate. Usually, however, the inflation rate has been either a little above or a little below the 2% official target. On occasion, notably in the economic downturn in 2009, there were fears that the inflation rate would become negative. Negative inflation, which involves a falling average price level, is called **deflation**. Make sure you don't confuse deflation with **disinflation**, which occurs when the rate of inflation is falling but is still positive.

The changes that have taken place in the UK inflation rate between January 2009 and January 2019 are shown in Figure 9.5. The diagram introduces you to the fact that changes in a **price index** are used to measure the rate of consumer price inflation. Nowadays, the dominant price index is the **consumer prices index** (CPI), though before 2011 the **retail prices index** (RPI) was also used. The CPI is used by the government for setting the inflation rate target which the Bank of England tries to hit. The CPI has also been used for the **indexation** of welfare benefits, though in recent years some state benefits were frozen as part of the Conservative government's austerity policy.

The ways in which the CPI and RPI have been used to measure the rate of consumer price inflation are explained in section 9.3 of this chapter. (Note: *indices* is the plural of *index*.)

> **TEST YOURSELF 9.3**
> Explain the difference between deflation and disinflation.

> **KEY TERMS**
>
> **price index** an index number showing the extent to which a price, or a 'basket' of prices, has changed over a month, quarter or year, in comparison with the price(s) in a base year.
>
> **consumer prices index** the official measure used to calculate the rate of consumer price inflation in the UK. It calculates the average price increase of a basket of 700 different consumer goods and services.
>
> **retail prices index** a measure formerly used to calculate the rate of consumer price inflation in the UK.
>
> **indexation** the automatic adjustment of items such as pensions and welfare benefits to changes in the price level, through the use of a price index.

Figure 9.5 Changes in the RPI and the CPI inflation rates in the UK, 2009–January 2019

In March 2018, the national statistician at the ONS wrote: 'Overall, RPI is a very poor measure of general inflation, at times greatly overestimating and at other times underestimating changes in prices and how these changes are experienced. In 2013, the RPI lost its status as a National Statistic. Our position on the RPI is clear: we do not think it is a good measure of inflation and discourage its use.'

Until 2011, the state pension went up each year in line with changes in the RPI. The government then replaced this with the CPI link, which has generally favoured the government rather than pensioners since, as Figure 9.5 shows, RPI inflation has usually been higher than CPI inflation.

The declining usage of the RPI as a measure of inflation has accompanied the growing use of measures such as 'core' inflation, 'headline' inflation and 'underlying' inflation. 'Core' inflation is calculated by stripping out volatile items such as food and fuel from the CPI measure of inflation. 'Headline' inflation, which is currently measured by changes in the CPI, may be temporarily influenced by factors that are mainly of a short-term nature. 'Underlying' inflation, by contrast, is measured by trying to get rid of the inflationary 'noise' created by such temporary price fluctuations. In this sense, 'underlying' inflation and 'core' inflation are much the same thing.

TEST YOURSELF 9.4

Table 9.2 shows both the unemployment rate and inflation rate for an economy between 2018 and 2020.

Table 9.2 Unemployment and inflation rates, 2018–20

	Unemployment rate (%)	Inflation rate (%)
2018	5.4	3.3
2019	4.8	4.0
2020	4.0	4.5

What can you conclude from the data?

QUANTITATIVE SKILLS 9.2

Worked example: calculating real values from nominal values

In Ruritania between 2018 and 2019, the rate of price inflation was 6% and the rate of increase of nominal GDP was 4%. What was the rate of increase of real GDP?

To answer this question, we use the equation:

$$\text{rate of increase of real GDP} = \text{rate of increase of nominal GDP} - \text{rate of price inflation}$$

Plugging the numbers given in the question into the equation, the rate of increase of real GDP = 4% – 6%, which equals –2%.

SYNOPTIC LINK
Inflation is explained in further detail in section 11.3 in Chapter 11.

TEST YOURSELF 9.5
Distinguish between the nominal value and the real value of an economic variable.

STUDY TIP
You don't need to possess detailed technical knowledge of the construction of price indices such as the CPI, but you should appreciate the underlying features of a price index (see section 9.3).

A satisfactory balance of payments

The **balance of payments** measures all the currency flows into and out of an economy in a particular time period, usually a month, quarter or year. An important part of the balance of payments is called the current account.

The **current account** of the balance of payments contains two main sections: the money value of **exports**, and the money value of **imports** (of both goods and services). Changes in these over a period extending from 2007 to 2019 are shown in Figure 9.6. Taken together, the money value of exports and imports make up the **balance of trade**. If the money value of imports exceeds the money value of exports, there is a **balance of trade deficit**; if the money value of imports is less than the money value of exports, there is a **balance of trade surplus**.

There are some other sections of the current account of the balance of payments, namely income flows and current transfers. These are explained in Chapter 14.

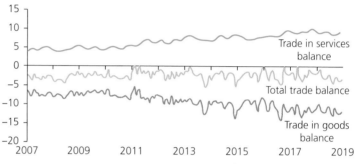

£bn, monthly data

Source: House of Commons Library, February 2019

Figure 9.6 Changes in the UK's balances of trade in goods and services, and total trade, 2007–January 2019

The word 'satisfactory' can be interpreted in different ways. People sometimes assume that a satisfactory balance of payments occurs only when the government achieves the biggest possible current account surplus (that is, when the value of exports exceeds the value of imports by the greatest amount). However, a country can enjoy a trading surplus only if at least one other country suffers a trading deficit. It is mathematically impossible for all countries to have a current account surplus at the same time. Therefore, most economists take the view that a 'satisfactory' balance of payments is a situation in which the current account is in equilibrium, or when there is a small surplus or a small but sustainable deficit.

Other macroeconomic objectives

Governments may also have other objectives of macroeconomic policy, such as **balancing the budget** and achieving a more equitable or fairer distribution of income. Since the 2008–09 recession, the objective of balancing or at least reducing the government's **budget deficit** has become a very important macroeconomic objective. This is explained in Chapter 13 on fiscal policy and supply-side policies.

The opposite has been true in recent years in relation to achieving a more equitable distribution of income. During the recession and its aftermath, income inequalities have widened, which most people regard as inequitable.

KEY TERMS

balancing the budget when government spending equals government revenue $(G = T)$.

budget deficit occurs when government spending exceeds government revenue $(G > T)$. This represents a net injection of demand into the circular flow of income and hence a budget deficit is expansionary.

STUDY TIP

Make sure you are aware that governments have policy objectives other than achieving economic growth, low unemployment, a low inflation rate and a satisfactory balance of payments.

SYNOPTIC LINK

Section 1.1 of Chapter 1 introduced you to the difference between positive and normative statements in economics. Section 7.1 of Chapter 7 explains how unequal and inequitable distributions of income illustrate the difference between positive and normative statements. At this stage, it would be useful to reread the relevant sections in both chapters.

Macroeconomic policy conflicts

Economists often argue that it is difficult, if not impossible, for a government to 'hit' all its desired macroeconomic objectives at the same time. Believing they can't achieve the impossible, policy-makers often settle for the lesser goal of 'trading off' between policy objectives. A **trade-off** exists when two or more desirable objectives are mutually exclusive. Because the government thinks it cannot achieve, for example, full employment and zero inflation, it aims for less than full employment combined with an acceptably low and sustainable rate of inflation.

Over the years UK macroeconomic policy has been influenced and constrained by four significant conflicts between policy objectives. The main **policy conflicts** and their associated policy trade-offs are:

301

KEY TERMS

trade-off between policy objectives although it may be impossible to achieve two desirable objectives at the same time, e.g. zero inflation and full employment, policy-makers may be able to choose an acceptable combination lying between the extremes, e.g. 2% inflation and 4% unemployment.

policy conflict occurs when two policy objectives cannot both be achieved at the same time: the better the performance in achieving one objective, the worse the performance in achieving the other.

- between internal policy objectives of full employment and growth and the external objective of achieving a satisfactory balance of payments (or possibly supporting a particular exchange rate)

| full employment and economic growth | policy conflict and trade-off | satisfactory balance of payments or exchange rate |

- between achieving full employment and controlling inflation

| full employment and economic growth | policy conflict and trade-off | control of inflation |

- between increasing the rate of economic growth and achieving a more equal distribution of income and wealth

| economic growth | policy conflict and trade-off | greater income equality |

- between higher living standards now and higher living standards in the future. This is an example of an 'intertemporal' conflict between enjoying something now, or in the future.

| current living standards | policy conflict and trade-off | future living standards |

Not all objectives conflict, however. Some economists believe that, with the 'right' policies, policy conflicts do not occur in the long run — that is, they are compatible.

Most economists agree that these policy conflicts and trade-offs pose considerable problems for governments in the economic short run, defined as a period in macroeconomics extending just a few years into the future. However, there is much less agreement about whether they need be significant in the long run — a period extending many years into the future. Pro-free-market economists often argue that if appropriate (and successful) supply-side policies are implemented, the main objectives of macroeconomic policy are compatible with each other and not in conflict in the long run. (Supply-side policies are explained in depth in Chapter 13.)

STUDY TIP

In Part 1 of this book, on microeconomics, you learnt that the short run is the time period in which at least one factor of production is held fixed and the long run is the time period in which all factors of production are variable. However, in macroeconomics, economists tend generally to use the terms in a looser way. For example, the macroeconomic 'short run' may extend to about 3 years into the future, with the 'long run' being any period longer than that. To complicate things still further, a period known as the 'medium term' is sometimes identified. This could be a period of about 18 months to 3 years into the future, separating the short run and the long run.

SYNOPTIC LINK

Policy conflicts are explained in further detail in section 11.4 of Chapter 11 on economic performance.

KEY TERMS

Keynesian economists followers of the economist John Maynard Keynes, who generally believe that governments should manage the economy, particularly through the use of fiscal policy.

pro-free-market economists opponents of Keynesian economists, who dislike government intervention in the economy and who much prefer the operation of free markets.

monetary policy the use by the government and its agent, the Bank of England, of interest rates and other monetary instruments to try to achieve the government's policy objectives.

fiscal policy the use by the government of government spending and taxation to try to achieve the government's policy objectives.

balance of payments equilibrium a situation in which a deficit or surplus on the current account of the balance of payments is exactly matched by capital inflows or outflows in the other parts of the balance of payments.

STUDY TIP

During your course of study, you should try to build a good knowledge of developments in the UK economy and government policies over the 15 years or so before you started studying economics. Knowledge of earlier economic history may also be useful.

How the importance attached to the different macroeconomic policy objectives has changed over time

The order in which the four main objectives of macroeconomic policy were listed at the beginning of this chapter shows a broadly **Keynesian** ranking of priorities. In the Keynesian era, which extended roughly from 1945 to 1979, UK governments implemented Keynesian macroeconomic policies. They believed that economic policy should be used to achieve full employment, economic growth and a generally acceptable or fair distribution of income and wealth. These were the prime policy objectives, which had to be achieved in order to increase human happiness and economic welfare — the ultimate policy objective. Controlling inflation and achieving a satisfactory balance of payments were regarded as intermediate objectives, or possibly as constraints, in the sense that an unsatisfactory performance in controlling inflation or the balance of payments could prevent the attainment of full employment and economic growth.

In the early 1980s, things changed. A new government in 1979, with Mrs Margaret Thatcher becoming prime minister, meant that UK governments were now **pro-free market** rather than Keynesian. In the 1970s inflation had threatened to escalate out of control, and in response UK governments placed control of inflation in pole position as a policy objective, relegating full employment to a lower position in the ranking of macroeconomic policy objectives.

Since then, UK governments have continued to give much more attention to the need to control inflation. Indeed, in 1993, the Conservative chancellor Norman Lamont stated that high unemployment was a 'price well worth paying' for keeping inflation under control. This view was echoed in 1998 when, under a Labour government, the governor of the Bank of England argued that 'job losses in the north were an acceptable price to pay for curbing inflation in the south'. These statements reflect the pro-free-market view that, in order to maintain a high and sustainable level of employment, inflation must first be brought under control.

The long and deep recession, which hit the UK (and many other countries) in 2008, has led to a partial revision of this view. For various reasons, which are explained in section 11.3 of Chapter 11 on economic performance, inflation has generally been successfully controlled in the UK in recent years. Chapters 12 and 13 explain how a combination of 'loose' **monetary policy** (i.e. very low interest rates) and 'tight' **fiscal policy** (i.e. cutting government spending in an effort to reduce the size of the budget deficit) have dominated recent UK macroeconomic policy.

It is also worth noting that, despite a rapid increase in the UK's balance of payments deficit on current account, achieving a satisfactory current account has not been viewed by recent governments as an important policy objective. All this may, of course, change.

A **balance of payments equilibrium** is a situation in which a deficit or surplus on the current account of the balance of payments is exactly matched by capital inflows or outflows in the other parts of the balance of payments.

The growth of Keynesian economics

Although the A-level specification only requires you to know about trends and developments in the economy which have taken place over the 15 years before you sit the examination, in order to understand the nature of modern macroeconomics, it is useful to go back to what was happening in the UK and world economies in the 1920s and 1930s. Most economists at the time, especially those in British and American universities, were free-market economists who believed that, in a competitive market economy, market forces would automatically deliver full employment and economic growth. In so far as governments needed to have a macroeconomic policy, it was generally believed that the policy should be restricted to maintaining the 'sound money' deemed necessary for a stable price level, and possibly to maintaining a fixed exchange rate.

However, the problem was that in the UK economy of the 1920s, and in the wider world economy (especially the USA) in the 1930s, free-market forces did *not* deliver full employment and economic growth. Instead, unregulated market forces seemed to have produced economic stagnation and mass unemployment. The most seminal event of the time was the Great Depression, which began around 1929–30 and lasted on and off for much of the following decade. Unemployment rose in 1933 to almost 25% in the USA, and in 1931 to 24% in the UK. Regional unemployment in towns such as Jarrow in northeast England rose to as high as 70%, though London, the southeast and the Midlands fared much better.

Free-market economists responded to the Great Depression by arguing that markets were not to blame for persistent large-scale unemployment. Instead, they believed that mass unemployment was caused by institutional factors, such as the power exercised by trade unions, which prevented markets from operating freely. In the free-market view, wage cuts were necessary to 'price the unemployed into jobs', but trade unions resisting wage cuts prevented this from happening.

In the late 1920s, John Maynard Keynes, who started his academic career as an economist in the free-market tradition, began to change his view on the main cause of unemployment. In response to an accusation of inconsistency, Keynes is reported to have said: 'When the facts change, I change my mind — what do you do, sir?'

Keynes believed that orthodox free-market economic theory failed to explain how the whole economy works, and that a better and more general theory was needed to explain mass unemployment. Keynes completed his new theory in 1936 with the publication of his great book *The General Theory of Employment, Interest and Money*, commonly referred to as Keynes's *General Theory*.

Keynes's *General Theory* marks the beginning of modern macroeconomics. For over a generation until about 1979, Keynesian economics was macroeconomics, and macroeconomics was Keynesian economics. In the three decades after the Second World War, Keynesianism became the new economic orthodoxy in the UK, the Netherlands and the Scandinavian countries. Economic policy in the USA also eventually became Keynesian, with the Republican president, Richard Nixon, famously stating in 1971 that 'we are all Keynesians now'.

- A policy objective is a target or goal that a government wishes to achieve.
- Over the years, the main policy objectives of UK governments have been to achieve economic growth and improve living standards and levels of economic welfare, to create and maintain full employment or low unemployment, to limit or control inflation, and to attain a satisfactory balance of payments.
- Governments may also have other objectives of macroeconomic policy, such as balancing the budget and achieving a more equitable or fairer distribution of income.
- Short-run growth or economic recovery is a movement from a point *inside* the economy's production possibility frontier to a point *on* the frontier.
- Long-run growth results from an outward movement of the production possibility frontier.
- The Beveridge definition of full employment relates to unemployment falling to 3% of the labour force.
- Free-market economists define full employment as occurring at the market-clearing real-wage rate, where the number of workers willing to work equals the number of workers whom employers wish to hire.
- Inflation is a general rise in average prices (a rise in the price level) across the economy.
- In the UK, controlling inflation means achieving a low inflation rate rather than absolute price stability.
- A satisfactory balance of payments is a situation in which the current account is in equilibrium, or when there is a small surplus or a small but sustainable deficit.
- Over the years UK macroeconomic policy has been influenced and constrained by four significant conflicts between policy objectives.
- The conflicts and their associated policy trade-offs have been: between achieving internal policy objectives of full employment and growth and the external objective of achieving a satisfactory balance of payments (or possibly supporting a particular exchange rate); between achieving full employment and controlling inflation; between increasing the rate of economic growth and achieving a more equal distribution of income and wealth; and between higher living standards now and higher living standards in the future.

9.2 Macroeconomic indicators

> **KEY TERM**
>
> **macroeconomic indicator** provides information from recent economic performance for judging the success or failure of a particular type of government policy, e.g. fiscal policy or monetary policy.

The A-level specification defines a **macroeconomic indicator** as data which is commonly used to measure the performance of an economy, such as real GDP, real GDP per capita, the consumer prices index, measures of unemployment, productivity and the balance of payments on current account.

Macroeconomic indicators provide governments and their policy-makers with information about the recent success or lack of success in achieving the target set for a particular type of economic policy, such as monetary policy or fiscal policy. The size and rate of change of the money supply is a commonly used monetary performance indicator. Likewise, the size and rate of change of the budget deficit is an indicator of fiscal policy performance.

Macroeconomic indicators also provide information about whether current policy is on course to hit the future target set for the stated policy. An indicator, such as information about labour productivity and productivity gaps, can also be used to compare the performance of the UK economy with that of competitor countries.

Some macroeconomic indicators are also related to targets which the policy-makers wish to hit in the future. For many years, a 2% rate of inflation, measured by the annual change in the consumer prices index, has been the policy indicator for the success of monetary policy. Likewise, achieving a budget surplus in good economic times, and limiting the structural budget deficit to below 2% of GDP in 2020/21 is the current target or future policy indicator of the success of fiscal policy.

Macroeconomic indicators can also be divided into *lead* and *lag* indicators:

- **Lead indicators** provide information about the future state of the economy (stemming from the way people are currently forming their expectations). Surveys of consumer and business confidence and investment intentions indicate the existence of a feel-good or feel-bad factor and provide information about the likely state of aggregate demand a few months ahead. Statistics for house-building starts and the number of people who have booked expensive summer or skiing holidays several months in advance also provide information about future spending, while data on commodity and input prices can signal future changes in retail price inflation.
- **Lag indicators** provide information about past and possibly current economic performance and the extent to which policy objectives such as economic growth and control of inflation have been achieved. Data on the level of GDP, and current and recent employment and unemployment figures, provide examples of lag indicators giving information about current and recent economic performance.

Macroeconomic indicators are almost always presented in the form of statistical data: for example, unemployment and growth figures in the case of lagged indicators, and projections about the number of house-building starts in the case of lead indicators. The accuracy of the information provided by performance indicators is thus highly dependent on the accuracy of the statistics available from the government and other sources.

TEST YOURSELF 9.7

Suppose there is an increase in people booking exotic foreign holidays for the summer ahead. Would this be a lead indicator or a lag indicator? Explain your answer.

CASE STUDY 9.3

David Smith's skip index and other confidence indicators

Every week David Smith, the economics editor of the *Sunday Times*, writes an Economic Outlook column—highlights can be accessed on David Smith's **economicsuk.com** website).

A few years ago, David Smith came up with the idea of a 'skip index', as an informal lead indicator of what might happen to the economy in the future. However, the accuracy of a skip index can be questioned. While an increase in the number of builder's skips might mean people are more affluent and spending the money on their houses, it might also mean that people cannot afford to move but their family is still growing and therefore they have to upgrade their house. A 'scaffolding index' might suffer from the same problem as a skip index.

Another possibility is a 'crane index'. This is a way to gauge prosperity by counting the cranes on the urban skyline. However, it is also possible to turn a crane index on its head. An increase in the number of tower cranes may indicate over-expansion or over-confidence — not necessarily economic growth. Another confidence indicator is frequency of receipt of unsolicited letters from estate agents, claiming for example that a 'Mr Jones' is desperate to buy a house in your road if you'll just give the agent a call.

Follow-up questions

1 Construct a skip index for your local community. What conclusions can you draw from the information you collect?
2 Can you think of any other things that could be used to gauge the state of consumer or business confidence in the economy?
3 Questionnaires and surveys are sometimes used for finding out what people think will happen to the economy in the future. Why should the information provided by such surveys be treated with caution?
4 Inspired by David Smith's skip index, a trade group, the Building Merchants Federation, now publishes a Builders Merchant Building Index (BMBI). Find out what the latest quarterly BMBI report has to stay about confidence in the building industry.

- A macroeconomic indicator is data which are commonly used to measure the performance of an economy, such as real GDP.
- Macroeconomic indicators provide governments with information about the recent success in achieving the target set for a particular type of economic policy, such as monetary policy or fiscal policy.
- Macroeconomic indicators also provide information about whether current policy is on course to hit the future target set for the stated policy.
- An indicator can also be used to compare the performance of the UK economy with that of competitor countries.
- Macroeconomic indicators can be divided into *lead* and *lag* indicators.
- Lead indicators provide information about the future state of the economy, stemming from the way people are currently forming their expectations.
- Surveys of consumer and business confidence and investment intentions provide information about the likely state of aggregate demand a few months ahead.
- Lag indicators provide information about past and possibly current economic performance and the extent to which policy objectives such as economic growth and control of inflation have been achieved.
- Data on the level of GDP and current and recent employment and unemployment figures are examples of lag indicators.
- Macroeconomic indicators are almost always presented in the form of statistical data: for example, unemployment and growth figures in the case of lagged indicators, and projections about the number of house-building starts in the case of lead indicators.
- The accuracy of the information provided by performance indicators is thus highly dependent on the accuracy of the statistics available from the government and other sources.

9.3 The uses of index numbers

Introduction to index numbers

Earlier in this chapter, we mentioned the difference between nominal GDP (or money GDP) and real GDP. To recap, real GDP, or real gross domestic product, is a measure of the total quantity of goods and services produced by the economy over a period of time, having got rid of the distortive effects of price changes or inflation.

Changes in real GDP, along with other economic variables, are usually expressed using **index numbers**. (Earlier in the chapter we explained how the consumer prices index (CPI) has largely replaced the retail prices index (RPI) as a measure of the price level and the rate of inflation.) Because index numbers frequently appear in the quantitative data you are expected to interpret in the course of your studies, it is especially important that you build up an understanding of how economic indices are constructed.

Economists frequently use index numbers when making comparisons over periods of time. An index starts in a given year, called the base year, which usually is given an index number of 100. In later years or months, an increase in the size of the variable causes the index number to rise above 100, while a fall in the size of the variable, compared to the base year, results in the index number falling to below 100. For example, an index number of 105 means a 5% rise from the base year, whereas an index number of 95 means a 5% fall.

> **KEY TERM**
> **index number** a number used in an index, such as the consumer prices index, to enable accurate comparisons over time to be made.

Objective test question: understanding data presented in index numbers, GDP per head

Table 9.3 shows index numbers for GDP per head for two countries, L and M, in 2010 and 2020.

Table 9.3 Index numbers for GDP per head, 2015 and 2020

	GDP per head	
	2015	**2020**
Country L	100	115
Country M	100	108

From the data, which one of the following is supported by the data:

A GDP per head was the same in both countries in 2015.
B GDP rose faster in country L than in country M.
C The rate of increase in GDP per head was greater in country L than in country M.
D GDP per head was higher in country L than in country M in 2020.

To answer the question correctly, it is important to appreciate that the data show GDP *per head of population*, and not the overall GDP figures for both countries. This means that although statement B could well be true, it cannot be concluded from the data, as the rate of population growth could be slower in country M than in country L. Statements A and D are wrong for a different reason, namely that there is insufficient information in the data to allow us to compare *across* the two data series. For statement A, the index number is the same in both countries, namely 100. The base year for both data series is probably 2015. The fact that both index numbers are 100 tells us nothing about whether GDP per head was the same in both countries in this year. For the same reason, we cannot conclude that GDP per head was higher in country L in 2020, simply because 115 is a larger number than 108. This means statement D is wrong. However, while we cannot compare *across* the two data series, we can compare *along* each series taken in isolation. The data allow us to conclude that GDP per head increased by 15% in country L between 2015 and 2020, but by only 8% in country M. This means that statement C is the correct answer.

Objective test question: interpreting macroeconomic data

Table 9.4 shows figures for population and index numbers for inflation (CPI) and money national income (GDP at current prices) in the years 2018 and 2019.

Table 9.4 Population size and GDP and inflation indices, 2018 and 2019

Year	GDP at current prices	Inflation index	Population size
2018	100	75	40 million
2019	106	125	42 million

In 2019, compared to 2018, which one of the following statements can be inferred from the data?

A Population grew by a slower rate than prices.
B The inflation price index increased by 25%.
C Money GDP per head rose by 6%.
D Real GDP increased.

Statement A provides the correct answer. The price level increased by nearly 67% ((50/75) × 100) but population grew by only 5%. Statement B is wrong because the starting-off price index was 75 and not 100. Statement C is wrong: money GDP did indeed increase by 6%, but the population grew in size by 5%, so the increase in money GDP *per head* is less than 6%. Finally, statement D is also wrong: if money GDP increased by 6% but the price level increased by nearly 67%, *real* GDP must have fallen.

CASE STUDY 9.4

The construction of the consumer prices index (CPI)

The following passages have been extracted from an article, 'Consumer price indices, a brief guide: 2017',
published by the Office for National Statistics (ONS) in 2017 and accessible on the ONS website: **www.ons.gov.uk**.

This article describes the main consumer price indices in the UK and explains how they are put together.
It focuses on the consumer prices index (CPI) including owner occupiers' housing costs (CPIH) but briefly
mentions the retail prices index (RPI).

Consumer price indices

Consumer price indices are important indicators of how the UK economy is performing. The indices are used
in many ways by the government, businesses and society in general. They can affect interest rates, tax
allowances, wages, state benefits, pensions, maintenance, contracts and many other payments. They also
show the impact of inflation on family budgets. The CPIH and CPI measure price changes, not price levels.
They are therefore expressed in terms of the comparison of prices relative to 2015, when the indices were
given values of 100.

Inflation figures

The CPIH is the most comprehensive measure of inflation. It extends the CPI to include a measure of the
costs associated with owning, maintaining and living in one's own home, known as owner occupiers' housing
costs, along with Council Tax. Both of these are significant expenses for many households that are excluded
from the CPI.

The RPI — a long-standing measure of UK inflation — does not meet the required standard for designation
as National Statistics. The RPI, its subcomponents and the RPIX continue to be published as they are tied to
long-term contracts, related for example to wage and saving contracts.

The shopping basket

A convenient way of thinking about the CPIH and CPI is to imagine a very large 'shopping basket' full of goods
and services on which people typically spend their money: from bread to ready-made meals, from the cost
of a cinema seat to the price of a pint at the local pub, from a holiday in Spain to the cost of a bicycle. The
content of the basket is fixed for a period of 12 months.

The cost of living

The CPIH and CPI are not 'cost of living' indices. The index simply indicates what we would need to spend
in order to purchase the same things we bought in an earlier period, irrespective of whether particular
products are 'needed' or are 'good for you'.

What's in the basket?

The CPIH and CPI include all types of household spending. It
is impractical and unnecessary to monitor the price of every
product sold in every single shop. The prices of similar items
can reasonably be assumed to move in line with one another in
response to market forces. It is therefore sufficient to compile
the index using prices of a large and varied sample of products in
selected locations. The goods and services for which prices are
recorded are called 'representative items'.

The CPIH, CPI and RPI are fixed quantity price indices: specific
items are chosen to represent price movements in the baskets;
prices are collected for those items only (700 representative items). Their movements are taken to represent
the price changes for all goods and services covered by the index, including those for which prices are not
specifically monitored.

Quality changes

It is important that the index calculations are based on like-for-like comparisons, of prices each month for each of the items in the basket. However, some brands or varieties of particular products priced at the start of the year may not be available in later months. Adjustments are also made, for example when a manufacturer changes the size or weight of a product.

Weighting

The quantities or 'weight' of the various items in the basket are chosen to reflect their importance in the typical household budget. We spend more on some things than others. So we would expect, for example, a 10% increase in the price of petrol to have a much bigger impact on the CPIH or CPI than a similar rise in the price of tea. For this reason, the components of the index are 'weighted' to ensure that it reflects the importance of the various items in the average shopping basket, and the amounts we spend in different regions of the country and in different types of shops.

Updating the shopping basket

It is important that the index is representative and kept up to date. The basket of goods and services is therefore reviewed every year, helping to ensure that the CPIH and CPI calculations more accurately reflect UK shopping and purchasing patterns.

Some changes to the basket are necessary each year due to changing markets, fashions and new products. Smart-phones and tablet PCs, for example, have been added in recent years. The basket is fixed for a period of 12 months.

The weights for the index are also changed each year to keep pace with general changes in our spending habits. Over the years people have tended to spend more of their money on electrical goods, travel and leisure while the proportion they spend on basics has fallen.

Calculating the index

After the price data have been checked and processed, the resulting price indicators are combined. Changes in prices of the individual goods and services in the index are measured by comparing them to their levels in the previous January. These are then weighted together using the weights for the current year to produce an overall average price change. The final stage in the calculation is to link the average price changes with the figures for earlier years. Only by 'chain-linking' the calculations in this way can the index take account of changes in the make-up of the shopping basket from year to year and provide like-for-like comparisons between different years — this procedure ensures that the index is not distorted when items are either removed from, or introduced into, the CPIH or CPI 'shopping basket'.

Follow-up questions

1 Distinguish between the price level and the rate of inflation.
2 What is meant by 'weighting' in the construction of a price index such as the CPI?
3 Why may changes in a price index such as the CPI not provide an accurate measure of the rate of inflation for an individual: for example, a pensioner?
4 Why has the consumer prices index (CPI) largely replaced the retail prices index (RPI) as a measure of the average price level?

TEST YOURSELF 9.8
What does a price index attempt to measure?

CASE STUDY 9.5

Spending by the average UK family

The goods and services in the CPI shopping basket and the weights attached to them are meant to reflect the spending patterns of the 'average British family'. In so far as there is such a thing, the ONS calculated in 2018 that in 2017 the average British household spent £554.20 a week in the financial year ending (FYE) 2017. After adjusting for inflation, household spending has not been this high since the FYE 2006. It is also a rise of £21.20 in real terms when compared with the previous year. In 2017 household spending exceeded pre-economic downturn levels for the first time.

By looking at headline economic indicators, we can put the latest household spending estimates into a wider context. Inflation, as measured by the CPI, including owner occupiers' housing costs (CPIH), grew from 0.7% in April 2016 to 2.3% in March 2017, the highest level of inflation seen since September 2013. Rising levels of inflation can encourage households to bring forward certain purchases; this in turn boosts economic growth. This could be one of the reasons behind higher levels of spending in FYE 2017.

GDP, a headline measure of how well the economy is performing, grew steadily for all quarters in FYE 2017. Quarter 1 (January to March) 2017 was the 17th consecutive quarter of growth, continuing the UK's period of growth since quarter 1, 2013. Employment also continued to grow during this period. The employment rate reached 74.8% in quarter 1, 2017; at that time, the highest rate since records began. The higher the number of people and households there are in work, the more households there are receiving a regular wage; this could be another factor that influenced higher levels of spending in this time period.

Median disposable income increased by £600 (or 2.3%) when compared with the previous year. This shows that households had more money to spend when compared with the previous year.

Alongside these main economic indicators, there are other indicators we can consider to help build a wider picture of the economy. In 2016, the household savings ratio fell to 7%, the lowest seen since 2006. This shows that households chose not to save their money during this time period, which could be attributed to the low base interest rate (Bank Rate) of 0.25% introduced in August 2016. A low interest rate is a disincentive to save but it is an incentive to spend. In particular, it can encourage households to buy more goods and services on credit, as well as taking out loans, which would influence higher levels of household spending.

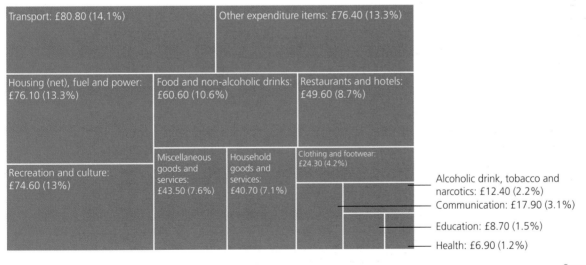

Source: ONS, 2018

Figure 9.8 How the 'average family' spent £554.20 a week in the financial year ending 2017

Follow-up questions

1 Why do rising rates of inflation encourage households to bring forward certain purchases? Give two examples of categories of spending that are likely to be brought forward.
2 Using examples taken from Figure 9.8, explain how higher levels of employment affect household spending.
3 What is the household saving ratio? How does a falling saving ratio affect household spending?
4 Figure 9.8 shows family spending on education in the financial year ending in 2017. Why do you think family spending on education was so low?

EXTENSION MATERIAL

Other economic indices

The Office for National Statistics publishes other economic indices besides the CPI and the RPI. In 2012, the ONS introduced a new price index to counteract criticisms that the main weakness of the CPI is that it does not reflect many of the costs of being a house owner, which make up about 10% of a typical family's average spending. The new index is called the CPIH where the letter 'H' stands for housing.

In recent years, as Figure 9.5 shows, the rate of inflation measured by changes in the RPI has been greater than the rate of inflation measured by the CPI.

The ONS also publishes a number of price indices which are not directly related to changes in consumer prices. These include producer price indices (PPI), which measure changes in input and output prices of goods bought and sold by UK manufacturers. Input prices are prices of materials and fuels bought; output prices, also known as 'factory gate prices', are prices at which goods are sold.

Other indices constructed by the ONS measure changes in a range of economic variables including output per worker or labour productivity mentioned earlier in this chapter. The ONS also publishes the index of production, which measures the volume of production at base year prices for the manufacturing, mining and quarrying, and energy supply industries.

EXTENSION MATERIAL

The 'Footsie' 100 index

Economic and financial indices are also published by non-government organisations. Perhaps the best known in the UK is the FTSE 100 index, often called the 'Footsie' index. The FTSE 100 is an index composed of the 100 largest companies listed on the London Stock Exchange (LSE). The index is seen as a good indicator of the performance of major public companies (PLCs). The FTSE Group which produces the index is 50/50 owned by the *Financial Times* and the London Stock Exchange (hence FTSE — FT and SE). Although the FTSE 100 is the most famous index the company produces, the FTSE Group also calculates other indices, covering markets around the world, every day. In the UK, the other FTSE indices include the FTSE 250 (the next 250 largest companies after the FTSE 100) and the FTSE All-Share index.

One point to note about the FTSE 100 index is that it was launched in 1984 with a base year value of 1,000. Usually, as we have seen, the base year index number in an economic index is 100. However, as the FTSE 100 index shows, this does not have to be the case. Also, unlike most other indices, including those published by the ONS, the FTSE 100 index has never been rebased. (Rebasing means that the base year used in an index is changed every few years, with the index number 100 being assigned to the new base year.) On 30 July 2018, the FTSE 100 index stood at 7,700.85. The fact that the FTSE index has never been rebased allows us to see the index as a barometer of UK economic performance over the last three decades.

Figure 9.9 shows how the FTSE 100 index has risen (and at times fallen) over the years between 1984 and 2018. However, the graph does not show how the composition of the UK's 100 leading companies has changed over that period. Companies are promoted into and relegated from the FTSE index every 3 months. Back in

1984, the index was dominated by the UK's leading manufacturing companies. This is no longer the case. Leading manufacturers have either disappeared or been taken over by foreign companies. To figure in the FTSE index, a company's shares have to be quoted on the London Stock Exchange. When a UK company is taken over and becomes a subsidiary of an overseas-based company, it disappears from the FTSE index. These days, the FTSE 100 companies are largely energy companies, retail companies and other service industry companies.

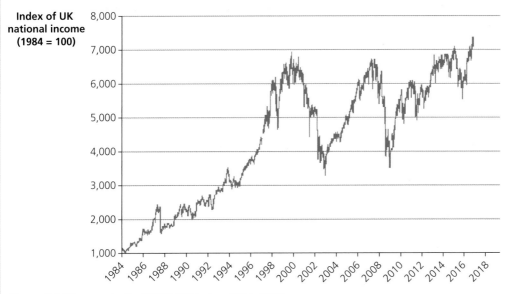

Figure 9.9 Changes in the FTSE 100 index, 1984–2018

SECTION 9.3 SUMMARY

- Changes in real GDP, and in other economic variables, are usually expressed using index numbers.
- An index number is a number used in an index, such as the consumer prices index, to enable accurate comparisons over time to be made.
- In 2017 household spending exceeded pre-economic downturn levels for the first time.
- Rising levels of inflation can encourage households to bring forward certain purchases.
- This in turn boosts economic growth.
- The number of people and households there are in work could be another factor that influences levels of spending.
- In 2016, the household savings ratio fell to 7%, the lowest seen since 2006.
- A low interest rate is a disincentive to save but it is an incentive to spend.

9.4 Uses of national income data

National income

Economists use the terms **national income** (NI) and **national product** (NP), which is also called **national output**, interchangeably. To produce the *flow* of national income or output, the economy must possess a *stock* of physical capital goods (the **national capital stock**) and a stock of **human capital**, together with stocks of the other factors of production: land and entrepreneurship. The national capital stock is part of the stock of **national**

wealth, which comprises all physical assets owned by the nation's residents that have value. The national capital stock includes capital goods, together with social capital such as the roads, hospitals and schools which are owned by the state. However, the national capital stock excludes consumer goods, which are a part of national wealth but not part of national capital. All capital is wealth, but not all wealth is capital.

KEY TERMS

national income the *flow* of new output produced by the economy in a particular period, e.g. a year, measured by the flow of factor incomes.

national product (also known as **national output**) the *flow* of new output produced by different industries in a particular period, e.g. a year.

national capital stock the stock of capital goods, e.g. buildings and machinery, in the economy that has accumulated over time and is measured at a point in time.

human capital the skills, knowledge and experience possessed by the population.

national wealth the stock of all goods that exist at a point in time that have value in the economy.

STUDY TIP

Make sure you don't confuse *wealth*, which is a stock at a point in time, with *income*, which is a flow generated over a period of time. Wealth is the stock of assets, or things that have value, which people own.

Figure 9.10 shows how we can relate a country's national income or output (for example, in 2020) to the national capital stock and the human capital stock. In the figure, national income in 2020 is shown as the area contained by the three rectangles *A*, *B* and *C*. We will now assume that at the beginning of 2020, the economy operates on its production possibility frontier. This means there is no unemployed labour, and the economy is working at full capacity to produce the flow of national income shown by *A* + *B* + *C*.

The national capital stock is the stock of capital goods that has accumulated over time in the economy. By contrast, national income is the flow of new output produced by the stocks of physical and human capital and other factors of production.

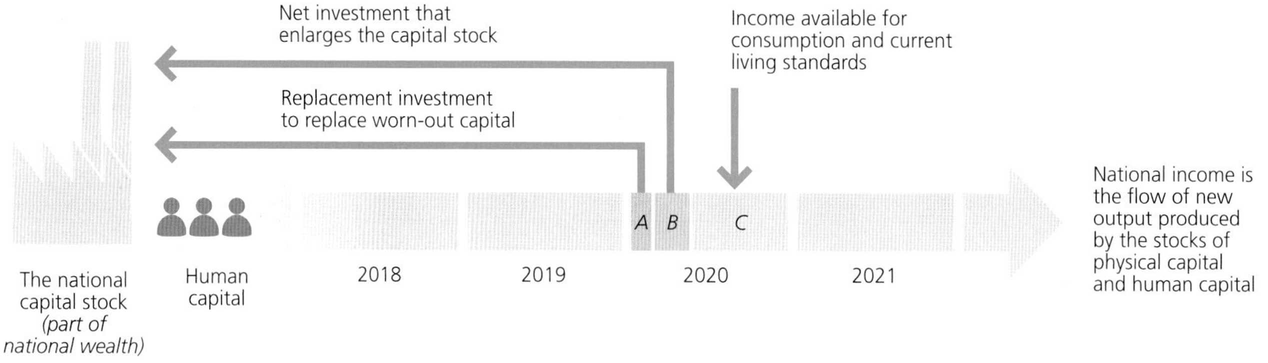

STUDY TIP

Make sure you understand the difference between stocks and flows.

Net investment that enlarges the capital stock

Replacement investment to replace worn-out capital

Income available for consumption and current living standards

National income is the flow of new output produced by the stocks of physical capital and human capital

The national capital stock (*part of national wealth*)

Human capital

2018   2019   *A B*   *C*   2021
                  2020

Figure 9.10 National income and the stocks of physical and human capital

TEST YOURSELF 9.9
Distinguish between positive and negative economic growth and explain how negative economic growth relates to recessions.

However, part of the national capital stock wears out in the course of producing 2020's national income. Worn-out capital (or the *depreciation* of the national capital stock) reflects *capital consumption*. To maintain the size of the capital stock, so that (in the absence of population growth and technical progress) the stock is capable of producing exactly the same size of national income in 2021 as in 2020, part of 2021's national output must be replacement capital goods. The spending on replacement investment is shown by area *A*. If this investment doesn't take place, the national capital stock shrinks in size. Negative economic growth occurs and the economy's production possibility frontier shifts inward.

Positive economic growth generally requires that investment takes place, over and above the replacement investment shown by rectangle *A* in Figure 9.10. The extra investment needed to enlarge the capital stock is shown by rectangle *B*. This is called net investment. Gross investment (shown by *A* + *B*) is the sum of replacement investment and net investment. Only net investment increases the size of the capital stock, thereby facilitating long-run (positive) economic growth.

KEY TERM
consumption total planned spending by households on consumer goods and services produced within the economy.

Rectangle *C* shows the fraction of national income available for **consumption** in 2020. A decision to sacrifice current consumption in favour of a higher level of future consumption means that more of society's scarce resources go into investment or the production of capital goods, enabling the national capital stock to increase in size. However, in the short term, the easiest way to increase living standards is to boost current consumption. This 'live now, pay later' approach sacrifices saving and investment, which ultimately reduces long-term economic growth.

TEST YOURSELF 9.10
What would happen to economic growth if gross investment were negative?

EXTENSION MATERIAL
The difference between national income and GDP

Students often confuse gross national income (GNI) with gross domestic product (GDP), though GDP is now the most commonly used measure of national income. Both reflect the national output and income of the economy. The word 'domestic' in gross domestic product indicates that GDP is the flow of output produced domestically within the economy. However, some British residents and companies receive income from assets they own in other countries. Likewise, some of the income produced within the UK flows out of the country to overseas owners of assets located within the UK. GNI and gross national product (GNP) take account of these income flows into and out of the economy; GDP does not.

Because it measures all the income available to spend in the UK, GNI is a better measure of the standard of living currently enjoyed by UK residents. However, GDP is a better measure of the productivity of industries actually located within the UK. Over the years, the UK invested and accumulated capital assets in other countries. As a result, income flows into the UK were larger than income flows leaving the UK. This meant that UK GNI and GNP was larger than UK GDP. Since 2006, however, in most years the reverse has been true — UK GDP has been larger than GNI and GNP. Thus in 2017 GNI was £2,008,593 million, but GDP was larger at £2,040,651 million.

The use and limitations of national income data to assess changes in living standards *over time*

Because GNP or GNI, GDP and other national income statistics are the main source of data on what has happened and what is happening in the economy, they are often used as indicators of economic growth, economic and social welfare and changing living standards, and for comparison with other countries.

To see how living standards change over time, we must look at figures for real per capita GNP, which is real GNP divided by the number of people living in the country. Rising real GNP per capita gives a general indication that living standards are rising, but it may of course conceal great and sometimes growing disparities in income distribution. This is especially significant in developing countries where the income distribution is typically extremely unequal and where only a small fraction of the population may benefit materially from economic growth.

Besides the problem of income distribution, a number of other problems surface when using national income statistics to measure living standards. The problems include:

- **The non-monetised economy.** In the UK, national income statistics under-estimate the true level of economic activity because housework and 'do-it-yourself' home improvement take place without money incomes being generated. When measuring national income, a decision has to be made on whether to estimate or to ignore the value of this production. The UK accounts can be criticised for estimating the value of some but not all of the non-monetised economy. 'Imputed rents' are estimated for the 'housing services' delivered to owner-occupiers by the houses they live in, based on an estimate of the rent paid if the house-owners were tenants of the same properties. But house-keeping allowances paid within households are not estimated, implying that housework is unproductive. Judgements such as these lead to the anomaly that national income appears to fall when, for example, a man marries his housekeeper or paints his own house, having previously employed a decorator!

- **The hidden economy.** Economic activity undertaken illegally in the **hidden economy** may be omitted. The hidden economy refers to all the economic transactions conducted in cash which are not recorded in the national income figures because of tax evasion. Because of its nature, it is impossible to make a completely accurate estimate of the size of the hidden economy. The gap between the GNP total obtained by the income and expenditure methods of measurement can be used to approximate the size of the hidden economy. The hidden economy probably equals about 10% of Britain's measured GNP, while countries such as Greece have hidden economies equal to 20–30% of GNP.

- **Quality changes.** Over time, the quality of goods changes for better or worse, presenting a particularly difficult problem in the construction and interpretation of national income figures. This is true also of services. When services such as public transport and health deteriorate, GNP may rise even though welfare and real living standards decline.

KEY TERM

hidden economy (also known as the **informal economy**, the **underground economy** and the **black economy**) all the economic transactions conducted in cash which are not recorded in the national income figures because of tax evasion.

- **Negative externalities.** National income statistics over-estimate living standards because of the effects of negative externalities such as pollution and congestion, and activities such as crime. What is in effect a welfare loss may be shown as an increase in national output, falsely indicating an apparent welfare gain. For example, the stresses and strains of producing an ever-higher national output leads to loss of leisure time, and people become ill more often. Loss of leisure and poorer health cause welfare to fall. But in the national accounts, these show up as extra production and as extra consumption of healthcare, both of which imply a welfare gain. Traffic congestion increases the cost of motoring, and hence the value of national income. Motorists would prefer uncongested roads and less spending on petrol and vehicle wear and tear.

The use and limitations of national income data to compare differences in living standards *between countries*

National income data also have limitations when comparing living standards in different countries:

- **Relative importance of the non-monetised economy.** Comparisons of national income per head between countries are misleading if the relative importance of the non-monetised economy differs significantly. There are also differences in the degree of statistical sophistication in data collection, particularly between developed and developing countries, and a lack of international uniformity in methods of classifying and categorising the national accounts. There are further problems in making comparisons when different commodities are consumed. Expenditure on fuel, clothing and building materials is usually greater in developed countries located in parts of the world with cold winters than in much warmer developing economies. However, greater expenditure on these goods may not indicate higher real incomes and living standards.
- **Exchange rates.** It is possible to compare GNP per capita in different countries by converting GNP figures for each country into a common currency such as the US dollar. However, such calculations suffer from the assumption that the exchange rates between local currencies and the dollar are correctly valued, in the sense that a dollar's worth of output in one country becomes immediately and accurately comparable with a dollar's worth of output in any other country. This can never be so. Exchange rates can only correctly reflect the values of internationally traded goods such as automobiles or internationally traded foodstuffs and raw materials.
- **Traded and non-traded goods.** The purchasing power of a currency over domestically produced goods and services, which do not enter into international trade or compete domestically with imports, may be completely different from the currency's purchasing power over imported goods. Exchange rate changes only reflect the price changes of internationally traded goods. In so far as there is a much wider gap in developing countries than in developed countries between the price changes of internationally traded and non-traded goods, GNP figures measured in US dollars tend to underestimate real levels of income and output in developing economies.

TEST YOURSELF 9.11
Why may changes in market exchange rates lead to misleading comparisons of the standard of living in different countries?

317

Purchasing power parity (PPP) exchange rates and comparing living standards

The correct solution to the problem outlined in the previous section is to establish **purchasing power parity (PPP) exchange rates**.

Calculations of GDP based on market exchange rates tend to over-estimate the cost of living in poorer developing countries. PPP exchange rates are based on the idea that, in the long run, exchange rates should move toward rates that equalise the prices of an identical basket of goods and services in any two countries. Stated simply, a dollar, or any other unit of currency such as the euro, should buy the same everywhere. Purchasing power is determined by the relative cost of living and inflation rates in different countries. Purchasing power parity means equalising the purchasing power of two currencies by taking into account these cost of living and inflation differences.

CASE STUDY 9.6

Market exchange rate versus purchasing power parity (PPP) exchange rates: which measurement should we use?

In everyday life it is usual to use a market exchange rate, the rate prevailing in the foreign exchange market, to calculate, for example, what a UK pound is worth in terms of US dollars. In some circumstances however, economists prefer to use PPP exchange rates — the rate at which the currency of one country would have to be converted into that of another country to buy the same amount of goods and services in each country.

In an article titled 'PPP versus the market', published in the March 2007 edition of *Finance and Development*, senior IMF official Tim Callen wrote:

> To understand PPP, let's take a commonly used example, the price of a hamburger. If a hamburger is selling in London for £2 and in New York for $4, this would imply a PPP exchange rate of 1 pound to 2 US dollars. This PPP exchange rate may well be different from that prevailing in financial markets (so that the actual dollar cost of a hamburger in London may be either more or less than the $4 it sells for in New York). This type of cross-country comparison is the basis for the well-known 'Big Mac' index, which is published by the *Economist* magazine and calculates PPP exchange rates based on the McDonald's sandwich that sells in nearly identical form in many countries around the world.
>
> Of course, any meaningful comparison of prices across countries must consider a wide range of goods and services. This is not an easy task, because of the amount of data that must be collected and the complexities in the comparison process. To facilitate price comparisons across countries, the International Comparisons Program (ICP) was established by the United Nations and the University of Pennsylvania in 1968. PPPs generated by the ICP are based on a global survey of prices. For the ongoing 2003–06 round, each of the participating countries (about 147) provides national average prices for 1,000 closely specified products.
>
> So which method is better? The appropriate way to aggregate economic data across countries depends on the issue being considered. Market exchange rates are the logical choice when financial flows are involved. For example, the current account balance represents a flow of financial resources across countries. It is appropriate to use the market exchange rate to convert these flows into dollars when aggregating across regions or calculating the global current account discrepancy. But for other variables, the decision is less clear cut. Take real GDP growth. International organizations use different approaches. The World Bank uses market-based rates to determine the weights in its regional and global aggregations of real GDP, whereas the IMF and the Organization for Economic Cooperation and Development use weights based on PPP. Each methodology has its advantages and disadvantages.

Advantages of PPP. A main one is that PPP exchange rates are relatively stable over time. By contrast, market rates are more volatile, and using them could produce quite large swings in aggregate measures of growth even when growth rates in individual countries are stable. Another drawback of market-based rates is that they are relevant only for internationally traded goods. Non-traded goods and services tend to be cheaper in low-income than in high-income countries. A haircut in New York is more expensive than in Lima; the price of a taxi ride of the same distance is higher in Paris than in Tunis; and a ticket to a cricket game costs more in London than in Lahore. Indeed, because wages tend to be lower in poorer countries, and services are often relatively labour-intensive, the price of a haircut in Lima is likely to be cheaper than in New York even when the cost of making tradable goods, such as machinery, is the same in both countries. Any analysis that fails to take into account these differences in the prices of non-traded goods across countries will underestimate the purchasing power of consumers in emerging market and developing countries and, consequently, their overall welfare. For this reason, PPP is generally regarded as a better measure of overall well-being.

Drawbacks of PPP. The biggest one is that PPP is harder to measure than market-based rates. It is a huge statistical undertaking, and new price comparisons are available only at infrequent intervals. The method of measurement does not cover all countries, which means that data for missing countries have to be estimated.

Follow-up questions

1 Access the OECD website at **https://data.oecd.org/conversion/purchasing-power-parities-ppp.htm** and identify the PPP exchange rates for the UK pound and the US dollar for the latest year on the chart.
2 Why do you thank that the US dollar has the same PPP exchange rate in every year in the chart?
3 Find out from the internet or from the business page of a recent newspaper the market exchange rate of the UK pound against the US dollar.
4 What conclusion(s) can you draw from comparing your answers for the two exchange rates?

CASE STUDY 9.7

The *Economist*'s Big Mac index

In 1986 the *Economist* magazine invented the Big Mac index as a light-hearted guide to whether currencies are at their 'correct' level. The Big Mac index is based on the theory of purchasing power parity (PPP), the notion that in the long run exchange rates should move towards the rate that would equalise the prices of an identical basket of goods and services (in this case, a Big Mac burger) in any two countries. 'Burgernomics' was never intended as a precise gauge of currency misalignment, merely a tool to make exchange-rate theory more digestible. The GDP-adjusted Big Mac index addresses the criticism that you would expect  average burger prices to be cheaper in poor countries than in rich ones because labour costs are lower. PPP signals where exchange rates should be heading in the long run, as a country like China gets richer.

Follow-up questions

1 Distinguish between a market exchange rate and a PPP exchange rate.
2 Why is a Big Mac burger a particularly suitable commodity for measuring a PPP exchange rate?
3 Name another commodity which might also be suitable for measuring a PPP exchange rate and explain why.
4 Find out from the Big Mac index whether the UK pound's exchange rate is currently overvalued of undervalued.

SYNOPTIC LINK

Exchange rates are explained in section 15.1 of Chapter 15 on the international economy.

SECTION 9.4 SUMMARY

- National income data are especially important for monitoring the performance of the UK economy.
- Economists use the terms national income (NI) and national product (NP) interchangeably.
- Gross domestic product (GDP) is now the most commonly used measure of national income.
- Because GNP or GNI, GDP and other national income statistics are the main source of data on what has happened and what is happening in the economy, they are often used as indicators of economic growth, economic and social welfare and changing living standards, and for comparison with other countries.
- National income statistics under-estimate the true level of economic activity because the non-monetised economy is under-represented.
- The hidden economy refers to all the economic transactions conducted in cash which are not recorded in the national income figures because of tax evasion.
- Standards of living reflect elements of quality of life and general economic welfare, as well as narrow GNP-related consumption.
- Comparisons of national income per head between countries are misleading if the relative importance of the non-monetised economy differs significantly.
- Purchasing power parity (PPP) exchange rates are the rates of currency conversion that equalise the purchasing power of different currencies by eliminating the differences in price levels between countries.

Questions

1 With the help of a *PPF* diagram, explain the difference between short-term and long-term economic growth.

2 Distinguish between an objective and an instrument of macroeconomic policy. Explain two macroeconomic policy objectives.

3 Explain **two** of the main conflicts affecting macroeconomic policy, and how a government might trade off between achieving these objectives.

4 Explain the differences between inflation, deflation and disinflation. When did deflation last occur in the UK economy?

5 What is the difference between a deficit and a surplus on the current account of the balance of payments? Which does the UK have today, and how large is it?

6 Briefly explain how a price index is constructed.

7 What is the purpose of a PPP exchange rate?

10

How the macroeconomy works: the circular flow of income, aggregate demand/aggregate supply analysis and related concepts

This chapter is about *macroeconomic theory*. The two main bodies of macroeconomic theory, or macroeconomic models, are explained in some detail. These are the circular flow and the aggregate demand/aggregate supply (*AD/AS*) models of the economy. The chapter then goes on to look at related macroeconomic concepts, such as the components of aggregate demand (consumption, investment etc.) and the multiplier concept. The following three chapters of the book, which cover economic performance, monetary policy and fiscal policy, will continue the task introduced in this chapter of applying macroeconomic theory to the analysis of current economic problems and the evaluation of government economic policies.

LEARNING OBJECTIVES

These are to remind you of the meaning of national income, and then to understand:

- the circular flow macroeconomic model of how the economy works
- the effect of changes in injections and withdrawals of demand on national income
- the accelerator and multiplier processes
- the aggregate demand/aggregate supply (AD/AS) macroeconomic model
- aggregate demand and aggregate supply in greater detail

10.1 The circular flow of income

National income revisited

In order to understand the meaning of the circular flow of income, it is useful to remind yourself of what we wrote about national income in the previous chapter. In Chapter 9, we explained:

- **What national income measures.** National income is the flow of new output produced by an economy in a particular time period, such as a year.
- **The difference between nominal and real national income.** The flow of new output is real national income, which comprises the actual goods and services that are produced. By contrast, nominal national income measures the flow of output at the current price level in the economy.
- **The role of real national income as an indicator of economic performance.** The *level* of real national income is an indicator of current living standards within the economy, and its *rate of change* measures the economic growth (or economic decline) occurring in the economy. The level and rate of change of real national income are used when comparing the country's economic performance with that of other countries.

National income = national output = national expenditure

It is also important to understand that there are three methods of measuring the flow of new output in an economy. Firstly, the flow of new output can be measured by adding together the incomes received by the different factors of production such as capital and labour. Measured in this way, the flow is called national income. Secondly, the flow can be measured by summing the totals of the actual goods and services produced by the economy. The flow is now called national output or national product. Finally, we can measure national expenditure. This shows how factor incomes such as wages and profits end up being spent on the goods and service produced by the economy.

Since they are three different ways of measuring the same things (the flow of new output), and provided that we ignore income flows into and out of the economy, it follows that national income, national output and national expenditure always equal each other and add to the same totals.

In summary:

- The **income approach** sums the factor incomes to the factors of production.
- The **output approach** adds up the 'value added' by each of the industries in the economy, such as agriculture, manufacturing and services.
- The **expenditure approach** sums consumption + investment + government expenditure + exports – imports.

The preliminary estimate of GDP is based solely on the output approach to measuring the flow of new output. The output approach measures gross value added (GVA) at a detailed industry level before aggregating to produce an estimate for the whole economy.

STUDY TIP
It might be useful at this stage to reread section 9.4 in Chapter 9 on the uses of national income data.

TEST YOURSELF 10.1
Distinguish between real and nominal national income and explain why real national income is a better indicator of economic performance than nominal national income.

The circular flow of income

Figure 9.10 in Chapter 9 depicts national income as the flow of new output moving along a horizontal arrow extending from the economy's national capital stock, shown to the left of the arrow. Look back also to Figure 6.1 in Chapter 6. The diagram shows households and firms functioning simultaneously in both the goods market, or market for output, and the economy's factor market or market for inputs into the production process. However, the roles of households and firms are reversed in these two sets of markets. Whereas firms are the source of supply in a goods market, in a factor market firms exercise demand for factor services supplied by households. We noted that:

'*The incomes received by households from the sale and supply of factor services contribute In large measure to households' ability to demand the output supplied by firms in the goods market. To exercise demand, which requires an ability to pay as well as a willingness to pay, households need an income, and for most people this requires the sale of their labour services in a labour market.*

The relationship between households and firms in the two markets is essentially circular. In goods markets, finished goods and services flow from firms to households, who spend their incomes on the goods. In labour markets, members of households earn the incomes they spend on goods by selling labour to their employers.'

This is the basis of the circular flow of income which we illustrate in the next three diagrams.

The simple circular flow model, illustrated in Figure 10.1, assumes that there are just two sets of economic agents in the economy: households and firms. The model pretends that the government and foreign trade don't exist. This is a model of a two-sector economy, or a **closed economy** with no government sector. The dashed flow lines in the figure show the real flows occurring in the economy between households and firms. Households supply labour and other factor services in exchange for goods and services produced by the firms. These real flows generate money flows of income and expenditure, shown by the solid flow lines.

> **KEY TERM**
> **closed economy** an economy with no international trade.

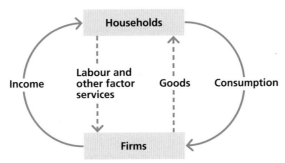

Figure 10.1 A simplified circular flow diagram of a two-sector economy

All the income received by households (shown by the left-hand flow curve of the diagram) is spent on consumption (shown by the right-hand flow curve).

Figure 10.2 is a more realistic version of Figure 10.1, because it shows households saving as well as consuming, and firms investing in capital goods. When households save part of their incomes, people are spending less than their incomes. **Saving**, which is an example of a leakage or **withdrawal** from the circular flow of income, is depicted by the upper of the two horizontal arrows in Figure 10.2. The lower of the two horizontal arrows shows **investment**, or spending on machinery and other capital goods, which is an **injection** of demand into the economy.

> **KEY TERMS**
> **saving** income which is not spent.
> **withdrawal** a leakage of spending power out of the circular flow of income into savings, taxation or imports.
> **investment** total planned spending by firms on capital goods produced within the economy.
> **injection** spending entering the circular flow of income as a result of investment, government spending and exports.

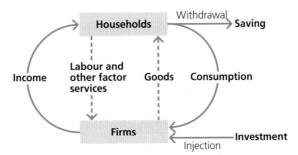

Figure 10.2 Introducing saving and investment into the circular flow of income

323

A first look at the concept of equilibrium national income

Equilibrium national income is the level of income at which withdrawals from the circular flow of income equal injections into the flow. And as we shall shortly see when taking a second look at the concept, it is also the level of output at which aggregate demand equals aggregate supply. Equilibrium income is not necessarily the same as **full employment income**. This is the level of income when the economy is producing on its production possibility frontier, with no spare capacity.

How a change in injections or withdrawals affects equilibrium national income

In circular flow theory, if planned saving (or the planned withdrawal of spending) equals planned investment (or the planned injection of spending into the flow), national income is in equilibrium, tending neither to rise nor to fall. However, if the withdrawal exceeds the injection, the resulting net leakage of spending from the circular flow causes output and income to fall. Likewise, if the withdrawal is less than the injection, the resulting net injection of spending into the economy causes output and income to rise.

Savings can be hoarded, or the funds being saved can be lent for others to spend. Hoarding — for example, keeping money under the mattress — means that a fraction of income is not spent. This can lead to deficient aggregate demand in the economy, which means there is too little demand to buy the output the economy is capable of producing. Because they cannot sell some of the goods and services they have produced, firms reduce their output and national income falls.

However, if all savings are lent, via financial intermediaries such as banks, for firms and other consumers to borrow and then to spend, planned saving may end up equalling planned investment. With this outcome, national income remains in equilibrium and there is no reason why the level of income should fall.

In the two-sector circular flow model, national income is in equilibrium when:

planned saving = planned investment

or:

$$S = I$$

However, because households and firms have different motives for making their respective saving and investment decisions, there is no reason why, initially, household saving should exactly equal the amount firms plan to spend on capital goods (that is, investment). Consider, for example, a situation in which planned saving is greater than planned investment ($S > I$). In this situation, the national income or output circulating round the economy is in disequilibrium, with withdrawals out of the system exceeding injections of spending into the flow of income, and national income will fall.

Bringing the government sector and the overseas sector into the circular flow model

The simple circular flow model we have looked at is unrealistic because it ignores how the domestic government and the rest of the world are sources of both injections of demand into, and withdrawals of demand from, the circular flow of income. Government spending is an injection of spending into the economy. In contrast, taxation, which takes spending power away from the people being taxed, is a withdrawal or leakage of spending. Exports and imports result from the fact that we live in an **open economy**: that is, an economy open to international trade. Exports, which result from people living in other countries buying goods produced in Britain, are an injection into the circular flow. By contrast, imports, or spending by UK residents on goods produced overseas, are a withdrawal from the circular flow. Spending on imports stimulates the economies of other countries rather than the UK economy.

Figure 10.3 shows the effect of bringing the activities of the government and overseas sectors into the circular flow model.

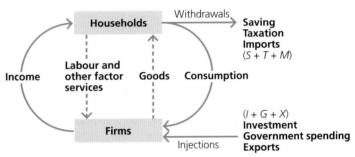

Figure 10.3 The circular flow of income in an economy with a government sector and an overseas sector

In this extended circular flow model, national income is in equilibrium, tending neither to rise nor to fall, when:

saving + taxation + imports = investment + government spending + exports

or:

$$S + T + M = I + G + X$$

However, whenever:

$$S + T + M > I + G + X$$

a net withdrawal or leakage of demand out of the circular flow occurs, which in Keynesian analysis causes the equilibrium level of national income to fall.

And when:

$$S + T + M < I + G + X$$

a net injection of demand into the circular flow occurs, which causes the equilibrium level of national income to rise.

KEY TERM

open economy an economy open to international trade.

STUDY TIP

Economists use the letters Y, C, S, I, G, T, X and M as shorthand, respectively for the macroeconomic variables income, consumption, saving, investment, government spending, taxation, exports and imports. Make sure you don't confuse S, used in the circular flow model as the shorthand for saving, with its microeconomic use as the shorthand for 'supply'. Section 10.2 also introduces the concept of aggregate supply, for which the shorthand is AS. Remember also that in Chapter 9 we used the letters NI as shorthand for national income.

325

Keynes and deficient aggregate demand

If planned saving by households exceeds planned investment by firms, there is a danger that deficient aggregate demand may cause the economy to sink into a recession. In the 1930s, during the Great Depression, John Maynard Keynes argued that if household savings are not lent to finance spending by others, particularly investment by firms, the level of income or output circulating round the economy falls. This reduces saving, until planned saving equals planned investment and equilibrium is restored, albeit at a significantly lower level of national income. The economy ends up in recession. Fairly recently, Keynesian economists used the same analysis as part of their explanation of the 2008–09 recession, arguing that a liquidity crisis and an associated collapse of consumer and business confidence were responsible for the collapse in aggregate demand.

Pro-free-market economists, who generally reject Keynesian theory, believe that deficient aggregate demand only exists as a *temporary* and self-correcting phenomenon. They argue that when deficient aggregate demand occurs, the rate of interest, rather than the level of income or output, falls, quickly restoring equality between saving and investment intentions. When interest rates fall, people save less because saving becomes less attractive. At the same time, firms invest more in new capital goods because the cost of borrowing has fallen.

Back in the 1930s, Keynes agreed that a fall in interest rates can bring about equality between saving and investment, but he believed the process to be slow. In the very long run it may work, but, in Keynes's memorable phrase, 'in the long run we are all dead'. Keynes argued that when planned leakages of demand from the circular flow of income exceed planned injections of demand into the flow, the level of income or output falls to restore equilibrium. According to Keynes, deficient aggregate demand is the cause of recessions.

Building and using economic models

Much of this chapter is about macroeconomic models: the circular flow model we have just explained, and the *AD/AS* model we are about to investigate, are the two macroeconomic models you need to understand. Model building is one of the most fundamental analytical techniques used by economists. Economic theory is based on developing economic models which describe particular aspects of the economic behaviour of individuals, groups of individuals and, in a macro context, the whole economy.

A model is a small-scale replica of real-world phenomena, often incorporating a number of simplifications. An economic model simplifies the real world in such a way that the essential features of an economic relationship or set of relationships are explained using diagrams, words and often algebra. Models are used by economists first to understand and explain the working of the economy, and second to predict what might happen in the future.

A good economic model simplifies reality sufficiently to allow important and often otherwise obscure economic relationships to be studied, away from irrelevant detail or 'background noise'. The danger is that reality can be oversimplified, with the resulting model failing to reflect in a useful way the world it seeks to explain. Economic modelling involves the art of making strong assumptions about human behaviour so as to concentrate attention and analysis on key economic relationships in a clear and tractable way, while avoiding an excessive oversimplification of the problem or relationship to be explained.

The ultimate purpose of model building is to derive predictions about economic behaviour, such as the prediction of demand theory that demand will increase when price falls. Economic controversy often exists when models generate conflicting predictions about what will happen in a given set of circumstances. For example, a model of the labour market which predicts that the supply of labour increases as wages rise carries the policy-making implication that a cut in income tax, being equivalent to a wage rise, creates an incentive to effort and hard work. Under alternative assumptions, the model could predict the opposite: that, as wages rise, workers begin to prefer leisure to work and react to the tax cut by working less.

It may often be possible to accept or dismiss a model of economic behaviour on the basis of common sense or casual observation of the world around us. Economists now usually go further, using sophisticated statistical tests to evaluate empirically the model's predictions. Good economic models or theories survive the process of empirical testing (which is part of a branch of the subject called 'econometrics'), whereas models or theories shown to be at odds with observed behaviour must be revised or discarded.

TEST YOURSELF 10.5
How is a recession defined in the United Kingdom?

STUDY TIP
Many macroeconomic questions can be addressed by using the circular flow model, the *AD/AS* model, or both.

SYNOPTIC LINK
Measures of economic performance in the next chapter, Chapter 11, and different economic policies discussed in Chapters 12 and 13, are explained and analysed using one or both of the macroeconomic models (circular flow and *AD/AS*) explained in this chapter.

EXTENSION MATERIAL

Circular flow and the Phillips machine

In the Meade Room in the Department of Applied Economics of Cambridge University stands a Phillips machine — a device so cunning and ingenious that it can predict the running of the national economy to within 4% accuracy. The prototype was an odd assortment of tanks, pipes, sluices and valves, with water pumped around the machine by a motor cannibalised from the windscreen wiper of a Lancaster bomber. Bits of filed-down Perspex and fishing line were used to channel the coloured dyes that mimicked the flow of income round the economy into consumer spending, taxes, investment and exports. A.W. 'Bill' Phillips and Walter Newlyn, who helped piece the machine together at the London School of Economics toward the end of the 1940s, experimented with treacle and methylated spirits before deciding that coloured water was the best way of displaying the way money circulates around the economy.

James Meade with the Phillips machine

Water flows through a series of clear pipes, mimicking the way that money flows through the economy. The machine lets you see (literally) what happens if you lower tax rates or increase the money supply or whatever; just open a valve here or pull a lever there and the machine sloshes away, showing in real time how the water levels rise and fall in various tanks representing the growth in personal savings, tax revenue and so on. This device was state of the art in the 1950s, but it looks hilarious now, with all its plumbing and noisy pumps.

One early demonstration of the machine displayed the difficulties that can arise when monetary and fiscal policy are not synchronised. Phillips asked one of his students to be chancellor of the exchequer and control taxes and spending; another to be governor of the Bank of England and control interest rates. Predictably, the policies were uncoordinated, and the upshot was that water overflowed on to the floor.

Read more about the Phillips machine in Tim Harford's book, *The Undercover Economist Strikes Back*, which is also available on a BBC radio podcast.

327

SECTION 10.1 SUMMARY

- National income is the flow of new output produced in an economy in a particular time period.
- Changes in real national income must not be confused with changes in nominal national income.
- A circular flow model of the economy shows the flows of income and spending around the economy.
- The circular flow model can illustrate injections into and leakages (or withdrawals) from income circulating round the economy and equilibrium national income.
- Economists use the letters Y, C, S, I, G, T, X and M as shorthand, respectively for the macroeconomic variables income, consumption, saving, investment, government spending, taxation, exports and imports.
- In a simplified circular flow model of the economy, equilibrium national income occurs when $S = I$.
- In a more realistic circular flow model of the economy containing a government sector and an overseas sector, equilibrium national income occurs when $S + T + M = I + G + X$.

KEY TERMS

aggregate demand total planned spending on real output in the economy at different price levels.

reflationary policies policies that increase aggregate demand with the intention of increasing real output and employment.

aggregate supply the level of real national output that producers are prepared to supply at different average price levels.

10.2 Aggregate demand and aggregate supply analysis

In the last 40 years or so, the *AD/AS* model has become the preferred theoretical framework that many economists use for explaining macroeconomic issues. For example, the model is useful for analysing the effect of an increase in **aggregate demand** (*AD*) upon the economy. This addresses a key issue: will expansionary fiscal policy and/or monetary policy increase real output and jobs (**reflationary policies**), or will the price level increase instead? As we shall explain, the answer to this key macroeconomic question depends to a large extent on supply-side factors as represented by the shape of the **aggregate supply** (*AS*) curve, in both the short run and the long run.

The meaning of aggregate demand

Aggregate demand is the total planned spending on the goods and services produced within the economy in a particular time period, such as a year. An *AD* curve is illustrated in Figure 10.4.

The four sources of spending included in aggregate demand, each originating in a different sector of the economy (households, firms, the government sector and the overseas sector), are shown in the equation:

$$AD = C + I + G + (X - M)$$

where C, I, G, X and M are the symbols used respectively for planned consumption, investment, government spending, exports and imports.

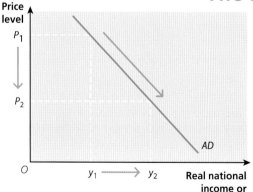

Figure 10.4 An aggregate demand (*AD*) curve

STUDY TIP

Make sure you don't confuse aggregate demand with national expenditure. Both are macroeconomic concepts, related to demand in the whole economy, or the economy in aggregate. However, aggregate demand measures *planned* spending, whereas national expenditure measures *realised* or *actual* spending, which has already taken place — for example, UK national expenditure in 2019.

STUDY TIP

Make sure you understand and can apply the aggregate demand equation:

$$AD = C + I + G + (X - M)$$

See also the section 10.3 of this chapter on the determinants of aggregate demand.

TEST YOURSELF 10.6

Distinguish between aggregate demand and national expenditure.

QUANTITATIVE SKILLS 10.1

Worked example: components of aggregate demand

Table 10.1 shows the components of aggregate demand for an economy in 2019 and 2020.

Table 10.1 Components of aggregate demand, 2019 and 2020 (£bn)

Year	Government and private consumption expenditure	Government and private investment expenditure	Exports	Imports
2019	1,000	150	300	200
2020	1,200	170	250	220

(a) What was the change in the level of aggregate demand between 2019 and 2020?

The information in Table 10.1 relates to the aggregate demand equation:

$$AD = C + I + G + (X - M)$$

Adding together the information in the columns, in 2019:

$$AD = £1,000bn + £150bn + £300bn - £200bn = £1,250bn$$

In 2020:

$$AD = £1,200bn + £170bn + £250bn - £220bn = £1,400bn$$

This means that between 2019 and 2020 aggregate demand increased by £150 billion.

(b) What was the change in net export demand between 2019 and 2020?

In 2019 net export demand $(X - M)$ was £300bn – £200bn, which was £100 billion.

In 2020 net export demand $(X - M)$ was £250bn – £220bn, which was £30 billion.

There was a balance of trade surplus in both years. The trade surplus fell by £70 billion between 2019 and 2020.

329

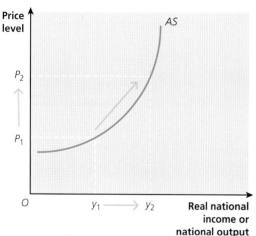

Figure 10.5 An aggregate supply (AS) curve

The meaning of aggregate supply

Aggregate supply is the level of real national output that producers are prepared to supply at different average price levels. An upward-sloping AS curve is illustrated in Figure 10.5.

The upward-slope of the AS curve is explained by two microeconomic assumptions about the nature of firms. These are:

- all firms aim to maximise profits
- in the short run, the cost of producing extra units of output increases as firms produce more output

At the average price level P_1 in Figure 10.5, the level of real output that all the economy's firms are willing to produce and sell is y_1. To persuade the firms it is in their interest to produce the larger output of y_2, the price level must rise. This is because higher prices are needed to create the higher sales revenues needed to offset the higher production costs that firms incur as they increase output, so that profits do not fall. In Figure 10.5, the average price level has to rise to P_2 in order to create conditions in which profit-maximising firms are willing and able to supply more output. If prices don't rise, it is not profitable to increase supply. Without a higher price level, profit-maximising firms, taken in aggregate, will not voluntarily increase the supply of real output.

Changes in the price level are shown by movements along the AD and AS curves

If you look back at Figure 10.4, you will see that as the price level in the economy falls from P_1 to P_2, the aggregate demand for real output increases. Likewise, as we have just explained, the aggregate supply curve in Figure 10.5 shows that as the price level in the economy rises from P_1 to P_2, firms are willing to supply more real output.

Factors that shift the AD curve and the AS curve

If either the AD curve or the AS curve shifts to a new position, the level of national income will change. Figure 10.6(a) shows the effect of a rightward shift of the AD curve, with the level of income moving from point X to point Z. By contrast, Figure 10.6(b) shows the effect of a leftward movement of the AS curve, with the level of income moving from point X to point V.

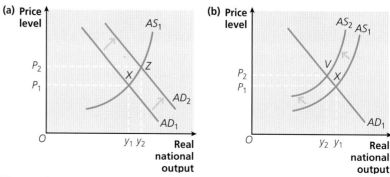

Figure 10.6 Shifts of, and adjustments along, AD and AS curves, showing movements to new levels of income

An *AD* curve will shift to a new position if there is a change in the value of any of the components of aggregate demand which we described earlier. Remember, these are consumption, investment, government spending, exports and imports.

The *AS* curve is constructed under the assumption that all the determinants of aggregate supply *other than the price level* remain unchanged. Should any of these determinants change, the *AS* curve shifts to a new position. The curve can shift either to the right (an increase in aggregate supply) or to the left (a decrease in aggregate supply). Figure 10.6(b) illustrates a decrease in aggregate supply, which results in inflation, with the price level increasing from P_1 to P_2.

> **TEST YOURSELF 10.8**
> Distinguish between an adjustment along, and a shift of, an aggregate supply curve.

> **KEY TERM**
> **long-run aggregate supply** the real output that can be supplied when the economy is on its production possibility frontier. This is when all the available factors of production are employed and producing at their 'normal capacity' level of output.

> **STUDY TIP**
> A *shift* of the *AD* curve, such as that illustrated in Figure 10.6(a), must not be confused with the *adjustment* that follows along the *AS* curve. In this case, the adjustment is called an expansion or extension of aggregate supply.
>
> The shift of the *AS* curve to the left, which we illustrated in Figure 10.6(b), is followed by a movement or adjustment up the *AD* curve. This time, the adjustment is called a contraction of aggregate demand. Other possibilities not shown in the graphs are a decrease in aggregate demand (or shift of the *AD* curve to the left) followed by a contraction of aggregate supply, and an increase in aggregate supply (shift of the *AS* curve to the right) followed by an expansion or extension of aggregate demand.
>
> As a practice exercise, try drawing diagrams to illustrate the events just described.

Introducing the long-run aggregate supply (*LRAS*) curve

Although we have not named them as such, the aggregate supply curves considered so far in this chapter are short-run aggregate supply (*SRAS*) curves. However, we now introduce the economy's **long-run aggregate supply** (*LRAS*) curve.

We have seen that in the short run, the aggregate supply or real output depends on the average price level in the economy. Other things remaining constant, firms are only prepared to supply more output if the price level rises. However, in the long run, aggregate supply is not influenced by the price level. Long-run supply reflects the economy's production potential. It is the maximum level of output that the economy can produce when the economy is on its production possibility frontier.

Producing on the production possibility frontier means that there is no spare capacity or idle resources in the economy. Thus, the vertical *LRAS* curve in Figure 10.7 is located immediately above the maximum level of physical output that the economy can produce. As Figure 10.7 shows, once the economy produces at full capacity, an increase in aggregate demand from AD_1 to AD_2 increases the price level from P_1 to P_2, but real output remains unchanged.

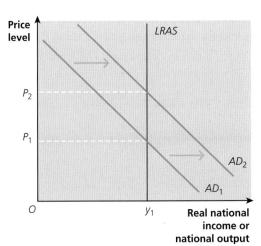

Figure 10.7 A shift of aggregate demand along a vertical *LRAS* curve

331

Underlying economic growth shown by a rightward shift in the *LRAS* curve

Short-run growth, which we will examine in Chapter 11 in the context of economic cycles, results mostly from temporary fluctuations in aggregate demand. By contrast, the underlying rate of growth, or trend growth rate, is the long-run average growth rate for a country over a period of time. Underlying growth is determined by the same factors that determine the position of the economy's production possibility frontier: the quantities of capital and labour and other factors of production in the economy, and technical progress. These also determine the position of the *LRAS* curve.

An increase in the quantity of available factors of production including labour, and improvements in technology that increase the productivity of labour, capital or land, shift the economy's production possibility frontier outwards. For the same reasons, the economy's *LRAS* curve shifts right. The shifts of the production possibility frontier and the *LRAS* curve to the right are both illustrated in Figure 10.8.

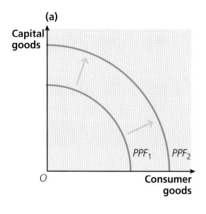
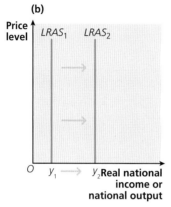

Figure 10.8 Underlying growth shown by an outward movement of an economy's production possibility frontier and by a rightward movement of its *LRAS* curve

A second look at the concept of equilibrium national income

There are two ways of approaching the concept of equilibrium national income (or macroeconomic equilibrium). We have already seen how national income is in equilibrium when planned injections into the circular flow of income equal planned withdrawals of demand from the flow of income circulating round the economy. Ignoring for the time being the distinction between short-run and long-run aggregate supply, the second approach defines equilibrium national income in the *AD/AS* model of the economy. Equilibrium national income occurs when the aggregate demand for real output equals the aggregate supply of real output, i.e. where *AD = AS*. This is illustrated in Figure 10.9 at point *X*, where the *AD* curve intersects the *AS* curve. The equilibrium level of real output is y_1, and the equilibrium price level is P_1.

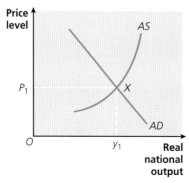

Figure 10.9 Equilibrium national income occurring when *AD = AS*

Demand-side and supply-side economic shocks

An **economic shock** is a sudden unexpected event hitting the economy, disturbing either aggregate demand (a demand shock) or aggregate supply (a supply shock). In some cases, an outside shock may affect both aggregate demand and aggregate supply. Thus, looking at the UK economy, the outbreak of a war in the Middle East, for example, may affect demand by causing a sudden collapse in consumer and business confidence, and aggregate supply via its effect on the supply and price of crude oil.

CASE STUDY 10.1

Economic shock caused by the El Niño effect

Above-average ocean surface temperatures develop every 3 to 7 years off the Pacific coast of South America and last about 2 years, causing major climatological changes around the world. This is the El Niño effect. The 2015–16 El Niño was one of the most severe events in the past 50 years and the largest since the 1997–98 El Niño that shocked global food, water, health, energy, and disaster-response systems.

Economists are increasingly interested in the relationship between climate — temperature, precipitation, storms, and other aspects of the weather — and economic performance. The extreme weather conditions associated with El Niño can constrain the supply of rain-driven agricultural commodities, lead to higher food prices and inflation, and may trigger social unrest in commodity-dependent countries that rely primarily on imported food.

An El Niño typically brings drought to the western Pacific (including Australia), rains to the equatorial coast of South America, and storms and hurricanes to the central Pacific. These changes in weather patterns have significant effects on agriculture, fishing and construction industries, as well as on national and global commodity prices.

Australia, Chile, India, Indonesia, Japan, New Zealand, and South Africa face a short-lived fall in economic activity in response to a typical El Niño shock. However, in other parts of the world, an El Niño event actually improves economic growth. Many countries experience short-term inflation pressures following an El Niño shock (its magnitude increasing with the share of food in the consumer prices index (CPI) basket), while energy and non-fuel commodity prices also rise around the world.

Much worse than El Niño is the effect of climate change and global warming on sub-Saharan economies. This has led to severe drought and desertification, which is dramatically increasing the area of the Sahara desert. African economies are on the verge of collapse and increasing poverty is fuelling attempted mass migration into the European Union and the growth of popularist political parties which are destabilising the democratic system in EU countries.

Source: IMF, March 2016

Follow-up questions

1 Would you classify the El Niño effect as a demand-side or as a supply-side economic shock, or as a mix of the two? Justify your conclusion.
2 Explain how the El Niño effect has affected global inflation.
3 In what ways, if any, has the 2018 hot summer in the UK had beneficial or adverse effects on the UK economy?
4 Do you agree that climate change and global warming in sub-Saharan Africa is having much more significant adverse effects on world economic performance than the El Niño effect in the Pacific Ocean? Justify your answer.

SECTION 10.2 SUMMARY

- The *AD/AS* model can be used as well as the circular flow model to show equilibrium national income (or macroeconomic equilibrium) in the economy.
- The *AD* curve shows total planned spending on real national output at different price levels.
- The *SRAS* curve shows how much output producers are prepared to supply at different price levels.
- It is important to distinguish between a *shift* of an *AD* or *AS* curve and the resulting *movement along* the curve that does not shift.
- A shift of the *AD* curve to the right is known as an increase in aggregate demand, while a shift to the left is a decrease in aggregate demand.
- A shift of the *SRAS* curve to the right is known as an increase in aggregate supply, while a shift to the left is a decrease in aggregate supply.
- Long-run aggregate supply (*LRAS*) is the maximum level of output that the economy can produce when on its production possibility frontier.

10.3 The determinants of aggregate demand

The components of aggregate demand

As we mentioned earlier in the chapter, consumption, investment, government spending and net export demand (spending on UK exports by residents of other countries minus spending on imports by UK residents) form the components of aggregate demand.

We shall now look in detail at the first two of the components of aggregate demand — consumption and investment.

SYNOPTIC LINK

We shall explain government spending's role as a component of aggregate demand in the section on fiscal policy in Chapter 13 and the role of exports and imports in the section on the balance of payments on current account in Chapter 14.

The determinants of consumption

Aggregate consumption is spending by all the households in the economy on consumer goods and services. Whenever members of households make decisions about whether or not to spend on consumer goods, they are simultaneously deciding whether or not to save. A determinant of consumption is also a determinant of household saving. If we assume a closed economy — pretending that there are no exports or imports — and that there is no taxation, then at any level of income, households can only do two things with their income: spend it or not spend it. Spending income is consumption, whereas not spending income is saving.

The determinants of income are described below.

Interest rates

The **rate of interest** rewards savers for sacrificing current consumption, and the higher the rate of interest, the greater the reward. Thus, at any particular level of income, the amount saved will increase as the real rate of interest rises and the amount consumed will fall.

Level of income

An important, and perhaps the main, determinant of both consumption and saving is the level of income. This is often called the Keynesian theory of consumption and saving. In 1936, in his explanation of the causes of the Great Depression, John Maynard Keynes wrote:

> The fundamental psychological law, upon which we are entitled to depend with great confidence…is that men are disposed, as a rule and on average, to increase their consumption as their income increases, but not by as much as the increase in their income.

In Keynes's view, as income rises, although absolute consumption rises, consumption falls as a fraction of total income, while the fraction saved increases. Therein lies the cause of recessions, according to Keynes: too much saving and too little spending.

Expected future income

The Keynesian consumption theory just explained is sometimes also called the 'absolute income' consumption theory because it assumes that the most important influence on consumption is the *current* level of income. However, the current level of income in a particular year may have less influence on a person's planned consumption than some notion of *expected* income over a much longer time period, perhaps extending over the individual's remaining lifetime or life cycle.

People plan a large part of their savings on the basis of a long-term view of their expected lifetime or permanent income, and of likely spending plans over the remaining length of an expected life cycle — this is the **life-cycle theory of consumption**. Temporary fluctuations in yearly income generally have little effect on forms of saving such as contributions to pension schemes and to the purchase of life insurance policies.

Wealth

The stock of personal wealth, as well as the flow of income, influences consumption and saving decisions. In countries such as the UK and the USA, houses and shares are the two main forms of wealth asset that people own. An increase in house prices usually causes homeowners to consume more and to save less from their current flow of income, partly because the wealth increase 'does their saving for them'. Rising house prices generally increase the amount of borrowing taking place in an economy, partly through house buyers taking out large mortgages to secure a house purchase. The additional borrowing finances extra consumption, not only on the houses themselves but on items such as furniture and new bathrooms and kitchens. Additionally, some owner-occupiers who do not wish to move house may take out a larger mortgage on the house they live in, and then spend what they borrow: for example, on new cars and holidays. This is called equity release. In this context, the word 'equity' means 'wealth'. Borrowing against the value of a house reduces the amount of equity 'locked up' in people's houses.

Rising house prices induce a 'feel-good' factor among property owners, which leads to a consumer spending spree in the shops. Conversely, falling house prices have the opposite effect, increasing uncertainty and precautionary saving via a 'feel-bad' factor.

When share prices rise, share owners also become wealthier and may finance extra consumption by using borrowed funds. However, this effect is less noticeable in the UK, where houses rather than shares are the main household wealth asset. Stock market crashes have the opposite effect to booming share prices, reducing the wealth of shareholders, and thence their consumption. In the summer of 2007, a dramatic fall in share prices occurred in the USA, and then in other countries, including the UK. A year later, in 2008, falling house and share prices, accompanied by a collapse in consumer and business confidence, ushered in recession in the USA and then in other countries such as the UK.

Consumer confidence

The state of consumer confidence is closely linked to people's views on expected income and to changes in personal wealth. When consumer optimism increases, households generally spend more and save less, whereas a fall in optimism (or a growth in pessimism) has the opposite effect.

Governments try to boost consumer (and business) optimism to ward off the fear of a collapse in confidence by 'talking the economy up' and by trying to enhance the credibility of government economic policy. If the government is optimistic about the future, and people believe there are good grounds for this optimism, then the general public will be optimistic and confident about the future. However, if people believe the government is pursuing the wrong policies, or if an adverse economic shock hits the economy in a way that the government can't control, confidence can quickly dissipate.

The availability of credit

Besides the rate of interest, other aspects of monetary policy, such as controls on bank lending, affect consumption. If credit is available easily and cheaply, consumption increases as people supplement current income by borrowing on credit created by the banking system. Conversely, a tight monetary policy reduces consumption. The financial crisis that occurred in 2007 and 2008, which arose from bad debts in the US sub-prime market, had this effect in the UK and the USA. In the so-called **credit crunch**, interest rates rose and the supply of credit dried up, with banks refusing to supply applicants with new credit cards or mortgages.

TEST YOURSELF 10.12
What is the difference between a stock and a flow?

KEY TERMS
availability of credit funds available for households and firms to borrow.

credit crunch occurs when there is a lack of funds available in the credit market, making it difficult for borrowers to obtain financing, and leads to a rise in the cost of borrowing.

Distribution of income

Consumption and saving are also influenced by the **distribution of income** within an economy. Rich people save a greater proportion of their income than poor people; redistribution of income from rich to poor therefore increases consumption and reduces saving.

Expectations of future inflation

It is not easy to predict the impact of inflation on consumption. However, uncertainty caused by fears of rising inflation increases precautionary saving and reduces consumption. It may also, however, have the opposite effect. Households may decide to bring forward consumption decisions by spending now on consumer durables such as cars or television sets, thereby avoiding expected future price increases. People may also decide to borrow to finance the purchase of houses if they expect property prices to appreciate at a rate faster than general inflation. In this situation, and particularly if the real rate of interest is low or negative, people often decide to buy land, property and other physical assets such as fine art and antiques as a 'hedge' against inflation, in preference to saving through the purchase of financial assets.

The determinants of savings

Saving is a decision by people to postpone their consumption. Whenever members of households make decisions whether or not to spend on consumer goods, they are simultaneously deciding whether or not to save. A determinant of consumption is also a determinant of household saving! Therefore all the factors we have listed in the previous section as determinants of consumption, are also determinants of saving. Consider the following equation:

$$Y = C + S$$

The equation is telling us that if we ignore taxation and spending on imports, people can only do two things with their income: spend it on consumption or save. We can rewrite the equation as:

$$S = Y - C$$

This is the definition of saving, namely income which is not spent on consumption.

TEST YOURSELF 10.13
Distinguish between saving and consumption.

EXTENSION MATERIAL

The personal savings ratio and the household savings ratio

The personal savings ratio measures the *actual* or *realised* saving of the personal sector as a ratio of total personal sector disposal income:

$$\text{personal savings ratio} = \frac{\text{realised or actual personal saving}}{\text{personal disposable income}}$$

The household savings ratio is used in a similar way. It measures households' realised saving as a ratio of their disposable income. However, the personal savings ratio and the household savings ratio are not the same. The personal sector is more than just households, including unincorporated businesses such as partnerships and charitable organisations such as independent schools.

Economists and the government are interested in how much of their incomes people plan to save and to consume in the near future, as this provides important information about what lies ahead for the state of aggregate demand. Because it is difficult to measure people's plans accurately, the personal savings ratio calculated for the most recent past period is generally used as an indicator of what people wish to do in the future.

The Office for National Statistics reported that the full-year household saving ratio fell to just 4.9% in 2017, down from 7% in 2016 — and the lowest annual reading since records began 1963. 'Household spending power has been flatlining for the last two years. That has forced consumers to run down savings and borrow more just to sustain sluggish growth in spending,' said Ian Stewart, an economist at Deloitte.

One of the factors affecting household savings is people's uncertainty about the future. People who fear job losses, or who expect to suffer a fall in future income, are likely to save more for precautionary reasons. They want a 'nest egg' to protect themselves from the loss of future income. This means that savings ratios generally rise in recessions, unless overridden by other factors such as the need to borrow more so as to maintain spending levels and current standards of living and lifestyles.

Source: ONS

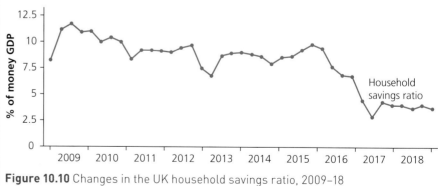

Figure 10.10 Changes in the UK household savings ratio, 2009–18

CASE STUDY 10.2

The 'credit crunch' and the financial crisis

The financial crisis which hit the world economy in 2007 started in the US housing market where banks had lent money to <u>sub-prime borrowers</u>. When these borrowers couldn't repay their loans, or even the interest on them, the banks were left with bad debts, as were other financial institutions that had bought 'packages' of bad debt from the banks.

This infected the entire financial system and meant that banks stopped lending to each other — creating the <u>credit crunch</u>. The first UK bank to be affected by the seizing up of financial markets was Northern Rock, which had to be rescued by the British government. (A few years later, the government sold the bank to Virgin Money.) A lack of mortgages meant the market began to stagnate and the properties that did change hands went for less than they would have done a few months previously. This increased the amount of <u>negative equity</u> in the economy.

Follow-up questions

1 Explain the underlined terms: sub-prime borrowers; credit crunch; negative equity.
2 Find out about how the UK housing market has fared since 2016.
3 Access Deloitte's chief economist Ian Stewart's article 'How to spot a bubble' on **https://blogs.deloitte.co.uk/mondaybriefing/2019/03/how-to-spot-a-bubble.html** Summarise the main message of the article.
4 It is generally agreed that the 2007 financial crisis was a major cause of the recession which hit the UK economy a year later in 2008. Why should a financial crisis be a cause of recession?

The difference between saving and investment

Economists make a clear separation between saving and investment, even though in everyday language the two terms are often used interchangeably. Whereas saving is simply income that is not spent on consumption, investment is spending by firms on capital goods such as machines and office equipment. *Physical investment* in new capital goods should not be confused with *financial investment*. The latter is the demand for financial assets such as shares and bonds, which is a form of saving.

As a simplification, economists often assume that households make saving decisions, while firms make investment decisions. Firms invest when they buy capital goods such as machinery. However, firms also save: for example, when they store profits in a bank account without spending them.

The determinants of investment

339

> **STUDY TIP**
> Make sure you don't confuse investment with savings.

A country's gross investment includes two parts: replacement investment (to make good depreciation or capital consumption), which simply maintains the size of the existing capital stock by replacing worn-out capital; and net investment, which adds to the capital stock, thereby increasing productive potential. Along with technical progress, net investment is one of the engines of economic growth.

The new capital goods created by new fixed investment often have an economic life extending many years into the future. The future is always uncertain and the further we go into the future, the greater the uncertainty. When deciding whether or not to go ahead with a fixed investment project in, for example, new machinery, firms need to form views on expected future sales revenue attributable to the investment project and expected future costs of production, resulting both from the rate of interest paid for borrowing the funds to finance the initial investment, and from the future maintenance costs.

Apart from the rate of interest, other factors that influence investment decisions include the following:

- **The relative prices of capital and labour.** When the price of capital rises (for example, when the prices of capital goods or rates of interest rise), in the long run firms adopt more labour-intensive methods of production, substituting labour for capital. A decrease in the relative prices of capital goods has the opposite effect. If the price of capital goods or interest rates falls, firms switch to capital-intensive methods of production, so investment increases.
- **The nature of technical progress.** Technical progress can make machinery obsolete or out of date. When this happens, a machine's business life becomes shorter than its technical life: that is, the number of years before the machine wears out. A sudden burst of technical progress may cause firms to replace capital goods early, long before the end of the equipment's technical life.
- **The adequacy of financial institutions in the supply of investment funds.** As mentioned, many investments in fixed capital goods are long-term investments that yield most of their expected income several years into the future. These investments may be difficult to finance because of the inadequacy of the financial institutions that provide investment funds. Banks have been criticised for favouring short-term investments and being reluctant to provide the finance for long-term investments. Likewise, the stock market may favour short-termism over long-termism, although in recent years the growth of new methods of lending to firms has provided an important source of medium- to longer-term finance. In recent years, private equity finance has emerged to provide an important source of medium- to longer-term finance.

Governments also lend funds to firms to finance investment projects, though at the same time they tax firms: for example, by levying corporation tax. Arguably, however, when choosing whether to invest in or support investment projects, governments may be better at 'picking losers' than 'picking winners'. In the past, UK governments have sometimes provided investment funds to rescue jobs in loss-making and uncompetitive industries that ought to be allowed to continue their decline. Government ministers and their civil servants may make bad investment decisions because, unlike entrepreneurs, they don't face the risk of being bankrupted as a result of poor decision making.

STUDY TIP
It is important to remember that capital is a *stock* concept, but investment is a *flow*.

TEST YOURSELF 10.14
Banks function as financial intermediaries. Explain what this means.

The accelerator process

The **accelerator** process stems from a simple and mechanical assumption that firms wish to keep a relatively fixed ratio, known as the capital–output ratio, between the output they are currently producing and their existing stock of fixed capital assets. If output grows by a constant amount each year, firms invest in exactly the same amount of new capital each year to enlarge their capital stock so as to maintain the desired capital–output ratio. From year to year, the level of investment is therefore constant. When the rate of growth of output *accelerates*, investment also increases as firms take action to enlarge the stock of capital to a level sufficient to maintain the desired capital–output ratio. When the rate of growth of output *decelerates*, investment declines.

EXTENSION MATERIAL

A numerical example of the accelerator

To illustrate the accelerator principle, we shall assume the economy's capital–output ratio is 4:1, or simply 4. This means that 4 units of capital are required to produce 1 unit of output. We shall also assume that the level of *current* net investment in fixed capital depends on the change in income or output in the *previous* year:

$$I = v(\Delta Y)$$

or:

$$I_t = v(Y_t - Y_{t-1})$$

where I_t is net investment this year, Y is current national income, Y_{t-1} is national income last year and v is the capital–output ratio. The **capital–output ratio**, v, is also known as the **accelerator coefficient**, or simply as the **accelerator**. We shall also assume no replacement investment is needed, and that the average capital–output ratio in the economy stays at 4.

Given these assumptions, consider the numerical example of the accelerator principle shown in Table 10.2.

Table 10.2 The accelerator: numerical example

Year	Net investment (£bn)		Capital output ratio (£bn)		Current income this year (£bn)		Income last year (£bn)
2017	40	=	4	×	(100	–	90)
2018	40	=	4	×	(110	–	100)
2019	80	=	4	×	(130	–	110)
2020	40	=	4	×	(140	–	130)

In each of the years from 2017 to 2020 national income grows. Between 2016 (the year preceding the data in the table) and 2017, income grows by £10 billion. Via the capital–output ratio, the £10 billion income growth induces net investment of £40 billion in 2017. The size of the capital stock increases by £40 billion, which enables the desired capital–output ratio to be maintained at the now higher level of income. In row 2, income continues to grow by £10 billion, so investment in 2018 remains at £40 billion. However, the next year is different. In 2019, shown in row 3, the growth of income speeds up or *accelerates*, doubling from £10 billion to £20 billion. Investment also doubles from £40 billion to £80 billion to maintain the value of the capital–output ratio. Thus, a £10 billion increase in income induces a £40 billion increase in investment. But in row 4, the growth of income falls back to £10 billion in 2020. Although income is still growing, net investment has fallen back to £40 billion.

This example shows how the accelerator gets its name. The figures show the rate of growth of income and output determining whether investment grows, falls or remains at a constant level.

In summary:

- if income grows by the same amount each year, net investment is constant
- if income growth speeds up or *accelerates*, net investment increases
- if income growth slows down or *decelerates*, net investment declines

Thus, as firms adjust the stock of capital to the desired level, relatively slight changes in the rate of growth of income or output cause quite large absolute rises and falls in investment. The acceleration principle therefore provides an explanation of why investment in capital goods is a more volatile or unstable component of aggregate demand than consumption.

SECTION 10.3 SUMMARY

- Aggregate demand is total *planned* spending on real output of all the economic agents in the economy. As an equation, $AD = C + I + G + (X - M)$.
- Consumption by households and investment by firms are two components of aggregate demand.
- Saving, or income which is not consumed, must not be confused with investment.
- Aggregate consumption and saving are determined by the rate of interest, the levels of current and future income, wealth, consumer confidence and the availability of credit.
- Investment is determined by factors such as the rate of interest, expected returns on capital, technical progress, the availability of finance, and the accelerator.
- The accelerator measures how a change in the level of investment in new capital goods is induced by a change in national income or output.
- The size of the accelerator depends on the economy's capital–output ratio.

10.4 Aggregate demand and the level of economic activity

What is economic activity?

Economic activity can mean many things, but we shall think of it as centring on the production and consumption of goods and services in the economy, together with the employment of the labour, capital and other inputs that produce output.

Aggregate demand and economic activity

AD/AS diagrams can be used to illustrate how changes in aggregate demand affect the level of real output, but they don't directly show the employment levels at each level of real output. However, the main link between aggregate demand and employment is simple. When real output increases, firms generally have to employ more workers to produce the additional goods and services that the output increase involves. Conversely, when real output falls, less labour is required to produce the smaller amount of goods and services now being produced.

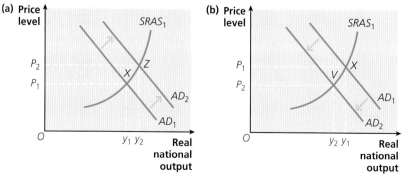

Figure 10.11 The effect of a change in aggregate demand on real output

Figure 10.11(a), which illustrates the effect of an increase in aggregate demand on real output, is the same as Figure 10.6(a). It shows how a rightward shift of the *AD* curve leads to an increase in real output. Figure 10.11(b), by contrast, shows how a leftward shift of the *AD* curve leads to a fall in real output. To put it another way, Figure 10.11(a) shows the expansionary effect of an increase in aggregate demand, while Figure 10.11(b) shows the contractionary effect of a decrease in aggregate demand. The expansionary effect is likely to increase employment; the contractionary effect is likely to lead to a fall in employment.

Two points to note about both diagrams:

- the greater the shift in aggregate demand, the greater the change in real output
- the extent to which real output changes also depends on the steepness of the *AS* curve

TEST YOURSELF 10.15

'Households save, but firms invest.' When do firms save?

Aggregate demand and the national income multiplier

KEY TERM

multiplier the relationship between a change in aggregate demand and the resulting generally larger change in national income.

The national income **multiplier** measures the relationship between an initial change in a component of aggregate demand, such as government spending or private-sector investment, and the resulting generally larger change in the level of national income.

Suppose, for example, that government spending increases by £10 billion, but tax revenue remains unchanged. The resulting budget deficit initially injects £10 billion of new spending into the circular flow of income. This spending increases people's incomes. If we assume that everybody in the economy saves a small fraction of any income increase and spends the rest, the £10 billion generates multiple and successively smaller further increases in income, until the next stage is so small that it can be ignored. Adding up the successive stages of income generation, the total increase in income is a multiple of the initial spending increase of £10 billion — hence the name 'multiplier theory'. If the size of the multiplier is 2.5, an increase in a component of aggregate demand, such as government spending, of £10 billion causes national income eventually to increase by £25 billion. Figure 10.12 illustrates the multiplier in an *AD/AS* diagram.

In Figure 10.12, an initial increase in government spending (ΔG) shifts the *AD* curve from AD_1 to AD_2. This then triggers the multiplier process, which leads to a further increase in aggregate demand to AD_3. If the size of the government spending multiplier is 2.5, then, as we have mentioned, the eventual increase in aggregate demand is two and a half times the size of the initial increase in government spending.

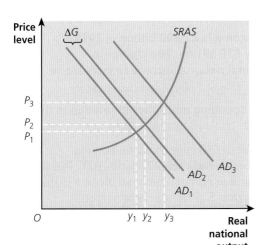

Figure 10.12 The national income multiplier illustrated on an *AD/AS* diagram

The multiplier relationship is shown in the following equation:

$$\text{multiplier} = \frac{\text{change in national income}}{\text{initial change in government spending}}$$

or:

$$\text{multiplier} = \frac{\Delta Y}{\Delta G}$$

343

As the quantitative skills example below shows, the size of the multiplier can be worked out providing we possess knowledge of both the change in aggregate demand and the resulting change in national income.

STUDY TIP
Make sure you don't confuse the multiplier with the accelerator.

The marginal propensities to consume and save

Before we explain the formula used for calculating the size of the multiplier, we shall first introduce you to the marginal propensities to consume and save. The **marginal propensity to consume** (*MPC*) is the fraction of any increase in income which people plan to spend on the consumption of domestically produced goods. For example, if people, on average, plan to spend 90p of an income increase of £1 on consumption, the *MPC* is 0.9. Likewise, **marginal propensity to save** (*MPS*) is the fraction of any increase in income which people plan to save rather than spend. If the *MPC* is 0.9, the *MPS* must be 0.1, and so on.

KEY TERMS
marginal propensity to consume the fraction of any increase in income which people plan to spend on the consumption of domestically produced goods and services.

marginal propensity to save the fraction of any increase in income which people plan to save rather than spend.

QUANTITATIVE SKILLS 10.2

Worked example: calculating the size of the multiplier

In an economy, nominal national income is £2,000 billion in 2020. Government spending increases by £10 billion. The change in government spending causes nominal national income to increase to £2,050 billion in 2021.

What is the size of the government spending multiplier in relation to the change in *nominal* national income?

The increase in government spending of £10 billion causes nominal national income to increase by £50 billion between 2020 and 2021. The size of the multiplier in terms of the growth in nominal national income is thus £50 billion divided by £10 billion, which is 5. This is a quite a large multiplier.

The different multipliers

Nested within the national income multiplier are a number of specific multipliers, each related to the particular component of aggregate demand that initially changes. Besides the government spending multiplier, there is an investment multiplier, a tax multiplier, an export multiplier and an import multiplier. Taken together, the government spending and tax multipliers are known as fiscal policy multipliers. Likewise, the export and import multipliers are foreign trade multipliers. An increase in consumption spending can also trigger a multiplier process.

The multiplier process can also work in reverse, reducing rather than increasing national income. This happens when government spending, consumption, investment or exports fall. It also happens when taxation or imports increase. This is because taxation and imports are withdrawals from the circular flow of income, rather than injections. The tax and import multipliers are always negative, meaning that an increase in taxes or imports causes national income to fall (and a decrease in taxes or imports causes national income to rise).

All the multipliers we have so far been considering are national multipliers. However, regional multipliers can also be important. A regional multiplier measures the relationship between an initial change in aggregate demand and the resulting change in regional income. Consider a situation in which central government spends on a subsidy paid to people in Cornwall. When the recipients of the subsidy spend the extra income they receive, most of it may be spent on goods and services produced in other parts of the UK, if not on imports. The regional multiplier, which reflects extra local spending within Cornwall, is likely to be very small.

TEST YOURSELF 10.16

The multiplier can refer to the effect of a change in the level of:

A exports on national income

B national income on investment

C consumption on saving

D saving on imports

Which is the correct answer?

STUDY TIP

It is useful to understand the government spending multiplier, the investment multiplier, the export multiplier and regional multipliers.

The multiplier formula

The formula for calculating the value of the multiplier is:

$$k = \frac{1}{1 - MPC} \text{ or } \frac{1}{MPS}$$

where k is the multiplier, MPC is the marginal propensity to consume, and MPS is the marginal propensity to save.

High marginal propensities to consume mean that, at each stage of the multiplier process illustrated in Figure 10.13, most new income is spent on consumption and only a small amount leaks into saving. In this situation, multipliers are relatively large. An initial increase in government spending or private investment has a larger multiplier effect than would be the case if the MPC were smaller. The eventual growth in income is significantly larger than the initial increase in aggregate demand. A low MPC (and a high MPS) produce the opposite effect: the eventual growth in income resulting from the multiplier process is not much larger than the initial increase in aggregate demand. In this situation, in which saving and the other leakages from the circular flow of income are quite high, multipliers are generally small, not significantly different from 1.

TEST YOURSELF 10.17

Distinguish between the multiplier and the accelerator.

The multiplier as a dynamic process

The multiplier process, which is essentially dynamic, taking place over time, resembles ripples spreading over a pond after a stone has been thrown in the water. However, the ripples in a pond last only a few seconds, whereas the ripples spreading through the economy following a change in aggregate demand can last for months and even years. Figure 10.13 illustrates the ripple effect. The diagram, which shows the government spending multiplier, can easily be adapted to illustrate the investment multiplier or any other national income multiplier. The assumption of quite a small *MPC* of 0.2 is realistic for the UK and many other developed economies because a large fraction of any increase in income leaks out of the circular flow of income in taxation and spending on imports, as well as into saving. As the next paragraph explains, this reduces the size of the multiplier to the small size of 1.25.

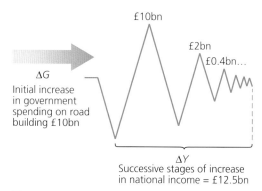

Figure 10.13 The dynamic nature of the multiplier process

In the first stage of the multiplier process illustrated in Figure 10.13, the £10 billion of extra government spending is received as income by building workers who, like everybody in the economy, spend 20 pence of every pound of income on consumption. (We are assuming the marginal propensity to consume (*MPC*) is 0.2 throughout the economy, which means that people plan to consume 20 pence out of an increase in income of £1.00. This means that at each stage of the multiplier process, 80% of an extra pound of income leaks into saving, taxation and imports, and is not spent on consumption.

At the second stage of the multiplier process, £2 billion of the £10 billion income is spent on consumer goods and services, with the remaining £8 billion leaking into savings, the payment of taxes and spending on imports.

At the next and third stage, consumer goods sector employees spend £0.4 billion, or 0.2 of the £2 billion received at the second stage of income generation.

Further stages of income generation then occur, with each successive stage being 0.2 of the previous stage. Each stage is smaller than the preceding stage, due to the fact that a large part of income leaks into savings, taxation and imports at each stage of the multiplier process.

Assuming that nothing else changes in the time taken for the process to work through the economy, the eventual increase in income Δ*Y* resulting from the initial injection of government spending is the sum of all the stages of income generation. In our example, the eventual increase in income (Δ*Y*) is larger than Δ*G*, which triggered the initial growth in national income, but the multiplier is quite small (1.25) because of the size of leakages out of the circular flow of income at each stage of the multiplier process.

TEST YOURSELF 10.18

Calculate the value of the marginal propensity to save and the value of the multiplier when the value of the marginal propensity to consume is:

(a) 0.9

(b) 0.1

(c) 0.5

Worked example: using the *MPC*

Calculate the size of the multiplier when, in a closed economy with no exports or imports, the size of the marginal propensity to consume (*MPC*) is (a) 0.6 and (b) 0.4.

(a) When the *MPC* is 0.6, the multiplier equals 1 divided by (1 − 0.6), which is 2.5.

(b) When the *MPC* is 0.4, the multiplier equals 1 divided by (1 − 0.4), which is 1.67.

Nominal national income, real national income and the size of the multiplier

It is important to understand the following relationship:

nominal national income = real national income × average price level

or, in shorthand:

$$Y = Py$$

The size of the multiplier depends on whether we are measuring the *nominal* national income multiplier or the *real* national income multiplier. In our earlier example, the size of the multiplier was 1.25 but this was the nominal national income multiplier. Provided the *SRAS* curve slopes upwards, as is the case in Figure 10.12, the size of the multiplier measured in real terms is always going to be smaller than the nominal national income multiplier. This is because part of the multiplier effect deflects into a rising price level. The growth of real income is restricted to the distance between y_1 and y_2, with the price level rising from P_1 to P_2. Indeed, if the *SRAS* curve is vertical rather than upward sloping, the size of the multiplier measured in real *income* terms would be zero. In this situation, the multiplier effect resulting from an increase in government spending would lead solely to inflation and *not* to rising real output.

TEST YOURSELF 10.19
Explain the difference between nominal national income and real national income.

SECTION 10.4 SUMMARY

- Economic activity centres on the production and consumption of goods and services in the economy, together with the employment of the labour, capital and other inputs that produce output.
- *AD/AS* diagrams can be used to illustrate how changes in aggregate demand affect the level of real output.
- *AD/AS* diagrams don't directly show the employment levels at each level of real output.
- When real output increases, firms generally have to employ more workers to produce the additional goods and services that the output increase involves. Conversely, when real output falls, less labour is required to produce the smaller amount of goods and services now being produced.
- An increase or decrease in any of the components of aggregate demand, such as government spending, usually leads to a multiplier effect.
- The multiplier measures the relationship between a change in any of the components of aggregate demand (*C*, *I*, *G* and *X* − *M*) and the resulting change in the equilibrium level of national income.

10.5 Determinants of short-run aggregate supply

As we mentioned earlier in the chapter, the price level and production costs are the main determinants of the *SRAS* curve. Changes in costs, such as money wage rates, raw material prices, business taxation and productivity, will shift the *SRAS* curve.

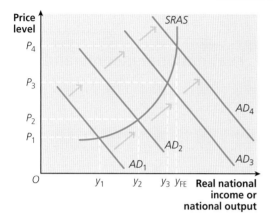

Figure 10.14 How an increase in aggregate demand affects real national income and the price level

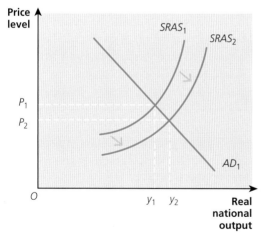

Figure 10.15 A rightward shift of the *SRAS* curve causing a fall in the price level

All of the *SRAS* curves drawn in this book are 'curved curves' or non-linear curves, which become steeper moving up the curve. This has important implications for monetary and fiscal policy, which are further explained in Chapters 12 and 13. As the *AD* curve shifts to the right along a non-linear *SRAS* curve, such as the one in Figure 10.14, whether or not real income or the price level increases depends on the steepness of slope of the *SRAS* curve.

When the *AD* curve shifts to the right from AD_1 to AD_2, the resulting increase in real output is proportionately greater than the increase in the price level. Real income increases from y_1 to y_2 and the price level rises from P_1 to P_2. This is because the *AD* curve is shifting along the relatively shallow section of the *SRAS* curve. But when the *AD* curve shifts rightward from AD_3 to AD_4, it is shifting along a much steeper section of the *SRAS* curve. As a result, most of the effect of the increase in aggregate demand falls on the price level rather than on real output. The effect is inflationary rather than reflationary. Indeed, if the *AD* curve were to shift any further to the right beyond AD_4, only the price level, and not real output, would rise. In the diagram, y_{FE} is the full-employment level of real income. In this situation, any further increase in aggregate demand results solely in a rising price level, or inflation. At full employment, real income cannot increase, at least in the short run, because the economy is producing at full capacity.

The *slope* of the *SRAS* curve must not be confused with a *shift* of the curve. The *SRAS* curve is constructed under the assumption that all the determinants of aggregate supply *other than the price level* remain unchanged. Should any of these determinants change, the *SRAS* curve shifts to a new position. The curve can shift either to the right (an increase in aggregate supply) or to the left (a decrease in aggregate supply). Figure 10.15 illustrates a rightward shift of the *SRAS* curve, or an increase in aggregate supply, which results in deflation, with the price level falling from P_1 to P_2.

Among the factors that cause a rightward shift of the *SRAS* curve are:

- a fall in businesses' costs of production; these include the costs of imported raw materials and energy
- a fall in unit labour costs, resulting from a fall in wage costs or an increase in labour productivity, the latter possibly caused by better labour training
- a reduction in indirect taxes such as VAT imposed on firms by the government
- an increase in subsidies granted to firms by the government
- technical progress which improves the quality and productivity of capital goods

A leftward shift of the *SRAS* curve would be caused by the opposite of these factors.

10.6 Determinants of long-run aggregate supply

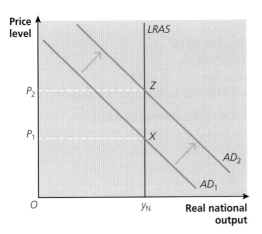

Figure 10.16 An economy's 'normal capacity' level of output

In the short run, the aggregate supply of real output depends on the average price level in the economy, and the position of the *SRAS* curve is determined by business costs. Other things remaining constant, firms are only prepared to supply more output if the price level rises. However, in the long run, aggregate supply is *not* influenced by the price level. Long-run supply reflects the economy's production potential. The *LRAS* curve is located at the **normal capacity level of output**, which is the level of output at which the full production potential of the economy is being used. To put it another way, it is the maximum level of output that the economy can produce when the economy is on its production possibility frontier.

The position of the *LRAS* curve

The position of the *LRAS* curve is determined by the same factors that determine the position of the economy's production possibility frontier. These include the following:

- The state of technical progress.
- The quantities of capital and labour and other factors of production in the economy.
- The mobility of factors of production, particularly labour.
- The productivity of the factors of production, particularly labour productivity.
- People's attitudes to hard work.
- Personal enterprise, particularly among entrepreneurs. The emergence of a large number of risk-taking entrepreneurs is especially important for shifting the *LRAS* curve to the right.
- Related to this, the existence of appropriate economic incentives.
- The institutional structure of the economy. This involves factors such as the rule of law and the efficiency of the banking system. Contract law is particularly important. If contracts are not legally enforceable, normal economic activity can break down, which shifts the position of the *LRAS* curve to the left. And as the financial crisis of 2007 and onward showed, the inability of banking systems to provide finance to businesses also shifted the *LRAS* curve leftward. This deepened and lengthened the 'great recession' in 2008 and 2009. Efficient contract law and an efficient banking system 'grease the wheels' of the economy, promoting long-run economic growth and an outward shift of the economy's production possibility frontier and a rightward shift of the *LRAS* curve.

QUANTITATIVE SKILLS 10.4

Worked example: interpreting data on the components of aggregate demand

Table 10.3 below contains data on the components of aggregate demand in 2018 in an economy experiencing positive economic growth

Table 10.3 Components of aggregate demand, 2018

	£bn at 2015 prices	% change in the year 2017/18
Household consumption	1,048	4.0
Investment	306	5.2
Government spending	292	3.4
Exports of goods and services	496	2.6
Imports of goods and services	570	7.1

Which one of the following is supported by the data?

A The economy enjoyed a balance of payments surplus on current account in 2018.
B Investment amounted to approximately 19.5% of aggregate demand in 2018.
C Exports of goods and services was the largest component of aggregate demand in 2018.
D The increase in the value of the components of aggregate demand in 2018 was solely due to inflation.

The only correct answer is statement B. To see that statement B is correct, you should make use of the aggregate demand equation: $AD = C + I + G + (X - M)$. The equation reminds you of the fact that imports of goods and services are a leakage of demand from the circular flow of income. All the other items in the left-hand column in Table 10.2 are positive components of aggregate demand. Adding these up gives you the total £2,142 billion, but you must now subtract the leakage of £570 billion to arrive at the aggregate demand total of £1,572 billion. Finally, the value of gross fixed investment as a percentage of aggregate demand is (£306bn/£1,572bn) × 100, which is approximately 19.5%.

Statements A, C and D are incorrect. Statement A is wrong because there was a current account deficit rather than a surplus in 2018 (£496bn – £570bn), which is a deficit of £74 billion. Consumption was the largest component of aggregate demand in 2018, so statement C is incorrect. Finally, Statement D is wrong because economic growth as well as inflation would have contributed to the increase in the value of the components of aggregate demand in 2018.

EXTENSION MATERIAL

A closer look at the 'normal capacity' level of output

Even when producing at 'normal capacity', the economy may still be capable of *temporarily* producing a *higher* level of real output. Figure 10.17 can be used to explain this possibility.

We shall assume that the economy is initially in macroeconomic equilibrium at point X in Figure 10.17, where curve AD_1 intersects both the $SRAS_1$ and the $LRAS$ curves. Since the economy is producing on the $LRAS$ curve, real output is at its 'normal capacity' level y_N. An increase in aggregate demand, caused perhaps by an expansionary monetary policy, shifts the AD curve rightward to AD_2, which brings about a new short-run macroeconomic equilibrium at point Y. In the new equilibrium, the level of real output has risen to y_2, which is above the 'normal capacity' level of output.

However, this level of output, in which the economy is producing above its production potential, cannot be sustained, unless of course the

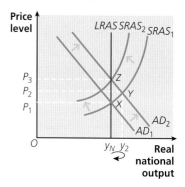

Figure 10.17 The economy can *temporarily* produce a level of real output higher than the 'normal capacity' level of output

LRAS curve itself shifts rightward. To understand why this is the case, we must remember that one of the determinants of the position of an *SRAS* curve is the level of money wages in the economy. A higher level of money wages shifts the *SRAS* curve upward or leftward, whereas lower money wages would shift the curve rightward. At Y_2 there are shortages of labour and other factors of production and so excess demand in the labour market and other factor markets leads to rising factor prices. To persuade workers to supply the extra labour needed for y_2 to be produced, given the fact that the price level has risen to P_2, money wages must also rise. As soon as this happens, the *SRAS* curve shifts to $SRAS_2$. As the backward-bending curved arrow lying along the horizontal axis shows, real output falls back from y_2 to the 'normal capacity' level of real output at y_N, located below point *Z* on the diagram.

TEST YOURSELF 10.20

Distinguish normal capacity income from full capacity income.

The Keynesian aggregate supply curve

The vertical *LRAS* curve is sometimes called the free-market *LRAS* curve. This label reflects the view commonly expressed by free-market economists that, provided markets function competitively and efficiently, the economy always operates at or close to normal capacity. In the short run, real output is influenced by the average price level, but in the long run, aggregate supply is determined by maximum normal production capacity, which determines the position of the *LRAS* curve.

These days, most economists agree that the *LRAS* curve is vertical. Some economists argue, however, that the *LRAS* curve has a different shape, the 'inverted L-shape' shown in Figure 10.18.

The inverted L-shaped *LRAS* curve is based on the explanation put forward by John Maynard Keynes of the Great Depression in the UK and US economies in the 1930s. Keynes argued that a depressed economy can settle into an under-full-employment equilibrium, shown for example by point *A* on the horizontal section of the *LRAS* curve. At point *A*, the level of real national output is y_1. Keynes believed that without purposeful intervention by the government, an economy could display more or less permanent demand deficiency. Market forces would fail to adjust automatically and achieve full employment. If the government could shift *AD* to the right along the horizontal section of the *LRAS* curve (mainly through expansionary fiscal policy), the existence of significant amounts of spare capacity would lead, in Keynes's view, to a growth in real output (and employment), without an increase in the price level. Eventually, when maximum normal capacity is achieved, the *LRAS* curve becomes vertical for the same reasons that the 'free-market' curve is vertical.

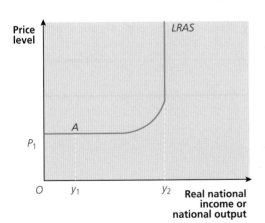

Figure 10.18 The Keynesian 'inverted L-shaped' *LRAS* curve

CASE STUDY 10.3

Keynes on 'Poverty in Plenty'

In 1934, in the depth of the Great Depression, and 2 years before he published his *General Theory of Employment, Interest and Money*, John Maynard Keynes gave a radio talk in which he expressed his view on the causes of unemployment. Keynes's talk was one of a series, entitled 'Poverty in Plenty', in which a number of economists and public figures gave their views on the title theme. At this time, the UK unemployment rate was 16.7%. Keynes started by summarising the common ground between himself and the other contributors. He then outlined what he saw as the main difference between the various contributors, before arguing that, in his view, the economic system was not self-adjusting. Here is what Keynes had to say.

Is the economic system self-adjusting?

We must not regard the conditions of supply, our ability to produce, as the fundamental source of our troubles. It is the conditions of demand which our diagnosis must search and probe for explanation. All the contributors to these talks meet to this extent on common ground. But every one of us has a somewhat different explanation of what is wrong with demand, and, consequently, a different idea of the right remedy.

Though we all start out in the same direction, we soon part company into two main groups. On one side are those who believe that the existing economic system is, in the long run, a self-adjusting system, though with creaks and groans and jerks, and interrupted by time lags, outside interference and mistakes.

On the other side of the gulf are those who reject the idea that the existing economic system is, in any significant sense, self-adjusting. They believe that the failure of effective demand to reach the full potential of supply, in spite of human psychological demand being far from satisfied for the vast majority of individuals, is due to much more fundamental causes.

The strength of the self-adjusting school depends on it having behind it almost the whole body of organised economic thinking and doctrine of the last hundred years. Now, I range myself with the heretics on the other side of the gulf. There is, I am convinced, a fatal flaw in that part of the orthodox reasoning which deals with the theory of what determines the level of effective demand and the volume of aggregate employment. The system is not self-adjusting, and, without purposive direction, it is incapable of translating our actual poverty into our potential plenty.

Follow-up questions

1 What is meant by 'effective aggregate demand'?
2 Suggest why there may be too little effective aggregate demand in an economy.
3 Why do free-market or anti-Keynesian economists believe the economic system is self-adjusting?
4 After the end of recession in 2009, the UK economy grew continuously, albeit at a slow annual rate of growth, until at least July 2019. Explain two causes of this growth.

TEST YOURSELF 10.21

Write short answers to the following questions.

(a) Is net national income the same as GDP?

(b) What is the difference between nominal and real national income?

(c) What is the difference between saving and investment?

(d) List the components of aggregate demand.

(e) What is deficient aggregate demand?

(f) Why is the *LRAS* curve usually assumed to be vertical?

EXTENSION MATERIAL

AD/AS analysis and the rate of inflation

Students are often puzzled by a particular feature of the *AD/AS* model as taught and learnt at A-level. If you look carefully at conventional *AD/AS* diagrams such as Figure 10.19, you will see that a leftward movement of the *AD* curve results in a *fall* in the price level: that is, deflation. However, we all know that except in a deep recession or immediately after a very large fall in world commodity prices, contractionary fiscal or monetary policy that shifts the *AD* curve to the left results not in falling prices, but in a slowdown in the rate of inflation, or disinflation. Average prices still rise, but at a slower annual rate of increase.

In Figure 10.20, by contrast, contractionary fiscal or monetary policy, and indeed a fall in any of the components of aggregate demand, reduces the rate of inflation (shown in Figure 10.20 by the symbol $\dot{P}$), but not necessarily the price level.

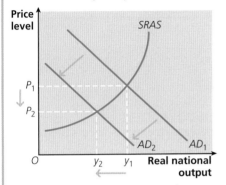

Figure 10.19 The traditional *AD/AS* model

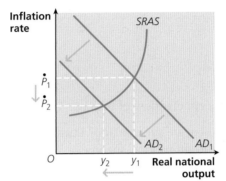

Figure 10.20 *AD/AS* analysis and the rate of inflation

TEST YOURSELF 10.22

Table 10.4 shows selected macroeconomic indicators for an economy in 2019 and 2020.

Table 10.4 Macroeconomic indicators, 2019 and 2020

	% change in real GDP	% change in prices	% change in earnings	(%) Unemployment rate
2019	4.2	4.6	9.4	8.4
2020	6.0	4.2	9.2	7.2

Explain why statement B of the following statements is correct, and also why the other three statements are incorrect.

A The price level fell between 2019 and 2020.

B Economic growth was accompanied by a falling unemployment rate.

C A fall in the rate of unemployment was accompanied by a falling price level.

D Earnings fell by 0.2% between 2019 and 2020.

- It is important to distinguish between a short-run aggregate supply (*SRAS*) curve and a long-run aggregate supply (*LRAS*) curve.
- *SRAS* curves generally slope upwards, but the *LRAS* curve is generally assumed to be vertical with its position determined by the economy's normal capacity level of output.
- The normal capacity level of output is the level of output at which the full production potential of the economy is being used
- A rightward movement of the *LRAS* curve illustrates long-term economic growth.
- Some Keynesian economists have argued that the *LRAS* curve is horizontal to the left of the full-employment level of real output, becoming vertical at the full-employment level of output.

Questions

1 Explain the meaning of the circular flow of income.

2 What are the components of aggregate demand? Illustrate how an increase in exports affects the position of the *AD* curve and equilibrium national income.

3 Explain how changes in the rate of interest affect consumption and saving.

4 Distinguish between the accelerator and the multiplier.

5 Explain the shape of the aggregate supply curve, both in the short run and in the long run.

6 Considering only the *SRAS* curve and not the *LRAS* curve, explain how an increase in aggregate demand may affect output and the price level.

11 Economic performance

This chapter returns to a number of topics mentioned briefly in Chapters 9 and 10. It focuses on the core macroeconomic topics of economic growth, unemployment and inflation, explaining and exploring the topics in greater detail than was the case in the earlier chapters. In particular, the *AD/AS* macroeconomic model introduced in Chapter 10 is used to analyse various issues related to each of the topics.

The chapter is about economic performance. A country's macroeconomic performance can be judged by how successful the economy is at achieving the four main objectives of macroeconomic policy outlined in Chapter 9. Can the economy achieve and then sustain a satisfactory rate of economic growth, relatively full employment, relative price stability and control of inflation, and a degree of trading competitiveness in international markets?

The meaning of economic performance having been explained here, Chapters 12 and 13 will go on to investigate how monetary policy and fiscal policy are used to try to improve economic performance.

LEARNING OBJECTIVES

These are to understand:

- the demand-side and supply-side determinants of economic growth
- the economic cycle and output gaps
- the benefits and costs of economic growth
- the effects of economic shocks on the economy
- the main types of unemployment
- demand-side and supply-side causes of unemployment
- how global events can impact on UK unemployment and inflation
- demand-pull and cost-push inflation, and the monetarist theory of inflation
- how changes in world commodity prices affect domestic inflation
- the effect of deflation on the economy
- how conflicts that arise from trying to achieve different macroeconomic policy objects affect economic performance in the short run and the long run
- the Phillips curve relationship

11.1 Economic growth and the economic cycle

Chapter 1 and Chapter 9 have already introduced you to economic growth. Chapter 1 defined economic growth and, with the help of a production possibility frontier, distinguished between short-term and long-run growth.

Short-run and long-run economic growth

As we explained in Chapter 1, the definition and the measurement of economic growth are not the same thing. The *definition* of economic growth was first introduced to you in Chapter 1, in the context of the outward movement of the economy's frontier. We defined economic growth as an increase in the *potential* level of real output the economy can produce over a period of time. The *measurement* of economic growth, by contrast, is performed simply by measuring the percentage annual change in real GDP, or possibly real GDP per capita. We then went on to distinguish between short-run and long-run economic growth, both of which are again illustrated in Figure 11.1.

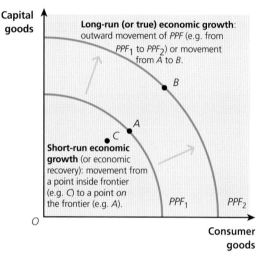

Figure 11.1 Short-run and long-run economic growth illustrated on an economy's production possibility frontier

Short-run growth brings idle resources into production and takes up the slack in the economy. By contrast, long-run economic growth, depicted by an outward movement of the economy's production possibility frontier, increases the economy's production potential.

TEST YOURSELF 11.2
Table 11.1 shows selected macroeconomic indicators for an economy in 2018 and 2019.

Table 11.1 Macroeconomic indicators, 2018 and 2019

	% change in real GDP	% change in prices	% change in earnings	Unemployment rate (%)
2018	4.2	4.6	9.4	8.4
2019	6.0	4.2	9.2	7.2

Explain why statement B of the following statements is correct, and also why the other three statements are incorrect.

A The price level fell between 2018 and 2019.

B Economic growth was accompanied by a falling unemployment rate.

C A fall in the rate of unemployment was accompanied by a falling price level.

D Earnings fell by 0.2% between 2018 and 2019.

Demand-side and supply-side determinants of short-run growth

Short-run economic growth, which takes up spare capacity within the economy, is primarily caused by **demand-side** changes in the economy. Anything which shifts the position of the aggregate demand (*AD*) curve is a demand-side influence on the economy. A rightward shift of the *AD* curve along an upward-sloping *SRAS* curve illustrates demand-side causes of short-run economic growth.

A good starting point for explaining demand-induced short-run economic growth is the aggregate demand equation, which we first mentioned in sections 10.2 and 10.3 of Chapter 10. To remind you, the aggregate demand equation is:

$$AD = C + I + G + (X - M)$$

where C, I, G and $(X - M)$ are the symbols used for the components of aggregate demand: consumption, investment, government spending and net export demand (exports minus imports). $(X - M)$ is also known as net trade.

If any of these components of aggregate demand change, the *AD* curve shifts to a new position. An increase in consumption, investment, government spending or net export demand causes the *AD* curve to shift to the right, as shown in Figure 11.2. What then happens in the economy depends on the shape and slope of the aggregate supply curve. Figure 11.2 shows an *SRAS* curve which is horizontal at very low levels of real income, then slopes upwards, and eventually intersects and crosses the economy's vertical *LRAS* curve.

If, initially, the level of real output is well below the normal capacity level of output (y_5 in Figure 11.2), a rightward shift of the *AD* curve from AD_1 to AD_2 increases real output, but has no effect on the price level. Real output increases from y_1 to y_2, but the price level stays the same at P_1. This is because the *SRAS* curve is horizontal at very low levels of real output.

However, as output rises, the *SRAS* curve begins to slope upward, which means that further increases of aggregate demand lead to inflation as well as rising real output. For example, when the *AD* curve shifts from AD_3 to AD_4, the price level rises from P_3 to P_4. And as the aggregate demand curve shifts closer to the normal capacity level of output, short-run economic growth is accompanied by higher rates of inflation. Short-run growth gradually absorbs the spare capacity in the economy until, when y_5 is reached (the normal capacity level of output), there are no longer any idle resources and the economy is producing on the *LRAS* curve. At this point, for growth to continue, short-run growth must give way to long-run growth.

To focus on the **supply-side** determinants of short-run economic growth, anything which shifts the position of the *SRAS* curve to the right will lead to short-run economic growth. This could be a fall in money wage rates or any other cost of production, a fall in taxes imposed on firms or an increase in subsidies paid to firms. However, the main impact of supply-side improvements is on the position of the *LRAS* curve, as we shall now explain.

> **KEY TERM**
> **demand side** relates to the impact of changes in aggregate demand on the economy. Associated with Keynesian economics.

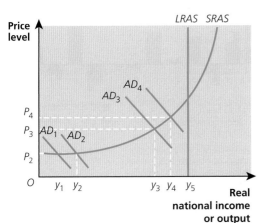

Figure 11.2 Comparing the effects on economic growth of rightward shifts of the *AD* curve

> **KEY TERM**
> **supply side** relates to changes in the potential output of the economy, which is affected by the available factors of production, e.g. changes in the size of the labour force, and the productivity of labour.

> **STUDY TIP**
> Make sure you understand the difference between aggregate demand and aggregate supply.

SYNOPTIC LINK
Chapter 10 explains the *AD/AS* macroeconomic model.

TEST YOURSELF 11.3
Distinguish between short-run and long-run economic growth.

CASE STUDY 11.1

Recession: 'now you see it, now you don't'

The Office for National Statistics (ONS) regularly revises its published statistics. When this happens, the beginning, end and depth of recessions (and of periods of positive growth) can change. Before revised statistics were published in 2013, the official view was that the UK economy had entered the second dip of a 'double-dip' recession. Some economists were even predicting that a 'third dip' was on the cards. The revised statistics — if they can be trusted — show that the 'double dip' did not happen.

The new statistics led to newspaper headlines such as 'The recession that never was: the small change which makes a big difference' in the *Daily Mail*. The data

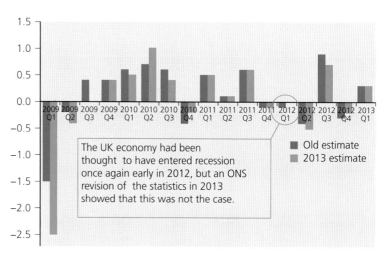

The UK economy had been thought to have entered recession once again early in 2012, but an ONS revision of the statistics in 2013 showed that this was not the case.

■ Old estimate
■ 2013 estimate

Figure 11.3 GDP, quarter-on-quarter growth, revised figures, 2013

in Figure 11.3, published by the ONS in June 2013, show what 'apparently' happened to quarterly UK economic growth between the second quarter of 2008 and the first quarter of 2013. The graph begins by showing the deep recession which lasted from the second quarter of 2008 until the end of the second quarter of 2009 (five quarters in total).

Figure 11.3 contains two sets of data. The blue bars in the graph show the ONS's estimate of quarterly growth published before June 2013. These data show the 'second dip' of a 'double-dip' recession occurring between the fourth quarter of 2011 and the end of the second quarter of 2012. But according to the revised data, shown by the green bars, there was zero growth in the first quarter of 2012: that is, neither positive nor negative. Hence the 'second dip' never happened and there was no 'double-dip' recession. However, the revised data also show the 2008–09 recession being deeper than previously thought.

A conclusion you may draw from this story is never to trust economic data. The ONS follows the 'continuous revision' method of publishing economic statistics. When new information comes to light, the data are revised. Back in April 2013 the *Daily Telegraph* had published an article under the headline: 'Never mind the triple-dip recession, the double dip may have been an illusion too', which anticipated the data revision.

Follow-up questions

1 Describe how a recession is defined in the UK and describe three of its features.
2 Find out how a recession is defined in other countries, including the USA.
3 Research what has happened to UK economic growth since this book was published.
4 How has the UK growth rate compared to that of the eurozone since the 2016 Brexit referendum?

TEST YOURSELF 11.4
'Some economists argue that recessions are necessary for restructuring the economy.' Evaluate this view.

Demand-side and supply-side determinants of long-run growth or trend growth

The trend growth rate

The economy's **trend growth rate** (or potential growth rate), which is often called the long-run growth rate, is the rate at which output can grow, on a sustained basis, without putting upward or downward pressure on inflation. Before the UK economy entered recession in 2008, the UK's trend growth rate was about 2.5% a year. At first sight, this growth rate appears low, especially when compared to higher trend growth rates in newly industrialising countries (NICs), and especially China. Nevertheless, the UK's trend growth rate was similar to the long-run growth rates of other developed economies in western Europe and North America. The absolute increase in real output delivered by a 2.25% growth rate may also exceed that delivered by a 10% growth rate in a much poorer country. Moreover, because of the compound interest effect, a 2.25% growth rate means that average UK living standards double every generation or so.

However, as we shall shortly see when we explain the **economic cycle**, since the end of the 2008–09 recession, UK trend growth has been below 2%.

The causes of long-run economic growth

We have already seen that short-run economic growth is caused by an increase in aggregate demand which makes use of spare capacity and takes the economy from a point inside the economy's production possibility frontier to a point on the frontier. By contrast, the main causes of long-run growth lie in the supply side of the economy.

In Figure 11.4, once full capacity is reached at the level of real output y_1 (the initial normal capacity level of output), for sustainable economic growth to continue the *LRAS* curve must shift rightward from $LRAS_1$ to $LRAS_2$. The new full-capacity level of real output is y_2. As Chapter 10 has mentioned, the determinants of long-run growth include improvements in technology resulting from investment and technical progress, increases in the size of the labour force, together with improvements in productivity, attitudes, enterprise, the mobility of factors of production and the economic incentives faced by entrepreneurs and the workers they employ.

To state it another way, the determinants of long-run economic relate to the economy's supply side. Supply-side reforms which increase labour productivity, bringing about higher output per worker, result from the investment decisions made by firms in pursuit of profit. These can be backed up and reinforced by successful supply-side policies undertaken by government.

However, aggregate demand still plays a role in bringing about long-run economic growth. This is because firms will only produce more goods and services if there is sufficient demand in the economy to absorb the extra output. Aggregate demand must increase to match the increase in aggregate supply.

KEY TERMS

trend growth rate the rate at which output can grow, on a sustained basis, without putting upward or downward pressure on inflation. It reflects the annual average percentage increase in the productive capacity of the economy.

economic cycle (also known as a **business cycle** or **trade cycle**) upswing and downswing in aggregate economic activity taking place over 4 to 12 years.

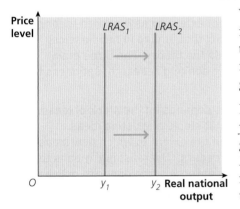

Figure 11.4 Long-run economic growth illustrated by a rightward shift of the *LRAS* curve

SYNOPTIC LINK
The roles of supply-side reforms and supply-side policies are examined in more detail in Chapter 13 on fiscal policy and supply-side policies.

Economic growth theories

As we have explained, long-run economic growth is caused by both supply-side and demand-side factors — though the former is the prime mover. However, sufficient aggregate demand has to be generated to absorb the extra output produced by the growth process. The immediate supply-side cause of long-run growth is *increased labour productivity*, which itself results from investment in, and accumulation of, capital goods and human capital, and from technological progress.

There are two main theories of long-term economic growth: neoclassical growth theory and new growth theory.

Neoclassical growth theory

The older theory, known as neoclassical growth theory, which was developed by Professor Robert Solow in the 1950s, argues that a sustained increase in investment increases the economy's growth rate, but only temporarily. The ratio of capital to labour goes up, the marginal product of capital declines and the economy moves back to a long-term path, which is determined by output growing at the same rate as the workforce, plus a factor to reflect improving labour productivity.

In neoclassical growth theory, the rate at which labour productivity improves is determined by technological progress. But the theory does not explain why technological progress occurs. Technological progress is assumed to fall on the economy 'like manna from heaven'. This is the theory's weakness. The causes or determinants of the ultimate engine of economic growth, namely technological progress, are exogenous to the theory (exogenous means 'outside'). Neoclassical growth theory therefore fails to provide a complete explanation of economic growth.

New growth theory

In recent years, neoclassical growth theory has been replaced to a significant extent by new growth theory. New growth theory is also called *endogenous growth theory*, reflecting the fact that, unlike in neoclassical growth theory, the determinants of technological progress are brought inside the theory. The three main sources of technological progress explained by new growth theory are profit-seeking research, openness to foreign ideas and accumulation of human capital:

- **Profit-seeking research.** The rate at which technological progress occurs depends on the stock of ideas. The flow of new ideas thought up by current researchers adds to the 'capital stock' of existing ideas. How many new ideas there are depends on the number of researchers, but the extent to which new ideas improve technological progress depends on whether or not 'over-fishing' occurs. 'Over-fishing' means that the discovery of new ideas makes it harder to find further new ideas. But conversely, the opposite may be true, as accumulating ideas may make researchers more rather than less productive. This is the so-called 'standing on the shoulders' effect. Paul Romer, one of the most influential developers of new growth theory, assumes that the this effect is dominant, which means that countries with more researchers can have higher growth rates.
- **Openness to foreign ideas.** Economic growth can derive either from domestic innovation or from technological transfer from other countries. In 1999, Cameron, Proudman and Redding argued that the rate at which technological progress occurs in a country depends on three factors: the domestic rate of growth of technology in the absence of technology transfer; the rate at which technology can be adopted from abroad; and the proportion of foreign technologies that can be adopted. This means that for a technology follower, technology grows at its own domestic rate of technology growth, plus some extra 'catch-up' generated by technology-leading countries.
- **Accumulation of human capital.** Human capital accumulates through educating and training a skilled workforce from among a country's indigenous population, and through migration from other countries. Migration adds to human capital provided migrants possess appropriate education and skills, or are willing and able to attain them. A high level of human capital is best regarded as a necessary but not a sufficient condition for successful economic growth. This is because technological change requires workers to possess the skills and aptitudes required for adapting to new technologies, rather than those that used to be necessary for old, declining technologies.

New growth theory suggests that appropriate government intervention can create the supply-side conditions which favour growth. These include:

- conditions that encourage profit-seeking research and appropriate accumulation of human capital
- externalities or external economies provided by the state which benefit private sector businesses
- patent legislation and a judicial system that enforces the law of contract and intellectual property rights, which create the incentive for firms to innovate

The costs and benefits of economic growth

For many people and most economists, achieving a satisfactory and sustained rate of economic growth is arguably the most important of all the macroeconomic objectives that governments wish to achieve. Without growth, other objectives, particularly full employment and competitive export industries, may be impossible to attain. And when growth becomes negative, as in the recession that started in the UK in 2008, people become all too aware of the rapid disappearance of the fruits of growth. For most people, standards of living fall, with the most unfortunate losing their jobs as the industries that used to employ them collapse or slim down.

However, in the long run, high rates of economic growth may not be sustainable. With countries in the developing world, particularly the 'emerging-market' countries, recently growing at a far faster rate than richer developed economies, maintaining global growth rates may not be sustainable. The rapid using-up of finite resources and the pollution and global warming that spin off from economic growth will result increasingly in desertification, water shortages, declining crop yields, famines and wars.

Some economists argue an opposite effect, namely that one of the benefits of growth, at least as far as advanced developed countries are concerned, is the development of environmentally friendly technologies. These reduce the ratio of energy consumption to GDP. Nevertheless, rich developed economies, especially the USA, continue to be, at least for the time being, the world's biggest consumers of energy and the biggest polluters.

Economic growth can have a number of costs that reduce economic welfare. Some of these, followed by some of the benefits of growth, are listed below.

Costs of economic growth

- Economic growth uses up finite resources such as oil and minerals that cannot be replaced.
- Economic growth leads to pollution and other forms of environmental degradation, with the Earth eventually reaching a tipping point, beyond which it cannot recover.
- Growth can destroy local cultures and communities, and widen inequalities in the distribution of income and wealth.
- Economic growth leads to urbanisation and the spread of huge cities, which swallow up good agricultural land.
- In its early phases, economic growth leads to a rapid growth in population, more mouths to feed, and more people who are poor.
- Growth produces losers as well as winners. Countries suffering low growth may enter a vicious circle of declining business confidence, low profits, low investment, a lack of international competitiveness, even lower profits, zero growth, and so on.

Benefits of economic growth

- Economic growth increases standards of living and people's welfare.
- Growth may lead to more civilised communities, who take action to improve the environment.
- Growth provides new and more environmentally friendly technologies.
- Economic growth has increased the length of people's lives and has provided the means to reduce disease.
- Economic growth provides a route out of poverty for much of the world's population.
- Economic growth produces a 'fiscal dividend', namely the tax revenues that growth generates. Tax revenues can be used to correct market failures and to provide infrastructure, thereby increasing the economic welfare of the whole community.
- For a particular country, economic growth can generate a 'virtuous circle' of greater business confidence, increased investment in state-of-the-art technology, greater international competitiveness, higher profits, even more growth, and so on.

SYNOPTIC LINK
Economic growth and economic development obviously overlap. Section 15.2 of Chapter 15 investigates economic development further. The chapter also describes alternatives to national income as measures of economic development, such as the United Nations Human Development Index (HDI).

The impact of growth on individuals, the economy and the environment

Some individuals, mostly the rich but also many of the less well-off, obviously benefit from the higher welfare and incomes, and the better prospects for the future that growth brings about. But others, including many of the poor, can suffer from loss of jobs and increased inequality that can also result from economic growth. For example, increased automation brought about by faster economic growth may reduce overall demand for labour.

Economic growth can also increase the international competitiveness of the economy, which implies that other less competitive economies will not enjoy so many of the fruits of rapid growth. The reverse, however, is true if other countries grow at a faster rate.

With regard to the environment, economic growth may have more costs than benefits, leading to an outcome in which growth becomes unsustainable. Growth may consume more and more finite resources, leading to resource depletion, and it leads also to resource degradation through pollution and loss of biodiversity.

STUDY TIP
Don't confuse *sustainable growth* with *sustained growth*. The latter simply means achieving a particular rate of economic growth (on average) over a number of years. For example, from the end of recession in 1992 until the onset of the next recession in 2008, the UK sustained an average annual growth rate of about 2.75% over this period. However, a growth rate which is sustained over quite a long period may nevertheless be unsustainable if it leads to environmental problems, the depletion of vital finite resources and the degradation of others.

○ **SYNOPTIC LINK**
See the section on environmental market failures in Chapter 8 (pages 238–241) and the extension material below on the environment and the sustainability of economic growth.

○ EXTENSION MATERIAL

The environment and the sustainability of economic growth

Nearly 50 years ago, the first oil crisis, in which the price of crude oil more than doubled, led to British people becoming aware of how the environment — in the guise of raw material and energy shortages — might severely limit a government's ability to achieve high employment levels and continuing economic growth.

Fuel shortages and increased energy prices drew people's attention to two publications of the then new but fast-growing ecology or environmentalist movement. The first of these was a document called 'A Blueprint for Survival', published in the January 1972 edition of the British journal *The Ecologist*, which was followed a few months later by the publication in New York of a vastly influential book, *The Limits to Growth: A Report for the Club of Rome's Project on the Predicament of Mankind*.

The authors of 'A Blueprint for Survival' wrote:

> The principal defect of the industrial way of life with its ethos of expansion is that it is not sustainable. Its termination within the lifetime of someone born today is inevitable — unless it continues to be sustained for a while longer by an entrenched minority at the cost of imposing great suffering on the rest of mankind. Our task is to create a society which is sustainable and which will give the fullest possible satisfaction to its members. Such a society by definition would not depend on expansion but on stability.

The Limits to Growth, published a few months later in 1973, suggested that humanity would soon face a threefold dilemma: the impending exhaustion of the world's non-renewable natural resources; the world's pollution problem becoming so acute that the capacity for self-cleaning and regeneration becomes exhausted; and as population continues to grow, a point being reached where humankind destroys itself through sheer weight of numbers. Commenting on *The Limits to Growth*, one reviewer wrote:

> Man is heading for disaster if, overall, mankind does not learn to limit economic growth. That such a thesis would be unpopular with economists was to be expected. All their training, their research and their ethos has been

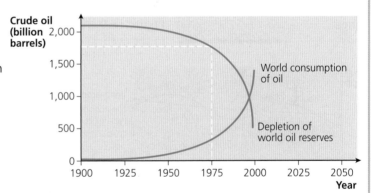

Figure 11.5 The gloomy prediction in the 1970s that exponential growth of oil consumption, matched by exponential depletion of known oil reserves, would lead to the world running out of oil by 2000

concerned with ways in which the economy can be stimulated and expanded. Practically no economist has given thought to the problems of economic stability. For one thing stability is read as stagnation, and for another it is hard for an economist to find anyone to employ him who is interested in economic equilibrium. It has no appeal to governments, board chairmen, company presidents or even to used-car salesmen.

The authors of 'A Blueprint for Survival' and *The Limits to Growth* based many of their forecasts and predictions on the assumption of accelerating rates of population growth and resource use. This is known as exponential growth. Figure 11.5 illustrates the forecast in 'A Blueprint for Survival' of exponential growth in demand for crude oil or petroleum and exponential decline in petroleum reserves. The dashed lines show the total world oil reserves that, in 1975, the authors of the 'Blueprint for Survival' estimated would be available for extraction.

The forecasts of resource use and depletion made in *The Limits to Growth* were rather more sophisticated, but they were still based on the assumption of exponential rates of growth of use and depletion. In their most optimistic scenario, the authors of *The Limits to Growth* argued that it might be possible to achieve a state of equilibrium, providing restrictions were placed on population growth and industrialisation — the two elements limiting growth which they argued principally cause resource exhaustion and pollution.

The economic cycle

Fluctuations in economic activity occur in two main ways: through seasonal fluctuations, and through cyclical fluctuations taking place over a number of years. Seasonal fluctuations are largely caused by changes in the weather. Examples include the effect of very cold winters closing down the building trade and seasonal employment in travel and tourism.

Upswings and downswings in economic activity which are longer than seasonal fluctuations are called the economic cycle. Economic cycles (also known as business cycles and trade cycles), which can be between approximately 4 and 12 years long, are caused primarily by fluctuations in aggregate demand. In recent years, supply-side factors such as supply shocks hitting the economy have also been recognised as causes of economic cycles.

Figure 11.6 shows two complete economic cycles, together with a line giving the economy's trend output, from which the economy's long-term growth rate can be calculated. **Actual output** rises and sometimes falls in the different phases of the economic cycle. Short-term growth, measured by the percentage change in real GDP over a 12-month period, also varies in the different phases of the economic cycle. In the cycle's upswing, growth is positive but, as Figure 11.6 shows, 'growth' becomes negative if and when a recession occurs in the cyclical downturn.

> **KEY TERM**
> **actual output** level of real output produced in the economy in a particular year — not to be confused with the trend level of output, which is what the economy is capable of producing when working at full capacity. Actual output differs from the trend level of output when there are output gaps.

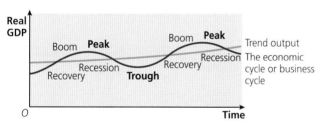

Figure 11.6 The phases of the economic cycle and the trend output line

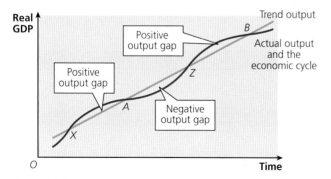

Figure 11.7 Upswings and downswings in the economic cycle, but no recessions

The phases of the economic cycle shown in Figure 11.6 are recovery, boom and the recessionary phase. Recovery occurs when real GDP begins to grow after the end of a recession, or at the end of the trough of the economic cycle. With continuing short-run growth in real output, recovery gives way to the boom phase of the economic cycle when the level of real output becomes greater than the trend level of output. The boom ends when the upswing of the economic cycle gives way to the next downswing, which is shown in Figure 11.6 by the economy entering a recession. (A severe recession lasting 2 years or more is sometimes called a depression. Unlike a recession, defined in the UK as real national output falling for 6 months or more, there is no generally accepted definition of a depression.)

In contrast to Figure 11.6, the next diagram, Figure 11.7, shows continuous *positive* economic growth with an absence of *negative* growth. In the downswings shown on the diagram, the rate of positive growth slows down, but negative growth does not occur.

Figure 11.7 illustrates what happened to economic growth in the years before the 2008–09 recession, and also in the recovery period after the recession, though in the latter period the underlying rate of growth was less than had been the case before the recession. In the recession itself, real output fell.

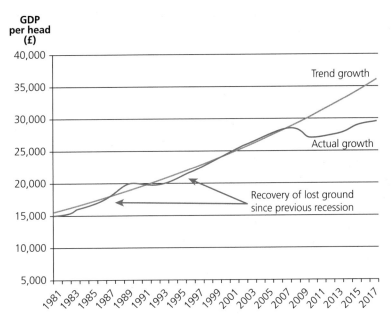

Figure 11.8 gives a better representation of what happened to economic growth before, after and during the 2008–09 recession. The graph shows that, unlike in the previous two recessions, which occurred at the beginning of the 1980s and the 1990s, the 2008–09 recession was much deeper, with real output only recovering to its pre-recessionary level in 2014 and remaining, even then, well below what would have been the level of output (shown by the blue line on the graph) had there been no recession. Indeed, the recession may have shifted the economy onto a new trend rate of growth much lower than the pre-recessionary trend growth line.

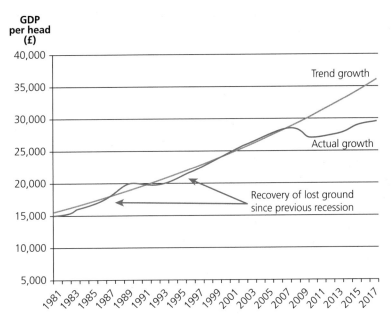

Figure 11.8 Has there been a change in UK trend growth since the 2008–09 recession?

The causes of change in the phases of the economic cycle

The principal explanations of the phases of the economic cycle are:

- **Fluctuations in aggregate demand.** In the 1930s John Maynard Keynes argued that economic recessions are caused by fluctuations in aggregate demand, which are caused by consumer and business confidence giving way to pessimism, and vice versa. This is still the prevailing view today.
- **Supply-side factors.** It is now recognised that supply-side factors can also trigger economic cycles. Edward Prescott and Finn Kydland, the 2004 Nobel Laureates in economics, have developed a theory of 'real business cycles', which argues that changes in technology on the supply side of the economy might be as important as changes in aggregate demand in explaining economic cycles.

Other factors that may cause or contribute to cyclical changes include:

- **The role of speculative bubbles.** Rapid economic growth leads to a rapid rise and speculative bubble in asset prices. When people realise that house prices and/or share prices rise far above the assets' real values, asset selling replaces asset buying. This causes the speculative bubble to burst, which in turn destroys consumer and/or business confidence. People stop spending and the economy falls into recession. The resulting cyclical instability is made worse by the excessive growth in credit and levels of debt, and 'animal spirits' and 'herding'. These terms are used to describe how, in financial markets, share prices and asset prices tend to 'overshoot' when traders suffer a bout of 'irrational exuberance', and then to 'undershoot' when the 'pricking' of the speculative bubble causes asset prices to collapse.

- **Political business cycle theory.** In democratic countries, general elections usually have to take place every 4 or 5 years. As an election approaches, the political party in power may attempt to 'buy votes' by engineering a pre-election boom. After the election, the party in power deflates aggregate demand to prevent the economy from overheating, but when the next general election approaches, demand is once again expanded.

- **Outside shocks hitting the economy.** Economic shocks, which were explained in Chapter 10, divide into 'demand shocks', which affect aggregate demand, and 'supply shocks', which impact on aggregate supply. In some cases, an outside shock hitting the economy may affect both aggregate demand and aggregate supply. A commonly quoted example is the effect on other countries of a war in the Middle East. The war might not only affect business confidence in a country such as the UK (a demand shock), but also lead to an oil shortage which increases businesses' costs of production. This would be a supply shock.

- **Changes in inventories.** Besides investing in fixed capital, firms also invest in stocks (inventories) of raw materials, and in stocks of finished goods waiting to be sold. This type of investment is called inventory investment or stock building. Although this accounts for less than 1% of GDP in a typical year, swings in inventories are often the single most important determinant of recessions. Firms hold stocks of raw materials and finished goods in order to smooth production to cope with swings in demand. However, paradoxically, changes in these inventories tend to trigger and exacerbate economic cycles. Stocks of unsold finished goods build up when firms over-estimate demand for finished goods. As the stocks accumulate, firms are forced to cut production by more than the original fall in demand. The resultant destocking turns a slowdown into a recession. In the USA, swings in inventory investment account for about half of the fall in GDP in recent recessions. Destocking has also made UK recessions worse.

- **The Marxist explanation.** Marxist economists explain economic cycles as part of a restructuring process that increases the rate of profit in capitalist economies. Under normal production conditions, a fall in the rate of profit caused by competitive pressure threatens to bankrupt weaker capitalist firms. Marxists believe that recessions create conditions in which stronger firms either take over weaker competitors, or buy at rock-bottom prices the assets of rivals that have been forced out of business. Either way, restructuring by takeover or bankruptcy means that the 'fittest' capitalist firms survive. In Marxist analysis, economic cycles are deemed necessary for the regeneration and survival of capitalism.

- **Multiplier/accelerator interaction.** Keynesian economists have argued that business cycles may be caused by the interaction of two dynamic processes: the multiplier process, through which an increase in investment leads to multiple increases in national income; and the accelerator, through which the increase in income induces a change in the level of investment. Thus the relationship between investment and income is one of mutual interaction:

STUDY TIP

The specification emphasises that destabilising speculation can cause economic cycles.

STUDY TIP
Go back and read Case study 10.1 in Chapter 10, which is about the effect of the regularly occurring El Niño climatic disturbance on the world economy

investment affects income (via the investment multiplier), which in turn affects investment demand (via the accelerator process), and in this process income and employment fluctuate in a cyclical manner.

- **Climatic cycles.** Stanley Jevons was one of the first economists to recognise the economic cycle in the nineteenth century. Perhaps taking note of the Bible's reference to '7 years of plenty' followed by '7 years of famine', Jevons believed a connection exists between the timing of economic crises and the solar cycle. Variations in sunspots affect the power of the sun's rays, influencing the quality of harvests and thus the price of grain, which, in turn, affects business confidence and gives rise to trade cycles. Although Jevons's sunspot theory was never widely accepted, the effect named El Niño, which figured in Case study 10.1 in the previous chapter, has renewed interest in Jevons's theory.

TEST YOURSELF 11.6
An economy had nominal GDP growth of 8% in the last year, an inflation rate of 5.5% and population growth of 2.5%. What was the approximate change in real GDP per capita over the year?

Indicators, besides changing GDP, which are used to identify phases of the economic cycle

Economic cycles are usually defined and measured in terms of changes in real output or real GDP. However, changes in other variables, including the rate of inflation, investment and unemployment, are also used to describe the phases of the economic cycle. In the upswing of the cycle, especially in the boom phase, excess aggregate demand begins to pull up the price level, a situation exacerbated by cost pressures when labour shortages lead to nominal wages and salaries rising faster than real wages. The reverse happens in the downswing. Business confidence is also higher in the upswing, leading to an increase in private sector investment. Conversely, a collapse of confidence in the cycle's downswing leads to investment projects being cancelled or postponed.

Employment increases (and unemployment decreases) in the recovery and boom phases of the cycle, though, as noted, eventual labour shortages may lead to a higher rate of inflation. In past UK economic cycles, though less so recently, the employment cycle has tended to lag behind the output or GDP cycle. Because people have votes, political parties tend to be more influenced by what is happening to jobs than to what is happening to GDP. The fact that the two cycles are out of phase, as illustrated in Figure 11.9, can lead to governments expanding the economy to reduce unemployment, even when real GDP began its recovery several months beforehand. This can increase inflation. Likewise, governments have sometimes taken demand out of the economy to try to temper a 'frothy' job market, even though real GDP has already begun to decline.

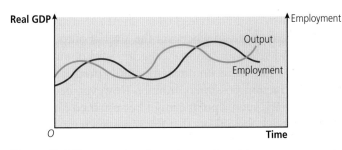

Figure 11.9 The output and employment cycles

The economic cycle and output gaps

Figure 11.10 illustrates **output gaps**, a feature of the economic cycle previously shown in Figure 11.7. If the economy's *actual* level of output were always to equal *trend* output, there would be no output gap. (In this situation, there would also be no economic cycles.) Output gaps occur when the level of *actual* real output in the economy is greater or lower than the *trend* output level at a particular point in time. When actual output is above trend output, there is a **positive output gap**. Similarly, when actual output is below trend output, there is a **negative output gap**. (Positive and negative output gaps are both illustrated in Figures 11.7 and 11.10, where the levels of actual output that the economy is producing are above and below the trend output line.) The UK government defines economic cycles as beginning and ending when there are no output gaps, whether or not a recession actually occurs. Thus, in Figure 11.7, an economic cycle beginning at point *X* would end at point *Z*. (Alternatively, points *A* and *B* could be used to mark the beginning and end of an economic cycle.)

KEY TERMS

output gaps show the level of *actual* real output in the economy either higher or lower than the *trend* output level.

positive output gap the level of *actual* real output in the economy is greater than the *trend* output level.

negative output gap the level of *actual* real output in the economy is lower than the *trend* output level.

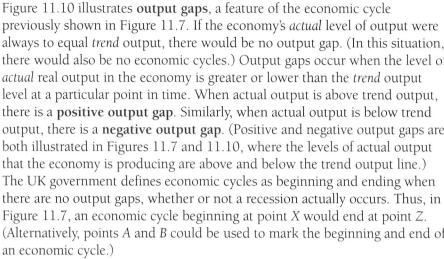

Figure 11.10 Negative and positive output gaps illustrated on an economic cycle diagram

TEST YOURSELF 11.7
What is another name for the economic cycle?

STUDY TIP
Don't confuse an *output gap* with a *productivity gap*, which is the gap between the levels of labour productivity in two countries. Make sure you understand the difference between positive and negative output gaps.

Output gaps and *AD/AS* gaps

Figure 11.11 *below* shows negative and positive gaps on an *AD/AS* diagram. The economy suffers a negative output gap whenever the level of output is to the left of the *LRAS* curve and *below* the 'normal capacity' level of output y_N. Positive output gaps occur when the economy temporarily produces at a point outside its current production possibility frontier. However, because this represents overuse of capacity, such a point cannot be sustained for long. In the context of the *AD/AS* model, this means that the economy temporarily produces a level of output to the right of the *LRAS* curve, and above the 'normal capacity' level of output y_N.

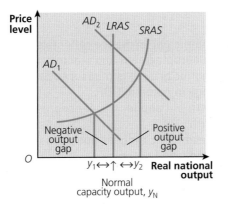

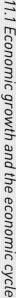

Figure 11.11 Negative and positive output gaps illustrated on an *AD/AS* diagram

Output gaps and the UK economy

Figure 11.12 illustrates how the UK economy performed between 2002 and 2019. When the vertical bars in the graph are positive, the UK experienced a positive output gap. When they were negative, the economy suffered a negative output gap.

Figure 11.12 UK's output gap measured as a percentage of potential GDP, 1980–2019

Source: IMF

In the years between 2000 and 2008 a positive output gap accompanied a booming economy. This was brought to a shuddering halt in the 2008–09 recession. In the subsequent economic recovery, the negative output gap gradually became smaller, until the IMF forecast a very small positive output gap in 2018. However, this does not indicate a return to economic boom. For many people, particularly those on low incomes and those who live in the more depressed parts of the economy, despite slow positive economic growth, real personal incomes have fallen in many of the years since recovery began. For low-paid workers, economic recovery did not improve their standards of living. The IMF's forecasts for future years after 2018 has hovered around an output gap of approximately zero, with the forecast for 2019 of a very small output gap.

11.2 Employment and unemployment

The meaning and measurement of unemployment

As with economic growth, we have already briefly discussed the meanings of employment and unemployment, together with the measurement of unemployment in Chapter 9. The main point we made was that the UK government has generally dropped the claimant count as a measure of unemployment, focusing instead on the Labour Force Survey (LFS) measure.

We explained that full employment does not necessarily mean that every member of the working population has a job. Rather, it means a situation in which the number of people wishing to work at the going market real-wage rate equals the number of workers whom employers wish to hire at this real-wage rate.

However, even this definition needs qualifying since, in a dynamic economy, change is constantly taking place, with some industries declining and others growing. This leads to two types of unemployment known as frictional and structural unemployment. We shall now look at these and other types of unemployment.

Voluntary and involuntary unemployment

In the next section, when we explain the different types and causes of unemployment, we shall discuss cyclical unemployment, or Keynesian unemployment as it is sometimes called. Writing in the 1930s, at the time of the Great Depression, Keynes argued that deficient aggregate demand in the economy results in **involuntary unemployment**. This is a situation in which the unemployed without jobs wish to work, but there are no jobs

> **STUDY TIP**
> Make sure you remember how unemployment is measured in the UK. You must be able to interpret claimant count and Labour Force Survey data.

> **KEY TERM**
> **involuntary unemployment** occurs when workers are willing to work at current market wage rates but there are no jobs available.

available because there is no demand for their labour. The unemployed
are willing, able and available to take up employment in any suitable job
at the going wage rate, but they cannot find employment. In this situation,
unemployment is caused by deficient aggregate demand. **Voluntary
unemployment**, by contrast, refers to a situation in which workers without
jobs are unwilling to take up employment at the going wage rate, often
choosing instead to receive benefits paid by the state rather than to seek
employment.

The types and causes of unemployment

The four types of unemployment we shall now explain are frictional,
structural, cyclical and lastly seasonal unemployment, which is the least
significant of the four, except of course for many of the workers who become
seasonally unemployed.

Frictional unemployment

Frictional unemployment, also known as **transitional unemployment**,
is 'between jobs' unemployment. As its name suggests, this type of
unemployment results from frictions in the labour market which create a
delay, or time lag, during which a worker is unemployed when moving from
one job to another. Note that the definition of frictional unemployment
assumes that a job vacancy exists and that friction in the job market, caused
by the immobility of labour, prevents an unemployed worker from filling the
vacancy. It follows that the number of unfilled job vacancies in the economy
can be used as a measure of the level of frictional unemployment. Frictional
unemployment is usually short term; if it persists, it becomes structural
unemployment.

Among the causes of frictional unemployment are geographical and
occupational immobilities of labour, which prevent workers who are laid off
from immediately filling job vacancies.

The geographical immobility of labour is caused by factors such as family
ties and local friendships discouraging people from moving to other parts
of the country, ignorance about whether job vacancies exist in other parts of
the country, and above all, the cost of moving and difficulties of obtaining
housing.

The occupational immobility of labour results from difficulties in training for
jobs that require different skills, the effects of restrictive practices such as a
requirement that new workers must possess unnecessary qualifications, and
race, gender and age discrimination in labour markets.

Redundant workers, who have been laid off by their previous employers
because they are no longer needed, may take time to find the types of work
they want at wage rates they are prepared to accept. They remain unemployed
whilst involved in job search. Likewise, young workers joining the labour
market for the first time, such as university graduates, may be frictionally
unemployed for a short time.

Imperfect information in the labour market, through which the jobless are unaware of jobs that are in fact available, tends to worsen frictional unemployment, as do incentive problems resulting from the fact that people may believe their pay will be swallowed up in taxes and loss of benefits.

The search theory of unemployment

The search theory of unemployment also helps to explain frictional unemployment. Consider the situation illustrated in Figure 11.13. A worker earning £1,000 a week in a skilled professional occupation loses her job. Although no vacancies apparently exist at present in her current line of work, there are plenty of vacancies for low-skilled office workers earning around £300 a week. Given this information, if on the day of her job loss the newly unemployed worker sets the weekly wage she aspires to at £1,000, she will choose to be unemployed, at least to start with, because she does not wish to fill a lower-paid vacancy. The lower weekly wage on offer, and perhaps poorer conditions of work and status associated with the lower-paid job, fail to meet her aspirations. She may also realise that she possesses imperfect information about the state of the job market. This means she needs to search the labour market to find out whether better-paid and higher-status vacancies exist, which she does not know about currently.

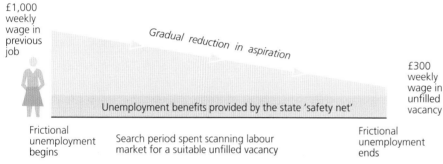

Figure 11.13 Search theory and frictional unemployment

Approached in this way, frictional unemployment can be viewed as a voluntary search period in which newly unemployed workers scan the labour market, searching for vacancies which meet their aspirations.

There are a number of ways in which a voluntary search period can end. First, in the example described above, the woman may eventually learn of a vacancy for which she is qualified, and which meets her initial aspiration. Indeed, the vacancy might have been there all the time but, until she searched the job market, she was unaware of its existence. Second, the vacancy may have arisen during her search period, perhaps because of a general improvement in the condition of labour markets. Third, she may end her voluntary unemployment if she decides, on the basis of her lack of success in getting a job, that her initial aspirations were unrealistically high and that she must settle for a lower-paid, less attractive job.

Long search periods, which increase the amount of frictional unemployment in the economy, result in part from the welfare benefit system. Without the receipt of welfare benefits, search periods would have to be financed by running down stocks of saving, or through the charity of family and friends. In this situation, the threat of poverty creates an incentive to search the job market more vigorously and to reduce the aspirational wage levels of the unemployed.

The availability of a state safety net provided by unemployment benefits and other income-related welfare benefits, together in some cases with redundancy payments, enable unemployed workers to finance long voluntary search periods. Because of this, many free-market economists support a reduction in the real value of unemployment benefits, together with restricting benefits to those who can prove they are genuinely looking for work. Free-market economists believe these policies create incentives for the unemployed to reduce aspirations quickly, which shortens search periods.

Structural unemployment

Structural unemployment, which is more long term than frictional unemployment, results from the structural decline of industries which are unable to compete or adapt in the face of changing demand or new products, and the emergence of more efficient competitors in other countries. Structural unemployment is also caused by changing skill requirements as industries change ways of producing their products. In the latter case, the structural unemployment is often called technological unemployment.

Technological unemployment results from the successful growth of new industries using labour-saving technology. In contrast to mechanisation (workers operating machines), which has usually increased the overall demand for labour, automation (machines operating other machines) reduces the demand for labour. Whereas the growth of mechanised industry increases employment, automation of production can lead to the shedding of labour, even when industry output is expanding.

Changes in technology can also lead to changes in the pattern of demand. In countries with hot climates, solar panels have been replacing electricity generated by coal, which leads to structural unemployment when fossil-fuel burning power stations close down.

The growth of structural unemployment in the service sector has partly been caused by the increasing use of information and communication technology (ICT) and automated services. Call centre employment has grown significantly in the service sector in recent years, though to some extent call centres have moved overseas to lower-waged countries such as India. Moreover, some companies which used to employ call centre workers now use automated communication software rather than humans to provide customer services.

It is not always easy to separate changes in structural unemployment from other causes of unemployment, particularly changes in aggregate demand. Manufacturing output grew in many of the years between 1993 and 2008, but manufacturing employment fell. However, during these years, there was a danger of exaggerating the growth of unemployment in manufacturing industries because many activities, ranging from cleaning to information technology maintenance, previously undertaken 'in-house' by manufacturing firms, were out-sourced to external service-sector providers.

STUDY TIP
Frictional and structural unemployment have supply-side causes which affect the position of the long-run aggregate supply curve.

TEST YOURSELF 11.8
Explain the difference between frictional and structural unemployment.

CASE STUDY 11.2

Under-employment and zero-hours employment contracts

In 2014 the UK prime minister announced: 'We have reached an important milestone, with more people in work than ever before in our history.' However, while unemployment had fallen since early 2012, under-employment had decreased to a lesser degree, to around a million people, or nearly twice the pre-recession level in 2007.

Across the UK the number of people who count as under-employed — people working part time because they cannot get a full-time job, or wanting more hours in their current job, has increased for both employees and the self-employed.

While there was a small fall in 2014 in involuntarily part-time work (people working part time because they cannot get a full-time job), there was a rise in the numbers who wanted more hours in their existing jobs. Overall, under-employment was still increasing.

However, by 2015, real wages had begun to rise, and at the time of writing in July 2019, it seems likely that they will continue to rise, albeit slowly, unless the UK economy is hit by an adverse economic 'shock' emanating, for example, from the eurozone, from China or from the protectionist policies introduced in the USA.

The problem of under-employment is exacerbated by zero-hours employment contracts. Zero-hours contracts do not guarantee a minimum number of hours of employment. The Office for National Statistics said the number of employment contracts without a minimum number of guaranteed hours increased to 1.8 million in the year to November 2017, up from 1.7 million in 2016. Summer-time seasonal employment in tourist trades bloats the number of workers on zero-hours contracts. On average, someone on a zero-hours contract usually works 25 hours a week. The majority are women and students, often aged under 25, or 65 and over. About a third of them want more hours, primarily in their current job, compared with 10% of other people in employment.

TUC general secretary Frances O'Grady has said: 'Zero-hours contracts sum up what has gone wrong in the modern workplace. They shift almost all power from the worker and give it to their boss.' But the government's business secretary has argued that 'Zero-hours contracts are valued by many employers and individuals who want flexibility in the hours they work, such as students, people with caring responsibilities and those who want to partially retire.' The shadow business secretary responded by saying: 'Ministers have watered down every person's rights at work and zero-hours contracts have gone from being a niche concept to becoming the norm in parts of our economy. Workers are unhappy that staff can simply be sent home if there is no work to be done.'

Follow-up questions

1 Why are women more likely than men to be under-employed?
2 Assess the advantages and disadvantages of zero-hours employment contracts.
3 Describe one other cause or low-paid work.
4 Should the government make zero-hours contracts illegal? Justify your answer.

EXTENSION MATERIAL

International competition and structural unemployment

The growth of international competition has been a particularly important cause of structural unemployment. During the post-Second World War era from the 1950s to the 1970s, structural unemployment in the UK was regionally concentrated in areas where nineteenth-century staple industries such as textiles and shipbuilding were suffering structural decline. This regional unemployment, caused by the decline of 'sunset industries', was more than offset by the growth of employment elsewhere in the UK in 'sunrise industries'. However, in the severe recessions of the 1980s and 1990s, and also in the 2008–09 recession, structural unemployment affected almost all regions in the UK as the **deindustrialisation** process spread across the manufacturing base. Decline of manufacturing industries as a result of international competition can also lead to structural unemployment in industries which service the manufacturing sector: for example, in private security firms.

Although manufacturing output grew in the 'boom' years before the 2008–09 recession, employment in manufacturing industries often fell. Recession and the growth of cyclical unemployment caused a further fall in manufacturing employment. However, there is a danger of exaggerating the decline in employment in manufacturing, because many activities, ranging from cleaning to ICT maintenance, which were previously undertaken 'in house' by manufacturing firms, have been outsourced to external service-sector providers.

Structural unemployment has occurred within the service sector as well as in manufacturing industries. For example, increasing use of ICT, automated services and the internet has meant that total employment has fallen in the travel agency industry. Call centre employment has grown significantly in recent years, though much of this growth has been in low-wage economies such as India. However, a decline has been forecast, partly because companies employ automated communication software rather than human beings to provide customer service and to answer telephone and internet queries.

> **KEY TERM**
> **cyclical unemployment**
> (also known as **Keynesian unemployment** and **demand-deficient unemployment**) unemployment caused by a lack of aggregate demand in the economy, occurring when the economy goes into a recession or depression.

> **KEY TERM**
> **deindustrialisation** the decline of manufacturing industries, together with coal mining.

> **STUDY TIP**
> A negative output gap is linked to cyclical unemployment.

Cyclical unemployment

Cyclical unemployment, as we have mentioned, is also known as **Keynesian unemployment**. During the Great Depression in the 1930s, Keynes — but not his opponents — believed that deficient aggregate demand was a major cause of persistent mass unemployment. Free-market economists generally agree that temporary cyclical unemployment may be caused by a lack of demand in the downswing of the economic cycle. However, Keynes went further, arguing that the economy could settle into an under-full employment equilibrium, caused by a continuing lack of effective aggregate demand. In contrast to frictional unemployment, which is voluntary, Keynes believed that cyclical unemployment is involuntary: that is, not caused by the workers themselves. As a result, the unemployed should not be blamed for their idleness.

Figure 11.14 illustrates cyclical unemployment in the context of the economy's *AD/AS* diagram. A collapse in business and consumer confidence causes the *AD* curve to shift left from AD_1 to AD_2. Keynesian economists argue that if prices and wages are 'sticky' (or inflexible), deficient aggregate demand and cyclical unemployment will persist, with the equilibrium level of national income falling from y_N to y_2.

However, anti-Keynesian or free-market economists reject this view. They assume that markets for both goods and labour are competitive; by reducing businesses' costs of production, falling wages shift the *SRAS* curve from $SRAS_1$ to $SRAS_2$. The price level falls to P_2 and output increases from y_2, back to the normal capacity level of output, y_N. According to the free-market view, cyclical unemployment is temporary and self-correcting — provided that markets are sufficiently competitive, and prices and wages are both flexible.

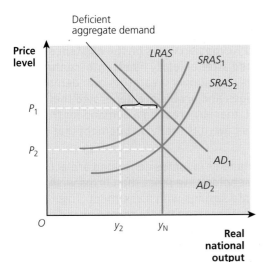

Figure 11.14 Cyclical unemployment caused by a leftward shift of aggregate demand

375

STUDY TIP

This is an example of applying *AD/AS* analysis to illustrate an important aspect of macroeconomics. There are many other economic problems and issues that can be analysed in a similar way.

TEST YOURSELF 11.9

The bar graph in Figure 11.15, for a particular year, shows an estimate of the percentage of workers structurally and cyclically unemployed in the Euro Area (eurozone), Japan and the USA in that year. What can you conclude from the data?

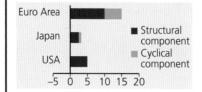

Figure 11.15 Structural and cyclical unemployment: selected areas

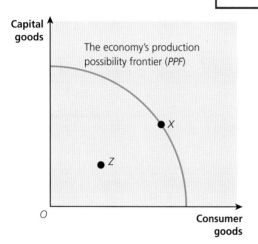

Figure 11.16 Cyclical unemployment and the economy's production possibility frontier

Figure 11.16, which shows the economy's production possibility frontier (*PPF*), illustrates another way of showing cyclical unemployment. All points on the production possibility frontier, including point *X*, show the economy using all its productive capacity, including labour. There is no demand deficiency and thus no cyclical unemployment. By contrast, deficient aggregate demand can lead to the economy producing inside its production possibility frontier: for example, at point *Z*. When this is the case, cyclical unemployment exists in the economy.

STUDY TIP

Figure 11.16 provides an example of how to use a production possibility curve to illustrate the point you are making. A PPF curve can also be used to illustrate scarcity, opportunity cost, choice, productive efficiency and economic growth.

EXTENSION MATERIAL

Say's Law

To explain the difference between the pre-Keynesian (free-market) and Keynesian views on the existence of deficient demand in the economy, we must introduce Say's Law, named after an early nineteenth-century French economist, Jean-Baptiste Say. In popular form, Say's Law states that supply creates its own demand. Whenever an output, or supply, is produced, factor incomes such as wages and profits are generated that are just sufficient, *if spent*, to purchase the output at the existing price level, thereby creating a demand for the output produced. Stated thus, there is nothing controversial about Say's Law; it is really a statement that is true by definition.

The controversial and critical issue concerns whether the *potential* demand or incomes generated are *actually* spent on the output produced. The pre-Keynesians believed that if households save more than firms wish to borrow to finance investment spending, the rate of interest falls to equate savings with investment. This adjustment mechanism means that Say's Law holds. Keynes disputed this, arguing that in recessionary conditions when business and consumer confidence is low, savings will exceed investment, and there will be a glut or excess of savings. Say's Law breaks down and the resulting deficient demand causes unemployment.

Seasonal unemployment

Seasonal unemployment is a special case of casual unemployment, which occurs when workers are laid off on a short-term basis at certain times of the year. It occurs in trades such as tourism, agriculture, catering and building. When casual unemployment results from regular fluctuations in weather conditions or demand, it is called seasonal unemployment.

> **KEY TERM**
>
> **seasonal unemployment** unemployment arising in different seasons of the year, caused by factors such as the weather and the end of the Christmas shopping period.

CASE STUDY 11.3

Beveridge and full employment

In his 1944 book, *Full Employment in a Free Society*, the British economist William Beveridge said that full employment 'means having always more vacant jobs than unemployed men, not slightly fewer jobs. It means that the jobs are at fair wages, of such a kind, and so located that the unemployed men can reasonably be expected to take them; it means, by consequence, that the normal lag between losing one job and finding another will be very short.'

Beveridge went on to say that full employment does not mean literally no unemployment: that is to say, it does not mean that every man and woman in this country who is fit and free for work is employed productively on every day of his or her working life. He argued that full employment would allow for no more than 3% unemployment due to frictions, but that there always had to be more vacancies than unemployed workers.

In terms of the categories of unemployment we have explained, Beveridge split his 3% unemployment into 1% seasonal, 1% frictional and 1% structural unemployment. In Beveridge's view, these frictions would mean that a worker was never unemployed for anything other than a very short period.

Beveridge also asked who is responsible for maintaining full employment. He believed that 'the ultimate responsibility for seeing that outlay as a whole, taking public and private outlay together, is sufficient to set up a demand for all the labour seeking employment, must be taken by the State'. Full employment required active government support to ensure that aggregate demand was sufficient to maintain employment opportunities for all those who desired to work.

Follow-up questions

1 What is the size of UK unemployment at the time you are reading this case study?
2 Which of the two definitions of full employment, the free-market definition or the Beveridge definition, has most influenced UK governments in recent years? Justify your answer.
3 Is there evidence of cyclical unemployment in the UK today? Explain your answer.
4 Why is seasonal unemployment not significant in the UK?

> **SYNOPTIC LINK**
> Read about the Beveridge definition and the free-market definition of full employment on pages 295–96.

Demand-side and supply-side factors affecting employment and unemployment

As we have explained, cyclical or Keynesian unemployment is caused by a lack of aggregate demand in the economy. This means that it is a demand-side form of unemployment, as for the most part is seasonal unemployment. By contrast, frictional and structural unemployment result from supply-side factors affecting the economy. Appropriate government policies to reduce the different types of unemployment depend on whether they are caused by demand-side or supply-side factors. Cyclical unemployment can be reduced through using fiscal and/or monetary policy to stimulate aggregate demand. However, supply-side policies should be used to reduce frictional and structural unemployment.

TEST YOURSELF 11.10
What is another name for cyclical unemployment?

The real-wage theory of unemployment

Nearly a century ago, large-scale persistent unemployment occurred in the United Kingdom, preceding the spread of unemployment worldwide in the Great Depression of the 1930s. Much of British unemployment in the 1920s probably resulted from the lack of competitiveness and decline of nineteenth-century staple industries such as shipbuilding and textiles. This problem was made worse by an overvalued exchange rate. However, free-market economists blamed a substantial part of the unemployment on excessively high **real wages**.

SYNOPTIC LINK
Overvalued and undervalued exchange rates are explained in Chapter 15.

Unemployment caused by excessively high wage rates is called **real-wage unemployment**, or classical unemployment. This type of disequilibrium unemployment is illustrated in Figure 11.17. In the diagram, full employment (equilibrium employment) is determined where the aggregate demand for labour equals the aggregate supply of labour, shown at point X, at the real wage rate w_{FE}. However, suppose wages are fixed at a higher real rate, at w_1 rather than w_{FE}. At this real wage rate, employers wish to hire E_1 workers, but E_2 workers wish to supply their labour. There is excess supply of labour in the labour market, equal to the horizontal distance between points Z and W: that is, $E_2 - E_1$. (Although Figure 11.17 is a macroeconomic diagram, depicting the economy's aggregate labour market, real-wage unemployment can also be thought of as a microeconomic phenomenon, related to individual labour markets that are in decline.)

Free-market economists argue that, as long as labour markets remain competitive, the resulting real-wage unemployment should be temporary. Competitive forces in the labour market should cure the problem, bidding down the real wage rate to w_{FE} and thereby eliminating the excess supply of labour. Full employment should quickly be restored when the number of workers willing to work once again equals the number of people that firms wish to hire.

But suppose labour market rigidity or 'stickiness', perhaps caused by trade unions, prevents the real wage rate falling below w_1. In this situation, the market mechanism fails to work properly, the excess supply of labour persists, and real-wage unemployment occurs. Pre-Keynesian free-market economists

KEY TERMS
real wages the purchasing power of the nominal (or money) wage; for example, real wages fall when inflation is higher than the rise in the nominal wage rate and real wages rise when the nominal wage rate increases more rapidly than inflation.

real-wage unemployment unemployment caused by real wages being stuck above the equilibrium market-clearing real wage.

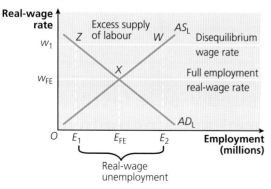

Figure 11.17 Real-wage unemployment in the economy's aggregate labour market

blamed trade unions and other causes of labour market imperfection for the mass unemployment that occurred between the First and Second World Wars. In their view, responsibility for unemployment lay with the workers in work and their trade unions who, by refusing to accept lower wages, prevented the unemployed from pricing themselves into jobs.

Many Keynesian economists believe real-wage unemployment to be involuntary unemployment, caused by wage stickiness or wage inflexibility over which workers have no control. By contrast, free-market economist argue that real-wage unemployment is voluntary unemployment on the grounds that workers and their trade unions should be prepared to accept wage cuts.

TEST YOURSELF 11.11
What is another name for real-wage unemployment?

The natural rate of unemployment

KEY TERMS

equilibrium unemployment exists when the economy's aggregate labour market is in equilibrium. It is the same as the natural *level* of unemployment.

natural rate of unemployment the rate of unemployment when the aggregate labour market is in equilibrium.

As we have already said, full employment does not necessarily mean that every single member of the working population is in work. Instead, it means a situation in which the number of people wishing to work at the going market real wage rate equals the number of workers whom employers wish to hire at this real wage rate. We then stated that even this definition needs qualifying, since in a dynamic economy there is always some frictional and structural unemployment brought about by the changes that are constantly taking place in the economy.

Frictional and structural unemployment make up what is called **equilibrium unemployment**. Equilibrium unemployment, which is also called the natural *level* of unemployment, exists even with the real wage rate at its market-clearing level. Expressed as a *rate* of unemployment, rather than as a *level*, this is the **natural rate of unemployment** (*NRU*).

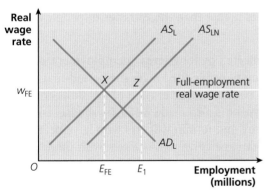

Figure 11.18 The natural *level* of unemployment, shown as OE_1 *minus* OE_{FE}, is made up of frictional and structural unemployment.

The natural *level* of unemployment is illustrated in Figure 11.18. It is shown by the distance E_1 minus E_{FE} (where E_1 indicates the number of workers willing to work at the full employment real wage rate W_{FE}, and E_{FE} is the 'full employment' level of employment). The natural level of unemployment is unemployment occurring when the aggregate labour market is in equilibrium, with the aggregate demand for labour equalling the aggregate supply of labour ($AD_L = AS_L$). In Figure 11.18, point X shows equilibrium *employment*, with the equilibrium wage rate or market-clearing real wage rate at w_{FE}. Full employment occurs when E_{FE} workers are hired. The distance between AS_L and the curve AS_{LN} shows the amount of frictional and structural unemployment in the economy at the full employment wage rate w_{FE}, namely the number of workers who are willing and able to work at this wage rate, but who for frictional and structural reasons cannot get jobs.

SYNOPTIC LINK
We develop the concept of the natural rate of unemployment in section 11.4 of this chapter when exploring possible conflicts between macroeconomic policy objectives.

The consequences of unemployment

The consequences of unemployment for the economy

Unemployment is bad for the economy as a whole, largely through the waste of human capital. When workers are unemployed, not all the economy's productive resources are used to produce output, which, if produced, could add to the material standards of living and economic welfare of the whole population. Instead, the economy produces inside its production possibility frontier and fails to operate to its potential.

Unemployment is also one of the factors that reduce an economy's international competitiveness. High unemployment can reduce incentives for firms to invest in new state-of-the-art technologies that generally lead to increased export competitiveness. The under-investment associated with high unemployment also results from a reduced need to invest in capital-intensive technologies when there are plenty of unemployed workers who are not only available but cheap to hire. In these circumstances, employers continue to use labour-intensive but antiquated technologies, particularly when high unemployment accompanies a stagnant economy, low profits and a climate of business pessimism.

Under-investment can also be caused by the higher business taxes that firms may have to pay to help finance the welfare benefits paid to unemployed workers. While it is true that the Jobseeker's Allowance can be claimed only in the first months of unemployment, in the UK the state continues to pay Universal Credit to families in which there is no wage earner, in order to save family members, particularly children, from the effects of absolute poverty. In 2013, at the time of the introduction of Universal Credit, which is replacing Income Support, the government introduced a benefit cap, which initially limited to £26,000 a year all the benefits an out-of-work family can receive. However, as part of the government's austerity programme, the benefit cap was reduced to £20,000 a year in the 2015 budget. The Conservative government has justified the cap on the grounds that families living solely on benefits should not receive welfare payments higher than the earnings of people on median incomes.

Economies are particularly badly affected by long-term unemployment. A worker may become effectively unemployable the longer the period that he or she is out of work: for example, because of the erosion of job skills and work habits. Long-term unemployment is also made worse by the fact that employers, who might otherwise hire and retrain workers who have been economically inactive for several years, perceive that workers with more recent job experience present fewer risks and are more employable. When inactive workers are seen as unemployable, the economy begins to behave as if it is on its production possibility frontier, even though there are plenty of unemployed workers notionally available for work. An increase in aggregate demand can then lead to inflation rather than to an increase in output and jobs.

Nevertheless, despite the disadvantages of high unemployment for the economy, many free-market economists believe a certain amount of unemployment is necessary to make the economy function better. In particular, by providing downward pressure on wage rates, unemployment can reduce inflation. Unemployment also contributes to a widening of income differentials between better-paid and low-paid workers. Some free-market economists argue that this is a good thing, believing that differences in pay are needed to promote incentives, which then create the supply-side conditions in which the economy can prosper.

The consequences of unemployment for individuals

Unemployment is obviously bad for the unemployed themselves and for their families, largely because of the way in which the low incomes that accompany unemployment lead to low standards of living. However, the costs of unemployment for the unemployed go further than this. Apart from situations in which the unemployed enjoy having 24 hours of leisure time each and every day, or when the so-called 'unemployed' are engaged in black economy activity, unemployment destroys hope in the future. The unemployed become marginalised from normal economic and human activity, and their self-esteem is reduced. Families suffer increased health risks, greater stress, a reduction in the quality of diet, and an increased risk of marital break-up and social exclusion caused by loss of work and income.

> **STUDY TIP**
> Don't confuse the *causes* and *effects* of unemployment.

Government policies to reduce unemployment

When governments intervene to reduce unemployment, the appropriate policy depends on identifying correctly the underlying cause of unemployment. For example, if unemployment is incorrectly diagnosed in terms of demand deficiency, when the true cause is structural, a policy of fiscal or monetary expansion to stimulate aggregate demand will be ineffective and inappropriate. Indeed, reflation of demand in such circumstances would probably create excess demand, which raises the price level with no lasting beneficial effects on employment.

In the long run, the only really effective way to reduce unemployment is to achieve successful economic growth, which increases firms' demand for new employees. This, however, is easier said than done. Free-market economists believe that growth is facilitated by anti-interventionist supply-side policies and by reducing intervention in markets. Chapter 13 explains this in detail. Keynesian economists, by contrast, argue that expansionary fiscal and monetary policy must be used to reduce demand-deficient or cyclical unemployment such as occurred during and after the 2008–09 recession.

Reducing frictional and structural unemployment

Governments can try to reduce frictional unemployment by improving the geographical and occupational mobility of labour, reducing workers' search periods between jobs, and by introducing supply-side policies.

Improving the geographical mobility of labour

Geographical mobility could be improved by making it easier for families to move house from one region to another: for example, by subsidising removal costs. However, the widening difference in UK house prices between south and north is in fact reducing the geographical mobility of labour. Government spending on rented social housing in areas where there are ongoing labour shortages would perhaps be the most effective way of improving the geographical mobility of labour, though for cost and other reasons, this policy is unlikely to be adopted, at least on a scale sufficient to have a significant effect.

Improving the occupational mobility of labour

Governments can improve the occupational mobility of labour by providing retraining schemes and introducing laws to ban professional and trade union restrictive practices that make it difficult for workers to move between jobs. Government retraining schemes are usually less effective than those run by private sector firms. But a problem is that employers in trades such as plumbing often prefer to avoid spending on training their employees, by poaching newly trained workers from the few employers who do invest in training their employees. As a result of this market failure, too few workers may end up being trained.

Reducing employment search periods

The introduction of the Jobseeker's Allowance (JSA) in 1996 was an attempt to reduce search periods between jobs. There have been two types of JSA, contribution based and income based, with the latter currently being merged into a new all-embracing benefit, Universal Benefit. The contributions-based allowance, based on having paid sufficient National Insurance contributions when working, can only be claimed for the first few months of unemployment, providing the claimant is actively seeking work. The allowance creates an incentive for the newly unemployed to accept lower wage rates and to speed up the search for vacancies that meet their (now reduced) aspirations.

Supply-side policies

Supply-side policies (explained in Chapter 13), which try to improve the competitiveness and efficiency of markets, are now used to reduce frictional and structural unemployment. In the past, deindustrialisation led to large-scale structural unemployment, concentrated in regions of decline such as coal fields and areas previously dominated by heavy industry.

Many traditional manufacturing industries and the coal industry have now largely disappeared in the UK, so there is less scope for further structural decline in these activities. The supply-side improvements of the 1980s and 1990s also created conditions in which service industries grew to replace manufacturing. As a result, more workers were able to move from declining industries into growing ones. However, as the recent and current financial services crisis shows, service industries such as banking have themselves become vulnerable to structural decline and to overseas location.

> **STUDY TIP**
> You must appreciate that unemployment has a variety of causes and hence the appropriate policies to reduce unemployment depend on the cause.

TEST YOURSELF 11.12

Table 11.2 shows changes in the UK index of production and total employment over the period from quarter 2 2007 to Quarter 2 2017.

Table 11.2 UK index of production and employment rate, 2007–17

	2007 Q2	2008 Q2	2009 Q2	2010 Q2	2011 Q2	2012 Q2	2013 Q2	2014 Q2	2015 Q2	2016 Q2	2017 Q2
Index of production (2010 = 100)	113.3	111.1	101.0	103.3	103.7	99.9	100.5	101.3	103.0	104.4	104.7
Employment rate (%)	72.7	72.9	70.8	70.4	70.5	70.9	71.3	72.8	73.4	74.4	75.1

With the help of the data, identify and explain **two** significant points of comparison between the changes in the index of production and the employment rate over the period shown.

SECTION 11.2 SUMMARY

- Full employment exists when the number of workers whom firms wish to hire equals the number of workers wanting to work at current market wage rates.
- Frictional unemployment is transitional and 'between jobs' unemployment. It is also voluntary and short term.
- Structural unemployment is usually long term and results from the structural decline of industries and from changes in required job skills.
- Cyclical unemployment is also known as Keynesian and demand-deficient unemployment.
- Keynesian economists argue that cyclical unemployment is involuntary, which means that the people who are unemployed are willing to work at current wage rates but there are not enough jobs available.
- Policies to reduce unemployment will be effective only if the causes of unemployment are correctly diagnosed.
- The costs of unemployment fall on the whole economy and on the unemployed and their families.
- Equilibrium unemployment, which is also known as the natural rate of unemployment, comprises frictional, seasonal and structural unemployment.
- The unemployment that exists when the labour market is in equilibrium is 'voluntary' unemployment.

11.3 Inflation and deflation

A brief history of recent inflation and deflation in the UK

In Chapter 10, we defined inflation as a persistent or continuous rise in the price level, or as a continuing fall in the value of money. Deflation is the opposite, namely a persistent tendency for the price level to fall or for the value of money to rise.

Fifty or so years ago in the 1970s, accelerating and highly variable rates of inflation caused acute problems in the UK economy. As a result, in the monetarist decade of the 1980s, the control of inflation was elevated to pole position among government macroeconomic policy objectives. Eventually, after 1980 when inflation touched 20%, the rate of inflation came down, though it increased again to 10% in 1990. Whether the fall in the rate of inflation was related to 'monetarist' monetary policy is debatable. Nevertheless, from 1993 until 2007, the UK inflation rate remained within 1% above or below the 2% inflation rate target set by the government, apart from on one occasion when it nudged over the 3% upper limit.

SYNOPTIC LINK
The meaning of monetarism is explained later in this section (page 388).

Until 2008, control of inflation was accompanied by arguably the longest period of continuous economic growth the UK has ever experienced, at least in modern times. Many other economies around the world, including the USA, experienced similar conditions of low inflation and steady growth; this period has become known as 'The Great Moderation'. However, in 2007 things started to go wrong. Along with other economies, the UK was hit by a sudden burst of cost-push inflation, mostly imported from the rest of the world via escalating oil, gas, commodity and food prices. Together with the credit crunch that began in the USA, severe cost-push inflation undermined business and consumer confidence. Then, in 2008, the problems in financial markets caused aggregate demand to collapse and the UK economy entered the deepest recession it has experienced since the Second World War. The rate of inflation began to fall, and some economists believed that deflation would replace inflation.

Although, the price level fell for a couple of months, this did not really constitute 'deflation' — defined as a persistent fall in the price level. Sharp, but probably temporary, falls in oil, gas and commodity prices were mainly responsible for the inflation rate dipping below zero, but most commentators were expecting positive inflation to return sooner rather than later. At the time of writing in July 2019, since 2015 inflation has been positive, generally fluctuating between 2% and 3%.

Inflation, deflation and disinflation

Until the 2008–09 recession and immediately after, the overall price level has seldom fallen in western industrialised countries since the 1930s. Since the Keynesian revolution, the phrase 'to deflate the economy' has been applied in a rather looser way to describe a reduction in aggregate demand and levels of economic activity, output and employment. A deflationary policy uses fiscal and/ or monetary policy to reduce aggregate demand, in order to take excess demand out of the system. In this situation, the rate of inflation is likely to fall, but remain positive. As explained earlier, this is known as disinflation. By contrast, *reflation* refers to an increase in economic activity and output, and a reflationary policy stimulates aggregate demand. Often, inflation is 'reflation gone wrong', stimulating the price level rather than real output and employment.

> **TEST YOURSELF 11.13**
> Explain the difference between deflation and disinflation.

Demand-pull and cost-push inflation

There are two basic causes of inflation: excess aggregate demand in the economy, and a general rise in costs of production. The former gives rise to **demand-pull inflation** (or **demand inflation**), while the latter is called **cost-push inflation** (or **cost inflation**). As the names imply, demand-pull inflation locates the cause of inflation in the demand side of the economy, whereas cost-push inflation has supply-side causes.

> **KEY TERMS**
> **demand-pull inflation** (also known as **demand inflation**) a rising price level caused by an increase in aggregate demand, shown by a shift of the *AD* curve to the right.
>
> **cost-push inflation** (also known as **cost inflation**) a rising price level caused by an increase in the costs of production, shown by a shift of the *SRAS* curve to the left.

Demand-pull inflation

As its name indicates, demand-pull inflation is caused by an increase in aggregate demand. If the economy is initially producing on the economy's *SRAS* curve, but below the normal capacity level of output (which means to the left of the *LRAS* curve), the price level has to rise to persuade firms to produce more output to meet the extra demand. In part, this is because firms incur higher costs when they produce more goods. For firms to maximise profit, higher prices are needed to reward firms for producing more output. Once the *LRAS* curve is reached, higher prices can temporarily encourage firms to produce beyond this point, but the increase in output cannot be sustained. The quantity of goods and services produced falls back to the normal capacity level of output, though there is no fall in the price level.

To remind you, the equation summarising the different elements of aggregate demand is:

$$AD = C + I + G + (X - M)$$

An increase in *any* of the components of aggregate demand, *C*, *I*, *G* or (*X* – *M*), can lead to demand-pull inflation. Increases in consumption spending (*C*) by households or current government spending (*G*) — for example, on public sector pay — may create the extra demand which pulls up the price level.

Investment spending and government spending on capital goods shift the *LRAS* curve rightwards. In the *long run*, a shift of the *LRAS* curve to the right can offset demand-pull inflationary pressures.

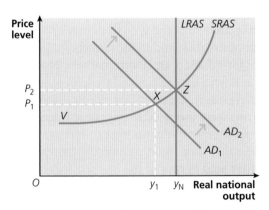

Figure 11.19 Demand-pull inflation illustrated by an *AD/AS* diagram

Aggregate demand/aggregate supply (*AD/AS*) diagrams can illustrate the main features of both demand-pull and cost-push inflation. Figure 11.19 illustrates demand-pull inflation.

In the graph, we have assumed that equilibrium national income is initially at point *X*. The *AD* curve is in the position AD_1; real output is at level y_1 and the price level is P_1.

Given this initial situation, any event that shifts the *AD* curve to the right — for example, to AD_2 — causes the price level to rise, in this case to P_2. In this example, real income increases to its normal capacity level of y_N. At the price level P_1, the economy's firms are only prepared to produce an output of y_1. This means that a higher price level is needed to create the conditions in which firms increase output from y_1 to y_N.

Figure 11.19 shows an economy initially producing below the normal capacity level of output, and then moving to normal capacity, once the *AD* curve has shifted right to *AD*$_2$. Following the increase in aggregate demand, equilibrium national income is at point *Z*, with the economy also on its long-run aggregate supply (*LRAS*) curve. In this situation, the economy is producing at normal capacity, so any further shift of aggregate demand to the right would result solely in the long run in demand-pull inflation, with no increase in real output (except possibly on a temporary basis).

Contrast this outcome with what would happen if the *AD* curve had initially been located substantially to the left of *AD*$_1$: for example, at point *V*. The economy would be in deep recession, suffering severe demand-deficient or cyclical unemployment. Given this initial position, a shift of aggregate demand to the right would increase output and employment, with relatively little effect on inflation to start with. Arguably, the adverse effect of a rising price level would be less significant than the boost to output and employment brought about by an increase in aggregate demand. However, as the increasing slope of the *SRAS* curve suggests, as the *AD* curve shifts right and moves closer to the *LRAS* curve, increasingly the *reflation* of real output (and employment) gives way to *inflation* of the price level.

Cost-push inflation

During the Keynesian era in the 1960s and 1970s, the rate of inflation increased even when there was little evidence of excess demand in the economy. This led to the development of the theory of cost-push inflation. Cost theories of inflation often locate the cause of inflation in structural and institutional conditions on the supply side of the economy, particularly in the labour market and the wage-bargaining process (known as wage-cost inflation), though rising prices of energy and/or commodities can also cause cost-push inflation (called import-cost inflation).

Cost-push theories generally argue that the growth of monopoly power in the economy's labour market and in its markets for goods and services is responsible for inflation. In labour markets, growing trade union strength in the Keynesian era enabled trade unions to bargain for money wage increases in excess of any rise in labour productivity. Monopoly firms were prepared to pay these wage increases, partly because of the costs of disrupting production, and partly because they believed that they could pass on the increasing costs as price rises when they sold output in the markets for their goods.

The *AD/AS* diagram in Figure 11.20 illustrates cost-push inflation. Once again (as is the case in Figure 11.19, which illustrates demand-pull inflation), equilibrium national income is at point *X*, with real output and the price level respectively at y_1 and P_1. In this case, the money costs of production that firms incur when they produce output rise: for example, because money wages or the price of imported raw materials increase. The increase in production costs causes the *SRAS* curve to shift left and up from *SRAS*$_1$ to *SRAS*$_2$.

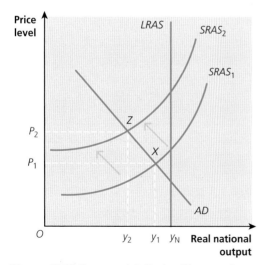

Figure 11.20 Cost-push inflation illustrated on an *AD/AS* diagram

As a result of the shift of the *SRAS* curve to the left, the price level increases to P_2, but higher production costs have reduced the equilibrium level of output that firms are willing to produce to y_2. The new equilibrium national income is at point Z. The economy could be in recession, in which case recessionary effects may moderate the cost increases.

Why it is important to diagnose correctly the causes of inflation?

Just as a government must correctly diagnose the cause or causes of unemployment when implementing policies to reduce the level of unemployment, so it (and its central bank) must first determine whether inflation is caused by excess demand or by cost-push factors when deciding on the appropriate policies to reduce or control inflation.

In the early 2000s, the Bank of England, which is responsible for counter-inflation policy, generally assumed that UK inflation is caused by excess aggregate demand. More recently, the Bank has acknowledged that rising import prices are responsible for cost-push inflation. Before then, the increase in aggregate demand that occurred in the 1990s and early 2000s was accompanied by an absence of cost-push inflationary pressure. This was partly due to the success of the supply-side policies implemented in the 1980s and 1990s. These policies, which are explained in Chapter 13, improved labour market flexibility partly by attacking the power of trade unions. The UK economy was also benefiting from the benign effect of globalisation, which at the time reduced the prices of imported manufactured goods.

As long as the assumption holds that inflation is caused primarily by excess aggregate demand, raising or lowering interest rates (that is, monetary policy) remains an appropriate policy for controlling inflation. The fact that interest rate policy kept the rate of inflation within the government's target range in virtually every month between 1997 and 2007 gave further support to the view held at the time that UK inflation had been primarily of the demand-pull kind.

However, as indicated, cost-push inflationary pressures have now become significant, particularly those stemming from the increased prices of imported energy and commodities such as copper. In this situation, raising interest rates to reduce aggregate demand can be an ineffective policy for tackling cost-push inflation, unless it is argued that the economy should suffer a severe recession in order to reduce the demand for imported oil, gas and industrial raw materials. If this argument is correct, UK governments now have to face up to the fact that they may lack the tools, apart from interest rates (and other monetary instruments which are discussed in Chapter 12), for controlling the rate of inflation.

How theories of the causes of inflation have changed over the years

Table 11.3 provides a summary of how theories of inflation have developed over the years, and of how the rate of inflation has changed in the UK in recent decades.

Table 11.3 Theories of inflation and details of recent UK inflation

Eighteenth century to the 1930s	The old quantity theory of money is dominant.
1930s	The problem of inflation disappears. Keynes's *General Theory* explains deflation in terms of deficient aggregate demand.
1940 and 1950s	Keynesians develop Keynes's ideas to explain how, in conditions of full employment, excess demand can pull up the price level through demand-pull inflation.
1950s	The early monetarist theory of inflation begins to develop when Milton Friedman revives the quantity theory of money (the modern quantity theory).
1950s–1960s	Many Keynesians switch away from the demand-pull to the cost-push theory of inflation.
1960s	The Phillips curve (explained in section 11.4) is introduced into the Keynesian demand-pull versus cost-push debate.
1968	The role of expectations in the inflationary process is incorporated into the monetarist theory of inflation. The theory of adaptive expectations is built into Milton Friedman's theory of the long-run Phillips curve.
1970s	The Phillips curve relationship appears to break down with the emergence of stagflation.
1980s onward	There is controversy once again between cost-push and demand-pull explanations of inflation, with New Keynesian explanations versus monetarist and free-market explanations, and the latter incorporating rational expectations into their models of the economy.
2008 onward	For a short period the problem of inflation largely disappeared, being replaced by the fear of deflation or a falling price level.
2015 onward	Deflation, which had been a temporary phenomenon, gives way to a low rate of inflation which continues at least until 2019.

The quantity theory of money and monetarism

Monetarism

Around 50 years ago, a group of generally pro-free-market economists became known as **monetarists**. Monetarist economists subscribe to the demand-pull theory of inflation, but they go one stage further by arguing that excess aggregate demand for output is caused by a prior increase in the money supply. To quote the leading monetarist economist Milton Friedman, monetarists believe that 'inflation is always and everywhere a monetary phenomenon'. Monetarist economic theory is known as **monetarism**. In its narrowest sense, monetarism is the theory that inflation is caused by an increase in the money supply. In a wider meaning, it is a name given to pro-free-market economic theories and policies.

> **KEY TERMS**
>
> **monetarists** economists who argue that a prior increase in the money supply is the cause of inflation.
>
> **monetarism** narrow monetarism centres on increases in the money supply as the prime cause of inflation. Broader monetarism focuses on the virtues of free markets in resource allocation.

The quantity theory of money

A very old theory that originated hundreds of years ago, the **quantity theory of money**, lies at the heart of the monetarist theory of inflation. Suppose the government creates or condones an expansion of the money supply greater than the increase in real national output. As a result, according to the quantity theory, households and firms end up holding excess money balances which, when spent, pull up the price level — provided real output does not expand in line with the increase in spending power. At its simplest, the quantity theory is sometimes described as too much money chasing too few goods.

The equation of exchange

The starting point for developing the theory is the **equation of exchange**, devised by an American economist, Irving Fisher, early in the twentieth century:

$$\text{money supply (stock of money)} \times \text{the velocity of circulation of money} = \text{price level} \times \text{quantity of output}$$

or:

$$MV = PQ$$

In the equation, for a particular time period, say a year, the stock of money in the economy (M) multiplied by the velocity of circulation of money (V) equals the price level (P) multiplied by the quantity of real output (Q) in the economy. On the left-hand side of the equation, the velocity of circulation (V) is the speed at which money circulates around the economy when people use money to buy goods. Monetarists argue that V is constant or at least stable. This means that, when M increases, it is spent on goods and services. If Q is unable to increase, the price level P is pulled up by excess demand. Keynesian economists, by contrast, believe that when M increases, it may be partially absorbed by a slowdown in V, which means that much of the extra money is not spent on consumer goods and services. (However, some of the extra money might be spent on investment in new capital goods, which would have a beneficial effect on aggregate demand and economic growth, stimulating Q rather than P.) In summary, PQ, on the right-hand side of the equation, can increase, either because real output increases or because the price level increases.

The equation of exchange is often written as $MV = PT$, where T stands for total transactions taking place in the economy. This is the version of the equation first stated by the American economist, Irving Fisher. A transaction occurs whenever a good or service is bought and sold. Total transactions include second-hand transactions as well as the exchange of new goods and services. Because of this PQ is a better measure than PT of expenditure on national output.

389

Why Keynesian economists generally reject the quantity theory of money

Keynesians generally reject the quantity theory of money as an explanation of inflation, or claim that it only provides an explanation of rising prices when a number of highly restrictive assumptions hold. There are three main ways in which Keynesians have attacked the quantity theory.

The velocity of circulation is not constant

Much of the debate between Keynesians and monetarists about the quantity theory has centred on the issue of whether the velocity of circulation of money (V) is constant. In ordinary language, V represents how often money is spent. Monetarists believe that, because money earns little or no interest, it is generally rational to spend quickly any extra money holdings, either on goods or on non-money financial assets such as shares, and not to hold idle money balances for any length of time. By contrast, Keynesians take the opposite view, arguing that under certain circumstances (particularly when share and bond prices are expected to fall), it is perfectly sensible to hold idle money balances. In this situation, to avoid capital losses they expect to suffer from falling financial asset prices, people decide to hold money instead as an idle wealth asset. They hang on to, rather than spend, their extra money holdings.

Under-full employment equilibrium

Keynesians also attack the quantity theory by arguing that if there is spare capacity and unemployment in the economy, an increase of the money supply may increase real income and output (y and Q) rather than the price level P. In the Keynesian view, market forces are too weak and take too long to return the economy to its normal capacity output. This means that the economy can get stuck in an under-full employment equilibrium.

Reverse causation

The two Keynesian attacks on the quantity theory we have so far examined accept the monetarist argument that changes in MV can cause changes in PQ, but they argue that an increase in the money supply (M) does not *necessarily* result in inflation (an increase in P). Instead an increase in the money supply may be absorbed in a slowing down of the velocity of circulation of money (V), or in a reflation of real income or output, which is a good thing.

The third Keynesian attack on the quantity theory is more deep-seated, since it is based on the idea of *reverse causation*. Instead of changes in the money supply causing changes in the price level, the true relationship is the opposite: changes in the price level cause the money supply to change. In this interpretation, inflation is caused by cost-push institutional factors in the real economy. The money supply then passively adapts, expanding to the level required to finance the level of desired transactions that the general public undertake at the new higher price level. In essence, the money supply accommodates itself to (rather than determines) the price level.

Keynesians agree with the monetarists over what they consider to be the rather trivial point that an increase in the money supply is needed to finance a higher price level and allow inflation to continue. However, the reverse causation argument rejects the view that an increase in the money supply is the cause of inflation. The monetarist response is that if the central bank were to exert control over the money supply, a temporary rise in the price level caused by rising costs could not persist.

Keynesians argue that if a government tightly restricts the growth of money to try to stem inflation, the main effect might be that the current level of transactions cannot be financed, so real activity will fall, resulting in higher unemployment. This effect occurred in the credit crunch that started in 2007, though the cause of the credit crunch lay not in tight control of the money supply by the government, but in a sudden collapse in the supply of money or liquidity emanating from the banking system itself.

TEST YOURSELF 11.16

Explain the meaning of the velocity of circulation of money.

The role of expectations in the inflationary process

It is now widely accepted by economists that people's expectations of *future* inflation can affect the *current* rate of inflation. Along with the quantity theory of money, expectations of future inflation are an important part of the monetarist theory of inflation. The leading monetarist Milton Friedman was one of the first economists to draw attention to the role of expectations in the inflationary process.

Theories of expectation formation are complicated. Two theories of expectations formation are described in the extension material which follows. However, the central idea is simple: if people expect that the rate of inflation next year is going to be high, they will behave in an inflationary way now, and their behaviour will deliver high inflation next year. Trade unions and workers bargain for higher wages, and their employers then raise prices, in anticipation of tomorrow's higher expected inflation rate. Workers and firms try to 'get their retaliation in first', to avoid being left behind when the inflation rate they are expecting eventually materialises.

Likewise, when people expect the inflation rate to fall, they behave in a way that enables low inflation to be achieved. Governments therefore try to talk down the rate of inflation by convincing people that government policies are credible and that the government (and its central bank) know how to reduce inflation. The UK government's decision to make the Bank of England operationally independent in 1997 was part of an attempt to convince people (and financial markets) of the *credibility* of government policies and of its determination to keep the rate of inflation low. However, when the Bank fails to hit the 2% inflation rate target, credibility is eroded.

Inflation psychology

One of the factors that has made inflation difficult to control in the UK has been the existence, built up over decades, of an 'inflation psychology'. Over the years, many groups in British society, including house owners, wage earners in strong bargaining positions, and also governments, have done extremely well out of inflation. Home owners with large mortgages, and also the government, have a vested interest in allowing inflation to continue in order to reduce the real value of their accumulated debt. (Indeed, property owners do even better when house price inflation exceeds the general rate of inflation. In this situation, the real value of houses increases while the real value of mortgages falls.)

Between 1997 and 2007 UK governments successfully cut through much of this inflation psychology by convincing people that inflation would remain low and around the target inflation rate of 2%. Because of this benign effect on people's behaviour and their expectations, it became much easier to control inflation. However, even in these years, some economists argued that circumstances could change quickly for the worse, and that inflationary dangers should be regarded as dormant rather than dead. In 2008 and 2011, inflation did indeed raise its ugly head once again and the same may be true in the future.

Two theories of expectations formation

The two theories about how people form their expectations of future inflation are called the *theory of adaptive expectations* and the *theory of rational expectations*. To understand the difference between the theories of adaptive and rational expectations, consider the situation of a gambler deciding whether to place a bet on a particular horse winning a race. Three races ago, the horse ended the race in fourth position, improving to third place two races ago, and to second place recently. Forming his expectations adaptively, the gambler decides to bet on the horse, expecting it now to win. But gambling on the basis of recent form alone could be less successful than a strategy that makes use of all the information available, including, of course, past form. Information about the quality of the jockey, and about other matters such as the qualities of the other horses and their jockeys, the length of the race, the state of the track, and perhaps 'inside information' provided by a stable lad, might lead to a more rational gambling decision.

This story does not mean that a gambler, forming expectations rationally, always wins his bets. He may win or lose, just as bets made on decisions formed adaptively, or by picking a name out of a hat, may be right or wrong. However, over a long sequence of races, it is likely that gambling decisions formed on the basis of rational expectations produce better outcomes than decisions formed adaptively or randomly. The more 'perfect' the information on which rational expectations are formed, the more likely it is that the expectations prove correct. It is less sensible to gamble on the basis of limited information when more up-to-date and relevant information is available.

Modern free-market economists believe that it is unrealistic to assume that a rational economic agent, acting on self-interest, forms expectations of future inflation solely on the basis of past or experienced inflation. Self-interest requires quick modification of economic behaviour in line with expectations formed on the basis of the most up-to-date information available.

The first stage in the development of the monetarist theory of inflation was Milton Friedman's revival of the quantity theory of money in the 1950s. The second stage, again developed by Milton Friedman, was the incorporation of the theory of adaptive expectation into the monetarist theory. We shall explain this shortly when we explain the Phillips curve.

The incorporation of the theory of rational expectations into the explanation of the inflationary process represents the third stage in the development of monetarist and free-market theories of inflation.

TEST YOURSELF 11.17
Is inflation always bad?

The consequences of inflation for the performance of the economy and for individuals

Inflation can impose serious costs on both the economy and individuals, and the seriousness of these costs depends on whether individuals successfully anticipate the inflation rate. If inflation could be anticipated with complete certainty, some economists argue that it would pose few problems. Households and firms would simply build the expected rate of inflation into their economic decisions, which would not be distorted by wrong guesses.

STUDY TIP
You should discuss the benefits and costs of inflation when explaining the effects of inflation on the economy.

When inflation is relatively low, with little variation from year to year, it is quite easy to anticipate next year's inflation rate. Indeed, creeping inflation, which is associated with growing markets, healthy profits and a general climate of business optimism, *greases the wheels* of the economy. Viewed in this way, a low rate of inflation — and not absolute price stability or zero inflation — may be a necessary side-effect or cost of expansionary policies to reduce unemployment.

However, rather than greasing its wheels, inflation may *throw sand in the wheels* of the economy, making it less efficient and competitive. If the 'sand-in-the-wheels' effect is stronger than the 'greasing-the-wheels' effect, the costs or disadvantages of inflation exceed the benefits or advantages.

A low but stable inflation rate may also be necessary to make labour markets function efficiently. Even if average real wage rates are rising, there will be some labour markets in which real wages must fall in order to maintain a low rate of unemployment. When prices are completely stable (that is, when the inflation rate is zero), to cut real wage rates, nominal wage rates have to fall. To save jobs, workers may be willing to accept falling real wages caused by money wage rates rising at a slower rate than inflation. However, workers are much less willing to accept cuts in money wage rates. Thus, with zero inflation, the changes required in relative real wage rates, which are needed to make labour markets function efficiently, fail to take place. Labour markets function best when inflation is low but stable. By contrast, absolute price stability produces wage stickiness, which results in unnecessarily high unemployment.

Some of the disadvantages of inflation

- **Distributional effects.** Weaker social groups in society, living on fixed incomes, lose, while those in strong bargaining positions gain. Also, with rapid inflation, real rates of interest may be negative. In this situation, lenders are really paying borrowers for the doubtful privilege of lending to them, and inflation acts as a hidden tax, redistributing income and wealth from lenders to borrowers.
- **Distortion of normal economic behaviour.** Inflation can distort consumer behaviour by causing households to bring forward purchases and hoard goods if they expect the rate of inflation to accelerate. Similarly, firms may divert funds out of productive investment in fixed investment projects into unproductive commodity hoarding and speculation. People are affected by *inflationary noise*. This occurs when changes in relative prices (that is, a rise or fall in the price of *one* good) is confused with a change in the *general* price level or inflation.
- **Breakdown in the functions of money.** In a severe inflation, money becomes less useful and efficient as a medium of exchange and store of value. In the most extreme form of inflation, a hyperinflation in which the rate of inflation accelerates to a minimum of several hundred per cent a year, less efficient barter replaces money and imposes extra costs on most transactions.
- **Reduced international uncompetitiveness.** When inflation is higher than in competitor countries, exports increase in price, putting pressure on a fixed exchange rate. Lower growth and rising unemployment are likely to result. With a floating exchange rate, the exchange rate falls to restore competitiveness, but rising import prices may fuel a further bout of inflation.

- **Shoe leather and menu costs.** Consumers incur shoe leather costs, spending time and effort shopping around and checking which prices have or have not risen. By contrast, menu costs are incurred by firms having to adjust price lists more often.

The consequences of deflation

Common sense might suggest that if inflation is generally seen to be bad, its opposite, deflation or a falling price level, must be good, both for the performance of the economy and for individuals. However, extended price deflation may bring its own problems. When people believe prices are going to fall, they postpone big-ticket consumption decisions: for example, replacing their cars. This may erode business confidence and trigger recession or deepen and lengthen an already existing recession. However, this assumes that falling prices are the result of a *bad* or *malign* deflation rather than a *good* or *benign* deflation.

The difference between the two is illustrated in Figure 11.21. A good or benign deflation, shown in Figure 11.21(a), results from improvements in the economy's supply side, which reduces business costs of production. Both the *SRAS* curve and the *LRAS* curve shift to the right and, assuming the *AD* curve does not itself shift, the price level falls, but output and employment rise. However, in the recessionary conditions existent in the UK economy in 2009, it was much more likely that a falling price level would signal a bad deflation. A bad or 'malign' deflation, shown in Figure 11.21(b), is caused by a collapse of aggregate demand, negative multiplier effects and possibly a credit crunch.

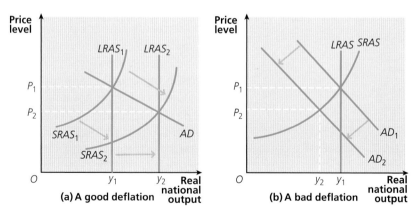

Figure 11.21 Good or benign and bad or malign deflations

STUDY TIP
Make sure you don't confuse deflation and disinflation.

CASE STUDY 11.4

Are lower prices a good thing? Not really

Deflation — if it gets out of control — can be just as bad as inflation. Like inflation, deflation is a form of monetary instability. It disrupts the price mechanism, so people become confused about the true value of things. Consumers see prices are going to fall, so they defer purchases and even procrastinate on other decisions, such as getting married, in the expectation that it will be cheaper later. Pay rises are few and far between. Economic growth is almost non-existent.

In a deflation interest rates may appear to be low, but may actually be high. This is explained by the difference between nominal interest rates and real ones. For example, if the Bank of England's base rate is 2%, and prices are falling at 3%, real interest rates are actually 5%. The cost of borrowing is, therefore, actually higher than people think. Owing £10 is a heavier burden at the end of the year than it was at the beginning. A factory must sell more widgets, a farmer more milk and a shop more goods to meet those monthly interest payments.

When people wake up to this, they might take steps to remedy the situation quickly. For individuals, the key is the housing market. If it cracks and those with huge mortgages — secured on a dwindling asset — suddenly put their homes up for sale, a deflationary spiral could erupt. In a period of deflation, the real value of people's debt rises; this reduces net wealth and often leads to lower spending.

Follow-up questions

1 Who may benefit from deflation in an economy?
2 What is a 'deflationary spiral'?
3 When house prices fall, young people who have only recently bought their first houses may fall into a negative equity trap. Explain what this means.
4 In the 2008–09 recession the UK government paid motorists £2,000 if they scrapped an old car which they owned. This was nicknamed 'cash for clunkers'. What was the economic aim of this car scrappage scheme?

The effect of world commodity prices on domestic inflation

More than 40 years ago, it was generally assumed that rising wage costs were the main cause of cost-push inflation in the UK. More recently, there has been less evidence of wage-cost inflation. When it occurs, it may be largely restricted to the effect of salary increases among bankers, top business executives, premier league footballers and the like far exceeding the rise in their labour productivity. Additionally, trade unions representing public-sector workers such as train drivers on the London Underground have contributed to cost-push inflation, though from 2008 to 2017 the wages of most ordinary workers rose at a slower rate than inflation, and in some cases not at all.

Cost-push inflation does still exist, but it is caused mainly by the rising prices of imported food, energy and raw materials, and to a lesser extent in recent years by rising prices of manufactured goods imported from China. The resulting import-cost inflation is shown by a shift of the *SRAS* curve to the left. Figure 11.22 shows in index number form how world commodity prices changed between January 2014 and February 2018.

Indices (Jan 2014 = 100)

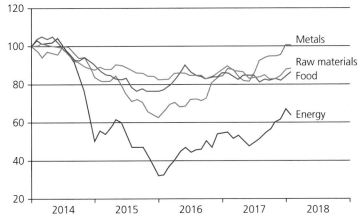

Source: World Bank Commodity Price Statistics

Figure 11.22 Changes in world commodity prices, January 2014–February 2018 (January 2014 = 100)

395

In 2014, the UK inflation rate was brought down by falling prices of imported food, energy and raw materials. However, this fall was short lived. Many commentators believe that with faster economic growth in commodity-consuming countries, especially emerging-market countries, and limited natural resources, 'spikes' in world commodity prices will frequently occur.

TEST YOURSELF 11.18

How does a fall in world commodity prices usually cause the UK rate of inflation to fall?

TEST YOURSELF 11.19

The data in Figure 11.22 are presented in the form of index numbers. Were the prices of food and all the other commodities the same in January 2014? Were energy prices lower than metal prices for most of the data period? Explain your answers.

How do changes in other countries affect UK inflation?

The answer to this question is partly provided by the information in the above paragraphs. However, other arguments can also be made.

First, the UK is now just a small part of a globalised system in which it has very little power to influence the state of the world economy. When times are good in the world economy, with rising demand for commodities and hence rising prices, the UK tends to import inflation from booming economies in the rest of the world. The prices of imported food and raw materials increase, which leads to the UK suffering import-cost inflation. Conversely, when times are bad in the world economy, with other countries experiencing recession, pressure on UK inflation is reduced. In the extreme, falling worldwide demand for UK exports, and the associated leftward shift of the *AD* curve, could lead to falling prices or deflation. Disinflation, which as we have seen is a fall in the rate of *positive* inflation, is, however, more likely to occur than *negative* inflation or deflation. Finally, a fall in the pound's exchange rate against other currencies contributes to imported cost-push inflation.

Second, two countries, the USA and China, are particularly significant in how they can affect the UK price level. It has been said that when 'America sneezes, the rest of the world catches a cold'. The USA is so important for the UK as a source of export demand, inward investment, and business and consumer confidence, that an American downturn can exert downward pressure on the UK inflation rate. Conversely, a booming American economy, as in 2018, tends to have the opposite effect.

China's influence on the UK inflation rate is a little different. For many decades, British consumers benefited from falling prices of manufactured goods imported from China. This reduced the UK's rate of inflation. However, more recently, costs of production have risen in China, partly as a result of increased wages paid to China's labour force. Rising prices of manufactured goods, imported from China and other emerging-market economies, are increasing retail prices in the UK. As yet, however, the effect has been mild.

Outside shocks spreading from other countries also affect UK inflation. A sudden rise in oil prices caused by events in the Middle East will increase UK inflation. Conversely, the rapid growth of oil fracking in the USA has dampened world oil prices.

STUDY TIP

Make sure you are aware of important events taking place in the world economy, particularly in the European Union and in the USA.

SECTION 11.3 SUMMARY

- Inflation is a continuing or persistent rise in the average price level.
- In the UK, the retail prices index (RPI) and the consumer prices index (CPI) are used for measuring inflation.
- The CPI is now used for the indexation of welfare benefits, as well as for setting the inflation rate target.
- Demand-pull inflation results from the fact that, when aggregate demand increases, firms are only prepared to produce and supply more output if prices increase.
- The monetarist theory of inflation, which stems from the quantity theory of money, is a version of the demand-pull theory.
- Cost-push inflation results from higher costs of production experienced by businesses.
- Demand-pull inflation and cost-push inflation can both be illustrated on *AD/AS* diagrams.
- Deflation is a continuing or persistent tendency for the price level to fall.
- Deflation is usually thought to be bad, but there can be good deflations.
- Disinflation, which is often confused with deflation, is a slowing down in the rate of inflation.
- It is important to diagnose correctly the cause(s) of inflation when selecting policies to reduce the rate of inflation.

11.4 Conflicts between macroeconomic policy objectives

In Chapter 9 we outlined the main conflicts between macroeconomic objectives, and the resulting policy trade-offs that can face governments, particularly in the short run. Over the years, UK macroeconomic policy has been influenced and constrained by four significant short-run conflicts between policy objectives. To recap, these conflicts have been between:

- the internal policy objectives of full employment and growth and the external objective of achieving a satisfactory balance of payments
- achieving low unemployment and controlling inflation
- increasing the rate of economic growth and achieving a more equal distribution of income and wealth
- higher living standards now and higher living standards in the future

With regard to the third trade-off, by taxing the rich more and then transferring the tax revenues to the poor in the form of welfare benefits, UK governments have tried to reduce income inequalities. However, free-market economists have argued that such policies reduce entrepreneurial and personal incentives in labour markets, which make the economy less competitive and the growth rate slower. In the free-market view, greater inequalities are necessary to promote the conditions in which rapid and sustainable economic growth can take place.

Moving on to the fourth trade-off, in the short term, the easiest way to increase living standards is to boost consumption. However, this 'live now, pay later' approach means sacrificing saving and investment, which in the long run may reduce economic growth.

When economic policy objectives are mutually exclusive, it is impossible for governments to achieve all of these objectives at the same time — at least in the short run. The result of this is that governments often trade off between policy objectives, attempting for example to combine *relatively* low unemployment with *relatively* low inflation on the grounds that full employment and absolute price stability cannot be achieved together.

Another possibility is that, over time, governments change their ranking of policy objectives. To win votes, a government may aim for low unemployment in the months before a general election, knowing that if the election is won, policy may have to be switched to the control of inflation. In the 5 years between the 2010 and 2015 UK general elections, the Conservative/Lib Dem coalition government started with policies of severe austerity which dampened growth and slowed down job creation. However, as the 2015 election approached, the austerity programme was replaced to a certain extent with more expansionary policies. Many commentators argued, however, that after the 2015 election, severe austerity policies would once again be resumed, which indeed they largely were.

Pro-free-market economists generally believe that successful supply-side policies, combined with supply-side reform in the private sector, facilitate the production of high-quality goods and services which people, in the UK and abroad, wish to buy. The recent success of car manufacturing in the UK is quoted as evidence. According to this supply-side view, in the long run, the sustained economic growth which results resolves short-run conflicts between policy objectives. The supply-side approach to economic policy is explained in Chapter 13.

STUDY TIP
It is useful to understand the difference, and also the links, between a policy conflict and trading off between conflicting policy objectives.

TEST YOURSELF 11.20
What is meant by a policy conflict?

How negative and positive output gaps relate to unemployment and inflationary pressures

The upper panel of Figure 11.23 shows an economy experiencing a volatile economic cycle. This means that the country's output gaps, both positive and negative are large, compared to those illustrated in the lower panel of the diagram which depicts a smoother or more stable economic cycle.

Assuming that inflation increases and unemployment falls when there is a growing positive output gap, and that the opposite is the case with a growing negative output gap, the policy conflict between achieving these two policy objectives is greatest, the more stark the difference between the size of the positive and negative output gaps.

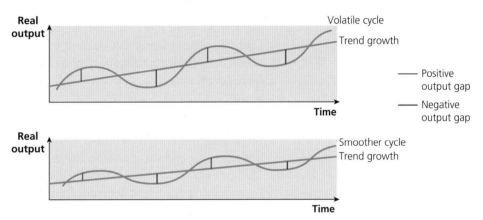

Figure 11.23 Output gaps and volatile and smooth economic cycles

TEST YOURSELF 11.21
Distinguish between a negative output gap and a positive output gap.

Policy conflicts and the Phillips curve
The short-run Phillips curve

The debate between economists over whether inflation is mostly caused by demand-pull or cost-push factors is sometimes conducted with the aid of a statistical relationship, the **Phillips curve**, which is illustrated in Figure 11.24.

KEY TERM
Phillips curve based on evidence from the economy, shows the apparent relationship between the rate of inflation and the rate of unemployment. Now known as 'the short-run Phillips curve'.

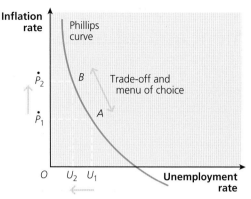

Figure 11.24 The policy choices indicated by the Phillips curve

The Phillips curve is named after the Keynesian economist A.W. Phillips, whom we mentioned on page 327 in chapter 10 in the context of the Phillips machine. Phillips argued that statistical evidence showed that in a period covering nearly a century, a stable inverse relationship existed between the rate of change of wages (the rate of wage inflation) and the percentage of the labour force unemployed. Later versions of the Phillips curve, such as the one illustrated in Figure 11.24, measure the inverse relationship between unemployment and the rate of price inflation.

The Phillips curve is a purported statistical relationship between two variables, and not in itself a theory of inflation. However, both the demand-pull and the cost-push theories of inflation can be used to explain the apparent relationship. In the demand-pull explanation, the factor causing unemployment to fall, moving up the Phillips curve, is excess demand, which pulls up money wages and the average price level. By contrast, in the cost-push explanation, falling unemployment means that trade union power increases, enabling unions to use their growing monopoly power over the supply of labour to push for higher wages.

Either way, the statistical evidence shown in the Phillips curve illustrates the conflict between full employment and control of inflation as policy objectives. It also suggests how the conflict can be dealt with. Suppose unemployment initially is U_1 and the rate of inflation is $\dot{P}_1$ with the economy at point A on the Phillips curve. (Note the symbol $\dot{P}$ is used to show the rate of price inflation.) By increasing aggregate demand, the government can move the economy to point B. The unemployment rate falls to U_2, but at the cost of a higher rate of inflation at $\dot{P}_2$. By using demand management policies, it appears possible for governments to trade off between increasing the number of jobs in the economy and reducing inflation. Points such as A and B on the Phillips curve represent a menu of choice for governments when deciding an acceptable combination of unemployment and inflation.

The long-run Phillips curve

Economists now generally recognise that the Phillips curve in Figure 11.24 is a short-run Phillips curve ($SRPC$), representing the short-run relationship between inflation and unemployment. In the next diagram, Figure 11.25, a vertical long-run Phillips curve ($LRPC$) has been added to the graph, intersecting the short-run Phillips curve where the rate of inflation is zero. The rate of unemployment at this point is the natural *rate* of unemployment (NRU), depicted by the symbol U_N. (As we explained earlier in the chapter, when expressed as the unemployment level, it is called the natural *level* of unemployment.)

Free-market economists argue that it is impossible to reduce unemployment *below* the natural level of unemployment, except at the cost of suffering an ever-accelerating and unanticipated rate of inflation. This would be likely to accelerate into a hyperinflation, which would then wreak severe damage on the economy. The explanation for this lies in the fact that the original Keynesian explanation of the (short-run) Phillips curve wrongly took into account only the *current* rate of inflation and ignored the important

> **TEST YOURSELF 11.22**
> Name the variables shown on the vertical and the horizontal axes of a Phillips curve diagram.

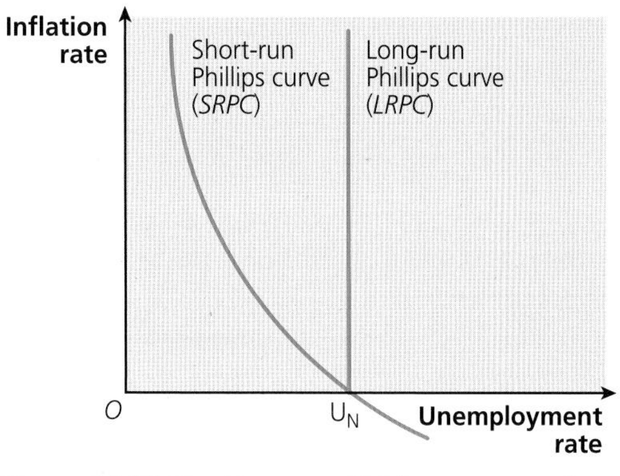

Figure 11.25 The long-run Phillips curve and the natural rate of unemployment

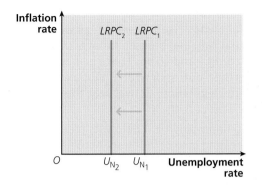

Figure 11.26 Successful supply-side policies shift the long-run Phillips curve to the left

influence of the *expected* rate of inflation. If the government increases aggregate demand with the aim of reducing unemployment below the natural level, people revise upwards their expectations of *future* inflation. This then leads to higher *current* inflation. Continuous upward revision of expected inflation, of course, leads to higher and higher rates of current inflation.

The immediate solution, according to free-market economists, is for the government to respond to its mistake in trying to keep unemployment *below* its natural level, by reducing aggregate demand so as to take unemployment back to its natural level. However, the long-term solution is to reduce the natural level itself. This can be done by implementing appropriate supply-side policies (see Chapter 13), which shift the long-run Phillips curve to the left. In Figure 11.26, the curve shifts from $LRPC_1$ to $LRPC_2$, and the natural rate of unemployment falls from U_{N1} to U_{N2}. In essence, supply-side economists argue that providing the 'correct' supply-side policies are implemented, the policy objectives of reducing unemployment and controlling inflation are compatible in the long run, though not necessarily in the short run.

The link between short-run and long-run Phillips curves

To explain Milton Friedman's theory of the long-run Phillips curve, we must re-introduce the role of expectations into the inflationary process, and also Milton Friedman's concept of the natural rate of unemployment (NRU). As we have noted, the original Keynesian explanation of the (short-run) Phillips curve wrongly took into account only the *current* rate of inflation and ignored the important influence of the *expected* rate of inflation.

To explain the link between short-run and long-run Phillips curves, we shall start by assuming, as a simplification, that the rate of growth of labour productivity is zero and that the rate of increase of prices (*price inflation*) equals the rate of increase of wages (*wage inflation*). In Figure 11.27, the economy is initially at point A, with the unemployment rate at its natural rate U_N. At point A, the rate of inflation is zero, as is the rate of increase of money wages. We shall also assume that people form their expectations of future inflation in the next time period solely on the basis of the current rate of inflation. Thus, at point A, current inflation is zero, so workers expect the future rate of inflation also to be zero.

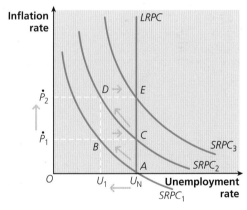

Figure 11.27 Long-run and short-run Phillips curves

We now assume that the government increases aggregate demand, to trade off along Phillips curve $SRPC_1$ to a point such as B in Figure 11.29, where unemployment at U_1 is below the natural rate, U_N. Inflation initially rises to $\dot{P}_1$ (say, 5%). But a point such as B is unsustainable. For workers to be willing to supply more labour, the real wage must rise, yet a rising real wage causes employers to demand less labour. In the short run, more workers may indeed enter the labour market in the false belief that a 5% increase in money wages is also a real wage increase. (This false belief is an example of *money illusion*, which occurs when people confuse the *real* values of economic variables with their *nominal* values.) Similarly, firms may be willing to employ more labour if they also suffer money illusion, falsely believing that rising prices mean that sales revenues are rising faster than labour costs.

This means that, to sustain an increase in employment above its natural level, workers and employers must suffer money illusion in equal but opposite directions, thereby keeping expectations of inflation, formed in the previous time period, consistently below the actual rate to which inflation has risen. However, as workers continuously adjust their expectations of future inflation to the rising actual rate and bargain for ever-higher money wages, the short-run Phillips curve shifts outward from $SRPC_1$ to $SRPC_2$ and so on. There is indeed a separate short-run Phillips curve for each expected rate of inflation. 'Further-out' short-run Phillips curves such as $SRPC_2$ and $SRPC_3$ are associated with higher expected rates of future inflation. Conversely, the short-run Phillips curve shifts inward when the expected rate of inflation falls.

Free-market economists argue that, in the long run, the only way to keep unemployment below its natural level is to permit the money supply to expand and finance an ever-accelerating rate of inflation. Actual inflation always has to be above the expected rate for workers and firms to be willing respectively to supply and to demand more labour. But if this happens, accelerating inflation will eventually create a hyperinflation, which, in the resulting breakdown of economic activity, is likely to increase the natural level of unemployment. Any attempt to reduce unemployment below its natural level is therefore foolhardy and irresponsible. In the short run it leads to accelerating inflation, while in the long run it perversely increases the natural level of unemployment (and the NRU) to unnecessarily high levels.

If the government realises it made a mistake when expanding the economy to point B, it can stabilise the rate of inflation at 5%. Workers and employers 'see through' their money illusion and realise that they have confused money quantities with real quantities. As soon as this happens, they refuse respectively to supply and to demand the labour necessary to keep unemployment below its natural level. The economy now moves to point C.

Short-run and long-run Phillips curves and economic policy

This section summarises points we have already made earlier in the chapter. These are:

- A downward-sloping short-run Phillips curve seems to indicate that governments can successfully trade off between the policy objectives of reducing unemployment and achieving stable prices. Looking back at Figure 11.24, expansionary polices can reduce unemployment from U_1 to U_2, provided the government accepts that the inflation rate must rise from to $\dot{P}_1$ to $\dot{P}_2$. Alternatively, if the government wishes to reduce the rate of inflation, it can do this if it is willing to accept a higher level of unemployment.
- However, with a vertical *LRAS* curve, such trade-offs are not possible. If the government expands aggregate demand in an attempt to reduce unemployment below its natural level, it will trigger an accelerating rate of inflation which will eventually destroy the policy. Reducing unemployment below its natural level is the 'wrong' way to reduce unemployment.
- According to free-market economists, the 'correct' way to reduce unemployment is to use supply-side policies, rather than demand management policies, to shift the *LRAS* curve leftward, thereby reducing the natural level of unemployment.

TEST YOURSELF 11.23
What are the different policy implications of short-run and long-run Phillips curves?

STUDY TIP
Make sure you understand the difference between short-run and long-run Phillips curves.

A further look at adaptive expectations and rational expectations

If expectations are formed rationally rather than adaptively, people don't suffer from money illusion and any attempt by a government to reduce unemployment below its natural rate fails, since 'artificially' stimulating aggregate demand leads solely to accelerating inflation. The correct way to reduce unemployment is to reduce the natural rate itself, rather than to increase demand to try to reduce unemployment below the NRU. To do this, the government should use appropriate free-market supply-side policies.

Modern free-market economists continue to accept the Friedmanite concept of the natural rate of unemployment. But whereas Milton Friedman believed that, in the short run at least, governments can trade off along a short-run Phillips curve and reduce unemployment below the natural rate, the theory of rational expectations rejects this possibility.

As a result, it is in workers' and employers' interests to realise instantly any mistakes made when forming expectations, and to see through any attempt by an 'irresponsible' government to reflate the economy beyond the level of output that is produced at the natural rate of unemployment. Free-market economists believe that in this situation, attempts by government to increase aggregate demand to stimulate output and employment are anticipated fully by private economic agents. Workers and firms modify their behaviour to offset or neutralise the effects intended by the government, so the increase in aggregate demand has no effect upon real economic activity and employment. For extreme neoclassical economists, this is the case in both the short run and the long run because they believe that market forces will ensure that output and employment are always at their natural or equilibrium levels.

Another important difference separating the adaptive and rational expectations of free-market economics is the length of time unemployment must remain above its natural rate as the cost or penalty of an attempt to reduce unemployment below the natural rate. In Friedmanite theory, the economy experiences a lengthy period of unemployment above its natural rate, to 'bleed' the system of inflationary expectations built up during the period of fiscal or monetary expansion.

In contrast to this 'gradualist' theory, rational expectations theory assumes that economic agents immediately reduce expectations of future inflation, provided they believe in the credibility of a tough free-market government's commitment to reducing inflation. Believing that the government means business in pursuing tight fiscal and monetary policies to control inflation, workers and firms immediately build a lower expected rate of inflation into their wage-bargaining and price-setting behaviour. Inflation falls quickly and fairly painlessly, without the need for a lengthy period of unemployment above its natural level. In effect, a firmly free-market government reduces inflation by 'talking down' inflation. However, if credibility in government policy were to disappear, its ability to control inflation would also be diminished. People would now expect higher prices, and would alter behaviour accordingly. Expectations of higher prices would become self-fulfilling.

Reconciling possible policy conflicts in the short run and the long run

In the short run, policy conflicts between reducing unemployment and achieving price stability might be reconciled in a highly depressed economy in which output is well below its normal capacity, as illustrated on a Keynesian AS curve (see page 351).

However, if the economy is initially producing on its vertical LRAS curve (or on the vertical section of a Keynesian AS curve) and with unemployment at its natural level, the short-run reconciliation is no longer possible. Instead the government should try to improve supply-side conditions in the economy in the hope of increasing labour productivity and making the economy more competitive in world markets.

- When economic policy objectives are mutually exclusive, it is impossible for governments to achieve all their policy objectives at the same time, so governments often trade off between policy objectives.
- A short-run Phillips curve illustrates the conflict between controlling inflation and reducing unemployment, but is not itself a theory of inflation.
- Monetarist and free-market economists argue that the long-run Phillips curve is vertical, located at the economy's natural rate, or level, of unemployment.
- Short-run reconciliation between conflicting possible objectives is possible, provided there is significant unused capacity in the economy.
- Free-market economists believe that long-run reconciliation is not possible and that in the long run governments should aim to increase aggregate supply in the economy.

Questions

1 Explain why it is important to identify correctly the cause of unemployment.

2 Do you agree that it is more important to reduce unemployment than to reduce inflation? Justify your answer.

3 Do you agree that it is supply-side, rather than demand-side, factors which have been the more important cause of UK unemployment in recent years? Justify your answer.

4 Explain the differences between inflation, deflation, disinflation and reflation.

5 Explain why the relationship between unemployment and inflation is likely to be different in the short run from the long run.

6 Evaluate the view that the avoidance of inflation should always be the major macroeconomic objective.

Financial markets and monetary policy

Like all the economies of nation states in the world today, the UK's economy is a monetary economy, in which most of the goods and services produced are traded or exchanged via the intermediary of money. This chapter begins by describing the nature and functions of money in the UK economy and then explains the structure of UK financial markets and the characteristics of some of the important financial assets that are traded in these markets. The chapter goes on to explain how bank deposits, which form the largest part of the money supply in modern economies, are created by the free enterprise banking system. It then surveys the changes that have recently taken place in UK monetary policy, showing how current monetary policy has developed out of the monetary policies implemented by UK governments and the Bank of England over the last 20–35 years.

LEARNING OBJECTIVES

These are to understand:

- the characteristics and functions of money
- the financial assets which have functioned as money, both in the present day and in the past
- the structure and functions of UK financial markets: money markets, capital markets and foreign exchange markets
- the relationship between asset prices and interest rates
- the roles of different types of bank: commercial banks, investment banks and central banks
- how a commercial bank creates credit and new bank deposits
- how the Bank of England, the UK's central bank, implements monetary policy
- the regulation of the UK's financial markets

12.1 The structure of financial markets and financial assets

Assets and liabilities

To understand fully the nature of financial markets, money and the monetary system, it is important to understand the two words: **assets** and **liabilities**. Banknotes and coins function as both financial assets and financial liabilities. A £10 note is an asset to the person owning it, since it gives the person £10 worth of spending power. However, it is a liability for the Bank of England which issued it. Many years ago, Bank of England notes were convertible into gold. The Bank had to meet this liability and, if asked by note owners, convert

405

banknotes into gold on demand. These days and more innocuously, the Bank's liability is to replace an old and dirty note, or a note mangled in a washing machine, with a brand-new note.

From a commercial bank's point of view, a loan (or credit) granted to a customer is an interest-earning asset, which the borrower is liable to repay. But the act of creating credit or a loan simultaneously creates a bank deposit owned by the customer to whom the loan is made. The bank deposit is the customer's asset, but it is a liability for the bank itself. The bank must honour cash withdrawals and cheques or debit card payments drawn on the deposit, which transfer ownership of part of the deposit to other people. The key point to remember is that the loan-creating process increases the bank's assets (i.e. the credit it creates) and its liabilities (i.e. customers' deposits) by equal amounts. The creation of credit (an asset from a bank's point of view) simultaneously increases by the same amount customers' deposits held in the bank (a liability from the bank's point of view).

In summary, when a bank creates an interest-earning asset (the credit it extends to its customers), it is simultaneously adding to its deposit liabilities, since it must now honour customers' withdrawals from their deposits of cash or payments they make to other people. The act of creating an asset simultaneously creates a liability. (It is worth remembering that liabilities (and capital) represent a bank's 'source of funds' whereas the assets show its 'use of funds'.)

The functions of money

Money is best defined by focusing on the two principal functions it performs in the economy. Money functions as:

- **A medium of exchange or means of payment.** The economy we live in is a monetary economy in which most of the goods and services produced are traded or exchanged via the intermediary of money, rather than through barter (that is, swapping goods). Whenever money is used to pay for goods or services, or for the purpose of settling transactions and the payment of debts, it performs this function.
- **A store of value or store of wealth.** Money is also an asset, something people own which has value. Most people store some of their wealth in the form of money in preference to holding other *financial assets*, such as stocks and shares, or *physical assets*, such as a house or car. When stored rather than spent, money's purchasing power is transferred to the future, although over time inflation may erode money's purchasing power.

The characteristics of money

Commodity money

Figure 12.1 shows the three main forms of money that have developed since money replaced barter. The earliest form of money was commodity money. Commodities that functioned as money had an intrinsic value of their own: they yielded utility and consumer services to their owners. Beads, shells, sharks' teeth and other commodities could be used for decorative purposes while being stored as wealth. Some commodities used as money, such as cattle, could be slaughtered and eaten.

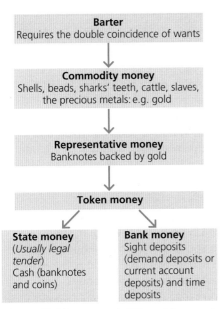

Figure 12.1 Barter and different forms of money

Representative money

As money evolved, gold and silver gradually replaced other forms of commodity money because they possessed, to a greater degree, the desirable characteristics necessary for a commodity to function as money: *relative scarcity, uniformity, durability, portability* and *divisibility*. All of these help to create confidence in money, which is necessary for its *acceptability*. Nevertheless, gold and silver are vulnerable to theft and are difficult to store safely. Eventually, wealthy individuals deposited the precious metals they owned with goldsmiths for safekeeping.

At the next stage, the goldsmiths developed into banks, and the receipts they issued in return for deposits of gold became the first banknotes or paper money. These notes were *representative money*, representing ownership of silver or gold. Early banknotes were acceptable as a means of payment because they could be exchanged for silver or gold on demand. They were issued on the whole by privately owned banks rather than by the state, although the state continued to issue gold and silver coinage. Although worthless in themselves, banknotes functioned as money because people were willing to accept them as long as there was confidence that notes could be changed into gold, which does have an intrinsic value.

Token money

Modern money is almost all token money with no intrinsic value of its own. It takes two main forms: *cash* and *bank deposits*. In England and Wales, the state, or rather its agent, the Bank of England, has a monopoly over the issue of cash (although in other parts of the UK, Scottish and Northern Ireland banks also have a limited ability to issue banknotes). However, cash is best thought of as the 'small change' of the monetary system — bank deposits form by far the largest part of modern money. Most modern money takes the form of bank deposits created by the private enterprise banking system.

Money's other functions

Money has two other functions which are less important for you to know. Money serves as:

- a measure of value
- a standard of deferred payment

Combined together, these are often called the 'unit of account' function. Money is the unit in which the prices of goods are quoted and in which accounts are kept. This allows us to compare the relative values of goods even when we have no intention of actually spending money and buying goods: for example, when we 'window-shop'. This is the measure of value function. Money's function as a standard of deferred payment allows people to delay paying for goods or settling a debt, even though goods or services are being provided immediately. Money acts as a standard of deferred payment whenever firms sell goods on credit or draw up contracts specifying a money payment due at a later date.

TEST YOURSELF 12.2

Why is most modern money token money?

What is money?

For most people, money is so desirable and so central to everyday life that what actually constitutes it hardly merits a second thought. For people living in England and Wales, money comprises coins and Bank of England notes, and any funds on deposit in banks such as HSBC and Barclays. Residents of Scotland and Northern Ireland would also include notes issued by local Scottish and Northern Irish banks. Building society deposits as well as bank deposits are now also regarded as money, although this has not always been the case.

Where do we draw the line as to what is money? Is a credit card money? What about foreign currency such as the US dollar or the Indian rupee, given the fact that we may not be able to spend a foreign banknote or coin in the UK? Do we include financial assets such as National Savings Securities, which possess some, but not all, of the characteristics of money?

Consider also the social relationship that takes place whenever modern banknotes are spent on goods or services. Why, for example, are shopkeepers prepared to hand over new and valuable goods to strangers, in exchange for grubby and unhygienic pieces of paper with no apparent intrinsic value of their own? The answer lies in a single word: 'confidence'. In a modern economy, people are prepared to accept such tokens in settlement of a contract or debt, because they are confident that these notes and coins will also be accepted when they decide to spend them.

TEST YOURSELF 12.3

A car is advertised for sale at a price of £25,000. This is an example of money's function as:

A a store of wealth

B a medium of exchange

C a measure of value

D a standard of deferred payment

Explain why C is the correct answer.

CASE STUDY 12.1

The development of modern money

Before the development of money, exchange and trade took place in simple and primitive village economies, where the exchange of goods and services was initially based on *barter* — the swapping of goods and services. However, barter is inefficient and impractical in a more complex economic system characterised by specialisation and trade. Successful barter requires a *double coincidence of wants*, which means that a person wishing to trade a television set for a refrigerator must not only establish contact with someone with equal but opposite wants (that is, an individual possessing a refrigerator who wishes to exchange it for a television set); they must also agree that the television set and refrigerator are of equal value (or how many TV sets equal one fridge — or vice versa).

Barter is inefficient because the time and energy spent searching the market to establish the double coincidence of wants results in unnecessary search costs (involving shoe-leather costs) and transaction costs. If trading products is inefficient, it inhibits the development of specialisation, division of labour and large-scale production. All of these contribute to the productive efficiency and range of consumer choice available in modern and sophisticated monetary economies.

Follow-up questions

1 Why does money provide a more efficient means of payment than barter?
2 What are the advantages and disadvantages of using cash as the main form of personal wealth?
3 Explain why the use of money as a medium of exchange enables an economy to benefit from specialisation and the division of labour.
4 Explain why precious metals, such as gold and silver, have often been used in economies as money.

SYNOPTIC LINK

At this stage, it might be a good idea to go ahead to section 12.3, pages 428–44, which explains how, through their ability to create credit, private enterprise banks such as Barclays create bank deposits, which make up the lion's share of modern money.

KEY TERM

money supply the stock of financial assets which function as money.

SYNOPTIC LINK

The terms 'monetarism' and 'monetarists' were explained in Chapter 11.

KEY TERMS

narrow money the part of the stock of money (or money supply) made up of cash and liquid bank and building society deposits.

broad money the part of the stock of money (or money supply) made up of cash, other liquid assets such as bank and building society deposits, but also some illiquid assets. The measure of broad money used by the Bank of England is called M4.

liquidity measures the ease with which an asset can be converted into cash without loss of value. Cash is the most liquid of all assets.

TEST YOURSELF 12.4

Only **one** of the following has increased the need to hold money on one's person:

A inflation

B increased use of credit cards

C increased use of automatic transfers between deposits

D increased use of ATM machines

Explain why only statement A provides the correct answer.

The money supply

Fifty or so years ago, before the advent of *monetarism*, few economists gave much attention to the precise definition of the **money supply** or stock of money in the economy. This reflected the Keynesian view that money did not matter in the macroeconomic management of the economy. However, when monetarism replaced Keynesianism as the prevailing orthodoxy in the 1970s, money did begin to matter — particularly in the years before monetarism itself drifted from favour around 1985. For a few years from the mid-1970s to the mid-1980s, during the 'monetarist era', control of the money supply became an important part of monetarist economic management in general and monetary policy in particular. During this period, monetarist economists devoted considerable attention to the problem of deciding which assets to include and exclude when defining the money supply.

Narrow money and broad money

Over the years, the Bank of England has used more than one definition of the money supply. These divide into measures of **narrow money** and **broad money**. Narrow money, which restricts the measure of money to cash and bank and building society sight deposits, reflects the medium of exchange function of money, namely money functioning as a means of payment. Broad money also includes other financial assets which, although stores of value, are too illiquid, at least for the time being, to function as media of exchange.

STUDY TIP

It is important to understand the meaning of the word 'liquidity' in the context of money, financial markets and monetary policy. **Liquidity** measures the ease with which an asset can be converted into cash without loss of value; cash is itself the most liquid of all assets. Assets that generally can only be sold after a long exhaustive search for a buyer are known as illiquid. Liquidity is also affected by whether or not the conversion can take place at a pre-known value. A share issued by a public company (PLC) is highly liquid in that it can quickly be sold on the stock exchange, but less liquid in the sense that the seller does not know the price the asset will fetch, in advance of the sale.

TEST YOURSELF 12.5

Is narrow money a good indicator of the store of value function of money?

TEST YOURSELF 12.6

Which of the following statements is true about a highly liquid asset?

A It generally has a very limited market for its resale.

B It cannot be sold on a market.

C It can be converted into a means of payment easily without loss of value.

D It has high transaction costs associated with its sale.

Explain why statement C provided the correct answer, and why statements A, B and D are wrong.

EXTENSION MATERIAL

Goodhart's Law

A significant problem that contributed to the decline of monetarism as a major force influencing UK governments stemmed from what has become known as Goodhart's Law. This 'law' is named after Charles Goodhart, formerly a professor at the London School of Economics and a member of the Bank of England's Monetary Policy Committee (MPC). Goodhart argued that, as soon as a government tries to control the growth of a particular measure of the money supply, any previously stable relationship between the targeted measure of money and the economy breaks down. The more successful the Bank of England appears to be in controlling the rate of growth of the financial assets defined as the money supply, the more likely it is that other financial assets, regarded previously as *near money* outside the existing definition and system of control, will take on the function of a medium of exchange and become money.

In this way, attempting to control the money supply is rather like a person trying to catch their own shadow. As soon as they move, their shadow also moves. Although what is defined as money may be controlled, when other financial assets become money, this becomes irrelevant. The difficulties of, first, defining the money supply and, second, exerting control over its rate of growth contributed to the downfall of monetarism after 1985.

The difference between equity and debt

The vast majority of people living in the UK today have some possessions which they own. For many adults, this includes the houses they live in, and financial assets, such as the money they possess and **shares** and **bonds**. Even their children own equity: for example, toys and a savings account given to them by grandparents. **Equity** is all the assets, physical and financial, which people own. **Debt**, by contrast, is what people owe: that is, their liabilities. For many adults, this is the mortgage on their house, which is money owed to a bank or building society, and credit card debt.

KEY TERMS

shares undated financial assets, sold initially by a company to raise financial capital. Shares sold by public companies or PLCs are marketable on a stock exchange, but shares sold by private companies are not marketable. Unlike a loan, a share signifies that the holder owns part of the enterprise.

bonds financial securities sold by companies (corporate bonds) or by governments (government bonds) which are a form of long-term borrowing. Bonds usually have a maturity date on which they are redeemed, with the borrower usually making a fixed interest payment each year until the bond matures.

equity the assets which people own.

debt people's financial liabilities or money they owe.

Positive and negative equity

The word 'equity' has two very different economic meanings. On the one hand, in the context of topics such as fiscal policy, poverty and the distributions of income and wealth, equity means fairness or justness. However, in the context of this chapter, equity means wealth. Consider the following situation.

Many of the parents of the students reading this book will have taken out a mortgage to finance the purchase of their house. The house is the parents' asset. However, the mortgage, or the money they have borrowed to finance house purchase, is the parents' liability. (Assets are everything you *own* that possesses value, while liabilities are everything that you *owe* to other people.)

In much of recent history, the value of mortgages has remained unchanged (or even fallen when part of the mortgages are paid off each year), but house prices have risen, at least in most parts of the UK. This means that owner-occupiers of houses have benefited from *positive equity* (what they own is greater than what they owe.)

However, in the financial crisis which hit the UK in 2007, house prices fell rapidly. This created the problem of *negative equity*, which occurs when what is owed exceeds the value of what is owned: that is, the amount owed on the mortgage is more than the value of the house. People in the negative equity trap often have crippling debt from which it is very difficult to escape.

Follow-up questions

1 Name **two** other assets, besides the houses they own, which are usually part of householders' equity.
2 Distinguish between positive and negative equity.
3 What is the negative equity trap?
4 In the years after 2007, young house buyers who had got onto the property ladder in the years just before the financial crisis were the main victims of the negative equity problem. Explain why this was so.

How can a recession lead to a negative equity trap?

Portfolio balance decisions

In old-fashioned English, a portfolio is a bag or piece of luggage in which people store things and transport them from one place to another. An art portfolio is the collection of drawings and paintings a student submits in order to gain an Art A-level pass. In financial jargon, a wealth portfolio contains the different wealth assets that an individual owns and holds at a particular point in time.

Everyone, except the completely destitute, makes decisions, consciously or subconsciously, on the form of asset in which to keep their wealth. In the first instance, people choose between holding physical assets (or non-financial assets), such as houses, and holding financial assets. (Physical assets such as property, fine art, classic cars and antiques can be attractive because they tend to go up in value or appreciate, thus providing a hedge against inflation.)

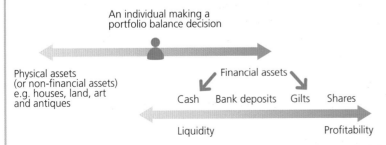

Figure 12.2 A spectrum of assets over which a portfolio balance decision may be made

When choosing the assets to hold, people make *portfolio balance decisions*. A portfolio balance decision is illustrated in Figure 12.2, which, besides making the distinction between physical and financial assets, arranges financial assets according to *liquidity* and *profitability*. As we have noted, liquidity measures the ease with which an asset can be converted into cash, and the certainty of what it will be worth when converted. We have seen that, provided it is generally accepted and can be used as a means of payment, cash is the most liquid of all assets. For the most part, bank deposits are not quite as liquid as cash, but they are sufficiently liquid to be treated as money. The other financial assets shown in Figure 12.2 are examples of non-money financial assets, in some cases being near-money. Shares and government bonds (gilt-edged securities, or gilts) are marketable (they can be sold second hand on the stock exchange), but they are less liquid than money. In contrast to money, which earns little or no interest, shares and gilts generally hold out the prospect of providing a profit for their owners.

Financial markets

> ### KEY TERM
> **financial markets** markets in which financial assets or securities are traded.

In section 3.1 of Chapter 3, we defined a market as a voluntary meeting of buyers and sellers. We went on to stress that markets do not have to exist in a particular geographical location, and in recent years, 24/7 global markets have grown up, facilitated by the development of the internet. This has enabled many markets to become truly global and to function on a worldwide basis.

This is certainly the case for some of the **financial markets** functioning in the UK: for example, the capital and foreign exchange markets and Lloyds insurance market. However, at the other extreme, some of the smaller financial markets, such as the market for Treasury bills and commercial bills, are restricted largely to trading in the City of London, the hub of UK financial markets.

> ### TEST YOURSELF 12.8
> What is the main difference between a financial market and a market for a good such as the car market?

Some of the main financial markets in the UK and global economies

A financial market is a market in financial assets or securities. (A security is so called because it secures a claim against a person or institution: for example, a share secures ownership of a fraction of the company which initially sold the share to the general public.) Financial markets, which are illustrated in Figure 12.3, can be classified in a number of ways, but one of the most fruitful is into markets for short-dated financial assets (often called **money markets**) and long-dated and undated financial assets (often called **capital markets**). There are also **foreign exchange markets**.

> ### KEY TERMS
> **money markets** provide a means for lenders and borrowers to satisfy their short-term financial needs. Assets that are bought and sold on money markets are short term, with maturities ranging from a day to a year, and are normally easily convertible into cash. The term 'money market' is an umbrella that covers several markets, including the markets for Treasury bills and commercial bills.
>
> **capital markets** where securities such as shares and bonds are issued to raise medium- to long-term financing, and where shares and bonds are then traded on the 'second-hand' part of the market, e.g. the London Stock Exchange.
>
> **foreign exchange markets** (forex, FX or currency markets) global, decentralised markets for the trading of currencies. The main participants in this market are large international commercial banks. Collectively, foreign exchange markets are the largest markets in the global economy.

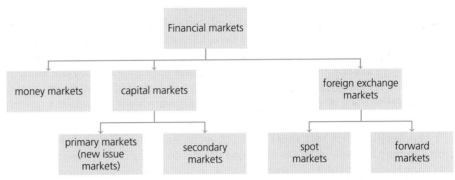

Figure 12.3 Some of the main financial markets in the UK and global economies

UK money markets

As we explain shortly, money markets provide mechanisms for banks to arrange their assets in terms of their liquidity or profitability, with highly liquid assets such as Treasury bills and commercial bills at the liquid end of the spectrum. Organising their assets in this way enables commercial banks to perform perhaps the most important banking function, namely that of a financial intermediary linking savers to borrowers.

A money market which has recently become extremely important in the operation of monetary policy is the London interbank market, in which the LIBOR interest rate is charged. (LIBOR is the London Interbank Offered Rate, which is a rate of interest charged when banks lend to each other, usually for very short periods of time.)

UK capital markets

In contrast to money markets, capital markets, which include the London Stock Exchange, provide the mechanism through which public limited companies (PLCs), which are arguably the most important form of business organisation in the UK, can raise the funds to finance their long-term growth. In addition, the part of the capital market known as the bond market performs a critical role in government finance: for example, by enabling a government to finance a budget deficit.

EXTENSION MATERIAL

Comparing money markets and capital markets

Table 12.1 enables us to compare the important similarities of, and also the important differences between, two of the most important money markets (the markets for commercial bills and Treasury bills) and the capital markets.

Table 12.1 Money markets and capital markets

	Money markets (markets for short-dated financial assets or securities)	Capital markets (markets for undated and long-dated financial assets or securities)
The private sector raising finance	Sale of commercial bills	Sale of new issues of shares Sale of new issues of corporate bonds
Central government raising finance	Sale of Treasury bills	Sale of new issues of government bonds (in the UK also known as gilt-edged securities or gilts)

The function of money markets is to supply both private-sector commercial firms and the government with a source of short-term finance. For a firm, bill finance is an alternative to a conventional bank loan. Bills are short-dated financial assets or securities, which mature within a year (and often within 3 months) of their date of issue. There are two main types of bill, or bills of exchange as they are known: *commercial bills* and *Treasury bills*. Commercial bills are sold by investment banks on behalf of client firms. Treasury bills, which are sold as new issues by the Bank of England on behalf of the government, provide the government with a method of financing the differences that emerge at certain times in the financial year between tax revenues and government spending.

Treasury bills are in fact short-dated government loans. (The word *bill* is used for a short-dated loan raised on a money market, whereas the word *bond* is used for a long-dated loan raised on a capital market.) The role of capital markets will be explained later in this section. Shares, **corporate bonds** and **government bonds** (gilt-edged securities or gilts) are the main securities traded on capital markets.

KEY TERMS

corporate bonds debt security issued by a company and sold as new issues to people who lend long-term to the company. They can usually be resold second-hand on a stock exchange.

government bonds debt security, in the UK known as gilt-edged securities or gilts, issued by a government and sold as new issues to people who lend long-term to the government. They can be resold second-hand on a stock exchange.

TEST YOURSELF 12.9

How is a bond different from a share?

STUDY TIP

Don't confuse a *public* company (PLC) with the *public* sector of the economy. Public companies are arguably the most important form of business organisation in the *private* sector of the economy.

The inverse relationship between bond prices and interest rates

Economics students are often confused by the relationship between the prices of bonds and long-run interest rates. To understand the relationship, consider Figure 12.4, which depicts the main characteristics of government bonds (in the UK, gilt-edged securities, or gilts) and the long-run rate of interest.

£100 is the price at which the bond was first sold on 6 April 2015 (the bond's **issue price**) and it is also the **maturity price** at which the bond can be **redeemed** 30 years later on 5 April 2045. However, it is not the second-hand price at which the bond can be bought or sold on the capital market (the stock exchange) on any day during the 30-year life of the bond. The second-hand price is determined by supply and demand, and can vary daily.

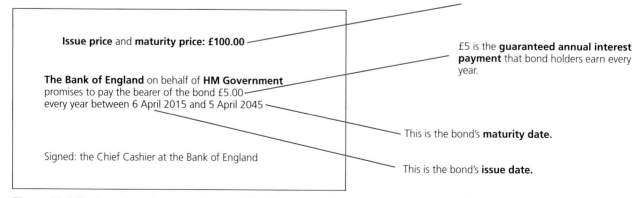

Issue price and maturity price: £100.00

The Bank of England on behalf of HM Government promises to pay the bearer of the bond £5.00 every year between 6 April 2015 and 5 April 2045

Signed: the Chief Cashier at the Bank of England

£5 is the **guaranteed annual interest payment** that bond holders earn every year.

This is the bond's **maturity date.**

This is the bond's **issue date.**

Figure 12.4 The key characteristics of a bond (in this case, a UK government bond or gilt)

Gilts (and also corporate bonds issued by private-sector companies) are *fixed-interest securities* sold by the government (or by companies) when they borrow in the long term. The bond in Figure 12.4 is a 30-year bond with a face value of £100 carrying a guaranteed annual interest payment, known as the coupon, of £5. Simple arithmetic will tell you that £5 is 5% of £100. Suppose, however, that after the bond has been sold on its day of issue for £100, its second-hand price on the London Stock Exchange or bond market *rises* to £200. This means that the bond's *yield* falls to 2.5% (£5 as a percentage of £200). (A bond's *yield* is in effect *the long-run rate of interest* earned by holder of the bond. It is determined primarily by the coupon and the price the holder paid for the bond.)

The guaranteed interest (or **coupon**) earned each year by gilt holders is paid in two instalments at 6-month intervals. Gilts and other bonds usually have a specific **maturity date**. In the case of the 4% Treasury Gilt 2016, the principal was repaid to gilt holders on 7 September 2016.

KEY TERMS

coupon the guaranteed fixed annual interest payment, often divided into two 6-month payments, paid by the issuer of a bond to the owner of the bond.

maturity date the date on which the issuer of a dated security, such as a gilt-edged security (long-dated) or a Treasury bill (short-dated), pays the face value of the security to the security's owner.

Suppose, by contrast, the bond's price falls to £50. This means that the bond's yield rises to 10% (£5 as a percentage of £50). Both these simple calculations illustrate the inverse relationship between bond prices and *long-run* interest rates. (However, if the calculation were made as the bond approached maturity, it would illustrate the inverse relationship between bond prices and short-run interest rates.) If bond prices rise, yields or long-term interest rates fall, and if bond prices fall, yields of long-term interest rates rise.

QUANTITATIVE SKILLS 12.1

Worked example: calculating the yield on a bond

The government sells a new issue of 50-year gilt-edged securities, each with a nominal value, or maturity value, of £100 and a guaranteed yearly interest payment (or coupon) of £2.50. Five years after the gilt was issued, its second-hand or market price on the stock exchange falls to £50.

Calculate the yield on the gilt-edged security at this date.

$$\text{yield} = \frac{\text{annual coupon payment}}{\text{gilt's current market price}} \times 100$$

$$= \left(\frac{£2.50}{£50}\right) \times 100$$

$$= \left(\frac{1}{20}\right) \times 100$$

$$= 5\%$$

Capital gains and losses and bond and share prices

In Quantitative skills 12.1, the fact that the gilt does not mature until 50 years after the date of issue means that an approaching maturity date has no noticeable effect on the gilt's current market price or on its yield. If, by contrast, the maturity date were next week, the market price would be very close to its maturity value (£50), and its yield would have converged to be very close to 2.5%.

For a gilt or a corporate bond with many years to go until maturity, another factor affecting changes in its market price is the expectation of making a capital gain (and the fear of suffering a capital loss). Suppose the current bond price is £100, but speculators *expect* the price to rise shortly to £150. If the bond can be bought now at or near its current price of £100, and its price does indeed shortly rise, speculators who buy the bond make a capital gain when selling the bond later: for example, for £150. If a sufficiently large number of speculators decide to buy the bond at or near the price of £100, increased demand for the bond pulls up the market price, until eventually it may indeed reach £150.

Conversely, a fear that the bond price will fall, say to £50, will induce speculative selling of the bond, which in turn causes the bond's price to fall. Provided a sufficiently large number of speculators behave in the same way, speculative buying and selling, in the hope of making a capital gain — or avoiding a capital loss — is an important determinant of short-run changes in bond prices. (Share prices are also affected in a similar way.)

There are some government bonds in existence (Consolidated Stock) which will never mature. Because there are no complications brought about by an approaching maturity date, the yield on Consolidated Stock, at any point in time, is the best indicator there is of the long-run interest rate on relatively risk-free assets at that time. Long-term interest rates on risky assets such as corporate bonds and on even riskier assets, such as Greek government bonds, will be higher.

TEST YOURSELF 12.10

Explain how a capital gain differs from a capital loss.

QUANTITATIVE SKILLS 12.2

Worked example: calculating a bond's current market price

The annual coupon payment on a 40-year bond issued last year is £8. When the bond was first sold, the long-run interest rate was 8%. The bond's maturity value is £100. Within the last year, long-run interest rates have fallen to 4%.

Calculate the approximate current market price of this bond on the stock exchange.

The calculation is as follows:

$$\text{yield} = \frac{\text{annual coupon payment}}{\text{bond's current market price}} \times 100$$

$$4 = \frac{£8}{\text{bond's current market price}} \times 100$$

$$\text{bond's current market price} = \frac{£8}{4} \times 100 = £200$$

A closer look at capital markets

Capital markets are made up of two parts: the *new-issues market* (or *primary market*) and the *second-hand market* (or *secondary market*). In the UK, the London Stock Exchange (LSE) functions as the main secondary market. There are, however, other secondary markets. These include the Alternative Investment Market (AIM), which is run by the London Stock Exchange, mainly for small PLCs, and second-hand trading, which takes place online and is outside the LSE's control. Many students confuse the capital market with the stock exchange. The LSE is indeed an important part of the capital market, but it is only a part, and the terms 'capital market' and 'stock exchange' are not interchangeable. On stock exchanges, previously issued shares and bonds are sold second-hand.

The relationship between the primary and the secondary parts of the main capital market is illustrated in Figure 12.5. The actual raising of new capital or long-term finance takes place in the primary market when public companies (in the private sector of the economy) or the government (in the public sector) decide to issue and sell new marketable securities. Companies can borrow long-term by selling corporate bonds, or they may sell an ownership stake in the company by issuing shares or equity. When selling corporate bonds, the company extends its debt, and the purchaser of the bond becomes a creditor of the company.

By contrast, new issues of shares are sold when a company 'goes public' for the first time, or when an existing public company decides to raise extra capital with a new equity issue. In the latter case, the new share issue is most often a rights issue, in which the company's existing shareholders are given the right to buy the new issue of shares at a discount.

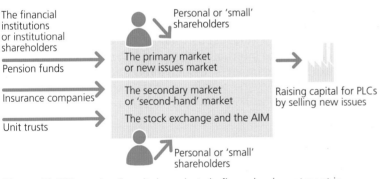

Figure 12.5 The role of capital markets in financing investment in British industry

New issues of shares are seldom sold directly on the stock exchange. Instead, the direct sale of new issues to the general public takes place in the primary market, usually being arranged by investment banks (whose functions are explained in section 12.2), via newspaper advertisements and the post. Though sometimes accused of being a mere casino devoted to the speculative buying and selling of second-hand shares, the secondary part of the capital market does perform an important economic role. Without the existence of a second-hand market, public companies or PLCs would find it difficult, if not impossible, to sell new share issues. The shares issued by private companies, which don't have a stock market listing, are generally illiquid and difficult to sell. But shares issued by listed public companies can be sold second-hand on the stock exchange. The stock exchange enables shares to be converted quickly into cash. Without the stock exchange, the general public would be reluctant to buy shares that could not easily be resold. An important source of funds necessary to finance the growth of a firm would be denied to public companies.

The principal function of the London Stock Exchange and other secondary capital markets is to increase the liquidity of second-hand securities (bonds and shares), making it easier for buyers to manage their investments and sell these securities when required. This in turn makes it more likely that those with surplus funds will be willing to buy new issues of shares and bonds, thus facilitating expansion in the economic activities of PLCs and government.

Foreign exchange markets

Over the last 60 years or so, foreign exchange markets have become more and more important in facilitating the growth of international trade and capital movements between countries. Arguably, the growth of international trade has been the main driver of economic growth, both in the world as a whole, and in trading nations such as the United Kingdom.

Foreign exchange markets are financial markets in which different currencies are bought and sold. International trade means that exporters and importers need to convert the funds they use to finance trade from one currency to another: for example, the UK pound sterling into euros or dollars. Foreign exchange can be traded on either the *spot market* or the *forward market*. Spot transactions involve the immediate exchange of foreign currency whereas forward markets involve the exchange of foreign currencies at some specified time in the future. Forward markets are used by, for example, exporters and importers to protect themselves against exchange rate risks.

12.2 Commercial banks and investment banks

The difference between a commercial bank and an investment bank

The main aim of almost all banks is to make profits for their owners. The Bank of England, the country's central bank (see section 12.3), though highly profitable, is an exception, since its aims are primarily to oversee the financial system and to implement the country's monetary policy. The most commonly used way of classifying banks other than the central bank is into commercial banks and investment banks.

Commercial banks

A **commercial bank** is often also known as a **retail bank** or a **'high street' bank**. UK examples include Barclays and HSBC. Commercial banks' customers are ordinary members of the general public and businesses. To make themselves attractive to customers, commercial banks have built up networks of branch banks, located in high streets and other shopping centres. However, with the development of electronic banking conducted over the internet and accessed on customers' computers and smartphones, most of the large commercial banks have been closing many of their branch banks.

In summary, commercial banks are commercially run financial institutions that:

- accept deposits from the general public that can be transferred by cheque, by debit card or through an online transfer of funds undertaken on the internet
- create deposits which are lent to customers who wish to borrow from their bank

Investment banks

Until fairly recently, **investment banks** were commonly known as merchant banks. Before the development of the internet, investment banks were clustered in the square mile of the City of London. This was partly because investment banks don't generally deal directly with ordinary members of the general public, so unlike commercial banks they do not need expensive branch networks.

Investment banks help companies, other financial institutions and other organisations (such as the government and its agencies) to raise finance by selling shares or bonds to investors and to hedge against risks. They do this by underwriting share issues. In return for substantial fees, investment banks guarantee to buy up all unsold shares in the event of the unsuccessful launch of a new share issue. Over recent decades, investment banks have earned large amounts of money, paid ultimately by taxpayers, through underwriting the privatisation of previously state-owned businesses, most recently the Royal Mail in 2013.

In addition, investment banks trade on their own behalf in shares, bonds and other financial assets. This trade also takes place with other investment banks and with other financial institutions such as insurance companies and pension funds.

KEY TERM

commercial bank (also known as a **retail bank** or **high street bank**) a financial institution which aims to make profits by selling banking services to its customers.

TEST YOURSELF 12.13
Distinguish between a retail bank such as HSBC and a central bank such as the American Federal Reserve Bank.

KEY TERM

investment bank a bank which does not generally accept deposits from ordinary members of the general public. Traditional 'investment banking' refers to financial advisory work, such as advising private companies on how to become a public company by floating on the stock market, or advising public companies on how to buy up another company. Investment banks also deal directly in financial markets for their own account.

Investment banks are essentially global banks, the largest of which trade in financial assets which are greater in size than the GDPs of most of the world's countries. Many of the largest investment banks have been formed through the merger of a retail bank and a previously smaller independent investment bank. A good example is provided by S.G. Warburg & Co., a London-based investment bank. Warburg was listed on the London Stock Exchange and was once a constituent of the FTSE 100 index. The bank was acquired by the Swiss Bank Corporation in 1995 and ultimately became a part of another Swiss investment bank, UBS.

Only two of the 'big three' US investment banks, J.P. Morgan and Goldman Sachs, have at all times remained independent of the retail banking sector. The 'top 10' global investment banks in 2017 are listed in Table 12.2.

Table 12.2 Top 10 global investment banks at October 2017

Investment banks
Goldman Sachs
Morgan Stanley
J.P. Morgan
Citigroup
Deutsche Bank
Bank of America Merrill Lynch
Credit Suisse
Barclays Capital
Wells Fargo
UBS

Source: Equity-Research.com, 2018

Although investment banks have headquarters in a range of countries which include the USA, the UK, France, Germany, Switzerland and Japan, they also have offices in all the world's financial centres, including the City of London and 'City-East' — that is, Canary Wharf to the east of the City proper. Indeed, all of the large global investment banks have a presence in London. These banks therefore contribute to UK economic activity, and help support the efficient functioning of the financial system. But investment banks also bring risks to the United Kingdom's financial system.

Investment banks and the problems of systemic risk

As we have noted, many banks carry out both retail and investment banking activities. However, this led to some of the difficulties and problems which appeared in the financial crisis that hit the global financial system in 2007. Perhaps the major problem results from the appearance of **systemic risk**. Systemic risk refers to the risk of a breakdown of the entire banking system rather than simply the failure of individual banks. This is a cascading failure caused by inter-linkages in the financial system, which may result in a severe downturn within the whole economy.

It is important to distinguish between systemic and one-off risks. In contrast to a one-off shock which affects only a single bank without rippling into the rest of the banking system, systemic risk affects the entire banking system and other financial institutions as well. The consequences of a systemic financial crisis can be devastating because of the role that banks and finance play in the wider economy.

> **KEY TERM**
>
> **systemic risk** in a financial context, this refers to the risk of a breakdown of the entire financial system, caused by inter-linkages within the financial system, rather than simply the failure of an individual bank or financial institution within the system.

Largely in response to these difficulties, national banking authorities are in the process of introducing regulations designed to separate 'high-street' and investment banking activities. Following the publication of the final version of the Vickers Report in September 2011, the retail banking activities of banks operating in the UK must be *ring fenced* from their investment banking activities by 2019.

Without ring fencing, an investment bank's mergers and acquisitions (M&A) department may acquire 'inside knowledge' about a company it is advising. This 'inside knowledge' could be very useful to the bank's own trading in the company's shares. An effective ring fence, which is also known as a firewall and a 'Chinese wall', is an internal device erected by the bank to separate different parts of a bank's activities.

TEST YOURSELF 12.14
How did the bank crashes which occurred during the 2008–09 recession partly result from the problem of systemic risk in the financial system?

How banks create credit and bank deposits

In contrast to cash, which is tangible and can be seen and touched, bank deposits are intangible. Customers only 'see' a bank deposit when reading the statement of a bank account, or when viewing the electronic display in a cash-dispensing machine. Bank deposits are the main form of money, and most transactions are paid for by transferring bank deposits from one account to another. Banks possess the ability to create new deposits, almost out of thin air, where none previously existed.

STUDY TIP
You should understand that bank deposits are the main form of money and that cash is a relatively small part of the total stock of money. If you read the second edition of the book *Where Does Money Come From?*, published by the New Economics Foundation in 2014, you will see that, at the time, 97.4% of the broad money measure M4 took the form of bank and building society deposits, together with other liquid assets, which means that only 2.6% of M4 was cash.

Many students are completely mystified as to how bank deposits are created. A good starting point for developing an understanding is provided by the following story.

Suppose we write our signatures on a scrap of paper, together with the words: 'We promise to pay the bearer £100'. We then give you the scrap of paper (a *promissory note* or 'I owe you'), and ask you to go to a shop and buy £100 worth of goods. Then, when the time comes to pay, you must give the scrap of paper to the shop assistant. Now we all know that, in real life, shops almost always refuse to accept such an 'I owe you'. But just suppose the shop did accept our scrap of paper, believing it could then use the note to buy goods from its suppliers. Our 'I owe you' note would have become money!

KEY TERM
credit when a bank makes a loan it creates credit. The loan results in the creation of an advance, which is an asset on the bank's balance sheet, and a deposit, which is a liability of the bank.

Now, while ordinary individuals cannot generally create money in the manner in which we have described, banks can. If the promissory note were to be headed 'Lloyds Bank promises to pay the bearer £100', as long as people believe that Lloyds will honour its promise, the 'I owe you' can function as money.

We explain the process through which banks create **credit** and new bank deposits in the next section on 'How banks create credit'. We explain credit creation, first (rather unrealistically) in the context of a 'monopoly bank', and then, more realistically, in the context of the real-world 'multi-bank' banking system.

TEST YOURSELF 12.15

What is the difference between an asset and a liability?

How banks create credit

The British banking system, and indeed that of most other countries, is a 'multi-bank' system in which there are a large number of commercial banks such as Barclays and Lloyds competing for business in pursuit of profit. Before we explain how banks in such a system create credit, we shall describe how credit would be created if there was just one commercial bank in the system. This often called a 'monopoly' banking system.

A 'monopoly' banking system

To illustrate the credit and bank deposit creating process, we are first going to assume the following:

- There is only one bank in the economy.
- The bank possesses only one reserve asset, namely cash, which it uses to meet any cash withdrawals (and running down of deposits) by customers.
- The bank decides that, to maintain confidence and always to be able to meet its customers' desire to withdraw cash out of their accounts, it must always possess cash equal to 10% of total customer deposits.

Although the first assumption is unrealistic, the retail banking system taken as a whole behaves as if there is just one bank. Shortly we explain how the end result of credit and deposit creation in the 'multi-bank' system in which we live is much the same as in the 'monopoly bank' system.

The assumption that there is only one retail bank means that, unlike in a system in which there are many banks, customers cannot withdraw and transfer cash from one bank to another. The second and third assumptions taken together mean that, for prudential reasons, the bank chooses to operate a cash ratio in which 10% of customers' deposits in the bank are backed by cash. Remember that most transactions are settled without any withdrawal of cash and, on most days, whilst some customers are withdrawing cash, other customers are depositing cash with the bank. This means that the bank does not need to back all its deposits with cash.

Suppose now that a member of the general public deposits £1,000 cash in the bank. From the bank's point of view, both its assets and its liabilities increase by £1,000. The cash is the bank's asset, but the £1,000 deposit credited in the customer's name is the bank's liability, since the bank is liable to honour any cash withdrawals made by the customer. The £1,000 is recorded in the bank's balance sheet in the following way:

Assets	Liabilities
Cash: £1,000	Deposit: £1,000
Total assets: £1,000	**Total liabilities: £1,000**

As things stand, all the bank's deposit liabilities are backed with cash (that is, the bank's *cash ratio* is 100%). If this remained the position, the 'bank' would not be a bank at all, but a safe-deposit institution, guarding, for a fee, the cash deposited by customers. The difference between a retail bank and a safe-deposit institution is that a bank uses the cash deposited with it as a *monetary base*, from which to launch the profitable loans it grants to customers.

Unlike the customer depositing cash, other customers may need to borrow from the bank. Provided they are creditworthy, the 10% cash ratio the bank has chosen to work with means that the bank is in a position to lend exactly £9,000 to these customers. This may take the form of an interest-earning advance on the assets side of the bank's balance sheet, which is matched by a £9,000 created deposit on the liabilities side of the balance sheet:

Assets	Liabilities
Cash: £1,000	Deposit: £1,000
Advances: £9,000	Created deposits: £9,000
Total assets: £10,000	**Total liabilities: £10,000**

Both the customers who made the initial deposit of £1,000 and the customers in receipt of the advances can draw cheques or make payments equal to £10,000 in total on their deposits. The initial £1,000 cash deposit has enabled total deposits to be increased to £10,000.

Although our assumption of a monopoly bank is completely unrealistic, it has allowed us to illustrate in a simplified way that the banking system *as a whole* can expand credit, bank deposits and hence the money supply to a multiple of the reserve assets (in this case, cash) that back the created deposits. The 'single-stage' creation of credit and deposits is possible in a 'monopoly bank' model because there is no danger that customers who have been granted loans will draw cheques on their deposits payable to customers of other banks. The main constraint on deposit creation is the need for the bank to hold sufficient cash to meet likely customer withdrawals. (A further constraint is the existence of customers who actually want to borrow from the bank. If no one is willing to borrow, the bank cannot expand its deposits by giving loans.)

A 'multi-bank' banking system

However, the real-world banking system contains more than one bank. Some of the biggest are HSBC, Barclays, Lloyds and TSB. We call this a 'multi-bank' banking system. When we drop the simplification of a 'monopoly bank' and assume a 'multi-bank' system similar to that in the United Kingdom, the general conclusions of our simple 'monopoly' model still hold. If the increase in cash deposits is spread over all the banks, deposits can expand to £10,000, provided every bank in the system is prepared to lend to the full extent that its chosen reserve ratio allows. But if only one bank is prepared to create deposits to the full, it will begin to face demands for cash that it cannot meet, losing some of its cash reserves to other banks. This will happen when the bank's customers make payments into the accounts of customers of the other banks. However, if all banks are prepared to expand deposits to the full, payments to customers of other banks will tend to cancel out. The banking system as a whole can expand deposits to £10,000, though some banks may gain business at the expense of others.

The above models illustrate how the supply of reserve assets, such as cash, available to the banks can limit their ability to create deposits. However, the banks' ability to create credit is also limited by their need to have sufficient capital. Since the financial crisis, central banks have imposed larger minimum required capital ratios on the banks and this has restricted their ability to lend.

If banks hold more capital, they are less likely to become insolvent if there is a fall in the value of their assets — for example, as a result of customers being unable to repay the money they have borrowed. This is the main reason why capital ratios are imposed.

STUDY TIP

In the real-world banking system, the cash ratio is much lower than 10%: for example, 5%. However, for illustrative purposes, we shall stick with the assumption of a 10% cash ratio as it makes the arithmetic in the calculations simpler. See Quantitative skills 12.3 for a calculation involving a 5% cash ratio.

STUDY TIP

In section 12.3, when examining the functions of a central bank (in the UK, the Bank of England), we explain how the central bank acts as a 'lender of last resort' to the banking system. To maintain confidence in the banks and to prevent a 'run' on an individual bank, the central bank is always prepared to supply cash at a price to a bank threatened by a sudden deposit withdrawal. However, this does not mean that the central bank will bail out a bank which has made bad investments and is making losses.

TEST YOURSELF 12.16

What is the link between a bank creating credit and a bank creating a new deposit?

QUANTITATIVE SKILLS 12.3

Worked example: calculating an increase in bank deposits

A customer makes a cash deposit of £100,000 in her bank. All the retail banks in the economy choose to keep 5% of their total assets in cash.

Calculate the maximum level of total bank deposits resulting from the deposit of £100,000 into the banking system.

A 5% cash ratio means that cash equals 0.05 of total deposits.

$$\text{total bank deposits} = \frac{\text{initial deposit}}{0.05}$$

$$= \frac{£100,000}{0.05}$$

$$= £2,000,000$$

The answer is £2,000,000. As all banks in the banking system have chosen to operate a 5% cash ratio, assuming that the banking system retains the extra cash, total bank deposits can increase to £2,000,000, following a deposit of £100,000 into the system. Notice that £100,000 is 5% of £2,000,000.

The structure of a retail bank's balance sheet

So far we have assumed that retail banks possess just two assets: cash and advances to customers. The left-hand column of Table 12.3 shows that, in fact, banks possess a range of other assets.

Table 12.3 The structure of a retail bank's balance sheet

Assets	Liabilities
Cash (notes and coins)	Share capital
Balances at the Bank of England	Reserves (retained profit)
Money at short and call notice (money lent to other banks via the interbank market)	Long-term borrowing (e.g. bonds issued by the bank)
Bills (commercial bills and Treasury bills)	Short-term borrowing from money markets
Investments (e.g. holdings of government bonds (gilts) and corporate bonds)	Customers' deposits (sight deposits and time deposits)
Advances (e.g. credit or loans and mortgages extended to the bank's customers)	
Fixed assets (e.g. bank buildings and other premises)	

In reality, banks possess *reserve assets* or *liquid assets* other than the cash we have already discussed. Two of these are items two to four in the left-hand column of Table 12.3. Nevertheless, cash is the most important reserve asset and source of liquidity in the banking system. The purpose of reserve assets is to allow banks to maintain liquidity and confidence and to meet any likely demands by customers for cash. In the event of a withdrawal of cash by customers, a bank must be able to turn reserve assets into cash without suffering a capital loss. To be as profitable as possible, a greedy or imprudent bank might be tempted to reduce cash and other liquid assets to a minimum, but this would run the risk of illiquidity and a loss of confidence among customers in the bank's ability to meet its liabilities. As was the case when the Northern Rock bank collapsed in 2007, a 'run' on the bank could then occur, leading to a 'crash'.

The liquidity–profitability trade-off

As we mentioned earlier, if a bank kept all its assets in the form of cash, it would not really be a bank at all, but a safe-deposit institution. The bank's profits, if it earned any, would come solely from the fees it charged customers for guarding their valuables. The bank's cash would be completely liquid, but not very profitable.

To make a profit, a bank has to make its cash go to work — in other words, be a monetary base upon which advances to customers are launched. Essentially, cash acts as 'high-powered' money which allows the banks to make advances to customers, creating deposits and increasing the total stock of money. The rates of interest that retail banks charge their customers on the advances granted to them are a major source of the banks' profits. Imprudent or greedy banks could be tempted to create far too many profitable advances — imprudent in the sense that the banks possess insufficient cash to meet customers' possible cash withdrawals. These banks would be operating on too low a ratio of cash and other liquid assets to the advances they have created. If a run on the banks occurred, the banks would crash.

Potential conflicts between liquidity, profitability and security

Prudent retail banking requires banks to operate on ratios of cash and other liquid assets to advances that maintain customers' confidence in the bank, while generating acceptable profits for the bank. In other words, prudent banking involves trading off liquidity against **profitability**. But taking the UK retail banking system as a whole, over the years, cash ratios fell below 5%. Some would say that this was a major contributing factor to the failure in the 2007–08 financial crisis of the Northern Rock and Bradford and Bingley banks and to the government's need to rescue much larger banks such as Lloyds TSB. Since the financial crisis, cash ratios have risen again toward 5%.

Besides trading off between profitability and liquidity, banks also have to make choices with regard to the **security** of their assets. The profitability for banks of loans granted to customers depends to a significant extent on the degree of risk attached to the loans. Non-secured loans are risky because if a customer defaults on the loan, the bank cannot recover any money. Because of the risk of non-repayment of unsecured loans, banks charge higher interest rates, and hence make more profit than is the case with secured loans. Mortgage loans granted to house purchasers are secured loans. If the borrower is unable to repay the loan or interest on the loan, the bank or building society which provided the mortgage can repossess the property which secures the loan. This reduces the risk in granting long-term mortgage loans.

Table 12.4 is similar to Table 12.3, but with the liabilities column deleted and a vertical arrow added to depict the liquidity–profitability trade-off.

Table 12.4 The liquidity–profitability trade-off

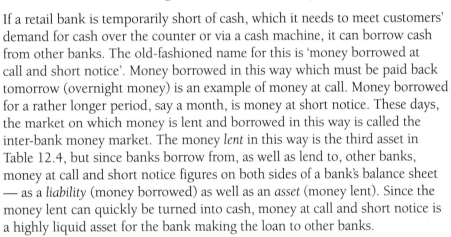

Assets	Liquidity
Cash (notes and coins)	
Balances at the Bank of England	
Money at short and call notice (money lent to other banks via the interbank market)	
Bills (commercial bills and Treasury bills)	
Investments (e.g. holdings of government bonds (gilts) and corporate bonds)	
Advances (e.g. credit or loans and mortgages extended to the bank's customers)	
Fixed assets (e.g. bank buildings and other premises)	Profitability

We have already explained why cash which is held in the tills and the cash machines that banks own is the most liquid asset of all. We have also explained why, at the other end of the spectrum, advances to customers are highly profitable, but illiquid. The other items in Table 12.4 deserve a brief explanation. The first of these is balances at the Bank of England. Just as members of the general public make payments to each other by shifting ownership of bank deposits from the person making the payment (the payer) to the person receiving the payment (the payee), so the retail banks settle debts between themselves in the same way. To do this, all the banks keep balances at the Bank of England. As a bank can instantly withdraw cash by running down its balance at the Bank of England, the balance is as liquid as cash.

If a retail bank is temporarily short of cash, which it needs to meet customers' demand for cash over the counter or via a cash machine, it can borrow cash from other banks. The old-fashioned name for this is 'money borrowed at call and short notice'. Money borrowed in this way which must be paid back tomorrow (overnight money) is an example of money at call. Money borrowed for a rather longer period, say a month, is money at short notice. These days, the market on which money is lent and borrowed in this way is called the inter-bank money market. The money *lent* in this way is the third asset in Table 12.4, but since banks borrow from, as well as lend to, other banks, money at call and short notice figures on both sides of a bank's balance sheet — as a *liability* (money borrowed) as well as an *asset* (money lent). Since the money lent can quickly be turned into cash, money at call and short notice is a highly liquid asset for the bank making the loan to other banks.

Retail banks also like to hold a portfolio of commercial bills and Treasury bills as a liquid asset (the fourth item in Table 12.4). When first issued and sold to the retail banks (by investment banks on behalf of businesses in the case of commercial bills, and by the Debt Management Office (DMO), an executive agency of the Treasury, on behalf of the government in the case of Treasury bills), bills typically have a life of 3 months before they mature. This means that for the bank purchasing a newly issued bill, the bank makes a profit because it buys the bill at a discount — the purchase price is lower than the bill's maturity value. The bank earns the bill's discount rate which is, in effect, the interest rate on the bill, and the money market on which commercial and Treasury bills are bought and sold is called the *discount market*. At any point in time, retail banks possess a portfolio of bills, some of which mature today or tomorrow, some in a week's time, and some in 3 months' time. From the bank's point of view, its bill portfolio provides it with liquid assets which are nevertheless profitable.

This is even more evident for the fifth set of assets in Table 12.4, namely investments. Because of a risk factor related to the fact that shares never mature and might have to be sold second-hand on a falling capital market, retail banks don't generally invest in company shares or equities. However, they do invest in corporate bonds issued by private sector PLCs, and even more so in government bonds (gilt-edged securities or gilts). When first issued, most gilts have a life of anything up to 50 years before they mature. However, because gilts are issued by the 'ship of state' and their maturity value and yearly interest payment (the gilt's coupon) are guaranteed by the government, banks usually regard gilts as being absolutely safe and profitable investments. For the banks which own them, gilts are profitable, but illiquid in the sense that the banks may suffer capital losses if they decide to sell the gilts on a falling second-hand market. From the banks' point of view, the risk of capital loss is greater than for bills.

> **TEST YOURSELF 12.18**
> Describe the liquidity/ profitability trade-off facing a commercial bank such as TSB.

SECTION 12.2 SUMMARY

- Banks can be divided into commercial banks and investment banks, though commercial banks can be better thought of as retail banks or 'high-street' banks.
- The growing size and role of investment banks or wholesale banks, both in the UK and in other economies, contributed to the global financial crisis which started in 2007.
- Investment banks are very difficult for national governments and central banks to control; some banks that conducted both retail and investment banking activities were deemed 'too big to fail'.
- By creating credit, giving loans, banks also create deposits, which are the main constituent of the money supply.
- The amount of credit a bank can create is affected by its liquidity and its capital.
- For banks, there are potential conflicts between liquidity, profitability and security.

12.3 Central banks and monetary policy

The main functions of a central bank

> **KEY TERM**
> **central bank** a national bank that provides financial and banking services for its country's government and banking system, as well as implementing the government's monetary policy and issuing currency. The Bank of England is the UK's central bank.

We have already mentioned that most banks are either commercial or investment banks, or both, whose main aim is to make a profit for their owners. Although it makes a considerable profit, the most significant exception is the Bank of England, which is the UK's **central bank**. For most of the period since its formation in 1694, the Bank of England was a private enterprise company. However, the Bank was nationalised in 1946 and its surplus profit goes to the state.

A central bank has two key functions: to help the government maintain macroeconomic stability and to bring about financial stability in the monetary system. With regard to macroeconomic stability, the Bank of England's remit is to deliver price stability and, subject to that, to support the government's economic objectives including those for growth and employment. The price stability remit is defined, not in terms of zero inflation, but by the government's inflation target, currently 2% on the consumer prices index (CPI). The remit emphasises the importance of price stability in achieving macroeconomic stability, and in providing the right conditions for sustainable growth in output and employment.

TEST YOURSELF 12.19
With an example of each, distinguish between a central bank and an investment bank.

TEST YOURSELF 12.20
What is the difference between a policy objective and a policy instrument?

Financial stability can be achieved, in part, through the central bank acting as lender of last resort to the banking system, and also, in part, by the central bank's monitoring and regulation of the financial system. The lender of last resort function is a standard function of central banks worldwide. It is commonly defined as the readiness of the central bank to extend loans to banks that are solvent but have short-term liquidity problems. By providing these funds, though at a price, the central bank aims to protect depositors and in the extreme case to prevent a systemic crisis in the financial system.

Central banks also carry out other related functions such as: controlling the note issue, acting as the bankers' bank, acting as the government's bank, buying and selling currencies to influence the exchange rate, and liaising with overseas central banks and international organisations.

We explained on page 427 how and why banks keep balances at the Bank of England, just as members of the general public keep balances in the retail banks themselves. This is the 'bankers' bank' function of the Bank of England. The government also has bank accounts at the Bank of England. However, the Bank's role as banker to the government has been significantly reduced; since May 1998 the Debt Management Office (DMO) has issued gilts on behalf of the Treasury, and in 2000 the DMO took over responsibility for issuing Treasury bills and managing the government's short-term cash needs.

Implementing monetary policy

Complementing the central bank functions we have just explained is the Bank of England's function of implementing monetary policy on behalf of the UK government.

Monetary policy is the part of economic policy that attempts to achieve the government's macroeconomic objectives using monetary instruments, such as controls over bank lending and the rate of interest. Before 1997, monetary policy was implemented by the Bank of England on a day-to-day basis but the Bank 'consulted' with the Treasury and in the end the Treasury had a veto over Bank Rate decisions (though the veto was never exercised). The Treasury, which is a part of central government, and the Bank of England were then known as the monetary authorities. But the Treasury abandoned its hands-on role in implementing monetary policy in 1997 when the government made the Bank of England operationally independent. Unless the Bank is put under pressure by the Treasury, there is now only one monetary authority: the Bank of England.

Objectives and instruments of monetary policy

To understand monetary policy, it is useful to distinguish between policy objectives and policy instruments.

- A policy *objective* is the target that the Bank of England aims to hit.
- A policy *instrument* is the tool of control used to try to achieve the objective.

Monetary policy objectives and instruments can be classified in different ways. Policy objectives can be divided into ultimate and intermediate objectives. Policy instruments separate into those that directly affect the supply of new deposits that the commercial banks can create and those that influence the creation of bank deposits by affecting the demand for loans or credit.

429

Monetary policy *objectives* and the role of the MPC

For over 35 years, control of inflation has been the main objective of UK monetary policy. The government needs to control inflation in order to create conditions in which the ultimate policy objective of improved economic welfare can be attained. With this in mind, the government, in the person of the chancellor of the exchequer, sets the inflation rate target, which since 2003 has been 2% CPI inflation, and instructs the Bank of England's **Monetary Policy Committee** (MPC) to operate monetary policy so as to 'hit' this target.

Monetary policy *instruments* and the role of the MPC

Monetary policy instruments are the tools used to achieve the objectives of monetary policy. In the UK, they can involve the Bank of England taking action to influence interest rates, the supply of money and credit, and the exchange rate.

Before 2009, UK monetary policy relied almost exclusively on the Monetary Policy Committee's use of **Bank Rate**, which is the Bank of England's key interest rate, to manage the demand for bank loans.

TEST YOURSELF 12.21
What is Bank Rate at the time you are reading this chapter?

Managing the demand for credit through the use of Bank Rate

In normal circumstances, monetary policy, rather than fiscal policy, is now used to manage the level of aggregate demand in the economy. To understand how monetary policy is used in this way, it is worth restating the aggregate demand equation:

$$AD = C + I + G + (X - M)$$

Whereas fiscal policy can affect aggregate demand by changing the level of government spending (G), monetary policy affects the other components of aggregate demand, C, I and ($X - M$).

Factors considered by the Monetary Policy Committee when setting Bank Rate

When deciding whether to raise or lower Bank Rate, or indeed to leave the rate unchanged, the MPC takes account of the current rate of inflation, the existence of inflationary or deflationary pressure, consumer and business confidence, the economy's growth rate, the levels of employment and unemployment, and a number of other economic indicators.

The committee is currently given a leeway of 1% above and 1% below the 2% CPI inflation rate, but if the inflation rate moves outside this band of flexibility, the governor of the Bank of England must write an open letter to the chancellor explaining why this has happened.

However, in the 2008–09 recession, negative economic growth and growing unemployment led to a situation in which controlling inflation as the main monetary policy objective was temporarily placed on the back-burner, with monetary policy being used instead to try to increase aggregate demand and bring about recovery from recession.

For several years before this, the objectives of monetary policy had been symmetrical in the sense that the Bank of England must stimulate aggregate demand, which will generally raise the rate of inflation, whenever inflation is expected to fall below the target rate, just as the Bank will try to decrease aggregate demand to reduce inflation whenever inflation is expected to exceed the target rate. Although the Bank's primary objective is price stability, it must also support the government's economic policy objectives, including those for growth and employment.

Contractionary monetary policy

In **contractionary monetary policy** interest rates are increased so as to take demand out of the economy. In Figure 12.6, higher interest rates shift the AD curve to the left. However, the extent to which the price level then falls (or, more realistically, the rate of inflation falls), and/or real output falls, depends on the shape of the economy's $SRAS$ curve. In Figure 12.6, the leftward shift of aggregate demand from AD_1 to AD_2 causes both the price level and real output to fall, respectively from P_1 to P_2, and from y_1 to y_2. This illustrates the possibility that a contractionary monetary policy, which aims to control the rate of inflation in the economy, might also cause the economy to sink into a recession. This is especially likely if the contractionary monetary policy triggers a large multiplier that shifts the AD curve even further to the left.

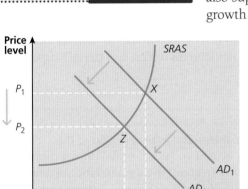

Figure 12.6 How an increase in the interest rate in a contractionary monetary policy causes the AD curve to shift to the left

How an increase in interest rates decreases aggregate demand

There are three main ways in which an increase in interest rates decreases aggregate demand:

- **Higher interest rates reduce household consumption** (C). First, higher interest rates encourage people to save, and higher saving means that less income is therefore available for consumption. Second, the cost of household borrowing increases, which increases the cost of servicing a mortgage and credit card debt. Borrowers have less money to spend on consumption because more of their income is being used for interest payments. Third, higher interest rates may cause asset prices, such as the prices of houses and shares, to fall. (An asset is something that has a value and can be sold for money). These falling prices reduce personal wealth, which reduces consumption. Fourth, falling house and share prices reduce consumer confidence, which further deflates consumption.
- **Higher interest rates reduce business investment** (I). Investment is the purchase of capital goods such as machines by firms. Businesses postpone or cancel investment projects because they believe that higher borrowing costs make the purchase of capital goods unprofitable. This is likely to be exacerbated by a fall in business confidence and increased business pessimism.

- **Changes in interest rates affect exports and imports via the exchange rate.** The third way in which an increase in interest rates leads to a decrease in aggregate demand works through the effect of higher interest rates on net export demand ($X - M$).
    - In the context of the UK balance of payments, a higher interest rate increases the demand for pounds by attracting capital flows into the currency. The increased demand for sterling causes the pound's **exchange rate** to rise, which makes UK exports less price competitive in world markets and imports more competitive in UK markets. The UK's balance of payments on current account worsens, which shifts the *AD* curve leftward.
    - By contrast, a fall in interest rates triggers a capital outflow in the balance of payments. The resulting increase in the supply of pounds on the foreign market leads to a fall in the exchange rate. Exports become more price competitive, and the current account of the balance of payments improves. Aggregate demand increases, and the *AD* curve shifts rightward.

> **KEY TERM**
> **exchange rate** the external price of a currency, usually measured against another currency.

> **STUDY TIP**
> 'Sterling' is the word often used for the pound in the context of the currency's role in the international economy: for example, the sterling price of imports. Economists often write about the demand for sterling.

Expansionary monetary policy

An **expansionary monetary policy**, the effect of which is illustrated in Figure 12.7, operates in the opposite way to that described above. A Bank Rate cut discourages saving, while stimulating borrowing, consumption and investment spending. Exports also increase. As already explained, lower interest rates cause the exchange rate to fall, making exports more price competitive and imports less competitive. The *AD* curve shifts to the right, with the size of the shift depending on the size of the multiplier. Finally, the extent to which real output increases or the price level rises depends on the shape and slope of the economy's *SRAS* curve, which in turn depends on the state of the economy. When the economy produces well below the normal capacity level of output, the *SRAS* curve is relatively 'flat'. In these circumstances, an expansionary monetary policy is likely to increase real output (and jobs), whereas the increasing 'steepness' of the *SRAS* curve as normal capacity utilisation approaches means that the stimulation of real output gives way to price inflation.

> **KEY TERM**
> **expansionary monetary policy** uses lower interest rates to increase aggregate demand and to shift the *AD* curve to the right.

The transmission mechanism of interest rate policy

The Bank of England argues that changes in Bank rate affects aggregate demand and inflation through a number of channels, which form the transmission mechanism of Bank rate policy. The flow chart in Figure 12.8 shows the routes through which changes in Bank Rate (the instrument of monetary policy, shown at point 1 in the diagram), eventually affect inflation (the objective of monetary policy, shown at point 11).

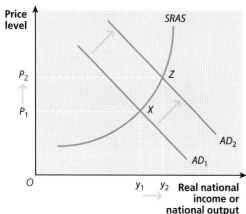

Figure 12.7 How a reduction in interest rate in an expansionary monetary policy causes the *AD* curve to shift to the right

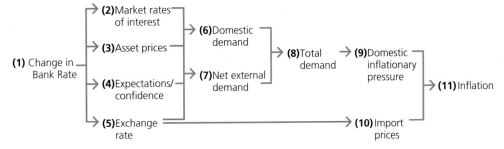

Figure 12.8 The transmission mechanism of interest rate policy

Official Bank Rate decisions (point 1 in Figure 12.8) affect market interest rates (point 2), such as mortgage rates and bank deposit rates set by commercial banks and other financial institutions. At the same time, policy actions and announcements affect expectations about the future course of the economy and the confidence with which these expectations are held (point 4). They also affect asset prices (point 3) and the exchange rate (point 5). (A rise or fall in the exchange rate also changes the prices of imports (point 10), which in turn affect the rate of inflation.)

These changes in turn affect aggregate demand in the economy (point 8). This comprises domestically generated demand (point 6) and net external demand (point 7), which is determined by export and import demand.

Domestic demand results from the spending, saving and investment behaviour of individuals and firms within the economy. Lower market interest rates increase domestic demand by encouraging consumption rather than saving by households and investment spending by firms. Conversely, higher market interest rates depress domestic spending. If Bank Rate falls, asset prices rise and people feel wealthier and generally more confident about the future. As a result, consumption increases.

Changes in aggregate demand affect domestic inflationary pressures (point 9). An increase in aggregate demand that exceeds the economy's ability to increase the supply of output creates demand-pull inflationary pressures.

Time lags in the transmission mechanism of interest rate policy

The Bank of England estimates a time lag of up to 2 years between an initial change in Bank Rate (point 1) and the resulting change in the rate of inflation (point 11). Output is affected within 1 year, but the fullest effect on inflation occurs after a lag of 2 years. In terms of the size of the effect, the Bank believes a 1% change in its official interest rate affects output by about 0.2–0.35% after about a year and inflation by around 0.2–0.4% per year after 2 years.

TEST YOURSELF 12.23
In relation to monetary policy, what is a transmission mechanism?

'Conventional' and 'unconventional' monetary policy

In recent years, the monetary policy that we have described so far in this chapter, which centres on lowering or raising Bank Rate in order to manage the level of aggregate demand, has become known as 'conventional' monetary policy. In the UK, this policy worked well for most of the first decade of the twenty-first century, but broke down in the financial crash and credit squeeze of 2007 and with the onset of recession in 2008.

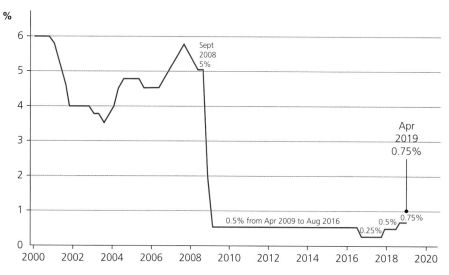

Source: Bank of England

Figure 12.9 Changes in UK Bank Rate, January 2000 to April 2019

Study Figure 12.9, which shows what happened to UK Bank Rate between January 2000 and April 2019. The data divide into two rather different halves. In the period before September 2008, extending back into the 1990s, Bank Rate was frequently changed, being raised or lowered in order to manage aggregate demand. However, in the months following September 2008, which was more or less the time that the recession started in the UK, Bank Rate was cut, first to a low of 0.5%, which lasted for several years, and then for a short period to 0.25%. Since then Bank rate has been increased on two occasions, and as Figure 12.9 shows, in April 2019 it stood at 0.75%.

At the time, the Bank Rate cuts were explained by some as a rather desperate attempt by the Bank of England to inject demand into the economy through the use of 'conventional' monetary policy. However, Bank Rate cuts failed to achieve this objective, and the economy experienced zero growth until late 2009 when recession gave way to a very slow economic recovery. Likewise, the Bank Rate increases which followed signalled 'conventional' monetary policy being used again to dampen inflationary pressures which were thought at the time to be re-emerging.

However, it was during this period that the Bank of England played down the role of 'conventional' monetary policy as a means of managing aggregate demand. Interest rate manipulation appeared not to be working, so the Bank began to use 'unconventional' monetary policy instruments to supplement the policy of keeping Bank Rate close to zero. Before we describe and explain these 'unconventional' instruments, we shall first introduce two concepts which help to explain why, in a deep recession, cuts in interest rates may fail to stimulate consumer spending. These are the concepts of 'zero lower bound' and the liquidity trap.

The zero lower bound

When Bank Rate is cut to a very low level, at or close to 0%, there comes a point at which a floor is reached. The Bank Rate floor is called the zero lower bound (ZLB). Once the zero lower bound is reached, it becomes impossible, in the Bank of England's view, to cut Bank Rate any further, which means that the 'conventional' monetary policy of reducing interest rates to stimulate aggregate demand is rendered ineffective.

The liquidity trap

Related to the zero lower bound is the liquidity trap, which describes a situation when cutting interest rates below a certain level fails to stimulate consumer spending. In a deep recession, it is likely to be the case that, however low Bank Rate is set, consumers refuse to borrow, and banks are too nervous to lend. Fear grips households and businesses, and spending in the economy dries up. A very low Bank Rate traps the country into a situation in which further cuts have little or no effect on the state of aggregate demand.

Quantitative easing

The main form of 'unconventional' monetary policy is called **quantitative easing** (QE). In 2009, the Bank of England's MPC began to use QE to influence commercial banks' ability to supply new loans to their customers. Quantitative easing, which is also known as the Asset Purchase Scheme, involves the Bank of England buying financial assets, usually government bonds or gilts, with new money the Bank has created electronically. The hope is that the financial institutions (banks, pension funds and insurance companies) which sell the bonds to the Bank of England will then lend the newly created money to businesses and individuals. The latter can then invest and spend more, hopefully increasing growth.

> **KEY TERM**
> **quantitative easing** when the Bank of England buys assets, usually government bonds, with money that the Bank has created electronically.

However, quantitative easing is by no means a new policy. Many monetary economists regard QE as simply a new name for an old policy called 'expansionary open market operations', which was used as far back as the 1930s.

EXTENSION MATERIAL

How quantitative easing works

To understand quantitative easing, you should be aware that monetary policy can operate in two contrasting ways: on the demand for money, or on the supply of money. Unlike changes in Bank Rate, which attempt to influence the demand for money and thence aggregate demand, the principal aim of quantitative easing (QE) is to increase the money supply directly. When QE was started in the UK in 2009, the Bank of England hoped that the new money would be quickly spent by the households and firms who received it, thereby reviving consumer and investment spending and stimulating economic growth.

People often think that QE increases the money supply through the printing of new banknotes. Indeed, when QE started in 2009, the metaphor was used of a central bank filling a helicopter with newly printed banknotes, before dropping the 'helicopter money' on the general public, who would then spend it.

However, QE is not as simple as this. To understand why, you should appreciate that as we explained earlier in the chapter, bank deposits, and not cash, make up the lion's share of the money supply. QE increases the deposits that commercial banks hold at the Bank of England — and these deposits are part of the money supply. At the next stage, holding more deposits at the Bank of England increases the commercial banks' ability to lend to the general public.

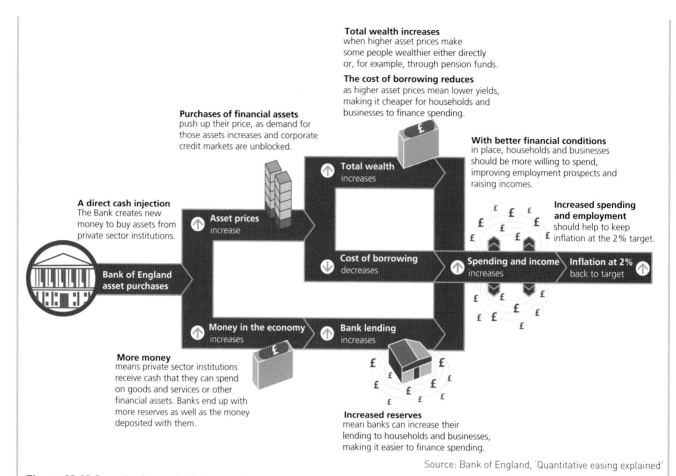

Total wealth increases
when higher asset prices make some people wealthier either directly or, for example, through pension funds.

The cost of borrowing reduces
as higher asset prices mean lower yields, making it cheaper for households and businesses to finance spending.

Purchases of financial assets
push up their price, as demand for those assets increases and corporate credit markets are unblocked.

With better financial conditions
in place, households and businesses should be more willing to spend, improving employment prospects and raising incomes.

A direct cash injection
The Bank creates new money to buy assets from private sector institutions.

Increased spending and employment
should help to keep inflation at the 2% target.

Asset prices increase

Total wealth increases

Bank of England asset purchases

Cost of borrowing decreases

Spending and income increases

Inflation at 2% back to target

Money in the economy increases

Bank lending increases

More money
means private sector institutions receive cash that they can spend on goods and services or other financial assets. Banks end up with more reserves as well as the money deposited with them.

Increased reserves
mean banks can increase their lending to households and businesses, making it easier to finance spending.

Source: Bank of England, 'Quantitative easing explained'

Figure 12.10 Quantitative easing's transmission route

The various stages through which QE proceeds are illustrated in Figure 12.10, published by the Bank of England. Explaining the flow chart in the diagram, the Bank wrote:

> Direct injections of money into the economy, primarily by buying gilts, can have a number of effects. The sellers of the assets have more money so may go out and spend it. That will help to boost growth. Or they may buy other assets instead, such as shares or company bonds. That will push up the prices of those assets, making the people who own them, either directly or through their pension funds, better off. So they may go out and spend more. And higher asset prices mean lower yields, which brings down the cost of borrowing for businesses and households. That should provide a further boost to spending.

> In addition, banks will find themselves holding more reserves. That might lead them to boost their lending to consumers and businesses. So, once again, borrowing increases and so does spending. That said, if banks are concerned about their financial health, they may prefer to hold the extra reserves without expanding lending. For this reason, the Bank of England is buying most of the assets from the wider economy rather than the banks.

> Normally, central banks do not intervene in private sector asset markets by buying or selling private sector debt. But in exceptional circumstances, such intervention may be warranted — for example, when corporate credit markets became blocked as the financial crisis intensified towards the end of 2008. Bank of England purchases of private sector debt can help to unblock corporate credit markets, by reassuring market participants that there is a ready buyer should they wish to sell. That should help bring down the cost of borrowing, making it easier and cheaper for companies to raise finance which they can then invest in their business.

STUDY TIP
QE is when a central bank creates money electronically which it uses to buy financial assets, mainly bonds. It is designed to support, but not to replace, Bank Rate policy.

QE1, QE2, QE3 and QE4

Quantitative easing was first used by the Bank of England in March 2009, though the USA had begun QE a few months earlier. In the UK there were initially three 'bouts' of quantitative easing, first in March 2009 (QE1), then in October 2011 (QE2) and finally in February and July 2012 (QE3), ending in November 2012. In the first three bouts, £200 billion, then £75 billion and finally £100 billion of 'new money' was unleashed into the banking system, making up a total of £375 billion.

In August 2016, the Bank of England said it would buy an additional £60 billion of UK government bonds (plus £10 billion of private sector corporate bonds), to address uncertainty over Brexit and worries about productivity and economic growth. Some economists called this QE4. By the end of 2016, therefore, a total of £445 billion of 'new money' had been released into the British economy (see Table 12.5).

Table 12.5 The four phases of quantitative easing in the UK between March 2009 and August 2016

QE1	£200 billion between March 2009 and January 2010
QE2	£125 billion between October 2011 and May 2012
QE3	£50 billion between July 2012 and October 2012
QE4	£60 billion from August 2016 + £10 billion purchase of corporate bonds from the private sector
Total amount	£445 billion, including corporate bond purchases

In recent years there has been some talk of the Bank of England reversing or 'unwinding' quantitative easing by selling back to the public some of the government bonds it accumulated while engaging in expansionary quantitative easing. This would be a form of contractionary monetary policy, taking demand out of the economy. However, with the uncertainty induced by the Brexit crisis, at the time of writing in July 2019, a reversal of QE has not yet taken place.

Has quantitative easing been successful?

It can be argued that QE1 worked in the sense that it prevented the 2008–09 recession from developing — as a result of collapsing aggregate demand — into a full-blown depression. It is debateable, however, whether the later bouts of quantitative easing had much effect in bringing about recovery from recession. From 2010 onward, the growth rate in the UK economy 'flat-lined', remaining very close to zero. When in 2013 a more substantial recovery did occur, further rounds of QE were not being implemented in the UK — at least until the time of the Brexit referendum in 2016.

It was also the case that, until early 2015, the continuation of QE in America stimulated growth in other countries, including the UK. (It is worth noting that QE was also started by the European Central Bank (ECB) in 2015 to try to offset the danger of negative growth returning to the eurozone economy.)

It could be argued that QE, along with 0.5% Bank Rate, was partly responsible for the rate of inflation being higher than it otherwise would have been. It was also the case that the increased bank lending made possible by quantitative easing went, not into cheap loans to small businesses and households, but into speculative activities undertaken by the banks themselves and by the big corporations which have most benefited from the cheap money sloshing around the British and American economies. House and land prices also went up. The asset-owning wealthy did much better out of quantitative easing than the poor who own few assets.

By reducing long-term interest rates and raising bond prices, QE also benefited the UK government. This was because QE made it much cheaper for central government to borrow to finance its large budget deficit and to pay interest on the national debt. House buyers have also benefited from the cheap mortgage loans made possible by the 0.5% Bank Rate and quantitative easing. On the other hand, savers and workers contributing to private pension schemes have suffered, although recent government policy has tried to counter this.

The *Bank of England Quarterly Bulletin* published in quarter 4, 2012 estimated that the £375 billion of QE up to that point had increased the supply of broad money in the UK by about £220 billion, or 15%, which in turn increased nominal GDP by nearly 6%. If this is true, then quantitative easing was indeed a factor causing recovery from recession. However, in an article titled 'Monetary impact of UK QE much smaller than claimed by BoE', which was published in January 2013, Simon Ward, the chief economist at Henderson Global Investors, argued that the first £375 billion of QE had delivered a monetary boost of only £78 billion.

EXTENSION MATERIAL

The Brexit vote and QE4

Immediately after the result of the Brexit referendum in 2016, the MPC acted quickly to stimulate the economy. In the following weeks, the Bank of England set out a package to prevent the economy from falling back into recession. First, Bank Rate was cut from 0.5% to 0.25% in the hope that ultra-low interest rates would ease borrowing costs. Second, the QE programme was restarted (QE4). This had two elements: £60 billion was made available to buy government bonds (a continuation of the QE 1, 2 and 3 approach); and £10 billion was allocated to buying corporate bonds to make it easier for business to raise finance for investment in the capital markets. Finally, the Bank introduced a new Term Funding Scheme which saw the Bank of England provide up to £100 billion of funding for commercial banks at interest rates close to 0.25%. The scheme was designed to make sure that commercial banks kept on lending to businesses, and if they reduced their lending, the rate of interest charged by the central bank would increase.

It is impossible to know what would have happened to the UK economy if the Bank of England had not taken swift action. Supporters of Brexit have been highly critical of governor of the Bank of England, Mark Carney, and of the mainstream economics profession, arguing that the warnings of economic catastrophe were part of the establishment's 'project fear', intended to scare the British people to vote to remain inside the European Union. The predictions of immediate economic collapse were incorrect for two reasons. First, if the majority of the British public voted to leave the EU, it is irrational for them to start hoarding cash in fear of an economic collapse. Second, after a volatile couple of days, the markets settled down as businesses and traders started to realise that the UK was going to remain a member of the single market for at least another 2 years and that the nature of the UK's departure was yet to be negotiated.

Nevertheless, what is clear is that in the 2 years following the Brexit vote in 2016 the UK's GDP growth slowed significantly. Due to the uncertainty surrounding the nature of future trade relationships, new business investment slowed. The 15% depreciation in sterling against the US dollar led to a hike in inflation, and higher prices of imported goods, mostly food and energy, hit households' standards of living. Consumer spending remained strong but much of this was financed by households taking advantage of the ultra-low interest rates and reducing their savings. Economists estimate that the UK's economy was 2% smaller than it would have been had the British people voted to remain. The supporters of Brexit dismiss these economists as part of a discredited profession that wrongly predicted the meltdown of the UK economy on 24 June 2016.

Forward guidance

A second 'unconventional' part of monetary policy became known as **forward guidance**. The policy, which was introduced by Mark Carney shortly after taking up his appointment as governor of the Bank of England, attempted to send signals to financial markets, businesses and individuals about the Bank of England's interest rate policy in the months and years ahead.

An aim of forward guidance was to increase the credibility of monetary policy. By using forward guidance, the Bank of England aims to calm uncertainty in otherwise jittery financial markets. If, for example, markets fear that low interest rates will move higher, interest rates on bonds and other credit instruments and agreements will rise and begin to discourage people and companies from taking out loans or spending money. But if the Bank of England signals that it intends to keep rates low, the Bank hopes to engineer an outcome in which interest rates are indeed kept low.

And by altering expectations favourably, forward guidance aims to improve the credibility of monetary policy, thereby enabling households and businesses to feel calmer about their future economic prospects. According to the Bank, forward guidance means companies and mortgage borrowers can estimate for how long low interest rates will be around. If this is achieved, forward guidance is a way of converting low short-term interest rates into lower long-term interest rates.

KEY TERM

forward guidance attempts to send signals to financial markets, businesses and individuals, about the Bank of England's interest rate policy in the months and years ahead, so that economic agents are not surprised by a sudden and unexpected change in policy.

EXTENSION MATERIAL

Forward guidance and the need for accurate economic forecasting

Mark Carney received considerable criticism for his attempts to pre-warn households, business and markets that changes in monetary policy were likely. In June 2014 an MP on the Treasury committee joked that forward guidance had led to the Bank of England acting like an 'unreliable boyfriend' by hinting that Bank Rate rises were imminent but failing to deliver. This sends confusing signals to the markets and merely increases the level of uncertainty.

When first announcing forward guidance in August 2013, Mark Carney said that the Bank would not consider raising Bank Rate from its low of 0.5% until the unemployment rate fell to 7% or below, which at the time the Bank forecast would happen in 2016. The forecast was wrong, and unemployment fell much faster than predicted, yet the MPC did not increase Bank Rate despite the rate of unemployment falling below 7% in early 2014.

If financial markets believed what Carney and the MPC were saying, the hope was that the markets would remain calm and orderly, and behave in a way which was consistent with the forward guidance strategy. There were, however, two dangers. First, the strategy could be knocked off course by an event such as a house price bubble hitting the UK economy (or, as happened, a faster than expected fall in unemployment).

Second, and related to this, financial markets might form their own expectations of what they thought was going to happen in the future. If markets believed that a bubble was going to occur, then, whatever the Bank of England's official policy, market operators might ignore the forward guidance strategy and raise interest rates anyway. Either way, if traders in financial markets perceive the strategy to be 'wishful thinking', forward guidance could damage rather than increase the credibility of the Bank of England in its management of the UK economy.

Forward guidance also loses credibility if the Bank of England repeatedly 'moves the goal posts' — that is, changes policy every few months in the light of unexpected events hitting the economy. This happened for the first time in January 2014, when UK borrowing costs shot up in expectation of a rise in Bank Rate, after the fall in unemployment had proved larger than Carney had expected. A few days later, Carney signalled the end of his forward guidance of linking interest rates to the unemployment rate, adding that the British economy was in a different place from where it had been in the previous summer. Thus, the Bank of England had overhauled its forward guidance strategy less than 6 months after it was first implemented.

Carney said that, instead of just considering the unemployment rate, the next phase of forward guidance would be determined by a range of 18 different indicators, which include productivity and the size of the output gap — the gap between potential and actual output. The Bank argued that a lack of inflationary pressure, spare capacity, and 'headwinds' at home and abroad, meant that 'Bank Rate may need to remain at low levels for some time to come'. Seeking to reassure businesses and households, the Bank's Monetary Policy Committee said that when rates did eventually go up, they would do so only gradually, settling around 2–3% — below the pre-crisis norm of around 5%.

Economists employed in the financial services industry were less than convinced. For example, Schroder's UK economist branded the new guidance as a 'bamboozling cluster bomb' which, on the one hand, highlights the degree of complexity in setting monetary policy, while, on the other hand, thoroughly confusing the average person. For cynics, forward guidance has introduced a new uncertainty for expectations on the future path of interest rates.

In general, the MPC is caught between trying to formulate monetary policy in a transparent manner that offers reassurance to markets, and the need to maintain short-term policy flexibility. Each month the MPC examines a variety of economic data and forecasts which can easily change given the unpredictable macroeconomic climate of recent years. It is extremely difficult for economic models to predict how monetary policy decisions may affect the economy in the next 2 years given the uncertainties surrounding Brexit and the possibility of a major trade war between the USA and China. Rather than attempting to give forward guidance and creating confusion, it might be better for monetary policy-makers to be clearer on the reaction function and how they will react to a given set of circumstances as they unfold.

The relationship between changes in interest rates and the exchange rate

A fall in UK interest rates causes financial capital to flow out of the pound and into other currencies in search of better rates of return. This reduces the demand for pounds and increases the supply of pounds on the foreign exchange market, which in turn causes the pound's exchange rate to fall. Changes in export and import prices brought about by a fall in the exchange rate affect inflation in two ways.

First, a falling exchange rate increases the prices of imported food and consumer goods. This increases the rate of inflation in the UK. At the same time, increased prices of imported raw materials and energy create cost-push inflationary pressures in the UK (import-cost-push inflation).

Second, a falling exchange rate reduces UK export prices, while raising the price of imports. This feeds into the inflationary process described above, by increasing the demand for UK exports and persuading some UK residents to buy more home-produced goods and fewer imports. This adds to demand-pull inflationary pressures. It is also likely to improve the UK's balance of payments on current account.

TEST YOURSELF 12.24
Explain the difference between Bank Rate's transmission mechanism and QE's transmission mechanism.

TEST YOURSELF 12.25
If the nominal interest rate is 6% and rate of inflation is 4%, what is the real rate of interest?

QUANTITATIVE SKILLS 12.4

Worked example: calculating real Bank Rate

In June 2014, Bank Rate was 0.5% and CPI inflation was 1.9%. What was Bank Rate expressed in real terms?

real rate of interest = nominal rate of interest – rate of inflation

Thus, in June 2014, Bank Rate expressed in real terms was 0.5% minus 1.9%, which is –1.4%.

SECTION 12.3 SUMMARY

- The main functions of the Bank of England are to implement the government's monetary policy and maintain the stability of financial markets.
- In recent decades, Bank Rate has been the main monetary policy instrument, aimed primarily at targeting the rate of inflation — that is, hitting a target of a 2% CPI rate of inflation. The target is set by the government and not the Bank.
- In an *AD/AS* diagram, monetary policy is illustrated by shifts of the *AD* curve to the right (expansionary monetary policy) and to the left (contractionary monetary policy).
- A 'good' deflation, caused by falling commodity prices and effective supply-side policies, might be deemed a success, but a 'bad' deflation, caused by a collapse of aggregate demand, would be a policy failure.
- In 2009, monetary policy switched away from relying solely on Bank Rate changes to a policy of quantitative easing (QE), through which the Bank of England buys bonds, reducing long-term interest rates and increasing the liquidity of financial markets.
- As well as QE, other 'unconventional' monetary policy instruments have been introduced, notably forward guidance, in 2013.

12.4 The regulation of the financial system

The meaning of regulation

We first explained regulation in section 8.8 of Chapter 8, when we said that governments use regulation to try to correct market failures and to achieve a socially optimal level of production and consumption. We also explained how regulation is used to limit and deter monopoly exploitation of consumers.

Regulation means imposing rules and sometimes laws which limit the freedom of individuals and businesses to make decisions of their own free will. *Financial regulation* involves limiting the freedom of banks and other financial institutions, and of the people they employ, to behave as they otherwise might wish to do.

TEST YOURSELF 12.26
Explain how regulation differs from deregulation.

Financial regulation in the UK

The recent history of financial regulation in the UK

Before 2001 the Bank of England largely controlled financial regulation in the UK. Back in 1985 a self-regulatory board, the Securities and Investments Board, was created with a limited number of regulatory powers. But after a series of scandals in the 1990s, culminating in the collapse of Barings Bank, there was a desire to bring to an end the self-regulation of the financial services industry and to consolidate regulatory responsibilities which previously had been split amongst multiple regulators.

In 1997, the name of the Securities and Investments Board was changed to the Financial Services Authority (FSA), an external regulator with a range of regulatory powers. The 1998 Bank of England Act, which also formally established the MPC and thereby radically changed the role of the Bank of England, transferred the responsibility for the supervision of deposit-taking institutions from the Bank to the FSA. However, the FSA did not start to exercise these powers until 2001 when the Bank of England was instructed to concentrate on banking, with its regulatory function taken away and given to the FSA.

But due to perceived regulatory failure of the banks during the financial crisis of 2007–08, the Treasury decided to abolish the FSA. It had been criticised for failing to spot the lending boom before 2007 and the subsequent bust, and for not curbing risky trading by banks, the end result of which was to see the collapse of banks such as Northern Rock and the Royal Bank of Scotland. The regulatory function of the FSA had lasted from 2001 until 2013, when the authority was eventually wound up.

With effect from 1 April 2013, some of the FSA's responsibilities were given to a new committee, the Financial Policy Committee (FPC) at the Bank of England, with the others being split between two new agencies, the Prudential Regulation Authority (PRA) — itself a part of the Bank of England — and the Financial Conduct Authority (FCA), which is not part of the Bank.

The Financial Policy Committee

Through the **Financial Policy Committee** (FPC) the Bank of England once again has responsibility for the Bank's second key function: maintaining financial stability. The FPC is primarily responsible for *macro*prudential regulation whereas the PRA and FCA are mainly responsible for *micro*prudential regulation. Macroprudential regulation is concerned with identifying, monitoring and acting to remove risks that affect the stability of the financial system as a whole. Microprudential regulation focuses on ensuring the stability of individual banks and other financial institutions; it involves identifying, monitoring and managing risks that relate to individual firms.

> **KEY TERM**
> **Financial Policy Committee** the part of the Bank of England charged with the primary objective of identifying, monitoring and taking action to remove or reduce systemic risks with a view to protecting and enhancing the resilience of the UK financial system. The committee's secondary objective is to support the economic policy of the government.

CASE STUDY 12.3

Macroprudential policy at the Bank of England

A vital element of recent reforms to the architecture of UK financial regulation is the creation of a macroprudential authority at the Bank of England — the Financial Policy Committee (FPC). In the 2008–09 recession, policy-makers around the world recognised that focusing separately on price stability and on microprudential regulation of individual firms and markets was not enough. A broader approach — macroprudential policy — was needed to ensure the resilience and stability of the financial system.

In the period leading up to the 2007–08 financial crisis, insufficient attention was paid to tackling risks and vulnerabilities across the financial system as a whole. The FPC fills that gap by identifying, monitoring and, crucially, taking action to remove or reduce systemic risks to the resilience of the financial system.

Under the Bank of England Act 1998, as amended by the Financial Services Act 2012, the Bank has a statutory objective to protect and enhance the stability of the financial system of the United Kingdom. The FPC is tasked with helping the Bank meet that objective and, subject to that, also supporting the government's economic policy, including its objectives for growth and employment.

The FPC has a statutory responsibility to identify, monitor and take action to remove or reduce risks that threaten the resilience of the UK financial system as a whole. This is supported by the objectives of the microprudential regulator, the Prudential Regulation Authority (PRA), which is part of the Bank of England. The PRA is responsible for the microprudential regulation of individual deposit-takers, insurers and major investment banks. The Financial Conduct Authority (FCA) is a separate institution responsible for ensuring that relevant markets function well, for conduct regulation and for microprudential regulation of financial services firms not supervised by the PRA, such as asset managers, hedge funds, many smaller broker-dealers and independent financial advisers.

One way in which the FPC can mitigate threats to the resilience of the financial system is by raising awareness of systemic risks among financial market participants. The FPC is required to publish a Financial Stability Report twice a year, which must identify key threats to the stability of the UK financial system.

At times, simply warning about risks may be sufficient to catalyse action within the private sector to reduce vulnerabilities. But experience from before the crisis showed that warnings alone are not always enough. The new legislation gives the FPC two main types of power: Recommendations and Directions.

Source: *Bank of England Quarterly Bulletin*, Quarter 3, 2013

Follow-up questions

1 What is the difference between macroprudential and microprudential regulation?
2 Explain the differences between the Bank of England's Monetary Policy Committee (MPC) and the Bank's Financial Policy Committee (FPC).
3 'The Bank has a statutory objective to protect and enhance the stability of the financial system of the United Kingdom.' Describe one event which might reduce the financial stability of the United Kingdom.
4 What is a systemic risk? Give an example of a 'systemic risk to the resilience of the financial system'.

KEY TERM

Prudential Regulation Authority the part of the Bank of England responsible for the microprudential regulation and supervision of banks, building societies, credit unions, insurers and major investment firms.

The Prudential Regulation Authority

The **Prudential Regulation Authority** (PRA) is responsible for the microprudential supervision of banks, building societies, credit unions, insurers and major investment firms. It sets standards and supervises financial institutions at the level of the individual firm. The authority regulates by setting standards which financial institutions are required to follow, and supervises by assessing the risks posed by individual financial firms and taking action to make sure they are managed properly. It aims to promote the soundness of banks and other firms providing financial services so that the stability of the UK financial system is enhanced.

> **KEY TERM**
> **Financial Conduct Authority** aims to make sure that financial markets work well so that consumers get a fair deal, by ensuring that the financial industry is run with integrity and that consumers can trust that firms have their best interests at heart, and by providing consumers with appropriate financial products and services.

The PRA may require individual institutions to maintain specified capital and liquidity ratios so as to try to ensure that, if a financial firm fails, it does so in a way that avoids significant disruption to essential financial services.

The Financial Conduct Authority

The aim of the **Financial Conduct Authority** (FCA) is to regulate the financial services industry in order to:

- *protect consumers* by securing an appropriate degree of protection for them
- *protect financial markets* so as to enhance the integrity of the UK financial system
- *promote effective competition* in the interests of consumers

However, the FCA is not without its critics and stands accused of being its own worst enemy, obsessed with media management rather than regulating markets. In March 2015 the authority was accused, in its search for flattering newspaper headlines, of creating a false market in insurance company shares — the very sin it is meant to prevent others committing.

Bank failures, liquidity assurance and moral hazard

A bank's capital is equal to the value of its assets minus the value of its liabilities, and if the value of its assets falls so that it runs out of capital, it is insolvent or bankrupt. A bank can also fail because it does not have sufficient liquidity. Insufficient liquidity makes a bank vulnerable to a run on the bank, which can cause the bank to fail, even if its assets are greater than its liabilities. However, the willingness of the central bank to act as lender of last resort and provide liquidity insurance increases confidence in the stability of the banks. It is necessary because the banks borrow short term (for example, overnight money borrowed on the inter-bank market), but lend long term (for example, mortgage loans which finance house purchase).

As the 2007–08 financial crisis showed, banks are sometimes tempted to take too many risks in pursuing the huge profits that lending long allows. They do this because they believe that the Bank of England, in its role as lender of last resort, and the government through its bailouts, will not allow banks to fail.

> **KEY TERM**
> **moral hazard** the tendency of individuals and firms, once protected against some contingency, to behave so as to make that contingency more likely.

This illustrates the problem of **moral hazard**. Moral hazard exists when a firm or individual pursues profit and takes on too much risk in the knowledge that, if things go wrong, someone else will bear a significant portion of the cost. Investing in high-risk assets can lead to high profits, but unless there is the possibility that financial institutions will be allowed to fail, there is insufficient incentive to act prudently.

When the Northern Rock bank got into financial difficulty in 2007, the Bank of England's initial reaction was to allow the bank to fail, as a way of teaching a lesson to other banks that might be taking excessive financial risks. However, the Bank soon realised that instead of promoting less risky behaviour, allowing a relatively small bank to fail could trigger a crisis within the whole commercial banking system, the effects of which would dwarf those of bailing out a reckless bank. The Bank of England quickly changed its policy and in effect nationalised the bank. Instead of allowing banks to go under, the Bank and the government started to bail out banks such as RBS, which failed in

October 2008 and was then part-nationalised. Rescuing banks deemed 'too big to fail' had replaced the policy of allowing banks to fail to teach others about the dangers of excessive risk taking.

However, the Bank of England's recognition of the problem of moral hazard did lead to other more robust measures being introduced, such as imposing 'firewalls' between the retail and the investment banking activities of the banks. In principle, such measures are meant to allow the riskier parts of the banks to fail without impairing the provision of their retail banking services.

Liquidity and capital ratios

Over time, banks have failed or required government assistance either because they lacked liquidity, or because they had inadequate capital, or through a combination of both of these contributory factors. Liquidity and capital are *distinct* but *related* concepts. Each plays an essential role in understanding a bank's viability and solvency.

We can use a family's finances to illustrate the differences between liquidity and capital. On the liquidity side, money in a family's bank account and any cash the family has on hand that can be used quickly and easily to pay its bills are measures of the family's liquidity position. On the capital side, the family's assets include not just the money in its bank account, but also its home, savings accounts and other investments. The family debts, or money it owes, such as a mortgage, are its liabilities. So the difference between the family's debts and its assets would provide a measure of the family's capital position.

We have already looked at a retail bank's **liquidity ratio** in the context of explaining how banks create credit and money. A bank's liquidity ratio is the ratio of cash and other liquid assets owned by the bank to its deposit liabilities. Liquidity is a measure of the ability and ease with which assets can be converted to cash. Liquid assets are those that can be converted into cash quickly, if needed to meet financial obligations. Examples of liquid assets are cash itself, balances held at the central bank, and holdings of short-dated government debt. To remain viable, a financial institution must have enough liquid assets to meet its near-term obligations, such as withdrawals of cash by depositors. Liquidity problems arise when a bank does not hold sufficient cash (or assets that can easily be converted into cash) to repay depositors and other creditors.

A bank's capital, which is the difference between the value of the bank's assets and its liabilities, represents the net worth of the bank or its value to those who own the bank. Alternatively, assuming the bank is a company, the bank's capital can be thought of as the shareholders' stake in the bank. Capital, which acts as a financial cushion that allows a bank to absorb unexpected losses, protects creditors in case the bank's assets fall in value. A bank's **capital ratio** is the amount of capital on a bank's balance sheet as a proportion of its loans. The ratio can be used as an indicator of a bank's financial health. Bank regulators are likely to require the capital ratio to be above a prescribed minimum level.

If banks do not have sufficient capital, they are at risk if the value of their assets falls. While *insufficient liquidity* makes a bank vulnerable to a run on the bank, *insufficient capital* exposes the bank to the risk of a fall in the value of its assets. If a bank invests in assets which fall in value because, for example, some customers default on their loans, this will result in losses and reduce the

KEY TERMS

liquidity ratio the ratio of a bank's cash and other liquid assets to its deposits.

capital ratio the amount of capital on a bank's balance sheet as a proportion of its loans.

bank's capital. If the reduction in the value of a bank's assets is so large that it wipes out the whole of the bank's capital, the bank is technically bankrupt and cannot continue trading.

In 2010 and 2011 the Basel III agreement was signed by the members of the Basel Committee on Banking Supervision, which include the Bank of England. The agreement, which is voluntary, is supposed to strengthen bank capital requirements by increasing bank liquidity and decreasing borrowing by banks. At the time of writing in July 2019 it is likely that the changes to capital ratios agreed in Basle III will finally be introduced by the beginning of 2022.

Systemic risk and the impact of problems that arise when financial markets affect the real economy

We defined and briefly explained systemic risk earlier in the chapter. We stated that financial systemic risk refers to the risk of a breakdown of the entire financial system, caused by inter-linkages within the financial system, rather than simply the failure of an individual bank or financial institution within the system.

The largest and most dramatic recent example of financial systems being threatened by systemic failure occurred in the so-called 'credit crunch', which began in 2007 and extended into 2009. The credit crunch, defined as 'a severe shortage of money or credit', began on 9 August 2007 when the French bank BNP Paribas told its depositors that they would not be able to take money out of two of the bank's funds because BNP Paribas could not value the assets in them, owing to a 'complete evaporation of liquidity' in the market.

This was the clearest sign yet that banks were refusing to do business with each other, which triggered a sharp rise in interest rates. However, the roots of the credit crunch were in place several years earlier.

Virtually all firms, large and small, require a reliable supply of credit or bank lending in order to remain in business. In 'normal' circumstances, the banking system provides this liquidity, which businesses, consumers and governments usually take for granted. Historically, the source of this liquidity was banks borrowing household savings, which the financial intermediaries then passed on through their lending for others to spend.

However, by 2007, banks throughout the world, but particularly in the USA, were raising the funds they lent to customers by borrowing from each other rather than from households. The funds were borrowed on the interbank market. In the USA, much of the borrowed funds were lent in the form of mortgages to low-income customers who were bad credit risks. These loans became known as *sub-prime* mortgages (in contrast to *prime* mortgages, which are secured loans granted to low-risk home owners). From a bank's point of view, a mortgage granted to a customer is an asset. For the borrower, it is a liability, since the house owner must eventually pay back the loan and pay interest in the intervening months and years. By definition, a sub-prime mortgage is a risky asset since there is a danger of the loan turning into a bad debt, which the bank that lent the money cannot recover.

In 2007, the credit crunch developed because the banks that had created sub-prime mortgages repackaged the risky assets and sold them on to other banks as if they were prime mortgages. In essence, banks were buying 'toxic debt' from each other, without understanding that the repackaged assets were

TEST YOURSELF 12.27
Distinguish between a capital ratio and a liquidity ratio.

extremely risky. As banks realised that many of their so-called 'assets' were more or less worthless, the situation quickly deteriorated and the supply of liquidity began to freeze. Banks became unwilling to lend to each other because they distrusted each other's creditworthiness. At the next stage, the credit crunch triggered a financial meltdown when banks either collapsed (Lehman Brothers in the USA) or were partly or completely nationalised by governments (Royal Bank of Scotland in the UK).

BNP Paribas's failure to honour its financial obligations started the credit crunch, and the financial crisis that followed eventually destabilised the real economies of many countries, including the USA and the UK. The financial crisis caused a collapse of aggregate demand, which in turn led to rising unemployment and recession. The credit crunch paralysed financial markets, threatening affected countries with the problem of systemic failure in their financial systems. Systemic failure was eventually largely averted through government and central bank intervention to rescue financial systems, but by this time much real economic damage had been done.

SECTION 12.4 SUMMARY

- A financial market is a market in which financial assets or securities are traded. The financial markets you need to know are money markets, capital markets and foreign exchange markets.
- In the light of what happened in the financial crisis and credit crunch after 2007, financial regulatory authorities have been set up in the UK to try to prevent systemic risk and moral hazard problems.
- Systemic risk in a financial context refers to the risk of a breakdown of the entire financial system, caused by inter-linkages within the financial system, rather than simply the failure of an individual bank or financial institution within the system.
- Moral hazard is the tendency of individuals and firms, once protected against some contingency, to behave so as to make that contingency more likely.
- The main authorities involved in financial regulation in the UK are the Bank of England's Financial Policy Committee (FPC), the Prudential Regulations Authority (PRA), which is also a part of the Bank of England, and the Financial Conduct Authority (FCA).

Questions

1 What is money? Explain how both the Bank of England and privately owned banks create money.

2 Explain how changes in Bank Rate may affect bank lending and the economy.

3 How has quantitative easing operated in the UK? Evaluate the case for and against the Bank of England extending quantitative easing.

4 Do you agree that monetary policy has been highly effective in the UK in recent years? Justify your answer.

5 Distinguish between capital markets and money markets. Explain how UK capital markets help both public limited companies (PLCs) and the government to undertake their functions.

13

Fiscal policy and supply-side policies

Fiscal policy is the part of economic policy in which the government attempts to achieve policy objectives using the fiscal instruments of government spending, taxation and the government's budgetary position (balanced budget, budget deficit or budget surplus). Supply-side economic policy is the set of government policies that aim to change the underlying structure of the economy and improve the economic performance of markets and industries, and also of individual firms and workers within markets. Supply-side fiscal policy is an important supply-side policy, but supply-side policies encompass more than just fiscal policy measures.

Section 13.1 offers an in-depth explanation of certain key aspects of fiscal policy. Section 13.2, which makes up the second half of the chapter, provides a similar coverage of supply-side policies.

LEARNING OBJECTIVES

These are to understand:

- what is meant by fiscal policy
- the difference between macroeconomic and microeconomic fiscal policy
- how fiscal policy can be used to influence both aggregate demand and aggregate supply
- how government spending and taxation can affect the pattern of economic activity
- the types of and reasons for public expenditure and taxation
- direct and indirect taxation, and progressive, proportionate and regressive taxes
- the principles of taxation
- the role and relative merits of different UK taxes
- budget deficits, surpluses and the national debt
- the role of the Office for Budget Responsibility
- the consequences of budget deficits and surpluses for macroeconomic performance
- supply-side policies and supply-side improvements
- the difference between free-market and interventionist supply-side policies
- the role of supply-side policies in reducing the natural rate of unemployment and in achieving the government's macroeconomic objectives
- the distinction between the microeconomic and macroeconomic effect of supply-side policies

13.1 Fiscal policy

The meaning of fiscal policy

Fiscal policy is the part of a government's overall economic policy that aims to achieve the government's economic objectives through the use of the fiscal instruments of taxation, public spending and the government's budgetary position. As an economic term, fiscal policy is often associated with Keynesian macroeconomic theory and policy. Between the 1950s and late 1970s, Keynesian governments used fiscal policy to manage the level of aggregate demand.

However, fiscal policy can also have microeconomic functions, especially when used to make markets more flexible and dynamic. At a micro level, government will use taxation and subsidies to influence consumer behaviour, and income tax and the welfare system to create incentives in the labour market.

How fiscal policy can be used to influence both aggregate demand and aggregate supply

Fiscal policy and aggregate demand

In order to explain demand-side fiscal policy, we need first to explain **balanced budgets**, **budget deficits** and **budget surpluses**. Using the symbols G for government spending and T for taxation and other sources of government revenue, the three possible budgetary positions a government can have are:

- $G = T$: balanced budget
- $G > T$: budget deficit
- $G < T$: budget surplus

A budget deficit occurs when public-sector spending exceeds revenue. It is important not to confuse *financing* a budget deficit with *eliminating* a budget deficit. A budget deficit can be eliminated by cutting public spending or by raising taxation, both of which can balance the budget or move it into surplus. Assuming a budget deficit persists, the extent to which spending exceeds revenue must be financed by public-sector borrowing.

From one year to another, it is the *change* in the budget deficit (or surplus) and not the absolute level that matters, though we shall explain later how a big budget deficit leads to a high level of government borrowing, which can lead to significant problems.

During the Keynesian era, a period which extended from around 1945 until the late 1970s, fiscal policy was used primarily to manage the level of aggregate demand in the economy. Keynesian fiscal policy, or **demand-side fiscal policy**, centred on the use of **deficit financing** to inject demand into the economy.

KEY TERMS

demand-side fiscal policy used to increase or decrease the level of aggregate demand (and to shift the *AD* curve right or left) through changes in government spending, taxation and the budget balance.

deficit financing deliberately running a budget deficit and then borrowing to finance the deficit.

TEST YOURSELF 13.1

Distinguish between 'demand-side' fiscal policy and 'supply-side' fiscal policy.

SYNOPTIC LINK

Pages 449–450 later in this chapter explain in detail the meanings of budget deficits and budget surpluses.

Deficit financing describes a situation in which the government runs a budget deficit, usually for several years, deliberately setting public-sector spending at a higher level than tax revenues and other sources of government revenue. For each of the years in which the government runs a budget deficit, the shortfall of tax revenue has to be financed through a positive borrowing requirement. The aim was to achieve full employment and to stabilise the economic cycle, without at the same time creating excessive inflationary pressures.

Keynesian fiscal policy was implemented with varying degrees of success in the decades before 1979. Some of the Keynesian views which strongly influenced the use of fiscal policy at the time were as follows:

- Left to itself, an unregulated market economy results in unnecessarily low economic growth, high unemployment and volatile business cycles.
- A lack of aggregate demand, caused by a tendency for the private sector to save too much and invest too little, can mean that the economy settles into an under-full employment equilibrium characterised by demand-deficient unemployment.
- By deliberate deficit financing, the government can, using fiscal policy as a demand management instrument, inject demand and spending power into the economy to eliminate deficient aggregate demand and achieve full employment.
- Having achieved full employment, the government can then use fiscal policy in a discretionary way (that is, changing tax rates and levels of public spending to meet new circumstances) to fine-tune the level of aggregate demand. For much of the Keynesian era, governments believed that fiscal policy could achieve full employment and stabilise the economic cycle, while avoiding an unacceptable rate of inflation.
- The overall stance of fiscal policy and, indeed, of economic policy in general, was orientated towards the demand-side of the economy. The more microeconomic elements of fiscal policy, such as transfers to industry, were aimed at improving economic performance on the supply side. But on the whole, supply-side fiscal policy was treated as subordinate to the macroeconomic management of aggregate demand and to the assumption that output would respond to demand stimulation. In any case, the microeconomic elements of Keynesian fiscal policy were generally interventionist rather than non-interventionist, extending rather than reducing the state's role in the mixed economy.
- Central to Keynesian fiscal policy was the assumption that the government spending multiplier has a high value. If the national income multiplier is quite large with respect to real output — for example, 3 — an increase in government spending of £10 billion increases aggregate demand and money national income by £30 billion. A relatively large multiplier means that changing the levels of government spending, taxation and the budget deficit (or surplus) can be quite effective in managing aggregate demand. However, real-world government spending multipliers are generally thought to be small, and in most cases are not significantly different from unity (1).

SYNOPTIC LINK

Refer back to Chapter 10 and refresh your knowledge of the national income multiplier in the context of shifts of the economy's aggregate demand curve.

Deficit financing and Keynesian macroeconomic policy

For many decades before the advent of the Keynesian era after the Second World War, UK governments believed they had a moral duty to balance their budgets. This has been called *sound finance* and *fiscal orthodoxy*. The orthodox view was that a budget surplus placed the government in the moral position of a thief, stealing from taxpayers. If the government ran a budget deficit, it would be in the moral position of a bankrupt, perceived as not being able to manage its finances. Since both these budgetary positions were regarded as wrong or undesirable, the government's fiscal duty was to aim for a balanced budget.

However, in the 1930s, John Maynard Keynes established a new orthodoxy that legitimised deficit financing and overturned the view that a government should always aim to balance its budget. The new Keynesian orthodoxy lasted until the late 1970s, when Keynesianism was replaced by a return to pro-free-market economics and a belief in balanced budgets.

Keynes argued that mass unemployment in the Great Depression was caused by deficient aggregate demand. He believed that, in the economy as a whole, too little spending was taking place because households and firms in the private sector were saving too much and spending too little.

In the 1950s and 1960s, Keynes's followers, the Keynesians, argued that, in this situation, if the government deliberately runs a budget deficit, the deficit can be financed by the government, first borrowing and then, in its public spending programme, spending the private sector's excess savings. This injects spending into the economy and (in Keynesian theory, at least) gets rid of demand-deficient unemployment.

In the UK, the Keynesian era lasted until the late 1970s, giving way then to a return of the free-market theory and policies that reject deficit financing and the use of fiscal policy to manage the level of aggregate demand.

SYNOPTIC LINK
Refer back to the extension material in Chapter 9 on 'The growth of Keynesian economics' (page 304) for further discussion of Keynesian economics.

CASE STUDY 13.1

Budget day

The UK government's financial year runs for the 12 months beginning 5 April. In October or November of the previous year, the chancellor of the exchequer reads his budget speech to the House of Commons outlining how the government proposes to collect tax revenue in the forthcoming financial year. Part of the budget speech, which is published in the 'Red Book' (formally called the Financial Statement and Budget Report (FSBR), but commonly named after the traditional colour of its cover), contains the chancellor's analysis of the state of the UK economy. This is the part of the budget which is of most interest to economists.

By contrast, the general public is more interested in the announcement of tax changes, some of which come into effect within hours of the budget speech. Modern chancellors often use the trick of announcing tax *increases* a few months earlier, in the Spring Statement). The chancellor hopes that taxpayers will not notice the announcement of these so-called stealth taxes because the higher tax rates will not be paid until a few months later. The extract below has been taken from the Treasury website.

History of the budget

The word 'budget' derives from the term 'bougette' — a wallet in which either documents or money could be kept. The longest Budget speech is believed to have been by William Gladstone on 18 April 1853, lasting four hours and forty-five minutes. The Budget box or 'Gladstone box' was used to carry the Chancellor's speech from Number 11 to the House for over 100 consecutive years. The wooden box was hand-crafted for Gladstone, lined in black satin and covered in scarlet leather.

451

Before going to Parliament to deliver the statement, the Chancellor holds up the red box outside Number 11 to waiting photographers. Chancellors are allowed to refresh themselves with alcoholic drinks during their Budget speech — no other Member of Parliament can do this! Traditionally, the Leader of the Opposition — rather than the Shadow Chancellor — replies to the Budget speech. This is usually followed by four days of debate on the Budget Resolutions (the basic parts of the Budget that renew taxes), covering different policy areas such as health, education and defence.

Follow-up questions

1 What is the purpose of budget day?
2 What is a 'stealth tax'? Why are stealth taxes unpopular?
3 On budget day, the government publishes an executive summary of the budget statement. Go to the Treasury website and download and read the executive summary of the most recent budget.
4 Budget day is usually the most important day in the year for UK fiscal policy. What is fiscal policy?

Using *AD/AS* diagrams to illustrate demand-side fiscal policy

To explain demand-side fiscal policy in more depth, it is worth reminding ourselves of the aggregate demand equation:

$$AD = C + I + G + (X - M)$$

Government spending (G) is one of the components of aggregate demand. An increase in government spending, and/or a cut in taxation, increases the size of the budget deficit (or reduces the size of the budget surplus). Either way, an injection into the circular flow of income occurs and the effect on aggregate demand is expansionary.

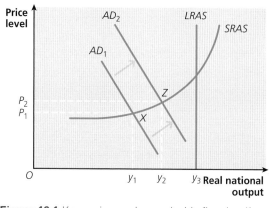

Figure 13.1 Keynesian or demand-side fiscal policy

Figure 13.1 illustrates the effect of such a reflationary or **expansionary fiscal policy**. Initially, with the aggregate demand curve in position AD_1, equilibrium national income occurs at point X. Real income or output is y_1, and the price level is P_1.

To eliminate demand-deficient (cyclical or Keynesian) unemployment, the government increases the budget deficit by raising the level of government spending and/or by cutting taxes. The expansionary fiscal policy shifts the AD curve right, from AD_1 to AD_2, and the economy moves to a new equilibrium national income at point Z.

However, the extent to which expansionary fiscal policy reflates real output (in this case, from y_1 to y_2), or creates excess demand that leads to demand-pull inflation (in this case, an increase in the price level from P_1 to P_2), depends on the shape of the $SRAS$ curve, which depends on how close, initially, the economy was to its 'normal capacity' level of output (y_3 in Figure 13.1). The nearer the economy gets to its 'normal capacity' level of output, depicted by the position of the $LRAS$ curve in Figure 13.1, the greater the inflationary effect of expansionary fiscal policy and the smaller the reflationary effect. Once the 'normal capacity' level of output is reached at y_3, a further increase in government spending or a tax cut solely inflates the price level. In this situation, real output cannot grow (except possibly temporarily), because there is no spare capacity. The economy is producing on its production possibility frontier.

Figure 13.1 can be adapted to illustrate the effect of a deflationary or **contractionary fiscal policy**. In this case, a cut in government spending and/or an increase in taxation shifts the AD curve to the left. The extent to which the demand deflation results in the price level or real income falling again depends on the shape and slope of the $SRAS$ curve.

TEST YOURSELF 13.2

Explain, using an *AD/AS* diagram, how a government can use fiscal policy to stimulate an economy in a recession.

EXTENSION MATERIAL

The multiplier and Keynesian fiscal policy

During the Keynesian era from the 1950s to the late 1970s, governments in many industrialised mixed economies, including the UK, based macroeconomic policy on the use of fiscal policy to manage the level of aggregate demand. This became known as **discretionary fiscal policy**. To achieve full employment, governments deliberately ran budget deficits (setting $G > T$). This expanded aggregate demand, but sometimes too much demand 'overheated' the economy. Excess demand pulled up the price level in a demand-pull inflation, or pulled imports into the country and caused a balance of payments crisis. In these circumstances, governments were forced to reverse the thrust of fiscal policy, cutting public spending or raising taxes to reduce the level of demand in the economy. The Keynesians used demand-side fiscal policy in a discrete way (supplemented at times by monetary policy), to 'fine-tune' the level of aggregate demand in the economy. Government spending and/or taxes were changed in order to stabilise fluctuations in the economic cycle, and to try to achieve the macroeconomic objectives of full employment and economic growth, without excessive inflation or an unsustainable deterioration in the balance of payments.

The larger the government spending multiplier, the smaller the increase in public spending needed to bring about a desired increase in national income. Similarly, the larger the tax multiplier, the smaller the required tax cut. It follows that if the government spending and tax multipliers are large (for example, equal to 5 as in our worked example in Chapter 10), and if the multipliers affect real output more than the price level, fiscal policy used as a demand management instrument can be an effective way of controlling the economy.

Unfortunately, real-world multipliers are unlikely to be much larger than 1 or unity. Small multipliers mean that demand-side fiscal policy has relatively little effect on the level of aggregate demand and thence on the economy.

A process known as **crowding out** may provide one reason for a small government spending multiplier. It is, of course, impossible to employ real resources simultaneously in both the private and the public sectors of the economy. This means that if more of the available factors of production are employed in the public sector, private-sector output must fall, assuming the economy is producing on its production possibility frontier. Employing more capital and labour in the public sector involves sacrificing the opportunity to use the same resources in private employment.

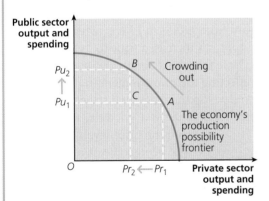

Figure 13.2 The crowding-out process

The production possibility frontier in Figure 13.2 shows maximum levels of output that can be produced with various combinations of public-sector and private-sector spending and output. Assuming there is full employment and the economy is initially at point A, an increase in public-sector spending from Pu_1 to Pu_2 crowds out or displaces private-sector spending, which falls from Pr_1 to Pr_2, shown at point B. Given these assumptions, the size of the multiplier with respect to real output is therefore zero. However, if the economy was initially producing at point C, inside the production possibility frontier, the multiplier is likely to be considerably larger with respect to real output. In this situation, the increase in public-sector spending from Pu_1 to Pu_2 absorbs idle or spare capacity in the economy, without reducing the resources available for the private sector to use. (Back in the 1930s, Keynes recommended fiscal expansion when the economy was in recession, or depression, but he did not advocate its use if the economy was already fully employed or operating at full capacity.)

KEY TERMS

discretionary fiscal policy involves making discrete changes to G, T and the budget deficit to manage the level of aggregate demand.

crowding out a situation in which an increase in government or public-sector spending displaces private-sector spending, with little or no increase in aggregate demand.

supply-side fiscal policy used to increase the economy's ability to produce and supply goods, through creating incentives to work, save, invest, and be entrepreneurial. Interventionist supply-side fiscal policies, such as the financing of retraining schemes for unemployed workers, are also designed to improve supply-side performance.

supply-side policies government economic policies which aim to make markets more competitive and efficient, increase production potential, and shift the $LRAS$ curve to the right. Supply-side fiscal policy is arguably the most important type of supply-side policy, but there are also non-fiscal supply-side policies.

SYNOPTIC LINK

Towards the end of the chapter we explain how supply-side fiscal policies relate to other types of supply-side policy.

STUDY TIP

Make sure you don't confuse demand-side fiscal policy and supply-side fiscal policy.

STUDY TIP

Most macroeconomic *PPF* diagrams show the trade-off between producing capital goods and consumer goods. Figure 13.2 is different, showing the trade-off between using scarce resources in the public sector or in the private sector.

SYNOPTIC LINK

Read about the government spending multiplier and other national income multipliers in on pages 343–44 of Chapter 10.

Fiscal policy and aggregate supply

It is misleading to associate fiscal policy exclusively with Keynesian demand management. After 1979, with the exception of the 2 years from 2008 to 2010 when Keynesian fiscal policy was revived to 'spend the economy out of recession', demand-side fiscal policy gave way to **supply-side fiscal policy**.

In demand-side fiscal policy, income tax cuts stimulate aggregate demand through shifting the *AD* curve to the right. In supply-side fiscal policy, by contrast, income tax cuts increase aggregate supply via their effects on economic incentives. Supply-side fiscal policy aims to increase the economy's ability to produce and supply goods, through creating incentives to work, save, invest and be entrepreneurial. (There are other important elements to supply-side fiscal policy, which include such interventionist policies as government spending on retraining schemes.) These policies will be covered in greater detail later in the chapter.

Using an *AD/AS* diagram to illustrate supply-side fiscal policy

Along with other **supply-side policies**, which we examine in some detail later in the chapter, supply-side fiscal policy was and is used to try and shift the economy's long-run aggregate supply (*LRAS*) curve to the right, thereby increasing the economy's potential level of output. The effect of successful supply-side fiscal policy on the *LRAS* curve is shown in Figure 13.3. The economy's *LRAS* curve shifts rightward from $LRAS_1$ to $LRAS_2$, which means that the 'normal capacity' level of output has increased (due to long-run economic growth) from y_{N1} to y_{N2}. (Note that the diagram also shows a rightward shift of the *SRAS* curve, reflecting the improvement in productivity and falling unit costs. You could also develop the diagram a stage further, by depicting the resulting fall in the price level, to show a 'good deflation', in which the price level falls because of the benign effects of successful supply-side policies and supply-side reform in the economy's private sector.) However, in normal circumstances, the improvements in the supply-side performance of the economy are accompanied by rising aggregate demand, which means that the effect is to moderate inflation rather than lead to deflation.

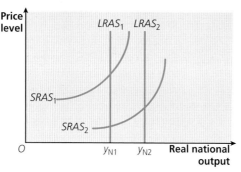

Figure 13.3 Supply-side fiscal policy shifting the *LRAS* curve to the right

Public expenditure and taxation

How government spending and taxation can affect the pattern of economic activity

Taxation raises the revenue required to finance government spending. Taxes and subsidies (which are a part of government spending) can also be used to alter the relative prices of goods and services in order to change consumption patterns and promote investment by firms in new capital goods.

Chapter 8 explained how governments collect tax revenue in order to finance the provision of goods such as roads and schools which otherwise would either be under-provided or not provided at all. Also, as we shall shortly explain, a large part of government spending transfers income and spending power between different groups in the economy: for example, from rich to poor.

Types of and reasons for public expenditure

Public expenditure has been classified into various categories. An important distinction is between investment by the government in new capital projects and infrastructure, such as new NHS hospitals and state schools, and expenditure to meet annual running costs from such projects, such as paying teachers' salaries.

A significant part of government expenditure takes the form of transfers: for example, the state pension and unemployment-related benefits. Unlike spending on capital projects and on the subsequent running costs, transfers do not involve a claim by the government on national output. Instead, spending by the government on transfers merely redistributes income and spending power from one part of the private sector to another — from taxpayers to recipients of state benefits and pensions.

A third type of public spending is interest payments on the national debt. This item of public spending rises when interest rates rise and also when the government runs a budget deficit which is financed by new government borrowing that adds to the national debt.

Public spending on social protection, health and education

Now study Figure 13.4, which shows estimated totals presented in the 2018 budget for different components of UK public spending, such as interest on the national debt in the tax year 2019/20. The largest areas of public spending have been on social protection, which encompasses the financial assistance and services provided to those in need or at risk of hardship, and on health and education. In the financial year 2019/20, spending on social protection was expected to be 30.4% of central government **total managed expenditure** (TME), with spending on health and education standing respectively at 19.7% and 12.2%. The three UK government departments involved are the Departments for Work and Pensions, Health and Social Care, and Education.

SYNOPTIC LINK
Refer back to Chapter 8 for an explanation of how both taxation and government spending relate to government policies to try to correct or eliminate market failures. Refer to Chapter 7 for an explanation of their links to altering the distribution of income and wealth and reducing poverty.

SYNOPTIC LINK
Read pages 470–71 later in this chapter which explain the link between budget deficits and the national debt.

KEY TERM
total managed expenditure the total amount that the government spends. It splits into the amount that government departments such as defence have been allocated to spend and spending that is not controlled by a government department, including welfare, pensions and national debt interest payments.

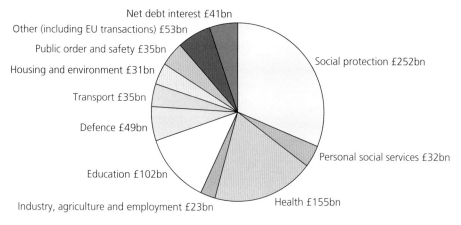

Total government expenditure (TME) £809bn

Net debt interest £41bn

Other (including EU transactions) £53bn

Public order and safety £35bn

Housing and environment £31bn

Transport £35bn

Defence £49bn

Education £102bn

Industry, agriculture and employment £23bn

Social protection £252bn

Personal social services £32bn

Health £155bn

Source: OBR and Treasury

Figure 13.4 Treasury estimates of government spending, 2019/20 (note the figures do not add up to £809bn due to rounding)

Spending on social security, which is part of social protection spending, increased after 2007 partly because the 2008–09 recession reduced incomes and, for a time, increased the number of unemployed. Pensioners now receive over half of all social security spending, with spending on the elderly forecast to continue to increase rapidly. This increase has been driven by steady growth in the number of pensioners, and by the 'triple lock' which protects pensioners from the effect of spending cuts.

The 'triple lock' guarantees that the state pension rises with whatever is highest out of wages increases, CPI inflation, or 2.5%. If this protection continues, the shares in total public spending of social security, the NHS and state education are likely to continue to rise. Robert Chote, the chairman of the **Office for Budget Responsibility** (OBR), has said the pensions 'triple lock' was pushing up government spending at a time when the population was ageing rapidly.

Health spending has also experienced significant growth over recent decades. From 2002 onward, Labour governments increased spending on the NHS, to around 7% of national income prior to the recession, but this is still below the OECD average. While other departments have experienced budget cuts as part of the government's austerity programme, spending on the NHS has effectively been frozen in real terms since 2010. However, despite a commitment in 2018 to increase spending on the NHS by £20 billion, increased population, longer life spans, and the cost of new drugs and medical technology mean that NHS spending levels are likely to lag behind demographics-driven demand.

The education budget also grew substantially under Labour governments from 2002 onward. As with the NHS and state pensions, spending on schools has been protected, but other areas of education spending have not. Higher education has seen the largest cuts in public spending, though this has been more than offset by an increase in fees paid by students.

One reason for the changes in government spending and taxation as ratios of GDP, which are shown in Figure 13.5, lies in changes taking place in employment and unemployment, which in turn relate to the economic cycle. As Figure 13.4 showed, spending on social security (under the heading 'Social protection'), which includes unemployment-related benefits, is by far the largest single category of public spending. When the economy booms,

KEY TERM

Office for Budget Responsibility advisory public body that provides independent economic forecasts and analysis of the public finances as background to the preparation of the UK budget.

unemployment falls, so spending on social security also falls. As a result, the cyclical component of the budget deficit becomes smaller. The reverse is true in a recession.

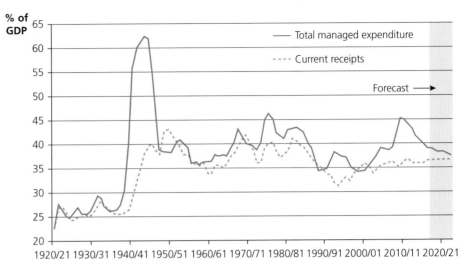

Source: Bank of England, ONS, OBR

Figure 13.5 Government spending and revenue as proportions of GDP, 1920/21 to 2020/21

Demand-led spending

The pattern of public spending, and also the extent to which certain types of public spending increase while others fall, depends in part on the extent to which spending is *demand-led*. Demand-led spending — for example, on unemployment benefits — is literally led by demand, increasing when unemployment grows and falling when unemployment drops. Although the rates at which unemployment benefits and pensions are paid, and the ages at which people qualify, can be changed, demand-led spending changes according to the phases of the economic cycle and, in the case of spending on the state pension, according to how long elderly people live.

QUANTITATIVE SKILLS 13.1

Worked example: calculating government spending percentages (1)

Calculate to two decimal places the percentage shares of spending on social protection and education in the estimates for total government spending in 2019/20.

According to the pie graph in Figure 13.4, the estimate for spending on social protection was £252 billion out of estimated total government spending of £809 billion. As a percentage, this is:

$$\frac{£252bn}{£809bn} \times 100 = 31.15\%$$

The estimate for spending on education was £102 billion out of estimated total government spending of £842 billion. As a percentage, this is:

$$\frac{£102bn}{£842bn} \times 100 = 12.61\%$$

> **QUANTITATIVE SKILLS 13.2**
>
> ## Worked example: calculating government spending percentages (2)
>
> **In 2018/19, the government expected UK public-sector current expenditure to be £712.5 billion and UK public-sector capital spending to be £82.8 billion. Nominal GDP was expected to be £2,044.47 billion.**
>
> **Calculate total planned government expenditure as a percentage of nominal GDP.**
>
> Total government planned expenditure = total planned current spending + total government capital spending. For 2018/19 this was £712.5 billion + £82.8 billion, which was £795.3 billion. The correct answer is:
>
> $$\frac{\text{total planned expenditure}}{\text{nominal GDP}} \times 100$$
>
> which is:
>
> $$\frac{£795.3\text{bn}}{£2,044.47\text{bn}} \times 100 = 38.9\%$$

Transfer payments made by the government

A large part of government expenditure takes the form of transfer payments: for example, the state pension and unemployment-related benefits. As the name indicates, in this context (though not in the way the term 'transfers' is used in the current account of the balance of payments), transfer payments are a redistribution of spending power from taxpayers in general to those receiving welfare benefits. By contrast, government spending on new hospitals or schools directly increases national output. As a generalisation, income taxes and transfers reduce the disposable incomes of those in work and increase the disposable incomes and spending power of those living on welfare benefits, who are very often out of work.

Transfers are the major part of the item 'social protection', which at £252 billion in 2019/20 dwarfed all other types of public spending, including health and education. When transfers, including debt interest, are excluded, government spending falls as a proportion of GDP. This figure is a more accurate measure of the share of national output directly commanded by the state (and thus unavailable for use in the private sector) to produce the hospitals, roads and other goods and services which government collectively provides and finances, for the most part, out of taxation.

Debt interest

Debt interest is made up of payments by the government to people who have lent to the state (i.e. to holders of the national debt). In 2019/20, interest payments on the national debt were expected to be £41 billion, or over 5% of public spending. This item of public spending, which rises when interest rates rise and falls when interest rates are cut, is a transfer from taxpayers in general to people who lend their savings to the government. Total interest payments are affected by the general level of interest rates, which are heavily influenced by the level of Bank Rate set by monetary policy. In terms of fiscal policy, if the national debt (relative to nominal GDP) can be reduced, debt interest as a fraction of nominal GDP also falls — providing interest rates don't rise.

Conversely, if the national debt rises faster than nominal GDP, debt interest rises as a fraction of real GDP — providing interest rates don't fall.

How taxation affects the pattern of economic activity

Figure 13.6 shows the total amount of revenue the UK government expected to collect from different taxes in 2019/20. By studying the pie graph, you can calculate the relative or proportionate importance of each tax. The three main categories of tax are taxes on income, taxes on spending or expenditure, and taxes on capital.

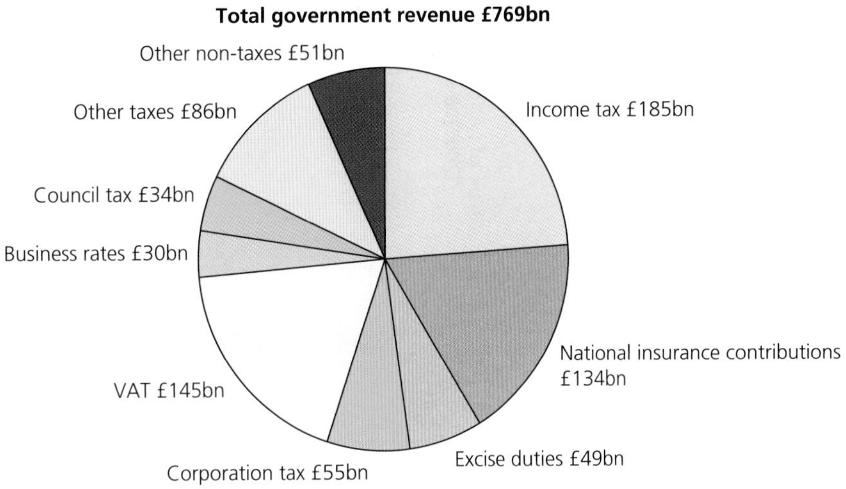

Total government revenue £769bn

Figure 13.6 Treasury estimates of tax revenue, 2019/20

Taxes on income include not only personal income tax (income tax in Figure 13.6) but also national insurance contributions and corporation tax. National insurance contributions (which in legal terms are not strictly a tax) are a second type of personal income tax, which may eventually be merged into personal income tax. Corporation tax is a tax paid by companies on their profits.

The two main indirect taxes are value added tax (VAT) and excise duties on goods such as motor fuels, alcohol drinks and tobacco. In 2019/20 these were expected to raise £156 billion and £50 billion in tax revenues.

Taxes on wealth and capital are not very important in the UK. Council tax, which is a tax on property, and business rates are the only wealth taxes shown in Figure 13.6. Inheritance tax, which is a tax on wealth given from the dead to the living, is included in the category 'Other taxes' in the pie graph. Much of income tax revenue is, of course, paid when people work for a living, producing useful goods and services. Wealth taxes, which by contrast stem from the ownership of assets such as houses and stocks and shares, reflect the accumulation or build-up of personal, household and business wealth in the economy.

Types of and reasons for taxation

A tax is a compulsory levy made by a government to pay for its activities. Taxes are therefore used to finance the different types of public expenditure we have just described.

Taxation is the principal source of government revenue for most economies. In the UK about 95.2% of total taxation is levied by, or collected by local government on behalf of, central government, with local government taxation (the council tax) accounting for the remaining 4.8%. In the financial year 2019/20, all but £54 billion of the total expected revenue of £810 billion was expected to come from taxation. The non-tax income was expected to come from other sources, such as interest and dividends which the government receives.

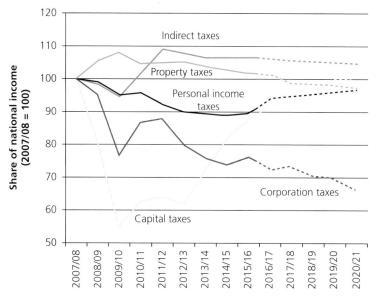

Figure 13.7, which has been taken from an Institute of Fiscal Studies (IFS) briefing note, 'The changing composition of UK tax revenues', shows how the composition of different categories of tax receipts have changed, or are expected to change, between 2007/08 and 2020/21.

Source: Institute for Fiscal Studies

Figure 13.7 Composition of UK government tax receipts, 2007/08 to 2020/21 (forecast)

Figure 13.8, taken from the *IFS Green Budget: February 2016*, shows revenues from excise duties as a percentage of national income from 1978/79 to 2020/21. In 2018/19 the UK government raised £49 billion from excise duties, but as can be seen in Figure 13.8 the long-term revenue received by the Treasury from these duties is in decline. In the future, with people choosing to live healthier lives and moving away from combustion engines and fossil fuels, the government is going to have to find new sources of taxation to finance public expenditure.

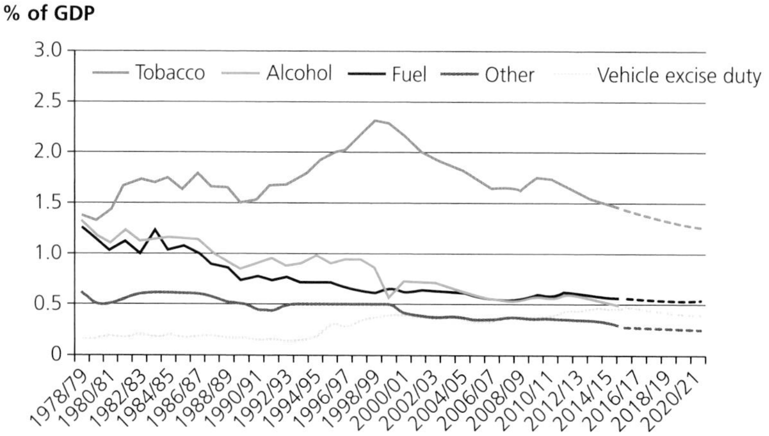

% of GDP

Source: Institute for Fiscal Studies

Figure 13.8 UK tax revenue from excise duties, 1978–2014 and forecast to 2020/21

We have previously given reasons for governments choosing to undertake different types of public spending, so these are also reasons for taxation. To repeat, governments tax in order to achieve economic goals such as altering the distributions of income and wealth and the management of aggregate demand. We shall now look at direct and indirect taxation, and progressive, proportionate and regressive taxes and the principles of taxation.

More detail on the structure of UK taxation

Some of the main taxes levied in the UK are described below.

Income tax

This is the UK's main direct tax, which is paid on earnings, pensions, benefits, savings and investment income, and rents. For most people, the first slice of income is untaxed. In the tax year 2019/20 in England, Wales and Northern Ireland, the personal tax allowance (untaxed income) for people with an income of £100,000 or less was £12,500, but for higher-income earners the personal tax allowance tapered away, dropping by £1 for every £2 earned over £100,000. In the same year, the standard rate of income tax (20%) was levied on individual income above the personal tax allowance but below £50,000. Higher rates of tax were levied on personal incomes above £50,000, namely 40% on the slice of income between £50,000 and £150,000, and 45% on income above £150,000.

National insurance

National insurance contributions (NICs), first started in 1911, were initially introduced to finance a government safety-net for workers who fell on hard times. Anyone needing cash for medical treatment, or because they had lost their job, could claim from the fund. Over the years, the system has changed. The national insurance fund is now used to help finance the NHS and welfare benefits, including unemployment benefit and the state pension. However, NICs are insufficient for this purpose and have to be supplemented from general taxation.

In strict legal terms, NICs are not a tax. Consequently, on a number of occasions UK governments have increased NICs, while leaving personal income tax rates and allowances unchanged, and then claimed that they have not increased income tax! Most people, however, regard NICs as a supplementary form of income tax. Over the years, NICs have generally been regressive, and this has reduced the progressivity of the direct tax system, provided we regard NICs as a form of tax.

In the future, income tax and national insurance could be merged by the Conservative government under plans to simplify the tax system. If this happens, it will be the biggest shake-up in the UK tax system certainly since the introduction of VAT in 1973, when it replaced an older percentage sales tax called purchase tax.

Corporation tax

This is a tax on company profits. It is levied at a lower rate than personal income tax. In recent years corporation tax rates have been cut. At present corporation tax is 19% but this will fall to 18% in April 2020.

Value added tax (VAT)

Unlike income tax and NICs, which are direct taxes, VAT is an indirect tax, currently paid at a standard percentage rate of 20% on spending on most goods and services. VAT is set at a lower rate of 5% on gas and electricity. It is not currently levied on books, children's clothes and food.

Excise duties

These are another form of expenditure tax (and indirect tax) paid on tobacco, alcohol, petrol and diesel fuel. Unlike VAT, which is an *ad valorem* percentage tax, these so-called 'sin taxes' are specific taxes or unit taxes levied on physical quantities of a good. For example, in 2019 an excise duty of £297.57 was levied on each hectolitre of wine with an alcohol content between 5% and 15%. With motor fuels, the excise duty levied on petrol is lower than that on diesel fuel. As inflation erodes the real value of excise duties, the government usually increases excise duties in the annual budget. Excise duties are generally regressive because they take a larger percentage of the income of the low-paid.

Stamp duty

Stamp duty land tax (SDLT) is paid on the purchase of property. The 2019 SDLT threshold was £125,000 for residential properties and £150,000 for non-residential land and properties.

Inheritance tax

When a person dies, inheritance tax, which is a tax on wealth, is paid on their estate at 40% on any value worth more than £325,000 during 2018/19. Conservative governments would like to reduce inheritance tax, and many of its supporters want the tax to be abolished.

Capital gains tax

This is levied on the profit a person makes when selling possessions or investments. The tax is paid on the increase in value from the date the assets were acquired to the date when they are sold or given away. Some forms of wealth are exempt from capital gains tax — for example, a main home or personal assets with a value of less than £6,000, or if the gain is less than £11,700 during the tax year.

Council tax

This is a tax charged by local authorities on the value of houses and flats to the people who live in the properties. Council tax rates are 'banded': the lowest rate is charged on Band A properties with a value of up to £40,000 (in 1993 when the tax was introduced), while the highest rate is paid on Band H properties with a value above £320,000 in 1993. Since they have never been revised, these bands are now hopelessly out of date. One result is that people living in £10 million-priced mansions pay the same council tax each year as households living in modest £350,000 properties. As a result, council tax has become a highly regressive tax.

> **KEY TERMS**
>
> **direct tax** a tax that cannot be shifted by the person legally liable to pay the tax onto someone else. Direct taxes are levied on income and wealth.
>
> **indirect tax** a tax that can be shifted by the person legally liable to pay the tax onto someone else, e.g. through raising the price of a good being sold by the taxpayer. Indirect taxes are levied on spending.

Direct and indirect taxation

Income tax is an example of a **direct tax** because the person who receives and benefits from the income is liable in law to have to pay the tax to the government; they cannot pass the tax on to someone else. Corporation tax and national insurance contributions are other examples of direct taxes.

By contrast, *most* taxes on spending, such as value added tax (VAT) and excise duties, are **indirect taxes**. This is because the seller of the good, and not the buyer who benefits from its consumption, is liable to pay the tax.

> **SYNOPTIC LINK**
>
> As discussed in Chapter 3, firms try to raise the prices they charge customers in order to recoup the tax revenue they pay to the government. When this happens, the buyers of the good indirectly pay some or all of the tax, via the higher prices the sellers now charge.

Progressive, regressive and proportionate taxation

If the government decides that the distributions of income and wealth produced by free-market forces are undesirable, taxation and transfers in its public spending programme can be used to modify these distributions and to try to reduce this market failure resulting from 'inequity'.

Progressive taxation

Until quite recently, British governments of all political complexions used progressive taxation and a policy of transfers of income to the less well-off, in a deliberate attempt — albeit with limited success — to reduce inequalities in the distribution of income. A tax is progressive when the proportion of income paid in tax rises as income increases. Progressive taxation, combined with transfers to lower-income groups, reduces the spending power of the rich, while increasing that of the poor. However, some taxes, particularly those designed to reduce consumption of the demerit goods alcohol and tobacco, are regressive and fall more heavily on the poor.

Regressive taxation

> **KEY TERM**
>
> **regressive taxation** when the proportion of income paid in tax falls as income increases.

Cigarette duty is an example of **regressive taxation**. The low-paid lose a greater proportion of their incomes in tax than rich people when buying cigarettes and alcohol. VAT is another example of a regressive tax.

To understand why the tax on cigarettes is regressive, compare two smokers, one with an income of £100 a week and the other with an income of £1,000 a week. Both smoke 20 cigarettes a week, which in 2018 cost £8.50, of which £6.98 was tax — both excise duty and VAT. This is 6.98% of the poor smoker's income, compared to 0.698% of the rich smoker's income. Additionally, because they recognise the health hazards of tobacco consumption, richer people, who may be better educated, have often given up or never started smoking. The regressive nature of taxes such as these partially offsets the fact that income tax is generally progressive.

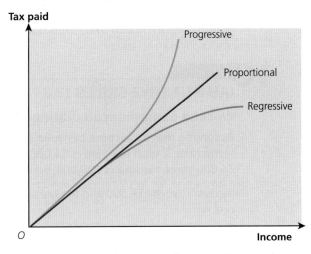

Figure 13.9 Progressive, proportionate and regressive taxation

Proportional taxation

In recent years, many economists and politicians, usually of a pro-free-market persuasion, have advocated the introduction of **proportional taxation**, which in the case of a proportional income tax is sometimes called a 'flat tax' (for example, income tax at the 'flat rate' of 10%). A proportional income tax system has been introduced in countries within central and eastern Europe that lack sophisticated tax-collecting government agencies but significantly benefits high income groups over the rest of society. The equity of a system that allows millionaires to pay the same rate of income tax as ordinary workers is questionable. This would result in governments facing significant budget deficits which in the long term would mean public expenditure needed to shrink.

Relating progressive, regressive and proportional taxation to marginal and average tax rates

For particular taxes such as income tax or inheritance tax, we can identify whether the tax is progressive, regressive or proportional by examining the relationship between the *average* rate at which the tax is levied and the *marginal rate*. In a progressive income tax system, the marginal tax rate is higher than the average tax rate, which means that the average rate, which measures the proportion of income paid in tax, rises as income increases. Conversely, in a regressive income tax system, the marginal rate of tax is less than the average rate, while the two are equal in the case of a proportionate tax.

For income tax, the average tax rate is calculated as total tax paid divided by total income. By contrast, the marginal tax rate is the tax paid on the last pound of income earned, calculated as the change in tax paid divided by change in income.

$$\text{average tax rate} = \frac{\text{tax paid}}{\text{income}} \text{ or } \frac{T}{Y}$$

$$\text{marginal tax rate} = \frac{\Delta \text{ tax paid}}{\Delta \text{ income}} \text{ or } \frac{\Delta T}{\Delta Y}$$

As a general rule, the average tax rate indicates the overall burden of the tax on the taxpayer, but the marginal rate may significantly affect economic choices and decision making. In the case of income tax, the marginal tax rate influences the choice between work and leisure when deciding how much labour to supply. It also influences decisions on whether to spend income on consumption or to save.

QUANTITATIVE SKILLS 13.3

Worked example: calculating the marginal tax rate

Assuming that all income between £30,000 and £38,000 is taxed at the same rate, if total tax paid is £4,000 when total income is £30,000 and £6,000 when income is £38,000, what is the marginal tax rate?

Income rises by £8,000 and the tax paid rises by £2,000. The marginal tax rate is:

$$\frac{\Delta T}{\Delta Y} \text{ or } \frac{£2,000}{£8,000}$$

which is 25%.

The principles of taxation

Taxpayers commonly view all taxes as 'bad', in the sense that they do not enjoy paying them, although most realise that taxation is necessary in order to provide for the useful goods and services provided by the government. A starting point for analysing and evaluating whether a tax is 'good' or 'bad' is Adam Smith's four **principles of taxation**, which are also known as the **canons of taxation**. Adam Smith suggested that taxation should be equitable, economical, convenient and certain, and to these we may add the principles of efficiency and flexibility. A 'good' tax meets as many of these principles as possible, although because of conflicts and trade-offs, it is usually impossible for a tax to meet them all at the same time. A 'bad' tax meets few if any of the guiding principles of taxation.

KEY TERM

principle of taxation (also known as a **canon of taxation**) a criterion used for judging whether a tax is good or bad.

- **Economy** means a tax should be cheap to collect in relation to the revenue it yields.
- **Convenience** and **certainty** mean that a tax should be convenient for taxpayers to pay and that taxpayers should be reasonably sure of the amount of tax they will be required to pay to the government.
- **Equity** means a tax system should be fair, although there may be different and possibly conflicting interpretations of what is fair or equitable. Specifically, a particular tax should be based on the taxpayer's *ability to pay*. This principle is one of the justifications of progressive taxation, since the rich have a greater ability to pay than the poor.

- **Efficiency** requires a tax to achieve its desired objective(s) with minimum undesired side-effects or unintended consequences. The disincentive effect on effort can be thought of as an unintended consequence of high rates of income tax.
- Finally, to comply with the principle of **flexibility**, a tax must be easy to change to meet new circumstances.

The role and merits of different UK taxes

A large proportion of people's income goes in paying taxes. Tax accounts for around a third of the money people earn. Direct taxes such as income tax and national insurance account for 20%. The rest goes mainly on VAT, duty on alcohol and petrol, council tax and other indirect taxes.

Taxation is the principal source of government revenue for most economies. In the UK about 91.1% of total taxation is levied by central government, with local government taxation (currently the council tax and business rates) accounting for the remaining 8.9%. In the financial year 2018/19, all but £51 billion of the total expected revenue of £769 billion was expected to come from taxation. The non-tax income was expected to come from other sources, such as interest and dividends which the government receives. UK governments have also received revenue from privatising state-owned firms and industries. However, in order to keep down the figure for public spending, UK governments perform the accounting trick of classifying these receipts as 'negative public expenditure' rather than as a source of government revenue.

We shall now look in turn at taxes on income, taxes on spending and taxes on capital and wealth.

Taxes on income

If you refer back to Figure 13.6, the chart shows that taxes on income, which are most important category of tax in the UK, include corporation tax and national insurance contributions as well as personal income tax. These are all direct taxes. This means that the person or organisation being paid the income is directly liable to pay the tax to the government. Failure to declare income is tax *evasion*. which is illegal.

With regard to some of the principles of taxation outlined earlier, for most wage and salary earners, income tax is cheap to collect, it is convenient and certain for the taxpayer, and, if progressive, it is equitable in the sense that it reflects taxpayers' ability to pay. In addition, when the basic tax threshold is set at a relatively high level, people who receive very low incomes can be taken out of the 'tax net', thereby paying zero income tax. (For most wage and salary earners, income tax is collected by the government through 'pay as you earn' (PAYE). This makes personal income tax cheap to collect, as employers bear most of the costs.)

Nevertheless, for some in society, income tax has been relatively easy to *avoid* and *evade*. By providing services such as plumbing and home-hairdressing, 'strictly for cash', those on relatively low incomes may successfully evade tax. Meanwhile, those at the top of the income pyramid find it relatively easy to avoid tax legally through signing up to 'tax-efficient' schemes provided by their financial advisers. Tax avoidance is not illegal but may allow some taxpayers to exploit unintended loopholes in the tax system.

The opportunities for avoiding and/or evading paying tax are, of course, among the disadvantages of income tax. Additionally, a highly progressive income tax may lead to undesirable 'unintended consequences' — for example, the disincentivising of hard work, risk taking and entrepreneurial effort. We return to this in the second half of the chapter, in our discussion of supply-side economic policies.

However, as Figure 13.6 clearly shows, personal income tax has long been the main source of government tax revenue in the UK. In part, this reflects the fact that for personal income tax, the 'tax base' is extremely wide in the sense that millions of people receive income that can be taxed. Total government revenue from the taxation of income is actually much higher than the revenue collected from personal income tax. Companies pay corporation tax on their income or profits and most of their employees pay national insurance contributions (NICs) as well as personal income tax to the government.

QUANTITATIVE SKILLS 13.4

Worked example: calculating the mean and median

Table 13.1 shows the weekly incomes of the 20 members of an economics class at an adult education college.

Table 13.1 Weekly incomes of an economics class

Class member	Weekly income (£)	Class member	Weekly income (£)
Student 1	220	Student 11	500
Student 2	1,000	Student 12	370
Student 3	800	Student 13	80
Student 4	340	Student 14	1,200
Student 5	620	Student 15	50
Student 6	800	Student 16	570
Student 7	400	Student 17	920
Student 8	680	Student 18	30
Student 9	730	Student 19	250
Student 10	690	Student 20	820

Calculate the mean and median weekly incomes for the class.

As we first explained in Chapter 3, the mean and the median are two kinds of 'average'. The mean class income can be calculated by adding up the incomes of all the members of the class (in this case £11,070) and dividing this number by 20 (the total number of class members). The mean value for all the members of the economics class is £553.50.

The 'median' is the 'middle' value in the list of numbers. To find the median, you should list the numbers in numerical order (£30; £50; £80; £220; £250; £340; £370; £400; £500; £570; £620; £680; £690; £730; £800; £800; £820; £920; £1,000 and £1,200), and then locate the middle value. In this example, because there is an even number of students in the class (20), there are two middle values, £570 and £620. The median is midway between the two: £595.

TEST YOURSELF 13.5

Chloé wants to achieve a mean score of at least 90% on her six economics multiple-choice tests. Her first five multiple-choice test scores are:

95%, 88%, 97%, 82%, 91%

What is the minimum score that Chloé needs to get on her last multiple-choice test in order to reach her target?

Taxes on spending

As Figure 13.6 again shows, after income taxes, VAT and 'excise duties' make up the second most important group of taxes in the UK. VAT is an *ad valorem tax*, whilst excise duties, such as the duty charged on spending on tobacco, are almost always *specific* or *unit taxes*, levied not on a good's price, but on the physical quantity of the good.

An advantage of taxes on spending, especially excise duties, is that they can be used to encourage people to switch their spending away from goods deemed to be undesirable to those regarded as 'good' for consumers — for example, away from demerit goods and toward merit goods. Some economists, mainly of a free-market persuasion, believe this to be a disadvantage rather than an advantage. They dislike governments exercising paternalism — that is, claiming to know better than ordinary individuals what is good for those whom they govern. VAT, by contrast, is a generally neutral tax, in that it is levied on spending on most goods and services, with the result that a change in the VAT rate has little effect on patterns of expenditure.

Many economists believe that, unless there is a good reason to affect people's choices through the tax system, the taxation of goods should conform to the principle of neutrality. Reasons for taxing some products at a higher rate than others could relate to demerit goods and externalities. Another reason could be to influence the distribution of income, imposing zero tax on basic necessities and high taxes on frivolous luxuries.

In any case, using indirect taxes to encourage people to alter their expenditure patterns becomes less effective if more and more goods are taxed at the same rate. Although this widens the 'tax base', which allows the government to collect more tax revenue, the tax becomes less useful as a tool for influencing the pattern of consumer spending.

Indirect taxes can also be evaded: for example, when a builder says he will not include VAT in the price he is quoting to a householder, as long as the householder pays in cash. However, it is generally less easy to evade and avoid indirect taxes than direct taxes.

QUANTITATIVE SKILLS 13.5

Worked example: calculating percentage change

Table 13.2 shows the changes in a government's total revenue from indirect taxes, expressed as index numbers, for the period from 2014 to 2019.

Table 13.2 Index of revenue from taxation, 2014–19

Year	Revenue from indirect taxation (2013 = 100)
2014	96
2015	94
2016	100
2017	102
2018	106
2019	104

Calculate to two decimal places the percentage change in revenue from indirect taxation between (a) 2014 and 2019, (b) 2016 and 2019.

Students often confuse percentage changes with changes in index points, possibly because percentages add up to 100%, while the base index number is normally 100. (There are exceptions — the base index number in the Financial Times/Stock Exchange index of the 100 leading shares (the FTSE 100 or 'Footsie 100' index) is 1,000.)

(a) Between 2014 and 2019 the index point values changed from 96 to 104, i.e. by 8 index points. However, this is *not* an 8% change. The percentage change is the change in index points divided by the initial index number, which is then multiplied by 100. In this case it is (8/96) × 100, which is approximately 8.33%.

(b) In this case, because we are comparing 104 with the base year index number of 100, the change in index points is 4 and the percentage change is 4%.

Taxes on capital and wealth

Taxes on capital and wealth are also direct taxes. Some taxes on capital and wealth can be avoided and evaded, but with others it is less easy to do so. Wealth in the form of cash can be 'money laundered' when given from one person to another, but on the other hand, wealth in the form of property is less easily hidden. If the taxman were to be given the authority, he could use a helicopter and data stored on the land registry to find out information about property values, and who owns the property. Having said that, successive British governments have shown little interest in updating property values. The last time houses were valued for the purpose of collecting council tax, which is the main UK tax on property, was back in 1991, since when house prices have risen rapidly in most UK regions, especially in London and the South East.

Some general comments on the structure of UK taxation

The financial crisis and the 2008–09 recession saw the government's tax revenues collapse and the budget deficit increase sharply. Tax receipts from capital taxes (which include stamp duties, capital gains tax and inheritance tax) declined rapidly and have taken over a decade to recover. Corporation tax revenues fell significantly during the recession and appear to be in long-term decline. Tax revenue from personal income (mostly income tax and national insurance) has struggled to recover from the crisis and is increasingly dependent on higher income groups.

Taxes on spending are now the main source of government tax revenue. Before the recession VAT was set at 17.5%. As a temporary measure it was cut in November 2008 to 15% to stimulate the economy, but since April 2012 it has been 20%. Likewise, property taxes (council taxes and businesses rates) have increased as a source of government revenue. Overall, regressive taxes, which affect the disposable income of low income groups have increased since the recession.

SYNOPTIC LINK

For a reminder of how taxes (and their opposite, subsidies) can affect resource allocation, refer back to the coverage of merit goods, demerit goods, public goods and externalities in Chapter 8. Consider also how you might apply the concept of allocative efficiency (equating a good's price with its marginal social cost of production) in your analysis of how taxes and subsidies can be used to correct market failure through improving resource allocation.

The role and merits of taxes in affecting the distribution of income and wealth

With regard to the distributions of income and wealth, in past decades UK governments used taxation and public spending to try to reduce inequality between rich and poor. More recently, although governments have been less concerned about reducing inequality, the combined effects of taxes and public spending have made the distribution of income much more equal than if governments did not intervene. Under the influence of supply-side thinking, government policy has been affected by the conflict between two of the principles of taxation mentioned previously: *efficiency* and *equity*.

Efficiency requires greater incentives for work and enterprise in order to increase the UK's growth rate. However, when progressive taxation and transfers to the poor are used to try to make the distribution of income more equitable, it can mean that people had less incentive to work hard and to take risks by engaging in entrepreneurial activity. Moreover, the ease with which the poor can claim welfare benefits and the level at which they are available can create a situation in which the poor rationally choose unemployment and state benefits in preference to low wages and work.

In this so-called dependency culture, the unwaged were effectively 'married to the state', but some of the poor, obviously not enjoying this marriage, drift into antisocial behaviour, attacking public property such as bus shelters as well as privately owned property.

The supply-side view

Many supply-side economists and politicians have argued that income tax rates and benefit rates should both be reduced. They believe that tax and benefit cuts would alter the work/leisure choice in favour of supplying labour, particularly for benefit claimants who lack the skills necessary for high-paid jobs. They believe that to make everyone eventually better off, it is necessary to increase the gap between the amount people earn when they are in work and what they receive when they are out of work. This means making those who are poor, because they are unemployed, worse off.

According to this view, increased inequality is necessary to create incentives to facilitate economic growth, from which all will eventually benefit. Through a 'trickle-down' effect, the poor eventually end up better off in absolute terms but, because inequalities have widened, they are still relatively worse off compared to the rich.

According to data from the ONS, inequality increased significantly in the 1980s and stabilised in the late 1990s. This was the intended outcome of government supply-side fiscal policy. In the first two decades of the twentieth century inequality has remained high, although it has narrowed in the years following the financial crisis because the incomes of high-income groups have fallen faster than those of low-income groups. Nonetheless, the UK remains one of the most unequal countries in Europe in terms of disposable income. According to the OECD, in 2014 the UK's Gini coefficient was 36% compared to France and Germany's 29% and Italy's 32.5%.

When considering the merits and demerits of different types of taxation, a starting point is to consider the extent to which a particular tax satisfies the various principles of taxation we have briefly explained. As we mentioned earlier, a 'good' tax meets as many of these principles as possible, whereas a 'bad' tax meets few, if any, of the guiding principles.

SYNOPTIC LINK
Income inequality is discussed in the context of the Lorenz curve and the Gini coefficient in Chapter 7.

TEST YOURSELF 13.6
Explain how equality and equity will be affected if a government cuts income tax rates and increases indirect taxes such as VAT.

STUDY TIP
Practise drawing the Lorenz curve to illustrate how pro-market supply-side polices have resulted in higher levels of income inequality in the UK. Remember always to integrate your diagrams into your written answers.

The budget deficit and the national debt

Revisiting the budget deficit

Towards the beginning of the chapter we took a first look at the budget deficit, together with budget surpluses and balanced budgets. We defined a budget deficit as the difference between government spending and revenue from taxes and other revenue sources when government spending exceeds revenue ($G > T$). In this section, we relate budget deficits to the national debt, before in the following sections taking a look at further aspects of budget deficits

The national debt

The **national debt** is a rather misleading term. It is *not* the debt of the whole nation, or even of the whole of the public sector (the public sector debt), with which it is often confused. Rather, the national debt is the total stock of central government debt — the accumulated stock of central government borrowing which has built up over the years and which the government has not yet paid back.

In the Keynesian era, when almost continuous deficit financing led to a steadily rising nominal national debt in the UK, the national debt was not regarded as a burden on the population and reduction of the national debt was not really a fiscal policy objective. However, during this period the national debt as a proportion of nominal GDP was falling because the economy was growing and experiencing inflation. By contrast, in more recent years — and related to the aim of trying to reduce the levels of both public spending and public-sector borrowing as proportions of national output — national debt reduction has become an important part of supply-side fiscal policy. Free-market supply-side economists are in favour of low levels of government spending and low levels of taxation, and are also, usually, in favour of the government running a balanced budget.

The relationship between the budget balance and the national debt

In recent decades, UK governments have usually run budget deficits. In this situation, the *flow* of public-sector borrowing which finances the budget deficit builds up a *stock* of accumulated debt. The central government's accumulated debt is the national debt.

Government ministers as high as the prime minister — the formal Head of the Treasury — sometimes confuse the two 'd' words: deficit and debt. In the depths of recession before 2010, both the budget deficit and the national debt (and the wider public-sector debt) were growing. More recently, the deficit fell by a third (a fact much trumpeted by the Treasury), but the national debt continued to grow. To understand the reason for this, you must first understand the difference between stocks and flows. A budget deficit is an example of an economic flow. This means that even when the deficit is falling, provided it is still positive (that is, not a budget surplus), the flow of new borrowing that finances the budget deficit adds to the stock of the national debt.

STUDY TIP
Make sure that you understand the difference between a flow and a stock, and that you are then able to provide other examples of economic flows and stocks.

TEST YOURSELF 13.8
Evaluate the view that budget deficits and government borrowing are a cause for concern.

It is useful also to distinguish between the *nominal* or *money* values of the budget deficit and the national debt as a percentage of nominal GDP — the 'debt to GDP' ratio. The debt to GDP ratio is an indicator of the burden of the national debt on the economy. With an understanding of these differences, you can appreciate that while the nominal national debt may be rising, the national debt as a percentage of nominal GDP may be falling. This happens when nominal GDP rises faster than the nominal debt, either because of economic growth (which is good) or inflation (which may be bad), or both.

Because it increases the national debt, a budget deficit generally increases the total interest payments the government has to pay to savers who have lent to the government. Conversely, a budget surplus allows the government to reduce the national debt by paying back a fraction of past borrowing. As mentioned in the previous section, changes in interest rates will also affect the outcome.

QUANTITATIVE SKILLS 13.6

Worked example: interpreting national debt statistics

In an economy, the cash value of the national debt increased from £1,000 billion in 2019 to £1,200 billion in 2020, while the nominal value of the country's GDP increased by 10% over the same period from its £1,600 billion value in 2019.

(a) What was the nominal national debt as a ratio of nominal GDP in 2019?
(b) What happened to this ratio over the year to 2020?
(c) What can we conclude about any change in the burden of the national debt over the year in question?

(a) In 2019 the ratio was £1,000bn/£1,600bn, which is 0.625 or 62.5%.
(b) During 2020, the ratio increased, calculated from £1,200bn/£1,760bn, which is 0.6818 or 68.18%.
(c) The burden of the national debt, measured by the nominal (or cash) value of the debt as a ratio of nominal national income, increased from 62.5% to 68.18%.

Cyclical and structural budget deficits and surpluses

KEY TERMS

cyclical budget deficit the part of the budget deficit which rises in the downswing of the economic cycle and falls in the upswing of the cycle.

structural budget deficit the part of the budget deficit which is not affected by the economic cycle but results from structural change in the economy affecting the government's finances, and also from long-term government policy decisions.

To understand fully the links between the government's budgetary position and the wider economy, it is useful to distinguish between the cyclical and the structural components of the budget deficit and borrowing requirement. The **cyclical budget deficit** is related to the level of aggregate demand in the different phases of the economic cycle. In a boom, when the economy is above its potential, tax receipts are relatively high and spending on unemployment benefit is low. The cyclical deficit falls in the boom, possibly moving into surplus. The reverse happens in the downswing in the economic cycle as tax revenues fall but public spending on unemployment and poverty-related welfare benefits increases. Government borrowing increases and the cyclical deficit gets larger.

The **structural budget deficit** is not related to the state of the economy. This part of the deficit does not disappear when the economy recovers. It thus gives a better guide to the underlying level of the deficit than the headline or cyclical figure. The structural deficit cannot be directly measured so it has to be estimated.

SYNOPTIC LINK

Chapter 15 looks at the problems confronting developing countries. Think about how a developing country that does not have comprehensive system of welfare or tax collection is prone to experiencing volatile fluctuations in economic activity.

As the name suggests, growth in the structural component of the budget deficit and borrowing requirement relates in part to the changing structure of the UK economy. (It also relates to government policy decisions: for example, those related to defence expenditure.) In recent years, a number of factors and trends have contributed to the growth of the structural budget deficit. These range from deindustrialisation and globalisation eroding the tax base, via the movement of industries to eastern Europe and Asia, through to an ageing population and the growth of single-parent families dependent on welfare benefits.

A growing structural deficit carries the rather dispiriting message that a government that seriously wishes to improve public sector finances will need to introduce significant tax increases or public spending cuts, or possibly both. This is what happened at the time of the rapid deterioration in the UK's public finances from 2008 onward.

The consequences of budget deficits and surpluses for macroeconomic performance

The Keynesian view

From the early 1950s to 1979, in the UK and in some other countries, mainly in western Europe and also the USA, Keynesian-inspired governments used discretionary macroeconomic policy, in the manner we described earlier, to manage the level of aggregate demand in the economy.

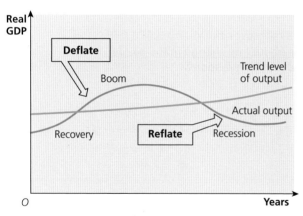

Figure 13.10 Deflating and reflating to 'smooth' the economic cycle

They did this by using contractionary fiscal and/or monetary policy to deflate aggregate demand in the boom phase of the economic cycle (see Figure 13.10), following this with expansionary fiscal and/or monetary policy to reflate (increase) aggregate demand to counter the downswing of the cycle. If successful, the economic cycle would be smoother and less volatile than would be the case had discretionary demand management not been used. And through better utilisation of labour and other resources throughout the cycle, the long-run trend rate of growth might improve. This is known as counter-cyclical demand management policy.

Automatic stabilisers

KEY TERM

automatic stabilisers fiscal policy instruments, such as progressive taxes and income-related welfare benefits, that automatically stimulate aggregate demand in an economic downswing and depress aggregate demand in an upswing, thereby 'smoothing' the economic cycle.

Reading through of our coverage of fiscal policy, you might have concluded that the fiscal policy choice facing a government lies between Keynesian-style discretionary demand management and the 'balancing the budget' approach advocated by many pro-free market supply-side economists. But in reality, there is an alternative approach that lies between these extremes, in which a government bases fiscal policy on the operation of **automatic stabilisers**. These dampen or reduce the multiplier effects resulting from any change in aggregate demand within the economy, thereby reducing the volatility of the 'ups' and 'downs' in the economic cycle. The 'ups' and 'downs' in the economic cycle are illustrated in Figure 13.11. The upper panel of the diagram shows economic cycles in an economy in which there are no automatic stabilisers. The lower panel depicts less volatile cycles brought about by the operation of automatic stabilisers.

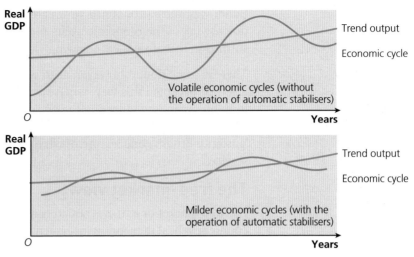

Figure 13.11 The shape of the economic cycle before and after the operation of effective automatic stabilisers

Suppose, for example, that a collapse of confidence or export orders causes aggregate demand to fall. National income then also begins to fall, declining by the initial fall in demand. But as national income falls and unemployment rises, *demand-led* public spending on unemployment pay and welfare benefits also rises. If the income tax system is progressive, the government's tax revenues fall faster than national income. In this way, increased public spending on transfers and declining tax revenues inject demand back into the economy, thereby stabilising and dampening the deflationary impact of the initial fall in aggregate demand, and reducing the overall size of the contractionary multiplier effect.

Automatic stabilisers also operate in the opposite direction to dampen the expansionary effect of an increase in aggregate demand. As incomes and employment rise, the take-up of means-tested welfare benefits and unemployment-related benefits automatically falls, while at the same time tax revenues rise faster than income. By taking demand out of the economy and reducing the size of the expansionary multiplier, automatic stabilisers reduce overheating in the boom phase of the economic cycle.

Developed economies and automatic stabilisers

It is now widely agreed that automatic stabilisers such as progressive taxation and income-related transfers contributed to milder economic cycles experienced by the UK, prior to 2008 at least. Before 1939, economic cycles — or trade cycles, as they were then known — were much more volatile, displaying greater fluctuations between boom and slump than in the years between the Second World War and 1973. Keynesians claimed that the relatively mild economic cycles prior to 1973 are evidence of the success of Keynesian demand management policies in stabilising cyclical fluctuations.

However, the economic cycle was relatively mild both in the UK and in countries such as West Germany, which did not use fiscal policy to manage aggregate demand in a discretionary way. This could suggest that the automatic stabilisers of progressive taxation and the safety net provided by welfare benefits for the poor — both of which were introduced widely in western industrialised economies after 1945 — were more significant than discretionary fiscal policy in reducing fluctuations in the economic cycle.

TEST YOURSELF 13.9
How might a period of strong economic growth affect the government's fiscal position?

473

Either way, most economists now agree that a deficit should grow in the downswing of the economic cycle, provided the deficit is matched by a surplus in the subsequent upswing.

There is some doubt, however, as to whether the former chancellor George Osborne accepted this view when starting and then continuing swingeing cuts in public spending following the crisis of 2007–08. Arguably, the Osborne cuts, continued by his successor Philip Hammond, created what is now called 'austerity Britain', one feature of which has been major cuts to social care and services.

The free-market view

Pro-free-market or anti-Keynesian economists are against the use of Keynesian counter-cyclical demand management policies. They argue, in the first place, that with discretionary demand management, governments may get their timing wrong — deflating when they should be reflating, and vice versa. This outcome might be especially likely if governments reflate aggregate demand to win votes in a general election, when economic conditions suggest that they should resist this temptation. The time lags between the change in the state of the economy and when the policy becomes effective also cause problems for policy-makers wishing to fine-tune the economy. Free-market economists believe that our knowledge of the economy is imperfect and that in the medium term market forces will drive the economy towards its normal capacity level of output, without government intervention. They believe that government intervention is likely to contribute to greater cyclical instability rather than reduce it.

In the second place, whether or not governments get their timing wrong, pro-free-market economists argue that when discretionary fiscal policy is used to try to 'smooth' the economic cycle, the long-run trend rate of growth is likely to fall.

Thirdly, and perhaps most importantly, free-market economists believe that the Keynesian use of demand-management policies in just an excuse for the growth of 'big government' which leads to 'crowding out', in which 'wealth-consuming' government spending replaces the profit motive and 'wealth-creating' private-sector activity. (At the extreme, this is a rather silly argument, as it implies that casinos are 'good' because they are in the private sector, but NHS hospitals are 'bad' because they are in the public sector.)

Financial crowding out

As explained earlier, resource crowding out occurs when resources used by the government cannot simultaneously be employed in the private sector. However, in the context of the possible harmful effects of large budget deficits, financial crowding out is more relevant. Financial crowding out results from the method of financing an increase in public spending. Public spending can be financed by taxation or borrowing. Taxation obviously reduces the spending power of the private individuals and firms paying the taxes. Suppose, however, that the government increases public spending by £40 billion, financing the resulting budget deficit with a sale of new bonds on the capital market, in the form of new sales of gilt-edged securities (gilts). In order to persuade insurance companies, pension funds and the other financial institutions in the market for gilts to buy the extra debt, the guaranteed annual interest rate offered on new gilt issues must increase. But the resulting

TEST YOURSELF 13.10
With the help of *AD/AS* diagrams, explain the difference between supply-side and Keynesian views of the effect of an increase in aggregate demand on the economy.

general rise in interest rates makes it more expensive for firms to borrow and to raise capital. Private-sector investment thus falls and financial crowding out has taken place. Higher interest rates are also likely to reduce household consumption.

Benefits and costs of budget deficits

When analysing the benefits and costs of budget deficits, Megan McArdle, a free-market economist, believes that we must again distinguish between the effects of cyclical and structural deficits. According to McArdle, Keynesian economists focus on cyclical deficits, which are not a big problem, whereas pro-free-market economists are more concerned about structural deficits, which can be a big problem.

When correcting cyclical fluctuation in the economy, government intervention may be effective, whether the intervention is based on discretionary demand management, or on the automatic fiscal stabilisers we described above. McArdle argues that this intervention can be thought of as 'Great Depression insurance'. In addition, the resulting debt is likely to be eaten away by inflation, so it will cost even less in real than nominal terms. Also, cyclical deficits should disappear as the economy recovers and in a boom a cyclical surplus should emerge, allowing some of the debt to be paid off.

The problem is the structural deficit: the mismatch between government spending and tax revenues that is unaffected by the phase of the economic cycle. The mismatch is manageable as long as the resulting growth of the national debt is roughly the same as or less than the rate of GDP growth. In this situation, even persistent structural deficits can be tolerated because the debt to GDP ratio will not increase. But when the structural deficit begins to exceed the rate at which the economy is growing, the economy rapidly runs into trouble. Interest payments begin to grow as a proportion of the overall budget, and as they get bigger, the size of the tax increases or spending cuts needed to close the budget deficit starts to grow. Higher taxes may reduce incentives and cuts in spending will often harm the most vulnerable.

So what about budget surpluses? On the plus side, budget surpluses may reduce inflationary pressures by taking demand out of the economy, and, as we have explained, they enable the national debt to fall. However, persistent budget surpluses may induce harmful deflation caused by excessive depression of aggregate demand. They can also mean that taxes are higher than necessary, reducing potential growth by damaging the supply-side performance of the economy.

TEST YOURSELF 13.11
Explain two reasons why a government will run a budget deficit to enhance the productive capacity of an economy.

TEST YOURSELF 13.13
Distinguish between cyclical and structural budget deficits.

TEST YOURSELF 13.12
In which one of the following situations is a government most likely to pursue a contractionary fiscal policy in order to decrease aggregate demand?

A When there is a negative output gap

B When the long-run trend rate of economic growth is too high

C When there is a low level of structural unemployment

D When inflationary pressures are operating in the economy

Explain why D provides the correct answer and why A, B and C do not.

The significance of the size of the national debt

Some economists and politicians argue that a large national debt is a burden on the economy because future generations of taxpayers end up paying interest to pay for profligate borrowing by current governments that have long ceased to exist. To assess the merits of this argument, it is useful to distinguish between the *reproductive* national debt and the *deadweight* national debt.

Suppose that the government sells gilts in order to finance the building of a motorway or some other capital investment or infrastructure project. Although the government is borrowing for a period of many years, the resulting liability is matched by a wealth-producing asset, the motorway. This type of 'reproductive' borrowing is not such a burden on future generations, since interest payments on the debt are in essence 'paid for' out of the motorway's contribution to future national output. (However, some capital assets such as schools and hospitals do not last 'for ever', whereas the debt incurred when they were built often does.)

In contrast, any long-term borrowing to finance *current* spending (for example, on wars, the salaries of public-sector employees or cash welfare benefits) can be regarded as a burden on future generations, whose taxes will be required to pay interest on the deadweight spending indulged in by the government today. Since the deadweight debt does not cover any real asset, interest payments end up being a burden on both current and future generations of taxpayers. Historically, however, the UK national debt grew fastest during the two world wars the country took part in during the twentieth century. On the one hand, spending on arms led to a massive growth in deadweight debt. But on the other hand, because the wars were won, the growth of the national debt saved the country from national enslavement. Despite the huge interest payments the UK would have to pay for many decades, arguably this was a price well worth paying.

The significance of the national debt is in part dependent on the size of debt as a percentage of GDP, and on whether the national debt can be 'rolled over'. We shall look at these in turn.

Debt as a percentage of GDP

If the rate of inflation is greater than the rate at which the budget deficit and borrowing requirement add to the nominal national debt, the money value of the debt as a proportion of money or nominal GDP falls. And if the rate of inflation is greater than the nominal interest rate which the government pays to debt-holders, the government gains and debt-holders lose. This is an example of inflation redistributing wealth from lenders (holders of the national debt) to borrowers (the government), thereby reducing the real burden of the debt to the government. But if holders of the national debt catch on to this, they will try to demand much higher nominal interest payments as a condition for continuing to lend to the government.

Rolling over the national debt

Each year, part of the national debt matures and, unless there is a budget surplus, the government must also sell new debt in order to raise the funds with which to repay the maturing debt. This is called renewing or 'rolling over' the national debt. If the government is forced to pay higher nominal interest rates to provide lenders with a real return on their savings, this can lead to the financial 'crowding out' that we described earlier.

The cost of *servicing* the national debt — represented by the interest payments to debt-holders — would not be a problem, first if the national debt were small, and second if all the debt were held *internally* by people living in the country. When the debt is internally held, servicing costs, apart from management costs, are really just a transfer from taxpayers (whose taxes are higher than they would be in the absence of debt interest payments) to debt-holders who have lent to the government. But when the debt is externally held by people living in other countries, the servicing burden of the national debt becomes significant for the country.

SYNOPTIC LINK
Chapter 12 explained how governments borrow money in the financial markets by selling bonds and gilts.

The Office for Budget Responsibility

The Office for Budget Responsibility (OBR) was created in 2010 to provide independent analysis of the UK's public-sector finances. The OBR produces medium-term forecasts of the UK economy twice a year in its *Economic and fiscal outlook*. By contrast, the Treasury compiles a monthly list of external economic forecasts, comparing them to those of the OBR. And instead of the chancellor making judgements based on Treasury forecasts, the OBR rules on whether the government's policy has a better than 50% chance of meeting the Treasury's fiscal targets.

CASE STUDY 13.2

The OBR as a fiscal watchdog

In 2012, Robert Chote, the OBR's chairman, explained the OBR's role as a 'fiscal watchdog':

The OBR is one of a new wave of independent fiscal watchdogs created in recent years. Academics have for some time thought that such bodies could help take some of the politics out of tax and spending policy in the same way that independent central banks had taken much of the politics out of monetary policy.

The core analytical argument for fiscal watchdogs is that, left to their own devices, democratic governments are prone to 'deficit bias' and 'pro-cyclicality' in their management of the public finances.

There are many possible reasons for such bias. Ministers may be seduced by their own rhetoric. Governments may be less forward-looking than voters, driven by elections and impatience. Finance ministries may be weaker than the large spending departments they are meant to control. You might expect outside scrutiny by unofficial bodies (such as the IFS) to be sufficient to counteract these tendencies. But governments can all too easily dismiss the scepticism of outside bodies by pointing out that government ministers have access to privileged information on the behaviour of tax revenues and public spending that outsiders lack.

The creation of the OBR was designed to breach that line of defence. We have been given a statutory entitlement to all the relevant information available within government necessary to fulfil our core duty — 'to examine and report on the sustainability of the public finances'.

In a high-profile speech in 2013, the then prime minister David Cameron said that, according to the OBR, there is 'no alternative' to the government's fiscal austerity programme. But the next day, the OBR published a letter sent to the prime minister taking exception to his claims. A spokesperson at the OBR said that this shows that the OBR is truly independent and a fiscal watchdog rather than a fiscal lapdog.

Follow-up questions

1 Define the terms 'deficit bias' and 'pro-cyclicality'.
2 Explain why it is desirable to take politics out of tax and public spending policy.
3 The OBR has claimed that it is a 'fiscal watchdog' rather than a 'fiscal lapdog'. What do these terms mean?
4 To what extent, if any, does an independent fiscal watchdog improve fiscal policy? Justify your reasoning.

SECTION 13.1 SUMMARY

- Fiscal policy and supply-side policy provide a way of managing the national economy.
- Fiscal policy uses government spending, taxation and the budgetary position to try to achieve the government's economic policy objectives.
- Keynesian fiscal policy (or demand-side fiscal policy) manages the level of aggregate demand.
- Changes in the government's budget deficit or surplus are important in Keynesian fiscal policy.
- Budget deficits and surpluses are *flow* concepts, and are the difference between the *flows* of government spending and tax revenue.
- The national debt is a *stock* concept, and is the historical accumulation of central government borrowing which has not as yet been paid back or redeemed.
- The size of the government spending multiplier affects the power of Keynesian fiscal policy.
- Government spending is a component of aggregate demand.
- Changes in government spending and/or taxation shift the *AD* curve.
- The effect on real output and employment then depends on the shape and slope of the *SRAS* curve, i.e. the amount of spare capacity in the economy.

13.2 Supply-side policies

Supply-side economics

Supply-side policies can best be understood if you first understand the meaning of **supply-side economics**. Back in 1983, Arthur Laffer, an eminent supply-side economist, wrote:

> Supply-side economics provides a framework of analysis which relies on personal and private incentives. When incentives change, people's behaviour changes in response. People are attracted towards positive incentives and repelled by the negative. The role of government in such a framework is carried out by the ability of government to alter incentives and thereby affect society's behaviour.

KEY TERMS

supply-side policies government economic policies which aim to make markets more competitive and efficient, increase production potential, and shift the *LRAS* curve to the right. Supply-side fiscal policy is arguably the most important type of supply-side policy, but there are also non-fiscal supply-side policies.

supply-side economics a branch of free-market economics arguing that government policy should be used to improve the competitiveness and efficiency of markets and, through this, the performance of the economy.

STUDY TIP

It is important to understand that, originally, supply-side economics was part of the free-market revival.

Supply-side economics and the free-market revival

Supply-side economics grew in significance in the 1980s as a part of the free-market revival. Free-market economists believe in the virtues of capitalism and competitive markets — a belief which is matched by a distrust and dislike of 'big government' and state intervention in the economy.

The original meaning of supply-side economic policy

When supply-side economics first came to prominence around 1980, it focused narrowly on the effects of fiscal policy on the economy. (Soon after, other supply-side policies were started, including privatisation and trade union reform.) As we have seen, during the Keynesian era most economists regarded fiscal policy — and especially taxation — as a demand management tool. In Keynesian economics, the government's budget deficit lay at the centre of fiscal policy. The Keynesians largely ignored the impact of public spending and tax changes on the supply side of the economy, focusing instead on how changes in government spending and taxation affect aggregate demand.

By contrast, supply-side economics initially grew out of the concern expressed by free-market economists about the microeconomic effects of demand-side Keynesian fiscal policy. Indeed, in many respects, supply-side economics is a revival of the old pro-free-market theory that largely disappeared from view during the Keynesian era. The central idea of supply-side economics is that a tax cut should be used, not to stimulate aggregate demand Keynesian-style, but to create incentives by altering relative prices, particularly those of labour and leisure, in favour of work, saving and investment, and entrepreneurship, and against the voluntary choice of unemployment.

The wider meaning of supply-side economic policy

Supply-side economic policy now encompasses more than just fiscal policy; it is the set of government policies which aim to change the underlying structure of the economy and improve the economic performance of markets and industries, and of individual firms and workers within markets. For the most part, supply-side policies are also *microeconomic* rather than simply *macroeconomic*, since, by acting on the motivation and efficiency of individual consumers, workers and entrepreneurs within the economy, the policies aim to enhance general economic performance and the economy's underlying production potential by improving microeconomic incentives.

Supply-side improvements

Economics students often confuse **supply-side improvement** (or supply-side reform) with supply-side policies. While the two are linked, they do not mean exactly the same thing.

- Supply-side improvements are undertaken by the private sector itself as a result of entrepreneurs realising they must make their firms more efficient and competitive, first to survive in the modern global economy, and second to make profits.
- The government's supply-side policies are part of the means of achieving this desirable outcome.
- In the free-market view, by financially propping up uncompetitive firms, interventionist supply-side policies are often counterproductive in that they don't bring about supply-side improvements.
- This is not necessarily true, however, in the case of interventionist policies which provide training, infrastructure and other external economies that reduce firms' costs.
- Pro-free-market economists generally prefer non-interventionist supply-side policies. By liberalising markets and setting them free, the government pursues the role of *enabler* rather than *provider*.

> **STUDY TIP**
> You should appreciate that many supply-side policies are microeconomic rather than macroeconomic.

> **KEY TERM**
> **supply-side improvements** reforms undertaken by the private sector to increase productivity so as to reduce costs and to become more efficient and competitive. Supply-side improvement often results from more investment and innovation, often undertaken by firms without prompting from the government.

The difference between free-market and interventionist supply-side policies

Supply-side economists, and free-market economists in general, believe that if markets are allowed to function competitively, the economy is usually close to full employment. However, due to distortions and inefficiencies resulting from Keynesian neglect of the supply side, towards the end of the Keynesian era economic growth and full employment were not achieved. To increase levels of output and employment (and to reduce unemployment), supply-side economists recommend the use of appropriate *microeconomic* policies to remove distortions, improve incentives and generally make markets more competitive.

During the Keynesian era, government microeconomic policy in the UK was generally interventionist, extending the roles of the state and of the planning mechanism. **Interventionist supply-side policies**, such as regional policy, competition policy and industrial relations policy (which were known collectively as industrial policy), generally increased the role of the state and limited the role of markets. The main interventionist supply-side policies supported by free-market economists are government provision of external economies that benefit private-sector firms. These policies include government provision of education and training, and investment in infrastructure projects such as motorways and high-speed trains.

By contrast, pro-free-market supply-side microeconomic policy is *anti*-interventionist, attempting to roll back government interference in the activities of markets and of private economic agents, and to change the economic function of government from *provider* to *enabler*. **Market-based supply-side policies** (or **non-interventionist supply-side policies**) include tax cuts to create incentives to work, save and invest, cuts in welfare benefits to reduce the incentive to choose unemployment rather than a low-paid work alternative, **privatisation**, **marketisation** (**commercialisation**) and **deregulation**.

In essence, the supply-siders, together with the other free-market economists, wish to create an enterprise culture. In this broad interpretation, supply-side policies aim to promote entrepreneurship and popular capitalism and to replace the dependency culture and statism that supply-side economists argue had been part of the Keynesian mixed economy. They believe that by creating incentives for businesses and workers, the potential output of the economy will increase and the underlying rate of economic growth will improve. Successful supply-side policies will in turn reduce both unemployment and inflation in the long term, and improve UK external performance, as reflected in the balance of payments on current account. This is because the supply-side reform produced by liberating markets is expected to produce conditions in which domestically produced goods are both price competitive and quality competitive in overseas markets.

However, to bring about the long-run improvements in economic performance required to achieve these ends, substantial and sustainable increases in labour productivity are required. This in turn requires successful reform of the supply side of the economy.

Earlier in the chapter, in the section 'Using an *AD/AS* diagram to illustrate supply-side fiscal policy' (page 454), we described briefly, with the help of Figure 13.3, how supply-side fiscal policy can be used to try to increase the potential output of an economy and hence its long-run rate of economic growth. At this point you should go back and read this section again.

KEY TERMS

interventionist policies occur when the government intervenes in, and sometimes replaces, free markets. Interventionist supply-side policies include government funding of research and development.

market-based supply-side policies (or **non-interventionist supply-side policies**) these policies free up markets, promote competition and greater efficiency, and reduce the economic role of the state.

privatisation involves shifting ownership of state-owned assets to the private sector.

marketisation (also known as **commercialisation**) involves shifting provision of goods or services from the non-market sector to the market sector.

deregulation involves removing previously imposed regulations. It is the opposite of regulation.

SYNOPTIC LINK

Interventionist supply-side policies are used to correct many of the market failures described in Chapter 8.

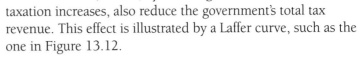

The Laffer curve

Supply-side economists believe that high rates of income tax and the overall tax burden create disincentives, which, by reducing national income as taxation increases, also reduce the government's total tax revenue. This effect is illustrated by a Laffer curve, such as the one in Figure 13.12.

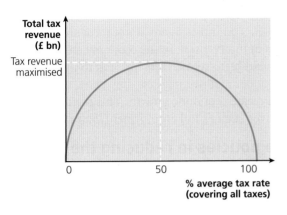

Figure 13.12 A Laffer curve

The Laffer curve, named after the leading supply-side economist Arthur Laffer, quoted earlier, shows how the government's total tax revenue changes as the average tax rate increases from 0% to 100%. Tax revenue must be zero when the average tax rate is 0%, but Figure 13.12 also shows that total tax revenue is assumed to be zero when the tax rate is 100%. With the average tax rate set at 100%, all income must be paid as tax to the government. In this situation, there is no incentive to produce output other than for subsistence, so with no output produced, the government ends up collecting no tax revenue.

Between the limiting tax rates of 0% and 100%, the Laffer curve shows tax revenue first rising and then falling as the average rate of taxation increases. Tax revenue is maximised at the highest point on the Laffer curve, which in Figure 13.12 occurs at an average tax rate of 50%. Beyond this point, any further increase in the average tax rate becomes counterproductive, causing total tax revenue to fall. (The tax rate which maximises total tax revenue is not necessarily 50%. It can vary through time.)

Supply-side economists argue that the increase in the tax burden in the Keynesian era, needed to finance the growth of the government and the public sector, raised the average tax rate towards or beyond the critical point on the Laffer curve at which tax revenue is maximised. In this situation, any further tax increase has the perverse effect of reducing the government's total tax revenue. Indeed, according to supply-side theory, if the government wishes to increase total tax revenue, it must cut tax rates rather than increase them.

A reduction in tax rates creates the incentives needed to stimulate economic growth. Faster growth means that total tax revenue increases despite the fact that tax rates are lower. Arguably, the effect is reinforced by a decline in tax evasion and avoidance, as the incentive to engage in these activities reduces at lower tax rates.

The role of supply-side policies in achieving the government's macroeconomic objectives

Chapter 11 on the measurement of macroeconomic performance introduced you to the government's macroeconomic performance and described how Keynesian and pro-free-market economists have different views on how best to achieve policy objectives such as full employment and control of inflation. At the risk of being too simplistic, Keynesian economists used fiscal policy, and sometimes monetary policy, to manage the level of aggregate demand. At times when it became impossible to achieve all the desired objectives simultaneously — and when policy conflicts arose — the Keynesians 'traded off' between objectives, but they still relied for the most part on demand-side economic policies.

However, Keynesian intervention went into decline when there was a simultaneous failure to achieve any of the prime policy objectives through demand management. Keynesian policies thus gave way to the free-market revival, and eventually to supply-side economics into which the free-market revival evolved.

Along with many other free-market economists, many if not most supply-side economists believe that government intervention in the economy should be minimised. The aim of policy should be to set markets free and to promote entrepreneurship, in the belief that competitive markets, low taxes, the profit motive and self-interest will then create economic growth. This then creates the conditions in which other objectives such as full employment 'naturally' result.

The role of supply-side policies in reducing the natural rate of unemployment

There can be no doubt that the transformation of Britain's economic performance…is above all due to the supply-side policies we have introduced to allow markets of all kinds to work better.

Nigel Lawson, Conservative chancellor of the exchequer, July 1988

The three panels of Figure 13.13 bring together three of the main elements of supply-side macroeconomics. The upper panel of the diagram depicts the economy's aggregate labour market, while the middle and lower panels respectively show the long-run vertical Phillips curve and long-run AS curve.

The upper and lower panels of Figure 13.13 respectively show equilibrium in the economy's aggregate labour market and in the economy's aggregate goods or product market. As the upper panel shows, the natural or 'equilibrium' level of employment E_{N1} is determined in the economy's aggregate labour market at real wage rate w_{FE}. When the labour market is in equilibrium, the number of workers willing to work equals the number of workers whom firms wish to hire.

The middle panel of the diagram shows the natural *level* of unemployment U_{N1} (or natural *rate* if stated as a percentage of the labour force) immediately below E_{N1} in the upper panel. Likewise, the natural level of real output (y_{N1}), which is the same as the 'normal capacity' level of real output, is shown in the lower panel of the diagram, where the long-run aggregate supply curve ($LRAS_1$) is positioned immediately below U_{N1} (in the middle panel) and E_{N1} (in the top panel).

Having set up the three panels of the diagram in Figure 13.13, we can now analyse how, according to the supply-side view, tax cuts can affect employment, unemployment and the 'normal capacity' level of real output in the economy. Suppose the government cuts *employers'* national insurance contributions. Employment costs fall and it becomes more attractive for firms to employ labour. As a result, in the upper panel of Figure 13.13, the aggregate demand for labour curve shifts *rightward* from AD_{L1} to AD_{L2}. Likewise, if income tax is cut, this will increase workers' disposable income

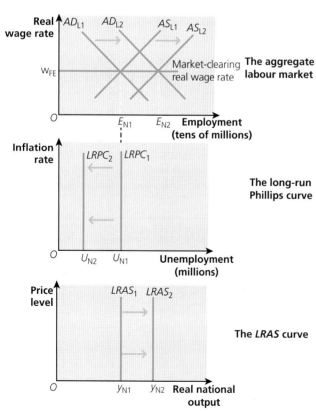

Figure 13.13 Bringing together the natural levels of employment and unemployment and *AD/AS* analysis in supply-side analysis

and thus the incentive to work, shifting the aggregate supply curve of labour *rightward* from AS_{L1} to AS_{L2}. Both these changes increase the economy's natural level of *employment*, which rises from E_{N1} to E_{N2}.

In the middle panel of Figure 13.13, the long-run Phillips curve shifts *leftward* from $LRPC_1$ to $LRPC_2$, which means that the economy's natural level of *unemployment* falls from U_{N1} to U_{N2}. Finally, the *increase* in the natural level of employment and the *fall* in the natural level of unemployment, depicted in the top two panels of the diagram, lead to a *rightward* shift of the long-run aggregate supply (*LRAS*) curve in the lower panel of the diagram. The curve shifts from $LRAS_1$ to $LRAS_2$, which means the economy can produce more output without running into the wall of inflation.

Monetary policy and supply-side policies

When supply-side policies were first implemented about 40 years ago, extreme supply-side economists argued that *neither* monetary policy *nor* fiscal policy should be used to manage aggregate demand. Instead, government activity should be restricted to creating the supply-side conditions (and 'sound' money) in which markets function competitively and efficiently. Most free-market economists now accept that monetary policy should be used to manage demand, but that it should be supportive, both of the supply-side reforms introduced over the years, and of any further supply-side changes to be made in the future. The essential tasks of monetary policy are to make sure there is just enough demand to absorb the extra output produced by the supply side of the economy, and to maintain the general public's confidence in 'sound' money by achieving a low, stable inflation rate.

UK governments (and the Bank of England) now realise that, because monetary and fiscal policy are interdependent rather than independent of each other, the success of monetary policy depends on the fiscal policy implemented by the Treasury. As we have seen, whenever it runs a budget deficit, the government has to borrow to finance the difference between spending and revenue. Conversely, a budget surplus enables repayment of past borrowing and a fall in the national debt. As we explained in Chapter 12, governments borrow in two main ways, by selling short-dated debt or Treasury bills, and by borrowing long-term by selling government bonds or gilts. Treasury bills are sold by the government to the banks, which create new bank deposits when they buy the bills. Because bank deposits are a form of money, this type of government borrowing increases the money supply and makes it difficult for monetary policy to control monetary growth.

By contrast, new issues of gilts are largely sold to non-bank financial institutions such as pension funds and insurance companies. To persuade these institutions to finance a growing budget deficit, the government may have to raise the rate of interest offered on new gilt issues. But higher interest rates discourage investment in capital goods by private-sector firms. (This is the financial crowding-out process referred to earlier in this chapter.)

Either way, government spending financed by borrowing has implications for monetary policy and produces an arguably undesirable result. Either the borrowing increases the money supply (which may be inflationary), or it raises interest rates (which may crowd out private-sector investment). The undesirable monetary consequences resulting from budget deficits and government borrowing explain why UK governments now try to make fiscal policy consistent with, and subordinate to, the needs of monetary policy.

SYNOPTIC LINK
At this point go back to Chapter 11 and read again the explanations on pages 379 and 385 respectively of the natural rate of unemployment (NRU) and the 'normal capacity' level of real output or GDP.

SYNOPTIC LINK
Refer back to Chapter 12 and make sure you understand how monetary policy impacts on the way the supply side of the economy performs.

Supply-side policies, the rate of inflation and the balance of payments

Supporters of the use of pro-free-market supply-side policies argue that by reducing business's costs of production and by reducing monopoly profits through making markets more price competitive, supply-side policies reduce cost-push inflationary pressures. By enabling productive capacity to grow in line with aggregate demand, successful supply-side policies also help to reduce demand-pull inflation pressures.

By creating 'lean and fit' firms, successful supply-side policies and supply-side reforms are also likely to improve the country's quality competitiveness. Highly competitive firms, which invest in product design and 'state-of-the-art' technology and methods of production, end up producing high-quality goods which customers demand. Taken together, increased price and quality competitiveness give the country a competitive edge, both in domestic and in overseas markets. With domestic customers switching to high-quality home-produced goods and overseas residents buying more of the country's exports, the country's balance of payments on current account should improve.

TEST YOURSELF 13.14
Explain how successful supply-side policies can improve the UK's balance of payments position on the current account.

TEST YOURSELF 13.15
Assess the view that a cut in income tax rates inevitably leads to an increase in total tax revenue.

SYNOPTIC LINK
By improving the economic performance of the domestic economy, supply-side policies aim to increase the international competitiveness of the country's exports, and thereby improve the balance of payments on current account (see Chapter 14).

EXTENSION MATERIAL

Expansionary fiscal contractionism

Figure 13.14 illustrates how the then chancellor George Osborne implemented fiscal policy in the period immediately after May 2010. Osborne believed that severe cuts in government spending would free resources for the private sector to use, and that the private sector would make better use of these resources than the government. If this was the case, workers who lose their jobs in the public sector would soon be employed more productively in the private sector. This view of how fiscal policy should operate has been called 'expansionary fiscal contractionism' (EFC) or 'expansionary austerity'. The expansionary fiscal contractionism hypothesis predicts that, given certain assumptions about how people behave, a major reduction in government spending that changes future expectations about taxes and government spending can expand private-sector spending, resulting in overall economic expansion.

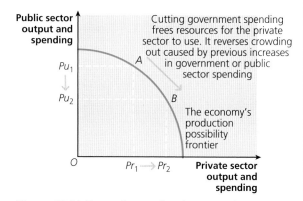

Figure 13.14 Expansionary fiscal contractionism

Not all economists accept the EFC hypothesis. Christina Romer at the University of California commented:

> Despite what I feel is overwhelming and compelling evidence that fiscal stimulus is expansionary, and fiscal contraction is, well, contractionary, many politicians claim the opposite is true...But even more striking are the number who assert forcefully that fiscal austerity — getting the budget deficit down immediately — would be good for unemployment and growth.

The 'trickle-down' effect

Along with other free-market economists, supply-side economists believe that, in the long run, expansionary fiscal policy leads to inflation, with no increase in real output. Some believe that although the rich benefit most from supply-side tax cuts, a 'trickle-down' effect means that the working poor also benefit. This is because the rich respond to tax cuts by employing more servants, nannies and gardeners, albeit generally on low wages.

But other economists question the strength and even the existence of trickle-down effects. J.K. Galbraith, for example, caustically quipped the less than elegant metaphor that if one feeds the horse enough oats, some will pass through to the road for the sparrows. Galbraith went on to state, 'We can safely abandon the doctrine that the rich are not working because they have too little money and the poor because they have too much.' And even if a trickle-down effect does operate, the widening income inequalities that are responsible for more of the poor being employed by the rich are viewed by Keynesian economists as far too inequitable or unfair.

CASE STUDY 13.3

Have UK politicians been influenced by supply-side theory?

On 18 December 2012, the then chancellor George Osborne spoke to a gathering of American supply-side economists at the Manhattan Institute for Policy Research in New York City. In answer to a question about the division between American Republicans and British Conservatives on the power of tax rate cuts to generate tax revenue, George Osborne replied:

> Well I'm a fiscal Conservative, and I don't want to take risks with my public finances on an assumption that we are at some point on the Laffer curve. What I would say is, let's see the proof in the pudding: in other words, I'm a low-tax Conservative, I want to reduce taxes, but I basically think you have to do the hard work of reducing government spending to pay for those lower taxes. If you want to cut taxes, cut welfare and cut spending, and that's what I'm doing.

Osborne seemed to be rejecting the 'extreme' supply-side argument, based on the Laffer curve, that tax cuts can be self-financing and that they are all that is needed for growth generation. Osborne, along with other Conservative members of the UK government between 2010 and 2016, was best seen as a 'moderate' rather than an 'extreme' supply-sider.

Many centrist Labour and Liberal Democrat politicians now also accept moderate supply-side arguments, though they continue to reject extreme supply-side calls for swingeing tax cuts and greater income inequality in order to incentivise the population. Especially since the emergence of problems caused by a large national debt, few politicians, except Jeremy Corbyn and his Momentum supporters on the left of the Labour Party, now call for continuous large budget deficits as the way to achieve growth and full employment, and there is much agreement that the tax structure should be used in a supply-side way to create incentives for work, entrepreneurship, saving and investment.

Follow-up questions

1 Explain, using the Laffer curve, how a government may aim to increase tax revenues by cutting taxes.
2 Describe the difference between 'extreme' and 'moderate' supply-side views on the role of tax cuts.
3 Which groups in society will be negatively affected by large cuts to public spending? Explain your answer.
4 Explain how the growth of the national debt has affected fiscal policy.

Microeconomic supply-side policies

So far, for the most part, we have been describing and explaining the macroeconomic effect of supply-side policies. This can give the misleading impression that supply-side economics and policies are mainly macroeconomic. However, the opposite is closer to the truth: most supply-side policies are based on microeconomic fundamentals such as the roles of self-interest and entrepreneurship.

The supply-side theory of the effects of taxation on labour market incentives, which lies at the heart of free-market supply-side economics, depends on the shape of the supply curve of labour.

Supply-side economists usually assume a conventional upward-sloping supply curve of labour. Such a curve, which is illustrated in Figure 13.15(a), shows that workers respond to higher wage rates by supplying more labour.

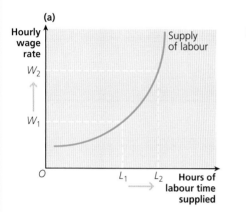
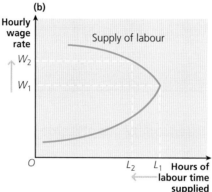

Figure 13.15 Microeconomic labour supply curves

Since a cut in the rate at which income tax rates are levied is equivalent to an increase in the wage rate, the upward-sloping supply curve implies that workers respond to cuts in the marginal rate of income tax by working harder. (The marginal rate of income tax is the percentage of the last pound of income paid in tax.) If this is the case, a reduction in income tax rates creates the incentive for workers to supply more labour (and for entrepreneurs to become more enterprising), while an increase in income tax rates has a disincentive effect on effort and the supply of labour.

However, the supply curve of labour need not necessarily slope upward throughout its length. The backward-bending labour supply curve in Figure 13.15(b) is another possibility. It shows that, above the hourly wage rate W_1, any further wage rate increase (or income tax decrease) causes workers to supply *less* rather than *more* labour. In this situation, workers prefer to enjoy extra leisure time rather than to work. Following an increase in the hourly wage rate from W_1 to W_2, the hours of labour time supplied fall from L_1 to L_2.

It is important to note that, if supply curves of labour bend backwards, the supply-side argument — that tax reductions increase national output and efficiency through their effect on labour market incentives — becomes much weaker. Far from encouraging people to work harder, a wage rise or income tax cut might have the opposite effect, causing people to work fewer hours and to enjoy more leisure time instead.

Examples of microeconomic supply-side policies

Industrial policy measures

- **Privatisation.** This involves the sale or transfer of assets such as nationalised industries from the public sector to the private sector.
- **Marketisation (or commercialisation).** This means shifting economic activity from non-market provision (financed by taxation) to commercial or market provision for which the customer pays.

- **Deregulation.** This involves the removal of previously imposed regulations in order to promote competition. Deregulation removes barriers to market entry to make markets contestable, and gets rid of unnecessary 'red tape' or bureaucracy, which had increased firms' costs of production.
- **Internal markets.** In the National Health Service and education, where the state continues to be a major producer and provider of services, internal markets can be introduced to provide a form of commercial discipline and to improve efficiency. In an internal market, which is a substitute for privatisation, the taxpayer continues to finance hospitals and schools, but hospitals and schools 'earn' the money according to how many patients and pupils they attract.
- **Subsidising spending on research and development.** This often takes the form of a cut in corporation tax rates to increase business profits. This provides firms with greater financial resources to boost investment and increase spending on research and development, which should lead to better products and higher sales in the long run.

Labour market measures

- **Lower rates of income tax.** Marginal rates of income tax can be reduced to create labour market incentives, and tax thresholds or personal tax allowances raised to remove the low-paid from the tax net.
- **Reducing state welfare benefits relative to average earnings.** Lower benefit levels create incentives to choose low-paid employment in preference to claiming unemployment-related benefits. In addition, welfare benefits can be made more difficult to claim, and available only to claimants genuinely looking for work. Making benefits less attractive may also reduce the unemployment trap.
- **Changing employment law to reduce the power of trade unions.** Possible changes include: removing trade unions' legal protection, restricting their rights, and extending the freedom for workers not to belong to unions, and for employers not to recognise and negotiate with unions; replacing collective bargaining with individual wage negotiation and employer determination of pay; and restricting the right to strike and to undertake industrial action.
- **Repealing legislation which limits employers' freedom to employ.** This makes it easier for employers to 'hire and fire' workers.
- **More flexible pension arrangements.** Workers may be encouraged to 'opt out' of state pensions and to arrange private pension plans so as to reduce the burden on taxpayers. They might be allowed to transfer private-sector pensions between employers when changing jobs.
- **Improving the training of labour.** This might involve establishing training agencies and academies to develop vocational technical education. However, UK governments have rejected the proposal to impose a 'training tax' on all employers to prevent free-riding by firms with no training schemes, which poach trained workers from firms that do train their workers.

Though not a government policy, the introduction of short-term employment contracts in labour markets replaced 'jobs for life' with short-term labour contracts. This, together with the promotion of profit-related and performance-related pay, has had a supply-side effect. 'Zero hours' employment contracts have been introduced by a large number of employers. Critics of these policies believe they lead to even greater poverty and inequality for ordinary workers in an increasingly casualised and exploited part-time labour force.

SYNOPTIC LINK
Chapter 8 explains how privatisation, marketisation and deregulation seek to increase levels of competition markets and make firms more efficient.

SYNOPTIC LINK
You should refer back to Chapter 6 on the labour market to review the theories of how labour markets operate.

Financial and capital market measures

- **Deregulating financial markets.** Financial deregulation has created greater competition among banks and building societies, and opened up the UK financial markets to overseas banks and financial institutions. These reforms have increased the supply of funds and reduced the cost of borrowing for UK firms. Financial deregulation and the removal of foreign exchange controls have also encouraged 'inward' investment by overseas firms such as Samsung and Nissan. However, very lightly regulated banks created by financial deregulation contributed significantly to the financial crisis which began in 2007 and then ushered in the 2008–09 recession.
- **Encouraging saving.** Governments have created special tax privileges for saving. They also encouraged saving by giving individual shareholders first preference in the market for shares issued when former nationalised industries such as British Gas were privatised. However, most individual shareholders quickly sold their shares to institutional shareholders, which negated one of the main reasons for privatisation. It is also worth noting that in recent years, very low interest rates, brought about by the government's monetary policy, have discouraged saving.
- **Promoting entrepreneurship.** Governments have encouraged the growth of popular capitalism and an enterprise culture. Company taxation has been reduced and markets have been deregulated to encourage risk taking.
- **Reducing public spending and public-sector borrowing.** This is intended to free resources for private-sector use and avoid crowding out.

A further look at market-based versus interventionist supply-side policies

The supply-side policies that we have described so far in this chapter have generally been market-based, in the sense that they have been used to 'free up' markets, to 'roll back' the economic functions of the state, and to replace public-sector economic activity with that of the private sector. Free-market economists seek to promote market conditions by designing policies which stimulate market forces in three main ways:

- tax cuts to create incentives to seek profits and work harder
- privatisation to unleash market forces by taking businesses out of the public sector
- deregulation to encourage enterprise and increase competition

This view of the supply side of the economy stems from the original use of the term 'supply-side economics' in the free-market revival 40 years ago.

However, interventionist policies can also be supply-side, provided that they aim to improve the efficiency and economic performance of individual firms, industries and markets. Interventionist supply-side policies include measures such as:

- government spending on education and training
- industrial and regional policy
- spending on infrastructure such as motorways
- subsidising spending on research and development (R&D)

Interventionist supply-side policies are based on the view that government intervention in the economy is needed to correct market failure and short-termism, which may reduce investment and growth, whereas more recent pro-free-market supply-side policies have generally aimed to correct and reduce government failure.

Some of the supply-side policies introduced and implemented by the Conservative/Liberal Democrat coalition government between 2010 and 2015 were interventionist rather than market-based. These included proposed public-sector investment in high-speed rail links between London, Birmingham and the north, together with George Osborne's plan, announced in 2014, to transform the north of England into an economic 'powerhouse' with investment of up to £15 billion to finance the building of infrastructure, besides the previously announced investment in High Speed 2 (HS2).

SECTION 13.2 SUMMARY

- Supply-side fiscal policy affects the position of the *LRAS* curve.
- In supply-side fiscal policy, tax changes are used to try to change incentives in the economy.
- Free-market supply-side economists argue that government policy should be used to improve incentives and the competitiveness and efficiency of markets.
- In its early years, supply-side economics focused on how, via increased incentives, tax cuts promote economic growth and are self-financing.
- The growth of supply-side economics has been part of the free-market revival.
- Supply-side economists are generally anti-interventionist and wish to reduce the economic role of the state. However, some supply-side policies, such as government financing of retraining schemes in labour markets, are interventionist.
- Supply-side policies contribute to supply-side reform and supply-side improvements.
- Most economists now accept the argument that the supply side of the economy is just as important as the demand side.
- Many supply-side policies are microeconomic rather than macroeconomic.

Questions

1 Explain the relationship between a budget deficit and the national debt.

2 Explain the role of fiscal policy in supply-side economic policy.

3 To what extent do you agree that supply-side improvements are needed if UK macroeconomic performance is to improve? Justify your answer.

4 Explain the difference between the cyclical and the structural components of a budget deficit.

5 Explain how automatic stabilisers operate.

6 Evaluate the impact of measures undertaken by governments to reduce the budget deficit.

7 Do you agree that supply-side policies on their own are sufficient to help the economy achieve a stable, sustainable and satisfactory rate of economic growth? Justify your answer.

14

The international economy: globalisation and international trade

Although we have made brief reference to aspects of the international economy in earlier chapters, particularly those on macroeconomics, we have not explained international economics in any systematic way. The purpose of the two remaining chapters in the book is to explain the key elements of the international economy and to examine their impact on the UK economy. This chapter looks first at globalisation, and then at trade and the balance of payments. This is followed in Chapter 15 by an explanation of exchange rate systems and a discussion of various international issues related to economic growth and the development of low-income countries.

LEARNING OBJECTIVES

These are to understand:

- the meaning of globalisation and its main elements
- the principle of comparative advantage and the case for free trade
- the different forms of protectionism
- patterns of trade, both globally and for the UK
- the main features of a customs union, the Single European Market (SEM) and the UK's membership of the European Union (EU)
- the role of the World Trade Organization (WTO)
- the different sections of the balance of payments account and the relationship between them
- the significance of balance of payments deficits and surpluses
- how deflation, import controls, devaluation and supply-side measures and policies can be used to try to correct a current account imbalance

14.1 Globalisation

The meaning of globalisation

Globalisation is the name given to the processes that integrate all or most of the world's economies, making countries increasingly dependent upon each other. Some economists argue that globalisation has occurred over centuries, going back at least as far as the creation of a system of relatively free worldwide trade in the nineteenth century. Perhaps it extends even further back to the Spanish and Portuguese occupation of much of South America.

KEY TERM

globalisation the process of increasing economic integration of the world's economies.

In the late nineteenth century and the period before 1914, communication and transport networks expanded throughout much of the world and international trade grew significantly. At the same time, older industrial countries, and particularly the UK, began to invest their surplus savings in capital projects located overseas rather than in their domestic economies.

However, these changes are better described as aspects of *internationalisation* rather than *globalisation*. Globalisation, which has come to mean rather more than mere internationalisation of economic relationships, began to feature in the economics literature of the mid-1980s. The use of the term has increased dramatically ever since.

Causes of globalisation

Recent globalisation has been made possible by improvements in information and communication technology (ICT), as well as by developments in transport and other more traditional forms of technology. Examples of globalisation include service industries in the UK dealing with customers through call centres in India, and fashion companies designing their products in Europe, making them in southeast Asia and finally selling most of them in North America.

Indeed, this textbook illustrates globalisation. The text on page ii of this book states that it is typeset in India and printed in Italy, while being written and published in England.

The main characteristics of globalisation

KEY TERMS

World Trade Organization an international body whose purpose is to promote free trade by persuading countries to abolish import tariffs and other barriers to trade. As such, it has become closely associated with globalisation.

multinational corporations enterprises operating in several countries but with their headquarters in one country.

Some of the main characteristics of globalisation are:

- the growth of international trade and the reduction of trade barriers, known as trade liberalisation — a process encouraged by the **World Trade Organization** (WTO)
- greater international mobility of both capital and labour
- a significant increase in the power of international capitalism and **multinational corporations** (MNCs) or transnational companies
- the deindustrialisation of older industrial regions and countries, and the movement of manufacturing industries to newly industrialising countries (NICs)
- more recently, the movement of internationally mobile service industries, such as call centres and accounts offices, to NICs
- a decrease in governmental power to influence decisions made by MNCs to shift economic activity between countries

TEST YOURSELF 14.1

Explain how, by reducing trade barriers, product markets have become more contestable.

Figure 14.1 (overleaf) depicts some of these characteristics or features of globalisation in the form of a 'mind map'.

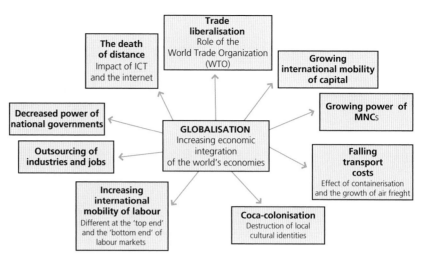

Figure 14.1 Some of the main characteristics or features of globalisation

The consequences of globalisation for less developed countries

Less developed countries are countries whose state of economic development is characterised by low national income per head, a high rate of population growth, low levels of human capital, high unemployment, poor infrastructure and overdependence on the export of a few primary commodities. Many nations in Asia, Africa and Latin America fit this model.

For the critics of globalisation, low-paid workers in sweatshops, farmers in the developing world being forced to grow genetically modified crops, the privatisation of state-owned industry in order to qualify for IMF and World Bank loans, and the growing dominance of US corporate culture and multinational companies symbolise what is wrong with globalisation in its effects on less developed countries.

According to this view, globalisation has led to a 'McDonaldisation' or 'Coca-colonisation' of significant parts of the world's economy, which involves the destruction of local and national products, identities and cultures by US world brands. This process is to some extent offset by a process known as 'glocalisation'. This word, which is a combination of the words 'globalisation' and 'localisation', reflects the idea that a global product or service is more likely to succeed if it is adapted to local practices and cultural expectations. An example of glocalisation is McDonald's restaurants offering menus to satisfy local tastes in different countries. In this sense, glocalisation is an extension of globalisation, being another way of extending the reach of global brands.

Closely related to the 'world brand' process, there has been controversy concerning the treatment of local labour by multinational corporations. On the one hand, companies such as Nike are accused of selling trainers and footballs in developed countries such as the UK, at prices far above the cost of raw materials and the low wages paid to workers in developing countries who make the goods. On the other hand, the multinationals argue that the 'low wages' they pay far exceed the local wages paid by indigenous firms. They believe this encourages local wages to rise. MNCs also claim to improve labour productivity, health and safety and other labour market conditions in the poor countries in which they operate.

The consequences of globalisation for more developed countries

The anti-globalisation argument that 'Coca-colonisation' of significant parts of the world's economy has had a harmful effect on the economies of less developed economies is not accepted by supporters of globalisation, who believe that people in the rest of the world demand the products supplied by global corporations because they consider them superior to traditional local produce.

The anti-globalisation lobby also believe that, by threatening to close down factories and offices in **more developed countries** and to move production to poor countries, MNCs may reduce wages and living standards in developed countries. The significance of this depends on the type of jobs that emerge in developed countries to replace those lost through deindustrialisation and globalisation. Are the new jobs being created in the highly skilled service sector, or are they menial, low-paid, unskilled 'McJobs'?

The arguments used so far in this and the previous section have been cast somewhat in a 'lose/win' or 'win/lose' format, implying that winners gain at the expense of losers. However, supporters of globalisation who believe that the world as a whole is a net winner from the globalisation process argue that globalisation stems in part from the massive increase in world trade that has taken place since the Second World War. This itself has only been possible because of increased trade liberalisation and the reduction of import controls and other forms of protectionism. They believe that free trade leads to a better allocation of resources and that additional benefits have been derived from international competition and the spread of technology making most people better off.

Dependency theory of trade and development

The belief that globalisation benefits most countries — less developed countries as well as more developed countries — has been attacked by supporters of the *dependency theory* of trade and development. Dependency theorists argue that many developing countries possess little capital because the system of world trade and payments has been organised by developed industrial economies to their own advantage. The terms of trade — the ratio of a country's export prices to its import prices — have generally moved in favour of industrialised countries and against primary producers. This means

> **KEY TERM**
> **more developed countries** countries with a high degree of economic development, high average income per head, high standards of living, usually with service industries dominating manufacturing, and investment having taken place over many years in human capital and infrastructure.

STUDY TIP

Use appropriate diagrams to explain how investment from an MNC can affect the economy of a less economically developed country. For example, a diagram showing a production possibility frontier shifting outward can be used to explain how the economy may experience economic growth, whereas a negative production externality can illustrate how pollution may be dumped on third parties in society. Remember always to integrate diagrams into written answers.

SYNOPTIC LINK

See page 511 for an explanation of 'North–North' and 'North–South' patterns of world trade.

KEY TERM

European Union an economic and partially political union established in 1993 after the ratification of the Maastricht Treaty by members of the European Community and since expanded to include numerous central and eastern European nations.

that, by exporting the same amount of manufactured goods to the developing world, a developed economy can import a greater quantity of raw materials or foodstuffs in exchange.

By the same token, the developing country must export more in order to buy the same quantity of capital goods or energy vital for development. Globally, the movement of the terms of trade in favour of developed nations has raised levels of income and standards of living in the richer countries at the expense of poorer developing countries. However, there have been exceptions, such as the oil-producing non-industrial countries, which have benefited from substantial increases in the price of oil over recent decades.

Economists of the dependency school argue that the transfer of wealth and resources to the richer countries is further promoted by profit flows and interest payments. On an international scale, dividends and profits flow to multinational corporations with headquarters in North America, western Europe and Japan from their subsidiaries in the developing world. Similarly, there is a flow of interest payments to western banks from loans originally made to finance development in developing countries. In most years, flows of dividends and interest payments from 'South' to 'North' exceed aid flows in the opposite direction. (The countries of the 'North' include the USA, the UK, Germany, France and Japan, and all other countries benefiting from a high degree of economic development. The 'North' gets its name from the fact that most of the countries which comprise the 'North' are geographically located to the north of most of the countries of the 'South'. The latter are poorer developing countries located in parts of the world such as sub-Saharan Africa.)

Is globalisation good or bad?

Free-market economists generally support globalisation and regard its growth as inevitable. They argue that the benefits of further global economic integration, which include the extension of political freedom and democracy as well as the economic benefits of more production and higher living standards, significantly exceed the disadvantages, such as the destruction of local cultures. However, opponents argue that globalisation is a respectable name for the growing exploitation of the poor, mostly in developing countries, by international capitalism and US economic and cultural imperialism.

Globalisation in the service sector

Until quite recently, it was said that manufacturing was much more internationally mobile than service-sector employment, but this is now disputed. Call centres became one of the fastest-growing sources of employment in the UK in the 1980s and 1990s. At that time, UK-based companies favoured locating call centres in regions of high unemployment (and relatively low wages) within the UK. To some extent this has now changed. Many call centres and back-office activities of firms in industries such as financial services have been moved to less developed countries, notably on the Indian subcontinent, and also to the eastern member countries of the **European Union** (EU), such as the Czech Republic. These movements result from the death of distance, which is an important part of the globalisation process. The rapid development of electronic methods of communication means that many service activities can now be located anywhere in the world, with little or no effect on a company's ability to provide the service efficiently to its customers.

Four factors encouraging the overseas location of call centres have been:

- relatively low wages in developing countries and in eastern and central Europe
- highly reliable and cheap telecommunications
- 24-hour shift employment to overcome the problem of time zones
- workers fluent in English, which is now the world's business language

However, for call centres, a fifth factor is often lacking: many overseas workers are insufficiently familiar with UK culture and habits, which leads to a communication problem. This has recently led to some call centres being relocated back to the UK. This disadvantage is much less significant for back-office employment: for example, employing people in India to administer a UK company's accounts.

Global labour and capital mobility

As the previous paragraphs indicate, globalisation involves moving capital to lower-cost labour much more than it involves allowing low-paid workers born in poor countries to enter rich countries in North America and Europe. However, since the late nineteenth century there has been a much greater movement of poor people into rich countries than ever before. To some extent, immigration controls introduced by countries such as the USA and Australia, which replaced an earlier completely free movement of labour, have slowed this process. But this has been offset by illegal immigration and the fact that rich countries informally encourage migration to fill the relatively low-paid jobs that their own citizens do not wish to do. MNCs recruit skilled labour from other countries and governments also encourage highly trained and talented individuals to migrate to fill skill shortages.

Enlargement of the EU is increasing both labour and capital mobility on a regional basis. Western European firms have been moving eastward, but this is balanced by workers from countries such as Poland and Hungary migrating westward. Nonetheless, it is still much easier in a globalised world for a brain surgeon or a highly paid business executive to move between countries than it is for a Chinese or Indian farm labourer.

Globalisation and the power of national governments

In recent decades, globalisation has considerably reduced the power of national governments, certainly in smaller countries, to control multinational firms operating within their boundaries. National governments have also lost much of the freedom to undertake the economic policies of their choice with respect to managing domestic economies. Governments enjoy less freedom to introduce tariffs and other import controls. At the same time, capital flows into and out of currencies severely constrain a government's ability to implement an independent monetary policy, even when the country's exchange rate is freely floating.

SYNOPTIC LINK
Chapter 15 looks at exchange rate systems and explains how central banks can set monetary policy to manage the value of their county's currency.

The role of multinational corporations in globalisation

As explained earlier, multinational corporations (MNCs) are business enterprises operating in several countries to manage production or to deliver goods and services, but with their headquarters in just one country. The growth of MNCs since the 1970s has driven globalisation in four main ways.

Economic integration and increased trade

MNCs have built global production platforms which enable specialisation and take advantage of the global division of labour. They have broken the production process down so that specialist workers in different geographical locations contribute value to the development of products. For example, the inscription on the back of Apple products states: 'Designed by Apple in California. Assembled in China.' The high-skilled development takes place in Silicon Valley in California, but the low-skilled assembly is undertaken where labour is significantly cheaper.

By organising global production platforms and supply chains which stretch across international boundaries, MNCs have increased the economic integration of different countries. Products are no longer made in one country and then exported across the world. Instead components are made in a variety of locations and assembled in different regional factories. The technological revolution in communication and transportation has allowed MNCs to coordinate global business activities and open up new markets. In turn, trade flows have increased as MNCs have moved products along their global supply chains.

Investment and technology transfers

MNCs think globally and seek to locate operations in countries that offer the best business opportunities. In the late 1990s the oil company British Petroleum changed its name to BP to reflect a new global identity. MNCs invest and create jobs in regions that appear attractive. By creating a business-friendly environment, since the 1990s the Chinese government has attracted foreign direct investment worth billions of dollars from MNCs. The Chinese currency has remained relatively weak against the US dollar and the abundant supply of cheap labour has meant that firms which have located low- and medium-skilled manufacturing in China have been able to reduce production costs significantly. Since 1990, hundreds of millions of Chinese workers have been lifted out of poverty as they have moved from subsistence farming to better-paid factory jobs.

The long-term investment flows undertaken by MNCs have seen technology transferred from developed economies such as the USA and the UK to the emerging market economies, most notably China and India. Capital equipment and advanced technology that was once located in Western economies has enabled countries in Southeast Asia to industrialise. In the long term, economic power is shifting from West to East. However, this has caused tensions, most notably between the US and Chinese governments. American firms have been unhappy with a lack of legal protection, and in some cases theft of intellectual property and the forced transfers of technology to China. US businesses have been forced to hand over proprietary technology in exchange for access to the Chinese mainland markets. This has eroded the technological advantages of US firms and allowed Chinese businesses to develop highly technical products without incurring research and development costs. This issue was an important part of the trade war that started in 2018 between the USA and China when President Trump argued, with some justification, that forced technology transfers amounted to illegal state aid by the Chinese government.

Changing employment patterns and global capitalism

The process of globalisation has seen MNCs transform employment patterns across the world. The long-term trend has been for manufacturing and industrial production to close down in the advanced Western economies and move to the emerging market economies in Southeast Asia. This has resulted in structural unemployment and large pockets of poverty in the industrial regions of North America and Europe, but the creation of hundreds of millions of jobs, lifting workers out of absolute poverty in China and India. MNCs have coordinated this process.

MNCs are profit-maximising enterprises and have used their leverage to demand a favourable business environment when deciding where to locate factories and offices. For decades governments across the world have been under pressure to cut corporate taxes, reduce social protection and workers' rights legislation, resist environmental protection and create a light-touch system of regulation. Globalisation has been driven by the demands of MNCs, which have affected inequality in two different ways. First, many of the poorest workers in the world have benefited from higher incomes as they have taken up jobs in factories. The higher incomes have reduced the level of inequality between the developed world and the emerging markets. This has, however, had its costs, such as environmental degradation, pollution, long hours and dangerous workplaces. Second, a significant number of the workers in the developed world have experienced stagnating living standards and lower real incomes as a result of well-paid employment disappearing and relocating to cheaper labour zones. In these economies, inequality has increased.

The global market place and international brands

MNCs compete against each other in markets around the world. They seek to operate a global scale of production which enables them to benefit from economies of scale and to reduce average production costs significantly. MNCs develop brands which are recognised across the world, although products are often tailored to suit the tastes of particular markets. Standardised products have eroded national boundaries. Consumer choice has widened, in the sense that a greater variety of global products are now available, but it has decreased as a result of local firms either disappearing or being assimilated into multinational conglomerates owned elsewhere. Globalisation means that MNCs sell to consumers in different continents the same clothes, cars, computers, phones, food and beverages.

TEST YOURSELF 14.2

MNCs invest in LEDCs and can increase employment, capital equipment, access to technology, pollution and environmental destruction, and worker exploitation.

To what extent does investment by an MNC in an LEDC increase living standards?

CASE STUDY 14.1

Economic nationalism and global production platforms

The global car industry is dominated by a few large firms. Modern cars are highly sophisticated products that contain thousands of component parts, from wind screens to satellite navigation systems, to airbags. To build vehicles, car makers have established complex supply chains across international borders so that they can source high-quality parts from specialist suppliers.

The US car makers, General Motors and Ford, have established production platforms across North America to build cars for the lucrative American markets. The North American Free Trade Agreement (NAFTA) sets out rules that firms selling in the USA, Mexico and Canada have to comply with several conditions to qualify for tariff-free trade. Under NAFTA rules, 62.5% of a vehicle has to be made in the USA, Canada or Mexico. Since the NAFTA trade bloc was established in 1994, car makers have located their factories in Mexico to take advantage of the lower labour costs. In Europe, German firms have invested in central and eastern Europe, as have Japanese companies in China. This allows firms which invest in this way to bring costs down so as to remain price competitive.

Global production platforms have enabled multinational companies to take advantage of specialisation and the division of labour and then to bring prices down for consumers. However, this has enraged economic nationalists such as US president Donald Trump. He argues that, through MNCs moving factories to Mexico, American communities in the US car industry's traditional heartlands in Michigan have lost thousands of jobs. This has created structural unemployment and large pockets of poverty. Economic nationalists believe that the US government needs to protect American jobs by forcing multinational firms to relocate factories back to the USA.

The Trump administration argues that the NAFTA trade deal disadvantages US workers. His advisors want to renegotiate the trade rules and compel car makers to produce 85% of vehicles in North America and at least 50% in the USA. Trump dislikes multilateral negotiations, favouring instead bilateral treaties because he believes the USA can secure more favourable terms by dealing with countries individually rather than in round-table talks. In discussions with the Mexican government, President Trump demanded the introduction of $16 hourly wage in all car factories across North and Central America to prevent Mexican firms from undercutting American competitors.

The nationalist 'America First' agenda may be popular in the US 'rust belt', which has faced many years of decline, but it is questionable whether the strategy will be successful in the long run. Forcing multinational firms to relocate factories in the USA will raise unit costs in a fiercely competitive industry. Import tariffs can be increased to protect US firms from competition, but consumers will experience higher prices. Furthermore, the managers at the car makers will deploy considerable resources into reorganising supply chains to comply with the new rules. This will divert funds away from projects that seek to improve production methods and develop new technologies. Finally, the $16 an hour wage may appeal to workers but in the long run it is likely to result in higher unemployment. Car firms originally located low-skilled manufacturing in Mexico to take advantage of lower labour costs. But by raising the wages to $16 an hour, firms will be incentivised to replace low-skilled workers with automated machinery. Multinational companies may also close factories in Mexico and build new ones in the USA to please President Trump, but it is unlikely that this will provide many new jobs for low-skilled American workers.

Follow-up questions

1 Define the term 'supply chain'.
2 Explain **two** ways in which a government can seek to protect domestic firms from competition.
3 Explain how building a global production platform enables a multinational corporation to reduce costs and increase profits.
4 Evaluate the effectiveness of President Trump's economic nationalist policies which aim to increase employment in the USA.

CASE STUDY 14.2

Has globalisation given way to de-globalisation?

Robert J. Samuelson of Investors.com recently asked: 'What has happened to globalisation?' Samuelson argued that for decades, growing volumes of cross-border trade and money flows have fuelled strong economic growth. But something remarkable is happening — the growth rate of trade and money flows is slowing and, in some cases, declining. Samuelson pondered whether these changes herald prolonged economic stagnation and rising nationalism or, optimistically, whether they make the world economy more stable and politically acceptable.

For workers employed or previously employed in US manufacturing industries, some aspects of de-globalisation are very attractive. Globalisation has sucked factory jobs out of North America. But now, the tide may be turning. Apple has announced a $100 million investment to return some Mac computer manufacturing to the USA. Though small, the decision may reflect a new trend.

General Electric's sprawling Appliance Park in Kentucky once symbolised America's manufacturing prowess, with employment peaking at 23,000 in 1973. Since then, jobs have shifted abroad or succumbed to automation. However, now General Electric is moving production of water heaters, refrigerators and other appliances back to Appliance Park from China and Mexico. Nor is GE alone. Otis is moving some elevator output from Mexico to South Carolina.

China's labour cost advantage has eroded. By 2020, China's manufacturing costs were projected to be US$6.5 billion. Although wages of US production workers average were much higher, other non-wage factors favour the USA. American workers are more productive; automation has cut labour costs, and cheap natural gas further lowers costs; finally, higher oil prices have boosted freight rates for imports.

Follow-up questions

1 What is meant by de-globalisation?
2 How may the growth in 'cross-border trade' promote globalisation?
3 Explain how the US government can use the threat of tariffs to encourage firms to relocate factories in the USA.
4 How may the movement of factories from Mexico to the USA increase the costs of production of multinational corporations?

SECTION 14.1 SUMMARY

- Globalisation is the name given to the increasing integration of the world's economies.
- Trade liberalisation, international capital and labour mobility, and the increased power of multinational corporations (MNCs) are important elements of globalisation.
- MNCs have driven many parts of the globalisation process.
- In recent years there has been an increase in support for economic nationalists who seek to reverse globalisation using protectionist policies.
- De-globalisation has seen MNCs close factories in less developed countries and relocate them in developed countries.

499

14.2 Trade

Imagine a small country such as Iceland in a world without international trade. As a closed economy, Iceland's production possibilities are limited to the goods and services that its narrow resource base can produce. This means that Iceland's average costs of production are likely to be high because the small population and the absence of export markets mean that economies of scale and long production runs cannot be achieved. At the same time, the consumption possibilities of Iceland's inhabitants are restricted to the goods that the country can produce.

Compare this with Iceland's position in a world completely open to international trade. In an open economy, imports of raw materials and energy greatly boost Iceland's production possibilities. In theory at least, Iceland can now produce a much wider range of goods. In practice, however, Iceland produces the relatively few goods and services that it is good at producing, and imports all the rest. By gaining access to the much larger world market, Iceland's industries benefit from economies of scale and long production runs. Likewise, imports of food and other consumer goods present Iceland's inhabitants with a vast array of choice and the possibility of a much higher living standard and level of economic welfare than are possible in a world without trade.

While the UK is a much larger country than Iceland, it still has a relatively narrow resource base. The arguments outlined above about using trade to widen production and consumption possibilities help to explain the role of international trade in the British economy. The UK's economy is dependent on foreign trade. Successive British governments have supported free and unrestricted trade and the UK has few restrictions on foreign trade and investment.

SYNOPTIC LINK

Chapter 4 explains how firms can reduce average costs by increasing their scale of production and benefit from global economies of scale. Earlier in this chapter we explain how MNCs have built global production platforms that enable them to operate on a global scale and benefit from global economies of scale. International trade enables consumers to buy products from MNCs and enjoy the benefits of lower average prices.

The model of comparative advantage

We shall follow the rather 'common sense' justification of the benefits of international specialisation and trade given above with a more rigorous explanation provided by the principle of comparative advantage.

To show how the principle of *comparative advantage* explains some of the benefits of international specialisation and free trade, it is helpful to look first at a related concept: *absolute advantage*.

Absolute advantage

A country has an **absolute advantage** if it can produce more of a good with a given amount of resources than another country. (Alternatively, we may say that it can produce the same amount of the product with fewer resources.)

To explain absolute advantage, we shall assume just two countries in the world economy, Atlantis and Pacifica. Each country has only 2 units of resource. Only two goods can be produced: guns and butter. Each unit of resource, or indeed a fraction of each unit (because we shall assume that resources or inputs are divisible), can be switched from one industry

KEY TERM

absolute advantage a country has an absolute advantage if it can produce more of a good than other countries from the same amount of resources.

to another, if so desired, in each country. Table 14.1 shows each country's production possibilities from 1 unit of resource.

Table 14.1 Production with 1 unit of resource

	Guns		**Butter**
Atlantis	4	or	2 tonnes
Pacifica	1	or	6 tonnes

Quite clearly, Atlantis has an absolute advantage in producing guns. It is four times better in gun production than Pacifica. However, this is not the case for butter production. Pacifica is three times better in butter production and so possesses an absolute advantage in this good.

Suppose that both countries devote half their total resources to each activity (that is, 1 unit of resource out of the 2 units available for each country). We shall call this *production without specialisation*. Without specialisation, Atlantis produces 4 guns and Pacifica produces 1 gun, which means that 5 guns are produced in total. Likewise, without specialisation, total butter production is 8 tonnes. Atlantis produces 2 tonnes and Pacifica produces 6 tonnes. Table 14.2 shows the outcome.

Table 14.2 Production without specialisation

	Guns		**Butter**
Atlantis	4	and	2 tonnes
Pacifica	1	and	6 tonnes
Total output without specialisation	5	and	8 tonnes

Now let's see what happens when each country produces only the good in which it has an absolute advantage. Table 14.3 shows that if Atlantis devotes both its resource units to guns, it produces 8 guns. Likewise, if Pacifica completely specialises, the country produces 12 tonnes of butter with its 2 units of resource.

Table 14.3 Production with complete specialisation

	Guns		**Butter**
Atlantis	8	and	0 tonnes
Pacifica	0	and	12 tonnes
Total output with complete specialisation	8	and	12 tonnes

The final table in this series, Table 14.4, shows how, when each country enjoys an absolute advantage in a different good, complete specialisation results in more of both goods being produced.

Table 14.4 Output gain from complete specialisation

	Guns		**Butter**
Atlantis	8	and	0 tonnes
Pacifica	0	and	12 tonnes
Total output without specialisation	5	and	8 tonnes
Total output with complete specialisation	8	and	12 tonnes
Output gains from specialisation	3	and	4 tonnes

In this example, specialisation produces a net output gain of 3 guns and 4 tonnes of butter. Since more has been produced, more can be consumed, and it is possible to make people better off.

However, for *output* gains to translate into gains from *trade*, two further factors have to be taken into account. First, administration and transport costs occur whenever trade takes place. As a result, the net gains from trade are:

(3 guns + 4 tonnes of butter) – transport and administration costs

Clearly, specialisation and trade are not worthwhile if transport and administration costs exceed the output gains resulting from specialisation.

Second, assuming that only two countries trade with each other, for output gains to transfer into *welfare* gains for the inhabitants of both countries, the goods being traded must be in demand in each of the importing countries. Given this assumption about demand, we shall further assume that each country exports its surplus to the other country once it has satisfied its own inhabitants' demand for the good in which it specialises. (This *double coincidence of wants* is not necessary when more than two countries trade together.)

But suppose Atlantis's inhabitants are vegans who refuse to eat animal products, while Pacifica's inhabitants are pacifists who hate guns. For Atlantis's inhabitants, butter is a 'bad' rather than a good. Likewise, guns are a 'bad' for Pacifica's residents. (A good yields utility or economic welfare to consumers, but a bad yields disutility or negative welfare.) Atlantis refuses to import butter, and Pacifica refuses to buy guns. Specialisation and trade do not take place. Without suitable demand conditions, the case for specialisation and trade disappears.

SYNOPTIC LINK
The extension material in Chapter 8, page 229, explains the distinction between 'goods' and 'bads' in the context of public goods and public bads.

> **KEY TERM**
> **comparative advantage** this is measured in terms of opportunity cost. The country with the least opportunity cost when producing a good possesses a comparative advantage in that good.

Comparative advantage

Absolute advantage must not be confused with the rather more subtle concept of **comparative advantage**. However, understanding absolute advantage is a stepping-stone to understanding comparative advantage. To explain comparative advantage, we shall change the production possibilities of both countries so that Atlantis possesses the absolute advantage for both guns and butter (which means that Pacifica has an absolute disadvantage in both goods). Table 14.5 shows how much 1 unit of resource can produce in each country.

Table 14.5 Production with 1 unit of resource

	Guns		Butter
Atlantis	4	or	2 tonnes
Pacifica	1	or	1 tonne

Although Atlantis is 'best at' — or has an absolute advantage in — producing both guns and butter, the country possesses a comparative advantage in the production of guns but has a comparative disadvantage in the production of butter. *This is because comparative advantage is measured in terms of opportunity cost, or what a country gives up when it increases the output of a product by 1 unit.*

The country that gives up least of the other commodity when increasing output of a particular commodity by 1 unit possesses a comparative advantage in that good. Ask yourself how many guns Atlantis has to give up in order to increase its output of butter by 1 tonne. The answer is 2 guns. But Pacifica only has to give up 1 gun to produce an extra tonne of butter. Thus Pacifica possesses a comparative advantage in butter production even though it has an absolute disadvantage in both products.

Table 14.6 shows the total output of guns and butter, if each country devotes 1 unit of resource to each industry.

Table 14.6 Production without specialisation

	Guns		Butter
Atlantis	4	and	2 tonnes
Pacifica	1	and	1 tonne
Total output without specialisation	5	and	3 tonnes

When one country possesses an absolute advantage in both products, as in the example above, its comparative advantage always lies in producing the good in which its absolute advantage is greater. Similarly, the country that has an absolute disadvantage in both activities possesses a comparative advantage in the product in which its absolute disadvantage is less. The table shows that Atlantis has a comparative advantage in gun production, while Pacifica's comparative advantage lies in butter production.

In this example, as Table 14.7 shows, complete specialisation results in more guns but less butter being produced, compared to a situation in which each country devotes half its total resources to each activity. Without specialisation, the combined output of both countries is 5 guns and 3 tonnes of butter. With complete specialisation, this changes to 8 guns and 2 tonnes of butter. While production of guns has increased, production of butter has fallen.

Table 14.7 Output gain from complete specialisation

	Guns		Butter
Atlantis	8	and	2 tonnes
Pacifica	0	and	1 tonne
Total output without specialisation	5	and	3 tonnes
Total output with complete specialisation	8	and	2 tonnes

When one country has an absolute advantage in both goods, complete specialisation in accordance with the principle of comparative advantage does not result in a net output gain. The output of one good rises, but the output of the other good falls.

Students are puzzled by this, thinking (wrongly) that because of the loss of output of one of the two goods, specialisation cannot lead to gains from trade. However, *partial* specialisation can produce a net output gain. For example, suppose Pacifica (which suffers an absolute disadvantage in both goods) specialises completely and produces 2 tonnes of butter. By contrast, Atlantis (which has the absolute advantage in both goods) devotes just enough resource (half a unit) to top up world production of butter to 3 tonnes. This means that Atlantis can still produce 6 guns using 1.5 units of resource.

Total production in both countries is therefore 6 guns and 3 tonnes of butter. At least as much butter and more guns are now produced compared with the 'no specialisation' outcome. This example shows that specialisation can produce a net output gain, even though one country is absolutely better at both activities.

TEST YOURSELF 14.3

Table 14.8 shows the production possibilities of two countries with 1 unit of resource.

Table 14.8 Production with 1 unit of resource

	Guns		Butter
Oceania	20	or	10
Eurasia	15	or	5

Which statement is correct? Explain why.

A Oceania has an absolute advantage in the production of both products so trade will not take place.

B Oceania has a comparative advantage in the production of both guns and butter.

C Oceania has a comparative advantage in the production of guns.

D Eurasia has a comparative advantage in the production of both guns and butter.

STUDY TIP

Make sure you don't confuse the 'terms of trade' with the 'balance of trade'. The balance of trade is a major part of the balance of payments on current account, which is explained later in this chapter. The balance of trade is the difference in value between a country's imports and exports. If the value of exports exceeds the value of imports, there is a balance of trade surplus. Conversely, if the value of exports is less than the value of imports, there is a balance of trade deficit.

EXTENSION MATERIAL

Adam Smith, David Ricardo and absolute and comparative advantage

Although he did not use the precise term, Adam Smith is credited with introducing the concept of absolute advantage in his great eighteenth-century book, *The Wealth of Nations*. Some years later, in the early nineteenth century, another distinguished classical economist, David Ricardo, developed Adam Smith's ideas into the principle of comparative advantage. Neither Smith nor Ricardo was interested solely in abstract economic theory. Instead, like many great economists, they wished to change society for the better by influencing the politicians of their day.

Smith and Ricardo believed in the virtues of a competitive market economy and industrial capitalism. Ricardo, in particular, believed that a single country such as the UK, and indeed the whole world economy, can only reach its full productive potential, maximising output, welfare and living standards, if the market economy is truly international. He argued that each country should specialise in the activities in which it possesses a comparative advantage, and then trade the output that is surplus to its needs in a world free of tariffs and other forms of protectionism.

The assumptions underlying the principle of comparative advantage

When arguing that definite benefits result when countries specialise and trade in accordance with the principle of comparative advantage, we made a number of rather strong but not necessarily realistic assumptions. Indeed, the case for trade — and hence the case *against* import controls and other forms of protectionism — is heavily dependent upon these assumptions. Likewise, some of the arguments in favour of import controls and against free trade, which we shall explain shortly, depend on showing that the assumptions necessary for the benefits of specialisation and trade to occur are simply not met in real life.

The assumptions underlying the principles of comparative advantage are as follows:

- Each country's endowment of factors of production, including capital and labour, is fixed and immobile between countries, although factors can be switched between industries within a country. In the course of international trade, finished goods rather than factors of production or inputs are assumed to be mobile between countries.
- There are *constant returns to scale*. In our example, 1 unit of resource is assumed to produce 4 guns or 2 tonnes of butter in Atlantis, whether it is the first unit of resource employed or the millionth unit. But in the real world, increasing or decreasing returns to scale are both possible and indeed likely. In a world of increasing returns to scale, the more a country specialises in an activity in which it initially has an absolute advantage, the more its productive efficiency and advantage increases. Countries that are 'best' to start with become even 'better'. But if decreasing returns to scale occur, specialisation erodes efficiency and destroys a country's initial advantage. A good example occurs in agriculture, where over-specialisation can result in monoculture or the growing of a single cash crop for export. Monoculture often leads to soil erosion, vulnerability to pests and falling future agricultural yields.
- Demand and cost conditions are relatively stable. Over-specialisation can cause a country to become particularly vulnerable to sudden changes in demand or to changes in the cost and availability of imported raw materials or energy. Changes in costs, and new inventions and technical progress, can quickly eliminate a country's earlier comparative advantage. The greater the uncertainty about the future, the weaker the case for a country specialising in a narrow range of products.

STUDY TIP

There are other justifications of specialisation and free trade beside the argument that global economic welfare increases if countries specialise and trade in accordance with the principle of comparative advantage. We mentioned a justification earlier in our discussion of widening production possibilities and consumption possibilities. A further justification, also mentioned briefly, is the ability to enjoy the benefits of economies of scale that lead to greater efficiency and lower average costs. (If you remember from Chapter 4, economies and diseconomies of scale are closely linked to increasing returns to scale and decreasing returns to scale.)

Comparative advantage and competitive advantage

Comparative advantage must not be confused with *competitive* advantage. A country, or a firm within a country, enjoys a competitive advantage when it produces better-quality goods at lower costs and better prices than its rivals. Competitive advantage is more similar to absolute advantage than to comparative advantage.

Dynamic factors that promote the growth of firms can create competitive advantage. Successful investment undertaken over many years equips a country with modern, 'state-of-the-art' production capacity, capable of producing high-quality goods that people want to buy. Properly funded and organised research and development (R&D) contributes in a similar way, while the stock of human capital resulting from investment in education and training adds to competitive advantage.

Factors that create competitive advantage can trigger a virtuous spiral of larger profits, higher investment, better products and greater sales, which in turn leads to even higher profits, and so on. Conversely, countries and firms that are not competitive may enter a vicious spiral of decline. Inability to compete causes profits to fall, which in turn reduces investment. The quality of goods declines and sales are lost to more competitive countries or firms. Profits again fall (maybe disappearing altogether), and a further round in the vicious circle of decline is unleashed.

Supporters of free trade argue that the increased competition between countries which an absence of import duties and other forms of protectionism creates are exactly the circumstances needed to foster the growth of competitive advantage. However, as we shall see in the next section, in our coverage of strategic trade theory, others argue that, if used *strategically*, protectionism is better at providing selected industries with a competitive advantage against the rest of the world.

The case for import controls and protectionism

Import controls can be divided into quantity controls such as import **quotas**, which put a maximum limit on imports, and **tariffs** or **import duties** (and their opposite, **export subsidies**), which raise the price of imports (or reduce the price of exports).

KEY TERMS

quotas physical limits on the quantities of imported goods allowed into a country.

tariffs (also known as **import duties**) taxes imposed on imports from other countries entering a country.

export subsidies money given to domestic firms by the government to encourage firms to sell their products abroad and to help make their goods cheaper in export markets.

Supporters of free trade believe that import controls prevent countries from specialising in activities in which they have a comparative advantage and from trading their surpluses. As a result, production takes place inefficiently and economic welfare is reduced. However, as already noted, the case for free trade depends to a large extent upon some of the assumptions underlying the principle of comparative advantage. Relax these assumptions and the case for free trade is weakened. Nevertheless, it should be remembered that the proponents of free trade also emphasise the dynamic benefits that result from opening up an economy to competition from abroad.

Below are some of the contexts in which import controls have been justified:

- **Infant industries.** As already explained, many economic activities benefit from increasing returns to scale, which mean that the more a country specialises in a particular industry, the more productively efficient it becomes. This increases its competitive advantage. Developing countries justify the use of import controls to protect infant industries from established rivals in advanced economies. It is argued that protectionism is needed while newly established industries develop and achieve full economies of scale.

- **Sunset industries.** A rather similar case to the infant industry argument is sometimes made in advanced industrial economies such as the UK to protect older industries from the competition of infant industries in developing countries. Some economists advocate the selective use of import controls as a potentially effective supply-side policy instrument to prevent unnecessary deindustrialisation and to allow orderly rather than disruptive structural change in the manufacturing base of the economy. According to this view, import controls are justified, at least on a temporary basis, to minimise the social and economic cost of the painful adjustment process, as the structure of an economy alters in response either to changing demand or to changing technology and comparative and competitive advantage. Labour is not perfectly mobile and import controls may help to reduce the incidence of structural unemployment.

- **Strategic trade theory.** The infant and sunset industry arguments are closely related to strategic trade theory, a relatively new theory that has grown in influence in recent years. Strategic trade theory argues that comparative and competitive advantage are often not 'natural' or 'God-given'. Rather, governments try to create competitive advantage by nurturing strategically selected industries or economic sectors. This justifies protecting the industries while competitive advantage is being built up. The skills that are gained will then spill over to help other sectors in the economy. Strategic trade theory also argues that protectionism can prevent exploitation by a foreign-based monopoly. Governments in more developed countries use two types of strategic trade policy to help declining industries such as textiles and shipbuilding:
  - trade adjustment assistance and other aid to workers and firms in these industries
  - subsidies on exports or taxes on imports and investment or adjustment assistance subsidies to protect the industries from foreign competition

  However, export subsidies, with few exceptions, such as agricultural products, violate World Trade Organization (WTO) rules. By contrast, less developed countries use strategic trade policies to protect and promote the growth of their infant industries.

- **Agricultural efficiency.** As noted earlier, monoculture, which might result from specialisation and trade, erodes efficiency and destroys comparative advantage that existed before specialisation took place. Decreasing returns to scale weaken the case for complete specialisation.

- **Changes in demand or cost conditions.** Over-specialisation may cause a country to become particularly vulnerable to sudden changes in demand or to changes in the cost and availability of imported raw materials or energy. Specialisation can lead to a lack of diversity in a country's economy. In this situation, countries could benefit from diversifying their economies, and import controls might lead to this outcome.

- **Anti-dumping.** When a country produces too much of a good for its own domestic market, the surplus may then be 'dumped' and sold at a price below cost in overseas markets. Import controls are often justified as a means to prevent this supposedly 'unfair' competition. Article 6 of the General Agreement on Tariffs and Trade allows countries to protect themselves against dumping where there is a material injury to the competing domestic industry.

- **Self-sufficiency.** Politically, it is often argued that protection is necessary for military and strategic reasons to ensure that a country is relatively self-sufficient in vital foodstuffs, energy and raw materials in a time of war.

- **Employment.** Trade unions argue that import controls are necessary to prevent multinational firms shifting capital to low-wage developing countries and exporting their output back to the countries from which the capital was moved. They further argue the case for employing labour, however inefficiently, in protected industries rather than allowing labour to suffer the greatest inefficiency of all: mass unemployment. This is an example of *second-best theory*. It stems from the fact that the 'first best' (free trade in a world of fully employed economies and perfect markets) is unattainable. Therefore, a country can settle legitimately for the second best. Employing resources perhaps inefficiently, protected by tariffs, is better than leaving resources, such as labour, unemployed. This justification for protecting domestic industries returned to prominence after the financial crisis in 2009. The 2016 election of Donald Trump in the USA saw the country move away from its traditional position as the champion of free trade and towards economic nationalism and protectionism. The Trump administration has started trade disputes with China and long-term allies Canada and Mexico as part of a strategy to bring factories and jobs back to the industrial regions that support the president's 'America First' agenda.

SYNOPTIC LINK

Unemployment is a significant cost of international trade. Many industries in the UK have closed down because British firms have been unable to compete with foreign competitors. Go back over Chapter 11 and look at how structural unemployment has affected the UK since the 1970s. Pay attention to the increase in UK unemployment in the early 1980s.

STUDY TIP

The case for free trade, or trade liberalisation, is the case against import controls and other forms of protectionism. Likewise the case for import controls is the case against free trade. However, remember that it is not unreasonable to argue that trade liberalisation is generally desirable but to accept that there are circumstances when protectionism may be justified. There is a wide spectrum of opinion amongst economists about the extent to which protectionist measures are economically justifiable.

Paul Krugman and strategic trade theory

In 2008, Paul Krugman, professor of economics at Princeton University in the USA, was awarded the Nobel prize in economics, in part for his pioneering work in developing strategic trade theory in the 1980s and 1990s. In contrast to the orthodox free-market approach to international trade, firmly grounded in the principle of comparative advantage, strategic trade theory argues that import controls can sometimes be justified. Krugman argued that rich, developed countries benefited from protectionism while they established their national wealth. However, they now put pressure on poor countries to abandon import controls and to allow overseas-based multinational corporations unlimited access to their economies. And as we mentioned earlier in the chapter, opponents of globalisation argue that free trade theory is used to justify first-world economic imperialism.

Below is an extract from the beginning of a paper Krugman wrote in 1987:

If there were an Economist's Creed, it would surely contain the affirmations 'I understand the principle of comparative advantage' and 'I advocate free trade'. For 170 years, the appreciation that international trade benefits a country whether it is 'fair' or not has been one of the touchstones of professionalism in economics.

Yet the case for free trade is currently more in doubt than at any time since the 1817 publication of Ricardo's *Principles of Political Economy*. This is not because of the political pressures for protection, which have triumphed in the past without shaking the intellectual foundation of comparative advantage theory. Rather, it is because of the changes that have recently taken place in the theory of international trade itself.

In the last 10 years the traditional <u>constant returns</u>, <u>perfect competition</u> models of international trade have been supplemented and to some extent supplanted by a new breed of models that emphasise <u>increasing returns</u> and <u>imperfect competition</u>. These new models call into doubt the extent to which actual trade can be explained by comparative advantage.

Showing that free trade is better than no trade is not the same thing as showing that free trade is better than sophisticated government intervention. The view that free trade is the best of all possible policies is part of the general case for laissez-faire in a market economy and rests on the proposition that markets are efficient. If increasing returns and imperfect competition are necessary parts of the explanation of international trade, we are living in a <u>second-best</u> world where government intervention can in principle improve on market outcomes.

Source: Paul Krugman, 'Is free trade passé?', *Journal of Economic Perspectives*, 1987.
The full article can be found online at: <u>www.aeaweb.org/articles.php?doi=10.1257/jep.1.2.131</u>.

Follow-up questions

1 What is comparative advantage?
2 Briefly define each of the terms underlined in the extract.
3 Do you agree that increasing returns to scale and imperfect competition weaken the case for unlimited free trade based on the principle of comparative advantage? Justify your answer.
4 What is first-world economic imperialism?

The causes and consequences of countries adopting protectionist policies

In this and the next two sections of the chapter, we bypass the justifications for tariffs put forward by economists such as Paul Krugman and return to the free-market case for free trade. Analysis of the welfare gains from free trade and the welfare losses caused by import controls centres on the concepts of consumer surplus and producer surplus that you learnt when studying Chapter 5.

If a country does not enter into international trade, which means its economy is *closed*, domestic demand for a good within a country can only be met

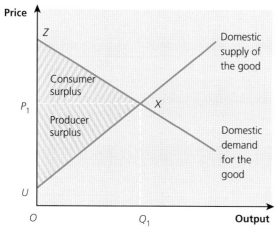

Figure 14.2 Consumer and producer surplus in a market closed to international trade

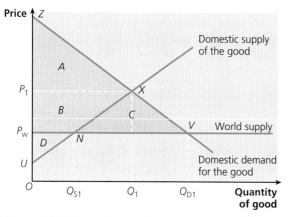

Figure 14.3 The welfare gains and losses resulting from the introduction of a tariff

by domestic supply (that is, by firms producing *within* the country). Such a situation is shown in Figure 14.2, where market equilibrium for the good occurs at point X. Consumers pay price P_1 for the good, and the quantity bought and sold is Q_1. Consumer surplus, which is a measure of consumer welfare, is shown by the triangular area bounded by points XZP_1. Likewise, producer welfare (producer surplus) is the triangular area bounded by points XP_1U.

But consider what happens in a world of completely free trade, in which domestically produced goods have to compete with cheaper imports. In Figure 14.3, imports are priced at the ruling world price of P_W, which is lower than P_1. In this situation, equilibrium now occurs in the domestic market at point V. Although domestic demand has increased to Q_{D1}, domestic supply (located where the domestic supply curve cuts the horizontal price line at P_W) falls to Q_{S1}. Imports (equal to $Q_{D1} - Q_{S1}$) fill the gap between domestic demand and supply.

To understand how imports affect economic welfare within the country, it is important to understand how consumer surplus and producer surplus change after the price of the good falls to the world price P_W. Consumer surplus increases by the wedge-shaped area bounded by the points P_WVXP_1. This divides into two parts, shown on the diagram by areas B and C. Look closely at area B. This shows a welfare transfer away from domestic firms to domestic consumers. The fall in the price from P_1 to P_W, brought about by lower import prices, means that part of the producer surplus that domestic firms previously enjoyed now becomes consumer surplus. The consumers 'win' and the domestic producers 'lose'.

But this is not the end of the story. Consumers enjoy a further increase in consumer surplus, which is brought about by receipt of area C. As a result, the total increase in consumer surplus exceeds the size of the welfare transfer from producer surplus to consumer surplus. A net welfare gain thus results, equal to area C, which makes up part of the consumer surplus that households now enjoy.

SYNOPTIC LINK

Chapter 5 on perfect competition, imperfectly competitive markets and oligopoly explains the key welfare concepts of consumer surplus and producer surplus.

STUDY TIP

You should practise drawing and explaining Figure 14.3 and the diagrams that follow to show the welfare gains and losses resulting from trade and import controls. Remember, however, the assumptions that underpin free-trade theory which we explained earlier. Question these assumptions and the case for free trade weakens.

How a tariff or import duty affects economic welfare

We shall now assume that domestic firms pressure the government to introduce a tariff to protect the home market. If the tariff equals the distance between P_1 and P_W, the domestic market for the good reverts to the original equilibrium position that existed before imports entered the country. But suppose the government imposes a smaller tariff, which is just sufficient to raise the price of imports (also allowing domestic producers to charge higher prices) to $P_W + t$ in Figure 14.4. At price $P_W + t$, domestic demand falls to Q_{D2}, while domestic supply rises to Q_{S2}. Imports fall from $Q_{D1} - Q_{S1}$ to $Q_{D2} - Q_{S2}$.

At the higher price, consumer surplus *falls* by the wedge-shaped area $P_W V Y P_W + t$, which equals the areas $D + A + B + C$. The higher price increases producer surplus by the area D, and the government gains tariff revenue shown by the area B. (The government's tariff revenue is measured by total imports, $Q_{D2} - Q_{S2}$, multiplied by the tariff per unit of imports, $P_W + t - P_W$.) The areas D and B are *transfers* of welfare away from consumers to domestic producers and the government respectively. The *net welfare loss* resulting from the tariff, which is the sum of triangles A and C in the diagram, is:

$$(D + A + B + C) - (D + B), \text{ which equals } A + C$$

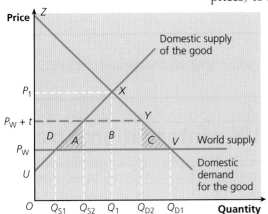

Figure 14.4 The effect of imposing a tariff.

Changing comparative advantage and the pattern of world trade

To many people living in industrial countries during the nineteenth century and the first half of the twentieth century, it must have seemed almost natural that the earliest countries to industrialise, such as the UK, had done so because they possessed a competitive and comparative advantage in manufacturing. It probably seemed equally natural that a pattern of world trade should have developed in which the industrialised countries in what is now called the North exported manufactured goods in exchange for foodstuffs and raw materials produced by countries whose comparative advantage lay in the production of primary products — in modern parlance, the countries of the South.

However, in recent years, the pattern of world trade has become quite different from the North–South exchange of manufactured goods for primary products that characterised the nineteenth century. In a North–North pattern of trade, which is illustrated in Figure 14.5, the developed industrial economies now exchange goods and services mostly with each other. However, a growing fraction of their trade, particularly in the case of imports, is with newly industrialising countries (NICs) or emerging markets, particularly India, China and South Korea. A group of countries known as the BRIC countries (Brazil, Russia, India and China) are responsible for exporting large quantities of goods and

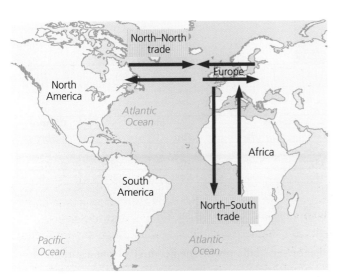

Figure 14.5 North–North and North–South patterns of trade

services to the North. India, China and South Korea now export manufactured goods to countries in the North such as the UK and the USA, and import raw materials or commodities such as copper from developing countries such as Zambia. They also import a growing fraction of the crude oil produced by oil-exporting developing countries such as Saudi Arabia and Venezuela.

The shift of manufacturing to China and other NICs reflects changing competitive and comparative advantage and the deindustrialisation of the UK, North America and some of the major European economies. Only a relatively small proportion of the trade of North countries is with poorer countries in the non-oil-producing developing world.

TEST YOURSELF 14.4
What is the difference between comparative advantage and competitive advantage?

The pattern of the UK's international trade

In July 2018, the House of Commons library in the UK parliament published a briefing paper written by Matthew Ward, titled 'Statistics on EU–UK trade'. The briefing paper, which was written before the proposed date for the UK leaving the European Union, stated:

> In 2017, the UK exported £274 billion of goods and services to other EU member states. This is equivalent to 44.5% of total UK exports. Goods and services imports from the EU were worth £341 billion (53.1% of the total) in 2017.

Goods and services (£bn)

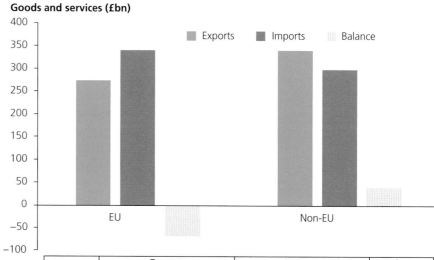

	Exports		Imports		Balance
	£bn	**%**	**£bn**	**%**	**£bn**
EU	274	44.5	341	53.1	–67
Non-EU	342	55.5	301	46.9	41
Total	616	100.0	642	100.0	–26

Source: ONS

Figure 14.6 UK trade with EU and non-EU countries, 2017

The UK had a trade deficit of –£67 billion with the EU in 2017 but a surplus of £41 billion with non-EU countries.

Goods and services (%)

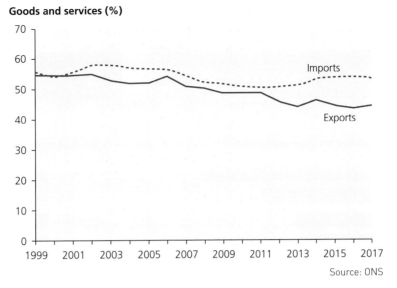

Source: ONS

Figure 14.7 Share of UK trade with the EU, 1999–2017

The share of UK exports going to the EU has declined gradually over recent years. In 2006, the EU accounted for 55% of UK exports. By 2017, this had fallen to 44%. The picture on imports is slightly less clear. In 2002, 58% of UK imports were from the EU. By 2010, this had fallen to 51% but has increased slightly more recently, reaching 54% in 2016.

The UK has had a trade deficit with the EU in every year since 1999, with the deficit bottoming out at about 4% of UK GDP in 2016. By contrast, the UK has had a surplus with non-EU countries since 2012, with the surplus reaching 2% of UK GDP in 2017.

Goods and services (% of GDP)

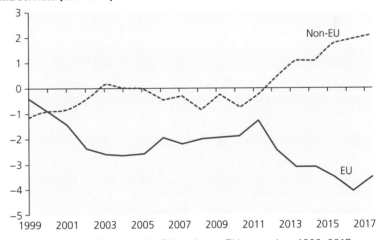

Figure 14.8 Balance of UK trade with EU and non-EU countries, 1999–2017

Figure 14.9 (overleaf) shows that four out of the top five of countries to whom the UK exported in 2018 were EU member states, though the USA was by far the main destination for British exports, leading Germany by nearly £20,000 million. On the import side, however, Germany topped the league of countries selling goods to Britain, sending to the UK more than £20,000 million more goods than second-placed China.

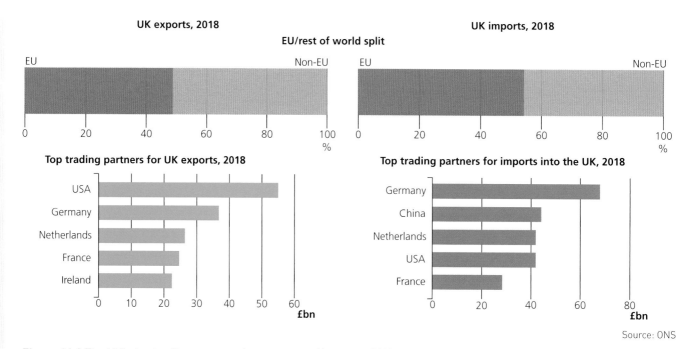

Top trading partners for UK exports, 2018

Top trading partners for imports into the UK, 2018

Source: ONS

Figure 14.9 The UK's top trading partners for exports and imports, 2018

Finally, Figures 14.10 and 14.11 show the commodity breakdown in the pattern of UK trade in 2018 for exports and imports of goods. The diagrams show the pattern of UK trade in terms of the different groups of goods which are traded.

Machinery and transport equipment headed the list for both exports and imports, with miscellaneous manufacturers and chemicals in second place respectively for exports and imports.

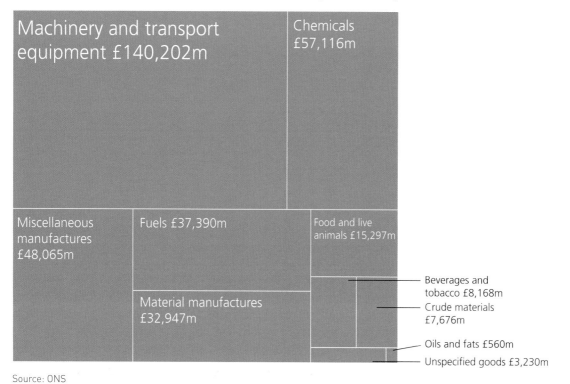

Source: ONS

Figure 14.10 The commodity breakdown for UK exports of goods, 2018 (total = £350,651m)

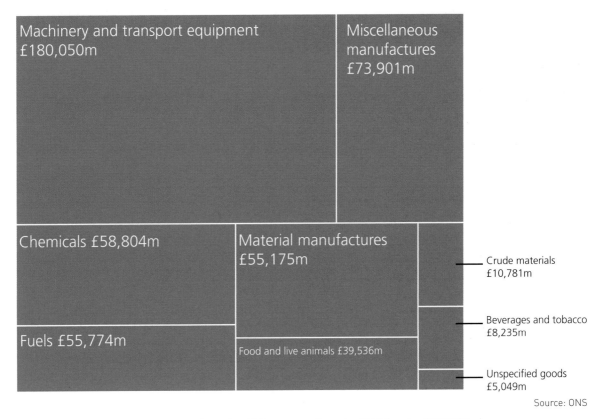

Source: ONS

Figure 14.11 The commodity breakdown for UK imports of goods, 2018 (total = £487,305m)

QUANTITATIVE SKILLS 14.1

Worked example: interpreting export and import statistics

Making use of the data in Figures 14.10 and 14.11, calculate the UK's trade deficit or surplus in 2018 for:

(a) **machinery and transport equipment**
(b) **chemicals**
(c) **fuels**

(a) £140,202m – £180,050m = deficit of £39,848m
(b) £57,116m – £58,804m = deficit of £1,688m
(c) £37,390m – £55,774m = deficit of £18,384m

Degrees of international economic integration

The main types of international economic integration are as follows:

- **Preference areas.** Countries agree to levy reduced, or preferential, tariffs on certain trade: for example, the EU's Association Agreements with certain developing countries.
- **Free trade areas.** Member countries abolish tariffs on mutual trade, but each partner determines its own tariffs on trade with non-member countries. A potential problem here is that traders try to import goods into the partner with the lowest external tariff and then re-export them to others tariff-free from there. To avoid this, complex rules of origin and border controls tend to govern intra-area trade to ensure that free trade refers only to the partners' produce and not to their imports.
- **Customs unions.** There are two main features of a customs union: first, a free trade area where member countries agree to abolish tariffs, quotas and other barriers to trade; second, a common external tariff wall set up on trade with non-member countries and coordinated centrally.
- **Common markets.** These are customs unions with additional provisions to encourage trade and integration through the free mobility of factors of production and the harmonisation of trading standards and practices.
- **Economic unions.** These add further harmonisation in the areas of general economic, legal and social policies, and the development of union-wide policies. Economic union may be supplemented by monetary union, which entails a common currency and monetary policy.
- **Political unions.** These are the ultimate form of economic integration. They involve the submersion of separate national institutions. Even within this category, however, several degrees of integration exist. For example, in the USA the states have substantial powers of taxation, whereas at the moment UK local government has few such powers (though Scotland now has some ability to raise its own taxes).

KEY TERMS

free trade area in a free trade area, member countries abolish tariffs on mutual trade, but each partner determines its own tariffs on trade with non-member countries.

customs unions trading blocs in which member countries enjoy internal free trade in goods and possibly services, with all the member countries protected by a common external tariff barrier.

TEST YOURSELF 14.5

Which of the following international organisations is protected by a common eternal tariff?

A a free trade area

B a customs union

C a preference area

D a monetary union

Free trade areas versus customs unions

Figure 14.12 illustrates the main difference between a customs union and a free trade area, and also the way in which the two forms of trading bloc are similar. The similarity lies in the fact that both organisations have internal free trade, at least in goods though not necessarily in services. However, the difference lies in the way tariffs are set against imports from non-member states. Members of a free trade area are free to set their own tariffs against non-members, but members of a customs union lose this freedom and have to abide by an external tariff common to all member states.

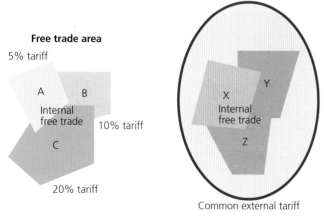

Figure 14.12 The difference between a free trade area and a customs union

The European Union as an example of international economic integration

The organisation which became the EU in 1993 was originally called the European Economic Community (EEC). The reasons why it was formed almost 60 years ago were partly economic and partly political. The economic reasons for the formation of the EEC stemmed from the benefits that all the member countries believed they could achieve from creating a large area of internal free trade.

On the political front, West Germany (as it was then called), which was one of the original six members of the new organisation, hoped that EEC membership would help to protect Germans from the military threat of Russian invasion. By contrast, France hoped that a stable and economically successful Germany would reduce the chance of another major war in Europe. This could best be achieved if EEC member states traded freely with each other.

On the economic front, France was willing to create free trade in manufactured goods (which would mostly benefit Germany), provided small French farms could be protected by a common external tariff from the competition of more efficient New World farmers in countries outside the EEC. Germany readily agreed to the creation of a protectionist common agricultural policy (CAP) as the *quid pro quo* of free trade in manufactured goods within the EEC.

Trade creation, trade diversion and the UK's membership of the European Union

There is some evidence that, as far as manufactured goods such as cars are concerned, the UK benefited from the trade-creating advantages of EU membership. But this is not true of many agricultural products, for which the UK has suffered the trade-diverting disadvantages of membership. This has involved a shift from a low-cost source outside the EU, such as Jamaican sugar cane, to a high-cost source within the EU, such as sugar beet grown in countries such as the UK and the Netherlands. Since joining the original EEC in 1973, and taking out the distorting effects of inflation, the British consumer has often had to pay higher prices for food than was the case before entry.

However, whether or not for the UK the trade-diverting disadvantages of EU membership exceed the trade-creating benefits, the UK will probably lose tariff-free access to the huge EU market, if and when it leaves. Supporters of leaving the EU claim that the UK could negotiate tariff-free access in the same way that non-members such as Switzerland and Norway have done. However, these are small countries and they have never been members of the EU. Will Germany, France and other EU countries be prepared to grant the UK similar privileged access if it decides to leave the EU? Perhaps not, but it should be remembered that the UK imports more from the EU than it exports and this may make it easier for the UK to persuade other EU countries to negotiate a free trade agreement.

The EU as an economic union

In the early 1970s, the United Kingdom's decision to join the EEC meant leaving a free trade area and joining a customs union which already possessed a number of common economic policies. Indeed, the fact that the word 'economic' is central to the European Union's original name clearly indicates that the union's founding fathers intended to develop the economic nature of the organisation well beyond a mere trading bloc.

British residents who have supported the UK's continued membership of the European Union are often known as Europhiles, while those who have wanted the country to withdraw membership are often known as Eurosceptics. Some, but not all, Eurosceptics would be happy for the UK to remain an EU member, but only if the union were to restrict its role to that of a glorified free trade area. However, for Europhiles, rolling back the clock in this way is completely unrealistic. To gain the benefits of free trade which the EU's huge internal market provides, their view is that the UK must accept the common economic policies. For a Europhile, the British government should work actively within the EU to make the common economic policies work better.

Since the creation of the EEC nearly 60 years ago, the EU has introduced a number of common economic policies. Of these, the common agricultural policy, or CAP, which began in 1962 is by far the most important (and expensive). Other common policies include the common fisheries policy, the EU competition policy and the EU regional policy. There was also an early attempt to introduce a common tax policy, centring on the introduction of VAT as the EEC's main expenditure tax. But member countries continue to levy their own national rates of VAT and tax harmonisation has not been developed much further.

Nonetheless, the creation in the late 1990s of the Stability and Growth Pact to constrain or limit government spending and borrowing in **eurozone** countries was an attempt to impose some elements of a common fiscal policy. In very recent years, the European Commission (the EU's executive body) and the European Central Bank (ECB) have imposed stiff conditions on countries in the eurozone, particularly Greece, when lending to them to bail out the huge national debts these countries incurred in the so-called eurozone crisis.

> **KEY TERM**
>
> **eurozone** (also known as the **euro area**) the name used for the group of EU countries that have replaced their national currencies with the euro. Before 2019, 19 of the then 28 EU countries were in the eurozone, though this may change in future years.

> **TEST YOURSELF 14.6**
>
> Which trading bloc has the highest level of economic integration?
>
> **A** North American Free Trade Agreement
>
> **B** European Union
>
> **C** Eurasian Customs Union
>
> **D** Eurozone
>
> Explain why the correct answer is D.

The World Trade Organization

To understand how the World Trade Organization (WTO) came into existence and its role today, it is useful to go back to events occurring in the 1930s and 1940s. In the 1940s, during the Second World War, it was widely believed (especially in the UK and the USA) that the worldwide Depression and mass unemployment of the 1930s had been made worse, and were possibly caused, by a collapse of international trade. 'Beggar my neighbour' protectionist policies, introduced by countries desperately trying to save local jobs, were blamed.

By 1945 the USA and the UK had decided to try to create a postwar world of free trade. Because this required international agreement, the General Agreement on Tariffs and Trade (GATT) was established as a multilateral agreement to try to liberalise world trade. To begin with, GATT was supposed to be a temporary organisation, to be replaced with a 'world trade organization' as soon as member countries could agree. However, because member countries were unable to agree, the 'temporary' organisation lasted much longer than intended. Indeed, GATT still exists today, though its functions have largely been taken over by the WTO.

Throughout their history, GATT and later the WTO organised rounds of talks among member countries to reduce import controls. The rounds, which took place at roughly 5-year intervals, were often named after the city or country in which the talks were initiated: for example, the Tokyo Round, the Uruguay Round and, more recently, the Doha Round. Out of respect, the Kennedy Round in the mid-1960s was named after the then recently assassinated American president. Each round of talks ends with an agreement to reduce import controls. GATT, and latterly the WTO, have then tried to get member countries to implement the tariff cuts they have agreed.

GATT and WTO agreements have been successful in reducing import controls on manufactured goods. There has been much less success in securing agreement to reduce tariffs and quotas on trade in services and agricultural goods. Recently, the WTO has tried to persuade the developed countries of the EU and the USA to open their markets to cheap food imports from the developing world. However, the most recent rounds of talks organised by the WTO at Cancún (in Mexico) and Doha (in Qatar) were not successful. Economists and politicians in many developing countries claim that this lack of success provides further evidence of globalisation and international organisations serving the interests of rich countries at the expense of the poor.

SECTION 14.2 SUMMARY

- International trade widens a country's production possibilities and also its consumption possibilities, and enables countries to benefit from specialisation and economies of scale.
- Absolute advantage means that a country is technically more efficient in producing a good than other countries — it can produce more of the product with the same amount of resources.
- A country has a comparative advantage in a product when its opportunity cost of production is lower than in another country.
- According to the principle of comparative advantage, specialisation and trade can lead to an increase in world output, which can translate into a net welfare gain. The theory shows that, provided each country has a comparative advantage in the production of a good, each country can benefit from specialisation and trade.
- Increased international competition and the potential for economies of scale can result in additional gains from trade.
- Import controls and other forms of protectionism have been justified by strategic trade theory, the protection of infant industries and a variety of other economic and non-economic arguments.
- The North–South pattern of world trade has largely given way to a North–North pattern.
- The European Union (EU) started life in the 1950s as the EEC, a customs union, but since 1993 it has been a much fuller economic union.
- Much of the UK's trade is with EU member states.

14.3 The balance of payments

The **balance of payments** is the record of all money flows or transactions between the residents of a country and the rest of the world in a given period of time. These transactions can be broken down into three main accounts:

- the current account
- the capital account
- the financial account

An overview of the UK balance of payments in 2017 is shown in Table 14.9.

Table 14.9 Selected items from the UK balance of payments (£m), 2017

The current account (mostly trade flows)	£m
Balance of trade in goods	−137,448
Balance of trade in services	+111,562
Primary income flows *(Net income flows)*	−32,058
Secondary income flows *(Net current transfers)*	−21,015
Balance of payments on the current account	**−78,959**
The capital account *(Transfers, which used to be in the current account)*	**−1,814**
The financial account *(Capital flows, which used to be in the capital account)* Net direct investment	+63,427
Net portfolio investment	−66,964
Financial derivatives and employee stock options	+9,848
Other capital flows *(including many short-term 'hot money' flows)*	−73,570
Drawings on reserves	+6,799
Net financial transactions *(This is the overall balance for the financial account.)*	**−60,460**
Net errors and omissions *(The financial account balance minus the current and capital account balances. It is required to compensate for inevitable mistakes and ensure that these three accounts sum to zero.)*	**+20,313**

Source: ONS, UK Balance of Payments, *The Pink Book*, 2018

(Note that the ONS has changed how it presents figures in the financial account. Figures that used to be shown as a plus are now shown as a minus and vice versa. Consequently, mathematically, the balances for the account as a whole no longer sum to zero.)

The difference between the current, capital and financial accounts of the balance of payments

The current account of the balance of payments

The balance of payments on the **current account** measures the flow and expenditure on goods and services, and shows the difference between the amount received from exports and the amount paid for imports. The current account is usually regarded as the most important part of the balance of payments because it reflects the economy's international competitiveness and the extent to which the country may or may not be living within its means. The current account is the main area of study at A-level and will be examined in detail in some of the following sections of this chapter.

> **TEST YOURSELF 14.7**
> The current account of the balance of payments comprises:
>
> **A** cash deposits held by high street banks with the central bank
>
> **B** government revenues from taxation minus its planned spending
>
> **C** all transactions involving money leaving or entering the country
>
> **D** trade in goods and services, primary income and secondary income
>
> Explain why the correct answer is D.

The capital account of the balance of payments

Several years ago, a change was made to the way the UK balance of payments is presented. The items in the capital account, a long-standing part of the balance of payments, were changed. Capital flows were moved out of the capital account and listed under a new heading: the financial account. The capital account now comprises various transfers of income that were part of the current account before the new method of classification was adopted. It is now a very small, and usually insignificant, part of the overall balance of payments account.

The financial account of the balance of payments

KEY TERM
financial account the part of the balance of payments which records capital flows into and out of the economy.

The balance of payments on the **financial account** has five main components which you can see toward the bottom of Table 14.9. It is worth noting that if a country is living beyond its means by running a current account deficit, the borrowing which finances the deficit is recorded in either the capital account or the financial account.

> **STUDY TIP**
> A detailed knowledge of the financial account is not needed at A-level, but we will take a look at capital flows later in this section and explain the difference between foreign direct investment (FDI) and portfolio investment.

The UK's balance of payments on current account

The four components of the current account

The main sections of the current account, which are shown in Table 14.9, are the balance of trade in goods, the balance of trade in services, **primary income** flows and **secondary income** flows. (These are summarised below in Table 14.10.) As we have already noted, the current account is usually regarded as the most important part of the balance of payments because it reflects an economy's international competitiveness and the extent to which the country is living within its means. If the currency outflows in the current account exceed the currency inflows, there is a **current account deficit**. If receipts exceed payments, there is a **current account surplus**.

KEY TERMS

balance of primary income inward primary income flows comprising both inward-income flowing into the economy in the current year generated by UK-owned capital assets located overseas, and outward primary income flows comprising income flowing out of the economy in the current year generated by overseas-owned capital assets located in the UK.

balance of secondary income current transfers, e.g. gifts of money, international aid and transfers between the UK and the EU, flowing into or out of the UK economy in a particular year.

current account deficit currency outflows in the current account exceed the currency inflows.

current account surplus currency inflows in the current account exceed the currency outflows.

In September 2014 the ONS changed the way in which it presents the statistics for the current account of the balance of payments. The item 'Balance of primary income' in Table 14.10 used to be referred to as 'Income balance', and the item 'Balance of secondary income' used to be referred to as 'Current transfers balance'. The titles 'Balance of trade in goods' and 'Balance of trade in services' did not change.

Table 14.10 Sections of the current account, 2017 (£m)

Balance of trade in goods	−137,448
Balance of trade in services	+111,562
Balance of primary income	−32,058
Balance of secondary income	−21,015
Balance of payments on the current account	**−78,959**

Source: ONS, UK Balance of Payments, *The Pink Book*, 2018

STUDY TIP

Make sure you understand the different items in the current account relating both to trade and to primary and secondary income flows.

For each of the sections of the current account, and for the current account itself shown in the bottom row of Table 14.10, a plus sign (+) indicates a credit item (net currency flowing into the UK), and a minus sign (−) indicates a debit item (net currency flowing out of the UK). The balance of trade in goods is sometimes called the balance of visible trade, and the balance of trade in services is part of the balance of invisible trade.

The story that can be read into the figures is quite worrying. Look carefully at Figure 14.13. Throughout the period shown the UK has run a persistent deficit on the current account. The value of sterling has depreciated significantly since 2008 but the UK has continued to run a large deficit. In 2016 the deficit on the current account was 5.9% of GDP, the largest of the G7 countries. The second largest was Canada at 3.3%. In the words of Mark Carney, the then governor of the Bank of England, the UK is reliant on the 'kindness of strangers' to finance the deficit. Put simply, the UK is living beyond its means and relies on investment flows from abroad which are secured against assets such as office buildings which are located in the UK.

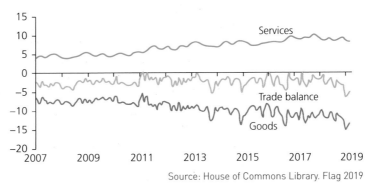

Source: House of Commons Library. Flag 2019

Figure 14.13 Changes in the UK trade balance, 2007–19

As Figure 14.3 shows, the UK balance of trade has been in deficit but relatively stable in recent years, with a goods deficit being partially offset by services surplus. The current account deficit, which is not shown in Figure 14.3, has widened because primary income deficit has been in growing. This means that foreigners who own assets in the UK are earning more from their assets than UK investors are receiving from their investments overseas. The primary income deficit has been the driving force behind the widening current account deficit. In earlier years, the UK had enjoyed a substantial surplus of investment income. The data is of course pre-Brexit. At the time of writing in July 2019, the UK is still in the European Union. Most but not all economists expect the current account to worsen if and when the UK leaves the EU.

The consensus view among economists has been that the size of the current account deficit is unlikely to cause a crisis in the near term, but is 'storing up big problems for the future'. If international investors lose confidence in the financial assets sold by the UK, the country will experience a dramatic fall in living standards because it will be unable to finance its trade deficit.

QUANTITATIVE SKILLS 14.2

Worked example: interpreting changes in the main sections in the current account

Table 14.11 shows selected components of a country's balance of payments on current account as a percentage of GDP in 2018 and 2019.

Table 14.11 Balance of payments: selected components, 2018–19 (% of GDP)

Year	Balance of trade in goods and services	Primary income balance	Secondary income balance	Current account balance
2018	−4.0	+2.0	−1.4	−9.0
2019	−3.9	−4.6	−1.3	−10.2

Do the data suggest that a main reason for the rise in the current account deficit as a percentage of GDP between 2018 and 2019 was a significant deterioration in the primary income balance?

The answer is 'yes'. Over the 2-year period, the current account deficit increased by 1.2% of GDP. Of the three components of the current account shown in the table, the balance of trade in goods and services deteriorated by 0.1% of GDP, while the secondary income balance improved by 0.1% of GDP. However, the primary income balance deteriorated by the significantly larger percentage of 6.6%, from +2.0% of GDP to −4.6%. This suggests that the deterioration in the current account balance was mainly caused by the deterioration in the primary income balance, though we cannot be absolutely sure because we don't know the sizes of all the items in the table.

The main sections of the current account

We shall now take a closer look at each of the four sections of the current account.

The balance of trade in goods

The **balance of trade in goods** shows the extent to which the value of exports of goods exceeds the value of imports, or vice versa. Table 14.12 does not indicate the total value of exports and imports, which were respectively £338,871 million and £476,319 million in 2017. The balance of trade in goods was therefore in deficit to the tune of £137,448 million. This figure is shown in the bottom row of Table 14.12.

The balance of trade in goods can also be disaggregated (broken up) into different forms of trade in goods, such as the balances of trade in manufactured goods and non-manufactured goods. Some of the different ways of disaggregating the balance of trade in goods are shown in Table 14.12.

Table 14.12 Selected items from the UK balance of trade in goods, 2017 (£m)

Balance of trade in food, drinks and tobacco	−24,170
Balance of trade in raw materials (basic goods)	−3,892
Balance of trade in oil	−8,020
Balance of trade in manufactured goods	−70,266
Balance of trade in all goods	**−137,448**

Source: ONS, UK Balance of Payments, *The Pink Book*, 2018

EXTENSION MATERIAL

Data presentation

Take note of the word 'Selected' in the captions of Tables 14.12 and 14.13. The word tells you that not all the items in the balance of trade in goods and the balance of trade in services are in the tables. Selections such as these try to separate the most interesting items from the 'background noise' of other perhaps less interesting items.

Table 14.12 shows that the UK is a net importer of primary products (food and raw materials), and was also a large net importer of oil in 2017. Up until 2005, the UK enjoyed a balance of trade surplus in oil, as a result of the development of the North Sea oil and gas fields in the 1970s and 1980s. However, depletion of these fields means that the UK now imports much of the energy it uses, including coal and natural gas as well as oil.

The balance of payments deficit in manufactured goods is significant. Apart from the periods during and immediately following the First and Second World Wars, for over 200 years Britain was a net exporter of manufactured goods. In the mid-nineteenth century, Britain was the 'workshop of the world'. This has now changed. In the early 1980s, the UK became a net importer of manufactured goods. The manufactured goods deficit is now huge, reflecting loss of competitiveness, the resulting deindustrialisation of the UK, and the fact that most manufactured goods are now produced in emerging-market countries, particularly in China.

The balance of trade in services

The decline of manufacturing and the growth of service industries mean that the UK now has a post-industrial and service-sector economy. This is reflected in the **balance of trade in services** shown in Table 14.13.

Table 14.13 Selected items from the UK balance of trade in services, 2017 (£m)

Balance of trade in transport	+8,015
Balance of trade in travel	−15,709
Balance of trade in telecommunication, computer and information services	+8,665
Balance of trade in insurance and pension services	+16,502
Balance of trade in financial services	+44,368
Balance of trade in intellectual property	+6,348
Balance of trade in all services	**+111,562**

Source: ONS, UK Balance of Payments, *The Pink Book*, 2018

Whereas most manufactured goods are internationally tradable, the same is not generally true for services such as retailing, car repair and hairdressing. Services like these are produced and consumed in the non-internationally traded economy, or sheltered economy. However, many services which were previously produced within the UK are now being imported. This is an important part of the globalisation process.

UK companies, which used to produce services 'in-house', now outsource or buy in the services from outside suppliers, often located in countries with cheap labour. UK-based companies are locating 'back-office' service activities overseas, including many financial and ICT-related services. Many call centres providing customer services and direct marketing services have moved to India.

Nevertheless, as Table 14.13 shows, the UK is still a significant net exporter of financial, insurance and ICT services. These industries illustrate the UK's competitive advantage in service-sector industries, though the picture is not as rosy in industries such as travel and tourism, where Britons now spend much more in other countries than overseas residents spend in the UK.

CASE STUDY 14.4

The UK financial services industry

We wrote this case study in the aftermath of the 2008–09 recession. Since then, with recovery under way, the future of the UK financial services industry may be more promising than was thought in 2010 and 2011 when the UK economy was 'flat-lining'. However, Britain's exit from the European Union may change this.

The financial services sector is a significant contributor to UK income and employment. Over a million people in Britain are employed in financial services, of which two-thirds are based outside London. Financial services is also one of the largest export industries in the UK. However, on the negative side, the growth of the financial services industry has led to an unbalanced economy.

The financial crisis that began in the summer of 2007 has, however, highlighted the need for a more resilient and sustainable financial services industry to support the broader economy. In addition to being an important part of the economy in its own right, the financial services sector provides essential credit and financial services to businesses and households.

During the period after 2000 the expansion of the financial sector was a significant influence on the growth rate of the economy overall. But the recent growth of the sector has been reversed, reducing GDP permanently by about 1.9%. The country will suffer a further loss of income as a result of the losses that banks have made, giving a total fall in national income of about 2.4%, and reducing government revenue by about 1% of GDP.

Follow-up questions

1 Explain **two** reasons for the temporary decline of the UK financial services industry after 2007.
2 'The growth of the financial services industry has led to an unbalanced economy.' What does this mean and how might the UK economy be 'rebalanced'?
3 Whereas many service industries are sheltered from international trade, this is generally not true for financial services. Explain why this is so.
4 If the UK has left the European Union by the time you have read the case study, describe how Britain's exit has affected the UK's financial services industry.

Primary income

Primary income flows are net income flows made up mostly of investment income generated from profits, dividends and interest payments flowing between countries. When we look later at the financial account of the balance of payments, we shall explain how UK-based multinational companies (MNCs) invest in capital assets located in other countries. The profit income generated from overseas investment flows back to the parent company and its UK shareholders. The investment itself is an outward capital flow, but the income it generates is current income, figuring in the current account of the balance of payments.

Profits also flow out of the UK to the overseas owners of assets located in the UK — for example, to Japanese or US multinational companies owning subsidiary companies in the UK. In Table 14.10, the item 'primary income flows' is largely determined by the difference between these inward and outward profit flows resulting from capital investment undertaken in the past. The fact that the UK's net income flows (primary income flows) were −£32,058 million in 2017 indicates that in that year, UK companies owned less profitable assets in the rest of the world than overseas-based MNCs owned in the UK. Until 2011, inward primary income flows had far exceeded outward flows, as can be seen in Figure 14.20. The collapse of foreign investment earnings was a main factor contributing to the current account deficit widening after 2011.

Finally, it is worth remembering that not all primary income flows are profit payments generated by multinational companies on their direct investments abroad. A significant proportion of the income flows are generated from portfolio investment, which is investment in financial assets such as shares and bonds. Interest and dividend payments within the international financial system contribute significantly to net primary income flows. By the time you read this book, further significant changes may have taken place in the UK current account. Make sure you keep up to date with these changes.

Secondary income

Secondary income flows are current transfers of income arising from such items as gifts between residents of different countries, donations to charities abroad, and overseas aid. Britain has long had a negative secondary income balance, caused by the UK's net contributions to the EU budget, overseas aid and, in some years in the past, the cost of maintaining armed forces in countries such as Afghanistan.

QUANTITATIVE SKILLS 14.3

Worked example: making calculations from balance of payments data

Table 14.14 shows the balance of payments on current account of a particular country.

Table 14.14 Balance of payment on current account, 2016–19 (£bn)

	2016	2017	2018	2019
Balance of trade in services (£)	+240	+120	+20	+30
Net primary income flows (£)	–30	–35	+10	–15
Net secondary income flows (current transfers) (£)	+5	–2	+12	–8
Current account balance (£)	+200	+100	+80	+100

Calculate the country's balance of trade in goods in each of the 4 years. Comment on your answers.

The calculations involve subtracting the balance of trade in services, net income (primary income) and current transfers (secondary income) from the current account balance in each of the 4 years. The answers are:

2016   –£15bn
2017   +£17bn
2018   +£38bn
2019   +£93bn

Over the 4-year period, the balance of trade in goods moved from a deficit of £15 billion in 2016 to a surplus of £93 billion. The current account as a whole and the balance of trade in services were in surplus throughout the period. Primary income flows were in deficit throughout the period (except for 2018), which means that more profits and other income were flowing into the country than flowing out. Secondary transfers switched from being positive to negative, and then to positive and negative again, but the secondary transfer flows were generally smaller than the net trade and primary income flows.

TEST YOURSELF 14.9

Figure 14.14 shows a country's trade deficit in goods and its current account balance for the years 2014–19. Suggest one possible reason which might explain why the trade deficit is smaller than the current account deficit.

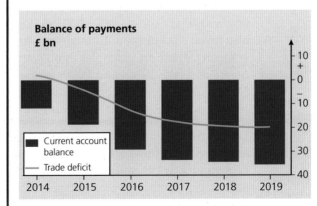

Figure 14.14 The balance of payments on current account and the trade deficit for a particular country, 2014–19

The financial account and investment flows between countries

As our discussion of primary income flows in the current account indicates, it is important to avoid confusing capital flows, which figure in the financial account of the balance of payments, with investment income, which is the lion's share of the primary income flows in the current account. As explained, outward capital flows generate inward flows of investment income in subsequent years. The capital outflow enlarges the stock of capital assets located in other countries, owned by residents and MNCs based in the country exporting the capital. Net capital flows are the difference between inward and outward capital movements. Positive net outward capital flows, over a period of years, mean that the country acquires capital assets located in other countries that are greater in value than the country's own assets bought by overseas companies.

The positive net investment income flow (in the current account) which occurred in years prior to 2012 suggests that, in these years, UK residents and MNCs had invested in a larger and more profitable stock of capital assets in the rest of the world than that acquired by overseas residents and MNCs in the UK. Following the UK's abolition of virtually all foreign exchange controls in 1979, the UK became a large net exporter of capital, presumably because owners of UK MNCs believed that investment abroad would be more profitable than investment within the UK. During the 1980s, the positive net capital outflow meant that the UK became a large owner of overseas capital assets. However, by 2010 the UK had once again become a net debtor nation. In 2016, the largest holders of foreign investment in the UK came from the USA (£3,294bn), France (£878bn), Germany (£858bn), the Netherlands (£566bn), Ireland (£551bn), Luxembourg (£489bn), Japan (£452bn) and Switzerland (£368bn).

Within the financial account of the balance of payments, we shall distinguish between long-term direct capital flows, long-term portfolio capital flows, and short-term speculative 'hot money' capital flows.

Long-term direct capital flows

Direct overseas investment involves acquisition of real productive assets, such as factories, oil refineries, offices and shopping malls, located in other countries. On the one hand, a UK-based MNC may decide to establish a new subsidiary company in the USA, for example. Direct investment can also involve acquisition, through merger or takeover, of an overseas-based company. These are examples of outward direct investment. Conversely, the decisions in the 1980s and 1990s by the Japanese vehicle manufacturers Nissan, Toyota and Honda to invest in automobile factories in the UK led to inward direct investment, or inward **foreign direct investment** (FDI).

Long-term direct capital flows can partly be explained by competitive advantage. The flows are a response to people's decisions to invest in economic activities and industries located in countries that have a competitive advantage. Comparative advantage may also rest in the same country. But since changes in competitive and/or comparative advantage usually take place quite slowly, long-term direct capital flows tend to be relatively stable and predictable.

KEY TERM

foreign direct investment
investment in capital assets, e.g. manufacturing and service industry capacity, in a foreign country by a business with headquarters in another country. Very often the overseas company establishes subsidiary companies in the countries in which it is investing.

Portfolio capital flows

These involve the purchase of financial assets (that is, pieces of paper or, increasingly these days, electronic claims laying claim to the ownership of real assets) rather than physical or directly productive assets. Typically, **portfolio investment** occurs when fund managers employed by financial institutions, such as insurance companies and pension funds, purchase shares issued by overseas companies, or securities issued by foreign governments.

The globalisation of world security markets or capital markets and the abolition of exchange controls between virtually all developed countries have made it easy for UK residents to purchase shares or bonds that are listed on overseas capital markets. This has led to a massive increase in portfolio investment. UK residents can now buy shares and corporate bonds that were previously only available on the capital market of the company's country of origin. Securities issued by foreign governments, such as US Treasury bonds, can also be bought.

The credit crunch that began in the USA in 2007, and the so-called 'financial meltdown' that followed, had a significant adverse effect on portfolio investment both within and between countries. Many financial assets, particularly those bought and sold by banks, became known as 'toxic assets'. This term arose from the fact that a potential purchaser of a package of financial assets offered for sale by a bank could not know in advance whether assets in the package were of high risk and potentially little value, or a sound investment (even the bank trying to make the sale might not know). In such conditions of imperfect information, trading in many types of financial asset collapsed.

Short-term speculative 'hot money' capital flows

Short-term capital movements, which are also called 'hot money' flows, are largely speculative. The flows occur because the owners of funds, which include companies and banks as well as wealthy private individuals, believe that a quick speculative profit can be made by moving funds between currencies. Speculating that a currency's exchange rate is about to rise, owners of funds move money into that currency and out of other currencies whose exchange rates are expected to fall. 'Hot money' movements are also triggered by differences in interest rates. Funds flow into currencies with high interest rates and out of currencies with lower interest rates. International crises, such as the outbreak of a war in the Middle East, also cause funds to move into the currency of a 'safe-haven' country, which is regarded as politically stable.

If the pool of hot money shifting between currencies were small, few problems would result. However, short-term capital flows have grown significantly over the last 65 or so years. A large-scale movement of funds from one currency to another creates an excess supply in the former currency and an excess demand for the second currency. To eliminate excess supply and demand, the exchange rates of the two currencies respectively fall and rise. As a result, the movement of funds between currencies produces the changes in exchange rates that speculators were expecting.

More importantly, a large-scale hot money flow of funds between currencies destabilises exchange rates, the current accounts of balance of payments and, indeed, domestic economies. Such destabilisation occurred late in 2008 and early in 2009 when owners of hot money shifted their funds out of the pound on a massive scale. However, in the next few years, market sentiment changed with the result that hot money flowed into the pound, at least until the middle of 2015. At the time of writing in 2019, the main 'hot money' flow is into the US dollar, forcing up its value. Things might, of course, have changed by the time you read this chapter.

Speculative capital flows between currencies such as the dollar, the pound and the euro, which occupy a central place in the finance of international trade, can destabilise the international monetary system. The most recent examples of destabilisation followed the credit crunch and the financial meltdown that were referred to earlier. Banks and other financial institutions, and also governments, in a range of countries (which included the UK) saw their international credit ratings downgraded. To fight the recession that was hitting their economies, governments built up massive budget deficits, which they tried to finance in part by borrowing overseas.

Finally, by the time you read this section, the UK's proposed exit from the European Union may also have led to considerable destabilisation of both the pound and the euro.

QUANTITATIVE SKILLS 14.4

Worked example: calculating missing statistics in a balance of payments table

Table 14.15 shows some of the items in the balance of payments for a country in 2019.

Table 14.15 Selected items from a balance of payments, 2019

Item	£m
Balance of trade in goods	+1,000
Balance of trade in services	?
Balance of trade in goods and services	**+600**
Primary income	−75
Secondary income	+30
Balance of payments on current account	**?**
Net direct investment	+300
Net portfolio investment	−100
Other items in the financial account	−550
Financial account balance	**?**

Assuming that 'net errors and omissions' and the 'capital account balance' are zero in the balance of payments, fill in the missing numbers in the table indicated by question marks, in each case including a plus or minus sign.

The missing numbers are shown in bold in Table 14.16.

Table 14.16 Selected items from a balance of payments, 2019: completed version

Item	£ million
Balance of trade in goods	+1,000
Balance of trade in services	−400
Balance of trade in goods and services	**+600**
Primary income	−75
Secondary income	+30
Balance of payments on current account	**+555**
Net direct investment	+300
Net portfolio investment	−100
Other items in the financial account	−550
Financial account balance	**−350**

Table 14.17 shows the components of the balance of payments on current account for an economy in 2019.

Table 14.17 Balance of payments current account, 2019

	£ million
Balance of trade in goods	–700
Balance of trade in services	–200
Primary income balance	230
Secondary income balance	–50

Calculate the value of the country's balance of payments on current account.

Applying *AD/AS* analysis to the current account of the balance of payments

In Chapter 10, the meaning of aggregate demand in the economy was explained, together with the aggregate demand equation: $AD = C + I + G + (X - M)$. We showed how, in an *AD/AS* graph, an increase in *any* of the components of aggregate demand (C, I, G or ($X - M$)) causes the aggregate demand (*AD*) curve to shift rightwards, leading to a new equilibrium national income.

We shall now apply *AD/AS* analysis to explain how a change in net exports, or ($X - M$), affects the national economy. As mentioned earlier, the current account includes non-trade items (investment income and transfers, or primary and secondary income) as well as exports and imports. However, for the rest of this section, we shall assume that exports and imports of goods and services are the only two sections of the current account of the balance of payments. Given this simplifying assumption, there is a current account surplus when net exports are positive (i.e. $X > M$), and a current account deficit when net exports are negative (i.e. $X < M$).

Exports are an injection of spending into the circular flow of income, whereas imports are a leakage or withdrawal of spending from the flow (refer to Figure 10.3 in Chapter 10 and to the accompanying explanation of the circular flow diagram).

Suppose initially that $X = M$, which means there is neither a surplus nor a deficit in the current account. Note also that in this situation, given the assumption of no non-trade flows in the current account, foreign trade injections into the circular flow of income exactly equal foreign trade withdrawals from the flow. When $X = M$, the current account has a neutral effect on the state of aggregate demand and on the circular flow of income.

However, at the next stage, overseas demand for British exports increases, but UK demand for imports remains unchanged. This means there is a net injection of spending into the circular flow of income. The current account moves into surplus, with $X > M$.

In the *AD/AS* diagram in Figure 14.15, the increase in exports shifts the *AD* curve to the right. What happens next in the economy depends on the shape and slope of the *SRAS* curve around the initial point of equilibrium

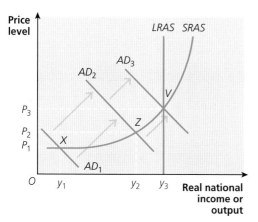

Figure 14.15 How an increase in exports can affect the national economy

national income. In Figure 14.15, equilibrium national income is initially at point X, which shows the economy in deep recession, suffering from deficient aggregate demand. In this situation, any event that increases aggregate demand increases the level of real output in the economy and causes demand-deficient unemployment to fall. An increase in exports is just such an event, shifting the AD curve from AD_1 to AD_2. This causes real output to rise from y_1 to y_2, though at the cost of some inflation, since the price level rises from P_1 to P_2.

Following the rightward shift of the aggregate demand curve to AD_2, equilibrium national income is now shown at point Z. As the $SRAS$ curve becomes steeper, moving up the curve, the diagram tells us that the main effect of a further shift of the AD curve from AD_2 to AD_3 falls on the price level rather than on output and jobs. Output increases, from y_2 to y_3, but the price level also increases to P_3. As full employment approaches, export demand becomes *inflationary* rather than *reflationary*.

Nevertheless, in this situation, the growth in export demand eliminates the demand deficiency previously existent in the economy. The economy ends up on its long-run aggregate supply ($LRAS$) curve, with equilibrium national income at point V.

At point V, what happens next in the economy depends on assumptions made about the nature of short-run and long-run aggregate supply. In Figure 14.15, when the economy produces on the vertical $LRAS$ curve, any further increase in the demand for exports leads only to the price level rising above P_3, without any sustained increase in real output. However, there is another possibility. Foreign demand for a country's exports may be a response to favourable supply-side conditions in the domestic economy which shift the $LRAS$ curve to the right. This means the economy can produce and supply the goods needed to meet the increase in export demand without generating inflation. This is the desired result of **export-led growth**. The German and Japanese economies enjoyed export-led growth from the 1960s to the 1980s, and China is now enjoying similar benefits. However, the worldwide growth of demand for Chinese exports has begun to cause inflation in the Chinese economy.

KEY TERM

export-led growth in the short run, economic growth resulting from an increase in exports, which is one of the components of aggregate demand. In the long run, economic growth resulting from the growth and increased international competitiveness of exporting industries.

STUDY TIP
You must be able to use the *AD/AS* model and the circular flow of income to analyse how changes in exports and/or imports affect macroeconomic performance: that is, economic growth, employment and inflation.

Deficits and surpluses on the current account

The current account measures trade flows and reflects an economy's international competitiveness. If a country is running a current account deficit, it means that its currency outflows are greater than its currency inflows, which generally means it is importing more than it is exporting. If one country is running a current account deficit, another country must be running a surplus, meaning that its currency inflows are greater than its outflows and it is generally exporting more than it is importing.

Look carefully at the current account balances from 2017 in Table 14.18. Over the last two decades, countries such as China and Germany have run persistent current account surpluses. They have successfully exported more products than they have imported, and they have experienced strong export-led growth. In contrast, the UK and USA have run persistent current account deficits, largely driven by very large deficits on the balance of trade in goods. The citizens of the UK and USA have enjoyed higher living standards but the current account deficits have been mainly financed by borrowing.

Table 14.18 Current account balance of selected countries, 2017 (£m)

China	+164,886
Germany	+291,458
United Kingdom	−98,374
United States	−449,137

Source: World Bank data

Do current account deficits pose problems?

While a short-run deficit or surplus on current account does not pose a problem, a persistent or long-run imbalance indicates fundamental disequilibrium. However, the nature of any resulting problem depends on the size and cause of the deficit: the larger the deficit, the greater the problem is likely to be. The problem is also likely to be serious if the deficit is caused by the uncompetitiveness of the country's industries. Although in the short run a deficit allows a country's residents to enjoy living standards boosted by imports, and thus higher than would be possible from the consumption of the country's output alone, in the long run, the decline of the country's industries in the face of international competition lowers living standards.

In a poor country, a current account deficit can be justified because of the country's need to import capital goods on a large scale to modernise the country's infrastructure and to promote economic development. However, there is always a danger, as the experience of countries such as Nigeria has shown, that the deficit soon becomes the means for financing the 'champagne lifestyle' enjoyed by the country's ruling elite.

Do current account surpluses pose problems?

While many people agree that a persistent current account deficit can pose serious problems, few realise that a balance of payments surplus on current account can also lead to problems. Because a surplus is often seen as a sign of national economic virility and success, a popular view is that the bigger the surplus, the better must be the country's performance.

Insofar as the surplus measures the competitiveness of the country's exporting industries, this is obviously true. There are, nevertheless, reasons why a large payments surplus is undesirable, though a small surplus may be a justifiable objective of government policy.

One country's surplus is another country's deficit

The balance of payments must balance for the world as a whole, so it is impossible for all countries to run surpluses simultaneously. Unless countries with persistently large surpluses agree to take action to reduce their surpluses, deficit countries cannot reduce their deficits. Deficit countries may then be forced to impose import controls from which all countries, including surplus countries, eventually suffer. In an extreme scenario, a world recession could be triggered by the resulting collapse of world trade.

At various times since the 1970s, the current account surpluses of the oil-producing countries have led to this problem, as have Japan's and more recently China's payments surpluses, which have been the counterpart to the US trade deficit. On several occasions, the US government has faced pressure from US manufacturing and labour interests to introduce import controls and other forms of protectionism. When introduced, US protectionism undoubtedly harms world trade.

Non-oil-exporting developing countries, almost without exception, also suffer chronic deficits, although these are very different from the US trade deficit. The imbalance of trade between more developed and less developed countries cannot be reduced without the industrialised countries of the 'North' taking action to reduce surpluses which have been gained at the expense of the developing economies of the 'South'.

A balance of payments surplus can be inflationary

A balance of payments surplus can be an important cause of domestic inflation because it is an injection of aggregate demand into the circular flow of income, which increases the equilibrium level of nominal or money national income. If there are substantial unemployed resources in the economy, this has the beneficial effect of reflating real output and jobs. However, if the economy is initially close to full capacity, demand-pull inflation results.

Three factors that influence a country's current account balance

We have made passing reference throughout section 14.3 to factors which might influence a country's current account balance. Three of these are productivity, inflation and the exchange rate, though primary income flows also need to be considered.

- **Productivity.** Improving labour productivity, or output per worker, is critical to the success of supply-side policies to improve both the price competitiveness and the quality competitiveness of a country's exports in international markets (see the later sections: 'Supply-side policies and the current account' and 'Export-led growth and the UK economy' on pages 539–40).
- **Inflation.** The key point here is not a country's *absolute* rate of inflation, but its rate of inflation *relative* to those of its trading competitors. If a country's inflation rate is higher than the inflation rates of competitor nations, the country's exports will lose their price competitiveness, which will lead to a deterioration in the country's current account balance. However, the price elasticities of demand for exports and imports may complicate things, as will be explained below.
- **Exchange rate.** Changes in the exchange rate of a country's currency have a rather similar effect to changes in its relative rate of inflation. In short, a rising exchange rate increases the foreign currency prices of the country's exports and reduces their competitiveness. Meanwhile, imports become more price competitive. The price elasticities of demand for exports and imports are relevant to the analysis of the effects of a change in a country's exchange rate. Note also that, with respect to a fall in the exchange rate, if a

rise in the domestic inflation rate relative to that of other countries exactly matches the fall in its exchange rate, the two effects cancel each other out, and the country's international price competitiveness remains unchanged.

Policies to cure or reduce a balance of payments deficit

Traditionally, it was thought that a government (or its central bank) can use three different policies to try to cure a persistent deficit caused by an overvalued exchange rate. These are the '3 Ds' of deflation, direct controls, and devaluation or currency depreciation, which are shown in Figure 14.16.

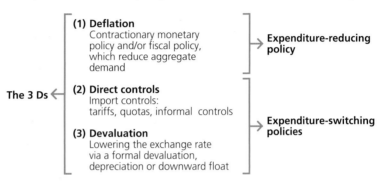

Figure 14.16 The '3 Ds' of deflation, direct controls and devaluation

A deflationary policy, which in this context refers to a reduction in the level of aggregate demand in the economy, reduces a current account deficit because for the most part it is an example of an **expenditure-reducing policy**. As aggregate demand falls, people's incomes fall and hence spending on imports is reduced. By contrast, import controls and devaluation are for the most part examples of **expenditure-switching policies** and affect the balance of payments by changing the relative price of home-produced and foreign goods.

Deflation as an expenditure-reducing policy

Deflationary policy involves using contractionary monetary and/or fiscal policy to reduce the demand for imports. For example, if the marginal propensity to import in the economy is 0.4, reducing aggregate demand by £10 billion should cause spending on imports to fall by £4 billion. This is an expenditure-reducing policy.

Although deflation is primarily an expenditure-reducing policy, it also has an expenditure-switching element. By reducing the rate of domestic price inflation relative to inflation rates in other countries, deflation improves the price competitiveness of exports and reduces that of imports.

However, in modern economies this is usually quite a small effect, and the main effect of deflationary policies, at least in the short run, is to reduce aggregate demand and depress economic activity in the domestic economy.

KEY TERMS

expenditure-reducing policy a government policy which aims to eliminate a current account deficit by reducing the demand for imports by reducing the level of aggregate demand in the economy. Conversely, to reduce a current account surplus, aggregate demand would be increased and spending on imports would rise.

expenditure-switching policy a government policy which aims to reduce a current account deficit by switching domestic demand away from imports to domestically produced goods. Conversely, to reduce a current account surplus, the policy would aim to switch domestic demand away from domestically produced goods toward imports.

Output, incomes and employment tend to fall rather than the price level. Falling demand for domestic output may force firms to seek export orders, so as to use spare production capacity. However, because exports are generally less profitable than domestic sales, a sound and expanding home market may be necessary for a successful export drive.

In summary, when deflating aggregate demand to achieve the external objectives of supporting the exchange rate and reducing a current account deficit, a government sacrifices the domestic economic objectives of full employment and economic growth. For this reason, governments may choose to use expenditure-switching policies of import controls and devaluation, in preference to expenditure-reducing deflationary policies. However, when an economy is overheating, expenditure-reducing measures are more appropriate than expenditure-switching policies. Reducing aggregate demand will help to control domestic inflationary pressures as well as to correct a balance of payments deficit.

Direct controls as expenditure-switching policies

Direct controls involve imposing quotas or even outright bans (embargoes) on imports. These directly cut or prevent expenditure on imports and, as a result, people switch their spending from foreign to home-produced goods. Together with import duties or tariffs, which make imports less price competitive, direct controls do not, however, cure the underlying cause of a current account deficit, namely the uncompetitiveness of a country's goods and services. Moreover, because a country essentially gains a 'beggar my neighbour' advantage at the expense of other countries, import controls tend to provoke retaliation.

Free-market economists believe that protectionism reduces specialisation and causes world trade, world output and economic welfare to fall. Because of this, international organisations such as the European Union and the World Trade Organization have reduced the freedom of individual countries to impose import controls unilaterally to improve their current accounts. However, the EU does use its common external tariff to provide protection for *all* its member states. As a member of the WTO, the UK government is unlikely to be able to use import controls to reduce a current account deficit.

However, the rules-based system of international trade has come under strain since 2016, especially with the election of Donald Trump in the USA. In 2018 the Trump administration introduced tariffs on imported products, most notably from China, made moves to renegotiate the North American Free Trade Agreement, and said the USA should consider leaving the WTO if it does not 'shape up' and treat the USA better.

Devaluation or currency depreciation as an expenditure-switching policy

The exchange rate is the value of one currency in terms of another currency. The word *devaluation* is used in a number of different ways. In a narrow sense, a country devalues by reducing the value of a fixed exchange rate or an adjustable peg exchange rate. (Fixed exchange rates and adjustable peg exchange rates are explained in section 15.1.) However, the term is sometimes used in a looser way to describe a *downward float* or *depreciation* of a floating exchange rate. In a floating exchange rate system, 'depreciation' is the correct term to describe a fall in the external value of a currency.

> ### SYNOPTIC LINK
> In Chapter 10 we looked at the components of aggregate demand and took a first look at policies such as fiscal policy that can be used by government to deflate the economy.

The word 'depreciation' can also confuse. Devaluation or a downward float causes an *external* depreciation of the currency; more units of the currency are needed to buy a unit of *another* currency. This should not be confused with an *internal* depreciation of the currency, occurring when there is inflation *within* the economy and the internal purchasing power of the currency falls as the price level rises.

In a fixed exchange rate system, an increase in the external value of a currency is known as a *revaluation*, whereas in a floating rate system it is known as an *appreciation* in the exchange rate.

If we assume the unavailability of import controls, if a country wishes to reduce a current account deficit, it must generally choose between *deflation* and *devaluation*, or *currency depreciation*. As with tariffs and export subsidies, a fall in the external value of the currency has a mainly expenditure-switching effect. By increasing the price of imports relative to the price of exports, a successful devaluation switches domestic demand away from imports and towards home-produced goods. Similarly, overseas demand for the country's exports increases in response to the fall in export prices.

Price elasticity of demand and devaluation

The effectiveness of a fall in the exchange rate in reducing a balance of payments deficit depends to a significant extent upon the price elasticities of demand for exports and imports.

As Figure 14.17 shows for the UK, when the demand for exports and the demand for imports are both highly price elastic, a fall in the exchange rate *is likely to* reduce a current account deficit.

Following a devaluation, the domestic price of imports into the UK rises from P_1 to P_2, while the overseas price of UK's exports falls from P_3 to P_4. As a result, UK residents spend less on imported goods following an increase in their relative prices. At the same time, residents of overseas countries spend more on the UK's exports, whose relative prices have fallen.

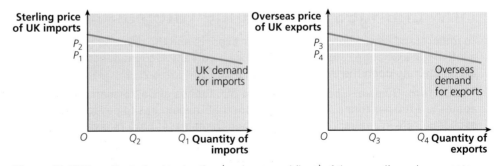

Figure 14.17 The effect of a devaluation (or downward float) of the pound's exchange rate on the current account of the UK balance of payments

On the import side, in Figure 14.17, spending falls from the rectangular area bounded by P_1 and Q_1 to the area bounded by P_2 and Q_2. Higher import prices mean that consumers switch to the now cheaper domestically produced substitutes.

In a similar way, expenditure on the country's exports increases from the rectangular area bounded by P_3 and Q_3 to the area bounded by P_4 and Q_4. Overall, the current account improves, assuming the demand for imports and the demand for exports are both price elastic.

SYNOPTIC LINK
Make sure you can apply the microeconomic concept of elasticity to macroeconomic analysis of the expenditure-switching policy of devaluation.

EXTENSION MATERIAL

The Marshall–Lerner condition

It is more difficult to see what may happen to the current account when, for example, the demand for exports is price inelastic but the demand for imports is price elastic. Fortunately, the *Marshall–Lerner condition* provides a simple rule to assess whether a change in the exchange rate can improve the current account. The condition states that when the *sum* of the export and import price elasticities is greater than unity (ignoring the minus sign), a fall in the exchange rate can reduce a deficit and a rise in the exchange rate can reduce a surplus. When, however, the export and import price elasticities of demand are both highly inelastic, summing to less than unity, a fall in the exchange rate can have the perverse effect of worsening a deficit (while a revaluation might increase a surplus).

The Marshall–Lerner condition is a *necessary*, but not *sufficient* condition for a fall in the exchange rate to reduce a payments deficit. For a devaluation or currency depreciation to be successful, firms in the domestic economy must have spare capacity with which they can meet the surge in demand brought about by the fall in the exchange rate. This means that if the economy is working at, or close to, full capacity, expenditure-reducing deflation and expenditure-switching devaluation should best be regarded as complementary policies rather than as substitute policies for reducing a current account deficit. Deflation *alone* may be unnecessarily costly in terms of lost domestic employment and output, yet may be necessary to provide the spare capacity and conditions in which a falling exchange rate can successfully cure a payments deficit. It may also be needed to offset the potential inflationary consequences of a fall in the exchange rate, which will erode the improvement in competitiveness resulting from the initial fall in the external value of the currency.

EXTENSION MATERIAL

How changes in exchange rates affect the prices of imports

To understand why, when the demand for exports and the demand for imports are both highly price elastic, a fall in the exchange rate *is likely to* reduce a current account deficit, consider the effect of a change in the exchange rate upon the UK prices of imports.

The UK firm, Quidsin supermarkets, buys 500 tonnes of Californian apples each month. The dollar price of the apples is $100 per tonne. The total amount that Quidsin has to pay for the apples, therefore, is $50,000. If the exchange rate in January is £1 = $1.50, then Quidsin will have to give up around £33,333 to acquire $50,000 (50,000 ÷ 1.50).

When the exchange rate changes a year later to £1 = $2.00, Quidsin now has to give up £25,000 to get the $50,000 that the supermarket chain needs to pay its suppliers. The strengthening of the pound's exchange rate has benefited Quidsin. The supermarket chain now has to give up fewer pounds to get the same amount of dollars. Quidsin's costs have fallen by around £8,333 a month.

However, 2 years later the situation changes again, with the exchange rate falling back to £1 = $1.50. This means that, once again, Quidsin has to give up £33,333 to acquire $50,000 (50,000 ÷ 1.50). Compared to a year earlier, Quidsin's costs have now risen by approximately £8,333.

The position for a UK business which *exports* rather than *imports* goods or services would be the exact opposite of the above.

The J-curve effect

Even if domestic demand for imports and overseas demand for exports are both price elastic and spare capacity exists in the economy, in the short run the balance of payments may deteriorate. It takes time for demand to respond to the price changes, and firms within the country may still be unable immediately to increase supply following a fall in the exchange rate. In the short run, the Marshall–Lerner condition (explained in previous extension material) may not hold because elasticities of demand are lower in the short run than in the long run. In these circumstances, the balance of payments may worsen before it improves. This is known as the *J-curve effect*, which is illustrated in Figure 14.18.

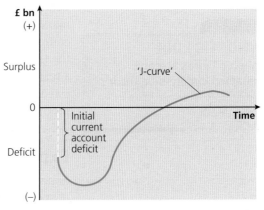

Figure 14.18 The J-curve effect

The initial worsening of the balance of payments that follows the fall in the exchange rate may reduce confidence in the idea that changing the exchange rate is the most appropriate method for reducing a deficit in the current account of the balance of payments. Falling confidence may, in turn, cause capital outflows to occur that destabilise both the balance of payments and the exchange rate. The J-curve effect thus reduces the attractiveness of exchange rate adjustment as an instrument to correct payments disequilibrium. Even when the benefits of a falling exchange rate are realised, they may be short-lived. The increased price competitiveness produced by the devaluation is likely to be eroded as increased import prices raise the country's inflation rate.

Nevertheless, if conditions are right, devaluation can reduce a current account deficit. Despite occurring on 'Black Wednesday', the pound's devaluation in September 1992 was extremely successful, at least for a number of years. There were two main reasons for this. First, expenditure reduction in the severe recession of the early 1990s created the spare capacity that enabled successful expenditure switching following the pound's devaluation. Second, the adoption and achievement of a low inflation target helped to prevent the benefits of the fall in the exchange rate being eroded by accelerating inflation.

In addition, the factories built in the UK by Japanese companies such as Honda and Toyota had just come on stream, producing goods of a quality that people wanted, in the UK and overseas. Some economists believe that the supply-side reforms that were introduced in the 1980s and 1990s also helped.

In contrast, the pound's devaluation of 2008 did not improve the UK's current account position. Despite the pound losing over 25% of its value against its major trading partners, the current account deficit did not shrink. Instead by 2010 the UK's deficit on the current account was larger than it had been in 2007. This was partly because in the years following the depreciation, the UK's major trade partners were in a deep recession, making it difficult for exporters to sell in these markets. Hence, a devaluation of a country's currency is in itself insufficient to eliminate a current account deficit because other macroeconomic factors are important.

Supply-side policies and the current account

SYNOPTIC LINK
Refer back to page 303 for a definition of balance of payments equilibrium.

Deflation, devaluation and direct controls (the '3 Ds') may be effective *short-term* policies for reducing current account deficits. However, it is now increasingly recognised that *long-term* improvement in trade flows requires appropriate and successful supply-side policies and supply-side improvements undertaken by firms within the economy.

The ability of the UK economy to deliver sustained growth of exports and meet the challenge of imported goods and services depends on making UK exports *quality competitive* as well as *price competitive*. A low exchange rate, low interest rates at which British firms can borrow and low domestic inflation all contribute to increased export price competitiveness. However, price competitiveness on its own is not enough. UK goods and services must also be quality competitive. This involves good design and well-made products.

SYNOPTIC LINK
Chapter 13 has already explained supply-side theory and supply-side policies in some depth.

Improved quality competitiveness may only be achievable in the long run if helped by appropriate government supply-side policies together with supply-side improvements undertaken by the private sector. Supply-side policies which promote greater investment in research and development and improved marketing strategies can have powerful long-term effects in improving quality competitiveness. Supply-side improvements, followed by an outward shift of the *LRAS* curve, provide the economy with an increased capacity — enabling a reallocation of resources towards exporting. Successful supply-side policies can also improve exports and lead to import substitution, by increasing labour productivity, which in turn is likely to improve the price competitiveness of UK exports.

Export-led growth and the UK economy

Export-led growth is a term first introduced about 45 years ago, in the context of speeding up the rate of economic growth in developing countries. The term is still widely used with regard to growth strategies in the developing world, but in recent years in the UK, together with the concept of investment-led growth, export-led growth has been more narrowly focused on how best to increase the competitiveness of UK exports and achieve sustained economic growth, without the UK economy slipping into recession. Perhaps not surprisingly, debate in the UK about how to achieve export-led growth became prominent when the economy appeared to be mired in recession in 2008 and 2009, and there seemed to be little hope of speedy economic recovery.

To remind you, short-term economic growth occurs whenever one or more of the components of aggregate demand increases. The components of aggregate demand are consumption (C), investment (I), government spending (G) and net export demand ($X - M$). In recent decades, short-term economic growth has been largely consumption-led, though in 2008 and 2009, via its fiscal stimulus, the Labour government tried to achieve government spending-led growth to 'spend the UK economy out of recession'.

Consumption-led growth

Consumption-led growth leads to two big problems. First, since much consumer spending is on goods and services produced in other countries, consumption-led growth 'sucks' imports into the economy, which may soon lead to a worsening deficit in the current account of the balance of payments. A growing payments deficit may then force the government and the Bank of England to deflate aggregate demand, which at best slows the rate of economic growth, and at worst triggers recession.

Second, and perhaps more significant, recent economic history has shown that consumption-led growth is unsustainable. This is because a rapid growth of consumption, fuelled by increased household debt and consumer borrowing, leads to speculative bubbles, particularly in the housing market. When these bubbles are eventually 'pricked', aggregate demand collapses, bringing to an end the 'boom' phase of the economic cycle. The rate of economic growth declines and perhaps becomes negative.

In this scenario, export-led growth and investment-led growth are seen as 'magic bullets' which, if they can be achieved, will increase productivity, competitiveness and supply-side reform within the economy, and allow sustained economic growth to take place. In such a situation, short-term economic growth, brought about by the increase in aggregate demand, will seamlessly move into sustainable long-term growth. This is because export-led growth and investment-led growth are associated with increased productivity and with the modernisation and enlargement of the economy's productive capacity.

Achieving export-led growth and investment-led growth is, however, much easier said than done. At the time of writing this chapter, the UK's continuing recovery from recession appears once again to be consumption-led, with little or no evidence of export-led or investment-led growth. Whether this heralds the eventual onset of another recession remains to be seen, and it must be remembered that adverse economic 'shocks' in the wider world economy can also lead to a collapse in aggregate demand in the UK economy.

Government policies to correct or reduce a balance of payments surplus on current account

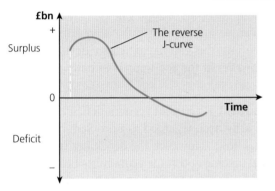

Figure 14.19 The reverse J-curve effect

The policies available to a government for reducing a balance of payments surplus are the opposite of the '3 Ds' of deflation, direct controls and devaluation, which are appropriate for correcting a payments deficit. The policies are the '3 Rs' of reflation, removal of import controls and revaluation:

- Reflating demand, via expansionary monetary policy or fiscal policy, increases a country's demand for imports.
- Trade can be liberalised by removing import controls.
- There have been calls on countries with large payments surpluses, such as Japan and China, to revalue in order to reduce global payments imbalances. But because there is much less pressure on a surplus country to revalue than on a deficit country to devalue, such calls have not usually been successful. It is also worth noting that, for a revaluation to reduce a current account surplus, the Marshall–Lerner condition must be met. In addition, a reverse J-curve, illustrated in Figure 14.19, may operate, causing the payments surplus to get bigger immediately after the revaluation, before it eventually starts to get smaller.

The significance of balance of payments deficits and surpluses for individuals

Earlier in this section we addressed the issue of whether balance of payments deficits and surpluses on current account pose problems for the country experiencing the deficit or surplus.

It was explained there that, while a short-run deficit or surplus on current account does not pose a problem, a persistent or long-run imbalance indicates fundamental disequilibrium. In the case of a deficit, the nature of any resulting problem depends on the size and cause of the deficit: the larger the deficit, the greater the problem is likely to be. The problem is also likely to be serious if the deficit is caused by the uncompetitiveness of the country's industries. Although in the short run a deficit allows a country's residents to enjoy living standards boosted by imports, and thus higher than would be possible from the consumption of the country's output alone, in the long run, the decline of the country's industries in the face of international competition lowers living standards.

While many people agree that a persistent current account deficit can pose serious problems, we also said that few realise that a balance of payments surplus on current account can also lead to problems. Because a surplus is often seen as a sign of national economic virility and success, a popular view is that the bigger the surplus, the better must be the country's performance. This is obviously true insofar as the surplus measures the competitiveness of the country's exporting industries. However, although a small surplus may be a justifiable objective of government policy, a large payments surplus should be regarded as undesirable. This is for two reasons:

- One country's surplus is another country's deficit. Since we don't trade with Mars or any other planet, the balance of payments must balance for the world as a whole. It is therefore impossible for all countries to run surpluses simultaneously. Unless countries with persistently large surpluses agree to take action to reduce their surpluses, deficit countries cannot reduce their deficits. Deficit countries may then be forced to impose import controls from which all countries, including surplus countries, eventually suffer.
- A balance of payments surplus is an injection of aggregate demand into the circular flow of income and this can be inflationary. If there are substantial unemployed resources in the economy, this can have the beneficial effect of reflating real output and jobs. However, if the economy is initially close to full capacity, demand-pull inflation results.

We noted earlier that, in recent years, the UK's current account deficit has increased in size. This has not necessarily been regarded as a problem because it has been financed by inward capital flows. However, the deficit has been increasing as a percentage of national income and some economists believe that, unless the deficit is reduced, it could lead to capital outflows as foreign investors question the ability of the UK to finance its growing overseas debts. It is not a deterioration in the balance of trade in goods and services that has been the main problem in recent years. As Figure 14.20 shows, a significant cause of the growing current account deficit is a deterioration in the primary income balance.

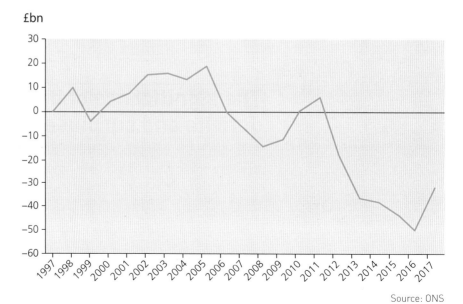

Source: ONS

Figure 14.20 The changes in the UK's primary income balance, 1997–2017

Primary income is the balance between the income (that is, profits, dividends and interest payments) received on the UK's foreign investments, and the income paid to overseas investors on their UK investments. Figure 14.20 shows that since 2011 there has been a significant deterioration of the UK's primary income position, which has widened the deficit on the current account. According to **www.parliament.uk**:

> … the deterioration in the primary account was driven by UK residents receiving lower income on their overseas foreign direct investments (FDI). This in turn was a result of both lower returns on those investments (thanks in part to economic weakness in the eurozone), and a reduction in the total stock of UK overseas FDI. In contrast, foreign residents have continued to expand their holdings of UK assets (something that may be linked to the relative strength of the UK's recovery and its status as a 'safe haven'), and have shifted the composition of their assets from low-yielding debt to riskier, higher-yielding equity, thereby increasing the rate of return on their holdings.

Implications for the global economy of other economies taking action to reduce their current account imbalances

As we have seen, countries are more likely to take action to try to reduce a current account deficit than to reduce a current account surplus. Indeed, surplus countries very often like to keep things exactly as they are, particularly if they benefit from artificial price competitiveness caused by an undervalued exchange rate.

Perhaps not surprisingly, corrective action by an economy to reduce the size of a current account deficit may have very little effect on other economies, first if the deficit is small, and second if the economy forms only a tiny part of the world economy. The same is not true, however, if the economy taking the corrective action is large.

The USA

The USA is the country which runs the largest current account deficit, importing far more than it exports. Many of these imports are cheap Chinese manufactured goods and components that American firms such as Apple design before they are assembled into finished consumer goods (often in China). China likes it this way because the USA provides a ready market for its exports. Many American importing firms and consumers also like it this way because they benefit from cheap components and consumer goods. (However, other American manufacturing firms and the workers they employ don't like it this way. Unless these firms move out of the USA and relocate in countries with cheap labour, they may be forced to go under, and either way, American workers will lose their jobs.)

To correct the deficit and to save American jobs, the US government may resort to protectionism. In the past the USA used its hegemony and power to engage in various forms of covert or hidden protectionism, such as preferential defence contracts to aircraft manufactures and subsidies to farmers. Such policies undoubtedly harm countries which sell goods to the USA. If a smaller and less powerful country were to take this action, it might suffer 'beggar my neighbour' retaliation, but the size and power of the USA generally make this impractical. In recent years the US has aggressively demanded better trading terms by breaking WTO rules and introducing tariffs on imported goods from China and the EU. It has upset traditional allies Mexico and Canada and demanded the renegotiation of NAFTA to better suit the interests of the USA.

The USA has never really deflated its economy in order to correct its payment deficit, but when the US economy does suffer from a downturn — for example, recession in 2008 and 2009 — other countries have faced a sudden loss of export markets. There is a saying: 'When America sneezes, the rest of the world catches a cold.' Because of the size of the US economy, countries which export to the USA are highly dependent on it continuing to grow. A recession in the USA tends to mean that other countries import recession from it, which is clearly not what those countries want.

Competitive devaluation

As we have seen, the other action a country can take to reduce a current account deficit is to devalue or encourage a depreciation of its exchange rate. Again, if this policy is viewed by other countries as an attempt to gain at their expense, it might lead to retaliatory devaluations and to an exchange rate war from which nobody benefits. Encouraging the dollar to fall has not always been an effective way of reducing the USA's balance of payments deficit. This is because other currencies, such as China's renminbi (RMB) or yuan, have at times been effectively 'pegged' to the dollar, which means that if the dollar's exchange rate falls, so does the RMB's exchange rate. However, China stunned financial markets in August 2015 by devaluing the RMB on two consecutive days in order to counter a slowdown in its growth rate. This is despite the fact that China had previously been reluctant to raise the RMB's exchange rate and lose its price competitive advantage.

In the case of the USA and China, the imbalance in the two countries' current accounts is largely resolved by large capital flows from China into the USA. For example, China has purchased large quantities of US government bonds. In 2015, China held US Treasury bonds worth more than $1.25 trillion. These capital flows finance the American trade deficit. Indeed, the world as a whole is generally willing to 'invest' in the USA, irrespective of the state of the US current account, because the US dollar is a reserve currency and is viewed as a 'safe haven'.

Smaller countries

For a smaller country such as the UK, a downward float of the pound's exchange rate might be a viable method of reducing a current account deficit. A fall in the pound's exchange rate would probably have relatively little effect on other economies. However, the effectiveness of a depreciation would depend on how big it was, on whether it provoked retaliation, and on the price elasticities of demand for the UK's exports and imports. A fall in the exchange rate might also provoke a 'hot money' flow out of the pound, leading to a further fall in the value of the currency that might then destabilise the UK economy.

- The balance of payments is the part of the national accounts that measures all the currency flows into and out of the country in a particular time period.
- The two main parts of the balance of payments are the current account and the financial account, which records most of the capital flows between countries.
- The financial account can be divided into direct investment, portfolio investment and short-term capital flows, which include many speculative or 'hot money' flows.
- There are two other much smaller sections of the balance of payments: the 'capital account' and 'net errors and omissions'.
- 'Hot money' flows can destabilise the exchange rate, the balance of payments and indeed the whole economy.
- The expenditure-reducing policy of deflation and/or the expenditure-switching policies of import controls and devaluation can be used to reduce a current account deficit.
- Sometimes deflation and devaluation should be used in tandem.
- Likewise reflation, removal of import controls and revaluation can be used to reduce a surplus.
- Supply-side policies can also help to reduce a current account deficit.

Questions

1 Do you agree that, for a developed economy such as the UK, the advantages of globalisation exceed any disadvantages? Justify your answer.

2 Explain the difference between absolute advantage and comparative advantage.

3 Assess the view that the progress made towards free trade has brought significant economic benefits both to the global economy and to the UK.

4 Explain the policies that may be used to reduce a deficit on the current account of the balance of payments.

5 Do you agree that supply-side reforms are needed if the UK's current account is to improve in the long run? Justify your answer.

6 Using a demand and supply diagram, explain how a trade deficit is eliminated in a freely floating exchange rate system.

15

Exchange rate systems and economic growth and development

Following on from Chapter 14, this is the second chapter in the book on international economics. Section 15.1 explains exchange rate systems. Exchange rate equilibrium cannot be fully understood without understanding the balance of payment equilibrium, and vice versa. The former is measured in terms of the relative prices of currencies, whereas the latter is stated in terms of the quantities of goods, services and financial flows between countries. Chapter 14 explained the balance of payments, but this chapter focuses on exchange rates. Section 15.2, the final part of the book, is significantly different, surveying the topic of development economics and some of the problems faced by the world's poorer economies.

LEARNING OBJECTIVES

These are to understand:

- how exchange rates are determined in a freely floating exchange rate system
- how a government and central bank can intervene to manage an exchange rate
- the advantages and disadvantages of freely floating and fixed exchange rate systems
- advantages and disadvantages of joining a currency union
- the impact of the eurozone on member countries
- the difference between economic growth and economic development
- the main characteristics of less developed economies
- the indicators of economic development
- the factors that affect growth and development
- the barriers to growth and development
- the policies that might be adopted to promote economic growth and development
- the role of aid and trade in promoting growth and development

15.1 Exchange rate systems

Introduction to exchange rates

So far in this book, we have made several mentions of exchange rates, particularly in the context of the balance of payments. This should not be surprising: whenever we discuss exchange rates, we usually have to make reference to the balance of payments, and vice versa.

Although domestic currencies are used to pay for internal trade within countries, imports are usually paid for in the currency of the country exporting the goods or services. An exchange rate measures how much of another currency a particular currency can buy; it is the external price of the currency quoted in terms of another currency. Exchange rates can also be measured against gold, or against a weighted average of a selection or 'basket' of currencies. Currencies are bought and sold in the foreign exchange market, which is now an international market, dominated by electronic trading. On a global scale, the market never closes, and ICT-based buying and selling takes place throughout the day and night.

> **SYNOPTIC LINK**
>
> Chapter 11 mentioned the relationship between the exchange rate and a country's international competitiveness and discussed how a falling exchange rate increases import prices and causes cost-push inflation.
>
> Chapter 12 explained the link between exchange rate and interest rates, in the context of monetary policy.
>
> Chapter 14 looked at globalisation, multinational corporations, trade and the balance of payments. Changes in the value of an exchange rate can have a major effect on all of these topics. The appreciation or depreciation of a currency affects economic activity because it changes the price of exports and imports.

The meaning and measurement of an exchange rate

> **KEY TERM**
>
> **exchange rate** the external price of a currency, usually measured against another currency.

These days the **exchange rate** of a currency is simply the external price of the currency in terms of another currency, such as the US dollar. The convention of quoting exchange rates in terms of the US dollar dates from the years after the Second World War. Before 1914 most exchange rates were expressed in terms of gold and only after 1945 did the dollar become the near universally accepted standard by which the external values of other currencies were measured.

In recent years, in response to the changing pattern of UK trade, the pound's exchange rate is as often quoted against the euro as it is against the dollar. The sterling exchange rate index (ERI) is also used to measure the pound's exchange rate. The ERI does not measure the pound's external value against a particular currency. Rather it is a trade-weighted average of the pound's exchange rate against a number of leading trading currencies, calculated to reflect the importance of each currency in international trade.

547

The real exchange rate

The different exchange rates mentioned so far are all *nominal* exchange rates. These must not be confused with a *real* exchange rate, which measures the weighted average value of a country's currency relative to a basket of other major currencies, adjusted for the effects of inflation. The real exchange rate of the pound, which is a measure of competitiveness, is calculated by the following formula:

$$\text{pound's real exchange rate} = \text{sterling index} \times \frac{\text{index of the domestic price level}}{\text{index of weighted foreign price levels}}$$

For simplicity, assume that the domestic price level rises by 10%, the foreign price level remains unchanged and the nominal value of the domestic currency depreciates by 10%; in that case, the real exchange rate remains unchanged. The price competitiveness of the country's products has not changed, and the improvement in competitiveness brought about by the fall in the nominal exchange rate has been exactly offset by a higher rate of domestic inflation.

QUANTITATIVE SKILLS 15.1

Worked example: calculating percentage changes in an exchange rate from data presented in index number form

Table 15.1 shows the value of a country's currency against other currencies, in index number form.

Table 15.1 Exchange rate index, 2016–19

Year	Exchange rate index (2017 = 100)
2016	96
2017	100
2018	106
2019	102

Calculate the percentage change in the country's exchange rate between: (a) 2016 and 2019, (b) 2017 and 2018.

(a) Between 2016 and 2019 the index changed by 6 points. The percentage change between these years was therefore (6/96) × 100, which is a 6.25% increase.

(b) In this example, because the comparison is with the base year index number (100), the change in index points and the percentage change are the same: a 6-point index number change and a 6% change.

TEST YOURSELF 15.1

Explain the difference between a currency's *nominal* exchange rate and its *real* exchange rate.

The different types of exchange rate system

Figure 15.1 shows the main types of exchange rate system. The two extreme types are freely floating exchange rates (also known as cleanly floating exchange rates) and rigidly fixed exchange rates. A fixed exchange rate is the most extreme form of managed exchange rates.

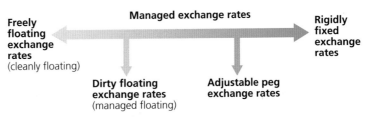

Figure 15.1 The different types of exchange rate system

TEST YOURSELF 15.2

What is the pound's exchange rate against the US dollar and the euro at the time you are reading this chapter? Is it a floating or a fixed exchange rate, and has the exchange rate been rising or falling in recent months?

The managed exchange rates, which lie between the extremes of freely floating and rigidly fixed exchange rates, take two main forms: adjustable peg and managed-floating (or dirty-floating) exchange rates. Adjustable peg exchange rates resemble fixed exchange rates in many respects, but the rate at which the exchange rate is fixed may be changed from time to time. A formal devaluation reduces the fixed exchange rate, while revaluation increases the fixed rate. With an adjustable peg system, there is usually a band in which the exchange rate is allowed to fluctuate.

Freely floating exchange rates

KEY TERM

freely floating exchange rate the exchange rate is determined solely by the interplay of demand for, and supply of, the currency.

In a regime of **freely floating exchange rates**, the external value of a country's currency is determined on foreign exchange markets by the forces of demand and supply alone. Toward the end of this section, we will remind you of how, in recent decades, capital flows and speculation have been extremely significant in influencing the supply of and demand for a currency, and hence its exchange rate. However, we will first simplify by assuming that a currency is demanded on foreign exchanges solely for the payment of trade and that trade flows alone determine exchange rates. We will also assume that any holdings of foreign currencies surplus to the immediate requirement of paying for trade are immediately sold on the foreign exchange market.

Explaining the slope of the demand and supply curves for pounds

Figure 15.2 Exchange rate equilibrium in a freely floating exchange rate system

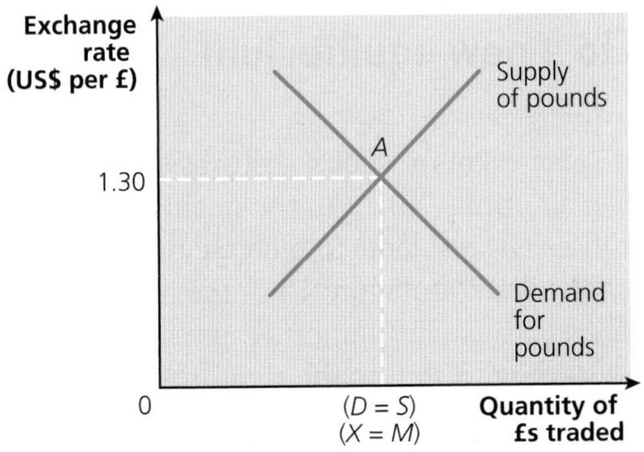

When the exchange rate of the pound falls, UK exports become more competitive in overseas markets. The volume of UK exports increases, leading to greater overseas demand for pounds to finance the purchase of these exports, provided that the demand for UK exports is price elastic. This explains the downward-sloping demand curve for pounds, which is illustrated in Figure 15.2.

But just as UK exports generate a demand for pounds on foreign exchange markets, so imports into the UK generate a supply of pounds. The explanation lies in the fact that UK trading companies generally pay for imports in foreign currencies. Importers must sell sterling on the foreign exchange market in order to purchase the foreign currencies needed to pay for the goods they are buying. As the pound's exchange rate rises, fewer pounds are needed to buy a given quantity of foreign currency. This means that the sterling price of imports falls. UK consumers are likely to respond to the falling price of imports by increasing total spending on imports (which happens as long as the demand for imports is price elastic). A greater total quantity of sterling must be supplied on foreign exchange markets to pay for the imports — even though the sterling price of each unit of imports has fallen. The result is the upward-sloping supply curve of sterling depicted in Figure 15.2. This shows

that at higher exchange rates, more sterling is likely to be supplied on the foreign exchange market.

Exchange rate equilibrium in a freely floating exchange rate regime

Exchange rate equilibrium occurs at the market-clearing exchange rate at which the demand for pounds on foreign exchange markets equals the supply of pounds. In Figure 15.2, this is determined at point A. The equilibrium exchange rate is $1.30 to the pound.

At this exchange rate, the money value of exports (paid in sterling) equals the money value of imports (paid in foreign currencies). And provided we assume that exports and imports are the only items in the current account, the current account is also in balance.

Because we are assuming away any complications introduced by capital flows, exchange rate equilibrium implies balance of payments equilibrium on current account and vice versa. As we stated in Chapter 14, the two equilibria are just different sides of the same coin: exchange rate equilibrium is price equilibrium, whereas current account equilibrium in the balance of payments (where $X = M$ in Figure 15.2) means that the quantity of the currency flowing into the country equals the quantity flowing out. Given the simplifying assumptions we have made, once the balance of payments is in equilibrium, there is no pressure for the exchange rate to rise or fall.

The adjustment process to a new equilibrium exchange rate

We shall now assume that some event or 'shock' disturbs the initial equilibrium — for example, an improvement in the quality of foreign-produced goods causes UK residents to increase demand for imports, whatever the exchange rate. In Figure 15.3, the increase in demand for foreign exchange to pay for imports causes the supply curve of the pound sterling to shift to the right from S_1 to S_2. (Remember, when more foreign currencies are demanded, more pounds must be supplied on the foreign exchange market.) In the new situation, the current account of the balance of payments is in deficit by the amount ($X < M$) in the diagram — as long as the exchange rate stays at $1.30. At the $1.30 exchange rate, UK residents supply or sell more pounds than before to pay for imports, but because overseas residents still demand the same quantity of UK goods (assuming that their views on the quality of UK goods relative to foreign goods have not changed), the overseas demand for pounds to pay for UK exports remains at its previous level.

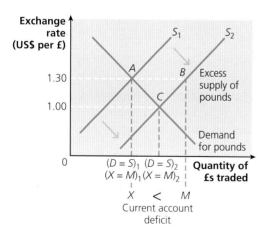

Figure 15.3 How a current account deficit is eliminated in a freely floating exchange rate system

At the exchange rate of $1.30 to the pound, there is now an excess supply of pounds on the foreign exchange market, equal to the distance B minus A. The market mechanism now swings into action to restore equilibrium — both for the exchange rate and for the balance of payments. When the excess holdings of pounds accumulated at the exchange rate of $1.30 are sold on the foreign exchange market, the pound's exchange rate falls. This increases the price competitiveness of UK exports while making imports less price competitive. The exchange rate falls until a new equilibrium exchange rate is reached at point C, where the exchange rate is $1.00 to the pound.

Note that the current account of the balance of payments is once again in equilibrium, but at $(X = M)_2$ rather than at $(X = M)_1$. This means that at the new equilibrium exchange rate ($1 to the pound), the money values of exports and imports are again equal in size, but the actual physical quantities of both exports and imports have increased.

Conversely, if the initial equilibrium is disturbed by an improvement in the quality of UK goods or services, the demand curve for the pound shifts to the right. This moves the current account into surplus, causing the pound's exchange rate to rise or appreciate in order to relieve the excess demand for pounds. Providing UK residents don't change their views on the relative quality of imports, the exchange rate rises until the balance of payments and exchange rate equilibrium are once again restored.

Advantages of floating exchange rates

Economists generally agree that, provided there are no distorting capital flows, freely floating exchange rates have the following advantages.

Automatically achieving balance of payments equilibrium

The exchange rate (which is the external price of the currency) should move up or down automatically to correct a payments imbalance. Provided the adjustment mechanism operates smoothly, a currency should never be overvalued or undervalued for long. In the event of an overvalued exchange rate causing export uncompetitiveness and a payments deficit, market forces should quickly adjust the exchange rate downward towards its equilibrium price, which also achieves equilibrium in the balance of payments. Similarly, undervaluation should be quickly corrected by an upward movement of the exchange rate.

Improving resource allocation

If the world's resources are to be efficiently allocated between competing uses, exchange rates must be correctly valued. For efficient resource allocation in a constantly changing world, market prices must accurately reflect shifts in demand and changes in competitive and comparative advantage that result from technical progress and events such as discoveries of new mineral resources. In principle, a freely floating exchange rate should respond and adjust to these changes. By contrast, a fixed exchange rate may gradually become overvalued or undervalued, as demand or competitive and comparative advantage move against or in favour of a country's industries. Similarly, different rates of inflation between countries mean that, over time, fixed exchange rates lead to a misallocation of resources between economies.

Freedom to achieve domestic policy objectives

It is sometimes argued that when the exchange rate is freely floating, balance of payments surpluses and deficits cease to be a policy problem for the government, as it is then free to pursue the domestic economic objectives of full employment and growth. Market forces 'look after' the current account of the balance of payments, leaving governments free to concentrate on domestic economic policy. If, in the pursuit of domestic objectives, the inflation rate is higher than in other countries, in a freely floating world the exchange rate simply falls to restore competitiveness.

Making it easier to control inflation

A government should benefit from a floating exchange rate because the exchange rate insulates the country against 'importing inflation' from the rest of the world. If inflation rates are higher in the rest of the world, a fixed exchange rate causes a country to import inflation through the rising prices of goods imported from high-inflation countries. By contrast, a floating exchange rate appreciates, which lowers the prices of imports, insulating the economy against importing inflation.

Ability to pursue an independent monetary policy

With a floating exchange rate, monetary policy can be used solely to achieve domestic policy objectives, such as the control of inflation. This is called an *independent* monetary policy. With a fixed exchange rate, as we explain later, interest rates may be determined by events in the outside world (and, in particular, by capital flows out of and into currencies), rather than by the needs of the domestic economy. To maintain a fixed exchange rate, interest rates may have to be raised to prevent the exchange rate from falling. In this situation, monetary policy is no longer independent, in the sense that it can no longer be assigned to pursuing purely domestic policy objectives. In a fixed exchange rate system, domestic policy objectives are often sacrificed to the pursuit of the external policy objective of maintaining an exchange rate target.

SYNOPTIC LINK
The external value of the currency is always going to affect the performance of a country's economy. Go back to Chapter 9 and recap your understanding of the main objectives of government policy and economic indicators.

TEST YOURSELF 15.5
Explain how a fall in the value of a country's currency can help the country to correct a trade deficit.

SYNOPTIC LINK
Refer back to the first macroeconomic policy conflict outlined on page 301 of Chapter 9.

SYNOPTIC LINK
Go back to section 11.3 of Chapter 11 and read over how inflation is measured in price indices. When the value of the sterling appreciates or depreciates, this impacts on the rate of inflation because the price of imports changes in the inflation price indexes.

Disadvantages of floating exchange rates

Freely floating exchange rates nevertheless have some disadvantages, particularly relating to the fact that, in the modern globalised world in which financial capital is internationally mobile, capital flows rather than exports and imports can be the main determinants of exchange rates. The main disadvantages of floating exchange rates are described below.

The adverse effects of speculation and capital flows

The argument that a freely floating exchange rate is never overvalued or undervalued for very long depends crucially upon the main assumption of the traditional theory of exchange rates, that currencies are bought and sold on foreign exchange markets only to finance trade. This assumption means that speculation and capital flows have no influence on exchange rates. But this is at odds with how the modern globalised economy works. These days, well over 90% of currency transactions taking place on foreign exchange markets stem from capital flows and from the decisions of individuals, business corporations, financial institutions and even governments to switch wealth portfolios between different currencies.

In the short run, exchange rates are extremely vulnerable to speculative capital or 'hot money' movements into or out of currencies. Just like a fixed exchange rate, a floating exchange rate can be overvalued or undervalued, which means it does not reflect the trading competitiveness of the country's goods and services. In this situation, speculators will buy currencies they perceive to be undervalued in order to make capital gains when selling the currencies at higher exchange rates in the future. Likewise, they will sell currencies they perceive to be overvalued in order to avoid capital losses when selling the currencies at lower exchange rates in the future.

(Arguably, however, fixed exchange rates are even more vulnerable than floating exchange rates to speculative capital flows. This is because fixed exchange rates often become overvalued or undervalued. In the case of an overvalued currency, speculators may sell the currency in order to make a profit by buying it back at a lower exchange rate after the currency has been devalued. However, if devaluation does not take place, the speculators can instead enjoy the 'one-way option' of buying back the currency at the exchange rate at which it was sold.)

International trading uncertainty

It is sometimes argued that, whereas fixed exchange rates create conditions of certainty and stability in which international trade can prosper and grow, the volatility and instability caused by floating exchange rates slows the growth of, and even destroys, international trade. The prospect of changes in the exchange rate means that companies cannot be sure how much domestic currency they will have to pay for imports or receive from exports, and this uncertainty can deter them from engaging in international trade. By inhibiting trade, resources may be misallocated and world living standards reduced.

(In reality, however, *hedging*, which involves the purchase or sale of a currency in the 'forward' market, say 3 months in advance of the actual delivery of the currency and payment for trade, reduces the trading uncertainties associated with floating exchange rates. Indeed, fixed and managed exchange rates may also cause uncertainty, especially when a currency is over or undervalued and a devaluation or revaluation is expected.)

SYNOPTIC LINK
Speculation and capital flows are recorded in the financial account of the balance of payments, which we explained in section 14.3 of Chapter 14.

TEST YOURSELF 15.6
What is meant by 'hot money'?

Floating exchange rates may cause cost-push inflation

Floating exchange rates sometimes contribute to cost-push inflation. Suppose a country has a higher rate of inflation than its trading partners:

● Trading competitiveness and the current account of the balance of payments both worsen, causing the exchange rate to fall in order to restore competitiveness.
● This may trigger a vicious cumulative downward spiral of faster inflation and exchange rate depreciation.
● The falling exchange rate increases import prices, which raise the rate of domestic cost-push inflation.
● Workers react by demanding pay rises to restore the real value of the eroded real wage.
● Increased inflation itself erodes the export competitiveness initially won by the fall of the exchange rate.
● This triggers a further fall in the exchange rate to recover the lost advantage, and so the process continues.
● The resulting downward spiral can eventually destabilise large parts of the domestic economy, causing unemployment and reducing economic growth.

Floating exchange rates may also cause demand-pull inflation

Floating exchange rates can trigger demand-pull inflation as well as cost-push inflation. With a floating exchange rate, there is no need to deflate the domestic economy to deal with a balance of payments deficit on the current account.

Suppose a large number of countries with floating exchange rates simultaneously increase aggregate demand. This can lead to excess demand on a worldwide scale, which fuels global inflation. This happened in the 1970s, when a worldwide expansion of demand created conditions in which oil and primary goods producers could raise prices and still sell in world markets. In countries such as the UK, the resulting inflation appeared to be import cost-push inflation, caused by the rising cost of imported energy and raw materials.

However, the true cause lay in excess demand created by the simultaneous effects of demand expansion and floating exchange rates, when world supply could not increase, at least in the short run, to meet the surge in global demand. Similarly, floating exchange rates allow an individual government to over-inflate its economy, provided it is willing to allow the exchange rate to fall.

In contrast, the commitment to a fixed exchange rate prevents a government unilaterally adopting an excessively expansionary monetary policy, since the resulting inflation will cause the balance of payments to deteriorate and put downward pressure on the exchange rate. To prevent this, interest rates will have to be increased, damping down the domestic inflationary pressures.

TEST YOURSELF 15.7
Use *AD/AS* diagrams to distinguish between cost-push and demand-pull inflation.

SYNOPTIC LINK
Refer back to the coverage of speculative 'hot money' capital flows in section 14.3 of Chapter 14.

STUDY TIP
Look up the relationship between changes in the value of sterling and the rate of UK inflation. Sterling has experienced at least two significant depreciations in recent years: 2008 and 2016. In the period after each depreciation the rate of inflation increased. Learn the value of sterling before and after each depreciation.

Fixed exchange rates

With a freely floating exchange rate system, a currency's external value rises or falls to eliminate a balance of payments surplus or deficit. By contrast, with rigidly **fixed exchange rates**, a currency's external value remains unchanged, while the *internal* price level, or more usually the level of domestic economic activity and output, adjusts to eliminate a balance of payments disequilibrium on current account.

As the extension material on pages 557–58 explains, there are few examples of fixed exchange rates today. Note also that so-called fixed exchange rates have seldom if ever been rigidly fixed. Modern fixed exchange rates are better thought of as adjustable peg exchange rates. We shall explain this term shortly.

KEY TERM

fixed exchange rate an exchange rate fixed at a certain level by the country's central bank and maintained by the central bank's intervention in the foreign exchange market.

STUDY TIP
A rigidly fixed exchange rate is an extreme form of a managed exchange rate.

Key features of a fixed exchange rate

Figure 15.4 illustrates the key features of a fixed exchange rate. In the first place, the country's government or its central bank announces that the exchange rate is being fixed at a particular rate and the central bank is then given responsibility for maintaining that rate. In the context of Figure 15.4, the Bank of England would announce that the pound's exchange rate is being fixed at US$1.30. $1.30 would be called the exchange rate's 'central peg', also known as the 'central rate', 'parity' or 'par value'.

Simultaneously, the Bank of England would announce 'ceiling' and 'floor' limits, set respectively just above and below the 'central peg'. Market forces (supply and demand on foreign exchange markets) then determine the currency's 'day-to-day' exchange rate.

Provided that the exchange rate remains inside the 'zone or band of flexibility' between the ceiling and the floor, central bank intervention is not needed. However, if either the demand curve for, or the supply curve of, the currency shifts to a new position, in the absence of Bank of England intervention, market forces might take the exchange rate above $1.32 or below $1.28. If this happens, the fixed exchange rate has effectively broken down. To prevent this happening, whenever the ceiling or floor looks as if it is going to be breached, the central bank intervenes.

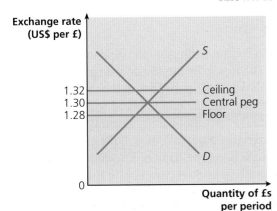

Figure 15.4 The ceiling, central peg and floor of a fixed exchange rate

Advantages of fixed exchange rates

Because the advantages and disadvantages of fixed exchange rates are closely related to but mirror those of floating rates, which we have already explained in some depth, we shall provide only a brief summary here.

The principal advantages of fixed exchange rates are:

- Fixed exchange rates attempt, not always successfully, to achieve certainty and stability in foreign exchange markets.
- Fixed exchange rates impose an anti-inflationary discipline on a country's domestic economic management and on the behaviour of its workers and firms.

Disadvantages of fixed exchange rates

By contrast, the principal disadvantages of fixed exchange rates are:

- Fixed exchange rates may *increase uncertainty* rather than *create certainty*. This is likely if a devaluation or revaluation is expected to occur in the near future.
- If the fixed exchange rate is significantly *overvalued*, it may impose the severe deflationary costs of lost output and unemployment, unless corrective action is taken to *devalue*.
- If the fixed exchange rate is significantly *undervalued*, inflation may be imported from the rest of the world, unless corrective action is taken to *revalue*.
- An independent monetary policy cannot be implemented.
- There may be recurrent balance of payments or currency crises in a country whose currency is overvalued.
- Resources may be tied up in official reserves (needed to support the fixed exchange rate), which could be used more productively elsewhere.
- Both overvaluation and undervaluation of the currency can lead to a misallocation of resources.

How governments can intervene to influence the exchange rate

These days, it is the country's central bank rather than its government that influences the exchange rate, though in a country such as the UK, the central bank (the Bank of England) takes strong notice of the wishes of the chancellor of the exchequer. We shall explain first how the central bank can try to maintain a fixed exchange rate, before extending the explanation to adjustable peg exchange rates in the extension material.

There are two main ways in which a central bank can intervene in markets to maintain a fixed exchange rate. The first is by buying or selling its own currency on the foreign exchange market. In Figure 15.4, if the exchange rate threatens to rise above the $1.32 ceiling, the Bank of England will sell its own currency on the foreign exchange market to offset excess demand for pounds that would otherwise pull up the exchange rate. Likewise, if the exchange rate is deemed likely to fall below its $1.28 floor, the Bank of England will step into the foreign exchange market and buy its own currency. In this case, by creating an 'artificial' demand for the pound, the Bank attempts to prevent an excess supply of pounds from pushing the exchange rate below the floor. The policy of buying and selling currencies to support an exchange rate is known as *exchange equalisation*.

The second method of supporting a fixed exchange rate is, in Britain's case, by the Bank of England raising or lowering Bank Rate to keep the pound's exchange rate between a ceiling of $1.32 and a floor of $1.28. Lower domestic interest rates might cause international holders of the pound to sell pounds and buy other currencies. This would cause the pound's exchange rate to fall, hopefully to a rate below the ceiling of $1.32. Conversely, an increase in UK interest rates attracts 'hot money' into the pound. Through the selling other currencies and the buying of the pound, short-run capital inflows raise the demand for pounds, hopefully taking the pound's exchange rate above its floor rate of $1.28.

In real life, both methods of intervention are likely to be used in tandem to support each other, particularly if an exchange rate crisis has led to a flow of money out the economy which threatens to destroy the fixed exchange rate. Perhaps the most important point to note is that when supporting a fixed exchange rate, a country's central bank may not be able to change its key interest rate (Bank Rate in the UK) to achieve purely domestic macroeconomic policy objectives such as economic growth and low unemployment.

Instead, the freedom to use monetary policy to achieve domestic objectives is sacrificed on the altar of supporting a fixed exchange rate. This fact of life probably explains why fixed exchange rates are rare today and why floating exchange rates are the norm. In 2019, however, there were still over 30 countries with formally or informally fixed exchange rates — most were pegged either against the euro (e.g. Denmark), or the US dollar (in Latin America).

> **SYNOPTIC LINK**
> If a government pursues a high exchange rate policy to combat inflation, this will have significant implications for the setting of monetary policy and the work of the central bank. Go back to Chapter 12 and read over section 12.3.

EXTENSION MATERIAL

Managed exchange rates

A rigidly fixed exchange rate is, of course, an example (the extreme example) of a managed exchange rate. However, there are two other examples of managed exchange rates: *adjustable peg* and *managed floating* or *'dirty' floating*. In both cases, a country's monetary authorities hope to achieve the stability and certainty associated with fixed exchange rates combined with a floating exchange rate's ability to avoid overvaluation and undervaluation by responding to market forces.

Adjustable peg exchange rates

An adjustable peg exchange rate is similar to a rigidly fixed exchange rate, except that the central bank may alter the exchange rate's central peg by devaluing or revaluing. If you look back at Figure 15.1, you will see that on the spectrum of exchange rates, an adjustable peg exchange rate is much closer to a rigidly fixed exchange rate than to a freely floating exchange rate. By contrast, a 'dirty-floating' (or managed-floating) exchange rate is much closer to a freely floating exchange rate.

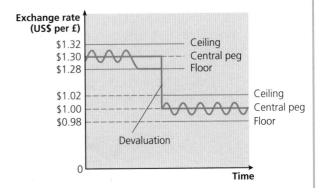

Figure 15.5 A devaluation of an adjustable peg exchange rate

Nevertheless, adjustable pegs are more flexible than the central pegs of rigidly fixed exchange rates, such as the old nineteenth-century gold standard. This is because the exchange rate can be adjusted upward or downward from time to time by the country's central bank. Adjustments take place because, over a period of time, exchange rates are likely to become over or undervalued as, for example, countries experience different rates of inflation. An upward revaluation corrects an undervalued exchange rate, whereas a downward adjustment or devaluation is used to correct overvaluation.

Figure 15.5, which is a development of Figure 15.4, illustrates devaluation of the pound in an adjustable peg exchange rate system. The exchange rate is initially fixed at a central peg of $1.30. As we explained earlier, the interaction of supply and demand for the currency on the foreign exchange market then determines the day-to-day exchange rate. Provided the exchange rate stays between a ceiling and a floor set at the time that the central peg was fixed, there is no need for central bank intervention. However, the graph shows the sterling exchange rate falling to the floor of $1.28, possibly because of a speculative capital flow against the currency. At this point the Bank of England intervenes, raising domestic interest rates to attract capital flows into the currency and purchasing the pound on the foreign exchange market using its foreign exchange reserves. By selling reserves and buying its own currency, the central bank creates an artificial demand for the pound, bidding up the exchange rate.

Persistent support for a currency almost certainly means that its exchange rate is overvalued, condemning the country to over-priced exports, under-priced imports and a persistent current account deficit. With the rigidly fixed exchange rate shown in Figure 15.4 this is the end of the story. The country's government has to deflate the domestic economy and/or impose import controls, since devaluation and revaluation are not permitted in a rigidly fixed system.

However, Figure 15.5 shows the Bank of England devaluing the exchange rate to a new central peg of $1.00 in an attempt to correct the fundamental imbalance. This illustrates the difference between adjustable peg and rigidly fixed exchange rate systems. But if a country makes frequent changes to the central peg, the benefits of having a fixed exchange rate are lost.

TEST YOURSELF 15.9
Suggest three reasons why a government might seek to manage its exchange rate.

Managed-floating or dirty-floating exchange rates

Fixed and adjustable peg exchange rate systems have now been abandoned throughout much of the world. Most exchange rates now float, though there is a difference between 'clean floating' and 'dirty floating'. Clean floating is the same as freely floating and pure floating — that is, there is no central bank intervention to prop up the exchange rate or to manipulate its value. In contrast to clean floating, 'managed floating' or 'dirty floating' occurs when the exchange rate is officially floating, in the sense that a country's monetary authorities announce that market forces are determining the exchange rate, but in fact they intervene unofficially behind the scenes, buying or selling their own currency in order to influence the exchange rate. (Countries around the world admit that they 'manage' their floating exchange rates. Arguably there are currently no countries that have a truly free-floating exchange rate system, with no central bank intervention at all.)

At the time of writing (in July 2019), it is probably true to say that for most of the period since September 1992, when the pound left an adjustable peg exchange rate system within the European Union, the pound's exchange rate has more-or-less freely floated. Nevertheless, the Bank of England does intervene on a daily basis, as part of a 'smoothing operation' through which it tries to iron out temporary fluctuations in the pound's exchange rate. In recent years, the UK has experienced two major currency crises. In the months after the 2008 financial crisis, sterling lost approximately 25% of its value against the US dollar; and after the Brexit referendum on 23 June 2016, the pound lost approximately 15% of its value against the US dollar.

STUDY TIP
Research the performance of the pound sterling since 2000 against the US dollar and the euro. Look carefully at how the value of the pound fluctuated throughout the period and examine the value of the currency in the months following the depreciations in 2008 and 2016.

Devaluation of the pound and UK economic performance

The devaluation of a nation's currency can be used by a government to reduce a current account deficit on the balance of payments and stimulate economic growth. In recent decades, three significant devaluations or depreciations of the pound have taken place. On each occasion, sterling lost almost a quarter of its value against the US dollar over a 6-month period. Each devaluation or depreciation took place for very different reasons and the impact on UK economic performance has varied.

The pound's ejection from the Exchange Rate Mechanism in 1992

The Exchange Rate Mechanism (ERM) was a system of adjustable peg fixed exchange rates set up by the European Union in 1979, within a newly created European Monetary System (EMS), in preparation for economic union within the EU. Having initially opposed membership of the ERM, the UK joined the system in 1990, but at a substantially overvalued exchange rate. On 16 September 1992 the British government was forced to abandon its economic policy and withdraw the pound from the Exchange Rate Mechanism, a currency system which was meant to stabilise the exchange rates of member countries.

When the pound joined the ERM in 1990, the 'high-pound' objective was meant to bleed inflation out of the economy by forcing British firms to make efficiency savings to stay price competitive in world markets. However, this harmed the British economy in two painful ways. First, the strong currency made imports cheap and exports expensive. Although this helped bring down the UK's rate of inflation, British firms struggled to survive in world markets. Second, the Bank of England raised interest to attract 'hot money' flows into the currency and maintain the high exchange rate. However, this put UK households with high levels of mortgage debt under tremendous pressure and choked off consumer spending.

When, in 1992, the markets forced the British government to devalue the pound, the UK economy was in a deep recession, which itself had been caused by the pound's overvaluation. At the time, the forced devaluation of the pound was seen as a national humiliation, with the result that the day on which it took place was nicknamed 'Black Wednesday'.

However, immediately after the devaluation, the economy started to grow. The low exchange rate made UK exports price competitive and in the following years the UK's unemployment rate fell and the current account deficit on the balance of payments was eliminated. Between 1992 and 1997, ONS statistics show that exports increased by 53% and the economy grew by 15.2%.

The departure from the ERM also had significant implications for UK monetary policy. The Bank of England no longer needed to maintain high interest rates to support a fixed exchange rate, so falling interest rates significantly reduced the cost of borrowing for both firms and households. Looser monetary policy created the conditions for increased consumer spending and business investment.

The Great Recession, 2008 and 2009

In the summer of 2008, the dollar exchange rate was £1 = $2.00. Then the banking crisis shook the world. The UK's banking system was at the centre of the worst economic crisis since the 1930s and the value of the pound crashed as 'hot money' flowed out of the pound and searched for safety in other currencies. By January 2009, the exchange rate had fallen to £1 = $1.30.

To stimulate the domestic economy, the Bank of England slashed Bank Rate to 0.5%, and in 2009 it started the unorthodox monetary policy of quantitative easing. The fall in the exchange rate, record low interest rates and the injection of billions of pounds of electronic money into the economy should, according to conventional economic theory, have stimulated the economy.

However, it took 7 years for the British economy to recover from the recession. After 2009, economic growth was weak and British firms failed to experience increased in demand in their export markets. The size of the deficit on the current account remained high, only reducing to 2% of GDP in 2011, 2 years after the devaluation. Fiscal austerity at home and the eurozone crisis abroad were major reasons why the UK recovery was so weak. However, the devaluation of sterling did eventually stimulate the economy in the same way that it had after earlier devaluations.

After the Brexit referendum in 2016

Following the publication of the 2016 Brexit referendum result, the pound's exchange rate fell against both the dollar and the euro. In January 2016, the exchange rate was £1 = $1.45. A year later in January 2017, it had fallen to £1 = $1.20. The devaluation had two predictable outcomes: cost-push inflation squeezed living standards. The CPI rate of inflation in the 2-year period after the devaluation increased to over 3% a year, but the current account deficit was little changed.

Some conclusions

The devaluations of 2008 and 2016 affected UK economic performance in a different way to what had happened after the earlier 1992 devaluation. In 1992, export competitiveness rapidly improved, export-led growth occurred, and the economy recovered quickly. By contrast, the falls in the value of the pound in the later cases did not lead to strong export-led growth or to the elimination of the current account deficit.

This difference was partly because the nature of global capitalism in the twenty-first century has changed. Modern global supply chains now require that the goods and services which British firms export are priced in US dollars and euros, and not in UK pounds.

As a result, a fall in the value of the pound has a limited effect on the price competitiveness of UK exports. The 2008 and 2016 devaluations or depreciations of the pound have not significantly boosted exports or decreased imports. Hence, the evidence appears to show that these devaluations brought limited gains for British exporters, while inflicting painful imported inflation on UK households.

Follow-up questions

1 Explain how a central bank will implement monetary policy to try to maintain a high exchange rate.
2 Explain how a depreciation in the value of a currency affects the rate of domestic inflation.
3 Suggest why a fall in the pound's exchange rate has not in recent years led to a significant increase in demand for UK exports.
4 Describe what happened to the pound's exchange rate during the year before you are reading this case study.

TEST YOURSELF 15.10
How does exchange rate stability affect businesses planning long-term investment projects?

STUDY TIP
Research the relationship between the Danish krone and the euro. Look carefully at the exchange rate of the currencies since 1999. The Danish krone has fluctuated throughout the period, but its movements have been very minor compared to that of, for example, the UK pound against the euro.

KEY TERM
currency union an agreement between a group of countries to share a common currency, and usually to have a single monetary and foreign exchange rate policy.

TEST YOURSELF 15.11
Explain how a country that joins a monetary union loses control of its monetary policy.

Currency unions, the euro and the eurozone

Currency unions

The United Kingdom comprises a number of countries, but all of them use the pound as a common currency. Likewise, the 50 states of the United States of America, plus the federal district of Washington DC, all use the US dollar. Both the UK and the USA are examples of a **currency union**, which is a group of countries using or sharing a single currency. A currency union is often known a monetary union.

In the 1990s, the UK, then being a member state of the European Union (EU), was given the choice of keeping its own currency (still within the EU), or of adopting the common European currency that at the time was being set up. If the UK had chosen the latter, it would have replaced the pound with the new common currency, the *euro*, and joined what became known as the *eurozone*.

The euro and the eurozone

The euro came into existence on 1 January 2002 when euro notes and coins entered circulation. However, economists usually date the euro's introduction as 1 January 1999, as this was the date on which the exchange rates of the 12 countries that became the first members of the eurozone (or euro area) were irrevocably fixed against each other.

In the early 1990s, the Treaty of the European Union (or Maastricht Treaty) had begun the process which eventually created monetary union within the eurozone. At the time, monetary union was considered necessary for two reasons. In the first place, although the Single European Act had eventually created almost completely free internal trade in goods and services, the need to exchange national currencies in this trade increased transaction costs. A single currency was thus deemed necessary to complete the single market. In the second place, upward and downward movements of EU national currencies led to undervalued and overvalued exchange rates within the trading bloc. Exchange rate fluctuations artificially increased the competitiveness of those countries benefiting from a falling exchange rate, while reducing the competitiveness of countries whose exchange rates were rising. Monetary union would create a level playing field for all member countries.

The UK government decided to keep the pound and not to replace it with the euro, which means that along with nine other EU member currencies, the pound was not in the eurozone. At the time of writing in July 2019, 19 EU member states were in the eurozone, together with non-member states such as Kosovo. Additionally, various other countries pegged their currencies against the euro.

Currency unions and economic integration

The euro was created to facilitate greater economic integration among EU member states. Indeed, the euro is regarded by many as a stepping stone to full monetary union between EU states and, possibly in the future, to a much fuller economic and monetary union (EMU). At this point it is worth noting that EMU can mean two different things. The official EU meaning is *economic and monetary union*. Defined in this way, EMU suggests that common monetary arrangements adopted by EU member countries are part of a grander scheme to integrate the national economies of member states. More narrowly defined, the acronym means *European monetary union*, which involves a common monetary policy applied to all EU member states adopting the euro. In the latter meaning, EMU can be interpreted simply as a step towards making the EU's single market work better and more efficiently.

The impact of the euro upon eurozone economies

When the eurozone first came into existence, it was claimed that member countries would benefit in the following ways: reduced transaction costs, elimination of currency risk, greater transparency and possibly greater competition because prices are easier to compare. According to Paul Krugman:

> The creation of the euro was supposed to be another triumphant step in the European project, in which economic integration has been used to foster political integration and peace; a common currency, so the thinking went, would bind the continent even more closely together.

But Krugman then stated:

> What has happened instead is a nightmare: the euro has become an economic trap, and Europe a nest of squabbling nations. Even the continent's democratic achievements seem under threat, as dire economic conditions create a favourable environment for political extremism. Who could have seen such a thing coming?

Mobility of labour

Krugman and many other economists did foresee chaos in some of the countries which use the euro because they realised that the eurozone is *not* an *optimal currency area* (see the extension material on page 563). The USA and the UK, which we mentioned earlier as common currency areas, are much closer to being optimal currency areas. Each uses a single currency, enjoys complete internal free trade, and has a fiscal policy as well as a monetary policy covering the whole of the union. The USA, in particular, also enjoys high mobility of labour which enables workers who lose their jobs in the poorer parts of the country to find jobs in richer states such as California.

Mobility of labour and a common fiscal policy are essential if a common currency area is to become an optimal currency area. Without outward labour mobility from poorer parts of the union to the richer parts or perhaps to other parts of the world, the main way a country can regain jobs that have been lost by lack of competitiveness is through a large fall in real wages to make the region more competitive. Without a single currency, a country could restore its competitiveness by devaluing its currency. But in a currency union this is impossible. A high degree of labour mobility is therefore needed to deal with the unemployment problem. Emigration can shrink the size of the labour force to match the number of jobs available. However, it is often the young and more dynamic workers who move and this can be counterproductive.

Importance of a common fiscal policy

A common fiscal policy is also particularly important, since it allows wealth to be transferred by a centralised fiscal authority from the richer to the poorer parts of the union. Transfers of wealth, via taxation and public spending, are essential to counter the fact that poorer parts of the union cannot achieve competitive advantage by devaluing their national currencies. Fiscal transfers can help to reduce inequality but can also be used to try to improve the competitiveness of the poorer regions: for example, by spending on improving infrastructure.

An optimal currency area thus requires coordination in fiscal policy as well as in monetary policy. The European Central Bank (ECB) achieves monetary policy coordination, but as Greece has found to its expense, there is no supranational authority in the eurozone similar to the ECB to coordinate fiscal policies and to facilitate significant fiscal transfers.

The lack of fiscal policy coordination has led to some eurozone countries having high levels of government debt. This has built up especially in the so-called 'club-med' countries, such as Greece and Portugal, in the southern eurozone. Governments in the poorer countries of the South believed they would always be bailed out painlessly by the richer governments of countries such as Germany and the Netherlands. Also, prior to the 2008–09 recession, 'club-med' countries could borrow cheaply on international capital markets. During that time, any euro-denominated debt was pretty much acceptable to investors, no matter which eurozone country issued the debt.

SYNOPTIC LINK
Go back to section 11.2 of Chapter 11 and recap your understanding of unemployment and the problem of labour immobility.

SYNOPTIC LINK
Fiscal transfers occur when a government uses the taxation and benefits system to transfer income and wealth from one section of society to another. This was covered in Chapter 7.

Conclusion: an incomplete single market

The single market means that in theory there is complete mobility of both labour and capital within the EU. In practice, however, labour mobility is limited, particularly in comparison with the USA where workers move in large numbers from state to state. With regard to capital, before the financial crisis in 2007 there was massive capital movement from Europe's core — mainly Germany — to its periphery, leading to an economic boom in the periphery and significantly higher inflation rates in the 'club-med' countries than in Germany. But when private capital flows from the core to the periphery came to a sudden stop in 2008, the southern countries were uncompetitive and left with prices and unit labour costs well out of line with those in the core. Suddenly the eurozone faced a major adjustment problem that it has yet to deal with fully. (So-called austerity measures appear to have had some success in countries such as Ireland, but less so in Greece.)

SYNOPTIC LINK

In section 14.2 of Chapter 14 we looked at trade blocs. Read over this section and ensure you can explain the difference between a customs union and a single market, and why the EU has an incomplete single market.

EXTENSION MATERIAL

Optimal currency areas

If several countries use the same currency, their inhabitants will benefit from efficiency gains. They no longer have to worry about possible future changes in exchange rates, and the costs involved in currency conversion. These gains will be greater the more economically interconnected the countries are, in terms of their trading relationship, the freedom of labour and capital to move between countries, and a unified fiscal policy covering all member countries. In these circumstances, the advantages of adopting a common currency can lead to benefits for all the member states within the currency union.

The 50 states of the USA satisfy most or all the requirements for benefiting from a common currency, namely a large amount of trade in goods and services, free movement of factors of production across the union, and a unified government budget with fiscal transfers from the richer to the poorer states.

The European countries that have adopted the euro as their common currency do not satisfy those requirements. Many economists believe that the eurozone countries adopted the single currency for political rather than economic reasons. Although the eurozone countries trade a lot with each other, capital and especially labour are not sufficiently mobile between countries, and the countries lack a unified 'government' budget.

The latter point is really significant. A common fiscal policy provides a mechanism for transferring resources — for example, in the form of subsidies or lower tax rates — from the more prosperous parts of the currency union to the less prosperous countries. This is what happens in the UK, for example, when taxes paid by Londoners are directed into public spending projects in Scotland, Wales and Northern Ireland. The UK and the USA are successful common currency areas, but the eurozone is much less successful, since it lacks a common fiscal policy.

SECTION 15.1 SUMMARY

- An exchange rate is the external price of a currency in terms of another currency.
- There are three main types of exchange rate: freely floating, fixed and managed floating.
- A freely floating (cleanly floating) exchange rate is determined by supply and demand.
- Provided there are no capital flows, a freely floating exchange rate should automatically eliminate a trade deficit or surplus.
- Free floating enables a country to pursue an independent monetary policy.
- There are, however, disadvantages with a freely floating exchange rate system, such as exchange rate instability or volatility.
- Speculative or 'hot money' capital flows also destabilise floating exchange rates, sometimes leading to severe overvaluation or undervaluation.
- In a rigidly fixed exchange rate system, the exchange rate cannot rise or fall to eliminate or reduce a payments surplus or deficit.
- The advantages of a fixed exchange rate relate closely to the disadvantages of a floating rate, while the disadvantages similarly relate to a floating system's advantages.
- Adjustable peg and 'dirty' floating are types of managed exchange rates.
- In an adjustable peg system, the exchange rate can be revalued or devalued to try to correct a fundamental payments imbalance.
- The euro has replaced national currencies for the majority of EU member states that are in the eurozone.
- In recent years there has been a eurozone crisis, partly caused by the fact that the eurozone is not an optimal currency area.

15.2 Economic growth and development

The difference between growth and development

SYNOPTIC LINK
Refer back to pages 355–62 in Chapter 11 for our first mention of economic growth and development.

In Chapter 11, we explained the concept of economic growth and mentioned the difference between economic growth and economic development. There we said that *economic growth* measures changes in the physical quantity of goods and services that an economy actually produces, or has the potential to produce, but that economic development goes further, encompassing not just the increase in *quantity* of output, but also its *quality* and contribution to human happiness.

Economic growth does not necessarily improve the economic welfare of all or most of the people living in a country. Consider, for example, the situation when the ruling elite in a country use the fruits of growth to buy military and police equipment which they then use to suppress and possibly kill those in the population who wish to change how the economy operates. Although economic growth has occurred, economic development has not.

As stated in Chapter 11, economic development can be measured by:

- a general improvement in living standards which reduces poverty and human suffering
- access to resources such as food and housing that are required to satisfy basic human needs
- access to opportunities for human development (for example, through education and training)

- sustainability and regeneration, through reducing resource depletion and degradation
- access to decent healthcare

STUDY TIP

Don't confuse *sustainable growth* with *sustained growth*. The latter simply means achieving a particular rate of economic growth (on average) over a number of years. For example, from the end of recession in 1992 until the onset of the next recession in 2008, the UK sustained an average annual growth rate of about 2.75%. However, a growth rate which is sustained over quite a long period may nevertheless be unsustainable if it leads to environmental problems, the depletion of vital finite resources and the degradation of others.

SYNOPTIC LINK

In Chapter 14 we looked at how multinational corporations have built global production platforms and located manufacturing factories in emerging market economies in Southeast Asia. Countries such as China and India have created hundreds of millions of industrial jobs which have lifted millions of people out of poverty.

SYNOPTIC LINK

Globalisation has increased the incomes of millions of workers in the emerging market economies and led to the transfer of advanced technologies and capital equipment to less developed countries. This has helped less developed countries to industrialise but also resulted in environmental destruction and high levels of pollution. Go back over section 8.4 in Chapter 8, and link the concepts of externalities to the topic of development.

TEST YOURSELF 15.12

Using a diagram, explain how an economy can grow in both the short run and the long run.

The main characteristics of less developed economies

The term 'less developed economies' covers a wide range of economies, from the extremely poor to what the United Nations calls higher middle-income economies. There are various ways of identifying the main characteristics of less developed economies, but we concentrate on only one, which was developed nearly 70 years ago by W.W. Rostow, an economic historian and political theorist.

- Rostow used the term 'traditional society' to describe economies that were completely lacking in economic development. He described these as very primitive and usually poor societies in which very little changes from generation to generation, and in which tradition, generally accepted customs and persistent relationships between people govern economic life. Traditional societies face a low limit to their total production which, because of limited available methods of production, is largely agricultural. Today, traditional societies survive very often as tribal societies in remote areas of countries such as Brazil and India, and in parts of Africa.

TEST YOURSELF 15.13
Explain how the taxation revenues of a country which exports large volumes of oil will be affected if the price of a barrel of oil suddenly falls significantly on world markets.

SYNOPTIC LINK
Go back to Chapter 1 and read over section 1.5. Use a production possibility diagram to explain why a country in the early stages of industrialisation will focus on capital investment to achieve a faster rate of economic growth in order to achieve higher living standards in the long run.

KEY TERM

indicators of development these include gross domestic product (GDP) per head, information on the distribution of income, mortality rates and health statistics.

- Higher up the ranking of less developed economies are what Rostow called 'traditional economies preparing for take-off'. These are economies which are becoming more productive and in which various preconditions for successful industrial growth are beginning to appear. Scope for commerce and trade appears, along with banks and other financial institutions for the mobilisation of savings into productive investment.
- At the next stage, Rostow identified economies taking off into self-sustaining growth. This involves change from a largely agricultural to an industrialised or manufacturing economy. Output increases, but only a small fraction of society benefits significantly from improved living standards. Growth takes priority over economic development.
- At the final stage, higher-income developing economies are the end result of continued self-sustained growth. At this stage of development, countries are in a position to choose to allocate the increased output their economies are producing to social welfare and to other aspects of what we now call economic development.

Rostow's description of economic growth and development has had many critics, who generally argue that it is historically and factually wrong and is too simplistic. Nevertheless, it serves as a starting point for understanding some of the key features of less developed economies and the stages they go through to develop into prosperous societies with high levels of consumption.

Indicators of development

Economists usually use gross domestic product per head or *GDP per capita* as their first **indicator of economic development**. Unfortunately, for most poor developing countries, GDP is usually greater than another national income indicator of development, *gross national income* or GNI. Profit outflows and interest payments out of developing economies to more developed economies, and to banks within these economies, explain why this is the case. (When national income statistics are used as indicators of development, GDP per capita or GNI per capita (where per capita means per head of population) should be used rather than 'raw' GDP or GNI statistics.)

But are measures of national income or output, whether GDP or GNI figures, the best measures of standards of living, economic welfare and economic development? To try to answer this question, it is useful first to identify three components of economic welfare:

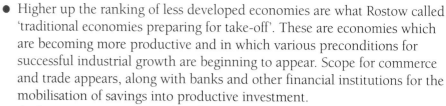

total economic welfare = economic welfare derived from goods and services purchased in the market economy + economic welfare derived from public goods and merit goods provided collectively by the state + economic welfare derived from quality of life factors, including external benefits minus external costs and intangibles

If used carefully, national income figures can provide a reasonable estimate of economic welfare derived from the first two of these three elements, both of which relate to the direct consumption of material goods and services. However, national income fails to provide a satisfactory indication of how externalities and other quality of life factors affect economic welfare and living standards.

Intangible factors, which are the third element in people's living standards, are largely ignored. These intangible factors include the value people place on leisure time and living close to work, and the externalities such as pollution and road congestion generated from the production and consumption of national income, which affect people's welfare and quality of life.

National income also fails to reflect the effect of the resource depletion and environmental degradation resulting from producing current income on humankind's ability to produce future income. This means that national income and GDP do not address the issue of sustainability.

In addition, whilst national income includes the value of the output of merit goods such as health and education, unless the data are disaggregated it is not possible to determine the extent to which the nation's resources are devoted to producing these services which are vital to economic development. Indicators such as life expectancy, infant mortality rates and literacy rates can be used to supplement national income per head in order to provide a better indicator of the quality of life enjoyed by people.

The United Nations Human Development Index (HDI)

The environmental pressure group Friends of the Earth has argued that measures of national income such as GDP were never intended to be indicators of a country's economic welfare or stage of development. Other indicators of development which are less dependent on 'raw' GNI or GDP are increasingly used to place a value on economic and social progress. One of the earliest of these was the *Measure of Economic Welfare* (MEW) developed by Nordhaus and Tobin in 1972. More recent attempts to adjust conventional national income figures to show developments in economic welfare include the **United Nations Human Development Index** (HDI) and the *Index of Sustainable Economic Welfare* (ISEW).

The HDI is constructed by measuring:

- life expectancy at birth
- mean years of schooling and expected years of schooling
- gross national income (GNI) per head of population, reflecting purchasing power parity (PPP) in US dollars

The maximum value of the HDI is 1 (or unity). The closer a country's HDI is to 1, the greater is its human development, measured in terms of the three indicators specified in the index.

Table 15.2 shows the 15 highest-ranked countries in the HDI for 2018, based on 2017 data, and also the 15 lowest-ranked countries.

In 2018 the Scandinavian country Norway led the way in the HDI 'top 15', with the USA and the UK respectively in thirteenth and fourteenth positions. At the other end of the spectrum, all the countries in the 'bottom 15' were located in sub-Saharan Africa.

In 2018, Iceland ranked in the 'top 15' in the HDI

The unadjusted HDI is by no means a perfect index of human development, however, since it ignores inequalities in the distribution of income. In 2010 the UN's *Human Development Report* developed the HDI by introducing a new *Inequality-adjusted Human Development Index* (IHDI). The IHDI estimates the actual level of human development (accounting for inequality) in each of the 189 countries included in the HDI. The HDI itself estimates the maximum IHDI that could be achieved if there were no inequality within countries. The greater the degree of inequality within a country, the greater the difference between the country's HDI and IHDI.

TEST YOURSELF 15.14
Explain two ways in which higher levels of education lead to higher living standards.

SYNOPTIC LINK
The Human Development Index was created to focus on people and their capabilities rather than solely on economic growth. Go back to section 7.2 in Chapter 7, which looked at the problem of poverty, and think about the countries shown in Table 15.2. How would you apply the concepts of absolute and relative poverty to the countries in the table?

CASE STUDY 15.2

Why GNP figures provide an inadequate indicator of economic development

The gross national product includes air pollution and advertising for cigarettes, and ambulances to clear our highways of carnage. It counts special locks for our doors, and jails for the people who break them. GNP includes the destruction of the redwoods and the death of Lake Superior. It grows with the production of napalm and missiles and nuclear warheads...and if GNP includes all this, there is much that it does not comprehend. It does not allow for the health of our families, the quality of their education, or the joy of their play. It is indifferent to the decency of our factories and the safety of our streets alike. It does not include the beauty of our poetry or the strength of our marriages, or the intelligence of our public debate or the integrity of our public officials...GNP measures neither our wit nor our courage, neither our wisdom nor our learning, neither our compassion nor our devotion to our country. It measures everything, in short, except that which makes life worthwhile; and it can tell us everything about America — except whether we are proud to be Americans.

US Senator Robert Kennedy, in 1967

Follow-up questions

1 Distinguish between GNP and GDP.
2 What are the thee methods of measuring national income?
3 Why was the United Nations' Human Development Index (HDI) created?
4 Taking into account what you have learnt earlier in your studies about negative externalities and demerit goods, to what extent does this extract support the view that national income is of little use in measuring economic development?

Table 15.2 The 'top 15' and the 'bottom 15' countries in the Human Development Index, published 2018

HDI rank	Country	Human Development Index (HDI) value, 2017	Life expectancy at birth (years), 2017	Mean years of schooling (years), 2017	Expected years of schooling (years), 2017	Gross national income (GNI) per capita (2011 PPP$), 2017	GNI per capita rank minus HDI rank	HDI rank 2016
Very high human development								
1	Norway	0.953	82.3	12.6	17.9	68,012	5	1
2	Switzerland	0.944	83.5	13.4	16.2	57,625	8	2
2	Australia	0.939	83.1	12.9	22.9	43,560	18	3
4	Ireland	0.938	81.6	12.5	19.6	53,754	8	4
5	Germany	0.936	81.2	14.1	17.0	46,136	13	4
5	Iceland	0.935	82.9	12.4	19.3	45,810	13	6
7	Hong Kong, China (SAR)	0.933	84.1	12.0	16.3	58,420	2	8
8	Sweden	0.933	82.6	12.4	17.6	47,766	9	7
9	Singapore	0.932	83.2	11.5	16.2	82,503	-6	8
10	Netherlands	0.931	82.0	12.2	18.0	47,900	5	10
10	Denmark	0.929	80.9	12.6	19.1	47,918	3	10
12	Canada	0.926	82.5	13.3	16.4	43,433	10	12
13	United States	0.924	79.5	13.4	16.5	54,941	–2	12
14	United Kingdom	0.922	81.7	12.9	17.4	39,116	13	14
15	Finland	0.920	81.5	12.4	17.6	41,002	10	15
Low human development								
175	Guinea	0.459	60.6	2.6	9.1	2,067	–11	177
176	Congo (Democratic Republic of the)	0.457	60.0	6.8	9.8	796	12	176
177	Guinea-Bissau	0.455	57.8	3.0	10.5	1,552	0	175
178	Yemen	0.452	65.2	3.0	9.0	1,239	5	172
179	Eritrea	0.440	65.5	4.0	5.4	1,750	–9	178
180	Mozambique	0.437	58.9	3.5	9.7	1,093	4	179
181	Liberia	0.435	63.0	4.7	10.0	667	9	180
182	Mali	0.427	58.5	2.3	7.7	1,953	–16	181
183	Burkina Faso	0.423	60.8	1.5	8.5	1,650	–7	182
184	Sierra Leone	0.419	52.2	3.5	9.8	1,240	–2	184
185	Burundi	0.417	57.9	3.0	11.7	702	4	183
186	Chad	0.404	53.2	2.3	8.0	1,750	–15	185
187	South Sudan	0.388	57.3	4.8	4.9	963	–1	186
188	Central African Republic	0.367	52.9	4.3	7.2	663	3	187
189	Niger	0.354	60.4	2.0	5.4	906	–2	188

Factors that affect growth and development

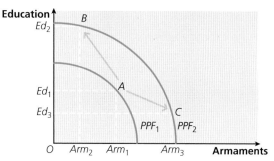

Figure 15.6 Economic growth and development in a country producing just two goods: education and arms

A large number of factors affect both growth and development. One of these that we have covered in some depth in Chapter 10 is investment. Investment in new capital goods and technical progress are two of the main factors leading to long-term economic growth and they are also necessary for economic development. Consider, however, Figure 15.6.

For the simplified economy depicted in Figure 15.6, the outward movement of the economy's production possibility frontier from PPF_1 to PPF_2 illustrates economic growth. However, the movement from point A on PPF_1 to point B on PPF_2 shows that the society is now using more of its available resources to educate its children and is actually devoting fewer resources than before to arms production. The resources devoted to education increase from Ed_1 to Ed_2, whereas those devoted to armaments fall from Arm_1 to Arm_2. Increased investment in the economy has led to economic development as well as economic growth.

By contrast, a movement from point A to point C illustrates economic growth, but almost certainly not economic development, as resources have been shifted from education to armaments. Although new investment has moved the production possibility frontier from PPF_1 to PPF_2, resources have also been shifted from education into arms production. Armament production increases from Arm_1 to Arm_3, but at the expense of education, the output of which falls from Ed_1 to Ed_3. The message is that economic growth can occur without economic development, and indeed at the expense of economic development.

Figure 15.6 also points to the fact that investment in **education and training** is usually an important part of both growth and economic development. Though often considered as meaning the same thing, education and training are in fact slightly different. Education furthers individual knowledge and develops a person's intellect. While a highly educated person is often more employable, however, education is not in itself about getting a job. By contrast, training is about getting a job, or about improving or diversifying skills when in a job. Training is undertaken in order to gain a specific work skill, the possession of which makes a person more employable, either in their existing line of work or through promotion or redeployment into a different type of work.

> **KEY TERM**
>
> **education and training**
> education develops individual knowledge and intellect, while training develops work skills. Both are necessary for economic growth and development.

> **TEST YOURSELF 15.15**
> Explain why a country with a low savings ratio and limited access to finance is going to struggle to achieve economic growth.

Barriers to growth and development

There are, of course, many barriers which prevent or reduce economic growth, and with it the chance for further economic development. Five of these are corruption, institutional factors, infrastructure, inadequate human capital, and a lack of property rights.

Corruption

Corruption, which can be defined as dishonest or illegal behaviour, often in the form of bribery, especially payments to powerful people such as government officials, prevents normal economic activity from taking place. Corruption and bribery, which are often endemic features of life in poor countries, but also in richer countries such as Russia, divert scarce resources away from more productive uses to protect less efficient resource use. Production costs and consumer prices also rise: for example, through 'back-handers' paid by customers to corrupt officials and to employees of firms with which they wish to do business.

SYNOPTIC LINK

It is very difficult for firms to raise capital for investment if potential lenders and investors believe that they are likely to lose money because of corruption. Go back to Chapter 12 where we covered financial markets and think about how trust and transparency are important for a firm seeking to raise finance from banks or capital markets.

TEST YOURSELF 15.16

Suggest two ways in which corruption will affect market transactions and incentives in an economy.

SYNOPTIC LINK

Paying bribes to corrupt government officials adds cost to businesses. In section 4.4 of Chapter 4, we looked at the firm's costs of production. Draw an average total cost curve showing the effect of corruption on a firm.

Institutional factors

Institutional factors, which can differ greatly between less developed and more developed economies, include countries' legal and judicial structures, public administration systems, the availability of, and access to, financial institutions such as banks and capital markets, the role, if any, of the civil service, attitudes to work, and the education and training systems.

The 'law of contract' is an important part of the legal and judicial systems of more developed economies, but contract law is much less well established in many less developed economies and indeed in eastern Europe. An efficient, policed and enforced 'law of contract' should be viewed as a necessary condition for businesses and consumers to 'do business with each other'. For example, without an enforced law of contract, firms may end up not supplying goods or services to consumers and other firms, even though the goods or services have been paid for. In this situation, business transactions may simply not take place.

SYNOPTIC LINK

The appropriate regulation of institutions and markets is necessary for a functioning economy. Go back to earlier chapters to read how UK governments have sought to regulate the British economy. In Chapter 8, section 8.7 we covered competition policy; Chapter 8, section 8.8 looked at regulation; and finally Chapter 12, section 12.4 explained the regulation of the financial system.

Poor infrastructure

It goes almost without saying that rich countries, over the course of their development over decades (and sometimes centuries), have built up an **infrastructure** of roads, railways, telephone and communication networks together with other key elements of a modern economy. Poorer developing countries lack such infrastructure, which is an important factor holding back their development. For example, a lack of roads raises firms' costs of production and makes it difficult or impossible for them to access raw materials and to develop their markets.

To a certain extent, as with other consumer and capital goods, developing countries can offset the disadvantage that lack of infrastructure creates, by using the fruits of technical progress to bypass old technology. A good example is provided by mobile phones. Use of these phones has become ubiquitous in many developing economies, which has circumvented the need to invest in an infrastructure of traditional 'land-line' or terrestrial phones. An example in the future could be investment in drone technology to bypass the need to build traditional roads.

Investment in infrastructure is often done by public-sector investment in social capital, rather than by the private sector. One reason for this is the fact that, being very expensive to undertake, the investment may only pay for itself after a long period of years. Linked to this, much infrastructure investment creates external economies for the private sector. It may be difficult or impossible for infrastructure providers to charge prices to the private-sector firms that yield sufficient profit, and even if prices can be charged, they might deter economic development.

Lack of human capital

Before beginning our coverage of development economics in this chapter, we had made scant reference to **human capital**. Our main reference, in Chapter 9, related the fact that investment in human capital, illustrated in Figure 9.10, can be as important as investment in physical capital goods such as machinery if long-run economic growth and development are to take place. The term 'human capital' is widely used to describe people at work and theircollective knowledge, skills, abilities and capacity to develop and innovate. It embodies their accumulated stock of skills and knowledge that are relevant to their employment.

Investments in both physical capital and human capital are of course *flows*, the purpose of which is to build up *stocks* of physical capital such as machines and trained labour that are needed for on-going growth and development to take place. The purpose of investment in labour training, and often investment in education in general, is to build up the stock of human capital.

We have already explained the meaning and importance of *property rights* in our discussion of market failure in Chapter 8. We wrote there that property rights can be defined as the exclusive authority to determine how a resource is used. In the case of a private property right, the owner of private property such as a bar of chocolate in a sweet shop has the right in law to prevent other people from consuming the bar unless they are prepared to pay a price to the owner.

The traditional and largely undeveloped societies that we mentioned earlier in this section often lack private property rights. Most resources are communally owned. While to some this represents an idyllic paradise economy, to others it is a major cause of a lack of economic development. According to this latter view, the establishment of, and ability to trade in, private property rights is a necessary pre-condition for successful economic development. Tradable private property rights underlie the development of capitalist economies, which are arguably the most successful in achieving economic development.

In contrast, the development of the Russian economy, prior to the collapse of communism, was based to a large extent on state ownership of property rights. Although this successfully created an industrial–military complex, it also created corruption and reduced individual incentives, and it was much less successful in delivering consumer goods to the general Russian population. The absence of sufficient private property rights not only diverted resources away from true economic development, but also led to the eventual disappearance of Russian communism. Unfortunately, it also led to the transfer of previously state-owned property rights to private-sector oligarchs such as Roman Abramovich and to other members of a new super-rich elite.

Policies that might be adopted to promote economic growth and development

According to the OECD, sustainable development can be interpreted in economic terms as 'development that lasts' — that is, a path along which the maximisation of human well-being for today's generations does not lead to declines in future well-being.

Macro and micro policies to promote economic growth

An obvious point from which to start our analysis of appropriate policies for promoting economic growth and development is the standard macroeconomic and microeconomic government policies explained in earlier chapters. These include demand-side fiscal policy and monetary policy and supply-side policies, all of which can be focused on achieving economic growth and development and overall economic stability.

The danger is that pursuing 'growth for growth's sake' might lead to outcomes in which the costs of growth, such as environment depletion and degradation, exceed the benefits of higher living standards and economic welfare that growth is supposed to bring about. If this is the case, growth may very well be at the expense of development.

Hence the need for appropriate microeconomic policies to reduce or correct the various market failures that growth may bring about. These can include the use of taxes and subsidies, respectively, to punish or deter the production of negative externalities and demerit goods, and to encourage the production of positive externalities and merit goods. Redistributive policies may also be deemed necessary to narrow the unjustifiable inequalities in the distributions of income and wealth, though, as we have seen, such policies may harm the

SYNOPTIC LINK

Go back to Chapter 11 and read over our explanation of economic growth. Then read over Chapter 12, section 12.3 which covered monetary policy and Chapter 13 which looked at fiscal policy and supply-side policy. Also, read Case study 8.5 in Chapter 8, which looks at atmospheric pollution caused by economic growth. Think carefully about how a government develops both short-term and long-term policies to promote economic growth.

KEY TERM

aid money, goods and services and 'soft' loans given by the government of one country or a multilateral institution such as the World Bank to help another country. Non-government organisations (NGOs) such as Oxfam also provide aid.

incentives provided by markets that many think are essential for sustained growth and development. However, there is a growing consensus that a high level of inequality is a barrier to growth and many would argue that an excessive degree of inequality is incompatible with development. An equitable distribution of income is generally regarded as a characteristic of a developed economy.

Economists and politicians sometimes argue that a higher level of state intervention is required to bring about growth and development in poor countries than in more developed economies. Believers in the virtues of free markets disagree, citing the many cases of government failure that state intervention brings about. In recent decades, pro-free-market approaches have generally gained the upper hand, though not completely so. The strategic trade theory justification of a degree of protectionism in developing countries is a case in point. In practice, there is a strong case for combining market-based instruments with some forms of government intervention.

Capital flight

Some problems which affect growth and development are much more serious in poor countries than in more developed economies. 'Capital flight', which is the sudden withdrawal of money out of a country, affects poor countries much more than it affects economies such as the UK. It occurs, for example, when the ruling elite within an economy move the profits they make from the country's industries into foreign bank accounts, instead of re-investing profits within the country to secure its further development. Capital flight, which is partly the result of free-market forces, can be reduced if not completely controlled by government and central bank intervention: for example, through the use of rigorously applied foreign exchange controls.

Capital flight is a major problem in sub-Saharan Africa as it impacts negatively on capital-scarce economies, such as Burundi, which generate very little saving from their own, generally very poor, populations. Trillions of dollars have flown out of Africa over the last four decades. Capital flight has accelerated since 2000, a period that has coincided with high profits being generated from the exploitation of Africa's mineral resources. Evidence suggests that capital flight has significantly undermined Africa's growth and development, through the siphoning of potential investment funds out of the continent.

The role of aid and trade in promoting growth and development

Economists often debate the issue of whether **aid** is more important than trade (or vice versa) in promoting economic development. The orthodox view in countries such as the UK and the USA is that free trade and trade liberalisation are more important than aid in this respect. Free-market economists believe that international specialisation and complete free trade, undertaken in accordance with the principle of comparative advantage, benefits all the countries involved.

The strategic trade theory argument

However, not all economists agree. The Korean economist Ha-Joon Chang has written that 'History debunks the free trade myth' (**www.theguardian.com/business/2002/jun/24/globalisation**). Ha-Joon Chang's view is that governments in already developed economies are fully in favour of free trade — but only if their countries face little or no competition from developing economies. As soon as such competition emerges, the rich countries 'pull up the drawbridge', arguing that protectionism is necessary to protect themselves from the 'unfair' competition coming from cheap labour countries. Rich countries also argue that they need protecting from countries in the much poorer developing world which steal their technology and clone their products, partly by ignoring international patent laws and other aspects of intellectual copyright. However, transfers of technology can be an important mechanism for stimulating the development of the world's less prosperous economies.

As we explained on page 509, strategic trade theorists such as Paul Krugman have also argued that developing countries can speed up the pace of development by first selecting, and then protecting, key industries deemed vital for successful economic growth.

The counter-argument

Having said this, there is plenty of evidence that the growth of free trade and improved transport links — brought about, for example, by the containerisation of cargo — have been major factors responsible for the huge growth in international trade over recent decades. Moreover, the argument for trade rather than aid is quite broad and is not necessarily just about free trade. Developing countries can benefit from preferential trading arrangements, both with each other, and also with richer developed countries. And countering the strategic trade theory argument, trade may allow a developing economy to build up its own industries and encourages investment in other activities that promote development, such as good governance, property rights, infrastructure and investment in human capital.

The various forms of aid

International aid provided by richer countries and directed at less developed countries takes many forms, some of which are not really aid at all:

- **Military aid** has to be spent buying the weaponry of the donor country, although it is questionable if this can be classified as aid.
- A **'hard' loan**, usually given in a hard currency, has to be paid back at a market rate of interest, which is aid in the loosest sense.
- A **'soft' loan**, by contrast, has a below-market rate of interest attached and may even be free in the sense that, although the loan must eventually be repaid, little or no interest is charged by the donor country.
- **Disaster relief** — much of this is dispensed by non-governmental organisations (NGOs) with their headquarters in developed economies. Sometimes this is matched by government-funded relief — for example, in 2015, in response to the devastating earthquake in Nepal, the UK government pledged to match every pound of disaster aid raised by NGOs, such as the Red Cross, with taxpayers' money. However, disaster relief, though very necessary to limit the human cost of events such as droughts and floods, is mostly a form of 'band-aid' relief, applying 'sticking plasters' to the results of natural disasters and civil conflict, but contributing little or nothing in itself to economic development. And in some cases, when drought and war are ongoing and seem never to end, as has been the case in Sudan, disaster relief may build up among sufferers a state of dependency on the generosity of those who feel honour-bound to continue to give. Several instances of corruption and sexual misdemeanour have

also been reported in recent years involving NGO officials exploiting aid recipients.

- **'Tied' aid** — this can take the form of either a 'soft' loan or a gift of money that has to be spent on the exports of the country granting the aid. Arguably, this can benefit the donor country as much as, if not more than, the recipient country.
- Richer donor countries can also give aid by **'lending' their experts** to a less developed country to offer advice on matters such as improving the country's governance, its methods of production, how to use advanced technology and the maintenance of transport links and other forms of infrastructure. In recent years, China has gone one stage further by using Chinese workers and managers to build roads and other types of infrastructure in a number of African developing countries — though in return the developing countries have agreed to sell their exports of minerals and other raw materials to China rather than to competitor countries.

> **SYNOPTIC LINK**
> Aid is often given to a less developed country with the intention of lifting people out of poverty. Go back to Chapter 7 and consider how effective various forms of aid are at alleviating poverty.

Effective and ineffective aid

Of course, economic aid of the right type does promote economic development. For example, in a country where domestic savings are low, aid can be used to finance the domestic accumulation of capital, and it can also provide vital foreign exchange to finance the import of capital goods and resources.

However, it has sometimes been argued that the export of high-technology capital goods in foreign aid programmes, from rich to poor countries, equips less developed countries with the 'wrong sort of technology'. One problem facing the poor country is that when a 'high-tech' piece of equipment breaks down, the country may lack people with sufficient expertise to repair it. Additionally, spare parts produced in developed economies may have to be bought and this uses up foreign exchange which is in short supply. Far better, it has been argued, for developing countries to focus on intermediate, less capital-intensive technology, rather than on advanced technology. Intermediate technologies are more suited to the often cheap and plentiful labour in poorer developing countries, while savings needed to finance the purchase of expensive capital goods and foreign exchange are scarce.

The fact that both trade and aid in developing countries are often 'skewed' to the purchase of high-technology goods often results from the desire of the countries' governments and ruling elites to invest in prestige projects such as a national airline which 'flies the flag' for the country.

Trade versus aid: a conclusion

In conclusion, free-market economists argue that trade is more important than aid in relation to economic development. Until quite recently, it was said that aid to Africa actually made the continent poorer rather than better off. This was contrasted with Asia where economic development

> **SYNOPTIC LINK**
> At this point it would be useful to read once again our coverage of globalisation and multinational corporations in Chapter 14. Think carefully about how the process of globalisation and MNCs have affected trade and global economic activity.

was the result of increased trade rather than aid. However, in its 2014 report, *Economic Development in Africa*, UNCTAD, the United Nations body responsible for dealing with development issues, particularly international trade, said:

> Africa has experienced high and continuous economic growth in the past decade, prompting analysts to argue that the continent has reached a turning point in its development history and is poised to play a more significant role in the global economy in the twenty-first century. Unlike in the 1980s and 1990s, Africa's average growth rate since the turn of the millennium has also been higher than the average growth rate of the world economy.

UNCTAD believes that international aid has played a significant role in economic development in Africa, although much aid has been disaster relief rather than true economic aid. China is now providing much of the aid given to African countries, albeit with many strings attached, such as the requirement to export minerals and other natural resources back to China.

SECTION 15.2 SUMMARY

- Economic development is not the same as economic growth.
- Free-market economists generally argue that reducing barriers to international trade is more important than aid in promoting economic development.
- Strategic trade theorists, by contrast, advocate the case for strategic protection in developing countries.
- Economic growth has costs as well as benefits, but costs are fewer and benefits greater when successful economic development takes place.
- Most economists agree that some forms of aid are good but that other forms are questionable in terms of promoting economic development.
- Trade may be a more significant cause of development than aid.

Questions

1 Distinguish between a floating and a fixed exchange rate.

2 Is the UK pound's current exchange rate floating or fixed?

3 Would you agree that there has been an exchange rate crisis in the UK in the period before and after Brexit? Justify your answer.

4 Using a demand and supply diagram, explain how a trade deficit is eliminated in a freely floating exchange rate system.

5 Explain the advantages and disadvantages of a floating exchange rate.

6 Distinguish between economic growth and economic development.

7 Explain **three** factors that might affect the growth and development of a country in sub-Saharan Africa.

8 Do you agree that national income figures provide an inadequate measure of economic development? Justify your answer.

Macroeconomics key terms

absolute advantage a country has an absolute advantage if it can produce more of a good than other countries from the same amount of resources.

accelerator a change in the level of investment in new capital goods induced by a change in national income or output. The size of the accelerator depends on the economy's capital–output ratio.

actual output level of real output produced in the economy in a particular year — not to be confused with the trend level of output, which is what the economy is capable of producing when working at full capacity. Actual output differs from the trend level of output when there are output gaps.

aggregate demand total planned spending on real output in the economy at different price levels.

aggregate supply the level of real national output that producers are prepared to supply at different average price levels.

aid money, goods and services and 'soft' loans given by the government of one country or a multilateral institution such as the World Bank to help another country. Non-government organisations (NGOs) such as Oxfam also provide aid.

assets things which people or organisations *own*.

automatic stabilisers fiscal policy instruments, such as progressive taxes and income-related welfare benefits, that automatically stimulate aggregate demand in an economic downswing and depress aggregate demand in an upswing, thereby 'smoothing' the economic cycle.

availability of credit funds available for households and firms to borrow.

balance of payments a record of all the currency flows into and out of a country in a particular time period.

balance of primary income inward primary income flows comprising both inward-income flowing into the economy in the current year generated by UK-owned capital assets located overseas, and outward primary income flows comprising income flowing out of the economy in the current year generated by overseas-owned capital assets located in the UK.

balance of secondary income current transfers, e.g. gifts of money, international aid and transfers between the UK and the EU, flowing into or out of the UK economy in a particular year.

balance of trade the difference between the money value of a country's imports and its exports. Balance of trade is the largest component of a country's balance of payments on current account.

balance of trade deficit when the money value of a country's imports exceeds the money value of its exports.

balance of trade in goods the part of the current account measuring payments for exports and imports of goods. The difference between the total value of exports and the total value of imports is sometimes called the 'balance of visible trade'.

balance of trade in services part of the current account, the difference between the payments for the exports of services and the payments for the imports of services.

balance of trade surplus when the money value of a country's exports exceeds the money value of its imports

balancing the budget when government spending equals government revenue ($G = T$).

Bank Rate the rate of interest that the Bank of England pays to commercial banks on their deposits held at the Bank of England.

bonds financial securities sold by companies (corporate bonds) or by governments (government bonds) which are a form of long-term borrowing. Bonds usually have a maturity date on which they are redeemed, with the borrower usually making a fixed interest payment each year until the bond matures.

broad money the part of the stock of money (or money supply) made up of cash, other liquid assets such as bank and building society deposits, but also some illiquid assets. The measure of broad money used by the Bank of England is called M4.

budget deficit occurs when government spending exceeds government revenue ($G > T$). This represents a net injection of demand into the circular flow of income and hence a budget deficit is expansionary.

budget surplus occurs when government spending is less than government revenue ($G < T$). This represents a net withdrawal from the circular flow of income and hence a budget surplus is contractionary.

capital markets where securities such as shares and bonds are issued to raise medium- to long-term financing, and where shares and bonds are then traded on the 'second-hand' part of the market, e.g. the London Stock Exchange.

capital ratio the amount of capital on a bank's balance sheet as a proportion of its loans.

central bank a national bank that provides financial and banking services for its country's government and banking system, as well as implementing the government's monetary policy and issuing currency. The Bank of England is the UK's central bank.

claimant count the method of measuring unemployment according to those people who are claiming unemployment-related benefits (Jobseeker's Allowance).

closed economy an economy with no international trade.

commercial bank (also known as a **retail bank** or **high-street bank**) a financial institution which aims to make profits by selling banking services to its customers.

comparative advantage this is measured in terms of opportunity cost. The country with the least opportunity cost when producing a good possesses a comparative advantage in that good.

consumer prices index the official measure used to calculate the rate of consumer price inflation in the UK. It calculates the average price increase of a basket of 700 different consumer goods and services.

consumption total planned spending by households on consumer goods and services produced within the economy.

contractionary fiscal policy uses fiscal policy to decrease aggregate demand and to shift the *AD* curve to the left.

contractionary monetary policy uses higher interest rates to decrease aggregate demand and to shift the *AD* curve to the left.

corporate bonds debt security issued by a company and sold as new issues to people who lend long-term to the company. They can usually be resold second-hand on a stock exchange.

corruption a barrier holding back economic growth and development, especially in less developed economies.

cost-push inflation (also known as **cost inflation**) a rising price level caused by an increase in the costs of production, shown by a shift of the *SRAS* curve to the left.

coupon the guaranteed fixed annual interest payment, often divided into two 6-month payments, paid by the issuer of a bond to the owner of the bond.

credit when a bank makes a loan it creates credit. The loan results in the creation of an advance, which is an asset on the bank's balance sheet, and a deposit, which is a liability of the bank.

credit crunch occurs when there is a lack of funds available in the credit market, making it difficult for borrowers to obtain financing, and leads to a rise in the cost of borrowing.

crowding out a situation in which an increase in government or public-sector spending displaces private-sector spending, with little or no increase in aggregate demand.

currency union an agreement between a group of countries to share a common currency, and usually to have a single monetary and foreign exchange rate policy.

current account measures all the currency flows into and out of a country in a particular time period in payment for exports and imports of goods and services, together with primary and secondary income flows (previously known as 'income flows and transfers').

current account deficit currency outflows in the current account exceed the currency inflows.

current account surplus currency inflows in the current account exceed the currency outflows.

customs unions trading blocs in which member countries enjoy internal free trade in goods and possibly services, with all the member countries protected by a common external tariff barrier.

cyclical budget deficit the part of the budget deficit which rises in the downswing of the economic cycle and falls in the upswing of the cycle.

cyclical unemployment (also known as **Keynesian unemployment** and **demand-deficient unemployment**) unemployment caused by a lack of aggregate demand in the economy, occurring when the economy goes into a recession or depression.

debt people's financial liabilities or money they owe.

deficit financing deliberately running a budget deficit and then borrowing to finance the deficit.

deflation a continuing tendency for the average price level to fall.

deindustrialisation the decline of manufacturing industries, together with coal mining.

demand-pull inflation (also known as **demand inflation**) a rising price level caused by an increase in aggregate demand, shown by a shift of the *AD* curve to the right.

demand side relates to the impact of changes in aggregate demand on the economy. Associated with Keynesian economics.

demand-side fiscal policy used to increase or decrease the level of aggregate demand (and to shift the *AD* curve right or left) through changes in government spending, taxation and the budget balance.

deregulation involves removing previously imposed regulations. It is the opposite of regulation.

direct tax a tax that cannot be shifted by the person legally liable to pay the tax onto someone else. Direct taxes are levied on income and wealth.

discretionary fiscal policy involves making discrete changes to *G*, *T* and the budget deficit to manage the level of aggregate demand.

disinflation a slowing down in the rate of inflation, e.g. from 3% to 2%.

distribution of income the spread of different incomes among individuals and different income groups in the economy.

economic cycle (also known as a **business cycle** or **trade cycle**) upswing and downswing in aggregate economic activity taking place over 4 to 12 years.

economic shock an unexpected event hitting the economy. Economic shocks can be demand-side or supply-side shocks (and sometimes both) and unfavourable or favourable.

education and training education develops individual knowledge and intellect, while training develops work skills. Both are necessary for economic growth and development.

equilibrium national income the level of income at which withdrawals from the circular flow of income equal injections into the flow; also the level of output at which aggregate demand equals aggregate supply.

equilibrium unemployment exists when the economy's aggregate labour market is in equilibrium. It is the same as the natural *level* of unemployment.

equity the assets which people own.

European Union an economic and partially political union established in 1993 after the ratification of the Maastricht Treaty by members of the European Community

and since expanded to include numerous central and eastern European nations.

eurozone (also known as **euro area**) the name used for the group of EU countries that have replaced their national currencies with the euro. Before 2019, 19 of the then 28 EU countries were in the eurozone, though this may change in future years.

exchange rate the external price of a currency, usually measured against another currency.

expansionary fiscal policy uses fiscal policy to increase aggregate demand and to shift the *AD* curve to the right.

expansionary monetary policy uses lower interest rates to increase aggregate demand and to shift the *AD* curve to the right.

expenditure-reducing policy a government policy which aims to eliminate a current account deficit by reducing the demand for imports by reducing the level of aggregate demand in the economy. Conversely, to reduce a current account surplus, aggregate demand would be increased and spending on imports would rise.

expenditure-switching policy a government policy which aims to reduce a current account deficit by switching domestic demand away from imports to domestically produced goods. Conversely, to reduce a current account surplus, the policy would aim to switch domestic demand away from domestically produced goods toward imports.

export-led growth in the short run, economic growth resulting from an increase in exports, which is one of the components of aggregate demand. In the long run, economic growth resulting from the growth and increased international competitiveness of exporting industries.

export subsidies money given to domestic firms by the government to encourage firms to sell their products abroad and to help make their goods cheaper in export markets.

exports domestically produced goods or services sold to residents of other countries.

financial account the part of the balance of payments which records capital flows into and out of the economy.

Financial Conduct Authority aims to make sure that financial markets work well so that consumers get a fair deal, by ensuring that the financial industry is run with integrity and that consumers can trust that firms have their best interests at heart, and by providing consumers with appropriate financial products and services.

financial markets markets in which financial assets or securities are traded.

Financial Policy Committee the part of the Bank of England charged with the primary objective of identifying, monitoring and taking action to remove or reduce systemic risks with a view to protecting and enhancing the resilience of the UK financial system. The committee's secondary objective is to support the economic policy of the government.

fiscal policy the use by the government of government spending and taxation to try to achieve the government's policy objectives.

fixed exchange rate an exchange rate fixed at a certain level by the country's central bank and maintained by the central bank's intervention in the foreign exchange market.

foreign direct investment investment in capital assets, e.g. manufacturing and service industry capacity, in a foreign country by a business with headquarters in another country. Very often the overseas company establishes subsidiary companies in the countries in which it is investing.

foreign exchange markets (forex, FX or currency markets) global, decentralised markets for the trading of currencies. The main participants in this market are large international commercial banks. Collectively, foreign exchange markets are the largest markets in the global economy.

forward guidance attempts to send signals to financial markets, businesses and individuals, about the Bank of England's interest rate policy in the months and years ahead, so that economic agents are not surprised by a sudden and unexpected change in policy.

freely floating exchange rate the exchange rate is determined solely by the interplay of demand for, and supply of, the currency.

free trade area in a free trade area, member countries abolish tariffs on mutual trade, but each partner determines its own tariffs on trade with non-member countries.

frictional unemployment (also known as **transitional unemployment**) unemployment that is usually short term and occurs when a worker switches between jobs.

full employment according to Beveridge's definition, full employment means 3% or less of the labour force unemployed. According to the free-market definition, it is the level of employment occurring at the market-clearing real-wage rate, where the number of workers whom employers wish to hire equals the number of workers wanting to work.

full employment income the level of income when the economy is producing on its production possibility frontier, with no spare capacity.

globalisation the process of increasing economic integration of the world's economies.

government bonds debt security, in the UK known as gilt-edged securities or gilts, issued by a government and sold as new issues to people who lend long-term to the government. They can be resold second-hand on a stock exchange.

gross domestic product the sum of all goods and services, or level of output, produced in the economy over a period of time, e.g. 1 year.

hidden economy (also known as the **informal economy**, the **underground economy** and the **black economy**) all the economic transactions conducted in cash which are not recorded in the national income figures because of tax evasion.

human capital the skills, knowledge and experience possessed by the population.

imports goods or services produced in other countries and sold to residents of this country.

indexation the automatic adjustment of items such as pensions and welfare benefits to changes in the price level, through the use of a price index.

index number a number used in an index, such as the consumer prices index, to enable accurate comparisons over time to be made. The base year index number is typically 100. In subsequent years, percentage increases cause the index number to rise above the index number recorded for the previous year, and percentage decreases cause the index number to fall below the index number recorded for the previous year.

indicators of development these include gross domestic product (GDP) per head, information on the distribution of income, mortality rates and health statistics.

indirect tax a tax that can be shifted by the person legally liable to pay the tax onto someone else, e.g. through raising the price of a good being sold by the taxpayer. Indirect taxes are levied on spending.

inflation a persistent or continuing rise in the average price level.

infrastructure for the most part, the result of past investment in buildings, roads, bridges, power supplies, fast broadband and other fixed capital goods that are needed for the economy to operate efficiently.

injection spending entering the circular flow of income as a result of investment, government spending and exports.

institutional factors examples include rules, laws, constitutions, the financial system and defined property rights.

interventionist policies occur when the government intervenes in, and sometimes replaces, free markets. Interventionist supply-side policies include government funding of research and development.

investment total planned spending by firms on capital goods produced within the economy.

investment bank a bank which does not generally accept deposits from ordinary members of the general public. Traditional 'investment banking' refers to financial advisory work, such as advising private companies on how to become a public company by floating on the stock market, or advising public companies on how to buy up another company. Investment banks also deal directly in financial markets for their own account.

involuntary unemployment
occurs when workers are willing
to work at current market wage
rates but there are no jobs
available.

Keynesian economists followers
of the economist John Maynard
Keynes, who generally believe
that governments should manage
the economy, particularly through
the use of fiscal policy.

Labour Force Survey a quarterly
sample survey of households
in the UK. Its purpose is to
provide information on the UK
labour market. The survey seeks
information on respondents'
personal circumstances and their
labour market status during a
period of 1–4 weeks.

less developed countries
countries considered behind in
terms of their economy, human
capital, infrastructure and
industrial base.

liabilities things which people or
organisations *owe*.

life-cycle theory of consumption
a theory that explains
consumption and saving in
terms of how people expect their
incomes to change over the whole
of their life cycles.

liquidity measures the ease with
which an asset can be converted
into cash without loss of value.
Cash is the most liquid of all
assets.

liquidity ratio the ratio of a bank's
cash and other liquid assets to its
deposits.

long-run aggregate supply
the real output that can be
supplied when the economy
is on its production possibility
frontier. This is when all the
available factors of production are
employed and producing at their
'normal capacity' level of output.

long-run economic growth
an increase in the economy's
potential level of real output,
and an outward movement of the
economy's production possibility
frontier.

macroeconomic indicator
provides information from recent
economic performance for
judging the success or failure of
a particular type of government
policy, e.g. fiscal policy or
monetary policy.

marginal propensity to consume
the fraction of any increase in
income which people plan to
spend on the consumption of
domestically produced goods and
services.

marginal propensity to save the
fraction of any increase in income
which people plan to save rather
than spend.

**market-based supply-side
policies** (or **non-interventionist
supply-side policies**) these
policies free up markets, promote
competition and greater efficiency,
and reduce the economic role of
the state.

marketisation (also known as
commercialisation) involves
shifting provision of goods or
services from the non-market
sector to the market sector.

maturity date the date on which
the issuer of a dated security, such
as a gilt-edged security (long-
dated) or a Treasury bill (short-
dated), pays the face value of the
security to the security's owner.

monetarism narrow monetarism
centres on increases in the money
supply as the prime cause of
inflation. Broader monetarism
focuses on the virtues of free
markets in resource allocation.

monetarists economists who
argue that a prior increase in
the money supply is the cause of
inflation.

monetary policy the use by the
government and its agent, the
Bank of England, of interest rates
and other monetary instruments
to try to achieve the government's
policy objectives.

Monetary Policy Committee
the part of the Bank of England
which implements UK monetary
policy. The UK government sets

the monetary policy objectives
or targets, currently a 2% CPI
inflation rate target, with the MPC
then implementing monetary
policy to try to 'hit' the target(s).

monetary policy instruments
tools such as Bank Rate which are
used to try to achieve monetary
policy objectives.

money primarily a medium of
exchange or means of payment,
but also a store of value.

money markets provide a means
for lenders and borrowers to
satisfy their short-term financial
needs. Assets that are bought
and sold on money markets
are short term, with maturities
ranging from a day to a year, and
are normally easily convertible
into cash. The term 'money
market' is an umbrella that
covers several markets, including
the markets for Treasury bills
and commercial bills.

money supply the stock of financial
assets which function as money.

moral hazard the tendency
of individuals and firms,
once protected against some
contingency, to behave so as to
make that contingency more likely.

more developed countries
countries with a high degree of
economic development, high
average income per head, high
standards of living, usually with
service industries dominating
manufacturing, and investment
having taken place over many
years in human capital and
infrastructure.

multinational corporations
enterprises operating in
several countries but with their
headquarters in one country.

multiplier the relationship
between a change in aggregate
demand and the resulting
generally larger change in
national income.

narrow money the part of the
stock of money (or money supply)
made up of cash and liquid bank
and building society deposits.

national capital stock the stock of capital goods, e.g. buildings and machinery, in the economy that has accumulated over time and is measured at a point in time.

national debt the *stock* of all past government borrowing that has not been paid back.

national income the *flow* of new output produced by the economy in a particular period, e.g. a year, measured by the flow of factor incomes.

national product (also known as **national output**) the *flow* of new output produced by different industries in a particular period, e.g. a year.

national wealth the stock of all goods that exist at a point in time that have value in the economy.

natural rate of unemployment the rate of unemployment when the aggregate labour market is in equilibrium.

negative output gap the level of *actual* real output in the economy is lower than the *trend* output level.

nominal GDP GDP measured at the current market prices, without removing the effects of inflation.

normal capacity level of output the level of output at which the full production potential of the economy is being used.

Office for Budget Responsibility advisory public body that provides independent economic forecasts and analysis of the public finances as background to the preparation of the UK budget.

open economy an economy open to international trade.

output gaps show the level of *actual* real output in the economy either higher or lower than the *trend* output level.

Phillips curve based on evidence from the economy, shows the apparent relationship between the rate of inflation and the rate of unemployment. Now known as 'the short-run Phillips curve'.

policy conflict occurs when two policy objectives cannot both be achieved at the same time: the better the performance in achieving one objective, the worse the performance in achieving the other.

policy objective a target or goal that policy-makers aim to 'hit'.

portfolio investment the purchase of one country's securities, e.g. bonds and shares, by the residents or financial institutions of another country.

positive output gap the level of *actual* real output in the economy is greater than the *trend* output level.

price index an index number showing the extent to which a price, or a 'basket' of prices, has changed over a month, quarter or year, in comparison with the price(s) in a base year.

principle of taxation (also known as a **canon of taxation**) a criterion used for judging whether a tax is good or bad.

privatisation involves shifting ownership of state-owned assets to the private sector.

profitability the state or condition of yielding a financial profit or gain.

pro-free-market economists opponents of Keynesian economists, who dislike government intervention in the economy and who much prefer the operation of free markets.

proportional taxation when the proportion of income paid in tax stays the same as income increases.

Prudential Regulation Authority the part of the Bank of England responsible for the microprudential regulation and supervision of banks, building societies, credit unions, insurers and major investment firms.

purchasing power parity (PPP) exchange rates the rates of currency conversion that equalise the purchasing power of different currencies by eliminating the differences in price levels between countries.

quantitative easing when the Bank of England buys assets, usually government bonds, with money that the Bank has created electronically.

quantity theory of money the oldest theory of inflation, which states that inflation is caused by a persistent increase in the supply of money.

quotas physical limits on the quantities of imported goods allowed into a country.

rate of interest the reward for lending savings to somebody else (e.g. a bank) and the cost of borrowing.

real GDP a measure of all the goods and services produced in an economy, adjusted for price changes or inflation. The adjustment transforms changes in nominal GDP, which is measured in money terms, into a measure that reflects changes in the total output of the economy.

real wages the purchasing power of the nominal (or money) wage; for example, real wages fall when inflation is higher than the rise in the nominal wage rate and real wages rise when the nominal wage rate increases more rapidly than inflation.

real-wage unemployment unemployment caused by real wages being stuck above the equilibrium market-clearing real wage.

recession in the UK and many other countries, a recession is defined as 6 months or more of negative economic growth or declining real national output.

reflationary policies policies that increase aggregate demand with the intention of increasing real output and employment.

regressive taxation when the proportion of income paid in tax falls as income increases.

retail prices index a measure formerly used to calculate the rate of consumer price inflation in the UK.

saving income which is not spent.

seasonal unemployment unemployment arising in different seasons of the year, caused by factors such as the weather and the end of the Christmas shopping period.

security secured loans, such as mortgage loans secured against the value of property, are less risky for banks than unsecured loans.

shares undated financial assets, sold initially by a company to raise financial capital. Shares sold by public companies or PLCs are marketable on a stock exchange, but shares sold by private companies are not marketable. Unlike a loan, a share signifies that the holder owns part of the enterprise.

short-run economic growth growth of real output resulting from using idle resources, including labour, thereby taking up the slack in the economy.

structural budget deficit the part of the budget deficit which is not affected by the economic cycle but results from structural change in the economy affecting the government's finances, and also from long-term government policy decisions.

structural unemployment long-term unemployment occurring when some industries are declining, even though other industries may be growing. Also occurs within a growing industry if automation reduces the demand for labour, and when production requires new skills not possessed by the workers who lose their jobs. Structural unemployment is associated with the occupational and geographical immobility of labour.

supply side relates to changes in the potential output of the economy, which is affected by the available factors of production, e.g. changes in the size of the labour force, and the productivity of labour.

supply-side economics a branch of free-market economics arguing that government policy should be used to improve the competitiveness and efficiency of markets and, through this, the performance of the economy.

supply-side fiscal policy used to increase the economy's ability to produce and supply goods, through creating incentives to work, save, invest, and be entrepreneurial. Interventionist supply-side fiscal policies, such as the financing of retraining schemes for unemployed workers, are also designed to improve supply-side performance.

supply-side improvements reforms undertaken by the private sector to increase productivity so as to reduce costs and to become more efficient and competitive. Supply-side improvement often results from more investment and innovation, often undertaken by firms without prompting from the government.

supply-side policies government economic policies which aim to make markets more competitive and efficient, increase production potential, and shift the *LRAS* curve to the right. Supply-side fiscal policy is arguably the most important type of supply-side policy, but there are also non-fiscal supply-side policies.

systemic risk in a financial context, this refers to the risk of a breakdown of the entire financial system, caused by inter-linkages within the financial system, rather than simply the failure of an individual bank or financial institution within the system.

tariffs (also known as **import duties**) taxes imposed on imports from other countries entering a country.

total managed expenditure the total amount that the government spends. It splits into the amount that government departments such as defence have been allocated to spend and spending that is not controlled by a government department, including welfare, pensions and national debt interest payments.

trade-off between policy objectives although it may be impossible to achieve two desirable objectives at the same time, e.g. zero inflation and full employment, policy-makers may be able to choose an acceptable combination lying between the extremes, e.g. 2% inflation and 4% unemployment.

trend growth rate the rate at which output can grow, on a sustained basis, without putting upward or downward pressure on inflation. It reflects the annual average percentage increase in the productive capacity of the economy.

United Nations Human Development Index an index based on life expectancy, education and per capita income indicators, which ranks the world's countries into four tiers of human development. These are: (i) very high human development; (ii) high human development; (iii) medium human development; (iv) low human development.

withdrawal a leakage of spending power out of the circular flow of income into savings, taxation or imports.

World Trade Organization an international body whose purpose is to promote free trade by persuading countries to abolish import tariffs and other barriers to trade. As such, it has become closely associated with globalisation.

Practice questions

Paper 1: Markets and market failure

Context 1

Total for this context: 40 marks

Mergers in the UK supermarket industry

Study **Extracts A**, **B** and **C**, and then answer **all** parts of Context 1 which follow.

Extract A: The percentage market shares in the UK grocery market of the 'Top Eight' UK supermarkets, for the 12 weeks ending 9 September 2018

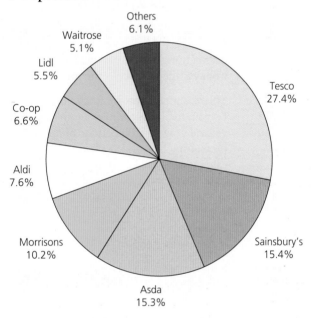

Source: News reports

Extract B: The Competition and Markets Authority's investigation of the proposed merger between Sainsbury's and Asda

In September 2018, the Competition and Markets Authority (CMA) published a first phase report on the proposed merger between Sainsbury's and Asda supermarkets. The CMA said it had found a realistic prospect of a significant lessening of competition in 463 places in the UK where local supermarkets' catchment areas overlapped. A key factor affecting the outcome for Sainsbury's and Asda would be the CMA's decision on whether to consider Aldi and Lidl stores, which are generally under 1,400 square metres in size, as direct competitors to larger Sainsbury's and Asda outlets.

585

5

The CMA pointed out that the companies are two of the largest grocery retailers in the UK, with overlapping stores in hundreds of local areas, 'where shoppers could face higher prices or a worse quality of service'. The two supermarket companies have said that the merger would allow them to pass on a 10% reduction in costs to shoppers in the form of lower prices. They pledged also to maintain their existing brands.

In the outcome, in April 2019 the CMA blocked the merger between Sainsbury's and Asda supermarkets. The CMA was unconvinced that the merger was in the best interest of shoppers, or indeed anyone other than the bosses of the two companies.

Source: News reports

Extract C: Mergers in the supermarket industry

Firms can grow in different ways. Horizontal growth occurs when firms undertaking similar activities merge. By contrast, vertical growth occurs when a firm grows by expanding back up its supply chain. A third type of growth, called conglomerate growth, results from the merger of firms in completely different industries.

Recent mergers in the supermarket industry exhibit all three of these kinds of growth. The merger between Sainsbury's and Asda would have been a horizontal defensive merger designed to protect both companies from competition from the much smaller German upstarts, Aldi and Lidl.

The recent takeover by Tesco, the UK's largest retail supermarket chain, of Booker, the largest wholesaler in the UK food market, was an example of vertical growth. Competition authorities such as the CMA have in the past been suspicious of vertical mergers, fearing, for example, that once Tesco came to own Booker, it might order its wholesaling subsidiary either to refuse to supply groceries to rival supermarkets such as Morrisons, or to charge artificially high prices to these rival firms. The CMA did, however, approve the merger, reflecting the view of some economists that because markets always operate in the interest of consumers, firms should be free to merge, without any interference by regulatory authorities.

Both the horizontal Sainsbury's–Asda merger, had it taken place, and the vertical Tesco–Booker merger can be seen as defensive reactions to the 2017 takeover by the internet-based company Amazon of Whole Foods Market. Because Amazon is globally very large and also an internet-based company, this could be game changing for the traditional supermarket industry. Amazon was the fourth biggest business in the USA, accounting for 43% of online sales in the States. Whole Foods Market was tiny in comparison. Prior to the merger, Amazon owned no supermarkets. This was therefore a conglomerate merger of firms in completely different industries.

Source: news reports

01 Using the information in **Extract A**, calculate the three-firm concentration ratio in the UK grocery market in September 2018. Give your answer, as a percentage, to 1 decimal place. **(2 marks)**

02 Explain how the data in in **Extracts A** and **B** indicate that the UK supermarket industry is a competitive oligopoly. **(4 marks)**

03 'Because Amazon is globally very large and also an internet-based company, this could be game changing for the traditional supermarket industry' (**Extract C**, lines 23–25).

With help of an appropriate diagram, explain how the entry of Amazon into the supermarket industry may affect competition and prices in the industry. **(9 marks)**

04 **Extract C** (lines 17–19) states that 'because markets always operate in the interest of consumers, firms should be free to merge, without any interference by regulatory authorities'.

Evaluate this statement. **(25 marks)**

Essay 1

'Traditionally, economic policy-makers have set out to change consumer behaviour by using taxation and subsidies to create incentives and disincentives, whereas behavioural economists seek to nudge consumers into making better decisions.'

(a) Explain three policies that behavioural economists have advocated to improve individual decision making. **(15 marks)**

(b) Evaluate the view that the UK government should only consider the insights of behavioural economics when choosing appropriate policies to use to reduce obesity levels in the British population. **(25 marks)**

Essay 2

(a) Explain why firms operating in perfectly competitive markets are price-takers, while a monopoly firm is a price-maker. **(15 marks)**

(b) 'Technological innovation means that the economy is constantly evolving. Firms such as IBM and Nokia once dominated the computer and mobile phone industries. However, technical innovation has contributed to new competitors entering the markets. The monopoly power of older firms has largely disappeared.'

Evaluate the view that, in the light of this information, competition policy is always unnecessary. **(25 marks)**

Essay 3

In recent years the British government has increased regressive taxes, such as VAT, and cut direct taxes, such as income tax.

(a) Explain the difference between equality and equity and how the taxation polices of British governments have affected both income equality and equity in the UK. **(15 marks)**

(b) Assess the case for the government using the taxation and welfare benefit system to create a fairer distribution of income in the UK. **(25 marks)**

Context 1

Total for this context: 40 marks

Negative interest rates

Study **Extracts A**, **B**, **C** and **D**, and then answer **all** parts of Context 1 which follow.

Extract A: Sveriges Riksbank base rate and changes in Swedish house prices, February 2013–February 2016

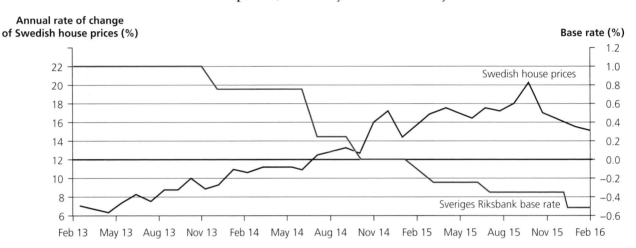

Source: News reports

Extract B: 'Nominal' versus 'real' interest rates

When a central bank, such as the Sveriges Riksbank in Sweden, changes its base rate (Bank Rate in the UK), it is changing a *nominal* rate of interest.

Although central banks can't directly set the *real* rate of interest, by taking account of the rate of inflation they can do this indirectly. For example, if the inflation rate is 2% but the central bank wants a real rate of interest of 5%, it   5
sets its base rate at 7%.

Source: news reports

Extract C: 'Conventional' and 'unconventional' monetary policy

In April 2015, the UK inflation rate turned negative, with the inflation rate falling to –0.1%. This was, however, only a 'blip', as a low rate of positive inflation was quickly restored. But economists were now recognising that when Bank Rate is close to zero, the policy of changing interest rates to influence and control aggregate demand is ineffective.   5

Bank Rate policy is now often called 'conventional' monetary policy. In response to the failure of conventional policy to bring about fast economic recovery, the Bank of England began to place more emphasis on various forms of 'unconventional' monetary policy such as quantitative easing and forward guidance.   10

Source: news reports

Extract D: What about fiscal policy?

In countries such as Sweden, though not the UK, negative interest rates have become part of the central bank's unconventional toolkit for stimulating economic growth when nominal interest rates are already very low.

With lacklustre growth and stubbornly low investment activity in many economies, policy-makers may want to do more, and monetary policy is far from the only option. Expansionary fiscal policy and appropriate supply-side policies provide other options for achieving improved economic growth. Government spending has a good track record when it comes to boosting growth, particularly when interest rates are low.

Supply-side reforms, ideally combined with fiscal policies, can also help to make economies more competitive and productive by improving the functioning of markets, upgrading educational systems, building critical infrastructure and unleashing entrepreneurship and innovation. Such measures will increase the potential for future growth.

5

10

Source: News reports

01 In February 2016 the rate of consumer price inflation in Sweden was +0.32%. Using this fact and the information in **Extract A**, calculate the real rate of interest in Sweden. **(2 marks)**

02 Do the data in **Extract B** support the view that a decrease in interest rates leads to an increase in house prices? **(4 marks)**

03 **Extract C** (line 6) states that 'Bank Rate policy is now often called "conventional" monetary policy.'

With the help of an *AD/AS* diagram, explain how cutting Bank Rate can affect aggregate demand and increase consumption spending in the economy. **(9 marks)**

04 **Extract D** (lines 6–7) states that 'Expansionary fiscal policy and appropriate supply-side policies provide other options for achieving improved economic growth.'

Using the data in the extracts and your knowledge of economics, evaluate the view that fiscal policy and supply-side policies should be used instead of, or as a complement to, monetary policy to achieve faster economic growth. **(25 marks)**

Essay 1

'When a country [the USA] is losing many billions of dollars on trade with virtually every country it does business with, trade wars are good, and easy to win' (US president Donald J. Trump, 2 March 2018).

(a) Explain, using an appropriate diagram, how tariffs might affect both domestic producers and consumers in the country imposing this form of protectionism. **(15 marks)**

(b) Assess the view that both producers and consumers in developed economies such as the USA have experienced greater benefits than costs from globalisation. **(25 marks)**

Essay 2

'Between 2008 and 2018 the UK pound lost approximately 35% of its value against the US dollar yet the UK has continued to run a large and persistent current account deficit.'

(a) Explain the factors which may result in a significant depreciation in the external value of a country's currency within a freely floating exchange rate system. **(15 marks)**

(b) Evaluate the policies that the UK government could pursue to eliminate its deficit on the balance of trade in goods and services. **(25 marks)**

Essay 3

'Unemployment is a serious economic problem in both developed economies and developing economies.'

(a) Explain how the activities of multinational corporations (MNCs) in developed economies such as the UK have led both to some workers losing their jobs, and also to the creation of new job opportunities. **(15 marks)**

(b) Evaluate the argument that, despite the harm they sometimes cause, multinational corporations have been a force for good in increasing living standards in the developing countries in which they operate. **(25 marks)**

Paper 3: Economic principles and issues

Multiple-choice questions

Microeconomics

1 The table below shows an individual's total utility from the consumption of glasses of lemonade.

Glasses of lemonade	Total utility (units of utility)
0	0
1	8
2	14
3	18
4	20
5	20
6	18

What is the marginal utility to the individual from consuming the fourth glass of lemonade?

A   0

B   2

C   18

D   20

2   The diagram below shows the production possibility frontiers for two countries, Oceana and Eurasia.

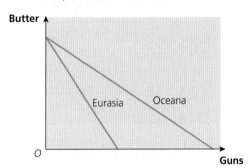

The opportunity cost of butter in terms of guns:

A   increases as more guns are produced

B   increases as more butter is produced

C   is greater for Oceana than for Eurasia

D   is greater for Eurasia than for Oceana

3   The diagram below shows the marginal revenue product of labour (MRP_L), the average cost of labour (AC_L), and the marginal cost of labour (MC_L) in a labour market with low barriers to entry for workers but a firm which can exercise monopsony power when employing labour.

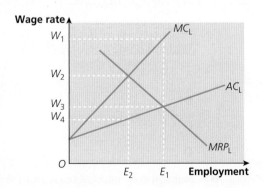

Where will a profit-maximising monopsony firm set the wage rate and the level of employment?

A W_1, E_1

B W_2, E_2

C W_3, E_1

D W_4, E_2

4 The diagram shows a firm's average and marginal revenue curves.

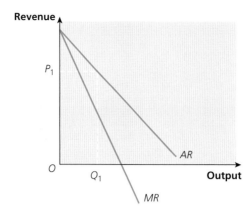

What is the price elasticity of demand at P_1?

A −1

B −2.5

C −0.25

D −0.75

5 The diagram below shows four Lorenz curves, W, X, Y and Z, and a line of complete equality.

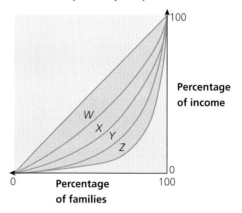

Which Lorenz curve would have the largest Gini coefficient?

A W

B X

C Y

D Z

6 Sales of new cars increase from 9,600 to 10,800 cars. The income elasticity of demand for new cars is +2.5. Workers' original income per annum is $21,000. What is the new average income per annum?

A $22,050

B $21,525

C $22,680

D $21,932

7   The diagram below shows the consequences of introducing an indirect sugar tax on fizzy drinks, with the market supply curve of fizzy drinks shifting from S_1 to S_2.

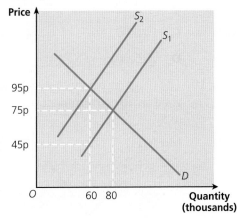

Once the tax has been paid to the government, what is the firm's total revenue?

A   £30,000

B   £12,000

C   £57,000

D   £27,000

8   The table below shows the price and quantity demanded of two goods, H and K.

Price of H ($)	Price of K ($)	Quantity demanded of good H	Quantity demanded of good K
40	50	80	60
36	40	96	84

When the price of H falls from $40 to $36, the cross elasticity of demand for K with respect to the price of H is:

A   −4

B   −2

C   +2

D   +4

9   The table below shows a firm's output and total costs.

Output	Total costs (£)
0	50,000
1,000	70,000
2,000	95,000
3,000	110,000
4,000	130,000
5,000	155,000

What is the average variable cost of producing 4,000 units of output?

A   £32.50

B   £12.50

C   £20.00

D   £25.00

10 The diagram below shows the impact of a subsidy imposed on a good by the government, which shifts the market supply curve from S_1 to S_2.

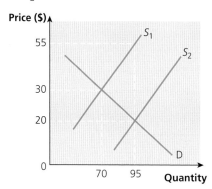

After the subsidy has been received, the revenue that firms receive from the sale of products is:

A $5,225

B $7,125

C $2,100

D $1,900

11 A local authority is deciding on how to allocate its budget to improve public transport in the area. It can afford to build only one of four capital infrastructure projects. The table below show the estimated private and external costs and benefits of each project.

	Private benefits (£m)	Private costs (£m)	External benefits (£m)	External costs (£m)
New tram system	200	160	75	40
New road bypass	175	250	100	20
New cycles lanes	60	40	25	30
New rail link	250	225	180	45

Which one of the projects should be chosen if the local authority wants to maximise economic welfare?

A   new tram system

B   new road bypass

C   new cycle lanes

D   new rail link

12 The diagram below shows the marginal private cost (*MPC*) and marginal social cost (*MSC*) and the marginal private benefit (*MPB*) and marginal social benefit (*MSB*) resulting from the production of a product.

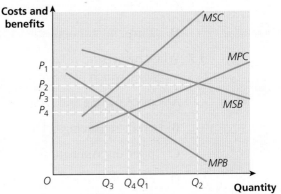

If the government intervenes in the market to achieve the optimal social output, where should the market operate?

A P_1, Q_1

B P_2, Q_2

C P_1, Q_4

D P_4, Q_4

13 A town which relies on tourism as its major industry has experienced problems with littering. If the local council wants to adopt a behavioural economic policy to address the problem, it should:

A place signs which state that the majority of people do not drop litter

B install CCTV and fine people caught dropping litter

C close the town centre at night

D deploy extra police to deter anti-social behaviour

14 The diagram below shows a firm operating in an imperfectly competitive market.

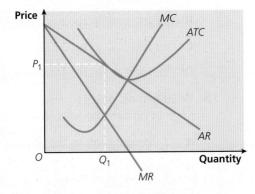

What does the diagram represent?

A an oligopoly firm pursuing a policy of limit pricing

B a monopoly firm experiencing X-inefficiency

C an oligopoly firm engaging in anti-competitive behaviour

D a firm in monopolistic competition making normal profits

15 When ownership resides with shareholders and control rests with manages, which of the following is most likely?

A price rigging and cartel activity

B profit-satisficing behaviour

C price discrimination

D profit-maximising behaviour

Macroeconomics

16 The table below shows the production possibilities of two countries, Oceana and Eurasia, if they divide their resources equally between the production of two goods, guns and butter.

	Guns	Tonnes of butter
Oceana	12,000	6,000
Eurasia	4,000	2,000

If Oceana decides to produce an extra tonne of butter, the opportunity cost in terms of guns will be:

A 2

B 3

C 1

D 0

17 Which represents a withdrawal from an economy's circular flow of income?

A an increase in the budget deficit

B an increase in the trade surplus

C an increase in income tax

D an increase in the level of investment

18 What is most likely to result from a sustained decrease in the world price of oil for a petroleum-exporting developing country?

A a deterioration in the government's finances

B an increase in the balance of trade in services

C an increase in the level of investment from MNCs

D an appreciation in the value of the currency

19 During the course of 2016 the value of the pound against the euro depreciated from £1 = €1.36 to £1 = €1.17. All other things being equal, this is most likely to result in:

A an increase in the size of the UK's budget deficit

B an increase in UK unemployment

C an increase in the rate of UK inflation

D UK exports becoming price uncompetitive in eurozone markets

20 A government makes the reduction of the natural rate of unemployment a major macroeconomic policy objective. Which of the following would be the most effective policy for the government to adopt to achieve its objective?

A a new bout of quantitative easing

B the introduction of tariffs on imported goods

C increasing the living wage

D raising the personal income tax threshold

21 The annual coupon payment on a 30-year bond issued in 2018 is £6. When the bond was first issued, the long-run interest rate was 4%. The bond's maturity value is £100. Within the last year, long-run interest rates have fallen to 3%.

Other things being equal, what will be the current market price of this bond?

A £150

B £200

C £106

D £103

22 The table below shows a price index in a country in the years from 2013 to 2018. What was the annual rate of inflation in the year 2018?

Year	2013	2014	2015	2016	2017	2018
Price index	98.7	100	97.3	101.6	104.5	109.1

A 4.2%

B 4.6%

C 4.4%

D 9.1%

23 Following a series of unsatisfactory annual stress tests on the UK's commercial banking system, the Bank of England's Financial Policy Committee decides that it needs to take action to maintain financial stability.

What is the Bank of England's most likely course of action?

A increase Bank Rate and introduce a new bout of quantitative easing

B decrease Bank Rate and introduce a new bout of quantitative easing

C cut liquidity ratio requirements and raise capital ratio requirements

D raise liquidity ratio requirements and raise capital ratio requirements

24 The diagram below shows two aggregate demand (*AD*) curves and two short-run aggregate supply (*SRAS*) curves for an economy.

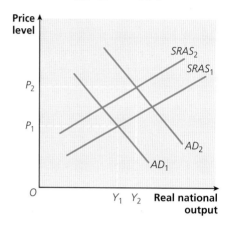

All other things being equal, which event is most likely to have resulted in the changes in real national output and the price level?

A a sustained depreciation in the external value of the currency

B a decrease in the rate of VAT

C an increase in investment spending

D an increase in demand for exported goods

25 The diagram below shows the market for steel after the introduction of a tariff.

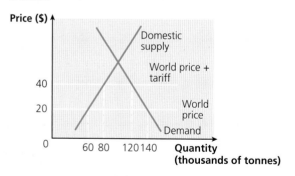

What is the percentage increase in domestic firms' total revenue following the introduction of the tariff?

A 62.5%

B 166.7%

C 125.5%

D 162.5%

26 The table below shows Bank Rate set by the central bank and the inflation rate over the period 2015–20.

	2015	2016	2017	2018	2019	2020
Bank Rate (%)	0.50	0.25	0.25	0.50	0.75	1.00
Inflation rate (%)	−3.00	1.00	2.00	2.00	5.00	3.00

Which one of the following can be concluded from the data?

A The economy experienced an extended period of disinflation.

B The economy had negative real interest rates in every year except 2015.

C The central bank used monetary policy to manage the exchange rate.

D The central bank raised Bank Rate in every year.

27 The table below shows the human development index rankings of four countries in the years 1990, 2005 and 2018.

	1990	2005	2018
Country W	0.361	0.378	0.429
Country X	0.215	0.327	0.342
Country Y	0.247	0.392	0.367
County Z	0.230	0.394	0.457

Which country experienced the highest rate of development over the period shown?

A Country W

B Country X

C Country Y

D Country Z

28 In 2018/19 the British economy is expected to grow below trend and government plans to spend £812.8 billion, of which £731.5 billion will be current spending and £81.3 billion will capital spending. The government expects to raise £787.3 billion in taxation receipts.

Which one of the flowing statements is false?

A The government is running a budget deficit.

B The national debt is going to increase in 2018/19.

C The government is running a structural deficit.

D The government could run a budget surplus in the later stages of the business cycle.

29 The table below shows the UK's income tax rates for the financial year 2018/19.

Taxable income	Tax band	Tax rate (%)
Up to £11,850	Personal allowance	0
£11,851 to £46,350	Basic rate	20
£46,351 to £150,000	Higher rate	40
Over £150,000	Additional rate	45

An individual worker earns £63,525. What percentage of their income does the worker have to pay in tax?

A 21.7%

B 25.7%

C 31.7%

D 34.7%

30 An economy has a £1,700 billion national debt and the government plans to run a budget deficit of £40 billion, but the economy is expected to grow by 3%.

All other things being equal, which of the following statements is correct?

A The national debt as a proportion of GDP is rising.

B The national debt as a proportion of GDP is falling.

C The budget deficit as a proportion of GDP is rising.

D The budget deficit as a proportion of GDP is falling.

Investigation question: Austerity Britain

Source booklet

Extract A The meaning of austerity

Extract B The effects of austerity

Extract C Selected economic data

Extract D Seaside towns and austerity

Extract A: The meaning of austerity

Austerity is a word that's been bandied about in the news for the past 10 years. The chancellor of the exchequer has now said that 'the end of austerity is in sight'. A few days earlier, the prime minister had declared at the Conservative Party's annual conference that 'people needed to know that austerity was over, and their hard work has paid off'. 5

But what exactly is austerity? Sadly, there isn't a single, simple definition of austerity. According to the *Sun* newspaper, austerity is: 'no weekends away and beans on toast for tea'. For some, such as ex-chancellor George Osborne, austerity means fiscal policy undertaken by government to reduce the budget deficit and the accumulation of the national debt. 10

In his 2010 budget, Osborne had outlined plans for £128 billion of 'fiscal consolidation' over the 5 years to 2015, made up of £29 billion of tax rises and £99 billion of spending cuts. This was the start of a major phase of public-sector austerity. The rate at which VAT is levied was increased from 17.5 % to 20 %, departmental spending was cut, with particularly heavy cuts imposed on education. Central government grants to local councils were halved, as were welfare payments, received mainly by the poor.

15

On the plus side, by 2018 the budget deficit as a share of GDP was back to pre-financial crisis level. The *current* budget deficit, which excludes government spending on infrastructure, has moved into surplus. However, there are still several billion pounds of welfare budget cuts scheduled in the coming years, which will make hundreds of thousands of families worse off. There will also be further cuts to many Whitehall departmental budgets (although the NHS has been promised a £20 billion increase by 2023).

20

Source: News reports, 2018

Extract B: The effects of austerity

Since 2010, austerity — primarily in the form of deep spending cuts with comparatively small increases in tax — has been the UK government's dominant fiscal policy, with far fewer measures undertaken to stimulate the economy. The stated aim of austerity was to reduce the deficit in the UK to give confidence to the markets in the hope of delivering growth to the economy. While austerity measures have had some impact on reducing the deficit, they have delivered little growth, and the national debt has risen. The policies have also had far-reaching impacts on the poorest people in the UK. In 2010, the government announced the biggest cuts to state spending since the Second World War, including significant cuts to social security and the planned loss of 900,000 public-sector jobs between 2011 and 2018.

5

10

Since the 2008 financial crisis began, those already in poverty have seen their impoverishment worsen, and many more have become potentially vulnerable to falling living standards. Millions are struggling to make ends meet. Just one example among many is the unprecedented rise in the need for emergency food aid, with at least half a million people using food banks each year.

15

The Institute for Fiscal Studies found that the net direct effect of tax and benefit changes will be to increase both absolute and relative poverty. Over the decade to 2020, an additional 800,000 children are expected to be living in poverty — almost one in four British children. Over the same period, an extra 1.5 million working-age adults are expected to fall into poverty, bringing the total to 17.5% of this group. When incomes are adjusted to account for inflation, absolute poverty has already seen its largest year-on-year increase in a decade.

20

Source: Oxfam case study, 'The true cost of austerity and inequality'

Extract C: Selected economic data

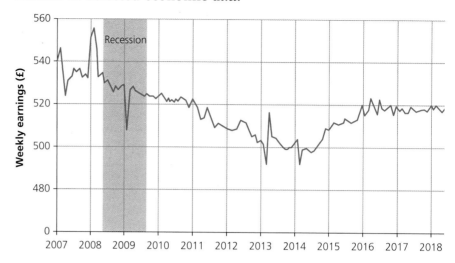

Source: ONS

Figure 1 Average weekly earnings in the UK, inflation adjusted, 2007–18

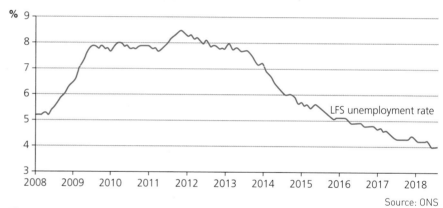

Source: ONS

Figure 2 LFS unemployment rate in the UK, 2008–October 2018

Note: Solid lines are actual percentages of people living in poverty, dashed lines are projections.
Source: House of Commons briefing paper, 2018

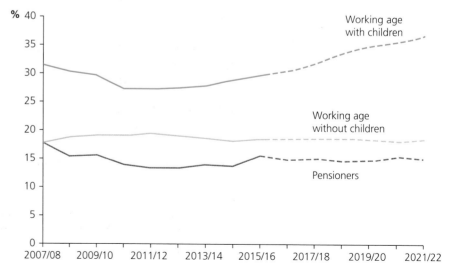

Figure 3 Percentage of people on relative low income, UK, 2007/08–2021/22, after housing costs have been taken into consideration

Extract D: Seaside towns and austerity

Coastal communities are lagging behind inland areas with some of the worst levels of economic and social deprivation in the country. Comparisons of earnings, employment, health and education in local authority areas have identified 'pockets of significant deprivation' in seaside towns and a widening gap with the rest the country. Around 85% of Great Britain's 98 coastal local authorities had pay levels below the national average for 2016. Average wages are £3,600 a year lower than the national average. 5

A Social Market Foundation report says that the economic gap between coastal and non-coastal communities has grown, and that this has been caused in part by poor infrastructure. Many coastal communities are poorly connected to major employment centres in the UK, which compounds the difficulties faced by residents in these areas. They lack local job opportunities and travelling elsewhere for work is also difficult. 10

Despite the evident social and economic problems which these places face, there is currently no official definition of a 'coastal community'. Arguably the government needs to do more to address economic problems in our coastal holiday resorts. Some coastal communities are pockets of significant deprivation surrounded by affluence — which leads to their problems being often overlooked by policy-makers. These forgotten seaside towns are home to some of the very poorest communities in the UK. 15

20

In an attempt to boost employment and encourage tourism, the government has pledged to give £40 million to coastal areas. Since 2012, the Coastal Communities Fund has invested £174 million into 295 UK-wide projects. Preferring to emphasise the positives, the coastal communities minister has said the latest round of funding 'will help attract even more visitors to the great British coast so that our coastal communities can thrive'. 25

Source: News reports, 2017

Total for this investigation: 50 marks

Austerity Britain

INVESTIGATION

Scenario

You are an economist employed by the Family Poverty Action Group, a pressure group which campaigns for government economic policies to help the poor, especially the young poor. The organisation has requested that you provide answers to three key questions.

Referring to the source booklet, study **Extracts A**, **B**, and **C** and then use these and your own economic knowledge to help you answer questions **31** and **32**. There is also an additional news report, **Extract D**, which is to be used with the other extracts to help answer question **33**.

31 To what extent, if at all, do the data support the view that the government's policy of 'fiscal consolidation' has caused austerity to occur in the UK? You must use the data in **Extract C** to support your assessment. **(10 marks)**

32 Explain why in recent years in the UK, the growth of poverty may have been caused by structural change taking place in the economy as well as by the policy of 'fiscal consolidation' implemented by successive governments. **(15 marks)**

33 Taking into account the news report concerning low living standards in UK seaside towns in **Extract D**, and the other evidence in the extracts, recommend **two** policies that the Family Poverty Action Group should advise the government to adopt in order to raise living standards and reduce poverty in UK coastal holiday resorts. Justify your recommendations. **(25 marks)**

Photo credits

The publishers would like to thank the following for permission to reproduce photographs:

Index

Page numbers in bold refer to key term definitions

Index